PRIVATE SECURITY

STANDARDS AND GOALS—FROM THE OFFICIAL PRIVATE SECURITY TASK FORCE REPORT

**A Special Edition
with an Introduction and
Discussion Questions by**

Arthur J. Bilek
Task Force Chairman

and

Preface by
Dr. Peter P. Lejins,
Foreword by
Clifford W. Van Meter

 anderson publishing co./cincinnati

© 1977 by

anderson publishing co.

ISBN: 0-87084-716-3

Preface

For three reasons I was very pleased to be asked to write a preface to this publication of the Report of the Task Force on Private Security of the National Advisory Committee on Criminal Justice Standards and Goals. First of all, I firmly believe that in our contemporary society the issue of providing security by private rather than public means is extremely important at the present time. It is rapidly gaining in importance, although so far relatively little analytical thought has been given to it. There is very little conceptualization on the subject and practically no theory building. And yet an activity of the magnitude of private security in this country, described so well by Governor Byrne, Chairman of the National Advisory Committee, can hardly be expected to develop rationally and be effective without a sound theoretical underpinning. Secondly, I believe that this Report is a good one and represents the most significant step so far in assessing the entire field of private security and proposing a set of standards for it. Thirdly, I believe that the purpose of this particular publication of the Report, which is intended to make it more accessible for educational programs in colleges and universities in the area of private security, is sound. In our complex society the planning, organization and management of private security facilities is by necessity a complex subject, requiring appropriately educated personnel at least for its top administrative and planning echelons.

In a very broad sense the field of private security today can be approached from two different perspectives. One is that of organizational and hardware technology; the other is a perspective on the role and function of private security in contemporary society, especially in its relationship to public security, provided by governmental agencies. The first of these topics is covered very excellently in this volume. In this Preface I would like to address myself primarily to the second of these perspectives.

Students of the history of criminal law, while fully recognizing the great variety in the patterns of its development, agree by and large that a major step toward the development of a "civilized" society has always been the change from the private resolution of conflicts, the private repulsion of attacks on one's legitimate rights, and private insurance of security for oneself and one's family to the ceding of the right to defend oneself to the government, which can settle such every day problems more objectively, with much greater authority, a greater reservoir of power and without excesses. The replacement of self protection by the rule of law enforced by the government has always been recognized as a major step in the development of modern society. Hobbes' *bellum omnium contra omnes* could be ended only by Rousseau's social contract, by which the citizens established a government and turned over to that government the protection of their legitimate rights. In this perspective the strong movement in modern society to return to private security poses a big question: Why? This single question mark must in fact be translated into a series of questions. Is there really a need to turn once again to private security as against governmental guarantees of one's rights? Is this due to the failure of the government to effectively guarantee these rights? If there is such failure, what are the reasons for it? Do these reasons stem from the essence of modern society, which makes this return to private security unavoidable? Or, is it some defect in our contemporary law enforcement system which can be remedied, and if so, how? These are the questions to be tackled by the planner of a criminal justice system who nowadays is faced with the basic issue of whether this justice system can be planned as a public system only or whether, in addition, a private security system should be planned for as well.

To the question—do we really have a trend toward a return to private security because of insufficient protection proffered by public law enforcement?—a twofold response suggests itself. On one hand it is obvious that a comprehensive study of these questions on the level of the best that contemporary social science research can offer, has not been done and is clearly called for. A program of research directed toward exploration of the issues raised in these questions might be looked for to give the answers. Some may feel that action has to be postponed until answers are obtained. On the other hand, one may feel that there are so many indicators that the assessment of the situation suggested by these questions is justified, that action does not need to be postponed. Our statistics show a long-term trend of steadily increasing adult criminality and juvenile delinquency. The growing concern of the public about the threat of becoming victims of criminal acts is also well documented. There seems to be ample evidence of the decreasing effectiveness of our law enforcement agencies in reaching the perpetrators of criminal acts and imposing the sanctions prescribed by law. Our statistics seem to show that an increasingly smaller percentage of perpetrators of burglaries, robberies, larcenies and many other offenses are found and convicted. As everybody in the field knows, the number of such offenses cleared by conviction is alarmingly small. The failure of prohibitions against gambling, drugs, prostitution, etc. because of the obvious inability to enforce the laws in this country is so obvious that it hardly needs substantiation. On the other hand, the search by the citizens for alternatives for the lacking protection by the governmental criminal justice system is also obvious. All over the country we find residential developments which have established their own private security systems, with guards patrolling the area and guard posts checking any potential visitor before admitting him to the compound. The widely publicized and supported movement toward hardening the target through the planning of business and residential communities, architectural design of residences, security lock and alarm systems which are suggested to the private citizens, all this represents a clear recognition that in our society public law enforcement cannot be relied upon for effective action against those who violate the criminal laws, and the system of general deterrence, or general prevention, does not work, hence the mechanical prevention of criminal acts must be the chief means for the private citizen to protect his rights.

Another indicator of the ineffectiveness of the public criminal justice system is the ever-increasing reliance on insurance as a way of compensation for losses sustained by the victims of crime rather than reliance on protection by the law enforcement agencies. One hears with increasing frequency of the attitude of the law enforcement officers that in the case of many crimes their main function is to officially register a criminal offense so that insurance can be properly claimed, without even an attempt to locate the perpetrator and interrupt his criminal depredations. Still another indicator is the practice of passing the losses from shoplifting and thefts by personnel on to the customers by raising prices, rather than by making a sustained effort to reduce thefts by enforcing the criminal law. Even when the businessman resorts to a combined system of passing some of the losses on to the customers but at the same time employs also a detective force in his store for the sake of prevention, he resorts to private security resources rather than relying on the public system.

In this discussion of protection by private versus public security, the following should be noted. It is true that a certain amount of private security has always been in use. Night watchmen, various kinds of guards, employed privately, etc., are reported throughout the history of Western Civilization. The issue here is not the existence of private security, but the extent to which it is relied upon and used.

The questions discussed so far were directed toward the comparative effectiveness of public versus private security in protecting the legitimate rights of the citizens. A series of broader questions was further suggested. It could be argued that the issue of effectiveness, while of course very important, is not the only one. There is also the question of the basic organizational pattern of governance of the society. Is the transfer of the guaranties of the rights of the individual to private initiative compatible with the organizational principles to which democratic societies, *e.g.* American society, subscribe? Could it be that immediate advantages of insuring security by private means in the long run lead to the weakening of the public government by transferring one of its basic functions to private enterprises? The old principle that every social organization is only as strong and as important as the functions which it performs, comes to mind. If one recognizes the strength of the argument just made, and at the same time does not feel that private security can be eliminated altogether, then the topic of the limits for private security obviously becomes very important. So far very little thinking has been done with regard to this point and thus another area for research and development suggests itself. Some formulation of general principles and the spelling out of the application of these principles to practical matters in planning for private security would be very helpful.

One of the specific issues with regard to private security's role in the society is the differential availability of private security to different strata of the population. Both proprietary private security and the services of the private security industry are clearly more available to the well-to-do classes and cannot be afforded by those with lesser incomes. This becomes an especially important issue when we remember that the crime rates are especially high in the impoverished and deteriorated sections of urban conglomerates. This availability of private security primarily to the more prosperous segments of the population has to be an important point in planning the role of private security in the society in general. Is it a sound basis to build on the assumption that public security is for the poor and private security for those who can afford it? Off hand it seems quite obvious that a truly democratic society can hardly be built on such a basis.

The role of the two major forms of private security which have presently crystallized—proprietary security and the private security industry or security services business—is another topic requiring attention. The term proprietary security refers to measures, personnel and equipment developed by a private individual or corporation to supplement the protection provided by the public law enforcement system. The term private security industry refers to business enterprizes which specialize in providing security to private individuals and corporations. Private security as business, of course, suggests itself as a more efficient and effective way of providing security than the systems developed by private individuals and corporations themselves, since it operates on a larger scale, has all the advantages of "mass production" and can better train personnel and secure the necessary equipment. The only exception might be presented by very large private corporations which, because of the scope of their operations, may enjoy the same advantages in developing their own security systems as the private security industry. Yet from the point of view of the relationship between government and the needs of the citizens for security, there is a considerable difference between the two plans. In proprietary security we have clearly a *supplementary* service, the principal tendency of which is to obtain as much as possible from the government and to provide only that which is absolutely needed but cannot be expected from the public law enforcement system. In the case of the private security industry, which, as all business, is motivated by profit and expansion, the tendency is not only to supplement public security, but to *substitute* for it. Thus the tendency is to replace the protection ordinarily offered by the government. Therefore the potential danger of radical changes in the governmental functions is much greater in the case of the private security industry than through proprietary security measures. In view of this, it is the growth of the private security services industry into a mammoth business with natural monopolistic tendencies which a political scientist engaged in the study of constitutional law and government administration and planning has to assess as a potential major change in the structure of government. The proprietary security measures, be they ever so great in the case of large corporations, promise to remain a much less important factor within the power structure of the country. This probably will remain so even if, for the needs of proprietary security, major hardware industries and educational and training systems for private security personnel are developed.

The issue of differential availability of private security to different socio-economic groupings in our society, as already mentioned above, is especially acute in the case of the private security services business, where profit is an important motive and the cost of services will put them out of reach for the impoverished strata of the population. It could be anticipated that with the growth of the private security industry, the governmental responsibility for the security of people who are unable to purchase it privately may turn into subsidizing such purchases rather than providing protection through public law enforcement.

The above remarks are not intended as a necessarily antagonistic stand toward the development of the private security services business or a warning against it. This is simply an attempt to point up the issues which are already coming up in connection with recent developments in this country and which should be given careful analytical consideration.

Arthur J. Bilek, Chairman of the Task Force on Private Security, should be complimented for his new role, regarding this Report, namely, that of an educator who, by his actions, is endeavoring to build a bridge between this technical material and those college and university classrooms which are striving to develop up-to-date programs for the preparation of personnel for the emerging field of private security.

Peter P. Lejins

Director,
Institute of Criminal Justice
and Criminology
University of Maryland

Foreword

It is a privilege for me to write the foreword to this book edited by my colleague Art Bilek who served as Chairman of the Private Security Task Force. Throughout the work of the Task Force it was apparent that material gathered could serve as a reference source for a wide variety of persons concerned about private security including legislators, practitioners, and students enrolled in private security and law enforcement courses.

Almost all government publications have one common deficiency which can be classified as "impersonal." The format for this text takes a step toward removing this shortcoming by establishing study questions which provide a format for discussion. The joining together of the content of the Task Force Report with the added discussion questions should enable students to obtain a better understanding of the issues identified by the Standard and Goal statements.

A myriad of problems faced the staff and members of the Task Force when the project began in March 1975. One of the steps in any planning process is the collection and analysis of data pertinent to the subject. This was a difficult task since the literature and research was sparce and difficult to gather. A major effort by my Research Associates, John Simmons and Dave Viar, did produce a respectable data base for the Report. However, the lack of literature and research in this field continues to be a restraint on those interested in developing a body of knowledge which can be identified as "private security."

The processes, both formal and informal, used to prepare the Report provide some insights into "how" and "why" the material emerged. Whenever possible, considering time and budget restraints, knowledgeable people in private security were utilized in the work of the Task Force. In some cases they recommended forceful and stringent statements, but, for the most part, advocated the use of modified statements that would not serve solely to rouse controversy which would obscure their original meaning and intent. Staff carefully codified and presented these inputs to the Task Force. The Task Force working first in committees and later as a whole, reviewed, discussed and amended these materials before adopting a Standard and Goal statement. The product of the Task Force deliberations was forwarded to the National Advisory Committee on Criminal Justice Standards and Goals along with the supporting commentaries. The National Advisory Committee reviewed the material *de novo* and in some cases referred the Standard and Goal statement back to the Task Force for modification and also made some suggested changes in commentaries. The staff then made the changes and resubmitted them to the Task Force for final decision. The Task Force was the final authority for conflicts except, as noted with Standard 4.11, the National Advisory Committee had the opportunity to express their views on unresolved differences. As a participant in the process, I was greatly impressed by the dedication and sincerity of both the Task Force and National Advisory Committee. However, in all candor, their interactions sometimes led to compromise Standard and Goal statements which did change the original intent of the Task Force.

One other process should be noted. After the Task Force and National Advisory Committee completed their work the material was turned over to the Editorial Staff of the National Advisory Committee. Since the Report is advisory by design they felt that terms, such as "must", "shall", "will", etc., were inappropriate and substituted terms such as "should" in lieu of the above phrases. A problem resulting from this procedure is that the final version of the Report does not differentiate between where the Task Force and National Advisory Committee originally used terms such as "should" and where the Editoral staff procedurally changed "shall", "must", and "will", to "should."

In conclusion, I am hopeful that an understanding of the process used to develop the Report will assist students in reviewing and discussing the material. If this text raises more questions than it answers, it will have served an important function in the definition and evaluation of the role of private security in the national program of crime prevention and crime reduction.

Clifford W. Van Meter
Director, Police Training Institute
University of Illinois

Introduction

Dilemmas, distortions and half-truths confront the student of private security. Critical analysis of the field evokes far more quesions than answers. Confusion and uncertainty clouds the decision-making process concerning the efficacy of alternate security options. Practices are defended and decried simultaneously. Despite a history almost as old as man, private security continues to function as anachronistically as if it had never met the tests of time.

Even a cursory overview of private security exposes a myriad of issues which demand contemporary response. A review of but a few gives ample support to the need for serious study, debate and resolution:

- If security officers are armed, they not only look more like public law enforcement officers, but the guard's self-image is impacted accordingly.

- The potential for security officers to successfully protect life and property against armed criminals is sharply diminished if the guards are unarmed.

- Is regulation by government or the marketplace more effective in enhancing private security's crime prevention role?

- Public law enforcement officers who "moonlight" as security guards may bring with them a high level of training, but are also accompanied by an "arrest" mentality which may result in more provocation than protection.

- Many arrests by security guards are not reported to the police, but complete reporting and prisoner turnover by private security would hopelessly innundate the nation's criminal justice system.

- Unwarranted shooting incidents involving carelessly screened, untrained guards outrage the public, but many businesses seek lowest-bid contracts with guard companies whose cut-rate overhead make such incidents possible.

An even more disturbing question, urgently in need of scientifically-validated research, asks whether private security actually has a meaningful, cost-effective impact on the safeguarding of persons and property from crime. Will a store with a guard be less likely to be subject to a robbery than an unguarded premise? What if a second guard is added? Or a third? If a building is equipped with a burglar alarm, what is the probability that it will be protected against illegal entry? 100%? 50%? 0%? Do special locking devices reduce the likelihood of burglary on every business in all neighborhoods? Which businesses? What neighborhoods? Despite these unanswered questions, in 1976 over a million persons were engaged in private security activities and security equipment and services costing over six billion dollars were purchased for the purpose of preventing criminal attack on people and property.

It was in this uncertain arena that the Private Security Task Force began its questions, probes and analyses. The Task Force Report is the first document of its kind in the private security field. In addition to its overview of American security history, practices and operations, the Report provides a basic primer of standards and goals for the entire security field. These standards and goals are supported by exhaustive research, new studies, wide-ranging professional input and extensive review and debate.

This special edition contains the entire content of the Private Security Task Force Report except for the appendices. No change has been made in any standard, goal, commentary or substantive text.

Over three hundred discussion and study questions covering all sections, chapters, standards and goals have been developed exclusively for this special edition. These study questions will provide the credit-earning student, the self-taught practitioner and the general reader with a thoughtful review of the Report's major recommendations, controversial areas and provocative findings. While certain study questions relate directly to specific textual content, other questions have no "school solutions" and demand involvement and contribution of the student's own ethics, outlook and experience.

New introductory material was also developed for this special edition by Dr. Peter P. Lejins and Director Clifford W. Van Meter. Dr. Lejins, a member of the National Advisory Committee on Criminal Justice Standards and Goals, reviewed the work product of the Private Security Task Force as it was presented in draft format to the National Advisory Committee. Various standards and commentary within the Task Force Report clearly bear his imprint. Additionally, Dr. Lejins was the developer and host of the First National Conference on Private Security held in 1975 at the University of Maryland. Dr. Lejins, currently the Director of the Institute of Criminal Justice and Criminology at the University of Maryland, shares with us in this special edition his critical insights into the issues and concerns of private security.

Clifford Van Meter, Executive Director of the Private Security Task Force, has contributed new comments on the Task Force and its work for this special edition. Director Van Meter, who formerly headed the Criminal Justice Program at Western Illinois University, now serves as Director of the Police Training Institute of the University of Illinois. As Executive Director, his personal dedication, administration and service provided both the raw input for the Task Force's initial considerations as well as the finished materials for their final decision-making.

While it was not possible to provide a dedication in the original Report presented to the U.S. Justice Department's Law Enforcement Assistance Administration, such action is appropriate in this special edition. It is most fitting that John A. Willis, who as Executive Vice President of Pinkerton's, Inc. was both my superior and mentor during my service as Chairman of the Task Force, should be cited for this honor. John Willis' sure-footed pragmatism and experience-tested wisdom generously support his competent professionalism. As the first chairman of the Guards and Investigators Committee of LEAA's Private Security Advisory Council, he shaped the guidelines that became the basis for the Council's model statute for security companies and personnel. A true security practitioner, he has spent his adult life learning, refining and contributing in the field of contractual security. Through his steadfast dedication to the tenets of integrity, professionalism and service, John Willis contributed directly to the contents of the Private Security Task Force Report just as he impacted countless security officials and operational personnel who came in contact with him over the years.

Arthur J. Bilek

Director, Corporate Security
CFS Continental, Inc.

Table of Contents

Chapter 5

Environmental Security

Part 4

Relationship Of The Industry With Others

Statement of the Administrator
From the Official Private Security Task Force Report

This volume, *Private Security,* is one of five reports of the National Advisory Committee on Criminal Justice Standards and Goals.

The National Advisory Committee was formed by the Law Enforcement Assistance Administration (LEAA) in the spring of 1975. Governor Brendan T. Byrne of New Jersey was appointed Chairman of the Committee. Charles S. House, Chief Justice of the Connecticut Supreme Court, was named Vice-Chairman. Other members were drawn from the three branches of State and local government, the criminal justice community, and the private sector. Four of the 12 members were elected officials of general government.

The purpose of the Committee was to continue the ground-breaking work of its predecessor organization, the National Advisory Commission on Criminal Justice Standards and Goals. In 1973 the Commission published a six-volume report setting forth standards and goals for police, courts, corrections, the criminal justice system, and crime prevention. Two years later, the National Advisory Committee addressed several additional areas of concern: juvenile justice and delinquency prevention, organized crime, research and development, disorders and terrorism, and private security. Task forces were established to study and propose standards in each of these areas. The task forces were comprised of a cross section of experts and leading practitioners in each of the respective fields.

The Committee reviewed the standards proposed by each task force and made suggestions for change, as appropriate. The process was a dynamic one, with an active exchange of views between task force and Committee members. In almost all instances, the Committee and the task forces ultimately concurred on the standards adopted. In a few cases, there were differences in philosophy and approach that were not resolved. Where such discrepancies exist, each view is presented with the Committee's position noted either in the Chairman's introduction or in a footnote to the particular standard.

Standards and goals is an ongoing process. As standards are implemented, experience will dictate that some be revised, or even discarded altogether. Further research and evaluation will also contribute to growing knowledge about what can and should be done to control crime and improve the system of criminal justice.

Although LEAA provided financial support to both the Committee and the task forces, the recommendations and judgments expressed in the reports do not necessarily reflect those of LEAA. LEAA had no voting participation at either the task force or Committee level. And, as with the 1973 report of the previous Commission, it is LEAA's policy neither to endorse the standards nor to mandate their acceptance by State and local governments. It is LEAA policy, however, to encourage each State and locality to evaluate its present status in light of these reports, and to develop standards that are appropriate for their communities.

On behalf of the Law Enforcement Assistance Administration, I want to thank the members of the National Advisory Committee and the task forces for their time and effort. Those members of the Committee who did "double-duty" as task force chairmen deserve special thanks.

I want to express LEAA's sincerest gratitude to the Chairman of the National Advisory Committee, Governor Byrne. Much of the success of this undertaking is directly attributable to his leadership, hard work, and unflagging good humor.

Finally, it is also appropriate to pay tribute to William T. Archey of LEAA for his outstanding and dedicated service to the Committee and for bringing this entire effort to such a successful conclusion.

RICHARD W. VELDE
Administrator
Law Enforcement Assistance Administration

Washington, D.C.
December 1976

Foreword
From the Official Private Security Task Force Report

There are more than 1 million people involved in private security in the United States. The private security industry is a multibillion-dollar-a-year business that grows at a rate of 10 to 12 percent per year. In many large cities, the number of private security personnel is considerably greater than the number of police and law enforcement personnel. Of those individuals involved in private security, some are uniformed, some are not; some carry guns, some are unarmed; some guard nuclear energy installations, some guard golf courses; some are trained, some are not; some have college degrees, some are virtually uneducated.

This report is the first attempt to codify standards dealing with all of the divergent persons and things associated with private security. There are great difficulties necessarily attached to such a project. Priorities of spending inevitably come into play, and the questions of whether uniform standards should apply to all those involved in private security or only to some, such as those who are armed, are vigorously debated.

The National Advisory Committee on Criminal Justice Standards and Goals is pleased to present this comprehensive report of the Task Force on Private Security. Crime prevention has long been a joint venture of the public and private sectors in the United States. There has, however, been relatively little research done over the years in the area of private security. This report, therefore, fills a long-standing void and provides a reference tool that will be most useful in evaluating the role played by private security in the law enforcement effort as well as in developing ways and means of improving the quality of private security services.

There is virtually no aspect of society that is not in one way or another affected by private security. A business may employ guards to protect persons and property from damage, injury, or loss. Special security services are obviously required in places of public accommodation, such as airports, schools, and commercial complexes. The pervasive involvement of private security plays a vital role in efforts to create a safe environment in which to work and live. The interrelation between public and private law enforcement agencies illustrates the obvious importance of striving to achieve uniformly high standards of quality for both personnel and performance.

This report deals not only with people involved in private security but also with things, such as burglar alarm systems and sophisticated and innovative concepts for environmental protection. As noted, this report is the first attempt to codify standards. There are included herein recommendations for the selection and training of private security personnel; the development of technology and procedures for crime prevention systems, such as burglar alarms; and the relationship of the private security industry with law enforcement agencies.

Discussion among members of the Committee included the questions of whether or not the standards and goals should apply to both large and national firms as well as the smaller security businesses and whether the standards and goals should be addressed exclusively to the problems presented by armed personnel. Also discussed and debated was the issue of whether or not governmental regulation of private security beyond that presently existing and on a uniform basis is indicated.

The Task Force concluded that in fulfilling the mission of improving the quality of private security, it was necessary to give equal importance to all firms, whether large or small, but to endeavor to establish standards and goals that would not have the effect of eliminating small businesses or pricing security services beyond the reach of the consumer. As to the personnel who implement the private security services, the Task Force determined that attention should be focused upon both armed and unarmed personnel, it being recognized that both play significant roles in crime prevention and control. The same philosophy resulted in a determination by the Task Force that the standards and goals would be made applicable to proprietary security personnel (those employees hired by a business to protect the assets of such business) as well as the contract security operation (those businesses that provide security services to others for a fee).

A minority of the Committee, considering these issues, determined that registration, etc., was not necessary for unarmed personnel. Those subscribing to this view believed that the unarmed security guard does not pose as great a potential hazard to the public that an armed guard does where an abuse of authority and power occurs. A particular fear was that across-the-board regulations would result in costs that would be prohibitive to the public as well as to some components of the private security industry that would not be able to carry the financial burden of meeting such standards. The minority viewpoint expressed in the Committee was that licensing by government in this area was inappropriate and that private security would be adequately supervised through the natural forces of civil liability remedies and free competitive enterprise.

In a subject as vast and complex as private security and in an innovative report such as this, it would be unrealistic and indeed surprising were there unanimity of thought. However, unanimity is not in and of itself important. What is important is that as a result of the work of this Task Force, all those involved in law enforcement and crime prevention now have an added tool with which to work. The Committee is content to leave to the States and to local governments final decisions on the priorities of spending and the determination of whether an orderly regulatory process necessitates the inclusion of all elements of the private security industry, whether armed or unarmed, and whether presently licensed or not.

The Committee pays tribute to the members of the Task Force who have worked so diligently and with such competence in this formidable project. This report is an integral part of the national effort to improve the quality of criminal justice.

BRENDAN T. BYRNE
Chairman
National Advisory Committee
on Criminal Justice Standards and Goals

Trenton, N.J.
December 1976

Preface
From the Official Private Security Task Force Report

Over the past 25 years, this country has become the unwilling victim of a crime epidemic. The present seriousness of the disease has outstripped even the most pessimistic prognosis. Coupled with a steadily rising numerical frequency of crimes is a savage viciousness that has rendered the American public almost immune from further shock. The ten-million-plus major felonies that annually occur have seriously debilitated the quality of life in the United States.

Citizens do not feel safe and, in fact, are not safe in their own homes or on their own streets. Businesses are rocked to bankruptcy by the high cost of crime committed by their own employees as well as by hordes of outsiders. Downtown areas at night are all but deserted. Large cities are viewed as jungles of criminality.

In a valiant but vain attempt to stem this massive tide of criminality, government officials, scholars, politicians, and a vast array of other professionals have responded with plans, programs, and projects all designed to reduce crime, ensure justice, and rehabilitate offenders.

One great hope was vested in increases in the numerical strength of the criminal justice system. More police, more prosecutors, more public defenders, more judges, more corrections workers, and more probation and parole officers soon swelled city, county, State, and Federal budgets but did not cause a reduction in crime.

A second approach involved upgrading the quality of the criminal justice system personnel. College education for police, training programs for prosecutors, sentencing conferences for judges, and seminars and institutes for corrections officers served to professionally upgrade criminal justice personnel but did not result in lowered crime or recidivism rates. Nor did the quality of justice noticeably improve.

Technology and applied sciences were also thrown into the fray, resulting in sophisticated police communications, computer-assisted court calendar control, and a wide variety of sociologically and psychologically oriented offender-adjustment programs.

Finally, millions of dollars were used to reshape the criminal justice system through the addition of new practices and the deletion of old processes. Thousands of projects—ranging from team policing to neighborhood legal aid services; from decriminalization of so-called victimless crimes to codified criminal statutes and new laws for new crimes; from diversion from the system at the police, prosecutor, judicial, and correctional stages to additional input into the system by more rapid police response; from methadone treatment centers for heroin addicts to satellite justice centers bringing criminal courts to the suburbs—were designed, heralded, and initiated. Unfortunately, although many of these programs were improvements over outdated practices, crime, the cost of crime, the damage from crime, and the fear of crime continued to increase.

One massive resource, filled with significant numbers of personnel, armed with a wide array of technology, and directed by professionals who have spent their adult lifetimes learning how to prevent and reduce crime, has not been tapped by governments in the fight against criminality. The private security industry, with over one million workers, sophisticated alarm systems and perimeter safeguards, armored trucks, sophisticated mini-computers, and thousands of highly skilled crime prevention experts, offers a potential for coping with crime that can not be equalled by any other remedy or approach.

The application of the resources, technology, skills, and knowledge of the private security industry presents the best hope available for protecting the citizen who has witnessed his defenses against crime shrink to a level which leaves him virtually unprotected.

Underutilized by police, all but ignored by prosecutors and the judiciary, and unknown to corrections officials, the private security professional may be the one person in this society who has the knowledge to effectively prevent crime.

Not represented on the boards or staffs of State Planning Agencies, rarely used by municipal or county planners, only infrequently consulted by elected officials, these members of a six-billion-dollar-a-year industry have crime prevention answers desperately needed by homes, schools, businesses, neighborhoods and communities.

This report is premised on the belief that the private security industry constitutes a massive resource that holds great promise for aiding the Nation in a joint effort to prevent and reduce crime. The purpose of this report is to propose how to upgrade the ability, competence, relationships, and effectiveness of that resource for the anticrime effort.

Up to the present, the anticrime role of private security generally has been ignored. Admittedly, there are important differences between the private security industry and the formal criminal justice system, although the two fields share many of the same goals. The private security industry exists to make a profit in return for the provision of services. It is not supported by public taxes. It is not an arm of the government.

Nonetheless, in serving its clientele, the private security industry serves all of society. Its personnel often are as much "on the line" as are sworn officers. The industry is responsible for the safety and wellbeing of the public in many locations and situations and for the protection of billions of dollars of assets and property.

There was no advisory task force on private security to assist the National Advisory Commission on Criminal Justice Standards and Goals when it undertook its historic work in 1971. The concept of proposing standards and goals for private security is of more recent origin.

The specific proposal to develop standards and goals for private security arose during the work of the Private Security Advisory Council, which recommended to Richard W. Velde, Administrator of the Law

Enforcement Assistance Administration, (LEAA), U.S. Department of Justice, that such a group be formed. (The Council advises LEAA on aspects of the private security industry.) When Mr. Velde decided in 1975 to initiate Phase II of the National Standards and Goals Program, the present Task Force on Private Security was included.

The members of the Task Force were drawn from a wide range of backgrounds, including the formal criminal justice community. Overall, the membership constituted a vastly experienced and highly qualified group of professionals. The Task Force was provided with a staff located at Western Illinois University, Macomb, Ill.

The standards and goals proposed can, if adopted, achieve greater and more effective use of the private security industry in the prevention and reduction of crime.

Little formal literature exists in the field of private security, a fact that both limited research in that area and added to the Task Force's sense of the significance of its study.

To ensure validity and acceptance as well as to forestall criticism and rejection, the Task Force vigorously and ardently pursued a course of open meetings and public discussions. Every identifiable national organization in the field was notified of the project and their assistance, contributions, and review were sought. Many detailed research projects on national, regional, and local levels involving thousands of participants and tens of thousands of data units were designed and implemented. Interim reports were issued and work-in-progress was made available to all interested parties. Non-Task Force members attended every meeting and entered into many discussions and debates on standards and commentaries. The end product reflects the conflux of a myriad of private security, public law enforcement, government, business, and public positions and opinions.

Special appreciation and thanks should go to the thousands of persons without whose assistance and cooperation this report would not have been possible:

• Task Force members.

• Mr. Clifford Van Meter, executive director, and the professional and clerical Task Force staff.

• Dr. Leslie F. Malpass, President, and Dr. Rodney J. Fink, Dean of College of Applied Sciences, Western Illinois University.

• Mr. Dennis Chesshir, Chairman of the Board, and Mr. O. P. Norton, Executive Director, and all of the members and staff of the American Society for Industrial Security.

• Citizens Crime Commission of Philadelphia.

• Mr. Irving Slott, Federal representative, Law Enforcement Assistance Administration.

• Consultants and contributors.

One final note of caution should be provided. As with the thousands of changes made in the criminal justice system, the application of private security know-how, manpower, and techniques to public crime prevention will not provide the ultimately desired goal of reducing crime to levels that are consistent with an orderly and free society unless certain other measures are also pursued. Although it is hoped that private security infusions will reduce the work load of the criminal justice system to manageable proportions, so that the enlarged, highly professionalized, and scientifically equipped police, courts, and corrections can best perform their vital missions, baseline change is necessary to bring the crime epidemic fully under control.

No group of individuals, since the beginning of time, has been able to exist without agreed-to rules and understandings. These rules must be the best product of society's combined competencies. The rules must be uniformly upheld and obeyed. The rule enforcers must be respected and assisted. Inappropriate rules must be promptly and correctly changed. Only then can a society of free men exist—persons exercising self-restraint and self-discipline in their conduct. Permissiveness, individual rights, and self-determination of which laws to obey and which laws to ignore must be replaced by responsibility, understanding, and obedience to the law. No police force can ever be large enough, no court system can provide adequate justice, no correctional scheme can afford the necessary services to cope with a society in which citizens do not respect or obey the laws.

The simple truth obscured by the massive anticrime program is that the criminal justice system, by and of itself, cannot and does not prevent crime and criminality. This vital goal can only be achieved by individuals not committing crime because of their respect for law and their acceptance of the ultimate wisdom of that behavior.

The report of the *Private Security Task Force* was developed in the hope that these standards and goals will provide the necessary impact to reduce crime to manageable levels, so that this Nation's citizens can then rebuild into our society the missing understanding and respect for law.

ARTHUR J. BILEK
Chairman
Task Force on Private Security

Chicago, Ill.
December, 1976

NATIONAL ADVISORY COMMITTEE ON
CRIMINAL JUSTICE STANDARDS AND GOALS

Chairman
Brendan T. Byrne
Governor of New Jersey

Vice Chairman
Charles S. House
Chief Justice, Connecticut
Supreme Court

Arthur J. Bilek
  Vice President
  Pinkerton's Inc.

Allen F. Breed
  Director, Department of
  Youth Authority,
  State of California

Doris A. Davis
  Mayor of Compton, Calif.

Lee Johnson
  Attorney General,
  State of Oregon

John F. Kehoe, Jr.
  Commissioner of
  Public Safety,
  Commonwealth of
  Massachusetts

Cal Ledbetter, Jr.
  Member, House of
  Representatives,
  State of Arkansas

Peter P. Lejins
  Director, Institute of
  Criminal Justice and
  Criminology, University
  of Maryland

Richard C. Wertz
  Executive Director, Commission
  on Law Enforcement and the
  Administration of Justice,
  State of Maryland

Jerry V. Wilson
  Institute for Advanced
  Studies in Justice
  Washington College of Law
  The American University

Pete Wilson
  Mayor of San Diego, Calif.

Counsel to the Committee
Barry H. Evenchick

Executive Coordinator
William T. Archey

Staff Consultant
Lynn Dixon

Administrative Assistant

Elsie E. Johnson

Secretary

Ann H. Kendrall

TASK FORCE
ON PRIVATE SECURITY

Chairman

Arthur J. Bilek
Vice President
Pinkerton's, Inc.

Walter J. Burns
Director, Operational Services
Division, Office of Federal
Protective Service, General
Services Administration

Sheriff Dale G. Carson
Sheriff of Duval County
Jacksonville, Fla.

Sidney H. Cates III
General Manager, GSS, Inc.
New Orleans, La.

Richard F. Cross
Vice President
The Bank of New York

Don R. Derning
Chief of Police
Winnetka, Ill.

Paul L. Douglas
Attorney General
State of Nebraska

R. Keegan Federal, Jr.
Judge of Superior Court
Stone Mountain Judicial Circuit
Decatur, Ga.

Robert C. Flowers
Executive Director
Criminal Justice Division
Office of the Governor
Austin, Tex.

Harold W. Gray, Jr.
Vice President and General
Manager, Pacific Fire
Extinguisher Co.
San Francisco, Calif.

John C. Klotter
Dean, School of Police
Administration
University of Louisville

Ian H. Lennox
Executive Vice President
Citizens Crime Commission of
Philadelphia

Joseph R. Rosetti
Director of Security
IBM Corporation

LEAA Representative

Irving Slott

TASK FORCE STAFF

Executive Director
Clifford W. Van Meter

**Administrative Assistant to
the Executive Director**

Sally Ann Jefferson

Research Associates

John E. Simmons
David L. Viar

Editor

Virginia M. Frankenberger

Clerical Staff

Jennifer M. Sharp
M. Gayle Walker

Staff Interns

David J. Ernat
Brian Hallwas
Jon St. Marie
Susan Stanley

EDITORIAL STAFF

CONSULTANTS AND CONTRIBUTORS

Consultants

Neil L. Austin
M. Cherif Bassiouni
Merril L. Boling
William C. Cunningham
Kenneth G. Fauth
Robert W. Jefferson
Arthur A. Kingsbury
Henry E. Metzner
Richard D. Nordstrom
Richard S. Post
Todd H. Taylor
Paul C. Thistlethwaite
Leon H. Weaver
Sorrel Wildhorn

Contributors

Charles Allen
John S. Ammarell
Frederick Aus
Melvin Bailet
Carl R. Ball
Michael B. Barker
Bernard M. Beerman
Richard Beliles
James W. Boyer
Arthur F. Brandstatter
Theresa Ann Buxton
Christopher A. Cardamone
Richard C. Clement
Russell L. Colling

Dennis M. Crowley, Jr.
T. L. Cumbow
Kenneth Dames
Anthony F. DeBlase
Garis F. Distelhorst
Robert O. Donnelly
William E. Douglas
Ernest Dunham
Paul F. Dunn
L. Chandler Eavenson
Thomas D. Fogarty
Robert E. Frederick
James C. Giese
Joseph Grealy
Frank P. Hayward
Claude E. Hinds
Peter House
Edward W. Hyde
Donald L. Janis
Robert Jensen
Carl W. Kellem
James A. Kelly
Thomas Kindler
Glen D. King
Alexander Laubach
Raymond B. Lauer
Howard L. Mai
Clark Martin
David L. Marvil
Joseph F. McCorry
Douglas Mikus
Frank Morn
Glenn R. Murphy
O. P. Norton

Keith C. Nusbaum
John C. O'Mara
John J. O'Neill
John Poile
Anthony N. Potter, Jr.
John W. Powell
Members of the Private Security Advisory Council
Members of the PSAC Committees on Alarms,
    Armored Cars, Environmental Security, Guards
    and Investigators, Law Enforcement/Private
    Security Relationships
Richard M. Rau
Richard Rifus
Robert R. Rockwell
Edward Rowley
Hugh E. Sabel
George Saunders
George Shollenberger
Lester D. Shubin
George A. Smith, Jr.
Milton L. Snyder
John X. Stefanki
Philip C. Stenning
Richard Stevens
Norman F. Stultz
John L. Swartz
Robert Tuckey
David Van Buren
Steven Van Cleave
Wayne Whatley
James B. White
Francis E. Wilkie
Gordon L. Williams
Herbert C. Yost

Statement to the Reader

This report is directed to the field of private security and its employers and employees; professional associations; educators; consumers; Federal, State, and local government officials; and the public.

To aid in the use of this report, the following chart is supplied listing the fields of interest and the standards and goals most aligned to those fields. Individuals are encouraged to identify their interest area on the chart and to read carefully those standards and goals indicated.

Area of Interest	Standards Relating to Interest
Alarm Systems and Personnel	2.5, 2.6, 4.1, 4.2, 4.3, 4.4, 4.5, 4.6, 4.7, 4.8, 4.9, 4.10, 4.11, 5.4, 6.1, 6.2, 6.3, 6.4, 6.5, 6.6, 7.1, 10.1, 10.2, 10.3, 10.4, 10.5, 10.6, 10.7, 10.8, 11.1, 11.2, 11.3, 11.4, 11.5, 11.6, 11.7, 11.8
Architects/Urban Planners	5.2, 5.3, 5.4, 5.5, 5.7, 5.8, 5.9, 5.10
Armored Car Services and Armed Courier Services	2.5, 2.6, 5.4, 6.1, 6.2, 6.3, 6.4, 6.5, 6.6, 10.1, 10.2, 10.3, 10.4, 10.5, 10.6, 10.7, 10.8, 11.1, 11.2, 11.3, 11.4, 11.5, 11.6, 11.7, 11.8
Citizens	4.10, 4.11, 5.1, 5.2, 5.3, 5.8, 5.9, 6.5, 6.6, 6.7, 6.8, 6.9, 7.1, 7.2, 7.3, 7.4, 9.3, 11.1, 11.4
Consumers	4.3, 4.4, 4.5, 4.7, 4.8, 4.9, 4.10, 5.9, 7.1, 7.2, 7.3, 7.4, 9.3, 10.1, 11.4
Courts	3.3, 7.3, 9.4
Detectives and Investigators	2.5, 2.6, 5.4, 6.1, 6.2, 5.3, 6.4, 6.5, 6.6, 7.1, 10.1, 10.2, 10.3, 10.4, 10.5, 10.6, 10.7, 10.8, 11.1, 11.2, 11.3, 11.4, 11.5, 11.6, 11.7, 11.8
Educators/Trainers	2.1, 2.5, 2.6, 5.5, 5.7, 5.10, 7.1, 8.3, 8.4, 10.3, 11.2, 11.3
Employers	1.1, 1.2, 1.3, 1.4, 1.5, 1.6, 1.7, 1.8, 2.1, 2.3, 2.4, 2.7, 2.8, 3.5, 5.2, 5.3, 6.1, 6.2, 6.3, 6.4, 6.5, 6.7, 6.8, 6.9, 7.1, 11.1, 11.4, 11.8
Federal Government	4.1, 4.6, 4.11, 5.2, 5.3, 5.8, 5.9, 6.1, 7.3, 9.6
Guards and Watchmen	2.5, 2.6, 5.4, 6.1, 6.2, 6.3, 6.4, 6.5, 6.6, 7.1, 10.1, 10.2, 10.3, 10.4, 10.5, 10.6, 10.7, 10.8, 11.1, 11.2, 11.3, 11.4, 11.5, 11.6, 11.7, 11.8
Law Enforcement Agencies	4.2, 4.5, 4.6, 4.7, 4.8, 4.9, 4.10, 4.11, 5.3, 5.4, 5.6, 5.7, 5.9, 6.1, 6.2, 6.3, 6.4, 6.5, 6.6, 6.7, 6.8, 6.9, 7.1, 7.3, 9.3, 11.5
LEAA	4.1, 4.6, 8.1, 8.2, 8.4

Area of Interest	Standards Relating to Interest
Local Government	4.6, 4.7, 4.8, 4.9, 4.10, 4.11, 5.1, 5.2, 5.3, 5.8, 5.9, 6.1, 6.5, 6.6, 6.7, 6.8, 6.9, 7.3, 9.1
Polygraphists	1.3, 3.1, 3.2, 3.3, 3.4, 10.1, 10.2, 10.3, 10.4, 10.5, 10.6, 10.7, 10.8
Professional Organizations	2.2, 3.1, 4.3, 4.6, 6.1, 6.2, 6.3, 7.1, 7.2, 7.3, 7.4
Security Consultants	3.5, 5.4, 5.5, 5.9, 5.10, 7.1
State Government	2.9, 2.10, 4.3, 4.6, 4.11, 5.2, 5.3, 5.8, 5.9, 6.1, 6.5, 6.6, 6.7, 6.8, 6.9, 7.3, 8.1, 9.1, 9.2, 9.3, 9.4, 9.5, 9.6, 10.1, 10.2, 10.3, 10.4, 10.5, 10.6, 10.7, 10.8, 11.1, 11.2, 11.3, 11.4, 11.5, 11.6, 11.7, 11.8

This project was supported by Grant No. 75–TA–99–0015, awarded by the Law Enforcement Assistance Administration, U.S. Department of Justice, under the Omnibus Crime Control and Safe Streets Act of 1968, as amended. Points of view or opinions in this document are those of the Task Force on Private Security and do not necessarily represent the official position of LEAA or the U.S. Department of Justice.

Part 1
Introduction

In the midst of this Nation's high priority struggle to prevent and reduce crime, a massive resource exists for crime prevention and reduction that holds promise of great assistance to the traditional criminal justice agencies. That resource is the private security industry.

Recently, several significant statistics relevant to the private security industry have emerged:

• The U.S. Department of Commerce, in a report released in 1976, estimated that ordinary crimes cost business more than $23.6 billion in 1975.

• *U.S. News and World Report* estimated that $6 billion was expended for private security in 1974.

• Research indicates that more than 1 million persons were employed in 1975 in the private security industry in the United States, as contrasted with 650,000 persons employed in local, State, and Federal law enforcement agencies, based on research conducted by the Law Enforcement Assistance Administration.

From these statistics, it can be reasonably concluded that:

• Crime against property and individuals results in businesses and citizens absorbing vast amounts of losses. No single component, such as the private security industry, law enforcement agencies, or the public, can independently effect the necessary improvements to combat this crime problem. All parties must coordinate their efforts.

• Billions of dollars are annually expended for private security services. If these resources are effectively used, the private security industry can have significant impact on crime prevention and reduction.

• There are more private security personnel than public law enforcement personnel in the United States. Combined, these personnel offer a large resource for the fight against crime.

This report represents the first national effort to set realistic and viable standards and goals designed for the objective of maximizing the ability, competency, and effectiveness of the private security industry for its role, indicated above, in the prevention and reduction of crime. All of the standards and goals contained in this report can assist in reaching this objective, but certain areas that require most improvement are:

• Government licensing and registration can be more effective in improving the private security industry and, thus, the protection of citizens.

• Architects, designers, and builders need to learn more about the use of private security crime prevention techniques in their work.

• Displacement of crime resulting from improved security measures in new developments should be identified through crime-impact statements.

• Private security industry salaries are not reflective of the responsibilities assumed by their personnel and should be adjusted accordingly.

• Training and education for private security personnel are inadequate, and should be upgraded and implemented industrywide.

• The false alarm problem needs to be remedied through improved application of alarm systems and better maintenance and use by consumers.

• The absence of input from private security professionals in local and State government should be remedied through the addition of this group to planning and development of crime-safe communities.

• Proper working relationships of police and private security need to be identified and implemented.

The standards and goals are aimed at increasing the crime prevention benefits of the private security industry, both to its clients and to the public. It is hoped that all segments of the industry, as well as local and State governments and concerned citizens, will evaluate and appropriately assist in implementing those standards and goals applicable to their specific situations and needs.

Structure of the Report

This report is divided into five major parts. Part 1 is an overview of the private security industry and is intended to establish the setting for the standards and goals that follow. The seven sections in this introductory material cover the following topics: (1) definition of the term "private security," and its use and scope within the report; (2) explanation of the background of the Private Security Task Force and its work; (3) discussion of the role of the private security industry in crime prevention and the criminal justice system; (4) definitions and functional descriptions of private security components encompassed by the report; (5) summary of research conducted to date by and for the private security field; (6) discussion of the history and development of the private security industry in the United States; and (7) discussion of unique security problems of specialized areas, such as airports, retail establishments, universities and colleges, and so forth.

The remaining parts of the report address specific topics and contain the standards and goals developed by the Private Security Task Force:

• Part 2 sets forth issues related to private security personnel. It includes chapters and standards and goals for selection, training, and appropriate conduct and ethics of private security personnel.

• Part 3, entitled "Crime Prevention Systems," includes chapters and standards and goals on the use of alarm systems and environmental security in crime prevention efforts.

• Part 4 addresses the relationship of the industry with others and includes chapters and standards and goals relating to law enforcement agencies, consumers of security services, and higher education and research.

• Part 5, entitled "Governmental Regulation," contains chapters and standards and goals concerning private security regulatory boards and licensing and registration of private security businesses and personnel.

Eleven appendixes are also included, containing research findings of studies conducted by the Private Security Task Force and model statutes developed by the Private Security Advisory Council.

Recognizing time restraints and budgetary limitations, the Task Force believed that only those areas that could be carefully studied should be included in the report. The areas covered in the above five parts, therefore represent the most important aspects of the private security industry that could be sufficiently and properly dealt with at this time.

SECTION 1

WHAT IS PRIVATE SECURITY?

Defining Private Security

Private security has many meanings for many people. Colloquially, the term "private security" describes individual and organizational measures and efforts (as distinguished from public law enforcement agency efforts) that provide protection for persons and property. It also describes business enterprises that provide services and products to achieve this protection.

A universally acceptable and explicit definition is difficult to construct because private security is not only identified with the performance of certain functions and activities of a public nature, but also encompasses many activities for the private sector. Development of a realistic working definition of private security is important, however, in order to establish parameters upon which to base use and understanding of the term and its components, as well as to indicate the intent and applicability of the standards and goals that follow. To this end, specific elements of private security are explored and analyzed to evolve the working definition adopted for this report by the Private Security Task Force.

Security. Ensuring the security of lives and property is the motivating force of private security. Richard S. Post and Arthur A. Kingsbury define the general concept of security as follows:

. . . security provides those means, active or passive, which serve to protect and preserve an environment which allows for the conduct of activities within the organization of society without disruption.[1]

This definition of security implies a stable, predictable, and orderly environment in which a person may pursue individual goals without fear of disruption through the use of protective measures. Within this context, security could be ensured by the actions of military forces, law enforcement agencies, fire departments, civil defense units, organized private enterprises, or individual self-help measures.[2] Although military, fire prevention, and civil preparedness activities contribute to a safer environment and many private security firms provide such services and products, these security-oriented elements broaden the concept beyond the purview appropriate to the development of this report's standards and goals. The involvement of law enforcement agencies (public security) in security matters is explored later in this section.

Hazards. Various types of hazards can, and do, occur that severely limit or disrupt security. Leon Weaver perceives security as protection of persons and property from a broad range of these hazards:

. . . including crime; fire and attendant risks, such as explosion; accidents; disasters; espionage; sabotage; subversion; civil disturbance; bombing (both actual and threatened); and, in some systems [of protection], attack by external enemies. Most security and protection systems emphasize certain hazards more than others.[3]

This range of hazards falls into two categories—natural and man-made. Private security, for the purposes of this report, is primarily concerned with man-made hazards—those that do not occur without introduction of the human element.

Among the man-made hazards are accidents, theft and pilferage; fraud; employee disloyalty and subversion; espionage; sabotage; strikes, riots, and demonstrations; and violent crime.[4] Because the purpose of the standards and goals is to promote the greater use and effectiveness of the private security industry in crime prevention, deterrence, and detection, only crime-related hazards are relevant to the working definition.

Protection and Detection Services. Most private security definitions include the concept of provision of protective services to safeguard life, property, and

---

[1] Post, Richard S., and Arthur A. Kingsbury, *Security Administration: An Introduction.* Springfield, Ill.: Charles C. Thomas, 1970, p. 5.

[2] Woodruff, R. S. *Industrial Security Techniques.* Columbus, Ohio: Charles E. Merrill, 1974, p. 2.

[3] Weaver, Leon. "Security and Protection Systems," *Encyclopedia Britannica.* Encyclopedia Britannica, Inc., 1975, vol. 16, pp. 453–455.

[4] Paine, D. *Basic Principles of Industrial Security.* Madison, Wis.: Oak Security Publications, 1972, p. 36.

interests against crime. Indeed, most persons perceive of private security, in this manner. Protection is delivered by devices, defensive means, and preventive activities—alarms, armored cars, guards, and so forth. However, protection is not the only service provided. Private security also includes detection services—the detecting of criminal or wrongful acts.[5] Thus, both protective and detective services are important elements of private security.

Specific Clientele. Private security can be further identified by its clients, which are specifically determined prior to receipt of protective or detective services. These specific clients may be businesses or individuals who obtain private security services (personnel or products) for the protection of lives and property in exchange for a fee.

For-Profit Orientation. One basic element of private security is the manner in which the crime-prevention security services rendered and security products supplied are funded: through payments by clients to organizations and individuals that operate for profit. Unlike other security-oriented services (e.g., law enforcement agencies, military forces, civil defense units), private security services are paid for, in most cases, by privately held dollars. The profit nature of private security and the source of those profits (clients) are basic elements of private security.

Delivery Systems. Security services are provided by private security through two distinct delivery systems—proprietary and contractual. Contractual security involves the provision of security services by a private organization on a contractual basis for the protection of assets and personnel belonging to a specific client. Proprietary security is defined as the method instituted, equipment owned, and personnel employed by a private entity for the exclusive protection of its assets and personnel. Both proprietary and contractual delivery systems are important elements of private security, as defined by this report.

Industry Diversity. Security services in the private security industry are provided by proprietary and contractual systems through a variety of sources for a wide range of clients. Figure 1 illustrates the industry components (both individuals and business and organizational entities) that provide the various security services (e.g., guards, investigators, armored cars) and products (e.g., alarms systems, intrusion detection devices) for specific, but varied, clients (e.g., individuals, financial establishments, governmental agencies). The private security industry encompasses not only proprietary and contractual se-

curity services, but also the manufacture, distribution, and sale of security products.

The RAND Corporation offered the following definition of private security:

The terms private police and private security forces and security personnel are used generically in this report to include all types of private organizations and individuals providing all types of security-related services, including investigation, guard, patrol, lie detection, alarm, and armored transportation.[6]

The RAND definition is inadequate for this report because it extends private security to essentially all police and security functions being performed by entities and individuals other than law enforcement agencies. Although their work is similar or identical to that of private security officers, certain groups of quasi-public police, such as housing authorities, park and recreation police, and so forth, are not included in the standards and goals unless they are paid by private funds. (This issue of quasi-public police, and other such exclusionary issues related to the scope of the Task Force standards and goals is discussed more extensively later in this section.) Further, the RAND definition omits key elements: The client relationship and the profit nature of private security.

For the purposes of this report, the Private Security Task Force formulated the following composite working definition of private security, based on various elements:

> **Private security includes those self-employed individuals and privately funded business entities and organizations providing security-related services to specific clientele for a fee, for the individual or entity that retains or employs them, or for themselves, in order to protect their persons, private property, or interests from varied hazards.**

The Task Force believed that this definition of private security best describes the missions and roles of private security as the term applies to the standards and goals.

Public and Private Security

The Post/Kinsbury and Weaver definitions of security indicated that both public and private sectors—government agencies, private organizations, and individuals—supply protective, deterrent, and detective services. However, public and private security

[5] Lord Hayter, "Introduction—Security and Society," *Security Attitudes and Techniques for Management.* London: Hutchinson and Company, 1968, p. XVII.

[6] Kakalik, J. S., and Sorrel Wildhorn. *Private Police in the United States: Findings and Recommendations.* R–869/DOJ. Washington, D.C.: U.S. Government Printing Office, 1972, vol. I, p. 3.

Figure 1. Private Security Service Overview

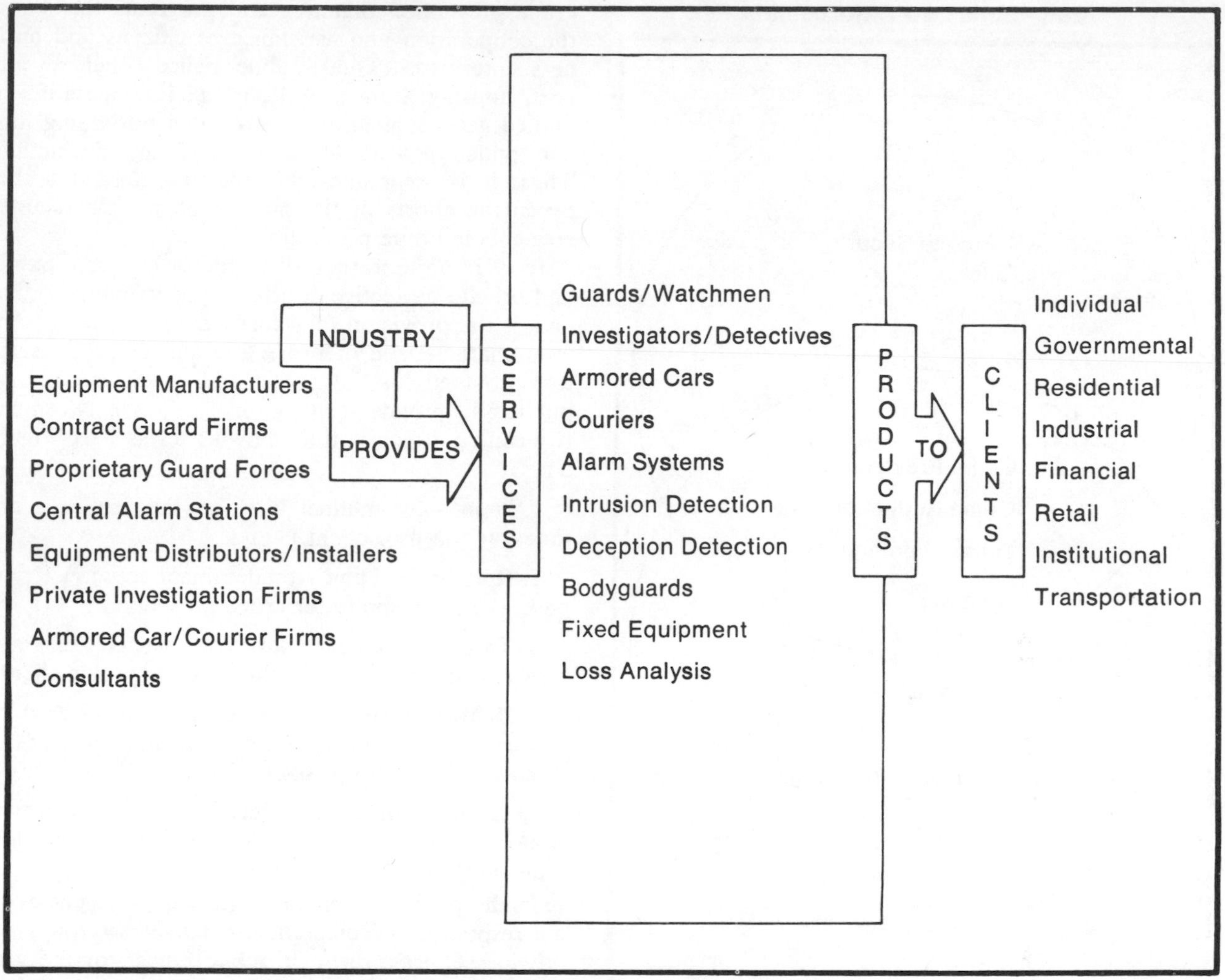

INDUSTRY	PROVIDES	SERVICES		PRODUCTS	TO	CLIENTS
Equipment Manufacturers		Guards/Watchmen				Individual
Contract Guard Firms		Investigators/Detectives				Governmental
Proprietary Guard Forces		Armored Cars				Residential
Central Alarm Stations		Couriers				Industrial
Equipment Distributors/Installers		Alarm Systems				Financial
Private Investigation Firms		Intrusion Detection				Retail
Armored Car/Courier Firms		Deception Detection				Institutional
Consultants		Bodyguards				Transportation
		Fixed Equipment				
		Loss Analysis				

differ in three basic areas: (1) the employer—publicly funded agencies and profit-oriented businesses and individuals, (2) the degree of statutory power possessed—great or limited police powers, and (3) the specific functions performed.[7] An exploration of such differences between public and private security offer further clarification of what is private security.

The terms public and private security can be distinguished primarily by the interests served—public or private. Private security basically is concerned with loss reduction and the prevention, deterrence, and detection of crime against private property—private interest concerns. On the other hand, public security (or public law enforcement agencies) mainly concentrate on the prevention and detection of serious crime, the investigation of criminal activities, traffic safety, and the apprehension of criminals—

public interest concerns.[8] (Of course, law enforcement agencies are often called upon to perform a wide variety of roles not necessarily limited to the previous functions.) Whether the provision of security serves primarily private or public interest concerns is a key distinction between the two.

Many security concerns and functions—crime prevention and reduction and order maintenance—are common to both the public and private sectors (see Figure 2), but the degree of emphasis placed on these common concerns and functions provides another distinguishing characteristic between the two. Private security focuses on the prevention and reduction of crime affecting private property. Public law enforcement primarily is concerned with order maintenance and criminal apprehension and enforces laws within a constitutionally and statutorily man-

[7] Ursic, H. S., and L. E. Pagano, *Security Management Systems.* Springfield, Ill.: Charles C. Thomas, 1974, p. 90.

[8] "A Design for Action by State and Local Government on Private Security, Private Security and the Public Interest." Berkeley, Calif.: Institute for Local Self Government, p. 85.

Figure 2. Common Objectives of Private Security and Public Law Enforcement

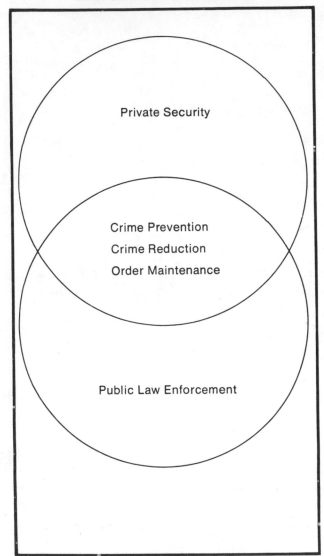

Private Security

Crime Prevention
Crime Reduction
Order Maintenance

Public Law Enforcement

dated criminal justice system. Although, in theory, the goal of public law enforcement agencies is to prevent and reduce crime through efforts tied to the criminal justice system, in practice, most of their resources are spent for response to, rather than prevention of, crime. (This issue, as well as the respective roles of the public law enforcement and private security sectors, is explored in greater depth in Section 3 of this introduction.)

Although the provision of protective services to the public or private sectors is a basic difference between public and private security, these sectors are often served by both security forces. Private security firms and individuals provide contractual security for governmental agencies, facilities, and installations—elements of the public sector. Similarly, law enforcement agencies, although primarily functioning in the

public sector, have increasingly become involved in crime prevention planning and programs that enlist the cooperation and assistance of citizens and business enterprises. Quasi-public police—such as airport, housing, transit, and park police, operating in limited geographical areas and often possessing limited police powers—further cloud the distinction. Thus, it is sometimes difficult to differentiate between the efforts of the public and private security elements in crime prevention.

It is important that distinctions between public and private protective efforts be understood. To that end, if the provision of security is viewed as a common characteristic of protection and detection services provided for the public and private sectors by public and private security, distinctions between the two can be drawn at the following levels (See Figure 3):

1. **Input**—the manner in which the service is initiated. (Citizen or client.)

2. **Role or Function**—predominant activity or purpose. (Crime response or crime prevention.)

3. **Targets**—the beneficiaries or objectives to which service is directed. (General public or specific client.)

4. **Delivery System**—the mechanism through which services are provided. (Government agencies or profit-oriented enterprises.)

5. **Output**—the end product of services performed. (Law enforcement/criminal apprehension or loss reduction/assets protection.)

In the public sector, law enforcement agencies do not respond to specific clients or interest groups but provide services, through public funds, for the general public. (However, public law enforcement does respond on an individual basis when delivering its services.) Additionally, although the goal of public law enforcement agencies is the protection of life and property, and much of their effort is spent on patrol activities, most of their output is directed toward enforcement of laws and the apprehension of law violators.

Private security services and products are provided by private, for-profit organizations for specific clients to effect crime prevention and reduction for selected targets (e.g., stockroom, loading platform, laboratory) and thereby reduce economic losses.

Scope of Private Security Services and Products

Private security provides a broad range of services to a clientele composed of individuals, institutions, businesses, and some governmental agencies. A number of authors described these services in terms of

Figure 3. Security Continuum

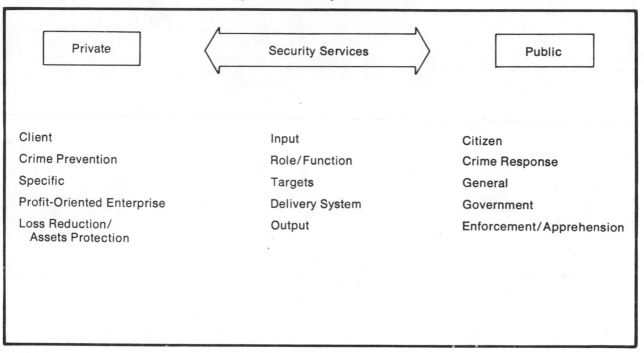

Private	Security Services	Public

Client	Input	Citizen
Crime Prevention	Role/Function	Crime Response
Specific	Targets	General
Profit-Oriented Enterprise	Delivery System	Government
Loss Reduction/ Assets Protection	Output	Enforcement/Apprehension

three functional areas: (1) information security, (2) personnel security, and (3) physical security.[9] Services performed in these functional areas include gathering information, maintaining order, and protecting persons and property through detection and prevention of crime.[10]

Information security includes those measures required to protect the confidentiality of information owned or held, such as:

1. Grading information according to its sensitivity and affording protection accordingly;
2. Providing physical protection;
3. Educating employees as to individual responsibilities;
4. Screening of employees and visitors; and
5. Control of access and personnel identification.[11]

Personnel security covers these measures necessary to protect the employees of a facility from the effects of:

1. Hostile propaganda and subversion;
2. Disloyalty;
3. Fires and other disasters;
4. Strikes, riots, and other disturbances; and
5. Injury and harassment.[12]

Physical security encompasses those measures necessary to protect the facility against the effects of unauthorized access, theft, fire, sabotage, loss, or other intentional crime or damage. Some of these measures include:

1. Prevention of unauthorized access by means of security officers, barriers, fences, lighting, and alarms;
2. Control of authorized entry by personnel identification;
3. Prevention of employee crime and pilferage;
4. Fire prevention and control;
5. Prevention of accidents;
6. Implementation of traffic control and parking regulations;
7. Implementation of security surveys;
8. Control of locks, keys, and safes;
9. Control of materials;
10. Procedures of control; and
11. Emergency measures.[13]

When an individual or business entity perceives a security need, a number of protective choices or alternatives are available. Figure 4 illustrates these

[9] Post and Kingsbury, *op. cit.*, p. 6.
[10] Ursic and Pagano, *op. cit.*, p. 95.
[11] Paine, *op. cit.*, p. 24.

[12] *Ibid.*, p. 25.
[13] *Ibid.*

Figure 4. Protective Services Alternatives

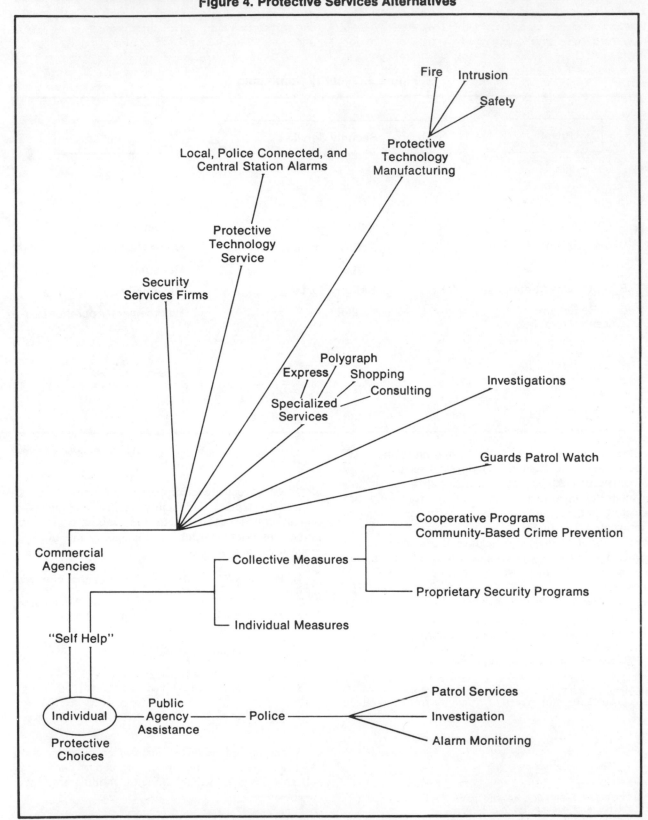

Source: Post, Richard S., from a paper presented to Task Force, April, 1975.

alternatives and the dimensions of services resulting from selection of an alternative.[14] Traditionally, one may turn to a public law enforcement agency for assistance; these agencies can provide patrol services, investigative services, and, in some communities, alarm monitoring. However, because of the magnitude of the crime problem and the mandate to provide protection to the public, it is increasingly difficult for law enforcement agencies to respond to every perceived security need.

In light of the limited availability of public assistance for perceived security needs, individuals and businesses engage in self-help measures. On occasion, these measures are encouraged by or incorporated with public law enforcement agencies. Examples of self-help measures would be an individual making his home more burglar resistant or joining together with neighbors to establish a cooperative community protective program. Or an individual may turn to commercial private security firms to meet perceived security needs.

The same self-help alternatives are exercised by business enterprises. A business may attempt to meet its security needs internally by creating a proprietary or inhouse security force or contract with a specialized firm to provide security services for a fee. A brief examination of the number of methods and devices available to an individual or business to meet security needs illustrates the diversity and complexity of private security.

Guard Services. One of the more traditional methods of providing security services is through the use of uniformed guards or watchmen. They are employed at retail stores, industrial plants, hospitals, airports, banks, railroads, warehouses, government facilities, educational institutions, apartment complexes, clubs, residential areas, special event sites and numerous other locations. The function of guards and watchmen is to protect persons or property during specified times or around-the-clock from damage, injury, loss, or other criminal acts. Their duties often include patrol and inspection, theft prevention and detection, traffic control, access control, and personal and physical safety.

Electrical Device Services. Another method for providing security services is through electrical and electronic devices. The use of this equipment has expanded rapidly over the last 15 years, and it is estimated that their increased use will ultimately curtail the growth rate of guard, armored car, and courier services.[15] One form of electrical security is central station alarm companies, which also provide alarm response and patrol and inspection services. One study estimates that there are aproximately 300 central alarm stations in the country, as well as nearly 4,000 local or regional installers of alarms.[16] The National Burglar and Fire Alarm Association estimates the number of central stations listed by Underwriters' Laboratories at 330, modified central stations at 700, and nearly 4,000 installation firms of local and/or police connected alarms.[17]

There are many other types of electronic security devices. For example, 1974 industry revenues for sales and service of access-control equipment have been estimated at $57 million.[18] The range of electronic security devices available is extensive:

1. Fire, smoke, water, heat and refrigeration sensors;
2. Outdoor perimeter control devices;
3. Motion-detection devices;
4. Proprietary alarms;
5. Safe- and vault-protection systems;
6. Vehicle tracking;
7. Closed-circuit television monitoring and surveillance;
8. Comprehensive security systems integrating many of the above devices as components; and
9. Access control systems.

Investigative Services. Many agencies and individuals provide criminal, civil, and general investigative services to business and management, including corporations, legal and financial firms, and private individuals. Investigative services may include preemployment investigation, surveillance, internal theft problems, undercover investigations, criminal investigations, polygraph examinations, and personal and property protection.

Armored Car and Courier Services. The security service provided by armored cars and couriers is distinguished from that provided by guards and watchmen in that armored cars usually use armed personnel, with the carrier assigned liability for valuables being transported from one location to another or while in storage. Armed couriers also transport valuables and are similarly liable for shipments. One study estimated 1975 revenues for these services at $385 million.[19] Another study estimated revenues for armored car services at $320 million in 1974.[20]

Ancillary Services. A number of ancillary services also are provided by security companies, including crowd control, canine patrol, and bodyguard and

---

[14] Post, Richard S. "Application of Functional Job Analysis to the Development of Curriculum Guidelines for the Protective Services Field." Unpublished Ph.D. dissertation, University of Wisconsin, 1974.

[15] Little, Arthur D., *Outlook for the U.S. Safety, Fire Protection and Security Business.* Cambridge, Mass.: ADLI, Jan. 1973, p. 23.

[16] Frost and Sullivan, Inc. *The Industrial and Commercial Security Market.* New York, Mar. 1975, p. 50.

[17] Distelhorst, Garis, Executive Director, National Burglar and Fire Alarm Association, Personal interview, Jan. 1976.

[18] Frost and Sullivan, Inc., *op. cit.,* p. 12.

[19] Little, Arthur D., Inc., *op. cit.,* p. 24.

[20] Nossov, *op. cit.,* p. 4.

escort services. The use of bodyguards for protection of corporate executives and their families, dignitaries, and VIP's is estimated to have grown between 10 and 20 percent in the last few years due to the increase in corporate extortion, executive kidnappings, and hostage situations.[21] The president of a contract security firm estimated the number of bodyguards nationally employed at 20,000, and this number is expected to increase to 70,000 by the end of the decade.[22] The FBI reports that in the first half of 1975 there were 124 hostage situations, eight resulting in deaths.

Private security firms also provide employees for positions that incorporate either implicit or explicit private security functions, e.g., guides, attendants, receptionists, hostesses, ushers, doormen, ticket takers, and so forth.

Issues in Defining Private Security

In order to formulate valid standards and goals for private security, it was necessary to develop an accurate and comprehensive definition of private security and to determine the appropriate parameters within which the standards and goals could be reasonably developed. As might be expected, in attempting to satisfy these requirements, a number of opposing viewpoints surfaced. It is necessary to examine these arguments or issues in order to reach satisfactory judgments regarding their relevancy to the inclusion or exclusion of certain segments of private security and the need for standards and goals.

One issue involves identifying a clear distinction between public and private security. As stated earlier, the Private Security Task Force differentiates between public and private security according to the source of funding—public and private. However, various professionals in the field consider the key distinction between public and private security to be whether or not personnel have police powers, i.e., the power of arrest. In many instances, publicly funded personnel possessing full police powers operate independently of public law enforcement agencies and perform security functions in limited areas, such as mass transportation, public housing, park districts, school districts, some colleges and universities, railroad police, port authorities, and toll roads. Many of these personnel use the title "police" and have statutory power of arrest independent of any local, State, or other law enforcement agencies. These individuals clearly are not sworn public law enforcement officers of city, county, State, or Federal law

enforcement agencies. Nevertheless, they clearly are sworn police officers with specific jurisdictional limitations on their powers of arrest, determined in most cases by statute or ordinance. Even though these personnel receive public funds, it is recognized that they perform similar and often identical services to those of private security personnel. Accordingly, these special police forces properly belong in special-function police categories.

Although not included within the scope of the standards and goals for the private security industry, special-function police personnel should make every effort to meet or exceed these standards and goals. In particular, the selection and training standards and the conduct and ethics standards should be adopted and met. These forces also should carefully review the chapter related to law enforcement agencies. In most cases, special-function police have been excluded from licensing and registration because the appropriate local, county, or State government already has the statutory authority to adopt the proper standards and goals relating to these personnel and activities. Similarly, security at government facilities provided by government employees is excluded. Not excluded is security at government facilities provided by contractual guard firms.

Arguments have been made for the exclusion of other private security personnel who have special police commissions or peace officer status. Private security personnel often derive their authority to carry firearms through designations such as special deputy sheriff, special police officer, and auxiliary police officer. Unlike the special-function police and special police forces, however, these personnel are funded by private sources. Furthermore, very little direct control is exercised over them by the public law enforcement agency granting the special powers. The police status is often confined to a very narrow spatial area, usually the place of assignment. Often the status is simply a mechanism to afford legal protection to the guard for apprehension and detention actions taken by private security personnel until law enforcement officials take formal custody of suspects.

Private security personnel with special police powers would be included in the scope of the standards and goals, depending upon the extent to which they meet the following criteria:

1. The personnel are primarily employees of a for-profit organization or contract guard firm, as distinguished from a nonprofit or governmental agency;

2. The personnel receive their salaries from the private sector; and

3. The personnel perform primarily private security (client-oriented) as opposed to public law enforcement (citizen-oriented) functions.

[21] Joseph, Raymond A. "Bodyguard Business Booms as Kidnapping and Crime Rates Rise," *The Wall Street Journal*, Nov. 20, 1975, p. 1.
[22] *Ibid.*

In a 1975 survey of licensed security personnel in New Orleans and St. Louis (Appendix 2), both cities granted police powers to all the licensed security personnel. In New Orleans, private security personnel are referred to as "special officers," and each special officer is granted limited police powers that extend to the actual premises of the company or beat assigned. In St. Louis, private security personnel are licensed as "watchmen" and, once licensed by the Board of Police Commissioners, are duly constituted police officers who may exercise police powers in an assigned, specified area. If the argument that all security personnel with police powers be excluded from these standards and goals was accepted, virtually all private security personnel in these two major American cities would be excluded—some 7,000 plus.

Another important issue questions whether the standards and goals should be equally applicable to contractual and proprietary security systems. Some private security community spokesmen advocate a differentiation between contractual and proprietary security personnel in the standards and goals. There is a differentiation made between contractual and proprietary delivery systems in some of the standards and goals, as appropriate, but generally proprietary private security personnel are treated exactly as are contractual security personnel.

Both contractual and proprietary private security personnel have a significant impact on crime prevention and are interrelated with the criminal justice system. For example, the rights of a citizen must be protected upon apprehension or arrest by private security personnel, just as when the arrest is made by a public law enforcement officer. Whether the private security personnel arresting the citizen are contractual or proprietary is not the issue; the major concern is that the citizen and his rights be treated according to the law.

Private security activities conducted within the generally recognized guidelines for the protection of individual rights best serve public interests. As the *RAND Report* (Vol. 1) pointed out, "there would be significant advantages in applying to private security work the same standards of conduct developed in constitutional decisions for arrest, detention, search, and interrogation by public police." [24] As in other areas, it is believed that no distinction should be made between whose conduct—contract or proprietary personnel—affects other's individual rights. Also, when discussing individual rights, no distinction should be made between ordinary citizens and employees. Private security personnel must recognize that both contractual and proprietary security employees, as well as other employees of organizations, retain their rights guaranteed by the Constitution and Bill of Rights.

The private security sector is a rapidly expanding force in our society. A clear understanding of its constituency and purpose must be developed if the standards and goals are to have an impact on the greater effectiveness of the private industry in crime prevention and reduction. Although some may disagree with certain aspects of the basic definition of private security presented, it is an accurate representation of the industry and vital to the development of meaningful response to the private security standards and goals. More specific definitions and functional descriptions of the major types of security-related services and the major clients or users of private security follow in sections 4 and 7 of this introduction.

---

[23] Kakalik and Wildhorn, *op. cit.,* p. 98.

SECTION 2

DEVELOPMENT OF STANDARDS AND GOALS FOR PRIVATE SECURITY

The Need for Standards and Goals

Residents of America's largest cities listed crime as the number one problem in their community in a nationwide poll conducted during the summer of 1975.[1] Crime has infiltrated every part of the Nation's structure—its cities and neighborhoods, its transportation and recreational areas, its schools and libraries, and its homes and commercial establishments. It has been estimated that before the end of 1976 one of every four Americans will be victimized by a crime.

Faced with alarming rises in crime and the constant fear of crime, Americans have reached out for protection beyond that which can be provided by the Nation's overcommitted, and often understaffed, public law enforcement agencies. As a result, the number of private security personnel now exceeds that of public law enforcement and the number of companies doing business in security products and services has increased dramatically, along with the number of businesses employing proprietary security forces. Recent statistics reveal that Americans pay more for private security services than Federal, State, and local governments pay for the criminal justice system.[2]

This significant growth has not been accompanied by a growth in measures devoted to evaluating and upgrading the private security industry in relation to its efficiency and effectiveness. The security industry is plagued by a variety of potential and actual problems, including low wages, poorly qualified and untrained personnel, abuse of authority, lack of regulation, and excessive false alarms, to name a few. Yet, little attention has been focused on providing effective remedies for these problems. In fact, there is an alarming paucity of research available for the purpose of studying and improving the operations of this vast industry.

Undoubtedly, the private security industry provides an important and necessary service in this country. Its rapid growth and increased revenues attest to its prominence as a vital force against crime. Although its benefits are directed primarily toward the private sector, it also provides certain public benefits and its potential for increased contributions to national crime prevention and reduction is apparent. Therefore, in the interest of the clients the private security industry serves, as well as the general public, uniform standards and goals to increase its efficiency and effectiveness as a crime-preventive force are essential.

The security industry itself has indicated a strong desire to establish standards to upgrade its operations. For example, in a 1975 survey of the membership of the American Society for Industrial Security, 87 percent of the respondents expressed a need for the development of a "set of standards."[3]

One security consultant recently described the problems of the industry as a "vicious circle"[4] (see Figure 5). Within this vicious circle, factors, such as low salaries, marginal personnel, lack of promotional opportunities, high turnovers, and little or no training, lead to one another and result in ineffective performance. To attract and keep highly qualified personnel, salaries must be commensurate with experience, training, education, and job responsibilities. However, competition by private security companies tends to keep wages low because of the bidding process. This, in effect, creates a vicious circle where higher caliber personnel cannot be provided unless there are higher wages, but the consumer has been reluctant to foot the bill. However, competition can still exist with a higher level of wages. In fact, a 1975 study of consumers of private security services in the Greater Philadelphia area revealed that 72 percent of the respondents (industrial, commercial, and financial businesses) indicated their willingness to expend additional funds for security if the quali-

---

[1] *Gallup Opinion Index.* Princeton, N.J., June 27–30, 1975.
[2] McKay, John. "A Challenge for the Crime Prevention Officer," commencement speech delivered to the 21st graduating class of the National Crime Prevention Institute, Louisville, Ky., 1975.

[3] Private Security Task Force, "American Society for Industrial Security Survey Results." See Appendix 1 to this report.
[4] Potter, Anthony. An address to the First Annual Conference on Private Security, University of Maryland, College Park, Md., December 1975.

Figure 5. Private Security Vicious Circle

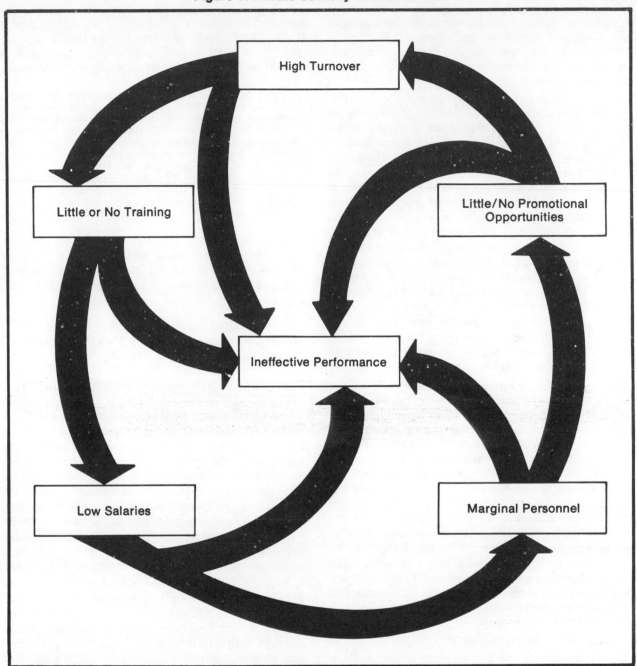

ficiations of personnel and/or quality of security service were improved.[5] The establishment of standards and goals is an important step toward improving quality and effectiveness in the private security industry, thus eliminating the vicious circle.

---

[5] Private Security Task Force, Survey of Consumers of Private Security Services in the Greater Philadelphia Area. See Appendix 3 to this report.

Law Enforcement Assistance Administration Role

Since 1968, the Law Enforcement Assistance Administration (LEAA), U.S. Department of Justice, has sponsored programs at all levels of government in its national commitment to reduce crime, protect society, and increase public safety. In 1970, LEAA recognized the impact of private security services upon crime prevention and funded a major study to describe the nature and extent of the industry.[6] The results of this study, published in 1972 by the RAND Corporation, included recommended policy and statutory guidelines for improving future operations and regulations.

LEAA was prompted in 1972 to establish a Private Security Advisory Council (PSAC), partly as a result of the RAND Corporation study and partly as a result of the demands of the alarm industry concern over the issue created by Federal funding of an alarm system in Cedar Rapids, Iowa, and the eventual disposition of this system to the municipal government. PSAC was formed to study and advise LEAA regarding various security issues, with the objective of enabling LEAA to better use and coordinate its resources in a comprehensive national effort to reduce crime. PSAC membership includes private security executives, criminal justice administrators, business leaders, and concerned citizens, and it has specific committees on (1) alarms, (2) environmental security, (3) guards and investigators, (4) law enforcement-private security relationships, (5) terroristic acts, and (6) armored car services (appointed in May 1976).

Acting on the recommendation of PSAC, LEAA Administrator Richard W. Velde publicly announced his intention of including the private security industry as a major part of the LEAA Phase II standards and goals effort at the December 1974 meeting of PSAC in Williamsburg, Va. Thus, in 1975 when LEAA created the second National Advisory Committee on Criminal Justice Standards and Goals, to provide direction and milestones for achievement of comprehensive improvement in the criminal justice system's capability to control crime, the Private Security Task Force was formed to develop private security standards and goals. The relationship between PSAC and the Task Force was made clear by selection of a common chairman and the dual membership by several persons on both PSAC and the Task Force.

Through the formation of PSAC and the subsequent inclusion of private security in the national standards and goals program, LEAA has acknowledged the belief that the crime prevention activities of the private security industry contribute substantially to this country's efforts to provide a safer environment for all Americans and that private security is a vitally important resource in crime prevention and control. As stated by LEAA Administrator Velde, the problem of crime in America is so large and so complex that the public and private sectors should be united in a partnership to reduce crime:

It is clear that the police, government, or its agencies cannot alone cope with the volume of crime in a way that is satisfactory to all. As law enforcement officials, we must recognize the multiplicity of factors that go into the process of preventing and controlling crime and delinquency and enlist—not turn away or discourage—the support of every public agency, social institution, private group and citizen to fight crime. In short, the criminal justice system must become partners with others. One of the areas in which this partnership must be formed and fostered is the private security community.[7]

LEAA's involvement with the private security community will not cease with this report. Through the continuing work of PSAC, further efforts will be undertaken to increase the effectiveness of the security industry in national crime prevention.

Issues Addressed Prior to Standards and Goals Development

The initial work of the Private Security Task Force focused on the resolution of certain important issues that would influence the structure of the report and the development of appropriate standards and goals. The first issue addressed was whether the emphasis of the report should be directed toward equipment or personnel. It became apparent that, in spite of great advances in technical devices, the industry was still largely personnel oriented. Furthermore, its most frequently cited problems and abuses were related to personnel. Therefore, the Task Force determined that the major thrust of the standards and goals development should be personnel oriented.

It was necessary to determine if there was a logical starting point for improvement of private security personnel and performance. Several alternatives were presented—improve and increase training, reduce the high turnover rate, remove marginal personnel, and increase salaries. Careful study of the question resulted in a determination that there was no single starting point for upgrading this complex industry, especially because many of its problems are self-perpetuating (see Figure 1). Therefore, the Task Force believed that the standards and goals should address all important problem areas.

Another issue that received serious consideration

[6] Kakalik, J. S., and Sorrel Wildhorn, *Private Police in the United States: Findings and Recommendations,* Vol. I, R–869/DOJ; *The Private Police Industry: Its Nature and Extent,* Vol. II, R–870/DOJ; *Current Regulation of Private Police: Regulatory Agency Experience and Views,* Vol. III, R–871/DOJ; *The Law and Private Police,* Vol. IV, R–872/DOJ; *Special-Purpose Public Police,* Vol. V, R–873/DOJ. Washington, D.C.: Government Printing Office, 1972.

[7] Velde, Richard W. Address by the Administrator of the Law Enforcement Assistance Administration at the annual meeting of the International Association of Chiefs of Police, Denver, Colo., Sept. 16, 1975.

was the potential economic impact of standards and goals on all sectors. Although a portion of the Nation's security business is dominated, in terms of market share, by a number of large national firms, there are thousands of small contract guard, investigative, alarm installation, response, and security equipment firms who handle an almost equal share of America's security business. Some of these smaller firms have expressed the opinion that to establish standards and goals across the board would merely enhance the market position of the larger firms, because only the larger firms have the extensive resources needed to implement the standards. In considering this issue, the Task Force determined that only those standards and goals that would not eliminate competent, small security businesses or make it impossible for small businesses to establish proprietary security forces would be adopted. In this regard, the Task Force was very careful to limit itself to requirements that are in the public interest and to consider at all times the value of maintaining competition in the private security industry. However, it was equally concerned with users' interests and the belief that citizens and clients must be afforded the same high quality of protection, whether delivered by large or small security firms.

A third issue facing the Task Force in its development of standards and goals involved armed versus unarmed personnel. Arguments were presented advocating the inclusion of only those private security personnel who are armed in its standards and goals. The Task Force rejected these arguments, however, because the value or effectiveness of private security personnel cannot be measured only in terms of the weapons they do or do not carry. The important issue is the nature of the private security functions that may or may not require the use or carrying of a firearm. Clearly, the nature of any private security activity is situation-specific—the activity tailored to specified needs. It is the optimum matching of the private security needs with appropriately selected personnel that will result in the highest quality protection. Thus, the dual objectives of the Task Force in resolving this issue were:

1. To provide guidelines pertaining to the nature of security functions, and

2. To describe reasonable criteria for the screening and hiring of armed versus unarmed personnel.

Finally, it was suggested to the Task Force that its study and report be directed solely at contract security—those businesses that provide security services to others for a fee. Remembering that the purpose of the report was to establish standards and goals that would improve the private security industry's role in crime reduction and prevention, the Task Force saw no valid reason for eliminating any

particular segment. Proprietary security personnel—employees hired by a business to specifically protect the employer's assets—perform the same functions as personnel who are hired by a contract security business. Although the differences between these two segments have been debated for years, the Task Force believes that there is more commonality than difference. This commonality was clearly visible in responses to the Task Force survey of the American Society for Industrial Security (Appendix 1). Except for wages, there were no significant statistical differences between the responses of people in contract security and those in proprietary security. Private security professionals basically have the same attitudes, opinions, and goals on important issues affecting the provision of security functions. Therefore, the Task Force decided to address itself in standards and goals development to all segments of the industry—both contractual and proprietary.

In addressing the basic issues presented above, the Task Force was cognizant of the valuable role that the private security industry is playing in the continuing fight against crime. It was also aware that the role of the Task Force was to make recommendations to facilitate the development of the industry's full potential to assist in reducing crime in the United States.

Procedure in Development of Standards and Goals

The following profile of procedures used by the Private Security Task Force to develop standards and goals indicates the thoroughness and comprehensiveness of the development process.

Initially, staff research was conducted to extract the suggestions and recommendations of professional associations, the Private Security Advisory Council, subcommittees of the Private Security Advisory Council, literature and publications concerning the field, and other research reports and studies. The staff summarized this material in the form of position papers. These position papers were presented for review to Task Force members at the July 1975 meeting.

After reviewing the staff's work, members of the Task Force removed, modified, or added material and expressed their views concerning the parameters of the report. Based on this input, the staff prepared a working outline of the Task Force Report, dated August 1, 1975. This report was reviewed by various subcommittees of the Task Force.

During August 1975, at meetings held in Louisville, Ky., Atlanta, Ga., and Philadelphia, Pa., further modifications were made of the working outline and an updated outline was prepared, dated September 15, 1975. This draft outline was distributed to approximately 150 leading private security practitioners throughout the United States, as well as to various professional security and law enforcement associations. Many of the recipients reproduced the material and sent it to colleagues and/or fellow members, thus assuring wide dissemination. One national publication, "Protection of Assets Manual," printed the outline in its entirety.

A large number of individuals throughout the private security industry made numerous suggestions to the Task Force, including approximately 50 persons sending detailed formally written comments to the staff. These comments were reviewed by the staff and members of the Task Force and proved very beneficial in the development of the final standards and goals. The staff of the Task Force also attended meetings of the Private Security Advisory Council and its various subcommittees, visited contract security operations, as well as companies employing proprietary security, and met with or had telephone contact with a cross section of security industry persons and people working in regulatory agencies. Many of the persons contacted or who contributed input are listed as consultants or contributors at the back of this report. Numerous other individuals provided specific input, on a one-to-one basis, through the staff and members of the Task Force.

Task Force meetings were held in April 1975 in Washington, D.C.; July and October 1975 in Chicago, Ill.; January 1976 in New Orleans, La.; April 1976 in San Francisco, Calif.; and finally in July 1976 in Atlanta, Ga. (The meetings were held at various locations to enable interested persons in different geographic areas to attend.) At these meetings, speakers representing broad constituencies were invited to appear before the Task Force and present their positions and, as appropriate, that of their association on matters related to the standards and goals effort. Their input was carefully reviewed by the Task Force and provided invaluable assistance in the development of the standards and goals.

The primary purpose for the six Task Force meetings, however, was to develop and vote on the standards and to review and discuss the standard commentaries. Recognizing the importance of the standards and goals, it was determined at the first meeting that a simple majority vote should not be sufficient for approval of a standard or goal; it was decided that no standard or goal statement could be approved unless it received at least 9 to 14 votes. After each standard and goal was approved, it was forwarded to the National Advisory Committee on Criminal Justice Standards and Goals (NACCJSG). Unless specifically noted within the report, the NACCJSG reviewed and approved each standard and goal.

Notices of all meetings of the Private Security

Task Force and the NACCJSG were printed in the *Federal Register* at least 15 days in advance of each meeting. All meetings were open to the public, and the Task Force received valuable input from numerous non-Task Force persons who attended the meetings. It was recognized that only through an open dialog, with as wide a participation as practical, could realistic and viable standards and goals be developed. To the best of its ability, the Task Force adhered to that principle.

Utilization of the Report

The Private Security Task Force report is designed as a reference tool and guiding document for use primarily by three major groups: (1) State and local criminal justice officials, (2) members of the private security community, and (3) consumers of private security services and citizens. It is intended to serve as a focal point for the greater interaction of the private security community with the criminal justice system and its component agencies.

State and local criminal justice officials should examine the standards and goals in order to adapt them to their local situations, for the increased coordination of private security services in crime prevention. The private security industry should find the standards and goals useful as a means of evaluating the industry's position and role in the criminal justice system and also as a means for improving the quality of its services and upgrading its image. Citizens and consumers of security services should read this report for a better understanding of the services and products available from the private sector, thus enabling them to explore new options in their individual efforts to reduce crime.

Limitations of the Report

Although the Task Force believes this report will be a significant contribution to the literature on private security and will serve as a useful planning document for private security practitioners, government officials, and citizens, it realizes that the report has certain limitations. The lack of definitive and comprehensive research regarding private security activities in the United States greatly handicapped the Task Force in its analysis of the industry. In an attempt to augment the available data, the Task Force undertook three major research activities. These research activities (reported in Appendixes 1, 2, and 3) are as follows: (1) "American Society for Industrial Security (ASIS) Survey Results," (2) "Characteristics of Licensed Private Security Personnel in Two American Cities: New Orleans, La., and

St. Louis, Mo.," and (3) "Survey of Consumers or Private Security Services in the Greater Philadelphia Area." Although the information obtained from this research was of great usefulness, more complete data need to be developed in various areas throughout the security industry.

The report is limited in the extensiveness of its standards and goals; many more could have been developed by the Task Force. However, it was believed that the main emphasis should be on the development of quality standard and goal statements and supporting commentaries in areas that the Task Force believed it had sufficient knowledge. Listing voluminous standards and goals that lacked adequate support was not the intent of the members of the Task Force. Staff and members of the Task Force, along with others who contributed to the process of standards and goals, singled out issues in which they had personal expertise for conversion into a standard or goal. Unfortunately, some of these issues were too narrow in scope to fit the structure of the report and,

in some cases, could not be supported in terms of the research available. These suggested standards are not included in the report.

Finally, limited time and financial resources made it difficult to address all of the recognized issues. With more time and financial support, a more thorough study could be made of additional problem areas. In view of the level of funding, available staff time, and short duration of the present project, the Task Force believed that inclusion of a smaller number of adequately documented standards and goals was a better approach than to attempt to treat all problem areas by including standards and goals that were neither viable nor relevant.

It is recognized that the report is limited in scope. Therefore, continuous analysis of the private security industry and its components is strongly encouraged. However, this report offers a starting point to provide positive direction toward the greater use of private security services in the major effort of crime prevention and crime reduction in this country.

SECTION 3

THE ROLE OF PRIVATE SECURITY IN CRIME PREVENTION AND THE CRIMINAL JUSTICE SYSTEM

Although the formal responsibility for crime control in this country rests with the traditional criminal justice system, many other organizations and citizens are involved in reducing and preventing crime. Indeed, the sheer magnitude of crime in our society prevents the criminal justice system by itself from adequately controlling and preventing crime. The cooperative efforts of every citizen, business, and institution are needed to effectively deal with the problem. As recently stated in *U.S. News and World Report,* "the number one need is to overcome the public's misconception that they can leave crime fighting entirely to the police." [1]

One major force that over the years has been consistently and directly involved with crime prevention is the private security community. As can be seen from the significant growth of the private security industry and the large amount of money expended for security services and products, the industry fulfills an important function in our society. Its importance is intensified through a look at the magnitude and impact of crime on the private sector.

U.S. News and World Report estimated total 1974 crime-related losses in the business community to be $21.3 billion.[2] Retail losses related to crime were estimated at $6.5 billion in 1975 by the U.S. Department of Commerce.[3] The FBI Uniform Crime Reports placed 1974 nonresidential losses from burglary at $423 million.[4] The Associated General Contractors of America estimates annual theft and vandalism of materials and supplies from construction sites at $100 million. The U.S. Senate Juvenile Delinquency Subcommittee Report estimates vandalism in the schools to be $500 million annually.[5] The Senate Select Committee on Small Business estimates cargo theft at $2.5 billion annually.[6]

Clearly, it is in the economic interests of the private sector to undertake additional protective measures, and, most often, the private security industry is called upon to provide this additional protection. Through its various components, the security industry provides crime prevention services and products aimed at reducing client losses and increasing profits. As stated by the head of a national security company, "A properly developed security plan is one of the wisest investments a company can make to assure continuity of earnings." [7]

The crime prevention role of private security also provides public benefits. For example, successful actions taken by the private sector to prevent and reduce crime against their property decrease the number of crimes to which public law enforcement agencies must respond, and thus frees valuable law enforcement resources for other important activities. Furthermore, there are many places frequented by the public where a public law enforcement presence cannot be established, and there are types of crime beyond the scope of the protective measures public law enforcement can provide, e.g., corporate theft, embezzlement, and retail trade. U.S. Bureau of the Census statistics reflect some 12.4 million commercial and business establishments in the United States.[8] The approximate 500,000 local law enforcement personnel in this country can not possibly provide protection for all of these establishments.

Although concerned with crime prevention, public law enforcement agencies have been mainly placed in a crime response mode by ever-spiralling crime rates and limited resources. Most public law enforcement agencies have neither the resources nor the time to engage in preventive activities, but, instead, must focus primarily on order maintenance and criminal apprehension. Moreover:

. . . there has never been a clearly defined role for the police to protect the public distinct from the role of the

---

[1] "The Losing Battle Against Crime in America," *U.S. News and World Report,* Vol. LXXCII, No. 25, Dec. 16, 1974, p. 43.

[2] *Ibid.*

[3] *Crime in Retailing.* Washington, D.C.: U.S. Department of Commerce, August 1975, p. VII.

[4] *FBI Uniform Crime Reports,* 1974.

[5] "School Crime at Crisis Stage," *Chicago Tribune,* January-February 1974, p. 25.

[6] Frost and Sullivan, Inc., *The Industrial and Commercial Security Market.* New York, March 1975, p. 55.

[7] "Crime Does Pay," *Fortune,* September 1974, pp. 45–60.

[8] "LEAA and the Regulation of the Private Security Industry," *NBFAA Signal,* 2nd Quarter 1975, p. 10.

police to serve the needs of the justice system by making arrests for crimes committed.[9]

In addresses to the International Association of Chiefs of Police and the National Burglar and Fire Alarm Association, LEAA Administrator Richard W. Velde accurately depicted both the role of public law enforcement as a criminal justice system component and the role of private security in crime prevention.

> The criminal justice system, and particularly our nation's police, do perform a rather narrow function that is largely a responsive one that follows the commission of crime. There are constitutional and statutory responsibilities in all the states that define the role of the police force and essentially they say that police are not in the crime prevention business.[10]
>
> The fact is, however, that the vast majority of these officers are in a response posture most of the time. They don't have the time to concentrate on crime prevention. The volume of crime prevention precludes them from devoting all but a relatively minor effort toward preventing it. It is obvious that they need help.[11]
>
> If there were no guards protecting our hospitals, hotels, office buildings, museums, schools, recreational areas and the like, and, if there were no alarm systems, these places would go virtually unprotected. There is no way that public law enforcement, as it is presently staffed, equipped and deployed, could provide much more than token protection.[12]

Significant crime prevention efforts are provided by private security interests, and interrelationships do exist between these interests and the criminal justice system, especially public law enforcement components. Ideally, public law enforcement and private security agencies should work closely together, because their respective roles are complementary in the effort to control crime. Indeed, the magnitude of the Nation's crime problem should preclude any form of competition between the two. Rather, they should be cognizant and supportive of their respective roles in crime control as advocated by LEAA Administrator Richard W. Velde:

> There is so much to be done in the area of crime prevention that I can think of no reason for competition between the police and private security in this area. In fact, I visualize a comprehensive program of modern, effective crime prevention in which private security and police departments cooperate with each other, exchange information, and utilize common bases of expertise and know-how. This will require, of course, mutual respect for each other's talents and capabilities.[13]

Velde's views are echoed by Richard S. Post:

The private security industry . . . their resources must be evaluated, regulated and integrated into community crime prevention programs.[14]

If this increased cooperation is to become a reality, the relationships between the two forces must be carefully examined and appropriate measures taken to resolve conflicts.

A survey of the membership of the American Society for Industrial Security (ASIS) indicates a positive relationship between the private security community and public law enforcement. The respondents classified relationships with public law enforcement as excellent (57 percent) and good (30 percent) for the most part. Additionally, 66 percent of the respondents believed that public law enforcement was supportive of private security efforts.[15] It should be noted, however, that these respondents were from the upper management/supervisory levels. The relationship may or may not be perceived the same at the operational level.

The Law Enforcement/Private Security Relationship Committee of the Private Security Advisory Council, on the other hand, in its examination of the relationship between private security and public law enforcement, found that friction between the two groups does exist. Specifically, the committee listed the following barriers to an effective relationship between the two sectors:

* Lack of mutual respect;
* Corruption;
* Lack of cooperation;
* Lack of two-way communication;
* Competition;
* Lack of knowledge by law enforcement of the function, mission and problems of private security;
* The failure of private security to speak with a unified professional voice; and
* The need for better formulated and articulated standards of professionalism on both sides.[16]

The level and intensity of existing problems in the above areas vary greatly. In some communities, private security and public law enforcement personnel enjoy a close, positive working relationship; in others, this relationship is strained and competitive. Time and financial constraints prevent a closer study of the relationship at this time; however, it is important to establish standards and goals designed to promote and ensure improved relationships at all levels in order to create a more effective interface between the public law enforcement and private security sectors.

---

[9] Post, Richard S. "Contemporary Protective Systems," *Security Register,* January-February 1974, p. 25.

[10] Velde, Richard W., address by the Administrator of the Law Enforcement Assistance Administration at the annual meeting of the International Association of Chiefs of Police, Denver, Colo., Sept. 16, 1975.

[11] *NBFAA Signal, op. cit.,* p. 11.

[12] *Ibid.*

[13] Velde, *op. cit.*

[14] Post, *op. cit.,* p. 27.

[15] Private Security Task Force, American Society for Industrial Security survey, p. 8. See Appendix 1 to this report.

[16] Private Security Advisory Council, Law Enforcement/Private Security Relationship Committee working paper, June 4, 1975.

The International Association of Chiefs of Police has recently taken a very strong, positive attitude toward the general function and value of private security services and toward improving relations and communication. This posture represents a significant step forward in the direction of cooperation and assistance between the two forces in their common struggle against crime. Such action can open the path to resolution of the problems that have hindered mutual cooperation and respect in the past.

One problem that has consistently caused friction between public law enforcement and private security is false alarms. It has been suggested that up to 90 percent of all alarm response calls received by law enforcement agencies are false alarms. Although this figure is a much-abused statistic, false alarms clearly create problems and conflicts. In fact, because of the frequency of false alarms, many law enforcement agencies give alarm response a low priority.

Although the largest percentage of false alarms appears to result from user error, inadequate installation and faulty equipment also cause them. For the most part, problems of installation and poor equipment are found in inexpensive systems, not in the more expensive, sophisticated installations, such as those used in banks and jewelry stores. Therefore, consumers should be educated on the nature and use of the alarm systems they purchase and should have reason to have confidence in their reliability. Public law enforcement agencies also should do their part by providing timely response to alarms and cooperating with the private security industry in informing users of the seriousness of false alarms.

The need for mutual cooperation and acceptance between the alarm industry and public law enforcement agencies was emphasized by Glen D. King, executive director of the International Association of Chiefs of Police, in an address before the 28th annual convention of the National Burglar and Fire Alarm Association:

. . . false alarms are the greatest single barrier to co-operation between professional law enforcement and the alarm industry. Every police administrator I have talked to about this problem agrees there have been too many words and too little action on both sides of this issue.[17]

Another substantive barrier to effective interaction between private security and public law enforcement agencies has been some law enforcement agencies' questioning of the qualifications of private security personnel to perform police-related functions. Whereas public law enforcement officers are subject to clearly defined controls concerning employment,

training, conduct, and so forth, private security employees are subject to little or no control in these areas. Furthermore, many consider their private security employment temporary. In the absence of minimum qualifications for employment and training, private security personnel, especially guards and watchmen, are often viewed with disrespect by public law enforcement personnel.

Greater respect by public law enforcement agencies for the crime prevention role of the private security sector can be achieved through standards and goals designed to upgrade the quality of private security personnel and encourage career paths in the field. ASIS has made significant efforts in this direction through its professional education programs. Respect for the crime prevention role of the industry is also fostered at the LEAA-sponsored National Crime Prevention Institute in Louisville, Ky. The institute, staffed by persons with law enforcement and private security experience, brings in private security leaders from various fields to address and discuss mutual problems with the law enforcement students. This interaction promotes not only greater respect but also a greater understanding of the function of the industry.

A misunderstanding on the part of public law enforcement agencies revolves around a belief that private security personnel are trying to provide public law enforcement services for profit. However, a survey of the ASIS membership found that the private security community clearly does not want to perform a public law enforcement role. For example, 74 percent of the respondents indicated that private security should not have the same legal authority as public police.[18] This viewpoint is further supported in a position paper by Claude E. Hinds, president of the World Association of Detectives, a group of principals and, in most cases, owners of private security firms:

Too long we have been looking to law enforcement for training, because nothing else was available. This practice has unfortunately contributed to the belief that we are basically concerned with enforcement of the law, when in fact we are not and don't wish to be. . . . Let me make it quite clear, we don't want to be Police Officers. When we employ an individual, we tell them they are not to consider themselves Police Officers. We do not want to enforce the law but feel that our primary goal is one of protection and prevention.[19]

It was noted in Section 1 that some private security personnel are granted limited police powers generally restricted to the premises of employment. However,

[17] King, Glen D. address delivered before the 28th annual convention of the National Burglar and Fire Alarm Association, Las Vegas, Nev., Mar. 20, 1975.

[18] Private Security Task Force, American Society for Industrial Security Survey, p. 8. See Appendix 1 to this report.

[19] Hinds, Claude E., World Association of Detectives. Position paper presented to Private Security Task Force, Chicago, Ill., July 11, 1975.

a major distinction between public law enforcement and private security powers is that police make arrests on behalf of the public and private security personnel make apprehensions on behalf of the client.

Another area of conflict between public law enforcement and private security is that of accountability. Public law enforcement officers are accountable to the public (citizens); private security personnel are primarily accountable to the individual or organization employing their services (clients):

> The client of the police officer, as it were, is the community. The community determines the rules under which the investigation, apprehension, and disposition of the case take place, and the officer, theoretically at least, is accountable to that system of rules and to the community.
>
> The private police agent, however, in dealing with the same acts that the public deals with, defined as crimes, is in the employ of a private individual or firm rather than serving the community. He is to a much greater extent not subject to the same rules for investigation and apprehension and he is accountable only to himself, his profession, and his employer.[20]

This accountability creates a situation in which persons are subject to investigation or apprehension by private security personnel for actions that would be considered criminal acts in the public sector. Many of these cases never enter the criminal justice system, and the employers or clients become a criminal justice system themselves, sitting in judgment. One study suggested that in 75 percent of the cases of internal employee theft, employees prefer restitution to criminal prosecution, and employers often accept this as a viable alternative.[21] It should be pointed out that restitution is a proper civil remedy. In fact, a criminal remedy without a civil remedy may be just as unjustified as the reverse. However, both are desirable in the interest of true justice, and many strongly believe that private security personnel should report all crimes.

Although the private security industry interacts most frequently with the public law enforcement component of the criminal justice system, it also interacts with other components. For example, when a shoplifter is observed committing the act by private security personnel of a retail establishment, security personnel may apprehend and detain the person until the police take formal custody. For purposes of prosecution and formal arraignment on charges of larceny, the store security agent becomes the complainant. The chief accuser and witness in a court of law also is the security person who observed the shoplifting incident.

Private security investigative personnel often work closely with investigators from law enforcement agencies and prosecutors' offices in investigating internal theft by employees, embezzlement, fraud, and external theft by organized criminal groups. For example, in large retail establishments (department stores, discount houses), security personnel have an interest in removing organized criminal rings that systematically prey upon the stores. The security personnel can exchange information among themselves and provide information to law enforcement investigators to assist them in the development of criminal cases. Law enforcement officers frequently provide information to the store security personnel regarding a suspect under arrest or investigation, who may have been involved in criminal offenses in their stores. Private security personnel commonly provide information to law enforcement agencies on criminal activities they observe or suspect that are not directly related to their assets-protection function, such as narcotics, gambling, and other vice offenses.

It is clear that the private security industry does indeed play a major role in crime prevention and interrelates with the criminal justice system. Its potential for significant contributions to national crime reduction is considerable. The standards and goals in this report will reinforce the primary role of private security in crime reduction and, at the same time, foster a public/private partnership in crime control by improving the quality and delivery of private security services.

One last important concern is the industry's need for criminal history information for purposes of preemployment screening. Because arrest data in many instances may be more significant than conviction data, this information should be provided to private security employers. Employers who hire personnel to protect their assets and to prevent crime need to have some means of researching their backgrounds and verifying their integrity. Law enforcement agencies have similar concerns, because some private security personnel receive limited police powers upon employment.

Private security organizations may be responsible for obtaining criminal history information concerning other employees as well: cashiers, tellers, sales clerks, and other persons responsible for monetary transactions and the handling of merchandise. In retail stores, for example, employee theft is a major contributor to sales shortages in excess of $2.3 billion annually, according to the National Retail Merchants Association.[22] Retailers believe there is

---

[20] Scott, Thomas M., and Marlys McPherson, "The Development of the Private Sector of the Criminal Justice System," *Law and Society Review*, November 1971, pp. 285–286.

[21] *Ibid.*, p. 287.

[22] Statement of the National Retail Merchants Association before LEAA regarding dissemination of criminal information records, Dec. 12, 1975, p. 2.

a compelling need to obtain conviction information on prospective employees:

In our view the pertinent question is ultimately one of suitability of a person to perform a certain job in which trust and deportment are the crucial requirements. . . . In addition to the need for verification of a prospective employee's honesty, we emphasize that persons convicted of certain crimes must be diverted from particular positions.[28]

The prudent provision of this information to private security organizations reduces the opportunity for the commission of crimes by excluding from certain positions those persons with a history of criminal activity in employment situations.

---

[28] *Ibid.*, pp. 3–4.

In summary, the crime prevention function of the private security industry is an effective complement to public law enforcement agencies. The industry provides services that cannot be furnished by public law enforcement because of limited resources and various other constraints. Significant benefits in national crime reduction and prevention are possible through the increased cooperation and coordination of the two forces. Existing barriers to closer unity between them must be removed if this goal is to be achieved. The development of standards and goals for the increased effectiveness of private security services is viewed as a method of facilitating a mutually productive working relationship in which conflicts can be resolved and progress toward cooperation and coordination enhanced.

SECTION 4

DEFINITIONS AND FUNCTIONAL DESCRIPTIONS OF PRIVATE SECURITY COMPONENTS TO BE COVERED IN THE REPORT

In Section 1 of this introduction, basic parameters were established to define the types of products, services, and activities referred to as "private security." The objectives of this approach are twofold:

1. To ensure the specificity of the standards and goals, and
2. To enable the private security industry, State and local criminal justice officials, and citizens to clearly understand the applicability of the standards and goals.

In this section, the private security industry is divided into major generic groupings that represent the primary components to which the standards and goals are directed.

Generally, considerable commonality exists in the definition of the functions and duties of police personnel across the country, and there is substantial consistency in job descriptions for law enforcement positions, such as patrolman, sergeant, and detective. Yet, a review of applicable licensing procedures, local ordinances, and State statutes throughout the country shows an absence of such commonality in the use of terms for private security personnel. In some instances, clear distinctions are made among such terms as private policeman, private patrol service, guards, and watchman, but there are many other instances of overlap and redundancy in job functions, responsibilities, and/or powers. For example, a position defined as an investigator in one State might be classified as a guard in another. The following definitions and functional descriptions, therefore, are necessary to avoid any misinterpretation in terminology and functions.

Major Private Security Components

In order to establish uniformity in the use of terms related to private security, four major industry components involving services and personnel are defined:

1. Guard and patrol services and personnel,
2. Investigative services and personnel,
3. Alarm services and personnel, and

4. Armored car and armed courier services and personnel.

Throughout this report, the term "private security personnel" refers to persons engaged in the performance of these services. Although there is considerable variance among States in the application of these terms, the important point is not the use of the terms but, rather, the functions they encompass. Admittedly, this breakdown of private security components is not exhaustive. Other related areas are discussed only peripherally in the first three sections of this introduction; still others are not identified specifically. However, States are encouraged to apply the standards and goals to those functions described in each of the four major private security industry components outlined below. Although the term private security "industry" is used, it is emphasized that proprietary security services are included in the standards and goals.

Guard and Patrol Services and Personnel

Guard and patrol services include the provision of personnel who perform the following functions, either contractually or internally, at such places and facilities as industrial plants, financial institutions, educational institutions, office buildings, retail establishments, commercial complexes (including hotels and motels), health care facilities, recreation facilities, libraries and museums, residence and housing developments, charitable institutions, transportation vehicles and facilities (public and common carriers), and warehouses and goods distribution depots:

• Prevention and/or detection of intrusion, unauthorized entry or activity, vandalism, or trespass on private property;

• Prevention and/or detection of theft, loss, embezzlement, misappropriation or concealment of merchandise, money, bonds, stocks, notes, or other valuable documents or papers;

• Control, regulation, or direction of the flow or movements of the public, whether by vehicle or otherwise, to assure the protection of property;

• Protection of individuals from bodily harm; and

• Enforcement of rules, regulations, and policies related to crime reduction.

These functions may be provided at one location or several. Guard functions are generally provided at one central location for one client or employer. Patrol functions, however, are performed at several locations, often for several clients.

Investigative Services and Personnel

The major services provided by the investigative component of private security may be provided contractually or internally at places and facilities, such as industrial plants, financial institutions, educational institutions, retail establishments, commercial complexes, hotels and motels, and health care facilities. The services are provided for a variety of clients, including insurance companies, law firms, retailers, and individuals. Investigative personnel are primarily concerned with obtaining information with reference to any of the following matters:

• Crime or wrongs committed or threatened;

• The identity, habits, conduct, movements, whereabouts, affiliations, associations, transactions, reputation, or character of any person, group of persons, association, organization, society, other group of persons or partnership or corporation;

• Preemployment background checks of personnel applicants;

• The conduct, honesty, efficiency, loyalty, or activities of employees, agents, contractors, and subcontractors;

• Incidents and illicit or illegal activities by persons against the employer or employer's property;

• Retail shoplifting;

• Internal theft by employees or other employee crime;

• The truth or falsity of any statement or representation;

• The whereabouts of missing persons;

• The location or recovery of lost or stolen property;

• The causes and origin of or responsibility for fires, libels or slanders, losses, accidents, damage, or injuries to real or personal property;

• The credibility of information, witnesses, or other persons; and

• The securing of evidence to be used before investigating committees, boards of award or arbitration, or in the trial of civil or criminal cases and the preparation thereof.

Detective or investigative activity is distinguished from the guard or watchman function in that the investigator obtains information; the guard or watchman usually acts on information (or events).

Alarm Services and Personnel

Alarm services include selling, installing, servicing, and emergency response to alarm signal devices. Alarm devices are employed in one of four basic modes: local alarm, proprietary alarm, central station alarm, or police-connected alarm. Alarm signal devices include a variety of equipment, ranging from simple magnetic switches to complex ultrasonic Doppler and sound systems. Various electronic, electromechanical, and photoelectrical devices and microwave Dopplers are also utilized.

Alarm personnel include three categories of employees: alarm sales personnel, alarm systems installers and/or servicers, and alarm respondents. Those persons in alarm sales engage in customer/client contact, presale security surveys, and postsale cutomer relations. Alarm installers and servicers are trained technicians who install and wire alarm systems, perform scheduled maintenance, and provide emergency servicing, as well as regular repair, of alarm systems. (Alarm installers and servicers may be the same depending on the employer.) Alarm respondents respond to an alarm condition at the protected site of a client. The alarm respondent inspects the protected site to determine the nature of the alarm, protects or secures the client's facility for the client until alarm system integrity can be restored, and assists law enforcement agencies according to local arrangements. The alarm respondent may be armed and may also be a servicer.

Armored Car and Armed Courier Services and Personnel

Armored car services include the provision of protection, safekeeping, and secured transportation of currency, coins, bullion, securities, bonds, jewelry, or other items of value. This secured transportation, from one place or point to another place or point, is accomplished by specially constructed bullet-resistant armored vehicles and vaults under armed guard. Armed courier services also include the armed protection and transportation, from one place or point to another place or point, of currency, coins, bullion, securities, bonds, jewelry, or other articles of unusual value. Armed courier services are distinguished from armored car services in that the transportation is provided by means other than specially constructed bullet-resistant armored vehicles. There are also courier service companies that employ nonarmed persons to transport documents, business papers, checks, and other time-sensitive items of limited intrinsic value that require expeditious delivery. Those services concerned merely with expeditious, unarmed delivery are not intended to be covered by this report's standards and goals.

The major distinction between the services provided by armored cars and armed couriers and those furnished by guards and watchmen is liability. Armored car guards and armed couriers are engaged exclusively in the safe transportation and custody of valuables, and the firms providing these services are liable for the face, declared, or contractual value of the client's property. These service companies are bailees of the valuable property and the guards and couriers are protecting the property of their employer. This liability extends from the time the valuables are received until the time a receipt is executed by the consignee at delivery. Except for war risks, the armored car company is absolutely liable for the valuable property during such protective custody.[1] Conversely, guards, watchmen, and their employers do not assume comparable liability for the property being protected.

Some opinions have been expressed that armored car and courier services should be excluded from the standards and goals, because they are already licensed and regulated by Federal and State government agencies—the Interstate Commerce Commission, State public service and public utilities commissions, and the U.S. Department of Transportation. Standards and goals applying to armored car and armed courier services do require special treatment, different in part from those applying to guards or watchmen. Because many armored car and armed courier service firms are intrastate only and do not operate interstate, they would be subject to licensing only by State public service and public utilities commissions. Furthermore, where armored car and armed courier service firms are subject to licensing and regulation, such regulation usually pertains only to the operation of the firm as a transportation company and not to such practices as personnel selection, training, conduct, and ethics. Therefore, it is important that the standards and goals in these areas be applied to armored car and armed courier service personnel and firms.

Other Components

It is recognized that there are private security components and practitioners in addition to those described here. As previously indicated, the majority of the standards and goals in this report apply to guards and watchmen, private investigators and detectives, alarm systems and alarm personnel, and armored car and armed courier services. This report also includes within the scope of private security the fields of:

• Detection-of-deception (polygraph examination, psychological stress evaluation, lie detection);

• Private security management (principals, owners, managers, and supervisors of security firms);

• Forensic science (practitioners in private practice); and

• Management consulting (private security specialists).

Some of these nondirect private security activities are subject to licensing and regulation by State and/or local government agencies. For example, 17 States require practicing polygraph examiners to be licensed, and 14 States restrict or prohibit detection-of-deception testing.[2] Additionally, in some jurisdictions, security firm owners and principals are required to obtain licenses, post bonds, and/or submit personal and corporate documentation to State and/or local government.

Developing specific standards and goals for these security-related activities was considered, but the time and financial resources were lacking to embark on such a project. Furthermore, the material available makes apparent that major research is needed before realistic and viable standards and goals can be developed for these activities. However, in a broad sense, many of the standards and goals do apply to these activities; for example, Chapter 3—Conduct and Ethics—is certainly applicable. From time to time throughout the report, specific mention is made of the relationship to the above fields, but the general intent is that the professionals in these areas will take the initiative to improve their activities by adopting the applicable standards and goals. Thus, those involved in the specific areas are encouraged to review, apply, and even exceed the standards and goals contained in this report.

---

[1] Position paper of the National Armored Car Association presented to the LEAA Private Security Advisory Council, Chicago, Ill., July 8, 1975.

[2] Barefoot, J. Kirk, ed., *The Polygraph Story*. Linthicum Heights, Md.: American Polygraph Association, 3d printing, October 1974, p. 2.

SECTION 5

SUMMARY OF RESEARCH IN PRIVATE SECURITY

Private Security Task Force Research

In its initial research, the Private Security Task Force found that it was entering a field that has not had extensive research and analysis. There are comparatively few books, articles, or scholarly treatises concerning the diverse and complex private security field. Recognizing the minimal amount of specific information available, the Task Force undertook over a half-dozen studies to provide a data base for its standards and goals. Summaries and information on the studies are contained in the Appendixes to this report.

On a national basis, the Task Force distributed questionnaires to the United States membership of of the American Society for Industrial Security to collect data concerning types of security functions performed by the members, education and training of personnel, uniforms, salaries, private security/public law enforcement relationships, and the need for a set of standards for private security (Appendix 1).

Regionally, the Task Force gathered information concerning the characteristics of licensed private security personnel in New Orleans, La., and St. Louis, Mo. (Appendix 2) and, in cooperation with an Ad-Hoc Committee of the Citizens Crime Commission of Philadelphia, conducted a survey of consumers in the Greater Philadelphia area to determine their attitudes toward the security services they were receiving (Appendix 3).

It should be recognized, however, that the Private Security Task Force studies and report are not the first of their kind. Several other valuable studies have been previously conducted on national, State, and regional levels and in foreign countries. These other reports and studies have been most useful in building a research base and assisting in the preparation of standards and goals by the Task Force. The Task Force does not necessarily support all of the findings and recommendations or the research methodology used in these other reports, yet their usefulness in studying the private security industry must be recognized.

Because of the lack of information and the need for further study, the Task Force believes it is necessary to outline the major studies that were brought to its attention. These other reports can be helpful to anyone conducting research on various aspects of security. Although an attempt is made to summarize their contents, these synopses may not reflect the specific nature of the studies.

Private Security Advisory Council Model Statutes

Although not studies in the traditional sense, the Private Security Advisory Council has prepared two model statutes, *A Model Burglar and Hold-Up Alarm Business Licensing and Regulatory Statute* and *Model Private Security Licensing and Regulatory Statute.* These model statutes were used extensively in the preparation of standards and goals and are included as Appendixes 10 and 11 to this report.

The Private Security Advisory Council and its various committees also have produced, and continue to produce, special-purpose documents related to private security interests. These reports can be obtained through the Law Enforcement Assistance Administration (LEAA) and the National Institute of Law Enforcement and Criminal Justice, LEAA, Washington, D.C. Some of these are referenced in the commentaries for standards and goals contained in this report.

National Research

At the national level, only one major study of the private security industry in the United States was conducted prior to establishment of the Private Security Task Force. This initial study was begun in 1970 by the RAND Corporation (1700 Main Street, Santa Monica, Calif. 90406) and took 16 months to complete. The study, supported by a grant from the National Institute of Law Enforcement and Criminal Justice, LEAA, U.S. Department of Justice, was primarily conducted by James S. Kakalik and Sorrel

Wildhorn. The purposes of this seminal study, as stated in the report, were twofold—"to describe the nature and extent of the private police industry in the United States, is problems, its present regulation, and how the law impinges on it. . . . [and] . . . to develop preliminary policy and statutory guidelines for improving its future operations and regulation."

In order to achieve its stated purposes, the RAND Corporation conducted interviews, undertook surveys, and used other generally accepted research techniques. The findings of this research were published in February 1972 in five volumes (*RAND Report*) as follows: *Private Police in the United States: Findings and Recommendations, The Private Police Industry: Its Nature and Extent, Current Regulatory Agency Experience and Views, The Law and Private Police, Special-Purpose Public Police.* These volumes cover the nature, size, growth, and operation of the industry and its personnel; the results of a survey of private security employees; licensing and regulation of the industry in every State and several cities; data on regulatory agency experience, complaints, disciplinary action taken, and the agency views on needed changes in regulation; the law as it relates to the private police industry, including a general discussion of the sources of legal limitations upon private police activities and personnel and sources of legal powers, and an examination of specific legal problems raised by these activities and relationships between the users and providers of private security services; descriptive information on certain types of public forces not having general law enforcement responsibilities, including reserve police, special-purpose Federal forces, special law enforcement agencies, and campus police; and, the overall findings and recommendations of the study.

State Research

In addition to the *RAND Report,* several studies, designed to study the industry in a single State, have also been conducted. The most comprehensive statewide study to date was conducted by the Institute for Local Self Government (Hotel Claremont Building, Berkeley, Calif. 94705). Completed in 1974, the report, entitled *Private Security and the Public Interest,* was funded by the California Office of Criminal Justice Planning and was directed by Robert E. Kandt.

The stated purpose of the California study was "to define and relate the problem of private security to California state and local governments in their legal obligation to provide for the public safety . . . to determine the actual and potential economic and

social impact of private security operations and their relationship to local government . . . [and to develop] a 'Design for Action.' " In achieving its purpose, the Institute conducted systematic research by surveying employees, employers/supervisors, and clients; interviewing regulatory agency personnel; studying ordinances and State laws; and using other generally accepted research techniques.

The 589-page report covers the present status and growth of the industry in California; patterns of relationships between private security firms and public police and sheriffs' departments and other elements of the criminal justice system; descriptive characteristics of the type of activities in which private security agencies engage; examination of present minimum qualifications for employment to determine their sufficiency in the public interest; suggested duties, responsibilities, powers, restraints, and regulations that should be proposed in the public interest; the legitimate role of private security services in protection of small business from crime; the status of regulation and control of the industry at both the State and local levels; and a suggested training program for private security personnel.

A statewide research project of a more limited scope was conducted in Virginia during 1972. "The Private Security Industry in Virginia" was prepared by the Research Department of the Division of Justice and Crime Prevention, Commonwealth of Virginia (8501 Maryland Drive, Richmond, Va. 23229).

The purpose of the study was to identify the private security industry in Virginia and the problems associated with its regulations. Using the *RAND Report* as a primary source and guide, the division conducted interviews, gathered and analyzed labor and census statistics, studied complaints received by various agencies, and gathered local ordinances and statutory material. The 115-page report contains statistical data on the number of security agencies and employees, a profile of private security personnel, training programs and policies within the State, an overview of State and local regulation, a brief summary of the law and the private security industry, and proposed model legislation.

State legislative committee staffs often conduct research and make reports concerning matters of legislative concern. One such report was prepared by the Florida Senate Judiciary Committee staff (Senate Office Building, Room 215, Tallahassee, Fla. 32304). The "Report on the Private Security Industry in Florida" was completed in September of 1974 and principally was prepared by Michael L. Ketchum.

Recognizing the enormous growth of the security industry in Florida and increasing problems this growth has caused, the Florida Senate Judiciary

Committee requested its staff to determine the seriousness of the problems and what measures should be taken to correct them. In conducting their study, the committee staff relied on a questionnaire mailed to all licensed security agencies in Florida; interviews with appropriate government agency personnel, heads of security agencies, State legislators, and journalists; news articles; the RAND Corporation study; and an investigation of security guard statutes from the other 49 States.

One other limited statewide-basis study was conducted by the Maine Criminal Justice Planning and Assistance Agency (295 Water Street, Augusta, Maine 04330). That agency conducted a survey of all licensed security agencies in Maine in 1975. The survey covered the employee-selection process, minimum employee requirements, training programs, weapons use, uniforms and badges, and State regulation. The report was designed to obtain certain statistical data but made no attempt to reach any conclusions or make recommendations as a result of the data collected.

Local and Regional Research

The first study of the private security industry, conducted in any regional metropolitan area, has received national attention. Covering the industry in the Greater Cleveland, Ohio, area, *The Other Police, Private Security Services in Greater Cleveland,* was published in 1975 by the Administration of Justice Committee of the Governmental Research Institute (Suite 511, Ten-Ten Euclid Building, Cleveland, Ohio 44115). This full-scale research project, directed by Dennis T. Brennan, was funded cooperatively by the A.H.S. Foundation, the Nationwide Foundation, the Oglebay Norton Foundation, and the General Electric Lamp Division.

The general purposes of the Cleveland study were "to portray the numbers, types, benefits, risks and regulations of Cuyahoga County, Ohio's private security forces . . . [and] to reduce the overall costs to society of current private security arrangements by evaluating alternative guidelines for improving the quality of such services."

One other regional study was published in 1975 by Public Systems Incorporated (1137 Kerns Avenue, Sunnyvale, Calif. 94086). Prepared for the City of St. Petersburg, Fla., and funded by a grant from LEAA and the Florida Governor's Council on Criminal Justice, the project was directed by Kai R. Martensen.

The purpose of the study was to identify and assess the private security resources operating within St. Petersburg and to draft an ordinance based on the study's findings and recommendations. To achieve this purpose, questionnaires were mailed to private security employers, employees, clients, and customers and to law enforcement agencies; a detailed analysis was completed regarding existing and proposed legislation and its impact on security operations; and three workshops were conducted with representatives from the private security industry and public police.

The 101-page study, entitled *Final Report, Private Security Survey and Ordinance for St. Petersburg, Florida,* includes a model regulatory ordinance and comments, a mandatory gun training program, a private security advertising ordinance, a survey of security resources, a model building security ordinance, questionnaire survey results, and a proposed State statute.

International Research

Three reports covering private security services in other countries were also brought to the attention of the Task Force. One concerned Canada, one dealt with security in the United Kingdom, and the last was a short paper emanating from the United Nations.

The Canadian report, *The Legal Regulation and Control of Private Policing and Security in Canada,* was prepared by Philip C. Stenning and Mary F. Cornish, Centre of Criminology, University of Toronto, under a student program financed by the Ministry of the Solicitor-General of Canada.

As the Canadian report states, its principal purposes were to make a preliminary examination of the legal regulation and control of the private security industry and to provide an information base and framework from which more detailed research could proceed. The major sources of information for this report were library research; a questionnaire sent to the seven existing provincial regulatory agencies for the industry; extensive interviews with industry representatives, regulatory agencies, local registrars, and law enforcement personnel; and a workshop conducted at the Centre of Criminology in October 1973.

In July 1971, the University of Cambridge, Institute of Criminology, conducted a conference on security. The papers presented at that conference were edited by Paul Wiles and F. H. McClintock and published in 1972 as *The Security Industry in the United Kingdom.* The 105-page document is not as comprehensive as other studies reported herein, but it does include some very valuable information concerning views of the private security industry within the United Kingdom.

Another report, which was the result of a conference, was released following the Fifth United Nations

Congress on the Prevention of Crime and the Treatment of Offenders, held in Geneva, Switzerland, in September 1975. The short working paper released following that assembly sketchily covers government regulation of security in many different countries and was designed to address the problem of establishing a framework of preventive cooperation and mutual support between the security industry and the appropriate public law enforcement authority. The congress also considered several resolutions addressed to various aspects of security and made recommendations concerning regulation.

SECTION 6

THE HISTORY AND DEVELOPMENT OF PRIVATE SECURITY IN THE UNITED STATES

Although the greatest growth in the private security industry has occurred in recent years, a review and understanding of the historical aspects that led to this growth are important. Through the review of the history, the present day state of the industry can be better understood.

Early History

The concepts and security practices that form the basis for modern American security can be traced to early England.[1] Colonists settling in a new and alien land banded together under a system of mutual protection and accountability that stemmed from early Anglo-Saxon times.[2] Prior to American independence, protection of the colonists and their property was the responsibility of town constables and sheriffs, supplemented in many towns, in English tradition, with watchmen who would patrol the streets at night. These watchmen remained familiar figures and constituted the primary security measure until the establishment of full-time police forces in the mid-1800s.

To ensure adequate protection, most local governments formalized the watch system and required each adult male inhabitant to serve a period of time as a watchman. A watchman's tour of duty usually began at 9 or 10 o'clock in the evening and ended at sunrise. During their tours of duty, the watchmen often encountered fires, Indian attacks, wild animals, runaway slaves, thieves, and grave robbers. They were expected to cope with these incidents and maintain order by quelling disturbances, arresting drunks, and enforcing the curfew. The watchman's job became increasingly difficult as industrialization and urbanization spread. Without training or legal support, and with little or no pay, most of those chosen to stand duty as watchmen would hire others to perform this unpleasant, thankless task. And, although the task of protecting their communities

had become more difficult and demanding, watchmen were vilified and downgraded in the eyes of their fellow colonists.[3]

As security problems kept pace with the rapid growth of the country, public pressure mounted for increased and more effective protection. Attempts were made to add daytime complements to support and supplement the night watchmen, but it soon became apparent that the watch system was neither adequate nor efficient. This realization led to the formation of public police departments with full-time, paid personnel. The first public police force in the United States was established in 1844 in New York City, and by 1856 police departments had been set up in Detroit, Cincinnati, Chicago, San Francisco, Los Angeles, Philadelphia, and Dallas. Although these early police departments were generally inefficient and often corrupt, and their personnel poorly trained, they represented a vast improvement over the old watchman system. The Civil Service Act of 1883 was instrumental in rectifying many problems of the early police departments.

The emergence of public police departments, however, did not mean the end of private citizen involvement in the protection of life and property. Public law enforcement agencies were in their most incipient stage and could not keep pace with the mounting problems of crime in their communities. The incidence of crimes against property had become acute. The coupling of these facts forced industrial and business organizations to recognize the need for some form of effective security to protect their assets. Thus, in the 1850's major components of the private security industry were developed in answer to this need.

Allan Pinkerton formed the North West Police Agency in 1855 to provide protection for six midwestern railroads, and the Pinkerton Protection Patrol in 1857 to provide a private watchman service.[4] For more than 50 years, Pinkerton's was the

---

[1] Green, G., and R. C. Farber, *Introduction to Security*. Los Angeles, Calif.: Security World Publishing Company, 1975, p. 23.

[2] Ursic, H. S., and L. E. Pagano, *Security Management Systems*. Springfield, Ill.: Charles C. Thomas, 1974, p. 12.

[3] Peel, J. D. *The Story of Private Security*. Springfield, Ill.: Charles C. Thomas, 1971, p. 16.

[4] Morn, Frank. "Discipline and Disciplinarians: The Problem of Police Control in the Formative Years," a paper presented at the annual meeting of the American Historical Association, Dec. 28–30, 1975, pp. 5–7.

only company in the country engaged in interstate activities, such as the provision of security for many of the railroads. Pinkerton's also provided security for industrial concerns and was even hired as an intelligence-gathering unit for the Union Army during the Civil War. Today, Pinkerton's, with numerous services and activities, is the largest security organization in the world.

In 1858, Edwin Holmes began the first central office burglar alarm operation, which evolved into Holmes Protection, Inc. When the American District Telegraph Company (ADT) was formed in 1874, use of alarms and detection devices spread to provide protective services through the use of messengers and telegraph lines. By 1889, the use of electric protection for industrial and commercial enterprises in New York City was well established.

In 1859, Washington Perry Brink formed his truck and package delivery service in Chicago. He transported his first payroll in 1891, thereby initiating armored car and courier service. By 1900, Brink had acquired a fleet of 85 wagons. Seventy-five years later his security business was grossing more than $50 million in revenue each year.[5]

During the 1800s, with the westward expansion of the United States, railroad lines moved into sparsely settled territories that had little or no public law enforcement. Trains were subject to attack by Indians and roving bands of outlaws who robbed passengers, stole cargo, dynamited track structures, and disrupted communications. In order to provide adequate protection of goods and passengers from the constant dangers, various States passed railway police acts that enabled private railroads to establish proprietary security forces, with full police powers, for the protection of assets. In many towns and territories, the railway police provided the only protective services until governmental units and law enforcement agencies were established.[6] By 1914, U.S. railway police numbered between 12,000 and 14,000.[7] Although railway police have been associated with public law enforcement for a long time, they are, in fact, private security forces granted law enforcement powers.

At the turn of the century, labor unions began to proliferate and to use strikes as a forceful tool for change. Because many factories were located in areas that had no effective public police forces capable of maintaining order, private security agencies were called in by management to quell the disturbances surrounding strikes and to protect lives and property. During this period, two firms were established that are now major security corporations. In 1909, Baker Industries, Inc., entered the fire control and burglary detection equipment business. That same year, the head of the FBI's predecessor agency, the Bureau of Investigation, formed the William J. Burns International Detective Agency, now a multinational corporation with 117 U.S. offices and more than 30,000 employees.

Industry Formation

Prior to and during World War I, the concern for security intensified in American industry, due not only to urbanization and industrial growth but also to sabotage and espionage by politically active nationalists. Security services expanded to meet the demands, but tapered off when demands lessened after the war, reaching a low point during the Depression era.

At the end of World War I, there were other significant developments in private security. A Burglary Protection Council was formed and held its first meeting in 1921, the results of which thrust Underwriters' Laboratories into the business of establishing specifications for, testing of, and certifying burglar alarm systems and devices.

During the 1940's, World War II proved to be a significant catalyst in the growth of the private security industry. Prior to the awarding of national defense contracts, the Federal Government required that munitions contractors implement stringent and comprehensive security measures to protect classified materials and defense secrets from sabotage and espionage. The FBI assisted in establishing these security programs. Additionally, the Government granted the status of auxiliary military police to more than 200,000 plant watchmen. Their primary duties included protection of war goods and products, supplies, equipment, and personnel.[8] Local law enforcement agencies were responsible for their training. As a result of the heightened emphasis on security within the government/military sphere, industry became increasingly aware of the need for plant security, and its value in protection of their assets.

After the war, the use of private security services and products expanded from the area of defense contractors to encompass all segments of the private and public sectors. For example, in 1954 George R.

[5] Kakalik, J. S., and Sorrel Wildhorn, *The Private Police Industry: Its Nature and Extent*, R–870/DOJ. Washington, D.C.: Government Printing Office, 1972, Vol. II, pp. 46–49.

[6] Position paper presented to the Private Security Task Force by the Police and Security Section of the Association of American Railroads, Washington, D.C., Dec. 5, 1975, pp. 2–3.

[7] Post, Richard S., and Arthur A. Kingsburg, *Security Administration: An Introduction*. Springfield, Ill.: Charles C. Thomas, 1970, p. 5.

[8] Green and Farber, *op. cit.*, p. 27.

Wackenhut and three other former FBI agents formed the Wackenhut Corporation as a private investigative and contract security firm. In just 20 years this firm has established itself as the third-largest contract guard and investigative agency in the country. Wackenhut also provides central station alarms, screening of passengers in airports, and, most recently, security services for the Trans-Alaska Pipeline.[9]

Wackenhut achieved its growth, in large part, through the acquisition of smaller contract security firms, as did the William J. Burns International Detective Agency. Baker Industries used this technique (notably in the acquisition of Wells Fargo) to expand beyond its electronic detection and equipment origins into guard, armored car, patrol, and investigation services. (Today Baker Industries' security guard and armored car service groups account for about 25 percent of its revenues.) Burns used its acquisitions and industry reputation to move into central station alarms and electronic security equipment. Pinkerton's, on the other hand, concentrated on guard and investigative services and achieved most of its growth internally.[10] Other companies developed along similar lines; these were selected merely to illustrate the historical growth patterns of the earliest private security firms.

Proprietary security, although not as visible as contractual and other forms of security, has experienced equal if not greater growth. From an historical aspect, the greatest growth occurred as a result of World Wars I and II, with the increased governmental concern for heightened security for contractors.

Although no accurate data are available, Federal Government regulation has been a significant factor in the growth of proprietary security over the years. Another major factor has been the increased awareness of companies of the importance of crime reduction and prevention as it relates to company property. In response to this need, both small and large companies have increased proprietary security functions. Thus, it can be concluded that the growth of proprietary security has paralleled that of contractual security.

Industry Composition

Several market studies suggest (on the basis of reported earnings of the publicly held corporations engaged in private security) that a half-dozen firms control more than 50 percent of the total market for protective services and products. This statistic, how-ever, does not present the true growth trends that are occurring.

One study indicates that since 1939, when industry records were first kept, more than 2,400 new firms have entered the private security field. The number of such firms doubled in the 9-year period from 1963 to 1972.[11] In Figure 6, some of the major firms are categorized according to security service and product lines [12] and shows that several companies are diversified in the types of services that they provide. More importantly, it illustrates that the growth of private security has become technologically intensive over time. A number of firms appearing in Figure 6 were not originally active in the traditional business areas of private security (i.e., guards, investigative, armored car and courier, and central station alarms). Moreover, some of these firms' major activities are in other industries, such as consumer products, electronics, data processing, and engineering.

An analysis of the data from a 1975 security survey in St. Louis (Appendix 2) offers further support that major firms do not control the private security marketplace. This survey indicated that there are only eight major national security firms or their subsidiary companies providing contractual guard, armored car and courier, investigative, and alarm services in this major market area. Their employees represent about 23 percent of the total number (1,962) of contractual, licensed private security personnel in St. Louis supplied by contractual security companies. The remaining 77 percent (1,511) are provided by 78 local contractual security companies.

Sufficient resources were not available to determine if this same situation exists throughout the United States. However, if St. Louis is representative of other market areas throughout the country, it is questionable whether a few major national firms consistently control more than half the total market for protective services and products. The number of guard, investigative, and other protective service contractual firms, as shown in Table 1, also suggest that smaller firms with fewer than 100 employees have experienced significant growth in this area.

---

[9] *1974 Annual Report to Shareholders,* the Wackenhut Corporation, Coral Gables, Fla., March 8, 1975.

[10] Kakalik and Wildhorn, *op. cit.,* pp. 46–49.

[11] Nossov, W., *The Security Enforcement Industry.* Merrick, N.Y.: Morton Research Corporation, October 1975, p. 51.

[12] The firms selected for Figure 1 were extracted from listings by the marketing reports of publicly held private security firms that account for a substantial share of the market for security service and product lines. In contract guards and investigators, for example, only those firms annually earning at least $7 million from these services were listed. These firms collectively, then, would be considered the major firms.

Figure 6. Major Publicly Held Firms by Type of Security Product and Services

Contract Guard & Investigative
Allied Security
ATO (Advance Industry Security)
Baker Industries (Wells Fargo)
Burns
Guardsmark
IBI Security
Loomis (Stanley Smith Security)
Pinkerton's
Servisco (N.B.)
Wackenhut
Walter Kidde (Globe Security)

Armored Car Services
Baker Industries
Loomis
Pittston (Brinks)

Courier Services
Bankers Utilities
Loomis
Pittston (Brinks)

Fixed Security Equipment
American Standard (Mosler)
ATO, Inc.
DieBold
Walter Kidde

Central Station Alarms
ADT
Baker Industries
Burns
Holmes Electric Protective
Honeywell
Morse Signal Devices
Wackenhut

Proprietary Alarm/Access Control Systems
ATO
Honeywell
Johnson Control
Pittway (ADEMCO)
Walter Kidde
Westinghouse

Closed-Circuit TV
Ampex
Babcock and Wilcox
Bell and Howell
General Electric
Honeywell
Motorola
Panasonic
RCA
Sony

Source: Research activities of the Private Security Task Force, 1975-1976.

Table 1. Number of Protective Service Establishments by Size of Employment

Firm employment	1967	1973	Unit change 1967–1973
1–3 employees	838	960	+122
4–7 employees	443	662	+219
8–19 employees	498	874	+376
20–49 employees	366	800	+434
50–99 employees	172	421	+249
100–249 employees	155	294	+139
250–449 employees	63	114	+51
500+ employees	23	57	+34
Total	2,558	4,182	+1,624

Source: *The Security Enforcement Industry,* the Morton Research Corporation, October 1975.

Technological Impact

Technology has played an important role in the growth of the private security industry. For example, with the application of advanced technology to the security industry, even one of the oldest security devices, the lock, was subject to revolutionary changes: combination locks, combination time locks, delayed-action time locks, combination locks with surveillance and electronic controls, and eventually access-control systems that use the technology of television and minicomputers.

The same advances in electronics technology that improved the quality of television and radio have had significant impact upon the security market, broadening it to include additional consumer areas. This new technology has fostered the development of large-scale, totally integrated security systems run by computers that control not only access but also refrigeration, heating, air-conditioning, and fire detection. The progression from vacuum tubes to transistors to today's subminiaturization age of hybrid integrated circuit technology has played a major role in the growth of the industry.

Additionally, technological advances have reduced component cost and size, leading to the introduction of security measures now commonly in use, such as low-light-level, closed-circuit television cameras and electronic article-surveillance devices. A number of recent technological advances in electronics and communications engineering have not yet been applied to the development of security products and systems. Electronic security will likely become more prevalent as applications are developed and become cost effective.

Other factors, in addition to the rising crime rate, account for this technologically intensive growth in private security services. For example, the Insurance Services Office recommends that insurance companies offer a premium credit or reduction when commercial and industrial property is protected by burglary and detection systems certified by Underwriters' Laboratories. The Federal Bank Protection Act of 1968 mandated increased security measures and equipment for Federal banks after they had sustained 23 deaths, 61 injuries, and $15 million in losses from robberies, burglaries, and larcenies in 1967.[13]

In some instances, the sheer magnitude of an organization's assets requires highly sophisticated security measures. For example, various art museums in the United States and Canada employ advanced security technology to protect their $7 billion collective investment. In fact, nearly half the budgets for special exhibitions at major art museums, as well as 10 to 20 percent of normal operating budgets, are expended for security measures.[14]

Most market estimates project that, with the "encroachment by electronic technology,"[15] growth rates for guard, armored car, and courier services will be modest compared to the 10 to 12 percent annual growth of the past few years.

Industry Trends and Revenues

The private security community is often referred to as the private security industry—and for good reasons. According to one 1974 estimate, expenditures for the provision of private security in this country has reached $6 billion annually.[16] This figure includes proprietary or inhouse security, as well as contractual private security products and services.

Quantifiable data concerning the size of the private security industry in terms of number of firms, personnel, and revenues vary within the research reports available. This is understandable because very little baseline data are available.

The following estimates give some idea of the magnitude of the security industry: Two recent market research studies place the estimate of security services and products provided to clients by private firms in 1975 at $3 billion. A study by Arthur D. Little, Inc., also estimated revenues of $3 billion in 1975 for "security products and services," based upon a growth rate of 12 percent per year.[17] Based upon estimated revenues of $2.5 billion in 1974 for "loss prevention products and services" and a projected growth rate of 10 percent annually, a study by Frost and Sullivan, Inc., estimated 1975 revenues of $2.8 billion.[18]

In a 1970 study of the nature and extent of private security, the RAND Corporation found that $3.3 billion was expended in 1969 for "security services within the private sector," including $1.6 billion for inhouse services.[19] This figure breaks down to $800 million for equipment, $540 million for contract guards, $128 million for armored car service, $120 million for central station alarms, and $80 million for investigative services.

Both the Arthur D. Little and Frost and Sullivan market research reports estimated that contract guard, investigative, and armored car and courier services account for approximately one-half of all revenues. A market study by Morton Research Corporation estimated total revenues for the provision of protective services at $2 billion in 1975, on the basis of total revenues of company growth trends and service sector growth patterns.[20]

A large number of persons are employed in private security. For example, the *RAND Report* (Vol.

[13] Davis, Alberts. "Bank Security—It is the Law," *Industrial Security*, October 1969, p. 5.

[14] Pfeffer, Irving, and Ernest B. Uhr, "The Truth About Art Museum Insurance," *Museum News*, Vol. 52, No. 6, March 1974, p. 23.

[15] Little, Arthur D., Inc. *Outlook for the U.S. Safety, Fire Protection and Security Business.* Cambridge, Mass.: ADLI, January 1973, p. 23.

[16] "The Losing Battle Against Crime in America," *U.S. News and World Report*, Vol. LXXCII, No. 25, Dec. 16, 1974, p. 32.

[17] Little, Arthur D., Inc. *op. cit.*, p. 23.

[18] Frost and Sullivan, Inc., *The Industrial and Commercial Security Market.* New York, March 1975, p. 2.

[19] Kakalik, J. S., and Sorrel Wildhorn, *Private Police in the United States: Findings and Recommendations*, R–869/DOJ. Washington, D.C.: Government Printing Office, 1972, Vol. I, p. 12.

[20] Nossov, *op. cit.*, p. 2.

I) stated that in 1969, 222,400 persons were employed in proprietary or inhouse security functions and 67,500 as contract guards and investigators.[21] Frost and Sullivan, in their 1974 study, indicated totals of 226,300 inhouse private security personnel and 71,200 contract guards and investigators.[22] The Morton Research Corporation report estimated the total number of private guards, watchmen, private police, and detectives at 350,243 in 1970, using occupational characteristics information from the U.S. Bureau of the Census.[23] This figure apparently includes persons employed in the primary occupation of the categories considered quasi-public police and guards and watchmen employed directly by governmental entities.

Various studies indicate that the number of private security personnel in this country currently by far exceeds the number of local sworn police personnel. For example, a recent study in Cuyahoga County (Cleveland, Ohio) found 8,900 private guards and detectives compared with 4,150 sworn police officers.[24] Considering that 1,000 of those police officers moonlight as private security officers, the number of private security personnel is even larger.

The contention that private security personnel outnumber public law enforcement officers is further supported by the results of Private Security Task Force surveys conducted in two cities—New Orleans and St. Louis.[25] Because police department licensing of private security personnel is required in these two cities, it was possible to obtain reasonably accurate figures for the number of licensed private security personnel. This 1975 study revealed that private security personnel outnumber public police. In New Orleans, there were 4,187 licensed private security personnel and 1,413 police officers. In St. Louis, the number of licensed private security personnel was 2,977; commissioned police officers numbered 2,177. In addition to the number of licensed private security personnel, approximately 45 percent of St. Louis police officers (1,000) have approved secondary employment in private security.

During the 15-year period from 1960 to 1975, there was a dramatic 2,312 percent increase in the use of contract guards in St. Louis, as measured by the change in numbers. At the same time, there was a significant decrease in the number of inhouse guards as a percentage of total private security personnel. During this same 15-year period in St. Louis, the number of private security personnel increased 263 percent, while the number of commissioned police officers increased only 11 percent.

The Private Security Task Force also gathered employment figures for private security. (A summary of that effort is in Appendix 9.) The most significant conclusion reached by this research was that there are at least a million persons presently employed in private security.

Although there are problems inherent in comparing sets of figures and determining the validity of data, the important point is that the delivery systems for providing private security services and products are a large-growth industry. Americans are spending increasing amounts of money, over and above public law enforcement expenditures, to protect themselves and their property.

Much of the growth of private security can be attributed to a rising crime rate, coupled with the fact that public law enforcement does not accommodate the specialized needs of business and industry for asset protection. The average annual growth rate of security services and products over the past several years of 10 to 12 percent has approximated the annual increase in the rate of crime, as measured by the FBI Uniform Crime Reports. According to preliminary reports for Crime Index offenses in 1975, crime in the United States rose by 9 percent in 1975, as compared with 1974.[26] Robbery and aggravated assault increased 5 percent each; larceny-theft, 12 percent; and burglary, 7 percent.

As crime-related losses in business communities grew to an estimated $21.3 billion in 1974, total expenditures for security were projected at $6 billion (contractual and proprietary).[27] The sales of contractual security services and products advanced rapidly in the 15-year period from 1958 to 1973: from $428 million to nearly $2 billion.[28] (See Figure 7.) In the 5 years from 1967 to 1972, total protective service receipts increased from $522 million to $1.4 billion.[29]

As mentioned earlier, market research studies by Arthur D. Little and Frost and Sullivan estimated the 1975 sales for security products and services at approximately $3 billion. Figure 3 outlines the major user segments of this market. These composite figures are based on the rather consistent market estimates

[21] Kakalik and Wildhorn, *op. cit.,* p. 11.

[22] Frost and Sullivan, Inc., *op. cit.,* p. 116.

[23] Nossov, *op. cit.,* p. 24.

[24] Brennan, Dennis T. *The Other Police.* Cleveland, Ohio: Governmental Research Institute, 1975.

[25] "Characteristics of Licensed Private Security Personnel in Two American Cities: New Orleans, Louisiana, and St. Louis, Missouri." See Appendix 2 to this report.

[26] *FBI Uniform Crime Reports,* January-June 1975.

[27] *U.S. News and World Report, op. cit.,* p. 32.

[28] Data for Figure 2 was compiled using Predicasts, Inc., data for security services and products, excluding fire-detection equipment. See J. S. Kakalik and Sorrel Wildhorn, *The Private Police Industry: Its Nature and Extent,* R–870/DOJ. Washington, D.C.: Government Printing Office, 1972, Vol. II, p. 31.

[29] Nossov, *op. cit.,* pp. 2–3.

Figure 7. Growth of Private Security (Sales of Products and Services)

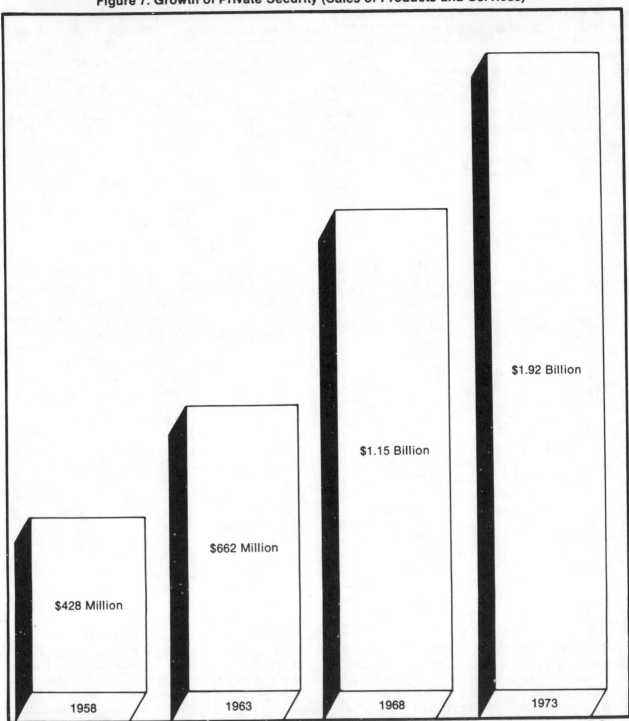

$1.92 Billion

$1.15 Billion

$662 Million

$428 Million

1958   1963   1968   1973

Source: RAND Corporation, *The Private Police Industry: Its Nature and Extent*, R-870/DOJ. Washington, D.C.: Government Printing Office, Vol. II, 1972, p. 31.

made by Predicasts, Inc., the RAND Corporation, A. D. Little, and Frost and Sullivan.

In reviewing Figure 8, it is significant to note the enormous cost of crime in selected areas of each market segment:

• Industrial and transportation segments account for 50 percent of the total market. The U.S. Senate Select Committee on Small Business fixes annual cargo theft at $2.5 billion.[30]

[30] Frost and Sullivan, Inc., *op. cit.*, p. 55.

Figure 8. Major Market Segments for Private Security Products and Services

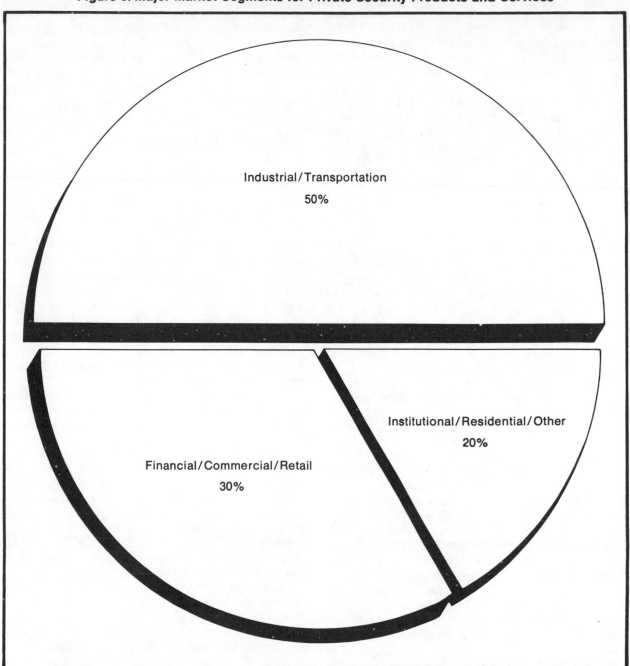

Industrial/Transportation
50%

Financial/Commercial/Retail
30%

Institutional/Residential/Other
20%

● Financial, commercial, and retail interests represent approximately 30 percent of the total market. The U.S. Department of Commerce cites $6.5 billion in retail losses from crime during 1975,[31] and the FBI Uniform Crime Reports placed nonresidential losses from burglary at $423 million in 1974.[32]

Discount department stores report that losses of cash and merchandise would reach $845 million in 1975.[33] And the hotel-motel industry estimates millions of dollars lost during 1975 to souvenir hunters alone.[34]

[31] *Crime in Retailing*. Washington, D.C.: Department of Commerce, August 1975, p. VII.
[32] *FBI Uniform Crime Reports*, 1974.

[33] *Store Thieves and Their Impact*, Mass Retailing Institute of New York, 1974.
[34] "Hotel-Motel Men Suffer in Silence," *Security Systems Digest*, Feb. 13, 1974, p. 1.

• Institutional, residential, and other areas comprise the remaining 20 percent of the market. The U.S. Senate Juvenile Delinquency Subcommittee Report estimates that the cost of vandalism in the schools—$500 million annually—is comparable to the "entire investment for textbooks for our nation's schools."[35]

The foregoing classification represents those industry segments that have remained the principal users of private security, but the industry has expanded and contracted over time to meet various other demands. For example, railway police reached a record number of between 12,000 and 14,000 personnel in 1914 as railroads spread across the country, but their number has now reduced to approximately 3,500.[36] The use of commercial aircraft skyjacking as a terrorist and extortion technique created an additional need in the transportation industry for private security personnel. The air transport industry has engaged in point-of-departure screening of airline passengers and baggage for explosive devices and weapons at all principal U.S. airports since December 1972. Largely as a result of these mandatory screening procedures, there has not been a successful skyjacking of a commercial aircraft in the United States since their institution.

Terroristic acts, however, have continued to increase in other segments of society. The FBI reported 42 persons killed, 242 persons injured, and $23.4 million in property damage from 1,574 bombing incidents in the first 9 months of 1975.[37] These figures show the largest increase in deaths, personal injuries, and property damage since 1972, when the FBI established the National Bomb Data Center to monitor such incidents. A majority of these bombings, especially those involving extensive property damage, were directed against corporations. Companies have had to initiate elaborate, and often costly, procedures to protect their assets and key executives. For example, private security firms, as mentioned in Section 1, provide an estimated 20,000 persons as bodyguards and frequently install electronic devices to aid in protecting corporate executives, other VIP's, and their families and personal property.

Despite its growth, periodic expansion into other areas, and increasingly sophisticated products, the private security industry continues to center most of its services in the areas from which it originated in the 1850s: guards, investigators, and armored car and courier services. These services, according to the Arthur D. Little, Inc., market report, continue to account for nearly 50 percent of industry revenues (Figure 9). The market study by Morton Research estimated the service mix among protective services, based upon the percentage of total receipts by type of service in 1974: detective agencies (including contract guards and watchmen), 61 percent; armored car services, 17 percent; burglar and fire alarm services, 22 percent.[38]

Security Trade Associations

The growth of private security services and products has been accompanied by a growth in security-related national trade associations. Currently, there are more than 30 private security trade organizations, plus a number of security committees or divisions of major national associations, such as the American Bankers Association, the Association of American Railroads, the National Association of Manufacturers, the American Hotel and Motel Association, the American Transportation Association, and the National Retail Merchants Association.[39] (See Appendix 5 for a listing of security-related associations.) There are also numerous State and regional security associations. Functionally, the trade associations cover the full range of private security activities, with one or more in areas such as alarms, armored cars, credit card fraud, private detectives, computer security, educational security, detection of deception, insurance, and security equipment.

The American Society for Industrial Security (ASIS), a professional society with a membership, in June 1976, of about 7,000 security executives, supervisors, and administrators, has made significant contributions to the professionalism of the private security industry. To further the objectives of crime prevention and the protection of assets, ASIS is concerned with all aspects of security in the private sector and emphasizes the education and professionalism of its members through publications, workshops, and seminars. The ASIS Foundation, Inc., was established as a separate organization in 1966 to receive grants and donations for programs to further upgrade security professionalism.

Conclusion

Private forces have been used to provide security in America from the earliest colonial times. Even with the establishment of public police forces, many businesses and industries sought the assistance of private security services to provide additional protection for their property and assets. Industrializa-

[35] "School Crime at Crisis Stage," *Chicago Tribune*, January-February 1974, p. 25.
[36] American Association of Railroads, *op. cit.*
[37] *FBI National Bomb Data Center Reports*, January-September 1975.
[38] Nossov, *op. cit.*, p. 5.
[39] *Security Letter*, Vol. V, No. 18, Part II.

Figure 9. Private Security Products and Services Revenues

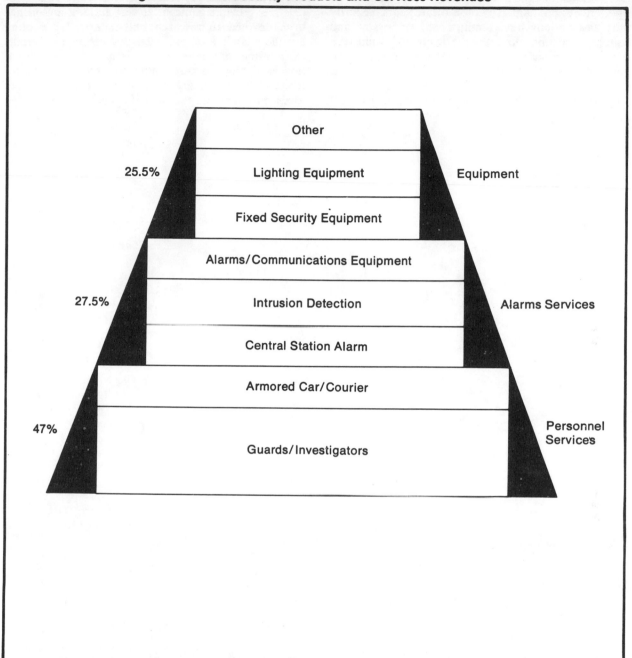

Source: A.D. Little, Inc., "Estimates of Sales to End User—1975," *Outlook for the U.S. Safety, Fire Protection and Security Business*, January 1973.

tion, urbanization, and prewar and postwar security demands intensified the need for additional protection. Many contractual private security companies and proprietary forces emerged in response to this need, resulting in a substantial growth of the industry. Advances in electronic technology have also contributed significantly to the industry's growth pattern.

Today, as a result of ever-rising crime rates, coupled with the enormous demands placed upon public law enforcement agencies and their lack of adequate resources to deal with these demands, private security has become a multibillion-dollar-a-year industry, and the number of private security personnel surpasses that of public law enforcement in many localities. Moreover, present crime and financial statistics indicate that the industry will continue to experience significant growth in future years. Security trade associations have similarly grown in size and number, and the American Society for Industrial Security has made significant strides toward professionalism of the field.

However, even though it can be established that the investment in private security services and products has grown significantly, very little attention has been devoted to research in this area, accounting for the inability to provide concrete figures on its exact extent and revenues. This paucity of information is highlighted throughout this report in the interest of establishing a reliable data base for future focus on upgrading the industry and its components.

SECTION 7

UNIQUE SECURITY PROBLEMS OF SPECIALIZED AREAS

- Airports/Airlines
- Commercial Complexes
- Educational Institutions
- Financial Institutions
- Health Care Facilities
- Hotels/Motels
- Housing
- Manufacturing
- Museums and Libraries
- Railroads
- Retail Establishments
- Special Events
- Transportation

Introduction

The major components of private security services and products and the major security user groups have been discussed in previous sections. Organizations, facilities, and business establishments utilize varying combinations of proprietary and contractual personnel, services, and hardware depending on their individual characteristics or security needs. This section presents a brief overview of selected areas to demonstrate both the prevalent use of private security services in specialized areas and the diversity of security problems encountered in protecting persons and property.

Airports and Airlines

The need for security at airports and airlines was dramatically brought to public attention by the sudden emergence of the skyjacking of commercial aircraft and by the bombings, bomb threats, and accompanying extortion attempts using aircraft and hostages in the late 1960's and early 1970's.

Between 1963 and 1967, there were only four attempted skyjackings of U.S.-registered aircraft. However, in the following 5-year period, 1968 to 1972, there were 134 attempted skyjackings of U.S.-registered aircraft; 82 of these were successful: the skyjackers were able to control the flight of the aircraft and either reach their destination or achieve

their criminal objective.[1] Although diversion of aircraft from international airports in New York, Miami, Los Angeles, and Chicago to destinations in Cuba and South America were the most frequent and highly publicized acts, attempted skyjackings also occurred during this period at 54 other U.S. airports.[2]

Disgruntled individuals, mentally deranged persons, inebriates, and practical jokers are frequently the perpetrators of bomb threats and skyjackings. Terrorist groups, however, have increasingly used these means to advance their causes. One of the most notable terroristic actions occurred in 1970 when Palestinian terrorists diverted three aircraft to Zerka, Jordan, and subsequently demolished them.[3] Sensational incidents such as this were responsible for the doubling of aircraft bomb threats the following year, according to the Federal Aviation Administration (FAA). (In 1971, 1,145 bomb threats were made against U.S. and foreign aircraft in the United States.[4])

In 1974, there were four bomb explosions at U.S. airports and two aboard U.S. aircraft.[5] In the same year, the FAA reported 1,453 bomb threats made against U.S. and foreign aircraft in the United States, including 48 attempts at extortion.[6] Additionally, 397 bomb threats were reported against domestic airports.[7] Of these, 89 percent were made by anony-

[1] U.S. Department of Transportation, Civil Aviation Security Service, Federal Aviation Administration, "Hijacking Statistics for U.S. Registered Aircraft." Washington, D.C., July 1975.

[2] Ibid.

[3] U.S. Department of Transportation, Civil Aviation Security Service, Federal Aviation Administration, "Worldwide Criminal Acts Involving Civil Aviation." Washington, D.C., July 1975.

[4] U.S. Department of Transportation, Civil Aviation Security Service, Federal Aviation Administration, "Bomb Threats Against U.S. Aircraft and Foreign Aircraft in the U.S." Washington, D.C., July 1975.

[5] Ibid.

[6] Ibid.

[7] U.S. Department of Transportation, Civil Aviation Security Service, Federal Aviation Administration, "Bomb Threats Against U.S. Airports—1974." Washington, D.C., July 1975.

mous persons using the telephone, and in 50 percent a specific area of the airport was designated.

The security problems associated with response to bomb threats are immense, because in only half of the incidents is an area of the airport specified, and very often little advance warning is given before the announced time of detonation. Air carriers experience delays in air traffic, and often it has been necessary to evacuate an entire section or terminal of an airport as a result. Some explosions have occurred without warning, causing serious injuries, loss of life, and extensive property damage. In December 1975, during the holiday traveling season, an explosion at a LaGuardia International Airport terminal in New York City killed 11 persons and injured 75. The boldness and tragedy of this bombing prompted the President of the United States to direct Cabinet-level officials to develop improved countermeasures against such terrorist actions.

Federal efforts and countermeasures had already been underway, however. Since 1972, the increasing frequency of skyjackings and bomb threats prompted the development of improved security measures and procedures for greater protection and safety of persons aboard aircraft and in airports. In December 1972, the FAA initiated compulsory screening of persons and carry-on baggage prior to entering the departure area of an airport. Federal legislation also was enacted providing specific criminal penalties for criminal actions against aircraft. Since the implementation of tighter security measures, there only have been two successful skyjackings of a common carrier aircraft in the United States—in November 1972 and September 1976.

The responsibility for screening passengers and baggage rests with the air carriers, and, in most of the major airports, this service is provided by contract security firms. Another FAA regulation requires that the airport manager provide a sworn law enforcement officer at the screening point to apprehend persons making threats or attempting to carry handguns, knives, explosives, or other dangerous weapons and articles aboard aircraft.

The FAA reports that approximately 165 million passengers and 125 million nonpassengers were screened at airport checkpoints during the first 10 months of 1975. Of that number, 9,766 persons were referred by the contract security screening personnel to law enforcement agencies, and 2,092 persons were arrested, including 1,131 for carrying weapons. The FAA further reports that, during this period, 1,600 handguns, 37,000 knives, 156 explosive devices, 22,700 rounds of ammunition, 2,485 assorted firearms (rifles, starter pistols, tear gas guns, and so forth), and some 45,000 other articles

considered dangerous were detected at the checkpoint by screening devices and searches.[8]

Although passenger checks are generally performed by employees of contract security firms, close cooperation is maintained with law enforcement agencies and airline and airport security personnel. Overall airport security is often provided by law enforcement officers, who are members of State, local, or county law enforcement agencies or who come under the aegis of a county commission, authority, or department established for the operation and maintenance of the airport facility. FAA regulations now require both scheduled airline carriers and airport managers to submit security programs to the FAA for approval.

Theft at airports is a major problem encountered by airline and airport security personnel. Aircargo theft is estimated to be in excess of $100 million annually [9] and is especially serious at those airport operations that have been infiltrated by organized crime. In addition, theft of passenger baggage, airline tickets, credit cards, merchandise from airport retail shops, and autos and their contents occur. Because of the large number of persons using airport facilities, order maintenance, crowd control, VIP escort, and traffic control functions must be provided by airline and airport security personnel. Extensive use is made of access-control systems and closed-circuit television monitoring.

The Air Transport Association of America has established 48 local security committees at principal airports in the United States. These security committees coordinate efforts to increase protection of aircraft and their crews, passengers, cargo, and baggage. Each committee is composed of representatives from every air carrier serving the airport, airport management, airfreight companies, catering services, every law enforcement agency serving the airport, and the Civil Aviation Security Service of the FAA.

A problem unique to airports and airlines is the potential for large-scale disaster—a plane crash resulting from heavy air traffic at major airports and extensive use of wide-bodied jet aircraft. Response to an aircraft disaster requires close cooperation among fire, medical, law enforcement, private security, and airport personnel in extinguishing fires, reaching and caring for victims, providing emergency medical treatment, and ensuring perimeter security to prevent looting and to expedite the movement of emergency personnel and vehicles. The FAA now requires, as part of its airport certification procedures, that an airport disaster plan be devel-

---

[8] Telephone interview with Civil Aviation Security Service, Federal Aviation Administration, Dec. 11, 1975.

[9] Frost and Sullivan, Inc., *The Industrial and Commercial Security Market.* New York: March 1975, p. 55.

oped. The Airline Pilots Association has been active in providing simulated aircraft disaster exercises to test the workability of these plans and to improve the coordination and mobilization of personnel and equipment at airports and crash scenes.

Commercial Complexes

Office Buildings

A large number of contractual and proprietary security forces perform a range of security functions, including guard, alarm, and armored car/courier services, at thousands of office buildings throughout the country. In addition to the need for security at manufacturing and distribution centers, corporations also must protect company assets and the lives and personal property of their employees, as well as ensure a safe working environment in leased or owned office buildings.

Some companies must establish and maintain specific levels of security in their offices and/or buildings to meet the requirements stipulated for certain government contracts. Similar security measures may be used for nongovernment work that the company deems highly sensitive, such as trade secrets.

Both innercity office buildings and commercial industrial parks (usually suburban office complexes that include nonmanufacturing businesses, such as research laboratories, sales facilities, medical buildings, and other professional and technical offices) are commonly constructed and owned by a private developer, who may either assume the responsibility of providing security for all buildings and tenants within the complex or assign the responsibility to the prime tenant of a particular building. The private developer is likely to use the services of a contract security firm to ensure the protection of the entire complex. A company designated as prime tenant of a building may lease excess office space to other firms and provide them with security of common areas in the office building, such as lobbies, hallways, restrooms, and so forth.

The major security problems encountered in office buildings include after-hours burglaries and theft; theft from a tenant by another tenant's employees; theft by service, maintenance, and custodial employees; assaults, rapes, and other crimes against persons; regulation and control of visitor traffic; bomb threats; protection of executive offices and personnel; and fire watch. The items most frequently stolen from office buildings include small office equipment, such as typewriters, calculators, and duplicating and photocopying machines; office furnishings; securities and valuable documents; blank

payroll checks; and checkwriting machines. General office or tenant space is protected primarily through the use of master key systems, card key readers, closed-circuit television (CCTV) on a limited basis, and security personnel.

Large commercial office buildings typically have elevator banks in lobby areas where access-control measures are essential to monitor visitor access. Many new office buildings are constructed according to the core-concept design, which places all elevators, restrooms, and service facilities at the center of the building and permits more flexible use of office space. This concept contributes to more effective control of lobby areas and visitor access by limiting the number of entrances and exits in the building.

Security measures designed to protect lobby areas and elevator banks may include the use of CCTV, guards, and receptionists who monitor visitor pass systems. In the evenings or after business hours, elevators can be equipped with key switch or programmable card key readers, which allow only authorized personnel to operate the elevators or to reach specified floors. In larger buildings, employees are issued programmable magnetic cards that can be used in conjunction with other access-control equipment and that contain magnetic codings for the doors to specific floors and offices.

The extent of use of other security devices and personnel depends on the size and location of the building, the number and nature of tenant businesses, and the crime rate of the surrounding area. Some corporate tenants need special security precautions because of threats of extortion resulting from actual incidents of arson and bombings against office tenants. Fire stairwells are a key security concern for many high-rise buildings, because local fire codes often require that doors to these stairwells be left unlocked.

Where security guards perform patrol functions in addition to access control, they generally follow programmed watchclock stations on tours of duty during the day and evening. In addition to CCTV, access-control systems, and the annunciation of intrusion and fire alarms, many of the newer and larger office buildings use central consoles to monitor heating, ventilating, and air-conditioning systems. These reduce manpower requirements, increase monitoring and detection capabilities, and permit faster response by security personnel.

Securities, cash, and valuable records and documents are generally stored in vaults that are often equipped with closed-circuit television or time-lapse cameras. In large companies, records on payroll, accounts payable/receivable, sales mailing lists, product information, customer lists, and other important information are kept on computers. Protection of computer processing centers, remote terminals, and the information contained in machine-readable form is a major security concern. Physical security measures—i.e., special access-control and locking systems, CCTV, and guard posts—are normally used to protect computer areas. Data base security involves the design of program verification and usage procedures by computer specialists.

Shopping Centers

The migration of central-city residents to the suburbs was largely responsible for the commercial phenomenon known as the shopping mall. These large shopping centers capitalized on the convenience of a large number of retail, entertainment, professional, and other business concerns in a central location with ample parking and easy access for thousands of customers. Shopping centers are microcosms of the communities in which they are situated and reflect many of their crime problems. Management of shopping centers has become a specialized field, and the International Council of Shopping Centers (ICSC) certifies the qualifications of managers for shopping centers of varying sizes.

Shopping malls are usually discussed in terms of gross leasable space, ranging from less than 100,000 square feet to more than 800,000 square feet. The major security problems of shopping centers are order maintenance in the common areas and traffic control. Each tenant is usually responsible for implementing security provisions within individual leased space. Security personnel are employed by virtually all open and enclosed shopping malls with more than 300,000 square feet of gross leasable space. About two-thirds of shopping centers with less than 300,000 square feet of leasable space also employ security personnel according to a 1975 ICSC survey of 117 shopping centers.

In shopping centers, various combinations of local law enforcement personnel and proprietary and/or contractual guard forces provide security. Some of the larger shopping centers are assigned local law enforcement officers, and in other jurisdictions security personnel of the shopping center are given limited police powers through local ordinance.

Shopping centers with less than 100,000 square feet of leasable space tend to use only part-time proprietary or contractual security personnel, whereas the larger shopping centers (more than 300,000 square feet) frequently use contractual security personnel on a part-time and seasonal basis to supplement proprietary security forces. In addition, the larger shopping centers generally have a director of security, and the proprietary security force is often supplemented with CCTV and supported by a communications system and mobile patrols of the parking areas.

Educational Institutions

Secondary Schools

Security in secondary school systems has received increasing national attention in the last few years. In addition to the number of incidents of crime and vandalism against schools, court-ordered desegregation of local school systems has resulted in security problems in both the schools and their surrounding communities. Several large city school districts have experienced violence as a result of these court actions.

Following their 1975 hearings and surveys, the U.S. Senate Subcommittee on Juvenile Delinquency estimated that vandalism in school systems amounts to $500 million annually—a figure the subcommittee stated was "comparable to the entire investment for textbooks for our nation's schools in 1972."[10] In compiling its estimates, the subcommittee noted that the cost of vandalism and stolen property in Chicago, Detroit, Los Angeles, and New York City school systems alone exceeds $10 million annually.

In addition to acts of vandalism and the violence related to court-ordered desegregation, crimes of violence in general are a significant problem in the schools. The Senate subcommittee conducted a survey of 757 public school districts for 1970 to 1973 and estimated that every year there are 70,000 serious physical assaults against teachers and literally hundreds of thousands of assaults on students, including at least 100 murders.[11] The report cited one incident in which an eighth grade pupil armed with .45-caliber and .38-caliber handguns killed his principal and wounded a school security officer.

Crime in secondary schools is not limited to large school systems. The Senate subcommittee found that the incidence of serious crime has substantially increased in suburban and rural school systems. Some school administrators feel that the open school concept, in which students are required to attend school only for classes, encourages an influx of idlers, drop-outs, and others, who may disrupt normal administrative and academic functions.

School systems have traditionally regarded order maintenance and theft problems as administrative concerns. But the rising incidence of these problems, combined with a school's civil liability for the safety of its students, has caused an increasing num-

---

[10] U.S. Senate Subcommittee on Juvenile Delinquency, *Our Nation's Schools—A Report Card: "A" in School Violence and Vandalism*. Washington, D.C., 1975.
[11] *Ibid.*

ber of school systems to view such occurrences as criminal in nature and has prompted development of comprehensive security programs.

The greater emphasis being placed on school security is evidenced by the recent formation of the International Association of School Security Directors, with members from some 300 school districts in the United States. Also, the American Society for Industrial Security has formed a specific division for school security—Educational Institutions. Finally, the United Federation of Teachers union in recent years has made security in the schools a negotiable item in its collective bargaining process for teacher contracts. Their concerns include improved security procedures, as well as adequate security personnel and equipment.

There are two primary objectives in school security: (1) protection of teachers and students and their personal property, and (2) protection of the school facilities and equipment. Law enforcement agencies have placed increasing emphasis on juvenile bureaus to deal with youthful offenders. But much of their work, similar to that of law enforcement agencies in general, is performed in a response mode, and little time is left to perform preventive work or to focus on the underlying specific problems of recurring incidents throughout the school systems. In New York City, for example, law enforcement officers were called to the schools on 5,530 separate occasions in the first 7 months of 1973.[12]

School systems have used varying combinations of contract and proprietary personnel to establish security programs. School security personnel have been given police powers in some States through county and local ordinances. Many of these personnel have primary jurisdiction over criminal incidents that occur in the schools. In the Broward County, Fla. (Ft. Lauderdale), school system, a staff of eight investigators is assigned to the director of internal affairs, who administers the school security program for the county. In the Fayette County, Ky., (Lexington) school system, the Division of Safety and Security is responsible for security in the county's 45 schools, which have more than 35,000 students and nearly 3,000 employees. The division is an organized law enforcement agency with jurisdiction over the elementary, junior high, and high schools; it employs only college-educated men and women.

Florida passed a Safe Schools Act in 1975 to provide funding to school systems for the development of crime prevention and safety programs, the provision of security personnel, and the installation of alarm systems. Another Florida law stipulates training certification for personnel engaged in school

---

[12] United Federation of Teachers, *Security in the Schools*, undated, p. i.

security functions. In addition, the State Department of Education is exploring the possibility of providing private security vocational training in 67 counties.

The increase in burglaries and arson, in addition to vandalism, has led many school systems to implement comprehensive intrusion-detection systems and to install nonbreakable windows. In Alexandria, Va., for example, a Law Enforcement Assistance Administration grant was made to the city for the installation of an intrusion-detection alarm system. This system has markedly reduced crime-related losses in the city's 22 schools, from a previous high of $180,-000 to approximately $20,000 annually.

Colleges and Universities

The security problems of colleges and universities are somewhat different from those of secondary school systems. One of the major differences is the almost continual use of facilities of a college or university. Except at community colleges, which generally close by midnight, access control is a major problem.

In addition, large numbers of residential housing units for students, faculty, and staff create a densely populated community within the city or town in which they are located. Some college or university campuses are larger than many towns. For example, the campuses of Michigan State University and the University of Michigan are larger in population than most cities in Michigan. Whether campuses are located on the periphery or near the center of cities, they do not escape the problems of the cities, particularly crime.

Initially, security at colleges and universities was an administrative function of the physical plant or buildings and grounds staff. Night watchmen or guards were used for fire detection and major crime prevention/detection patrol. The need for organized, well-trained security personnel at colleges and universities was dramatically demonstrated in the late 1960's. Campus demonstrations, student strikes, and forceful occupation of school buildings by students often resulted in local and State law enforcement agencies being called. But few long-term countermeasures were developed to provide an ongoing security capability to successfully prevent or contain such outbreaks of violence and confrontation. The intervention of police agencies on the campus was viewed by many students, faculty, and administrators as unwarranted.

Today, however, both students and administrators are increasingly demanding and providing comprehensive security programs to protect colleges and universities from property thefts and violent crimes that have overflowed from the cities onto the campuses. (Unlike secondary schools, vandalism—with the exception of graffiti—is not a major problem.) The primary concern, according to a recent survey of some 700 attendees at security conferences sponsored by the National Association of College Auxilliary Services, is safety of individuals. There has been a dramatic increase in the past few years in armed robberies, assaults, muggings, and rapes at college campuses throughout the country. On some campuses, the students have organized rape-crisis centers to provide counseling and assistance to rape victims; on other campuses, male students have formed protective night escort services for female students.

In more recent years, population density created by the construction of high-rise dormitories has posed new problems in providing protection for students and their personal property. This high concentration of students makes it virtually impossible for them to be familiar with all other residents of the dormitory, and, thus, it is easier for an intruder to assume the identify of a student. In answer to this problem, many colleges have installed extensive locking and access-control systems to restrict access to residential areas.

In addition to theft of student property, college campuses sustain significant losses from theft of college property, most commonly audiovisual and laboratory equipment, typewriters, calculators, and educational materials such as books and art objects. Another major concern is theft of examinations.

Similar to secondary schools, higher education institutions have used combinations of contractual and proprietary security personnel and hardware for the protection of the campus and its residents. One of the major constraints in the use of electronic security is the 24-hour access to some areas of the campus, such as athletic and student unions, that are heavily trafficked and typically have several entrances and exits. However, closed-circuit television and alarm systems have been installed in bursar's and cashier's offices on many campuses because of the rising number of armed robberies and robbery attempts. These areas generally serve as central collection points for all cash funds from campus facilities, such as student unions, snack bars, cafeterias, housing, and so forth.

Many administrators also believe that the installation of electronic sensor detection devices in libraries has significantly reduced the number of thefts of library books. When these devices are used only at main entrances and exits, however, theft of books may still occur, because other exits (i.e., fire doors) are not monitored.

Campuses have increasingly moved toward the establishment of proprietary security forces and the appointment of directors of security. The over-

whelming majority of proprietary forces on publicly funded campuses have some power of arrest or police authority. Approximately 40 States have legislation providing police authority for proprietary security personnel on campus. Most of these States restrict such police powers to public institutions of higher education, but some States, such as Massachusetts and New Jersey, also make these powers available to private institutions. On some campuses, security personnel obtain police powers on a provisional basis from local law enforcement agencies.

At some larger institutions, the security personnel are responsible for comprehensive law enforcement, traffic and fire safety, and loss-prevention functions. At the University of Connecticut, for example, the Public Safety Division maintains a fire department, mounted patrol, locksmith and key control, ambulance service, and campus transportation system, in addition to its police functions.

A recent trend in campus security has been the active involvement and participation of students in crime prevention with the security personnel. On some campuses, students are used on an informal basis to assist in crowd control and traffic direction at large public events, such as concerts and sporting contests. On other campuses, there is more formal organization of student patrol or student marshal programs. One such program at Syracuse University uses students to patrol parking areas and general residence halls. They are equipped with two-way radios and arm patches identifying them as "student security services." At the University of Georgia, the campus security department is comprised entirely of students. In this program, security personnel must have undergraduate degrees and be pursuing graduate degree programs in police science or criminal justice. Some universities offer incentives to campus security workers by providing free tuition or tuition assistance.

Financial Institutions

The security and stability of the Nation's financial institutions (commercial banks, savings and loan associations, credit unions, loan companies, and brokerage houses) are critical to a lasting and healthy economy. In contrast to the many indirect losses sustained by other businesses, most losses in the financial community are direct financial losses: theft of cash, stocks, and bonds; check and credit card fraud; and embezzlement of funds.

From 1958 to 1967, commercial and mutual savings banks grew at an average rate of 40 percent, according to the American Bankers Association. Today they number approximately 40,000. During the growth period, crimes against these institutions increased by more than 200 percent. In 1967, 23 persons were killed and 61 persons were injured as a result of bank robberies, burglaries, and larcenies,[13] and $15 million in losses were sustained.

A wide variance in the number and type of security measures employed by banks caused great concern to Government agencies that regulate federally insured financial institutions. Surveys by the FBI, resulting from investigations of bank robbery statute violations, disclosed that many banks had totally inadequate protective and preventive measures against these crimes. In 1968/1969, the Federal Home Loan Bank Board conducted a survey of 194 banks that revealed that fewer than 50 percent had alarm systems, only 17 percent used cameras, and just over 10 percent used security guards. The same agency surveyed 60 banks that had been burglarized and found that 20 had installed alarm systems, only 3 monitored the premises with cameras, and again just over 10 percent used security guards.[14]

The significant increase in bank robberies, larcenies, and burglaries, and the lack of standardized or adequate protective measures, led Congress in 1968 to enact the Bank Protection Act. This act required federally insured banks and savings and loan institutions (provisions were subsequently extended to federally insured credit unions) to (1) designate a security officer, (2) cooperate with and seek security advice from the FBI and other law enforcement agencies, and (3) develop comprehensive security programs and implement protective measures to meet or exceed certain federally approved standards. The act is monitored and administered by four federal regulatory agencies: the Federal Reserve Board, the Federal Savings and Loan Insurance Corporation, the Office of the Comptroller of the Currency, and the Federal Deposit Insurance Corporation. In a graduated sequence, beginning in July 1968 and ending in February 1970, each federally insured financial institution covered by the act was required to (1) develop, for approval by its board of directors, a written security plan or program meeting nine minimum requirements, (2) appoint a security officer, (3) file a formal report with the appropriate regulatory agency on current security measures at bank facilities, and (4) install and maintain vault area lighting systems, tamper-resistant exterior doors and window locks, and alarm systems.

The net effect of the Bank Protection Act was a mandated increase in the range of security services and hardware utilized by most financial institutions. Market research studies, in fact, reflect a sharp rise in spending by banks in 1969 and 1970 for fixed security equipment, electronic surveillance equipment, and proprietary and contractual alarm systems and security guard forces. Banks and other financial institutions represent a major segment of the market for fixed security equipment such as vaults, lockboxes, tamper-resistant locking systems, and automatic and drive-in teller equipment. In addition, financial institutions are a major market for armored car and courier services.

Compliance with the Bank Protection Act requirements was facilitated by development of bank security manuals and security seminars by the Bank Administration Institute and American Bankers Association. The American Society for Industrial Security also sponsored workshops on providing security for and combatting crimes against banks and financial institutions. Many bank administrators found these to be useful tools, especially when security officers designated under the act had no training in security or law enforcement and devoted only partial time to security activities.

Despite these expanded security measures, violations of bank robbery statutes, which the act was designed to reduce, increased significantly in both number and dollar losses. The FBI reports that in 1974 there were 3,517 robberies, 408 burglaries, and 328 larcenies, with losses totaling $40.3 million— more than double the amount of losses prior to the enactment of the Bank Protection Act.[15] Bank officials, however, point out that the security measures specified in the act have had a preventive and deterrent effect and that approximately 60 percent of these crimes occurred in urban banks in the 10 most populated States.

The Bank Protection Act did not address forgeries, fraud, and embezzlement, although losses to financial institutions from these actions far exceed losses from robberies and burglaries. Enormous losses are incurred each year as the result of fraudulent use of credit cards and checks. Added to these are the estimated $40 million worth of stock certificates and $25 million in government bonds that are lost or stolen each year.[16]

Indicative of the concerns of the Securities Exchange Commission are recent amendments to the Securities and Exchange Act of 1934 that require that every member of a national securities exchange, broker, dealer, registered transfer agent, and registered clearing agency fingerprint partners, directors, officers, and employees. The amendments also direct every national securities exchange, member thereof, registered securities association, broker, dealer, municipal securities dealer, registered transfer agent, reg-

---

[13] Davis, A. S. "Bank Security—It is the Law," *Industrial Security,* October 1969, p. 4.
[14] *Ibid.*

[15] *FBI Uniform Crime Reports,* 1974.
[16] Chamber of Commerce of the United States, *Deskbook on Organized Crime,* Rev. ed. Washington, D.C., 1972, pp. 51–52.

istered clearing agency, participant therein, member of the Federal Reserve System, and bank whose deposits are insured by the Federal Deposit Insurance Corporation to report to and inquire through the National Crime Information Center (NCIC) regarding missing, lost, counterfeit, or stolen securities. Also, stock exchanges and the Securities Exchange Commission are urging brokerage houses to increase protective measures for negotiable stocks and bonds, because many of them store a substantial number of negotiable documents on their premises.

The U.S. Department of Commerce states that losses from fraudulent use of credit cards cost banks about $420 million in 1973.[17] A wide variety of fraudulent practices contribute to these losses: false applications; cards issued but never received by applicants because of error or theft during the manufacturing process or mailing; and cards lost or stolen in lodging or restaurant establishments, from automobiles, and by pickpockets. In addition, merchants and waiters sometimes use a customer's credit card to cut a blank charge slip at the time of sale, and later submit a receipt to cover a cash sale, the proceeds of which they keep. Stolen credit cards are often sold to other persons or presented at automatic tellers for cash withdrawals.

Legislation enacted in recent years has been directed specifically toward the reduction of fraudulent credit card offenses. For example, most States have adopted major provisions of the model State credit card crime act; this, according to the Association of Credit Card Investigators, has had a measurable effect on both the deterrence of credit card fraud and the prosecution of offenders. Similarly, prior to the 1970 amendment of the Federal Truth-in-Lending Act, which prohibited the indiscriminate mailing of credit cards, many banks incurred losses in the range of several million dollars from mass mailing of bank credit cards. Banks continue to experience other credit card-related offenses, however, and some bank security officials feel that they do not receive sufficient cooperation or resources from law enforcement agencies in the investigation of such crimes.

Although the introduction of computers in banking greatly assisted data processing operations, it also indirectly aided individuals defrauding banks through checking account schemes. Approximately 26 billion checks are written and processed each year, and losses from check frauds amount to about $1 billion annually.[18] Check fraud is committed in a number of ways: by forging signatures on stolen checks, by altering face amounts on legitimate checks, by forging bank officials' signatures of approval on large checks to be drawn on accounts with insufficient funds, through the theft of blank payroll checks and check-writing machines, and through the practices of kiting.

Kiting has become particularly difficult to detect since the advent of computerized banking. It involves the use of two or more banks to make simultaneous deposits and withdrawals and thereby obtain credit before sufficient time has elapsed to clear the checks. Prior to the use of computers, bank personnel were able to scrutinize such transactions at the time of processing. However, kiting practices can now be detected only by using special computer programs to monitor unusually large transactions and continuous activity involving accounts with small running balances.

Some of the more important regulations set forth by the Bank Protection Act include the maintenance of bait money for potential robberies, the periodic removal of excess cash from tellers' windows and bank premises, and the development of security-conscious opening and closing procedures and stringent security inspections. The act also requires that bank security officers be trained to use security devices and to follow specified procedures in the event of a robbery; however, many of them undertake far more comprehensive training. This broader perspective is significant, because bank security programs must be closely interfaced with all aspects of banking operations, not just limited to areas where money and valuables are exchanged or stored.

In addition to the changes occurring as a result of the Bank Protection Act, the movement toward electronic funds transfer systems, which include such activities as remote tellers and automatic bank machines, is having a major impact on the banking industry. This movement toward making banking activities more accessible to citizens provides unique challenges to bank security officers. Adjustments in security programs need to be made to meet the new marketing activities of financial institutions. Some bank security officers indicate that these changes will require more and, in many cases, new and different training for their security guards, tellers, and other banking personnel.

Health Care Facilities

A recent security research report indicates that there are more than 31,500 health care facilities in the United States.[19] Indeed, health care is big business—the fifth largest industry in the Nation.[20] Health

---

[17] U.S. Department of Commerce, Bureau of Domestic Commerce, *The Cost of Crimes Against Business.* Washington, D.C., November 1974, p. 4.

[18] Chamber of Commerce, of the United States, *A Handbook on White Collar Crime.* Washington, D.C., 1974, p. 33.

[19] Frost and Sullivan, Inc., *op. cit.,* p. 22.

[20] Colling, Russell L., "Hospital Security," *Security World,* Vol. 3, No. 6, June 1966, p. 14.

care facilities include publicly and privately owned hospitals, clinics, nursing homes, outpatient trauma centers, and physicians' office complexes. Hospitals represent the most significant element of health care and have the most serious security problems. Hospital/health care security can be defined broadly as a system to create and maintain a safe environment for patients, visitors, and employees, and to protect physical assets (medical equipment, supplies, buildings, and personal property).

Hospital security is distinct from many other forms of private security because of its openness—24-hour-a-day operation, few locked doors, and campus-type construction.[21] Unlike retail stores, banks, schools, and some industrial plants, the hospital cannot shut down at the end of the day and establish security barriers against entry. The hospital must remain open to admit the sick and injured, to permit patients to have visitors, and to carry on the normal business of gift shops, pharmacies, and doctors' offices. Because of the necessary openness of health care institutions, access control is more difficult and must be tempered in accordance with the objectives of medical care and the institution's public relations program.

Because the goal or end product of health care is life preservation, security restrictions that are perceived even remotely as impediments to this primary goal are often unacceptable to administrative and medical staffs. For example, rigid check-out/check-in procedures for surgical equipment or supplies are often viewed as hindrances to prompt medical treatment.[22] Further, for the patient's well-being, health care institutions generally encourage visitors, a practice that poses security problems and risks.

In a 1972 security survey of 196 hospitals in 30 States, visitor control was cited by the respondents as the most formidable security problem to be overcome.[23] The same survey revealed that internal theft ranks as the second most troublesome security problem. In descending order, the items most frequently stolen are linens, cash and personal effects, office supplies and equipment, housekeeping supplies, food, radios and television sets, and drugs.[24]

Additional security problems relatively unique to hospitals and other health care facilities include the heavy daily flow of people (patients, visitors, medical personnel, and other employees) and vehicular traffic, a substantial number of female employees (on some night shifts, hospital staffs are often 95 percent female), a high percentage of professional staff who often are disinclined to adhere to security procedures, and large quantities of consumable items (drugs, linens, food, medical supplies, and equipment) that make property inventory and accountability difficult.

Health care security administrators generally agree that their major crime and security hazards are theft of materials, drugs, and personal property and the possibility of fires or explosions. They also indicate that crimes against persons are frequently committed in and around medical centers. Of concern are not only simple assaults but also violent crimes, such as rape and aggravated assaults on patients, nurses, and visitors. Hospitals and health care facilities feel a strong responsibility to protect patients and employees, as indicated by one hospital administrator:

The patient entering a hospital expects to be medically treated with the highest quality of care, to be safe from intrusion or theft, to be protected from personal injury and to be treated not only as a guest, but as a human being who has entrusted his life and his possessions to complete protection.[25]

Officers of the International Association for Hospital Security stress the importance of preemployment screening and training for health care security personnel to reduce crime problems and security-related incidents. Areas for security improvement frequently mentioned by hospital security administrators include:

1. Better accounting control procedures for medical supplies and equipment, and

2. Access to criminal history records for preemployment screening purposes to reduce the potential for employee theft of cash, property or drugs, or assaults and sex crimes committed against patients or employees.

Further recognition of the unique security problems of hospitals and other health care facilities is supported by the American Society for Industrial Security, which has a health services division.

Hotels and Motels

During the past decade, crime in lodging establishments has climbed to dangerous heights, both in terms of the number of incidents and the severity of the incidents. Formerly, a retired police officer was sufficient to control hotel crime. Today, security staffs of over 25 personnel cannot prevent crimes against guests and the establishment in some major city properties.

Coupled with the national rise of law suits against hotels and motels has been an unprecedented increase in civil filings against these establishments, charging

[21] Glassman, Stanley A. and William J. Fitzgerald, "Contemporary Changes in Hospital Security," *Security Management,* September 1974.

[22] Colling, *op. cit.,* p. 15.

[23] Burns Security Institute, *National Survey on Hospital Security.* Briarcliff Manor, N.Y., October 1972, p. 2.

[24] *Ibid.,* p. 3.

[25] Olmstead, John A. "The Legal Aspects of Hospital Protection," *Security Management,* September 1974, p. 25.

that security negligence resulted in harm to a guest, a tradesman, or an employee. In many of these cases, a new innkeeper's case law is developing as the hotels appeal adverse court decisions.

Not only are insurance costs skyrocketing because of this increase in hotel crime, but, in some instances, hotel liability insurance is becoming difficult to obtain.

With guests fearful of leaving downtown hotels because of the risk of street crime, huge losses sustained from employee theft, and the growing frequency of guestroom thefts and attacks on guests, hotel and motel operators are turning to private security to develop professional responses to these many problems.

Hotel and motel security spokesmen agree that a major crime problem exists with internal employee theft. Because some employees of lodging establishments must have master or submaster keys in order to perform their routine daily functions, they have access to secured hotel/motel property, as well as to the personal property of guests or residents. Thus, an employee may have innumerable opportunities to steal from guest rooms and/or hotel/motel property. The items most frequently stolen include money, linens, silver, foodstuffs, liquor, and other articles that can be easily concealed when taken from the premises. The most significant internal-theft losses are associated with functions such as cash handling, housekeeping activities, receiving and storage functions, laundry services, and restaurant/bar services.

External theft also represents a substantial share of the crime problems cited by hotel/motel industry spokesmen. Guests who steal property from their rooms and professional thieves and burglars using illegally obtained master keys account for external losses. The American Hotel and Motel Association estimates that millions of dollars worth of property is lost through guests who take items as souvenirs.

Motels, for the most part, have been able to avoid one difficulty that has traditionally plagued the hotel industry: skips or nonpaying guests. Motels typically require guests either to pay in advance for their lodging or to establish valid credit, whereas in most hotels room charges and other costs incurred by the guests are paid upon checkout. Certain problems are common to both hotels and motels, however, and these include the theft of money, jewelry, credit cards, and other valuables from their guests; acts of vandalism; and the vice problems frequently associated with such semipublic facilities.

The increase in the number of armed robberies at motels has prompted many to follow the lead of hotels and install closed-circuit television monitoring systems in lobby and cashier areas. It is ironic that efforts to make hotels and motels more convenient for guests inadvertently increase their vulnerability to clandestine activities; elevators and parking garages provide thieves with greater access to unprotected areas and less possibility of detection. Consequently, an increasing number of hotels and motels are also making use of monitoring systems in parking areas, ancillary lobbies, and elevators; they also have begun to use central access-control systems for guest rooms.

Hotels and motels in resort areas encounter security problems of a slightly different nature because most of their guests are occupied with recreational or sightseeing activities and spend considerable time away from their rooms. Similarly, hotels and motels that regularly host large conventions and conferences must adapt their security procedures to accommodate the special demands created by such situations.

In general, the security practices established at a particular hotel or motel are the responsibility of the individual owner or franchise holder. The large, national lodging chains usually have corporate security staffs to provide support and guidance to franchise owners. The corporate security staff conducts security surveys; investigates specific loss problems; establishes guidelines for security policies and staffing; makes recommendations on cash-handling procedures, preemployment screening techniques, and emergency plans; and maintains liaison with local law enforcement agencies.

Hotel/motel industry executives and security directors agree that greater emphasis should be placed on security in training managers, owners, and franchise holders. Clearly, providing free movement and open facilities to guests must be balanced with the implementation of procedures and measures to minimize criminal opportunities. Industry spokesmen believe that sound security measures not only will increase the safety of guests but also will raise the profitability of hotel and motel operations. In particular, industry officials believe that degree programs in hotel and restaurant management should include courses in security as part of the core curriculum.

Housing

Although crimes of violence have received considerable attention because of their dramatic and tragic nature, reported burglaries of residential dwellings now account for more than $600 million in property losses annually. In addition, victimization studies conducted for the Law Enforcement Assistance Administration (LEAA) indicate that the incidence of crime actually committed is two to three times higher than that officially reported to law enforcement. Possible reasons for this underreporting of crime include a sense of despair on the part of citizens victimized more than once and a lack of citizen confidence in the ability of law enforcement agencies to solve crimes and recover stolen property.

Traditionally, people's homes have been considered their castles, but many homes are now becoming fortresses to protect residents and their personal property from criminals. Only affluent persons can afford to install sophisticated burglar alarm systems and other advanced technological protective devices. But increasing numbers of homeowners are installing special locks, floodlights, and less expensive burglar alarms to protect their homes and families. Contract security firms offer residential patrol services to augment law enforcement protection in many communities. Some homeowners associations and developers of more exclusive residential developments hire their own security personnel to perform patrol services and to monitor central gate entrances, and many new real estate developments advertise such security features as major selling points.

The high incidence of burglary and muggings has also resulted in increased security measures in private high-rise apartment and condominium complexes, with emphasis on controling the access of nonresidents. Access-control measures include the use of doormen in vestibules, external door locks to interior hallways controlled remotely by tenants, and monitoring of entrance areas with closed-circuit television (CCTV) often connected to a master antenna system to allow tenants to view visitors from their dwellings. Some newer high-income apartment and condominium complexes have installed extensive alarm, monitoring, and access-control systems that are manned on a 24-hour basis by central console operators.

Recent studies by the U.S. Department of Housing and Urban Development indicate that crime is considerably higher in public housing with low- and medium-income and senior citizen residents than in other residential areas. These studies reveal that crime rates in some public housing projects are two to four times higher, with higher rates of victimization per household or dwelling unit. These studies also indicate substantially higher rates of multiple victimization of the same dwelling unit—a large number of residences experiencing more than one burglary.

Many public housing authorities have implemented some of the same protective measures being used by private apartment buildings and high-rise complexes, including access control and CCTV monitoring. However, housing authority administrators point out that they are limited in the protective measures they can undertake because public housing is often a low priority item in municipal budgets. Housing authorities in larger cities with many housing projects often maintain proprietary or quasi-public security forces. Many of these security personnel have full or limited police powers, are armed, and provide the primary law enforcement response within the area encompassed by the various housing projects under housing authority control. In some cities, housing authority police departments that operate their own investigative units are as large as medium-sized local law enforcement agencies.

Smaller housing authorities, or those with limited funds for security, organize tenant patrols or use contract security firms to provide protective services. Tenant patrols are made up of volunteers or minimally paid tenant-residents who patrol the housing project in the evening hours. Some of these tenant patrols have portable radios to communicate directly with the police department when a suspicious person or criminal incident is observed. Housing authority administrators cite two major drawbacks to the use of tenant patrols: (1) tenants are often reluctant to take action against their neighbors for fear of retaliation; (2) little legal protection is afforded members of the tenant patrol should they intervene in a crime situation.

In addition to burglaries, muggings, rapes, and assaults, public housing authorities also must contend with a considerable amount of vandalism. They attribute much of this to the vandals' attitude that they are destroying someone else's property and not their own. Because much of the vandalism is caused by juveniles living in the housing projects, the establishment of recreation programs and youth activities programs has considerably decreased the incidence of vandalism in some projects.

In the past several years, LEAA has emphasized improved design of buildings and residential and commercial developments to create safer environments and to minimize opportunities for the commission of crimes. Several pilot studies and demonstration programs indicate that architectural features, lighting, building layout, and site design can affect the incidence of crime. LEAA's Private Security Advisory Council includes an Environmental Security Committee to study ways to reduce crime through improved environmental security design. Among the items under consideration are requiring crime impact statements prior to approval of building plans and granting certificates to builders who provide certain security protective devices, features, and standards in building residential units.

Manufacturing

Manufacturing consistently accounts for nearly one-quarter of the gross national product. The net production of the manufacturing industry at $326 billion in 1974 makes it the largest contributor of all industries to the gross national product—nearly double that of retail trade.[26] At the 313,000 manufactur-

---

[26] Telephonic interview with Bureau of Economic Analysis, U.S. Department of Commerce, January 1976.

ing plants throughout the country, goods and products shipped from production facilities were valued at $757 billion in 1972 and nearly 18 million Americans, representing one-fourth of the total labor force, were employed in manufacturing.[27] The term "manufacturing" encompasses a range of primary products, including those related to food processing, transportation (automotive, aerospace, shipbuilding), textiles, primary metals (steel and aluminum), fabricated metal products, machinery, consumer electrical products, and heavy durable goods.

The U.S. Department of Commerce estimates that manufacturers incurred losses of more than $2.8 billion in 1974 from crime, which represents an increase of 60 percent since 1971.[28] Manufacturing losses result from internal employee theft and pilferage, external theft of production materials and finished products, arson, and burglary and sabotage of machinery and equipment.

Internal theft by employees is a major contributor to manufacturing crime losses. The items most frequently stolen include tools; electronic components; assembly parts; consumable items such as cleaning supplies, oils and greases, paints, wire, and so forth; plumbing and electrical supplies; and manufactured products, including consumer products that can be readily used by employees. External theft losses include not only cartons and containers of finished products but also raw materials in usable form; silver, gold, and other precious metals; small machinery and power tools; and office equipment from administrative offices located at production facilities.

In manufacturing complexes, the areas most vulnerable to the theft of finished products are warehouses, loading docks, shipping and receiving areas, and distribution centers. The Office of Transportation Security, U.S. Department of Transportation, has conducted studies that demonstrate that most cargo theft occurs in and around these areas during normal operating hours and is accomplished by persons and vehicles authorized to be in the area. This finding implies a considerable degree of collusion among employees and outside individuals.

The security priorities of the manufacturing industry are as varied as the types of products manufactured. For example, the drug industry is vitally concerned with the protection of chemical substances used in the production of drugs and the prevention of theft or loss of narcotics and dangerous drugs as well as their diversion into illegal distribution channels. On the other hand, the chemical industry places heavy security and safety emphasis on preventing fires and explosions.

A major security concern of manufacturing firms engaged in Department of Defense (DOD) contract work is the protection of classified information and materials. They must adhere closely to prescribed Government regulations for safeguarding classified information, documents, materials, end products, and storage and work areas. The security programs and policies at these manufacturing plants are mandated by the DOD regulations, and the plants are subject to inspections by the Office of Industrial Security, U.S. Defense Supply Agency. Such inspections typically focus on visitor control, document flow, guard assignments and responsibilities, classified material destruction, and records of accountability. Extensive background checks must be conducted on applicants by security personnel prior to their employment to ensure they meet Government security clearance standards.

In addition to the protection of classified information, manufacturing plants often use production processes and techniques that are patented or considered to be trade secrets of the firm. Special procedures are undertaken to protect these production areas, formulas, materials, blueprints, and so forth from observation or theft by visitors and unauthorized persons.

Production areas, in general, are protected by plant security personnel to prevent disruption of work flow or damage to materials and to facilitate product delivery schedules. The responsibilities of security guards in manufacturing plants often include the monitoring of electrical and utility systems for failure or malfunction of automated machinery, fire prevention, and inspections for Occupational Health and Safety Act (OSHA) violations. These responsibilities, coupled with crime prevention and detection functions, essentially comprise manufacturing security, which is often referred to as "plant protection."

A major emphasis of plant security programs is the regulation and screening of visitors; service, repair, delivery, and maintenance personnel; vendors; truck drivers; and employees. Access control at manufacturing plants may include the use of card key and color-coded photo identification badge systems for restricted areas; closed-circuit television monitoring on shipping and receiving platforms and in high-security storage and production areas; perimeter fencing and high-intensity lighting; vehicle and pedestrian checkpoints and security barriers; and employee and visitor parcel inspections. Other security concerns are the prevention of crimes such as petty thefts and assaults among employees and the protection of employees, vehicles, and their contents in parking areas.

[27] U.S. Department of Commerce, Bureau of Census, *Census of Manufacturers*. Washington, D.C., 1972.

[28] U.S. Department of Commerce, Bureau of Domestic Commerce, *The Cost of Crimes Against Business*. Washington, D.C., November 1974, p. 15.

In many large corporations, a director of security is responsible for managing an overall corporate security program. The corporate director of security administers a central security staff that provides support services to subsidiary companies and production plants; conducts internal investigations and analysis of major thefts, security violations, losses, and reported shortages; establishes corporate security policies and employee security-awareness training; and inspects security operations at manufacturing plants and facilities.

At the plant level, there frequently is a supervisor of security who may report to either the corporate director of security or to the plant manager. The plant security supervisor is responsible for most of the daily physical security operations.

Security expenditures are often a function of the plant's profit center costs.[29] In smaller corporations, the security director at the corporate level is responsible primarily for security policies and internal investigations, and the plant manager assumes the security responsibility. In other instances, each plant has a security manager with no centralized corporate security function or the plant manager provides security services through contract security firms.

Guards were first used in plants on a large scale prior to World War I amid concerns of sabotage and espionage by politically active nationalists. During World War II, many proprietary security forces were established in manufacturing plants, and more than 200,000 plant guards were granted the status of auxiliary military police because their primary duties included the protection of war goods and products, supplies, equipment, and personnel.[30] Larger manufacturers have continued to maintain proprietary security forces, but recently there has been an increased use of contractual security guards because proprietary security programs have become more expensive with the rising costs of employee fringe benefit programs. Plant managers and facility security supervisors often have corporate authorization for entering into contracts for plant protection services. In these instances, contract guards may be supervised by a small proprietary force and follow procedures established at the corporate level.

Plant security personnel maintain liaison with local, county, and State law enforcement agencies in the investigation of internal theft and criminal incidents that occur on the premises. Defense industry security personnel maintain an active liaison with the Federal Bureau of Investigation and the Defense Investigative Service, Office of Industrial Security, and are required to report all security violations and theft of classified materials and products to the Defense Supply Agency.

Museums and Libraries

Museums

In 1974 the aggregate investment of fine arts museums in the United States and Canada was estimated to be several billion dollars, including permanent collections of artifacts and art objects of $4.5 billion, loan collections worth $550 million, and special exhibitions that average $300 million per year.[31] Although fine arts museums have a favorable loss experience from an insurance point of view, the annual insurance premiums for their collections are estimated to be $12 million.[32] Nearly half of the total budget for special exhibitions at major art museums, as well as 10 to 20 percent of normal operating budgets, is expended for security measures.[33]

The criminal problems most frequently encountered by fine arts museums are theft of collection pieces and the inadvertent purchase of works of art fraudulently presented as authentic or that have been stolen. Museums also experience order-maintenance and vandalism problems, but the trend toward charging admission fees has reduced these problems. The most common thefts involve small items that are easily concealable and items that can easily be converted to cash. In some cases, precious metals and gems are cut away from artifacts, reset, and sold. The theft of less valuable items and small concealable items occurs during the hours when the museum is open to patrons, but the theft of the more valuable items generally occurs at night.

Thefts of major works of art involve a complex distribution channel often consisting of a thief, a receiver of the stolen art, a middleman, and a final purchaser. A black market exists through which the art is eventually resold to museums or private collectors after first being purchased by antique or art dealers. The return of stolen art is often impeded because once a dealer has purchased a work of art, few people question the integrity of the dealer. They assume that any work of art purchased from the dealer is authenticated and not stolen. In some cases, invaluable masterpieces have been stolen and held for ransom. Museum directors and art curators point out that the loss of a work of art or an artifact can never really be valuated because the historical, cultural, and artistic value is inestimable.

The problem of stolen or fraudulent art is met in various ways. In the art museum, a registrar has the

[29] "Crime Does Pay," *Fortune,* September 1974, p. 55.
[30] Green, G., and R. C. Farber, *Introduction to Security.* Los Angeles, Calif.: Security World Publishing Company, 1975, p. 27.

[31] Pfeffer, Irving, and Ernest B. Uhr, "The Truth about Art Museum Insurance," *Museum News,* March 1974, p. 23.
[32] *Ibid.*
[33] *Ibid.*

responsibility for authenticating all acquisitions. Although there is no centralized place for documenting losses or cataloging permanent collections, INTERPOL, the international police organization, investigates international art thefts and distributes circulars on stolen art to member police organizations and art museums. Many museum directors have expressed a need for a central art registry, but some observers point out that museums normally do not disclose information concerning their sources of art acquisitions because of the competition for major works. The International Art Registry in New York City provides a service to collectors, dealers, and artists in photographing and classifying works of art for the purposes of documenting authenticity, ensuring value, and avoiding purchase of fraudulent works.

Fine arts museums employ proprietary and contractual security personnel and make extensive use of intrusion- and fire-detection systems. Many thefts occur at fine arts museums with no extensive technical security systems in operation. The areas of concern in the museum are vaults, reserve collections, study collections, and public exhibition sections. Three major types of surveillance and protection systems are used in museums: (1) perimetric, used to protect the perimeter areas; (2) volumetric, used to detect motion and entry into a showcase or room; and (3) fixed point, used to protect individual pieces. Both contractual and proprietary alarm systems are used, with some museums using central consoles and video monitoring manned by their personnel for faster response time in the event of an incident.

Another problem faced by all type of museums is the display of controversial exhibits. These pose a threat that activist groups may threaten to carry out wanton destruction of museum pieces. An example of this might be a Russian cultural exhibit on loan to U.S. museums threatened by radical religious or nationalist groups.

Libraries

Libraries experience a major problem with the theft of books. It is difficult to assess the dollar volume of losses incurred by libraries due to book theft because many libraries infrequently or never take inventory. As with works of art, the value of certain library losses cannot accurately be estimated, for example, the theft of special collections, rare or historic books, and out-of-print or irreplaceable books, manuscripts, and periodicals. Generally, these invaluable books and periodicals are kept in closed stacks and are subject to restricted-use policies and close supervision. The introduction of electronic marking of books and the use of detection sensors at main exits have significantly reduced the incidence of book theft.

Such systems are generally used in conjunction with security personnel. Security personnel also are maintained in libraries to deter disorderly behavior and vandalism and to maintain a fire and security watch during night hours when patrons are not using the facilities.

The mutilation of books is also a problem but has been minimized somewhat by providing photocopying machines at the libraries so that material can be reproduced rather than removed from the books. Larger circulation libraries sometimes have extensive intrusion- and fire-detection systems. One method that is being used to retrieve library books is the amnesty system whereby overdue books are allowed to be returned without penalty.

Railroads

Security of America's railways is provided by perhaps the oldest and most highly organized segment of the private security industry, the railroad police.

Today the railroad police represent an essential element of the industry and work closely with local, State, and Federal law enforcement agencies. Although the Nation's 3,500 railroad police are paid from corporate funds, at least 40 States have given them broad police powers. Because of this dual responsibility to the rail industry and the public, railroad police have been termed "parapublic." [34] In fact, railroad police are proprietary private security operations that have been granted certain law enforcement powers.

The Police and Security Section of the Association of American Railroads describes the basic objectives of the railroad police as:
- Protection of life and property;
- Prevention and suppression of crime;
- Investigation of criminal acts committed on or against the railroad, patrons, or employees;
- Arrest of criminal offenders;
- Supervision of conduct on railroad property;
- Performance of certain nonpolice services such as accident and claims investigation and safety management.

Railroad security executives cite cargo theft, vandalism, and theft of metals as their industry's major security problems. Total losses incurred for these acts were reported as $11.5 million in 1975 for 32 rail carriers, representing approximately 73 percent of U.S. and Canadian mileage.[35]

[34] "The Railroad Police," paper prepared by a subcommittee of the Police and Security Section, Association of American Railroads, December 1975, p. 2.
[35] "Monthly Statistical Report of Railroad Police Activities —December 1975," Association of American Railroads.

Certain security difficulties are unique to railroads, as illustrated by the following examples:

• A freight car loaded at one part of the country may move over several different railroads to its final destination in another part of the nation. The cargo is not examined unless an exception to a seal is noted during the movement or the car is listed on a special bulletin as a high-value load.
• Many railroads pass through the most crime-ridden areas of our largest cities.
• It is impossible to fence or adequately patrol the approximately 400,000 miles of railroad rights-of-way.
• Most criminals causing major problems are not railroad employees; therefore, internal controls do not suffice.
• Many thefts occur in large rail yards which are difficult to monitor with conventional hardware.
• The number and size of rail yards also make them difficult to cover by saturation of manpower.
• Metals belonging to railroads are easily stolen and "fenced." Examples are copper communication wire, brass rail car bearings and steel track material.
• The physical nature of railroads makes them vulnerable to acts of vandalism by trespassers, especially by juveniles.[36]

Security techniques utilized by railroad police to prevent and control crime as well as to enhance security include:

• Radio-equipped foot and vehicle patrol, including canine patrols;
• Patrol by helicopter and fixed-wing aircraft;
• Fixed-surveillance stakeouts;
• Undercover operations;
• Exchange of intelligence information with public law enforcement agencies;
• Employee security-consciousness programs;
• Criminal investigations aimed at prosecuting persons found responsible for crimes against railroads;
• Task force approaches involving the movement of many railroad police officers into a specific problem area to perform a tactical mission;
• Public relations and education programs aimed at community awareness and support of railroad police activities;
• Installation protection, including closed-circuit television, electronic security, sophisticated locking devices and gate controls.[37]

Railroad security administrators suggest that engineering improvements to cars and trailers may aid in preventing cargo theft and vandalism. Specifically, they cite problems with door construction of boxcars and trailers, container locking mechanisms, boxcar and trailer locking devices, and cable seals.

The need for further research is also apparent in other areas specific to railroad security, including:

• Night lighting (portable and permanent) for operational surveillance;
• Helicopter patrol for theft and vandalism surveillance;
• Canine units for trailer terminals and rail yard patrol;
• Closed-circuit television in trailer terminal operations;
• Photographic methods for trailer terminal operations (use of Regis Scope, etc.);
• Sensor device use on rail car and trailer shipments;

• Use of computers for determining claim and theft patterns;
• Use of screened rail cars to protect auto shipments from vandalism and theft.[38]

The private security industry should examine the excellent relationship that exists between railroad police and law enforcement agencies to determine how the industry's relationship with public law enforcement can be improved.

Retail Establishments

Retail establishments comprise perhaps the largest segment of business with which the average citizen comes in contact on a daily basis. Retail establishments include not only general merchandise department stores and speciality and apparel shops but also drug and food stores, appliance and furniture stores, radio and television stores, hardware stores and lumberyards, restaurants and fast-food shops, automobile dealers, and gasoline service stations. The U.S. Department of Commerce estimates that retail merchants lost $5.8 billion to crime in 1974, an 11 percent increase over 1973.[39] This loss is almost twice that experienced by other industries such as manufacturing, wholesaling, services, and transportation.

The types of retail businesses that absorb the greatest losses are general merchandise and apparel, $3.5 billion; food stores, $1.2 billion; and drugstores, $600 million.[40] Loss figures in retail businesses are generally reported in terms of gross sales or receipts and inventory shortages as a percentage of them. (Inventory shortage refers to the value of merchandise on the shelves being less than the book value at time of inventory.) Using these indices as a basis of comparison, small businesses, according to the Small Business Administration, suffer losses from crime that are 3.2 times the average and 35 times that of businesses with receipts of more than $5 million.[41] The small businesses are least able to absorb such losses or to expend money for adequate protective measures.

Stolen retail merchandise can be easily converted to cash or readily usable and consumable by thieves. The categories of merchandise representing the highest loss items for department stores include junior sportswear, young men's and women's high fashion

---

[36] "The Railroad Police," p. 5.
[37] Ibid., p. 6.

[38] Ibid., p. 7.
[39] U.S. Department of Commerce, *Crime in Retailing.* Washington, D.C., August 1975, p. vii. Figure cited excludes eating and drinking places, automobile dealers, building material dealers, and gasoline service stations.
[40] Ibid., p. 2.
[41] U.S. Department of Commerce, Bureau of Domestic Commerce, *The Cost of Crimes Against Business.* Washington, D.C., November 1974, p. 8.

clothing, costume and fine jewelry, leather and fur goods, cosmetics, phonograph records and tapes, and small electronic items such as hand calculators and portable radios. Based on the shortages in the financial and operating results of its membership in 1974, the National Retail Merchants Association estimates that the average shortage ratio for retail sales is 2 percent.[42] The average shortage ratio per type of retail business varies from 1 to 5 percent, with some of the high-loss items ranging as high as 10 percent. An average shortage ratio of 3 percent in drugstores is nearly at the margin of profit, any higher level of loss would force an owner out of business or into uncompetitive higher prices.[43] High-loss items for drugstores include cosmetics, costume jewelry, candy, toys, drugs, and phonograph records and tapes.

Reported crimes committed against all types of retail establishments in order of frequency are shoplifting, burglary, vandalism, bad checks, employee theft, and robbery.[44] It has been suggested that the frequency of employee theft is much greater than is indicated because a large percentage of employee theft is never uncovered or reported. For some retail merchants, however, robbery and bad checks are the major problems. Small food chainstores, gasoline service stations, and fast-food outlets are frequently subject to armed robberies.

According to FBI statistics, reported chainstore robberies increased 167 percent from 1968 to 1973.[45] A survey of crime in the Nation's five largest cities, conducted by LEAA concluded that victimization rates for retail establishments were substantially higher than for other types of businesses: 70 percent of the retail businesses reported being robbed or burglarized as opposed to about 50 percent of all commercial establishments.[46] Most food stores offer a check-cashing service for their customers, and the U.S. Department of Commerce estimates that $500 million were absorbed in losses in 1974 as a result of bad checks cashed at food stores.[47] Although merchants are sometimes able to recover losses from bad checks, the Federal Government will not honor forged Government checks, nor reimburse merchants for counterfeit bills.

The principal crime affecting retail stores is shoplifting (28 percent of all losses) according to the Small Business Administration, but many large department stores in major cities place the figure much higher. In New York City, more than 50,000 shoplifters are apprehended each year; certain of the major national department and catalog outlet stores apprehend a total of more than 50,000 shoplifters per year in their many stores across the country. Reported incidences of shoplifting rose 73 percent in the 5-year period between 1967 and 1972.[48] A shoplifter profile, developed by the National Retail Merchants Association from a survey of general merchandise department and speciality stores, reflects that approximately half the shoplifters are under 18 years of age; they are almost equally male and female; the average amount recovered per shoplifter apprehended is $27.78.[49] Some independent sources, however, cite the loss figure at nearly double this amount.

Young shoplifters often steal on impulse, as a result of peer group pressure, or because of alcohol or drug addiction. There are also professional shoplifters who selectively shop stores for specific high-value items that are easily convertible to cash through an organized fencing operation. Shoplifting techniques include concealing items in handbags and shopping bags, stealing additional items identical to the one purchased, occupying the salesclerk with a special order or request while others remove items, wearing stolen garments under and over clothes, and exchanging shabby or inexpensive street clothing for expensive store clothing in fitting rooms. Modern merchandising techniques create a significant security problem in retail operations by emphasizing customer accessibility to merchandise. As a result, many displays are highly vulnerable to theft.

Retail security personnel generally classify merchandise shortages in terms of external and internal theft. Forms of external theft by customers, in addition to shoplifting, include ticket switching of lower price sales tickets to higher price items, price writeover on sales tickets to simulate price markdowns, and return of previously stolen merchandise for refunds. External theft activities are often inadvertently facilitated by operational practices within the stores. For example, a limited number of sales personnel typically cover large areas of merchandise in discount and department stores. They are unfamiliar with some of the merchandise and would not recognize ticket switching or price writeovers on unfamiliar items. Similarly, store policies that allow items from

[42] National Retail Merchants Association, "Crime Against General Merchandise and Department Stores for 1974." New York, July 1975.

[43] U.S. Department of Commerce, Bureau of Domestic Commerce, *The Cost of Crimes Against Business*. Washington, D.C., November 1974, p. 20.

[44] *Ibid.*, p. 18.

[45] *Ibid.*, p. 10.

[46] U.S. Department of Justice, Law Enforcement Assistance Administration, *Crime in the Nation's Five Largest Cities*. Washington, D.C., April 1974.

[47] U.S. Department of Commerce, Bureau of Domestic Commerce, *The Cost of Crimes Against Business*. Washington, D.C., November 1974, p. 20.

[48] U.S. Department of Commerce, *Crime in Retailing*. Washington, D.C., August 1975, p. 4.

[49] National Retail Merchants Association, "Crime Against General Merchandise and Department Stores for 1974." New York, July 1975.

one department to be rung up in another department contribute to these forms of theft. External theft also occurs during the movement of merchandise, through hijackings, and by intentional shortages produced when vendors deliver goods to the store. Large retailers with their own credit card plans also experience losses through various types of customer credit card fraud.

Many retail security experts and store executives believe that the problem of internal theft by employees is as great as or greater than shoplifting and other forms of external theft. Although the Small Business Administration indicates that only 13 percent of retail losses are due to employee theft, others estimate that it accounts for as much as 50 to 60 percent of all retail losses. Employee theft occurs primarily by sales, stockroom, cashier, shipping and receiving, and delivery and mail order personnel who steal actual cash and store merchandise. For example, a salesperson may ring a sale on the cash register lower than the list price of the item and pocket the difference when the customer pays in cash. A salesperson may act in collusion with a customer who is shoplifting, ticket switching, or writing over prices on sales tickets. A buyer may take a markdown on items without recording them or act in collusion with vendors in shorting goods or taking kickbacks on inflated prices. Store personnel may also be responsible for the creation of fraudulent charge accounts or merchandise department accounts in computers.

For large retailers, a major internal theft problem exists in the flow and movement of merchandise from vendors to distribution centers, to stores, and to departments within the stores. Merchandise is often either removed before it is delivered or delivered intact but stolen by the receiving clerk or department checker who lists the load as being short. Home and C.O.D. deliveries are also sources of internal theft by employees and common carriers under contract to retailers. Similar to cargo theft, the volume and size of many thefts suggest extensive employee collusion on a significant number of documented external thefts and unexplained large shortages.

The kinds of protective measures undertaken by retailers vary significantly depending upon the size, location, and type of retail establishment. Small- and medium-sized retail establishments commonly utilize mirrors, closed-circuit television on a limited basis, trained guard dogs, store detectives from contract guard firms, merchant patrols provided by either a contractual firm or organized by area merchants, and alarm systems. Small- and medium-sized retail services account for a significant part of the revenues of the alarm industry. Jewelry stores are particularly susceptible to robberies and burglaries because of the high value and low bulk and weight of their merchandise, and they make extensive use of sophisticated intrusion-detection systems. High-value merchandise is also stored in large vaults, and even the smallest retailer commonly uses a safe to store money until receipts can be deposited.

Large retail establishments, such as general merchandise department stores and chain discount houses, often employ a full-time proprietary or contractual security force of uniformed guards, fitting-room checkers, and store detectives. In a survey of 41 member companies ranging in annual sales volume from $20 million to $100 million, the National Retail Merchants Association found that the average for total security expense expressed as a percentage of sales was 0.5 percent, compared to an average overall security payroll expense of 0.38 percent.[50] The same survey reported one full-time security person for every 27 employees in the reporting companies.

The proprietary retail security force generally employs an aggressive apprehension and prosecution policy against shoplifters, although shoplifter-arrest policies often vary according to local court policies on dealing with shoplifting offenders. Security personnel must see the shopper actually steal the merchandise or run the risk of false arrest.

Other retail security operations include the use of electronic article-surveillance devices installed at exits to scan packages for electronically sensitized price tags, honesty or test shopping, in which stores are selectively shopped by outside persons to detect shoplifting occurrences and employee security violations, undercover operatives in high-shortage or -loss areas, and rewards to employees who provide information on employee theft.

Historically, the principal functions of retail security departments have centered around the apprehension of shoplifters. In recent years, however, the mission of such departments has expanded to include preventive measures and shortage control. Security personnel spend a significant part of their time developing loss-prevention and security-education programs for employees, monitoring internal procedures with merchandising and auditing personnel, and coordinating their efforts with other store personnel.

Retail security personnel feel strongly that criminal history information on applicants should be made available to retail establishments because of the high incidence of employee theft and because "the pertinent question is ultimately one of suitability of a person to perform a certain job in which

---

[50] *Ibid.*

trust and deportment are the crucial requirements."[51] Other needs cited by retail security experts include improved merchandise display techniques, more sophisticated electronic control of merchandise, greater cooperation with law enforcement agencies, and consumer campaigns to stress the impact of shoplifting on price increases.

Special Events

In most major U.S. cities, the private security industry plays a significant role in order maintenance and traffic control at large public gatherings, such as sporting contests, entertainment events, trade association shows, conventions, parades, festivals, and civic functions. In the past, the facilities available for large events such as these were usually stadiums, armories, exhibition halls, and special-purpose public arenas. In recent years, however, many cities have constructed large multipurpose facilities that may be leased to organizations on a long-term seasonal basis (for example, to a professional football, basketball, or hockey franchise) or on a short-term basis for events such as dog shows, auto and boat shows, concerts, and college athletic contests.

In most large multipurpose facilities and stadiums, a small security force is maintained as an integral part of the facility's operations. Professional sports organizations often employ contract security personnel as well. The size of the security force varies considerably, as many of the facilities require an event's promoter or the lessee to provide adequate security. In these cases, the facility's security personnel coordinate and direct contract security firm personnel who have been hired by the promoter.

The major functions of proprietary or contractual security personnel at public gatherings include maintaining order; preventing the admission of nonpaying persons or persons using counterfeit tickets; preventing theft from patrons and their automobiles; preventing internal theft by employees such as concession stand attendants, ushers, and ticket takers; providing first aid for injured patrons; and regulating pedestrian and vehicular traffic. Security personnel work closely with local law enforcement agencies in traffic control and in dealing with problems that are special to large gatherings of people, such as apprehension of pickpockets and ejection of disorderly or abusive persons. In some cities, a local law enforcement presence is required at such events by local ordinance; in other cities, the facility managers routinely hire off-duty law enforcement officers to supplement security personnel and provide a law enforcement presence for arrest situations.

The number of patrons at a special event can vary considerably. For example, a football game in some stadiums can attract more than 75,000 persons; a basketball game at a civic center arena might attract 10,000 persons one night and a concert the next evening at the same arena draw only 1,000. There is also notable variation in crowd behavior at public functions. Security directors and operations managers of such facilities agree that sporting events attract a crowd different from that of other events. Sports spectators tend to exhibit more antisocial behavior, i.e., they get caught up in the emotion, competition, and aggressiveness of an athletic contest. The major problems at sports events involve restricting patrons from bringing alcoholic beverages into the facility and restraining spectators who become abusive to other patrons or athletic participants.

Security directors attempt to forecast the number of security personnel required for an event by monitoring advance ticket sales and gauging the type of crowd the event is likely to attract. Rock music concerts, in particular, pose a difficult security problem for most facilities. The patrons are generally young persons who become emotionally excited, and the events are very often sold out in advance. Persons who do not possess tickets for the event will often attempt to crash the ticket gates in large numbers to gain entrance to the concert or will mill about outside the facility in a disorderly manner.

Exhibitions and trade shows present security problems other than order maintenance and traffic control. A major problem is the protection of high-value merchandise and exhibits from theft and vandalism and regulation of access control. These events are generally open for patrons during the day and evening, and the merchandise, display articles, and booths must be protected at night and when access is restricted to exhibitors and officials. Special precautions must be taken during the assembly and dismantling of exhibits and trade shows to prevent theft by commercial thieves posing as truckers and exhibitors.

Transportation

Cargo Movement

The movement of goods and merchandise by the Nation's transportation system—air, rail, motor, and marine carriers—is one of the largest industries in the United States. Manufacturing and industrial operations depend on the transportation industry to

---

[51] Statement of the National Retail Merchants Association at Law Enforcement Assistance Administration, U.S. Department of Justice hearings on dissemination of criminal information records, Dec. 12, 1975.

supply them with raw materials for production, as well as to distribute and deliver merchandise to customers. Most of these materials and goods are transported by common carriers rather than company-owned transportation fleets. There are, for example, approximately 15,500 interstate motor carriers subject to the economic control and regulation of the Interstate Commerce Commission (ICC) and thousands more intrastate motor carriers not under ICC control. The term "cargo" is commonly applied to anything that enters and is moved by the Nation's transportation system—beginning at the shipper's loading platform and terminating at the consignee's receiving dock.[52]

The term "cargo theft" refers to the theft of entire shipments, containers and cartons, as well as pilferage of smaller amounts of goods or contents. Annual losses due to cargo theft from all modes of transportation are estimated at $1.5 billion, with nearly $1 billion of that amount attributable to theft from motor carriers.[53] The types of cargo most frequently stolen from motor carriers include food, clothing and textiles, tobacco and liquor, appliances, electrical and electronic supplies and components, automotive and other vehicle parts, and paper, plastic, and rubber products. The Office of Transportation Security, U.S. Department of Transportation (DOT), estimates that the sources of cargo theft/losses are hijacking (5 percent); breaking and enterings and external theft (10 percent); and internal theft, collusive theft, and unexplained shortages (85 percent). Cargo theft occurs at all points of the distribution system, including warehouses, receiving and shipping platforms, storage areas, depots, distribution centers, terminals, and piers.

It is estimated that organized crime activities account for 15 to 20 percent of the value of all cargo theft. Organized crime is involved in actual theft and redistribution of stolen goods as well as in the consumption of goods in the businesses it controls or owns.[54]

The remainder of the theft occurs primarily as the result of employee collusion among themselves or with persons outside the transportation system and organized fences. Transportation security experts point to the large dollar amount and size of cargo thefts as indications of the extent of employee collusion. Fences are often organized along both geographic areas and product lines; the operation can be very small, with a single person acting as a broker, or quite large, with several persons having cash readily available for the purchase of stolen goods. Thieves can generally expect to receive from fences anywhere from one-third of retail value to 10 cents on the wholesale dollar depending on the type of goods and the prevailing market.

Most of the stolen cargo ends up back in the transportation system, and legitimate businesses and dealers are often the recipients, either knowingly through collusion or unknowingly through the alteration of shipping invoices and so forth. Examples of legitimate dealers as receivers of stolen cargo are discount houses, wholesalers, salvage companies, and meat and food distributors.

The precise amount of direct financial loss to the transportation industry due to cargo theft is questioned because the figures cited are largely estimates. Some of the problems in arriving at accurate statistics include the reporting of goods as stolen that are subsequently found, the resolution of many claims shortly after they are reported, and the variance in assigning either wholesale, retail, or invoice values to the reported losses. The DOT is confident of its estimate of $1.5 billion, because it has been collecting statistics regularly over the past 3 years. (ICC-regulated carriers must report quarterly on freight loss and damage claims.)

Transportation security officials point out that argument over statistics only downplays the true impact of cargo theft on the transportation industry. For example, losses are generally expressed as a ratio of insurance claims to gross operating revenue, and, at an average of 1 to 2 percent, many firms view the losses as a simple cost of doing business. But security officials point to the high indirect losses that result from cargo theft: higher premium and deductible rates for insurance and difficulty in obtaining insurance coverage, lost time on cargo theft claims, delayed and lost sales by consignees, lost business by carriers, and increases in the price of goods and freight rates to absorb the loss in operating expenses.[55]

Security measures undertaken by the transportation industry include the use of proprietary and/or contract guards in shipping, receiving, and storage areas; access-control systems and perimeter fencing and lighting; closed-circuit television systems and alarms; and special security seals and alarms on trucks. Some high-value shipments are monitored through the use of transmitters on the vehicle or by a directional monitoring receiver in a helicopter. As part of the DOT's National Cargo Security Program, a demonstration program in Los Angeles monitors truck movements through electronic sign-

---

[52] U.S. Department of Justice and U.S. Department of Transportation, *Cargo Theft and Organized Crime*. Washington, D.C., October 1972, p. 1.

[53] Figures supplied by Office of Transportation Security, U.S. Department of Transportation, January 1976.

[54] U.S. Department of Justice and U.S. Department of Transportation, *Cargo Theft and Organized Crime*. Washington, D.C., October 1972, pp. 25–26.

[55] *Ibid.*, pp. 3–8.

posts in selected locations. High-security storage bins or areas have been established by various modes of carriers for high-value and high-loss classes of commodities; security guards, electronic surveillance, and intrusion-detection systems are used extensively in these high-security areas. Due to the high incidence of employee involvement in cargo theft, security officials believe that obtaining criminal history information on applicants for employment is essential to screening out potential thieves.

DOT makes several publications available on cargo theft countermeasures. These publications were developed from a series of studies that DOT conducted on pilferage, theft, and hijackings. In addition, DOT administers a special City Campaign Program in 15 key cities that are heavily industrialized and are prominent transportation centers for goods; these cities represent the major motor carriers shipping the largest volume of goods. In this program DOT establishes working relationships among carriers and government and law enforcement agencies, with emphasis on prevention of theft and prosecution of perpetrators as well as on increased accountability of goods.

The American Trucking Association has a Trucking Industry Committee on Theft and Hijacking that sponsors preventive programs for its member State trucking associations. Similarly, the Transportation Cargo Security Council is involved in the analysis of cargo theft and the development of preventive programs. The membership of this independent organization includes carriers, shippers, consignees, insurers, and labor groups.

Mass Transit Systems

Millions of Americans depend on public transit systems as their primary or only mode of transportation. Public transit systems evolved from the congested living conditions in major cities at the beginning of the 19th century with the establishment of horse-drawn streetcars that were eventually replaced by cable and electric cars, buses, and the rapid transit system of today. Gradually, these early transit systems began to experience the crime problems of the congested urban environment in which they operated, including vandalism, roving gangs of youths, and pickpockets. By the early 1900's several States had authorized transit companies to establish security forces, some with full police authority. As crime has increased in the Nation over the last 20 years, it has increased at comparable levels in transit systems. Consequently, most transit systems have established full-time security forces with full or limited police powers.

A 1970 survey, conducted by the American Transit Association of 37 transit systems in the United States and Canada, estimated that between 33,000 and 37,000 criminal incidents occur each year on transit systems.[56] The same survey placed the value of property loss and destruction due to vandalism on transit systems at between $7.7 and $10 million annually.

The major types of criminal incidents occurring on transit systems are robberies and assaults of operators, passengers, and fare collectors; rapes and murders; voyeurism; and theft of autos and their contents at park-and-ride facilities. Armed robberies of bus drivers, a major problem in the 1960s in many cities, have been sharply reduced with the introduction of exact fare procedures. Some researchers suggest that the amount of serious crime against patrons of mass transit may be even higher than recorded, because incidents involving victims who were waiting for buses or walking to rapid transit system stations are not recorded as crimes in the transit system.

Criminal acts most frequently occur in the mass transit systems located in or adjacent to high-crime areas. Crime against patrons most often is committed while they are waiting for transit vehicles, particularly on platforms and in stations of rapid transit systems. Crime also occurs at station entrances and exits, stairwells, ramps, and tunnels as well as on transit vehicles.[57] The American Transit Association has suggested a model for calculating exposure to crime in transit systems based upon the average amount of time spent in the transit system by patrons.

With the transportation of goods, direct financial loss is of primary concern, but in mass transit systems the primary financial concern is the indirect loss of declining passenger revenues as a result of fear of crime. Although the correlation between the actual amount of crime and the level of passenger revenues has not been precisely documented, it is known that patrons stop using mass transit or become reluctant to use it when their perceptions of crime are high. Research conducted in various studies indicates that security concerns are the reasons most often cited by patrons for avoiding the use of mass transit during off-peak evening hours. Several researchers suggest that patrons perceive far more crime than actually occurs. In addition to serious crime, offenses of antisocial behavior such as drunk-

[56] Thrasher, E. J. et al., *Vandalism and Passenger Security. A Study of Crime and Vandalism on Urban Mass Transit Systems in the United States and Canada.* Washington, D.C.: American Transit Association, September 1973.

[57] Carnegie-Mellon University Transportation Research Institute, "Extrapolating What We Know to the New Generation of Automated Small Vehicle Systems," *Security of Patrons on Urban Public Transportation Systems.* Pittsburgh, Pa., pp. 33–37.

enness and abusive conduct and language add to the displeasure of riding mass transit.

Mass transit officials are taking added measures to deal with crime, particularly because it is the only transportation available to many persons. Also, efforts to increase ridership as an energy-saving measure will be unsuccessful if people are afraid to use transit systems.

Transit officials and transportation planners are relying on the use of improvements in security personnel, hardware, and architectural design to cope with rising crime problems. The major objectives are to increase visibility in passenger waiting areas, to reduce patron waiting time, and to provide quick detection of and response to criminal incidents.[58] There is considerable debate over not only the proper composition of and police authority for transit security forces but also the degree of interface with local law enforcement agencies. One problem in this regard is that crimes can occur in the transit system and offenders be pursued into nontransit system areas, or crimes occur while vehicles are passing from one jurisdiction (local or State) to another. In answer to these problems, transit security forces are attempting to develop new techniques and strategies for deployment of manpower. One study conducted for the Chicago Transit Authority found that 60 percent of the criminal offenders were caught when crimes were reported within 4 to 5 minutes.[59] Achieving this type of response requires improved technology applications in emergency communications and surveillance.

Technological applications to security in transit systems may involve the installation of closed-circuit television in waiting areas and on vehicles and the use of telephones and other emergency communications devices by patrons. Installation of these devices is expensive because of the number of transit facilities and vehicles in a given system, the susceptibility of the devices to vandalism, and the need to monitor them on a regular basis to ensure their effectiveness. Most security applications are directed to rapid transit systems rather than buses. A new system being developed for the Chicago Transit Authority by the Carnegie-Mellon University Transportation Research Institute is designed to deal primarily with platform crime through the use of closed-circuit television and emergency telephones that are activated by the public with alarm buttons.

Architectural design for security is included in the planning of new rapid transit systems; visibility has been improved and vandalism reduced in existing transit systems with the use of unbreakable glass as see-through barriers and increased use of high-intensity lighting. Transportation planners also believe that with the increased automation of transit systems demand-responsive schedules can be developed to reduce passenger waiting time.

---

[58] Carnegie-Mellon University Transportation Research Institute, "The Impact of Public Perception of Crime on Mass Transit Patronage," *Security of Patrons on Urban Public Transportation Systems.* Pittsburgh, Pa., p. 18.

[59] Shellow, R. et al., *Improvement of Mass Transit Security in Chicago.* Pittsburgh, Pa.: Carnegie-Mellon University Transportation Research Institute, June 1973.

Part 2
Private Security Personnel

Chapter 1
Selection of Personnel

INTRODUCTION

Private security personnel now outnumber public law enforcement officers in this country. The dramatic growth rate of the private security industry over the past 15 years has far surpassed that of public law enforcement. This rapid increase can be attributed primarily to the growing concern of Americans for the welfare of their personal, business, and industrial holdings in light of constantly spiraling crime rates.

As crimes against property and person continue to rise and place staggering demands upon public law enforcement agencies, the private security industry should be prepared to take on added responsibilities to both its clients and the public. To meet these responsibilities, it should examine its past performance and current operations and identify goals and standards that will lead to provision of higher quality services. Because the ability of the industry to provide its services depends largely on the competence of its personnel, improvements in the quality of service directly correlate with improvements in the quality of personnel.

Both in numbers and dollars, personnel is the most significant part of the private security industry. As indicated in Appendix 9, recent estimates suggest that more than a million persons in this country are employed primarily in the occupation of private security. Countless others profess private security to be a form of secondary employment. These personnel account for approximately half the total expenditures for providing private security services, an estimated $3 billion annually. The magnitude of these figures alone shows the potential for improving private security's effectiveness through its greatest resource—its personnel. To advance its professional status and to meet the challenge of crime, the private security field should focus on the quality of its personnel.

The selection process is a crucial step in determining personnel quality. Inferior or improper selection methods lead to inferior personnel. Therefore, the standards in this chapter are devoted to the establishment of sound, realistic personnel selection guidelines that successfully can be used by the private security industry as a whole and by individual employers.

Goal 1.1 provides the basis for the selection process. It stresses the selection of employees who are qualified, efficient, and career minded. It also points out the importance of developing incentives to attract the most qualified personnel for all levels of operation. Because personnel are the foundation of the private security industry, the importance of their careful selection cannot be overemphasized. Unqualified personnel may make errors of judgment; inefficient workers reduce productivity; uninterested personnel will have high absenteeism; and all of these, in turn, ultimately will result in high turnover rates and poor-quality services. On the other hand, qualified personnel who can do the job assigned and enjoy their work will not only perform more effectively but also create a favorable public attitude toward private security.

If the industry is to attract and retain high-quality personnel, employment incentives should be developed. Goal 1.2 indicates that salaries for private security personnel need to be commensurate with job qualifications and competitive with salaries for other occupations. Career paths also should be developed in order to attract and motivate quality personnel. Such career path development is particularly important at the entry level.

Preemployment screening is a vital component of the selection process. Because of the nature of the private security employee's obligations to the public, to his employer, and to private security clients, the applicant's capability and integrity should be determined prior to employment and/or assignment. Preemployment screening procedures should include face-to-face interviews, honesty and other job-related tests, and intensive background investigations. Although the preemployment screening process is costly, it can prevent even more costly and sometimes dangerous errors stemming from the employment of dishonest or incapable personnel.

An exchange of job-related information pertaining to prospective personnel can aid in the process of preemployment screening. High mobility of employees between companies is a problem in the industry, but if employers exchange data about previous work performance and other selection criteria, the selection process can be greatly improved and an atmosphere of mutual cooperation both within and outside the industry can be established.

Along these same lines, it also is a recognized need that private security employers have access to criminal history records to assist in the selection process. As set forth in the selection standards, governments should cooperate with employers in making this information available.

Private security employers need to cooperate with the Federal Government by complying with equal employment opportunity guidelines. Statistics indicate that females and minority group members are becoming an increasingly significant part of the private security labor force. These trends should be encouraged and supported by selection standards that preclude discrimination based on sex, race, creed, or age. Minority members can increase the pool of qualified applicants for private security employment.

Another valuable screening tool is the employment application. A common problem in the selection process has been the rapid transition from the time the applicant walks in the door, to assignment, to the job. Although there is a recognized need to place personnel on the job rapidly, appropriate applications should be used and essential information verified prior to employment. The application form is particularly valuable during preemployment screening to furnish helpful information to assist in background investigations.

Perhaps one of the most important standards for the selection process is the establishment of minimum preemployment qualifications. Too often employers view the selection process as merely a vehicle for finding "bodies" to fill predetermined slots. Qualification standards are either ill conceived or nonexistent. Clearly, the lack of minimum standards has had a detrimental effect on the industry's image and, even more importantly, on its ability to deliver efficient, effective services. If this image is to be improved and the quality of services upgraded, minimum qualifications should be adopted throughout the private security industry.

The qualifications listed in Standard 1.8 are considered by this report to be the minimum requirements for prospective private security personnel.

They basically establish age, education, conviction record, and physical criteria for operational-level personnel. As are the public police, the industry is evaluated by citizens on the basis of one-to-one contact with an employee. Private security personnel functioning at the operational level day after day establish the image of the industry. These representatives of the industry should possess, at the minimum, basic qualifications indicating their suitability to carry out the protective duties for which they were employed.

In summary, personnel selection is the basic component for increasing the industry's effectiveness in crime prevention. Implementation of personnel selection standards can form the basis for other components, such as training, ethical behavior, education, and acceptance and approval by regulatory boards. The selection of quality personnel who are well suited to the job smooths the way for implementing all other industry standards and is important for the industry's ability to maintain good relationships with public law enforcement agencies, consumers of security services, governmental agencies, the public, and others. Therefore, strengthening personnel ultimately will result in the increased ability of the private security industry to prevent crime in the Nation.

Considering the significant crime deterrent potential of personnel selection standards, it is important that employers, consumers of security services, public law enforcement officials, and government agencies recognize their specific roles and responsibilities in the selection process. Private security employers, of course, have the most obvious role because they directly implement the standards through acceptance or rejection of applicants. Consumers of security services, however, also can assume a significant part in implementing personnel selection standards by demanding that employers follow established guidelines. Because government agencies, especially regulatory boards, hold licensing and/or registration powers, they also can demand adherence to standards before granting licenses and/or registrations. Law enforcement officials can cooperate within their legal and ethical constraints to provide private security employers with vital information to assist background investigations. The smooth integration of these standards into the selection process will depend on how well each of these agencies and individuals carries out its role.

Goal 1.1

Selection of Qualified Personnel

Primary emphasis in the screening process should be placed on selecting qualified personnel who will perform efficiently and preferably make a career in private security.

Commentary

Private security has experienced significant national growth and has become a multibillion-dollar-a-year business, but it is generally recognized that its personnel quality is often inferior and personnel turnover rates exceedingly high. Actions to correct this situation can be made at the personnel selection level.

As pointed out in *Effective Personnel Security Procedures,* executives in all fields need to take action to improve the personnel situation:

Some facts are so obvious as to force consensus. The accepted fact that people are the most important asset of any company is seldom challenged by any top executive. The lag between the acceptance of this fact and the implementation of procedures that would attest to such comprehension tends to prove again that many executives agree in principle but fail to follow through in practice.

Criteria need to be established to select persons who are qualified, efficient, and career oriented. Applicants with these characteristics are likely to perform well because they possess the necessary knowledge, capability, and desire. They also are more likely to remain employed through a working career because a person who is qualified for a job and does it well obviously will obtain satisfaction from it.

As it is recognized that no satisfactory indicators (tests or screening processes) presently exist for identification of persons who meet the above standards, it is strongly recommended that a team of experts in the fields of private security and behavioral science work together to develop such indicators. Until appropriate test instruments are developed, however, the employer should rely on his best professional, subjective judgment and on the preemployment screening techniques described in the following standards to obtain personnel who are qualified, efficient, and career oriented.

One significant step that can be taken immediately is to provide more incentives to attract the most competent personnel. According to the *RAND Report* (Vol. II), a survey of private security employees indicated that 40 percent accepted a private security position for the following reason: "I was unemployed, and this was the best job I could find." Management should be made aware of this lack of incentive and should promote benefits to attract more competent personnel.

65

Incentives also are needed to attract career-oriented personnel at all levels. *Career Development for Law Enforcement* notes that "career-development emphasis is placed on developing managers and not on career growth of all employees per se." If the present high turnover rate of private security personnel is to be curbed, career growth needs to be emphasized at all levels. The lack of potential career growth is especially evident at the operational levels.

If the private security industry is to improve its competitive position in the marketplace and provide better services to the public, it should actively seek quality personnel and screen out those who are unqualified, inefficient, and uninterested. Only in this way will the industry be able to meet the increasing need for higher quality services.

Selected References

1. Gorrill, B. E. *Effective Personnel Security Procedures.* Homewood, Ill.: Dow Jones-Irwin, Inc., 1974.

2. Green, Gion, and Raymond Farber. *Introduction to Security.* Los Angeles: Security World Publishing Company, 1974.

3. Kakalik, James, and Sorrell Wildhorn. *The Private Police Industry: Its Nature and Extent.* Washington, D.C.: Government Printing Office, Vol. II, R-870/DOJ, 1972.

4. Pitchess, Peter J. (Project Director). *Career Development for Law Enforcement.* Washington, D.C.: Technical Assistance Division, Law Enforcement Assistance Administration, U.S. Department of Justice, June 1973.

Related Standards

The following standards and goals may be applicable in implementing Goal 1.1:

1.2 Commensurate Salaries
1.3 Preemployment Screening
1.4 Employer Exchange of Information
1.5 Equal Employment Opportunity
1.6 Application of Employment
1.7 Availability of Criminal History Records
1.8 Minimum Preemployment Screening Qualifications
2.1 Training in Private Security
2.3 Job Descriptions
2.7 Ongoing Training
2.8 Training of Supervisors and Managers
3.1 Code of Ethics
3.4 Employer Responsibilities
8.3 Noncredit and Credit Seminars and Courses
8.4 Degree Programs for Private Security
9.6 Regulatory Board Access to Criminal Record Information
11.2 Registration Qualifications
11.6 Registration Renewal

Goal 1.2

Commensurate Salaries

In an effort to reduce the attrition rate of the industry, salaries for private security personnel should be commensurate with experience, training and/or education, job responsibilities, and other criteria related to the job performed.

Commentary

To attract and keep high-quality personnel, most private businesses offer competitive salaries commensurate with an individual's experience, education, skills, responsibilities, performance, and other job-related variables. Many also offer merit or incentive pay plans and other benefits to raise performance levels and to promote job satisfaction.

In contrast, private security personnel—who assume important responsibilities in the performance of their duties and often must make serious decisions affecting the safety of life and property—often are only paid minimum wages regardless of qualifications or other job-related criteria. There is also a noticeable lack of incentives or opportunities for advancement for private security personnel. These factors have created serious problems in attracting and retaining quality personnel.

Unless salaries and incentives for private security personnel are upgraded, many qualified applicants may look elsewhere for employment. "A Survey of

Experiences, Activities, and Views of the Industrial Security Administration Graduates of Michigan State University" indicated that 32 percent of the graduates were not employed in the private security field because of "lack of employment opportunities" and 22 percent because of "better pay and/or opportunities in other fields." Fewer than half the qualified graduates actually took jobs in industrial security.

Present high attrition rates also indicate that wages and incentives need improvement if quality personnel are to remain employed in the private security industry. It would be more cost effective in the long run to offer competitive salaries rather than to absorb the high costs of constant personnel turnover. The present attrition rate in the industry is primarily caused by resignations rather than by deaths or retirements.

If these conditions are so well known and so commonplace, why, then, are private security salaries so low? The following excerpt from an article in *Security World* portrays one view—that qualification standards are not adequate:

The only qualification for the lowest salaried guard is that he is alive and breathing . . . any additional abilities raise the price significantly.

Management personnel in all aspects of the industry, who were interviewed in an attempt to discover the reason for the lack of adequate salaries, indicated that low salaries are due to clients or higher management personnel being unwilling to pay for higher quality security services. Accepting their statements at face value places heavy responsibility for low salaries on persons outside the industry. The private security industry, however, cannot take a passive position; it should take the initiative to adequately inform the public of the dangers inherent in this situation. In many instances, private security personnel have sole responsibility for protecting assets worth millions of dollars; in other cases, they are armed with weapons that can cause serious injury or death. Rather than merely providing low-cost protection, the private security industry should inform the public of these facts.

Attempting to identify a recommended national minimum wage would, at best, be questionable because local salaries are related to multiple factors, such as general economic aspects of the area, labor pool availability, and competitive aspects of private security services. However, the following data were gathered from three different sources to illustrate the need for wage improvement in the industry:

The Other Police reported that security guards received only $80 to $84 weekly gross pay in the Cleveland, Ohio, area in 1974. However, on a more positive note, it also reported that in 1969 573 of 3,888 guards had salaries in excess of $10,000 a year.

Members of the American Society for Industrial Security provided the data on wages documented in Table 1.1. It readily can be seen that operational-level personnel, both proprietary and contractual, receives minimal wages.

Table 1.2, from *Security Letter,* indicates that salary problems are not limited to the operational levels of the private security industry. Compared to national salary medians for comparable employment, the security executive earns less than most of his counterparts in other occupations.

It is recognized that salaries must be upgraded in order to attract and maintain high-quality personnel and that no realistic, nationwide minimum wage can be recommended due to varying economic, labor, and competitive factors. Therefore, it is recommended that major efforts be initiated by the security industry to make salaries commensurate with experience, training and/or education, job responsi-

bilities, and other job-related criteria. Only in this way can the high personnel attrition rate found in the industry be reduced and the quality of both services and personnel be maintained.

Selected References

1. Brennan, Dennis T. *The Other Police.* Cleveland, Ohio: Governmental Research Institute, 1975.

2. "Exclusive Fourth Annual Report on Compensation of Corporate Loss Prevention Management," *Security Letter,* Vol. V, No. 14, Part II.

3. Larkins, Hayes Carlton. "A Survey of Experiences, Activities, and Views of the Industrial Security Administration Graduates of Michigan State University." Unpublished master's thesis, Michigan State University, 1966.

4. Private Security Task Force. "American Society for Industrial Security (ASIS) Survey Results." (See Appendix 1 to this report.)

5. Schnabolk, Charles. "Protection Against a Guard Force," *Security World,* May 1971.

Related Standards

The following standards and goals may be applicable in implementing or providing additional information regarding Goal 1.2:

1.1   Selection of Qualified Personnel
1.3   Preemployment Screening
1.5   Equal Employment Opportunity
1.6   Application of Employment
1.8   Minimum Preemployment Screening Qualifications
2.1   Training in Private Security
2.2   Professional Certification Programs
2.3   Job Descriptions
2.4   Training Related to Job Functions
2.5   Preassignment and Basic Training
2.6   Arms Training
2.7   Ongoing Training
2.8   Training of Supervisors and Managers
2.10 State Boards to Coordinate Training Efforts
3.1   Code of Ethics
3.4   Employer Responsibilities
8.3   Noncredit and Credit Seminars and Courses
8.4   Degree Programs for Private Security

Table 1.1. Comparison of Wage Data for Subcategories of Private Security Personnel, Proprietary and Contractual*

Question 16: What is the approximate monthly wage for the following security personnel within your enterprise?

	None Employed		Less than $500		$501–$750		$751–$1000		$1001–$1250		More than $1250		No Response	
	Prop. %	Cont. %	Prop. %	Cont. %	Prop. %	Cont. %	Prop. %	Cont. %	Prop. %	Cont. %	Prop. %	Cont. %	Prop. %	Cont. %
Unarmed uniform guards	16	9	7	39	24	29	18	4	5	1	1	1	29	17
Armed uniform guards	18	15	3	19	17	30	15	6	6	1	1	1	40	28
Investigators/detectives	14	16	1	0	9	18	12	18	14	6	12	3	38	39
Middle management/supervisors	3	5	0	0	4	7	14	25	27	26	36	18	16	19
Owner/general manager	7	7	0	0	0	1	2	3	6	9	49	46	36	34

* Sample size: Proprietary N = 888; contractual N = 469.
Source: Private Security Task Force. "American Society for Industrial Security (ASIS) Survey Results," (See Appendix 1 to this report.)

Table 1.2. National Salary Medians of Selected Job Titles

Job Title	Small Companies*		Medium Companies*		Large Companies*	
	No.	$	No.	$	No.	$
Plant/Factory Manager/Superintendent	61	18,000	105	21,300	120	32,000
Chief Internal Auditor	84	17,500	87	20,400	79	24,800
Credit and Collections Executive	73	14,500	90	21,700	92	25,100
Labor Relations Executive	54	21,800	55	27,000	57	33,100
Chief EDP Executive	88	18,400	115	22,200	70	31,500
Director of Security	50	15,000	76	18,100	59	22,000
Director of Safety	112	16,500	78	19,500	63	23,000
Employee Training Manager	119	18,300	51	21,300	51	23,100
Personnel Director	173	18,700	105	23,000	51	31,400
Personnel Assistant	145	11,700	75	13,100	82	14,700
Office Services Executive	88	15,100	81	18,600	66	23,200

* Size designations of small, medium, and large generally are related to sales: less than $100 million (small), $100 to $500 million (medium), and more than $500 million (large). In some cases, however, payroll, production, and number of employees were used to determine classification. Salaries do not indicate the wide variance possible according to specific situations, organizational policies, and exceptional individuals.

Source: "Exclusive Fourth Annual Report on Compensation of Corporate Loss Prevention Management," *Security Letter*, Vol. V, No. 14, Part II.

Standard 1.3

Preemployment Screening

In order to determine whether prospective personnel are trustworthy and capable, preemployment screening should be initiated. Preemployment screening should include screening interview, honesty test, background investigation, and other appropriate job-related tests.

Commentary

The *U.S. Atomic Energy Commission Regulatory Guide* (Nuclear Regulatory Commission) of January 1974 clearly states the rationale for this standard:

> Preemployment screening provides a means to determine whether a prospective security employee is trustworthy and capable of performing the security tasks that will be assigned to him.

Private security work demands that employees be both reliable and capable when carrying out assigned tasks and meeting emergencies. Individuals who are dishonest, corrupt, lazy, or emotionally or physically unstable, for example, are unfit for employment in the field.

The intent of this standard is to preclude the employment and/or assignment of personnel until a reasonable preemployment screening has been conducted. Preemployment screening techniques should be used to detect characteristics that would prevent or hinder satisfactory job performance. Individuals who display such characteristics should be rejected for employment. In a field as vital to the safety of individuals and property as security work, the time to discover persons unsuited for the job is before they are hired. This timely discovery can eliminate costly, dangerous, and even deadly mistakes. For example, a newspaper article from Phoenix, Ariz., April 20, 1975, reported that a 70-year old guard was killed trying to stop a grocery store robbery. The article explained that the security guard had informed his employing agency that he was 50 years of age. Some form of preemployment screening possibly could have eliminated exposing this guard to the hazard that ultimately caused his death.

Many employers accept statements made on application forms without attempting verification. These employers are failing in their responsibilities to both their clients and the public.

Although a thorough, complete screening process is desirable, the extent of preemployment screening is logically controlled by a number of factors, such as the following:

1. The amount of time available for the screening process, from the time of application to the time the employee is scheduled to start work;

2. The amount of funds an employer can economically allocate for the screening process; and

3. The availability of the needed information.

71

Employers often are required to fill vacancies on very short notice. Several security workers interviewed indicated they started work within 24 to 72 hours after applying. Obviously, no thorough screening process can be accomplished in this timeframe. In these instances, however, requiring proof of birth, education certificates, and names and addresses of references would be an improvement over mere acceptance of application form statements without verification.

Economically, the employer must logically limit the scope of screening because of employment instability in some segments of the private security industry. The *RAND Report* (Vol. I) indicated turnover rates as high as 200 percent, and other studies have documented similarly high rates. Although other sections of this report deal with this problem, its effect on the screening process must be recognized; high turnover rates result in added expense to screen new applicants for vacated positions. Although full field investigations and extensive credit and criminal record checks may not always be economically feasible because of high turnover, employers must take reasonable screening steps to ensure that capable, trustworthy employees are hired.

Availability of necessary information is another limiting factor. The private security industry has very limited access to criminal justice records. Also, in many States, fingerprint record searches on new security personnel take 6 to 9 months.

Despite the above limitations, every effort should be made by employers to develop complete and effective preemployment screening procedures. Use of screening interviews, honesty tests, and background investigations as measures of trustworthiness and capability is recommended. The specific extent and method of implementation of these screening techniques should be tempered by logic and economics. Used together, however, these three techniques form a sound nucleus for preemployment screening.

Screening Interview

The screening interview is a two-way communication—employer to applicant and applicant to employer. Although somewhat subjective, it allows both parties to assess the job situation. Employer questions should include:
1. Why do you want the job?
2. What are your career objectives?
3. What interests you about the job?
4. Other job-related questions.

The employer should clearly indicate to the applicant the requirements, positive and negative aspects, salary and fringe benefits, and other pertinent factors about the job.

The screening interview also allows the employer to assess the applicant's character. Although such an assessment is admittedly highly subjective, the applicant's demeanor and attitude during the interview may indicate the need for more careful background investigation or even psychological testing.

Honesty Test

For the purpose of this standard, honesty tests refer only to written tests that allow employers to gain insights into a prospective employee's honesty without extensive costs. In general terms, honesty tests are designed to measure trustworthiness, attitude toward honesty, and the need to steal.

Several paper-and-pencil honesty tests were reviewed for this report, this independent evaluation determined that the tests appear to have high face validity. Several validity and reliability studies supporting such tests have been published in scholarly journals. However, it should be noted that much of the supporting evidence is based on subsequent detection-of-deception examinations of persons who had taken the written honesty tests. Nevertheless, honesty tests used with background investigations should furnish a reliable method of determining honesty.

Background Investigation

Background investigations should be conducted prior to employment and/or assignment. The employment application information stated in Standard 1.6 and the qualifications stated in Standard 1.8 provide guidance regarding background investigations. Valuable background data can also be obtained through employer exchange of information (Standard 1.4).

Too often, employers do not conduct any background investigations or investigations are sketchy. Many employers use only the telephone and/or form letters for background information. Such methods do not provide sufficient data for effective verification and evaluation. Although costly, field investigations should be encouraged to provide valuable information about an individual's character and ability that cannot be gained by other means.

Other Screening Considerations

Job-related psychological tests and detection-of-deception examinations are additional processes that could be included in the screening process. Job factors such as access to funds and other property, control of personnel, whether armed, and so forth, should determine the types of job-related tests that can best serve the employer and the public. It is shocking to realize that many armed guards are not screened to determine if they have major psychological problems that would clearly render them unacceptable for employment involving carrying a deadly weapon. Obviously, extreme care should be taken to ensure that all screening measures are job-related and are not an invasion of the applicant's individual rights. It is also important that all screening methods be administered and evaluated by competent personnel and the results carefully protected from illegal release.

Properly conducted, preemployment screening will aid employers in selecting capable and trustworthy employees. By eliminating those unsuited for private security work, such screening processes also will lead to increased productivity and lower turnover rates.

Selected References

1. Brennan, Dennis T. *The Other Police*. Cleveland, Ohio: Governmental Research Institute, 1975.

2. Kakalik, James S., and Sorrell Wildhorn. *Private Police in the United States:* Findings and Recommendations. Washington, D.C.: Government Printing Office, Vol. I, R-869/DOJ, 1972.

3. General Services Administration, Office of Federal Protective Service Management. "Instructions for Using Guideline Specifications for Incentive-Type Protection Services Contracts," February 1973.

4. U.S. Atomic Energy Commission. *U.S. Atomic Energy Commission Regulatory Guide,* 5.20. January 1974.

Related Standards

The following standards and goals may be applicable in implementing Standard 1.3:

1.1 Selection of Qualified Personnel
1.4 Employer Exchange of Information
1.5 Equal Employment Opportunity
1.6 Application of Employment
1.7 Availability of Criminal History Records
1.8 Minimum Preemployment Screening Qualifications
2.3 Job Descriptions
2.4 Training Related to Job Functions
3.1 Code of Ethics
9.6 Regulatory Board Access to Criminal Record Information
11.2 Registration Qualifications
11.3 Qualifications for Armed Security Personnel
11.7 Suspension and Revocation

Standard 1.4

Employer Exchange of Information

Employers should cooperate in exchanging information on previous work performance and other data relating to selection criteria.

Commentary

Although the current legal restraints on pre-employment screening may seem overwhelming, much improvement can be made. One area in which there is great potential for improvement involves employer cooperation in exchanging previous work performance information and other data related to selection criteria. Studies made for this report (Appendix 2) of licensed private security workers in New Orleans, La., and St. Louis, Mo., revealed that 15 percent and 20 percent, respectively, of the employees had previous private security employment. Based on these percentages employer cooperation could be extremely important in obtaining previous work performance records and other data for almost one of every five applicants, giving the employer a practical frame of reference to establish the applicants suitability for the job.

Mutual cooperation among private security companies can help improve overall personnel quality. Employers often possess information about a former employee's work performance or character that would be helpful and pertinent to another employer in the personnel selection process, because there is an extremely high movement of individuals from one employer to another in the private security industry. Thus it is especially important to share such information when the person being considered is unsuited for private security employment. For example, a private security employee fired for stealing should not be placed in another private security position where theft is again possible.

An exchange of information among employers can not only speed the selection process but also help professionalize the private security industry and protect clients and the public. Because of the competitive nature of the industry, however, many argue that such an exchange of information is unrealistic and could hurt a cooperating company if others fail to do likewise.

The need for total cooperation must be understood and petty jealousies put aside for the betterment of the industry. Employers should realize that the 'advantages from cooperative efforts benefit everyone involved. Indeed, because such cooperation can help eliminate unqualified, inefficient, and untrustworthy personnel, the industry, the public, clients, and employers would all benefit through increased efficiency and more effective crime prevention. Even applicants would benefit, because prompt exchange of information between employers can help qualified personnel quickly gain employment in new locations and continue their career in private security.

It is the responsibility of the prospective employer to initiate the actions necessary for any exchange of information. If an applicant indicates previous private security employment on the application form, the employer should contact the previous employer for information regarding past work performance and other selection criteria. As referred to in *Security Management Systems,* information about the following personal characteristics should be exchanged:

1. Honesty
2. Dependability
3. Loyalty
4. Judgment
5. Initiative
6. Appearance

Where permitted by law, information should be exchanged on the following additional items:

1. Arrest and/or conviction information,
2. Use of drugs and/or alcohol,
3. Poor interpersonal relations with clients or fellow workers,
4. Poor credit rating,
5. Improper use of force, and
6. Psychological unsuitability.

Cooperative arrangements for exchange of information can also be made between the public law enforcement and private security sectors. The previously mentioned studies (Appendix 2) show that 6 percent of the private security personnel in New Orleans and 7 percent in St. Louis had previous public law enforcement experience. Many applicants for law enforcement employment likewise have experience in private security. Cooperation in exchanging pertinent work-related data about former employees could enhance the screening process for both sectors. The constant interaction, in both operational and administrative matters, between public and private security personnel should provide a strong motivating influence of mutual interest in the effort to obtain high-quality personnel.

Selected References

1. Ursig, Henry S., and Leroy E. Pagano. *Security Management Systems.* Springfield, Ill.: Charles C. Thomas Publisher, 1974.

2. Private Security Task Force. "Characteristics of Licensed Private Security Personnel in Two American Cities: New Orleans, La., and St. Louis, Mo." (See Appendix 2 to this report.)

Related Standards

The following standards and goals may be applicable in implementing Standard 1.4:

1.1   Selection of Qualified Personnel
1.2   Commensurate Salaries
1.3   Preemployment Screening
1.5   Equal Employment Opportunity
1.6   Application of Employment
1.7   Availability of Criminal History Records
1.8   Minimum Preemployment Screening Qualifications
3.2   Conduct of Private Security Personnel

Standard 1.5

Equal Employment Opportunity

Employers should comply with equal employment opportunity guidelines and other Federal, State, or local guidelines that preclude discrimination based on sex, race, creed, or age.

Commentary

Many minority group members are qualified for jobs in the private security field. Sound personnel procedures require that employers seek qualified personnel regardless of sex, race, creed, or age, because these factors are of no importance to the employer's responsibility to select applicants who can perform effective and efficient security services. Private security employers should, therefore, constantly seek ways to attract qualified minority applicants for open positions.

The Federal Government, through legislation and administrative regulations, provides equal employment opportunity (EEO) guidelines for employers, such as the rules and regulations of the Equal Employment Opportunity Commission and the Civil Rights Act of 1964. These guidelines are provided to promote job opportunities for minority groups and to eliminate discriminatory hiring and employment practices. Private security employers should develop procedures to ensure that their selection activities are within these guidelines. They also should keep abreast of court and administrative decisions to make certain their current selection practices do not violate the law.

By examining past employment records, individual employers can determine if qualified minority workers are applying for jobs and being utilized within their work forces. If these records indicate a lack of minority employees, steps should be taken to ensure that current hiring practices are free of discrimination based on sex, race, creed, or age.

An attempt at evaluating past equal opportunity employment practices of the private security industry as a whole would, at best, be speculative, because only recently have accurate statistics become available. However, a representative indication of the present status of minority employment within the industry can be obtained from pertinent studies and reports and may prove helpful for comparative analyses. Perhaps the most current of such studies are those conducted for this report (Appendix 2) of licensed private security workers in New Orleans, La., and St. Louis, Mo.

Most Federal, State, and local EEO guidelines suggest that the proportion of minorities employed by an agency equal the proportion in the available labor market. The studies mentioned above found that 52 percent of the private security workers in New Orleans are Caucasian, 40 percent are black, and 8 percent are classified as "other," which in-

76

cludes Spanish-Americans. In St. Louis, 50 percent of the private security workers are Caucasian and 50 percent are black. These percentages are proportionate with race ratios in the two cities.

The study also gathered information on the age of private security employees in two cities. The following table, based on the data developed in the study, illustrates that age is apparently not a criterion for denial of employment in either city.

Age at Time of Employment	New Orleans %	St. Louis %
24 and under	21	13
25 to 34	25	21
35 to 44	18	22
45 to 54	19	22
55 to 64	13	16
65 to 74	4	5
75 and over	0.5	0.2

Note. Figures do not add to 100 percent due to rounding.

The study also found that females account for 7 percent of the private security personnel in both New Orleans and St. Louis. Because women only recently have begun to enter police and security work, this data are difficult to evaluate. Undoubtedly, changing social attitudes and the women's liberation movement will make more and more qualified women available in the private security labor market. The following excerpts from the *RAND Report* (Vol. II) and the *Wall Street Journal* indicate their potential is already being realized by private security employers:

Many of the larger private security firms claim that the relative demand for, and employment of, female security workers has risen over the past several years, especially in hospitals, educational institutions, and retail trade. (*RAND Report*, Vol. II)

Female guards gain more acceptance in private security firms

Leading companies say 10% to 15% of their guards are female, up from less than 5% a few years ago. Guardsmark, Inc., with 11% women, pays its agents an extra commission for persuading clients to use them. Burns International runs ads to lure women to the jobs. "Clients are a little hesitant at first," says a Burns official, "but when they see women on the job, they love them."

Women are still used mostly in airports. Wackenhut Corp. says only 5% of its nonairport guards are women, though 15% of its total guard force is female. Guardsmark has

women heading security teams at electrical plants, a brewery. (sic) In three Wells Fargo offices women have risen to management rank. But only five of Brink's Inc.'s 1,800 guards are women.

One security-firm executive explains, "By hiring women we double the limited labor pool available at the relatively low wages guards get paid." (*Wall Street Journal*)

In order to obtain the ever-increasing numbers of personnel needed by the industry, private security employers should continue and expand their efforts to hire qualified personnel regardless of race, age, sex, or creed.

Selected References

1. Equal Employment Opportunity Commission. *Rules and Regulations*. Washington, D.C.: Oct. 27, 1971.

2. Kakalik, James S., and Sorrell Wildhorn. *The Private Police Industry: Its Nature and Extent*. Washington D.C.: Government Printing Office, Vol. II, R-870/DOJ, 1972.

3. Private Security Task Force. "Characteristics of Licensed Private Security Personnel in Two American Cities: New Orleans, La., and St. Louis, Mo." (See Appendix 2 to this report.)

4. Robinson, Katherine. "Promising Career Areas for Women," *Reader's Digest*, November 1974. (Condensed from *The Saturday Evening Post*.)

5. Rosen, Benson, and Thomas H. Jerdee. "Sex Stereotyping in the Executive Suite," *Harvard Business Review*, March-April 1974.

6. *The Wall Street Journal*. Vol. LV, No. 201, July 29, 1975, p. 1.

7. Title VII *Civil Rights Act, 1964*. Washington, D.C.: Government Printing Office.

Related Standards

The following standards and goals may be applicable in implementing Standard 1.5:
1.1 Selection of Qualified Personnel
1.2 Commensurate Salaries
1.3 Preemployment Screening
1.4 Employer Exchange of Information
1.6 Application of Employment
1.7 Availability of Criminal History Records
1.8 Minimum Preemployment Screening Qualifications
2.4 Training Related to Job Functions
3.1 Code of Ethics

Standard 1.6

Application for Employment

An employment application should be used to provide a basis for the screening process and should reveal the following information:

1. Full name,
2. Aliases,
3. Proof of age,
4. Statement of U.S. citizenship or work permit number for aliens,
5. Current residence and phone number,
6. Prior residences,
7. Educational background,
8. Previous employment,
9. Physical conditions as they relate to the job,
10. Military service,
11. Record of traffic and criminal convictions and pending criminal charges and indictments,
12. Credit information relevant to the job, and
13. A set of fingerprints.

Commentary

The employment application form often is the only formal document that appears in an employee's personnel file. It is the only document that many employers have providing information about the applicant's work history, educational preparation, and former residences. Particularly during the pre-employment screening process, it often is the only information employers have readily available to assist investigations.

Every applicant should be required to complete all items on the application, as well as provide the following documents:

1. Proof of age;
2. Proof of education;
3. Armed Forces of the United States Report of Transfer or Discharge (DD214), if appropriate; and
4. Other job-related documents.

The reference to other job-related documents needs some clarification. For example, if a jurisdiction requires a certain amount of training and the applicant states that training has been completed, it is appropriate to ask for the training certificate.

A set of fingerprints is necessary in conjunction with the employment application for three main purposes: (1) to positively determine if the applicant has a criminal conviction record; (2) to give the employer an opportunity to verify the information on the application by a fingerprint check, if needed; and (3) to provide a document for positive identification in the situation in which the employee was killed on the job in a manner preventing routine identification, such as death by explosion.

A good employment application is an important part of the screening process. It not only provides a basis for background investigations, but also guards against verbal misrepresentation by the applicant. For example, *The Other Police* cites a case of a five-time convicted felon who, by simply stating he had no criminal record, was able to get four out of six jobs he sought. A written application form would have made it more difficult for this applicant to misrepresent himself, if for no other reason than the psychological implications of a written statement. "Internal Control of Employee Dishonesty," a master's thesis from Michigan State University, points out that a good personnel screening process will, in itself, serve as a psychological deterrent for undesirable applicants.

It cannot be assumed that all applicants will complete the application form acurately. Therefore, a personal interview to review the document should be standard procedure. In the interview, unclear responses can be clarified and the employer can obtain any additional background information needed for investigations.

The employer must assume certain responsibilities in using application forms. For example, it should be clearly stated on the application form that falsification of material information on the application is grounds for denial of employment or dismissal after employment. The employer should verbally call this to the applicant's attention. In addition, the employer should constantly review the forms in use to ensure compliance with equal employment opportunity guidelines and the individual's right to privacy.

The style and format of employment application forms vary. The employer may wish to devise a form or use a prepared standard form. In either case, the application should be carefully reviewed to ensure that the questions are pertinent to the job to be performed and reveal all necessary information. The time spent in verifying the application's completeness and accuracy will increase the employer's capability to eliminate unsuitable applicants and select the most qualified personnel.

Selected References

1. Brennan, Dennis T. *The Other Police*. Cleveland, Ohio: Governmental Research Institute, 1975.

2. Myers, David Jeffrey. "Internal Control of Employee Dishonesty." Unpublished master's thesis, Michigan State University, 1968.

3. Private Security Advisory Council to the U.S. Department of Justice, Law Enforcement Assistance Administration. "A Report on the Regulation of Private Security Guard Services including a Model Private Security Licensing and Regulatory Statute." May 1976. (See Appendix 11 to this report.)

4. Van Meter, Clifford W. (Project Director). *Pilot Study for Feasibility of Regionalization of Components of the Criminal Justice System in Gallatin, Hamilton, Hardin, Pope, and Saline Counties Illinois*. Macomb, Ill.: Western Illinois University 1972.

5. Wilson, O. W. *Police Administration*. New York: McGraw-Hill Book Company, 2d ed., 1963.

Related Standards

The following standards and goals may be applicable in implementing Standard 1.6:

1.1 Selection of Qualified Personnel
1.2 Commensurate Salaries
1.3 Preemployment Screening
1.4 Employer Exchange of Information
1.5 Equal Employment Opportunity
1.7 Availability of Criminal History Records
1.8 Minimum Preemployment Screening Qualifications
11.2 Registration Qualifications
11.3 Qualification for Armed Security Personnel

Standard 1.7

Availability of Criminal History Records

Criminal history records for offenses, specified by statute or other authority as grounds for denying employment, should be made available to employers to assist them in the screening of private security personnel.

Commentary

Access to criminal history records is one of the key issues in personnel screening. Many employers have expressed concern over their inability to obtain information from the National Crime Information Center and local and State systems.

Section 524(b) of the Crime Control Act of 1973 mandates procedures to ensure security and privacy of criminal history information:

All criminal history information collected, stored, or disseminated through support under this title shall contain, to the maximum extent feasible, disposition as well as arrest data where arrest data is included therein. The collection, storage, and dissemination of such information shall take place under procedures reasonably designed to insure that all such information is kept current therein; the Administration shall assure that the security and privacy of all information is adequately provided for and that information shall only be used for law enforcement and criminal justice and other lawful purposes. In addition, an individual who believes that criminal history information concerning him contained in an automated system is inaccurate, incomplete, or maintained in violation of this title, shall, upon satisfactory verification of his identity, be entitled to review such information and to obtain a copy of it for the purpose of challenge or correction.

The *Federal Register,* Feb. 14, 1974 (39 F.R. 5636), published Criminal Justice Information Systems Rules and Regulations to obtain comments before finalizing them. Hearings were held in Washington, D.C., and San Francisco, Calif., in the spring of 1974.

On May 20, 1975, the *Federal Register* (40 F.R. 22114) published a set of rules and regulations promulgated by the Law Enforcement Assistance Administration (LEAA), U.S. Department of Justice. These rules and regulations greatly restricted private security employers' access to criminal history information. This denial of access was thought to be unrealistic and unresponsible by many individuals, companies, and associations. Concerns raised by the private security field and input from LEAA's Private Security Advisory Council lead LEAA to reconsider its original position on this point. Accordingly, in December 1975, special hearings were held in Washington, D.C., with many private security professionals testifying. Based primarily on these hearings, a new set of rules and regulations was promulgated by LEAA and printed in the Mar. 19, 1976, *Federal Register* (41 F.R. 11715). The portion of these rules and regulations directly related to this standard is section 20.21(b):

(b) Limitations on dissemination. By December 31, 1977, [the States must] insure that dissemination of nonconviction data has been limited, whether directly or through any intermediary only to:
(1) Criminal justice agencies, for purposes of the administration of criminal justice and criminal justice agency employment;
(2) Individuals and agencies for any purpose authorized by statute, ordinance, executive order, or court rule, decision, or order, as construed by appropriate State or local officials or agencies;
(3) Individuals and agencies pursuant to a specific agreement with a criminal justice agency to provide services required for the administration of criminal justice pursuant to that agreement. The agreement shall specifically authorize access to data, limit the use of data to purposes for which given, insure the security and confidentiality of the data consistent with these regulations, and provide sanctions for violation thereof;
(4) Individuals and agencies for the express purpose of research, evaluative, or statistical activities pursuant to an agreement with a criminal justice agency. The agreement shall specifically authorize access to data, limit the use of data to research, evaluative, or statistical purposes, insure the confidentiality and security of the data consistent with these regulations and with section 524(a) of the Act and any regulations implementing section 524(a), and provide sanctions for the violation thereof.
These dissemination limitations do not apply to conviction data.

These rules and regulations do not authorize dissemination to private security personnel of nonconviction data but do authorize release of conviction data. Further, criminal history record information, including arrest data, that relate to an individual currently processing through the criminal justice system (i.e., no final disposition) may be available to employers.

After Dec. 31, 1977, each State will have to specifically allow access to nonconviction data for entities other than criminal justice agencies by statute or ordinance, executive order, or court rule. Private security professionals should take the initiative, on a State-by-State basis, to encourage government officials to specifically allow private security employers access to nonconviction data to assist them in the screening process.

Although each State must determine the parameters for releasing nonconviction information, one guideline is offered for consideration: Considering the role of private security personnel in crime prevention, that many of them are armed, and that on some assignments they may be in a position to control the individual freedoms of the public, employers of private security personnel should have access to the same criminal history records that are used in the preemployment screening of public law enforcement officers. This would provide a uniform frame of reference for government officials and private security employers.

The fact that an applicant has an arrest or conviction record should not be automatic grounds for disqualification. In some instances, particularly with regard to minor offenses, persons with records may perform most satisfactorily in private security services. However, it is important that employers have access to the information to enable them to make sound determinations regarding both employment and job assignment. Employers should also assume the responsibility to ensure that the information is used only for the intended purpose—to determine an individual's suitability for private security employment.

Selected References

1. Crime Control Act of 1973, Public Law 93–83, Aug. 6, 1973.
2. U.S. Department of Justice. "Criminal Justice Information Systems," *Federal Register,* Vol. **39**, No. 31. Washington, D.C.: Government Printing Office, Feb. 14, 1974.
3. ———. "Criminal Justice Information Systems," *Federal Register,* Vol. 40, No. 98. Washington, D.C.: Government Printing Office, May 20, 1975.
4. ———. "Criminal History Records," *Federal Register,* Vol. 41, No. 55. Washington, D.C.: Government Printing Office, Mar. 19, 1976.
5. Kakalik, James S., and Sorrel Wildhorn. *Private Police in the United States: Findings and Recommendations,* Vol. 1, R–869/DOJ. Washington, D.C.: Government Printing Office, 1972.

Related Standards

The following standards and goals may be applicable in implementing Standard 1.7:
1.1   Selection of Qualified Personnel
1.3   Preemployment Screening
1.4   Employer Exchange of Information
1.5   Equal Employment Opportunity
1.6   Application of Employment
1.8   Minimum Preemployment Screening Qualifications
3.2   Conduct of Private Security Personnel
3.3   Reporting of Criminal Violations
9.6   Regulatory Board Access to Criminal Record Information
11.2   Registration Qualifications
11.3   Qualifications for Armed Security Personnel

Standard 1.8

Minimum Preemployment Screening Qualifications

The following minimum preemployment screening qualifications should be established for private security personnel:

1. Minimum age of 18;

2. High school diploma or equivalent written examination;

3. Written examination to determine the ability to understand and perform duties assigned;

4. No record of conviction, as stated in Standard 1.7;

5. Minimum physical standards:

a. Armed personnel—vision correctible to 20/20 (Snellen) in each eye and capable of hearing ordinary conversation at a distance of 10 feet with each ear without benefit of hearing aid

b. Others—no physical defects that would hinder job performance.

Commentary

In order to improve the effectiveness of private security personnel, minimum preemployment screening qualifications should be established. At present, criteria for employment vary among employers, if they exist at all. This standard proposes a set of criteria that can be used by all private security employers in their preemployment screening.

The qualifications suggested are minimum. Certain employers may wish to establish stricter criteria, depending on the nature of assignment. Also, the qualifications are directed to operational personnel and generally would be inappropriate for supervisors, managers, and other specialized personnel whose duties would require more advanced knowledge and/or experience.

Age Requirements

A minimum age of 18 is recommended for all personnel. Public law enforcement agencies have constantly been hampered in recruitment by the lack of opportunity to employ sworn personnel immediately upon completion of high school. Likewise, the private security industry should not restrict itself from obtaining qualified personnel by setting unrealistic minimum or maximum ages. Many individuals are capable of performing as efficiently at age 18 as at age 21. The military services, for example, have effectively used personnel in security positions under the age of 21 for many years.

Because the establishment of career paths is an important need in the industry, age requirements need to be low enough to attract qualified applicants before they are committed to other careers. It is likely that an individual reaching age 21 would have already identified career aspirations, and a job in private security would, at best, be only a secondary interest. As mentioned previously in Goal 1.1, personnel will function more effectively when they are performing the job they want to do.

Educational Requirements

The *RAND Report* (Vol. I) stated that, in response to a survey questionnaire, two-thirds of the regulatory agencies indicated that minimum educational requirements should be mandatory for private security personnel. Of the two-thirds favoring minimum educational requirements, one-third indicated that private security personnel should be high school graduates. Others thought education beyond high school would be a more appropriate requirement for some categories. For example, two recommended college education for investigators; two proposed polygraph-school graduation for lie-detection examiners; one believed that supervisors should have some college training. Significantly, one-third of the survey respondents thought no minimum educational requirements should be established.

For the purpose of this standard, educational requirements are classified in two main categories: (1) basic educational qualifications and (2) ability to understand and perform duties assigned. The basic educational qualifications can be met by a high school diploma or an equivalent written examination designed to measure basic educational aptitudes. The employer should be careful, however, to utilize only those tests that have been proven valid and reliable.

The second educational requirement—the ability to understand and perform duties assigned—is determined through a written examination. Here, again, the employer should use only validated tests. Furthermore, there should be a close cause-effect relationship between the tests and the job description in accordance with the following Equal Opportunity Employment Commission guideline on employment testing procedures:

> The Commission accordingly interprets "professionally developed ability test" to mean a test which fairly measures the knowledge or skills required by the particular job or class of jobs which the applicant seeks, or which fairly affords the employer a chance to measure the applicant's ability to perform a particular job or class of jobs. The fact that a test was prepared by an individual or organization claiming expertise in test preparation does not, without more, justify its use within the meaning of Title VII (Civil Rights Act of 1964).

The two categories of educational requirements are not mutually inclusive or exclusive. For example, a high school graduate might have psychological characteristics that would indicate this person should not be armed. Conversely, a person who did not graduate from high school but passes the equivalent written examination might be found to be psychologically qualified to carry a weapon. A high school diploma, in and of itself, should not necessarily be a prerequisite for armed personnel, but regulatory agencies, for administrative reasons, may set such a requirement.

The National Advisory Committee on Criminal Justice Standards and Goals (NAC) did not agree with the Task Force's position that a high school diploma or equivalent written examination should be a minimum preemployment screening qualification for all private security personnel. Although agreeing that this requirement was appropriate for armed guards and certain security activities, the NAC believed that a written examination to determine if an individual had the ability to understand and perform the duties involved was adequate for other security assignments. The NAC believed that individuals who were competent to perform these other security assignments would be denied employment in the field if the high school education level requirement was a minimum standard. However, it is the opinion of the Private Security Task Force that the basic knowledge engendered by a high school diploma (or equivalent written examination) is important for emergency situations that may arise. The written ability examination may not test for those skills outside the private security employee's job description, and he may, therefore, not be able to handle the emergency situation. Also, in the furtherance of the development of a professional private security industry, high-school-level education is considered necessary in the judgement of the Task Force.

Conviction Records

Conviction records, except for certain minor offenses, should preclude private security employment. Standard 1.7 discusses this topic fully and points out the responsibilities assumed by private security personnel to the public and to the role of crime prevention. For the public to have confidence in private security personnel, employers should select persons of high moral integrity. In order to facilitate implementation of this standard, this report calls for the cooperation of government agencies in supplying pertinent conviction records.

Physical Requirements

Physical requirements should not be unnecessarily restrictive. In most cases, specific physical qualifications, such as height and weight, would be inappropriate. The results of a study released by the International Association of Chiefs of Police and the Police Foundation, and published in the Dec. 1, 1975, issue of *Crime Control Digest,* confirm that height requirements, for example, have little relation to performance and tend to unnecessarily reduce the available pool of qualified applicants:

> The authors . . . say that they found no data, either from their survey of five police departments or from their search of literature on the subject, that show that the height of a police officer does affect performance. . . .
>
> . . . Height requirements can vastly reduce the pool of applicants who have personal qualities needed by police departments.
>
> For example, 56 percent of young adult males and 99 percent of young adult females would be excluded from employment by a minimum height requirement of 5 feet 9 inches.

Although the authors of this study were hampered in their research by the lack of a large comparative population, the results point the way to a selection system without height requirements.

However, private security employers should not totally disregard physical standards or take them lightly. One employer cited in the *RAND Report* (Vol. 1) said, "Some standards are a joke. While we require a physical exam for employment, if the man can take three steps he passes the physical." In general, physical requirements should be determined by the nature of the job the applicant would be performing. Any physical defect that would interfere with ability to perform assigned duties would disqualify the applicant.

Differentiation should be made physical qualifications for armed personnel and others. Obviously, good eyesight and hearing are vital to anyone who carries a weapon; therefore, specific vision and hearing qualifications should be established for armed private security personnel in consideration of protecting both themselves and the public.

Selected References

1. Kakalik, James S., and Sorrel Wildhorn. *Private Police in the United States: Findings and Recommendations,* Vol. 1, R–869/DOJ. Washington, D.C.: Government Printing Office, 1972.

2. "No Effect on Performance Seen But Study Said Handicapped," *Crime Control Digest*. Washington, D.C.: Washington Crime News Services, Dec. 1, 1975.

3. Private Security Advisory Council. "Model Private Security Licensing and Regulatory Statute." Washington, D.C.: Law Enforcement Assistance Administration, 1975.

4. Private Security Task Force. "Characteristics of Licensed Private Security Personnel in Two American Cities: New Orleans, La., and St. Louis, Mo." (See Appendix 2 to this report.)

5. Schnabolk, Charles. "Protection Against a Guard Force," *Security World*, May 1971.

Related Standards

The following standards and goals may be applicable in implementing Standard 1.8:

1.1   Selection of Qualified Personnel
1.2   Commensurate Salaries
1.3   Preemployment Screening
1.4   Employer Exchange of Information
1.5   Equal Employment Opportunity
1.6   Application of Employment
1.7   Availability of Criminal History Records
2.3   Job Descriptions
11.2   Registration Qualifications
11.3   Qualifications for Armed Security Personnel

Chapter 2
Personnel Training

INTRODUCTION

Training is a vital determinant of job performance. Yet, every major research project reviewed and every study conducted for this report point to a serious lack of personnel training at all levels of private security. This situation needs to be reversed if the industry is to assume a respectable and effective role in crime prevention.

Chapter 1 emphasizes the importance of personnel to the private security industry and outlines the steps necessary to select qualified personnel who have strong potential for providing security services efficiently and effectively. Although the selection of well-qualified personnel is crucial for the advancement of private security, equal emphasis must be given to the importance of training the selected personnel in order that they might be provided with the knowledge, skills, and judgment needed for effective performance. The aim of this chapter is to establish realistic standards that promote the development, implementation, and maintenance of training programs for all private security personnel.

As noted in the licensing and registration chapters of this report, private security regulatory agencies at the State level can play an important role in encouraging and enforcing training. If States take the initiative to require training, they should be responsible for using whatever resources that are appropriate to ensure that such training becomes available. As will be discussed later, two standards focus on the role of State participation in the administration, guidance, and delivery of private security training. However, the industry itself has a major role in seeing that training is provided. Private security companies should strengthen and expand their training programs and create new training opportunities. Cooperation among companies and personnel also can help ensure that a wide variety of training becomes available for all employees.

In developing training programs, it is important, at the outset, to recognize that all levels of training are interrelated. Preassignment and basic training for operational personnel is, in and of itself, an important and progressive step. But the full potential of such training cannot be realized unless supervisors and managers are trained to lead and motivate their personnel. Recognizing this relationship, Goal 2.1 provides a framework for the standards that follow. Based on the great responsibilities assumed by private security personnel in both crime and noncrime situations, the goal calls for training at all levels of the industry and stresses the need to allocate the resources necessary to make such training applicable and meaningful.

To achieve this objective, the industry must do more than provide the most minimal of training services. Unfortunately, the attitude of a former contract guard supervisor illustrates that of many employers:

> Everyone wants trained guards. Untrained employees are . . . a cause for wasted money and lost business and a danger to themselves and others. But, the demand for manpower is so great, the wages and bids so low, that training standards have to be altered, with a little misrepresentation to salt it. (Institute for Local Self-Government, *Private Security and the Public Interest,* Berkeley, Calif.)

If the industry is to improve its capacity for crime prevention and gain the respect and confidence of the public, these negative attitudes need to be replaced through positive training measures. Although the problems of low wages and high training costs are recognized, the private security industry cannot afford to let these factors blunt the overriding need for training at all levels.

The professional certification programs outlined in Goal 2.2 can do much to promote training throughout the industry. These programs offer great potential for increasing the professionalism of the industry through training. However, in developing certification programs, the private security professional associations need to be aware that certification should be job related in order to have significant impact.

Job-relatedness is essential for the success of any training program. In this respect, Standard 2.3 stresses the importance of preparing job descriptions as the first step in developing meaningful training programs. Because private security personnel perform extremely varied services, clear job descriptions are invaluable tools for selecting and assigning personnel and for developing training programs related to the specific functions of each type of security position. Once the activities and responsibilities of a job are identified, the objectives and content of training programs fall readily into place and courses can be designed, presented, and evaluated, as outlined in Standard 2.4.

The second step in program development is establishing standards for training. Standard 2.5 contains guidelines for preassignment and basic training. A minimum of 8 hours of preassignment training is recommended for all private security personnel, including investigators or detectives, guards or watchmen, armored car personnel and armed couriers, alarm system installers or servicers, and alarm respondents. In addition, during the first 3 months of assignment, these personnel should be required to complete a basic training course of a minimum of 32 hours.

Comments from the industry during the preparation of the training standards indicate that Standard 2.5 will provoke mixed reactions. Many individuals in the industry will accept and support it as a reasonable and viable standard. Some will argue that the requirements are overly optimistic and may cause financial hardship on smaller companies. Others will assert that the requirements are totally inadequate and should include extensive contact hours and a broader curriculum. These types of reactions were anticipated in establishing this standard.

The private security industry performs a necessary and important function in our society, and it is not the purpose of this standard to set overly stringent requirements that would drive competitive companies from the business. But the compelling need to upgrade training throughout the industry cannot be ignored. Therefore, considering the present state of training, it is believed that Standard 2.5 provides a realistic starting point for improving the quality of private security services through the training of its personnel. It also is believed that, in the long run, the cost of training will pay for itself through greater efficiency and effectiveness.

Disagreement exists in the private security industry over the need for minimum training requirements for unarmed personnel, but there is no disagreement over the need to train armed personnel. Although it may never have to be used, an employee's firearm carries the potential for serious repercussions. Its misuse can result in difficult legal consequences, injury, or death. It is imperative that any armed employee know how, when, and where to use his weapon. Standard 2.6 specifies that all armed personnel complete appropriate firearms training prior to assignment and meet proficiency requirements at least once a year. A recommended course outline is presented in the standard.

Preemployment and basic training provide operational personnel with the basic knowledge, skills, and judgment needed to perform their jobs effectively. However, ongoing training is also needed by personnel to develop additional skills, to acquire added knowledge, and to guard against laxness in job performance. It is not recommended that private security companies establish a formal, inservice, classroom training program as is common in public police departments. Rather, as stated in Standard 2.7, rollcall training, training bulletins, and other less formal methods should be used so that ongoing training is available when needed.

Supervisory and managerial employees also need job-related training. Standard 2.8 addresses this need. It is not presently possible to clearly delineate the diverse nature of the duties and responsibilities of all supervisors and managers. Therefore, at present, employers should take the initiative to provide training for supervisors and managers according to their specific functions. Appropriate prior training, education, and professional certificates should be acknowledged as fulfillment of training requirements for these personnel, and research should be undertaken to develop training methods best suited to meet their specific needs.

As noted earlier, State regulatory agencies should become involved in encouraging and enforcing training requirements. Standard 2.9 gives State regulatory agencies the authority and responsibility for accrediting training schools, approving curriculums, and certifying instructors. Where in existence, a State private security regulatory agency could best manage these responsibilities. Standard 2.10 recommends that appropriate State regulatory agencies and boards also coordinate efforts to establish a delivery system for private security training programs through optimum use of existing educational and vocational personnel and facilities.

In summary, adequate training for private security personnel at all levels is a matter of immediate concern. If the industry is to meet the increasing demands placed on it because of rising crime and overburdened law enforcement agencies, it should concentrate on positive measures for advancement. One such measure—and a crucial one—is training. The steps outlined in this chapter offer a realistic approach to the development of solid, meaningful training programs for all private security personnel. The time and money spent to implement them will be a wise investment in the safeguarding of lives and property.

Goal 2.1

Training in Private Security

The responsibilities assumed by private security personnel in the protection of persons and property require training. Training should be instituted at all levels to insure that personnel are fully prepared to exercise their responsibilities effectively and efficiently.

Commentary

The demand for private security services has reached new heights in the United States. Due to rising crime trends, the Nation is increasingly aware of the need for additional protection of life and property. Private security personnel are called upon more and more to fulfill this need, and in so doing, assume major responsibilities to employers and the public. Many times, when performing their varied duties, security personnel are confronted with problems that call for instantaneous action. The magnitude of their responsibilities is clearly stated in *The Police Yearbook, 1975*:

> The huge numberical [sic] superiority of private guards working daily in the community makes it inevitable that in many instances concerning criminal or emergency situations a private guard will be the first concerned individual on the scene. His reaction to the situation could make the difference between successfully protecting the lives and property or disaster.

Clearly, private security employees should be trained in view of the serious consequences that could arise from misaction or inaction. Supervisory and managerial employees also need training to deal effectively with the problems of operational personnel. The decisions they make are no less important than those made at the operational level. Through training, supervisors and managers can develop the ability to maximize security resources, and thereby improve the overall operations of the industry.

Previous research has revealed that training for private security personnel is either minimal or nonexistent. Recent studies support these findings. For example, a survey of members of the American Society for Industrial Security revealed that only 68 percent of the respondents provided formal training for new employees and only 48 percent required annual formal training. The results of the "Survey of Consumers of Private Security Services in the Greater Philadelphia Area" were even more discouraging: Only 18 percent of new security personnel and 23 percent of supervisors received classroom training. Also, approximately 50 percent of the respondents answered "did not know" or failed to respond to the questions about training. Significantly, the same respondents ranked "inadequate training" as their most frequent and important problem.

The important responsibilities of private security

personnel demand that this situation be changed. To make better use of private security resources in crime prevention and to protect consumers, employers, and the public, as well as employees themselves, training should be instituted at all levels of the private security industry.

To attain this goal, all employers should allocate the necessary personnel and physical resources to make training relevant and meaningful. Security companies also should develop more cooperative efforts—for example, combined training would be cost effective and encompass a larger number of personnel. Finally, governmental agencies also should take an active role by setting progressive training requirements and taking a responsibility for delivery of training.

Failure to reach the goal of increased training will have a serious detrimental impact on the credibility and reliability of the private security industry. Conversely, its attainment should lead to increased acceptance of the industry as a viable crime prevention force.

Selected References

1. Kakalik, James, and Sorrel Wildhorn. *Private Police in the United States: Findings and Recommendations,* Vol. I, R–869/DOJ, Washington, D.C.: Government Printing Office, 1971.

2. Paulson, S. Lawrence (ed.). "Remarks by Thomas F. Jones," *The Police Yearbook, 1975.* Gaithersburg, Md.: International Association of Chiefs of Police, Inc., 1975.

3. Pitchess, Peter J. (project director). *Career Development for Law Enforcement.* Washington, D.C.: Technical Assistance Division, Law Enforcement Assistance Administration, U.S. Department of Justice, June 1973.

4. Private Security Task Force. "American Society for Industrial Security (ASIS) Survey Results." (See Appendix 1 to this report.)

5. Private Security Task Force. "Survey of Consumers of Private Security Services in the Greater Philadelphia Area." (See Appendix 3 to this report.)

Related Standards

The following standards and goals may be applicable in implementing Goal 2.1:

1.1   Selection of Qualified Personnel
1.2   Commensurate Salaries
2.2   Professional Certification Programs
2.3   Job Descriptions
2.4   Training Related to Job Functions
2.5   Preassignment and Basic Training
2.6   Arms Training
2.7   Ongoing Training
2.8   Training of Supervisors and Managers
2.9   State Authority and Responsibility for Training
2.10 State Boards to Coordinate Training Efforts
3.1   Code of Ethics
4.3   Certified Training of Alarm Sales and Service Personnel
4.5   Training and Instruction of Alarm Users by Alarm Companies
6.1   Interaction Policies
8.3   Noncredit and Credit Seminars and Courses
8.4   Degree Programs for Private Security
11.2 Registration Qualifications
11.3 Qualifications for Armed Security Personnel

Goal 2.2

Professional Certification Programs

Professional associations should study the feasibility of developing voluntary certification programs for private security managerial personnel.

Commentary

Certification programs can strengthen the role of private security personnel and increase the professionalism of the industry. In addition, such programs encourage training and motivate career-minded employees. Other professional groups have used certification as a means of promoting personnel quality. Private security professional organizations should follow their example.

The benefits of certification to both employers and employees are apparent. Employers could use certification as an independent evaluation of a person's qualifications for employment and/or promotion. Employees would benefit, because, in effect, certification would be an endorsement of competence, providing the opportunity for better positions.

The industry has indicated support for pursuing the establishment of certification programs. The American Society for Industrial Security (ASIS) surveyed 5,000 of its members in the spring of 1975. Responses were received from 40 percent (2,031) of its members, with 91 percent (1,815) indicating that there should be a professional certification pro-

gram for security personnel. Additionally, 89 percent (1,657) indicated they would consider applying for security certification, and 86 percent (1,697) responded in favor of ASIS having the responsibility for conducting the program. (See Table 2.1 for details of the survey.)

The development of certification programs that will be accepted as valid and reliable is a recognized problem. To achieve validity and credibility, the legal, medical, and teaching professions have established a pattern that can be useful as a model. Their requirements incorporate three key concepts: (1) an appropriate educational background; (2) appropriate examinations, developed through input from professional organizations; and (3) legal sanctions. From a practical and historical perspective, the legal sanction concept has been the key ingredient. Legal sanctions are not recommended as part of the private security certification programs. However, the remaining two components seem appropriate for a realistic private security certification program.

Perhaps the most difficult problem in developing certification programs will be providing validated, job-related certificates that receive general recognition. If, for example, an employer required certification as an employment prerequisite, the certification program administrators would have to be able to provide information indicating that the certificate is job related. If the certificate does not become a

Table 2.1. American Society for Industrial Security (ASIS) Survey Results on Need for Professional Security Certification

Question 1. There should be a professional security certification program for security personnel.

a Strongly agree	b Moderately agree	c Slightly agree	d Slightly disagree	e Moderately disagree	f Strongly disagree
1,226	467	122	21	29	117
Total	Agree.... 1,815 (91.6%)			Disagree.... 167 (8.4%)	

Question 2. ASIS should have the responsibility for conducting a professional security certification program.

a Strongly agree	b Moderately agree	c Slightly agree	d Slightly disagree	e Moderately disagree	f Strongly disagree
1,007	501	189	63	43	167
Total	Agree.... 1,697 (86.1%)			Disagree.... 273 (13.9%)	

Question 3. Upon establishment of a certification program, would you consider applying for Security Certification?

a Strongly agree	b Moderately agree	c Slightly agree	d Slightly disagree	e Moderately disagree	f Strongly disagree
1,127	389	141	34	37	141
Total	Agree.... 1,657 (89.1%)			Disagree.... 202 (10.9%)	

Source: American Society for Industrial Security. "A Proposal to Establish a Program for Certification of Security Professionals." Washington, D.C.: ASIS, 1975.

generally accepted credential, it will serve no useful purpose.

ASIS, through its Professional Certification Board, has developed "A Proposal to Establish a Program for Certification of Security Professionals," which should provide a useful guide for other professional security organizations wishing to set up certification programs. The requirements for testing, experience and education, and endorsement are as follows:

II. TESTING REQUIREMENT

A. Successful achievement of passing grades on a battery of eight (8) tests, each approximately fifty (50) minutes in length shall be necessary. This battery, chosen from a list of nineteen (19) tests, shall include three (3) required and five (5) optional tests on the theory and principles in the following fields of security, protection and loss prevention:

1. MANDATORY SUBJECTS

   A. Security Management
   B. Physical Security
   C. Investigations

2. OPTIONAL SUBJECTS

   A. Legal Aspects of Security
   B. Protection of Proprietary Information
   C. Transportation and Cargo Security

   D. Fire Resources Management
   E. Restaurant and Lodging Security
   F. Banking Security
   G. Educational Institutions Security
   H. Protection of U.S. Classified Defense Information
   I. Protection of Special Nuclear Materials and Facilities
   J. Retail Security
   K. Computer Security
   L. Health Care Institutions Security
   M. Disaster Control
   N. Public Utilities Security
   O. Alcohol and Other Drug Abuse Control
   P. Credit Card Security

B. Actual testing shall be accomplished at least annually in each A.S.I.S. region and in conjunction with the annual national seminar of the American Society for Industrial Security.

C. Certification fees shall be established, based upon the costs of the certification program.

III. EXPERIENCE AND EDUCATION REQUIREMENTS

A. An earned associate degree from an accredited college and eight (8) years security experience, at least half of which shall have been in responsible charge of a security function, or

B. An earned bachelor's degree from an accredited college or university and five (5) years security experience, at least half of which shall have been in responsible charge of a security function, or

C. An earned master's degree from an accredited college or university and four (4) years security experience, at least half of which shall have been in responsible charge of a security function, or

D. An earned doctoral degree from an accredited college or university and three (3) years security experience, at least half of which shall have been in responsible charge of a security function, or

E. Ten (10) years security experience, at least half of which shall have been in responsible charge of a security function.

F. "Responsible Charge" shall mean that charge exercised by an individual who makes decisions for the successful completion as to specific methods or techniques. An applicant need not have held a supervisory position, as long as the position(s) on which the application relies shall have included responsibility for independent decisions or action.

IV. ENDORSEMENT REQUIREMENT

A. Each applicant for certification as a Certified Protection Professional shall be endorsed by either a member of the Professional Certification Board or a person who shall himself already have been certified as a Protection Professional. Endorsement of an application for certification shall signify that the person making the endorsement shall have satisfied himself that the statements made by the applicant upon the application for certification are complete and accurate; and, that in the considered opinion of the person making the endorsement, the applicant is fully qualified for consideration for certification.

Another certification program, which may be used for reference purposes, is that initiated by the International Association for Hospital Security to provide basic training for operational hospital security personnel. A senior member of the International Association for Hospital Security must certify to the association's training committee that a person has completed the 40-hour basic course and recommend that person for certification. Russell Colling, co-chairman of the training committee, stated that 21 persons had been certified and 130 enrolled for certification as of Jan. 1, 1976.

Other private security associations should initiate activities to develop similar programs for their diverse operational and management people. The professional associations that take the initiative and explore the feasibility of developing certification programs will provide positive leadership for the ultimate goal of professionalizing the industry.

It is recognized that providing a validated and generally accepted certification program would re-quire innovative planning and monetary resources. For example, the ASIS Professional Certification Board estimates expenditures of $90,000 for the first year, $53,000 for the second year, and $44,300 for the third. Persons responsible for the development of such programs can obtain assistance in budgetary estimates and developmental factors from organizations, such as the American Bar Association, American Medical Association, International Association of Chiefs of Police, and others that have initiated certification programs.

To achieve this goal, the concentrated efforts of a wide variety of private security interests is necessary. The leaders of professional associations and their members should coordinate their efforts with respected individuals in the security field to provide meaningful, validated, job-related certification programs that receive general acceptance by all parties. The establishment of accepted certification programs could be a positive contribution to the professionalization of the private security industry.

Selected References

1. American Society for Industrial Security. "A Proposal to Establish a Program for Certification of Security Professionals." Washington, D.C.: ASIS, 1975.

2. ————. "Charter for ASIS Program for Certification of Protection Professionals." Approved by ASIS Board of Directors, Sept. 8, 1975.

3. International Association for Hospital Security. "Basic Training Certification." Chicago, Ill.: Merchandise Mart Station, P.O. Box 3776.

Related Standards

The following standards and goals may be applicable in implementing Goal 2.2:

Standard 2.3

Job Descriptions

Private security employers should develop job descriptions for each private security position.

Commentary

Private security is a complex and diverse field, with personnel assigned to numerous kinds of security functions. Problems in selecting personnel and establishing training program curriculums arise unless employees, employers, and persons responsible for training have carefully prepared job descriptions as resource documents.

The job description is a valuable asset to the private security executive. In the preemployment screening process, it provides a method of determining if an applicant's qualifications match job requirements. In the assignment process, it promotes productivity, by placing the right person in the right job. Finally, used in the training process, it ensures that curriculums correspond to the jobs to be performed.

Unfortunately, many security positions currently do not have adequate job descriptions. A recent survey of the members of the American Society for Industrial Security indicated that only 66 percent of the firms had job descriptions for all security job functions, 18 percent had descriptions for most functions, 6 percent had descriptions for a few functions, and 10 percent either had no job description or did not respond. The survey did not ask respondents to submit copies of their job descriptions, but a cursory review of various job descriptions indicated that many are perfunctory.

As a general guide, the data recorded in job descriptions should relate to two essential features of each position: (1) the nature of the work involved, and (2) the employee type who appears best fitted for the position.

With respect to the nature of the job, the following data should be included:

1. The job title;
2. Classification title and number, if any;
3. Number of employees holding the job;
4. A job summary, outlining the major functions in one to three paragraphs;
5. A job breakdown, listing the sequence of operations that constitute the job and noting the difficulty levels;
6. A description of equipment used;
7. A statement of the relationship of the job to other closely related jobs;
8. A notation of the jobs from which workers are promoted and those to which workers may be promoted from this job;
9. Training required and usual methods of providing such training;
10. Amounts and types of compensation;
11. Usual working hours; and

94

12. Peculiar conditions of employment, including unusual circumstances of heat or cold, humidity, light, ventilation, or any others.

With respect to the employee, the data generally available should include:

1. Necessary and special physical characteristics;
2. Necessary physical dexterities;
3. Emotional characteristics, such as disposition, mood, introversion, or extroversion;
4. Special mental abilities required;
5. Experience and skill requirements.

This outline is not intended to be all inclusive or all exclusive but is presented to highlight the depth to which job descriptions should be prepared if they are to be effective. It was noted, however, that some job descriptions reviewed included nonsecurity functions, such as running errands. This practice should be discouraged, because it detracts from the overall effectiveness and morale of private security personnel.

In summary, the preparation of high quality job descriptions is a critical step in the personnel selection, assignment, and training processes. Without job descriptions, the employer, employee, and person responsible for developing training programs are at a tremendous disadvantage. Further, the need to relate training to the job is vital if training is to carry more significance than mere hours spent sitting in a classroom.

Selected References

1. Longenecker, Justin G. *Principles of Management and Organizational Behavior*. Columbus, Ohio: Charles E. Merrill Books, Inc., 1964.

2. Mager, Robert F., and Peter Pipe. *Analyzing Performance Problems or "You Really Oughta Wanna."* Belmont, Calif.: Fearon Publishers, 1970.

3. Pitchess, Peter J. (project director). *Career Development for Law Enforcement*. Washington, D.C.: Technical Assistance Division, Law Enforcement Assistance Administration, U.S. Department of Justice, June 1973.

4. Private Security Task Force. "American Society for Industrial Security (ASIS) Survey Results." (See Appendix 1 to this report.)

5. Yoder, Dale. *Personnel Management and Industrial Relations,* 4th ed. Englewood Cliffs, N.J.: Prentice Hall, Inc., 1956.

Related Standards

The following standards and goals may be applicable in implementing Standard 2.3:

1.1 Selection of Qualified Personnel
1.2 Commensurate Salaries
1.3 Preemployment Screening
1.8 Minimum Preemployment Screening Qualifications
2.1 Training in Private Security
2.2 Professional Certification Programs
2.4 Training Related to Job Functions
2.5 Preassignment and Basic Training
2.6 Arms Training
2.8 Training of Supervisors and Managers
3.2 Conduct of Private Security Personnel
3.3 Reporting of Criminal Violations
3.4 Employer Responsibilities
3.5 Maintaining Data on Criminal Activities
6.3 Policies and Procedures
6.6 State Regulation of Private Security Uniforms, Equipment, Job Titles
8.2 National Private Security Resource and Research Institute

Standard 2.4

Training Related to Job Functions

Private security employers should ensure that training programs are designed, presented, and evaluated in relation to the job functions to be performed.

Commentary

The purpose of training is to provide the trainee with the necessary skills, knowledge, and judgment to perform specific job functions. However, all too often training subjects are determined, lesson plans prepared, and tests given without any direct cause-effect relationship to actual job performance. In fact, private security employers, eager to place personnel on the job, often are more concerned with successful completion of a course of instruction than with its content. As a result, much of the limited amount of security training that has been offered to date is largely haphazard, with little regard to the job to be performed.

To be truly effective, as well as meaningful, training must not occur in a vacuum. Instruction needs to be job related, not merely training related. Although theoretical discussions are interesting, private security personnel should be provided with information that they can directly apply to the performance of their duties. For example, training for guards in the subject of procedures for bomb threats should relate to the level at which the guards will be functioning (i.e., movement of people from the area, who to notify when the threat is received), and not be limited to a theoretical discussion of how bombs are constructed and detonated. Unless the curriculum is geared to preparing personnel for their specific job assignments, the purpose of training will be lost in its mechanics.

To ensure that training fulfills its purpose, several factors need to be considered in the process of its development. One key factor is the preparation of job descriptions. As discussed in Standard 2.3, job descriptions pave the way for training programs that are meaningful and relevant to the jobs to be performed. The following guide is provided to further assist in designing, presenting, and evaluating effective training programs.

Prior to Determining Curriculum

1. Review job descriptions prepared for the positions in which the students are or will be employed.

2. Conduct a job analysis to provide a systematic and precise identification of the skill requirements of the various job categories identified through review of job descriptions.

3. Determine the frequency and importance of the functions so that appropriate training time can be assigned to prepare the student for the job.

During Curriculum Preparation

1. Ensure that each job function is identified in both the curriculum and individual lesson plans within the broad curriculum.

2. Ensure that the teaching objective is to prepare the student for the job to be performed and not simply to successfully complete the course's final test.

3. Contact present employees who perform the functions, their supervisors, and others who can provide input into the subject matter.

During Curriculum Presentation

1. Use audiovisual resources, practical exercises, and case studies to relate the subjects to the actual job functions students will be performing.

2. At the conclusion of each section of the curriculum, develop a feedback mechanism to ensure that the students are prepared for the next phase of instruction. For example, in preparing the student to perform the job function of "controlling personnel access to a given location," the student could receive information in the following order:

   a. Legal and/or policy authority to restrict access,

   b. Techniques for gaining cooperation from others without the use of force,

   c. Use of minimal force to stop persons from gaining access, and

   d. Procedures to follow if someone has illegally gained access.

During Curriculum Evaluation

1. Ensure that the testing procedures are aimed at determining the students' understanding of the material, so that it can be applied to the job rather than being mere recitation of abstract facts.

2. Allow students an opportunity to review their performance on the test and reinforce any training deficiencies through explanations or retraining, if needed.

3. After the students are on the job, check their performance through contact with them and their supervisors.

4. As necessary, provide input at the appropriate place (i.e., curriculum preparation) to ensure that training remains job related. This is extremely important because job functions change from time to time and training should adapt to these changes.

The above guide is intended to serve only as an explanation of the broad scope of the standard. Obviously, implementation will be a more complicated process, involving a wide variety of resources, such as private security personnel, training consultants, psychologists, and others. Persons responsible for training are encouraged to build and expand training programs in response to the various job-related needs of personnel, remembering that job performance—not test performance—determines the final effectiveness of any training program.

Selected References

1. Epstein, Sidney, and Richard S. Laymon. *Guidelines for Police Performance Appraisal, Promotion and Placement Procedures.* Washington, D.C.: Law Enforcement Assistance Administration, 1973.

2. Fine, Sidney. *Functional Job Analysis.* Washington, D.C.: UpJohn Institute, 1971.

3. Landy, Frank J., and James L. Fair. *Police Performance Appraisal.* University Park, Pa.: Pennsylvania State University Press, 1975.

4. The National Commission on Productivity. *Opportunities for Improving Productivity in Police Services.* Washington, D.C.: National Commission on Productivity, 1973.

5. Wilson, Brooks W. *The P.O.S.T. Training Program—A Review and Critique.* Sacramento, Calif.: The Commission on Peace Officer Standards and Training, 1972.

Related Standards

The following standards and goals may be applicable in implementing Standard 2.4:

1.2	Commensurate Salaries
1.3	Preemployment Screening
1.5	Equal Employment Opportunity
2.1	Training in Private Security
2.2	Professional Certification Programs
2.3	Job Descriptions
2.5	Preassignment and Basic Training
2.6	Arms Training
2.7	Ongoing Training
2.8	Training of Supervisors and Managers
2.9	State Authority and Responsibility for Training
2.10	State Boards to Coordinate Training Efforts
3.2	Conduct of Private Security Personnel
8.2	National Private Security Resource and Research Institute
8.3	Noncredit and Credit Seminars and Courses
8.4	Degree Programs for Private Security
11.2	Registration Qualifications
11.3	Qualifications for Armed Security Personnel

Standard 2.5

Preassignment and Basic Training

Any person employed as an investigator or detective, guard or watchman, armored car personnel or armed courier, alarm system installer or servicer, or alarm respondent, including those presently employed and part-time personnel, should successfully:

1. Complete a minimum of 8 hours formal preassignment training;

2. Complete a basic training course of a minimum of 32 hours within 3 months of assignment. A maximum of 16 hours can be supervised on-the-job training.

Commentary

Other standards have highlighted the lack of training in the private security industry. This lack has inspired much criticism, most of it directed specifically at the failure of the industry to properly and adequately prepare its operational-level personnel. *The Other Police,* a report on the Ohio private security industry, contains a section entitled "Training: Infrequent, Incomplete, and Misdirected." It points out that fewer than 25 percent of Ohio's guards hold training certificates from the Ohio Peace Officer Training Council and that training throughout the State is decreasing instead of increasing.

Lack of private security training also tends to generate friction with public law enforcement agen-

cies. For example, law enforcement officers, working in the same community with private security guards, investigators, and so forth, often look down on their abilities and question their judgments, because private security personnel are untrained. The public law enforcement sector has made tremendous progress in the past decade in both adequacy of training and quality of courses, but the private security industry has barely taken a step in this direction.

A survey of members of the American Society for Industrial Security (ASIS) indicated a present range of 4 to 80 hours of training for newly hired personnel. Table 2.2, from the *RAND Report* (Vol. II), further illustrates the wide range and general inadequacy of initial training in a sample of 11 private security companies.

Other findings from the *RAND Report* (Vol. II) indicate that a large percentage of private security guards do not know their legal powers to detain, arrest, search, or use force. Frequently, in fact, they lack understanding of the basic policies and procedures of their functions. The following comment from a former guard, who was beaten during a robbery, vividly illustrates the need for additional training:

For $1.60 per hour I wouldn't stick my neck out again. Anybody who does is crazy. I stand around looking cute in my uniform. Don't let anybody tell you a guard doesn't need training. If I'd had it I might had known what the hell was going on.

Private security professionals do recognize the importance of training. The previously mentioned ASIS survey revealed that 76 percent of the respondents believed training standards were "very important"; 15 percent, "somewhat important"; and 1 percent, "not important." Yet, until specific standards are required, private security training is not likely to improve.

Preassignment Training

This standard recommends that training requirements be initiated for all operational private security personnel. A RAND survey of private security personnel in California revealed that 65 percent of the respondents had received no training prior to beginning work. Because the instruction received at this stage familiarizes the employee with the responsibilities of the job and establishes certain basic skills and concepts, it is recommended that every private security employee successfully complete 8 hours of preassignment training before commencing work.

Due to the complexity of functions performed by private security personnel, the final determination of subject content for preassignment training will need to be made by employers and regulatory agencies; however, the following topical outline is recommended as a general guide. It is based on a model originally prepared by the Private Security Advisory Council, included in their *Model Private Security Licensing and Regulatory Statute,* and designed for guards. Obviously, some additions in content were necessary to expand it to meet the broader spectrum of personnel included in this standard.

Private Security 8-Hour Preassignment Training Course

Section I—Orientation: 2 hours that include the following topics:

- What is security?
- Public relations.
- Deportment.
- Appearance.
- Maintenance and safeguarding of uniform and/or equipment.
- Notetaking/Reporting.
- Role of public law enforcement.

Section II—Legal Powers and Limitations: 2 hours that include the following topics:

- Prevention versus apprehension.
- Use of force.
- Search and seizure.
- Arrest powers.

Section III—Handling Emergencies: 2 hours that should include appropriate topics pertinent to the job functions to be performed by the employee:

- Crimes in progress.
- Procedures for bomb threats.
- Procedures during fires, explosions, floods, riots, and so forth.
- Responding to alarms.

Section IV—General Duties: 2 hours that should include the appropriate topics pertinent to the job functions to be performed by the employee:

- Fire prevention and control.
- Inspections.
- Interviewing techniques.
- Patrol.
- Safeguarding valuable property.
- Safety.
- Surveillance.

The following model preassignment training programs are intended to explain how the program could be implemented for guards or watchmen or alarm respondents. Again, specific recommendations are not established because of the complexity of training needs, but the outline may prove helpful as a general guideline. The hour designation used in all training standards is a 50-minute block of instruction that is standard for training and education curriculums.

Model Preassignment Training Program for a Guard or Watchman

Section I—Orientation (2 hours)	Minutes
• What is security?	15
• Public relations	15
• Deportment	15
• Appearance	10
• Maintenance and safeguarding of uniforms and/or equipment	20
• Notetaking/Reporting	15
• Role of public law enforcement	10

Section II—Legal Powers and Limitations (2 hours)	
• Prevention versus apprehension	40
• Use of force	25
• Search and seizure	15
• Arrest powers	20

Section III—Handling Emergencies (2 hours)	
• Procedures for bomb threats	40
• Procedures during fires, explosions, floods, riots, and so forth	60

Table 2.2. Current Private Security Guard Training Programs

Program	Initial Prework Training								Initial On-the-Job Training				Total Initial Training (hours)
	Talking with Supervisors (hours)	Read Manual	View Films/ Slides (hours)	Class (hours)	Test	Firearms Range	Trained on Previous Job	Total (hours)	By Supervisor (hours)	By Fellow Employee (hours)	Written Post Orders	Total (hours)	
Company A: Small Contract Guard Firm	½ to 1	None	None	None	None	N/A	None	½ to 1	8 to 16	None	Yes	8 to 16	8½ to 17
Company B: Small Contract Guard Firm	1 to 2	Yes	None	None	Yes	Yes	None	2½ to 3½	8 to 16	None	Yes	8 to 16	10½ to 19½
Company C: Medium Contract Guard Firm	1 to 3	Yes	1½	None	Yes	Yes	None	5 to 7	8 to 16	None	Yes	8 to 16	13 to 23
Company D: Large Contract Guard Firm (full- and part-time)	1 to 2	Yes	2	None	Yes	Yes	None	6½ to 7½	1 to 8	None.	Yes	1 to 8	7½ to 15½
Company E: Large Contract Premium Guard Firm	1 to 2	Yes	2	40 to 80	Yes	Yes	None	46½ to 87½	1 to 8	None	Yes	1 to 8	47½ to 95½
Company F: Large Contract Guard Firm													
a. Regular	None	Yes	1	9	None	Yes	None	12	1 to 8	None	Yes	1 to 8	13 to 20
b. Temporary	3 to 4	None	1	None	None	None	None	4 to 5	½	None	None	½	4½ to 5½
Company G: Large Contract Guard Firm													
a. Regular	None	Yes	None	10	Yes	Yes	None	11	½ to 1	None	Yes	½ to 1	10½ to 11
b. Temporary	None	None	None	8	None	None	None	8	½	None	None	½	8½

Company H: Small Contract Patrol Guard Firm	1 to 2	None	None	None	Yes	None	3 to 4	16	None	Yes	16	19 to 20
Company I: Inhouse Guards (Bank)	2 to 4	Yes	None	None	Yes	Occa-sionally	5 to 7	80 to 120	None	Yes	80 to 120	85 to 127
Company J: Inhouse Guards (Research)	1 to 4	Yes	None	None	N/A	None	3 to 6	None	160	Yes	160	163 to 166
Company K: Inhouse Guards (Manufacturing)	½ to 1	Yes	None	None	N/A	Manda-tory	½ to 2	None	24	Yes	24	25½ to 26

Source: Kakalik, James S., and Sorrel Wildhorn. *The Private Police Industry: Its Nature and Extent.* Vol. II, R–870/DOJ. Washington, D.C.: Government Printing Office, 1972, p. 33.

Section IV—General Duties (2 hours)

- Patrol   40
- Fire prevention and control   30
- Safety   30

Model Preassignment Training Program
for an Alarm Respondent

Section I—Orientation (2 hours)	Minutes
• What is security?	15
• Public relations	10
• Deportment	10
• Appearance	10
• Maintenance and safeguarding of uniforms and/or equipment	30
• Notetaking/Reporting	15
• Role of public law enforcement	10

Section II—Legal Powers and Limitations (2 hours)

- Prevention versus apprehension   25
- Use of force   25
- Search and seizure   30
- Arrest powers   20

Section III—Handling Emergencies (2 hours)

- Crime in progress   20
- Responding to alarms   80

Section IV—General Duties (2 hours)

- Interviewing techniques   40
- Patrol   30
- Safeguarding valuable property 30

Model Preassignment Training Program
for an Armored Car Guard [1]

Section I—Orientation (2 hours)	Minutes
• Protective transportation:	50
History of armored car industry	
Basic elements of service	
Interface with the financial community	
• The company:	
History of employer	15
Organizational structure	15
Wages and benefits	20
Driver/guard	
Messenger/guard	
Custodian/guard	

[1] This model preassignment training program was prepared by the Training Committee of the National Armored Car Association at the request of the Private Security Task Force.

Section II—Legal Powers and Limitations (2 hours)

- Parameters of operation
  - We are not policemen or stationary guards   10
  - Theory of bailment   10
  - Use of selective force in defensive role   25
  - Weapons philosophy   25
  - Physical force and its operational application   20
  - Restraints in dissemination of confidential information   10

Section III—Handling Emergencies (2 hours)

- Emergency situations (an overview)
  - Defining the threat   30
    - Robbery
    - On the sidewalk
    - In customer's premises
    - In the truck
  - Political terrorists versus conventional criminal   70
    - Extortion
    - Abduction
    - Ambush
    - Bomb threats

Section IV—General Duties (2 hours)

- Fire procedures   25
- Traffic accidents   25
- Rules and regulations 40
  - Uniforms
  - Equipment (familiarization)
    - Armored truck
    - Handtruck
    - Seals and bags
    - Terminals
    - Vaults
    - Security areas
- Deportment   10

In implementing the suggested preassignment training programs, the following factors should be noted:

1. All topics in Sections I and II should be covered in some portion of the 2 hours assigned.

2. Only pertinent topics in Sections III and IV need to be included in the 2 hours assigned.

3. Supervised, on-the-job training cannot be used to meet preassignment training.

4. Lectures, films, programmed learning, and other training methods can be used.

Basic Training

Upon successful completion of preassignment training, the employee should be allowed to begin work, but training should not stop at this point. Additional training is needed to provide the skills, knowledge, and judgment necessary for efficient, effective job performance. Although the importance of this training cannot be overemphasized, it is recognized that the high cost of training may place a heavy economic burden on some employers. Therefore, a realistic minimum of 32 hours of basic training is recommended in addition to preassignment training. This training should be completed over a 3-month time period and may include a maximum of 16 hours on-the-job training.

Although many may believe that the 32-hour training standard is totally inadequate, it is a progressive step in terms of the amount of training presently provided. Admittedly, it is far short of the 400 hours recommended in 1973 for sworn police officers by the National Advisory Commission on Criminal Justice Standards and Goals. It should be understood, however, that Federal, State, and local tax dollars support training for public law enforcement officers, but only limited monetary resources are available to provide training for private security personnel. Ultimately, a large portion of the cost would have to be borne by the consumer. Although, in some instances, employees are required to pay the cost of their own training, this practice is discouraged unless such training is personally sought by the individual to prepare himself for private security employment. The 32-hour minimum basic requirement is believed to be economically feasible for implementation by all; those employers financially capable of providing additional training should surpass the 32-hour minimum.

Basic training requirements, as stated in this standard, should apply to both presently employed and part-time personnel. Because of the prevalent lack of training throughout the private security industry, many present employees are not adequately prepared for the responsibilities of their positions. Thus, they should be required to have the same training as newly hired personnel if uniform quality of performance is to be achieved. Part-time employees also assume the same responsibilities and need the same amount of training.

By allowing 16 hours of the basic training to be completed on the job, employers can maximize the training effect. However, it is very important that close supervision is provided for employers to meet the intent of the standard. With appropriate supervision, an employee can effectively relate classroom instruction to the specific job performed. In this manner, training can take on added significance and reality.

Responsibility for implementation of private security basic training would rest with employers and State regulatory agencies. As with preassignment training, these persons ultimately would have to determine the actual subjects presented in basic training. However, to provide general guidance in determining curriculums, the following topical outline for a 32-hour basic course of training is offered:

Private Security 32-hour Basic Training Course

Section I—Prevention/Protection

- Patrolling.
- Checking for hazards.
- Personnel control.
- Identification systems.
- Access control.
- Fire control systems.
- Types of alarms.
- Law enforcement/Private security relationships.

Section II—Enforcement

- Surveillance.
- Techniques of searching.
- Crime scene searching.
- Handling juveniles.
- Handling mentally disturbed persons.
- Parking and traffic.
- Enforcing employee work rules/regulations.
- Observation/Description.
- Preservation of evidence.
- Criminal/Civil law.
- Interviewing techniques.

Section III—General emergency services

- First aid.
- Defensive tactics.
- Fire fighting.
- Communications.
- Crowd control.
- Crimes in progress.

Section IV—Special problems

- Escort.
- Vandalism.
- Arson.
- Burglary.
- Robbery.
- Theft.
- Drugs/Alcohol.
- Shoplifting.
- Sabotage.

- Espionage.
- Terrorism.

To allow flexibility for individual situations and yet provide reasonable controls, the following items should be considered:

1. A minimum of 4 classroom hours should be provided in each of the sections.

2. A maximum of 16 hours supervised, on-the-job training should be permissable.

The following models explain how the basic training course can be implemented:

Model 1. Maximum classroom hours

| | Classroom hours | |
Section	Minimum	Maximum
• Prevention/Detection	4	16
• Enforcement	4	16
• General/Emergency services	4	16
• Special problems	4	16

Discussion: The maximum of hours in each section can be modified in any way that is appropriate to the training needs; however, 4 classroom hours should be provided in each section. For example, an alarm response runner could follow these courses:

Section	Classroom hours
• Prevention/Detection	20 or 16
• Enforcement	4 or 5
• General/Emergency services	4 or 5
• Special problems	4 or 6

(May use any combination provided a minimum of 4 classroom hours are in each section and the total hours are 32.)

Model 2. Minimum classroom hours

Section	Classroom hours
• Prevention/Detection	4
• Enforcement	4
• General/Emergency services	4
• Special problems	4

(Should include 16 hours of supervised on-the-job training.)

Discussion: In many cases needs can best be met by training the employee in the job setting after providing basic knowledge and skills. This model provides the necessary latitude for these situations.

Model 32-hour Basic Training Course for Armored Car Guards [2]

Section I—Prevention/Detection

[2] Prepared from model 32-hour basic training course presented to the Task Force by the Training Committee of the National Armored Car Association.

(Operating procedures)—6 hours	Minutes
• Crew operations	100
In the terminal	
On the street	
On customer's premises	
• Armored truck and equipment drills	50
• Packaging	25
• Receipting system	50
• Reporting and forms preparation	25
• Police liaison	50

Section II—Enforcement (Robbery and loss)—4 hours

	Minutes
• Case studies of attacks on men and equipment	50
• Role playing	150

Section III—General/Emergency services (Emergency response)—6 hours

	Minutes
• Trauma treatment (10-minute medicine)	100
Gunshot	
Explosion	
Burns	
Vehicle accidents	
CPR training	
• Basic firefighting techniques	25
• Basic self-defense	75
• Bomb threats	50
Bomb recognition	
Vehicle inspection	
Tactical reaction to a bomb	
Bomb call threat to terminal	
Customer premises threat	
Suspicious device located	
On the vehicle	
In the terminal	
In customer's premises	
• Use of communications	50

Section IV—Special problems (Emergency drivers)—4 hours

	Minutes
• Defensive driving	40
• Philosophy of offensive driving	30
Counterambush	
Urban	
Rural	
• Night driving	30
• Hands-on driver training	100

(Should include at least 12 hours of supervised on-the-job training to include examination and course evaluation.) (Note: A number of industry representatives indicated that more than 12 hours of supervised on-the-job training would be provided to meet employees' needs.)

Discussion: Because the vast majority of armored car guards are armed (and to meet the firearms training of Standard 2.6), the Training Committee of the National Armored Car Association included the following outline as part of the basic training program:

Firearms Training
>Company and industry policy on use of weapons
>Legal limitations
>Firearms safety
>Care and cleaning
>Basic revolver training
>>Combat firing
>>Use of gunports
>>Use of shotgun
>>Qualification and certification

The previous models provide the extremes of the standard. The 32 hours of training could be implemented in a variety of ways, with the following factors in mind:

1. The total basic training program encompasses 32 hours.

2. The minimum classroom hours are 16.

3. The maximum supervised on-the-job training is also 16.

4. The ratio between the minimum classroom hours and the maximum supervised, on-the-job training can vary (e.g., 20 classroom hours and 12 on-the-job training hours).

Several final points involving this training standard are offered for purposes of clarity:

1. The issue of an exemption from the requirements of this standard—a "grandfather" clause—for all private security personnel was considered and rejected because the training standard is a basic minimum and all personnel should receive it.

2. Formal or classroom training, both for preassignment and basic, can be lectures, films, slides, programmed instruction, and the use of other training media.

3. Supervised, on-the-job training means that personnel receive close observation and supervision. Merely being assigned to a job cannot be called on-the-job training.

4. The 3-month period to complete training is included to allow employers the flexibility to group personnel into training sessions that best meet the employers' and employees' needs, and also to minimize the economic losses caused by training persons who leave after a short period of time.

5. At least 1 hour for examinations should be included in the training curriculum and should be taken as a reduction in the supervised, on-the-job training hours. Depending on the delivery system, it may be advisable to have a testing block of time for each section.

6. Part-time personnel means all personnel who work less than full-time and includes personnel listed as temporary, half-time, and so forth.

7. Some may view the 8-hour preassignment training as totally inadequate preparation before starting employment. More preassignment training, as appropriate is encouraged. Many subjects in the basic course could be included in an expanded preassignment course.

As stated earlier, many security professionals would believe that the training recommended is minimal and that additional specialized training would be needed, depending on the skills, knowledge, and judgment required for certain assignments. For example, private investigators and detectives may require more training than this standard specifies. The specific amount of time and course content would have to be determined on an individual basis. The following list is presented to illustrate the types of specific subjects that could be included in the additional training:

- Background investigation.
- Civil court procedures.
- Civil damage suits.
- Criminal court procedures.
- Collection and preservation of evidence.
- Crime prevention.
- Custody and control of property.
- Fingerprints.
- Followup investigations.
- Identification of persons.
- Industrial investigations.
- Insurance investigations.
- Interviews.
- Investigation and security as a professional vocation.
- Investigator's notebook.
- Mock crime scene.
- Modus operandi.
- Motion and still cameras.
- Obtaining information from witnesses.
- Plaintiff investigations.
- Preemployment investigations.
- Preliminary investigations.
- Preventive security.
- Principles of investigation.
- Purpose of private investigation.
- Report writing.
- Retail store investigation.
- Rules of evidence.
- Search and seizure.
- Sources of information.
- Surveillance and stakeout.
- Taking statements.

- Testifying in court.
- Undercover assignments.

Although many of these topics may seem more important to public law enforcement investigators, they are also relevant to private investigators. For example, many cases developed by private investigators end up in civil court while others are filed in criminal court. Thus, the training of private investigators should properly prepare them for this eventuality.

Guards or watchmen, couriers, alarm system installers or repairers, and alarm respondents may also require additional training, and similar, expanded subject outlines can be developed to provide the needed training. The use of investigators and detectives as one example should not be construed as an indication that they are the only categories of private security personnel who might need specialized training.

Selected References

1. Brennan, Dennis T. *The Other Police.* Cleveland: Governmental Research Institute, 1975.
2. Criminal Justice Institute: "88-Hour General Security Program." Detroit: Criminal Justice Institute.
3. Eversull, Kenneth S. "Training the Uniformed Officers," *Security World,* May 1967.
4. Ford, Robert E. (supervising ed.). *TIPS: A Continuous Program of Training and Information for Private Security.* Santa Cruz, Calif.: Davis Publishing Company, Inc., 1975.
5. Kakalik, James S., and Sorrel Wildhorn. *The Private Police Industry: Its Nature and Extent,* Vol. II, R–870/DOJ. Washington, D.C.: Government Printing Office, 1972.
6. Kelly, James. Address before the Private Security Advisory Council, Chicago, Ill., July 11, 1975.
7. National Advisory Commission on Criminal Justice Standards and Goals. *Police.* Washington, D.C.: Government Printing Office, 1973.
8. National Council on Crime and Delinquency. "Minimum Standards for the Training of Private Security Guards." Hackensack, N.J.: National Council on Crime and Delinquency, May 1973.
9. Norell and Acqualino. "Scarecrows in Blue," *The Washingtonian,* August 1971.
10. O'Hara, Charles E. *Fundamentals of Criminal Investgation,* 3d ed. Springfield, Ill.: Charles C Thomas Publishers, 1973.
11. Post, Richard S. "Application of Functional Job Analysis to the Development of Curriculum Guidelines for Protective Services Field." Ph.D. dissertation. Madison: University of Wisconsin, 1974.
12. Private Police Training Institute. "The Course Outline." Louisville, Ky.: Jefferson Community College, 1975.
13. Private Security Advisory Council. *Model Private Security Licensing and Regulatory Statute.* Washington, D.C.: Law Enforcement Assistance Administration, 1975.
14. Private Security Task Force. "American Society for Industrial Security (ASIS) Survey Results." (See Appendix 1 to this report.)
15. "Survey of Security Instruction Time," *Security World,* February 1972.
16. Vanderbosch, Charles G. *Criminal Investigation.* Gaithersburg, Md.: International Association of Chiefs of Police, 1968.
17. Wilson, O. W. *Police Administration.* 2d ed. New York: McGraw-Hill, Inc., 1963.

Related Standards

The following standards and goals may be applicable in implementing Standard 2.5:

1.2	Commensurate Salaries
2.1	Training in Private Security
2.3	Job Descriptions
2.4	Training Related to Job Functions
2.6	Arms Training
2.7	Ongoing Training
2.8	Training of Supervisors and Managers
2.9	State Authority and Responsibility for Training
2.10	State Boards to Coordinate Training Efforts
3.1	Code of Ethics
4.3	Certified Training of Alarm Sales and Service Personnel
8.2	National Private Security Resource and Research Institute
8.3	Noncredit and Credit Seminars and Courses
8.4	Degree Programs for Private Security
11.2	Registration Qualifications
11.3	Qualifications for Armed Security Personnel

Standard 2.6

Arms Training

All armed private security personnel, including those presently employed and part-time personnel, should:

1. Be required to successfully complete a 24-hour firearms course that includes legal and policy requirements—or submit evidence of competence and proficiency—prior to assignment to a job that requires a firearm;

2. Be required to requalify at least once every 12 months with the firearm(s) they carry while performing private security duties (the requalification phase should cover legal and policy requirements).

Commentary

Armed personnel are defined as persons, uniformed or nonuniformed, who carry or use at any time any form of firearm. The serious consequences, for both employers and employees, when untrained personnel are assigned to jobs that require firearms are obvious. These consequences can be generally outlined as:

1. Self-injury because of mishandling of the weapon;

2. Injury to others, often innocent bystanders, because of lack of skill when firing the weapon; and

3. Criminal and/or civil suits against both employers and employees resulting from the above actions.

A 1974 study by the Institute for Local Self Government revealed that 45 percent of licensed California private security agency heads admitted to providing no formal preassignment instruction in firearms use, and 40 percent indicated a lack of weapons retraining. Even more revealing and disturbing, 55 percent of the employees surveyed said they sometimes carry firearms, but only 8 percent had received firearms training in their present jobs.

The *RAND Report* (Vol. II) indicated that 49 percent of private security personnel carried firearms, but only 19 percent had received any firearms training in their present jobs. The following statement from the *Philadelphia Magazine* pointedly reveals one employee's feelings:

One guard who shot two people within two weeks in Philadelphia complained that the detective agencies were "taking young jitterbugs off the street, putting guns in their hands and giving them no training. The companies are cleaning up, man, and they ought to spend some of that money to train us."

Statistics and reports, such as the above, emphasize the vital necessity of adequate training for all personnel who are to carry firearms in their private security duties, even if they are instructed never to use them. Employers cannot ignore this need or

107

attempt to evade it, as was done in the following example: An article in the January 1973 issue of *Police Weapons Center Bulletin* reported that a Virginia firm was manufacturing fake replicas of standard police revolvers and marketing them to security agencies for issuance to guards. According to the article, 30 private security agencies had purchased these replicas to equip their guards, thus eliminating the problem of issuing real firearms to untrained or semitrained personnel. The consequences of this action could be tragic. No firearms should ever be issued to private security personnel, unless the weapons are authentic and employees are well trained in their use and legal implications.

The intent of this standard is that employees should not be allowed to carry firearms while performing private security duties unless they can demonstrate competency and proficiency in their use. In attempting to construct an appropriate training course for firearms instruction, many existing courses were reviewed. The recommended course that follows is designed for persons armed with revolvers and may require modification for other weapons or for adaptation to local situations. Dick Mercurio, training coordinator, Southwestern Illinois Law Enforcement Commission, indicated that persons were trained in 1974 and 1975 with about a 90 percent successful completion rate by generally following this classroom-range outline. In general, the recommended course includes 6 hours of classroom and 18 hours of range firing.

CLASSROOM

Topic I Legal and policy restraints—3 hours
1. Rights of private security personnel to carry weapons and powers of arrest
2. Statutory references
3. Policy restraints

Topic II Firearms safety and care and cleaning of the revolver—2 hours
1. Nomenclature and operation of the weapon
2. Performance of cartridge
3. Safety practices on duty and at home
4. Range rules
5. Care and cleaning of the weapon

Topic III Successful completion of written examination—1 hour
1. At least 20 questions on the above topics with a minimum passing score of 70 percent
2. Should be designed so that persons with other and/or prior experience can demonstrate competence in the subject areas.

RANGE [1]

Topic I Principles of marksmanship—2 hours
1. Shooting stance
2. Gripping and cocking the revolver
3. Sighting
4. Trigger control
5. Breathing control
6. Speeding loading and unloading techniques

Topic II Single action course—8 hours
- Distance: 25 yards
- Target: silhouette
- Rounds fired for qualification: 30
- Minimum passing score: 18 hits (60 percent)
- Stages of the course:
  1. Slow fire—consists of 10 shots fired in a total time of 5 minutes.
  2. Time fire—consists of two strings of 5 shots each. Each string is fired in a time limit of 20 seconds.
  3. Rapid fire—consists of two strings of 5 shots each. Each string is fired in a time limit of 10 seconds.
- Courses fired:
  1. Slow fire practice—30 rounds
  2. Time fire practice—6 strings—30 rounds
  3. Rapid fire practice—6 strings—30 rounds
  4. Practice course—30 rounds
  5. Record course—30 rounds

Topic III Double action course—8 hours
- Distance: as outlined below
- Target: silhouette
- Rounds fired for qualification: 72
- Minimum passing score: 43 hits (60 percent)
- Stage of the course: 7 yard line—Crouch position
  a. First phase:
     (1) load; draw and fire 1 and holster on the whistle command (6)
     (2) load; draw and fire 2 and holster on the whistle command (6)
     (3) repeat (1) and (2), using weak hand (12)
  b. Second phase:
     (1) strong hand—time 30 seconds—load; draw on the whistle, fire 6; reload and fire 6 more (12)
     (2) weak hand—time 30 seconds—

---

[1] The training hours for the range may seem excessive. However, it must be remembered that many of the personnel may have had no previous firearms training. Other factors that cause delays, such as the number of shooting positions available in relation to the number of students, should also be considered. The outline for the range course was supplied by Dick Mercurio, training coordinator, Southwestern Illinois Law Enforcement Commission.

load; draw on the whistle, fire 6; reload and fire 6 more (12)

- Courses fired: The above courses will be fired fired 4 times in the following sequence:
  1. A practice course (72)
  2. Skip loading with 3 rounds each string (24)
  3. Preliminary record course (72)
  4. Firing for record (72)

The purpose of range training is to ensure that private security personnel meet minimum proficiency requirements. If, for example, a student qualifies during the preliminary or practice rounds, it may be appropriate to remove him from the range course and give the instructor more time with students who are having difficulties. However, no person should be considered proficient, and assigned to a job that requires a firearm, unless he meets the minimum qualifications outlined.

Although not specifically stated in the standard, all instructors should be qualified through the National Rifle Association or other comparable qualifications programs.

In summary, the following requirements should be stressed for personnel carrying firearms:

1. Competence in the classroom subjects (minimum score of 70 percent) and proficiency with the weapon (minimum score of 60 percent) should be met before assigning any personnel to jobs that require firearms.
2. Personnel should be trained in the use of any weapon they carry.
3. They should meet the weapon proficiency requirements at least once every 12 months.

One study, *Private Security Survey and Ordinance for St. Petersburg, Florida,* recommended a more stringent requirement for point three—retraining courses to be held at 6-month intervals.

Employers also should consider preparation of a firearms policy form, including safety rules, policies regarding discharge of weapons, and other pertinent matters. Employees would be required to sign the form every 3 or 4 months, indicating they understand the policies. Their supervisors also would be required to sign the form. This system has been used for a number of years in the military services and has been an effective reminder of firearms policy.

No amount of required training can guarantee that weapons abuses will be eliminated or that accidents will cease to occur. However, a firearms training program, as outlined, can reduce the incidence of these types of problems. The necessity of training is apparent; the risks are too great without it. The private security industry should immediately provide training for all of its armed personnel.

Selected References

1. Chapman, Samuel G., and Thompson S. Crockett. "Gunsight Dilemma: Police Firearms Policy," *Police,* March–April 1963.

2. Institute for Local Self Government. *Private Security and the Public Interest.* Berkeley, Calif.: Institute for Local Self Government, 1974.

3. International Association of Chiefs of Police. "A Questionable Practice: Security Officers 'Armed' with Fake Weapons," *PWC Bulletin,* January 1973.

4. Kakalik, James S., and Sorrel Wildhorn. *The Private Police Industry: Its Nature and Extent,* Vol. II, R–870/DOJ. Washington, D.C.: Government Printing Office, 1971.

5. Mallowe, Mike. "Willie Lee Weston Is Armed and Dangerous," *Philadelphia Magazine,* August 1975.

6. Martensen, Kai R. "Private Security Survey and Ordinance for St. Petersburg, Florida." Sunnyvale, Calif.: Public Systems Incorporated, 1975.

7. Silvarman, Allen B. I. "Firearms Training," *Security Distributing and Marketing,* December 1974.

8. Strobl, Walter M. "Private Guards: Arm Them or Not," *Security Management,* January 1973.

Related Standards

The following standards and goals may be applicable in implementing Standard 2.6:

1.2 Commensurate Salaries
2.1 Training in Private Security
2.3 Job Descriptions
2.4 Training Related to Job Functions
2.5 Preassignment and Basic Training
2.7 Ongoing Training
2.8 Training of Supervisors and Managers
2.9 State Authority and Responsibility for Training
2.10 State Boards to Coordinate Training Efforts
3.1 Code of Ethics
3.4 Employer Responsibilities
8.2 National Private Security Resource and Research Institute
8.3 Noncredit and Credit Seminars and Courses
8.4 Degree Programs for Private Security
11.2 Registration Qualifications
11.3 Qualifications for Armed Security Personnel
11.4 Permanent Registration Card
11.6 Registration Renewal

Standard 2.7

Ongoing Training

Private security employers should ensure that private security personnel are given ongoing training by using rollcall training, training bulletins, and other training media.

Commentary

A survey of the members of the American Society for Industrial Security revealed information pertinent to this standard. To the question, "Do you require formal training on an annual basis for all security personnel?" 48 percent of the members responded "yes," 46 percent responded "no," and 6 percent did not respond. It appears that less than half of the private security industry has taken the necessary steps to provide some form of ongoing training for its personnel.

Preassignment and basic training standards contained in this chapter are designed to give private security personnel the basic skills, knowledge, and judgment needed to perform their duties. But situations and conditions change. Therefore, ongoing training also is needed to keep employees currently informed on issues, such as changes in company policies, legal aspects of their jobs, and technological improvements, relating to their job functions. Also, employees may forget certain important aspects of

their training and need to have their memories refreshed.

Several methods can be used to provide training on a continuing basis. One method that has been effective for public law enforcement agencies is rollcall training: Personnel receive 15 or 20 minutes of training at the start of a shift. The supervisor usually provides training through lectures, handouts, or other techniques meeting specific needs. The programs can be repeated the necessary number of times.

Another useful ongoing training method is the training bulletin. Such bulletins can be read by personnel during free time, on- or off-duty, with the supervisor answering any questions later. These bulletins can provide inexpensive ongoing training for private security workers. Other possible ongoing training media include slides, audio cassettes, video tapes, films, and correspondence courses.

A unique training program in California provides constant updating via recorded training messages. By dialing a phone number, an employee can hear these messages at any time. The messages also are made available in printed form.

Although not all inclusive, the above training methods show the scope of possibilities. Still other possibilities for providing ongoing training should be explored. The best ongoing programs will draw on the strong points from all types of training delivery systems. For exmple, a slide presentation could be prepared to illustrate a new report form, be supplemented by a training bulletin, and finally discussed at rollcall.

To ensure that employees understand the content of ongoing training, a feedback system should be developed. Feedback can be provided by question-and-answer sessions after rollcall training, true-false or short-answer questions relating to training bulletins, practical exercises, specific responses for programmed instruction courses, and other appropriate techniques.

Ongoing training should not be confused with inservice training. There are certain basic differences between the two. Ongoing training, unlike inservice training, is not classroom-oriented, and does not require a specific number of hours during a specific timeframe. It is a flexible, continuous program that should be individualized. For example, if an employee is efficiently and effectively performing all job functions on a routine basis, there is little need for training. However, if some aspects of the job are not performed routinely, the information received in preassignment or basic training should be reinforced periodically. The main thrust of ongoing training should be to provide training on important subjects that are not part of the day-to-day routine.

The structured formalized classroom nature of most inservice training programs in terms of regulated subject selection and specified classroom hour requirements precludes the type of individualized instruction needed for private security personnel. For example, in a traditional inservice course, the subject of legal aspects of the job may call for classroom time of 2 hours. Depending on the security function being performed, this time requirement may be too little, about right, or too great for an individual employee. Also, because of the structured timeframe, the training may not be presented until after the employee has experienced an on-the-job need for the information.

Inservice training is also considered impractical for private security personnel for the following reasons:

1. Inservice training may not be economically feasible.

2. Employees who are performing their services efficiently and effectively may not need formal inservice training.

3. Formal inservice training often is used to avoid continuous ongoing training.

In summary, the need for training is continuous. Rollcall training, training bulletins, and other training media should be used on a continuous basis to provide private security personnel with the necessary skills, knowledge, and judgment to perform efficiently and effectively.

Selected References

1. Berg, Harold. "Training on Patrol: A TOP Program," *The Police Chief,* November 1974.

2. Higginbotham, Charles E. "Roll-Call Training: A Worldwide Technique," *The Police Chief,* May 1975.

3. Holden, E. W. "The Deeper Look: Guard Forces Are Alive and Breathing," *Security World,* January 1972.

4. Potter, Anthony N., Jr. "Effective In-Service Training," *Security World,* October 1971.

5. Private Security Task Force. "American Society for Industrial Security (ASIS) Survey Results." (See Appendix 1 to this report.)

6. United Security Personnel Training. "Your Career as a Security Officer." Knoxville, Tenn.: United Schools, Inc., 1975.

7. ———. *Security Officer Training Book.* Knoxville, Tenn.: Training Consultants, Inc., 1975.

Related Standards

The following standards and goals may be applicable in implementing Standard 2.7:

1.1   Selection of Qualified Personnel
1.2   Commensurate Salaries
2.1   Training in Private Security
2.2   Professional Certification Programs
2.4   Training Related to Job Functions
2.5   Preassignment and Basic Training
2.6   Arms Training
2.8   Training of Supervisors and Managers
3.4   Employer Responsibilities
8.3   Noncredit and Credit Seminars and Courses
8.4   Degree Programs for Private Security

Standard 2.8

Training of Supervisors and Managers

Private security employers should provide effective job-related training for supervisory and managerial employees. Appropriate prior training, education, or professional certification should be accepted to meet this requirement.

Commentary

Because the quality of an organization is determined largely by personnel quality, all personnel should be well trained for their respective roles. Training should not stop at the basic level but should be available and encouraged at all levels.

Private security supervisory and managerial personnel perform important functions, yet there is a definite lack of advanced training for them. Previous private security training is not likely to have prepared them for the responsibilities they now face.

The Police Manager states qualities of a successful police manager that are also applicable to private security supervisors and managers:

1. **Patience**—the manager must be calm and steadfast, despite opposition to his beliefs, opinions, and attitudes.
2. **Wisdom**—the manager must have the ability to judge fairly and equitably the behaviors and actions of his subordinates.
3. **Virtue**—the manager must show moral excellence, not only by word of mouth, but by his everyday actions in dealing with department problems and his private life.

4. **Empathy**—the manager must learn to accept and understand the feelings of his subordinates, and he must constantly seek the positive features of those around him.
5. **Kindness**—the manager must attempt to be kind and gentle in all of his dealings with his fellow man.
6. **Trust**—the manager must develop confidence in his subordinates, not just respect their position or knowledge, but he must allow them to achieve their personal goals, as well as those of the organization.
7. **Knowledge**—the manager must constantly attempt to upgrade his knowledge about the technical aspects of his job, about the management theories being developed and implemented in government and industry, and he must constantly be aware of the facts as they occur within his own police department.
8. **Self-control**—the manager must restrain his own emotions.

Many of these qualities can be developed, or in some cases originated, through training. Supervisors and managers need supervisory training if they are to have a positive influence on the personnel they direct. A recent study, "Survey of Consumers of Private Security Services in the Greater Philadelphia Area," contained questions designed to determine current levels of training for supervisors. The survey results are summarized as follows:

1. Only 23 percent of the supervisors received classroom training.

2. Only 42 percent of the supervisors received on-the-job training.

3. 26 percent of the respondents felt that the

amount of training supervisors receive is "inadequate."

Admittedly, the number of respondents to this survey (163) is small and the geographical area limited, but the results do illustrate the lack of supervisory training in the private security industry. It is encouraging to note that 59 percent of the respondents believed that the best security supervisors are persons who "have specialized training, education, or experience in security services."

Defining the scope and depth of supervisory responsibilities, as related to training, is not possible because of the wide variations of duties, assignments, and responsibilities. Some suggestions are:

1. Private security supervisors and managers should perform line functions, such as organizing, directing, and controlling uniformed and nonuniformed personnel.

2. Supervisors and managers should include persons in an organization who have, as an assigned duty, the overall responsibilities for security services.

3. All other supervisors and managers in an organization, regardless of their functions, should be familiar with the responsibilities and duties of private security supervisors and managers.

4. The current lack of training for security supervisors and managers calls for employers to undertake the steps necessary to provide training opportunities.

5. At some future time, requirements for supervisors' and managers' training should be designed along lines simliar to those established for preassignment, basic, and firearms training.

Although the private security industry offers few training opportunities for supervisors and managers, they are available from other organizations. The Traffic Institute at Northwestern University and the Southern Police Institute, School of Police Administration at the University of Louisville, for example, provide excellent training programs. College and university credit and noncredit courses for supervisors and managers should be accepted as fulfilling the requirements of this standard.

There is a definite need, however, for advanced training, specifically geared to the needs of private security supervisors and managers. Employers should actively seek such training for their personnel. Existing management training schools might be encouraged to develop appropriate courses of study. In the meantime, employers should encourage their supervisors and managers to use existing training opportunities.

Professional private security associations can also encourage training for supervisors and managers. For example, the certification efforts of the International Association for Hospital Security have made a significant contribution to the training of security personnel working in health care facilities; the American Society for Industrial Security, through its professional board certification program, has encouraged high-quality training at all levels of the industry.

The complexities of the problems related to private security supervisors and managers, from identifying who they are through enunciating their training needs, are beyond the scope of this report. Research is needed to determine curriculum issues, to design delivery systems for training, and to evaluate ongoing training activities. However, at this time, employers should make every effort to give supervisors and managers the training they need, and employees themselves should seek any available training to increase their efficiency and effectiveness.

Selected References

1. American Society for Industrial Security. "Charter for ASIS Program for Certification of Protection Professionals," Approved by ASIS Board of Directors, Sept. 8, 1975.

2. Boyd, Bradford B. *Management Minded Supervision*. New York: McGraw-Hill, Inc., 1968.

3. Iannone, N. F. *Supervision of Police Personnel*. (2d ed.) Englewood Cliffs, N.J.: Prentice-Hall, Inc., 1975.

4. Kassoff, Norman C. *Organizational Concepts*. Washington, D.C.: International Association of Chiefs of Police, 1967.

5. Kazmier, Leonard J. *Principles of Management* (2d ed.). New York: McGraw-Hill, Inc., 1-964.

6. Lynch, Ronald G. *The Police Manager*. Boston, Mass.: Holbrook Press, Inc., 1975.

7. McGregor, Douglas. *Leadership and Motivation*. Cambridge, Mass.: The MIT Press, 1972.

8. Pfiffner, John M., and Marshall Fels. *The Supervision of Personnel* (3d ed.). Englewood Cliffs, N.J.: Prentice-Hall, Inc., 1964.

9. Private Security Task Force. "Survey of Consumers of Private Security in the Greater Philadelphia Area." (See Appendix 3 to this report.)

10. Scholz, William. *Communication in the Business Organization*. Englewood Cliffs, N.J.: Prentice-Hall, Inc., 1962.

11. Vogel, T. E. "Management in Security," *Security World,* May 1969.

Related Standards

The following standards and goals may be applicable in implementing Standard 2.8:

1.1   Selection of Qualified Personnel
1.2   Commensurate Salaries
2.1   Training in Private Security
2.2   Professional Certification Programs

Standard 2.9

State Authority and Responsibility for Training

A State government regulatory agency should have the authority and responsibility to accredit training schools, approve training curriculums, and certify instructors for the private security industry.

Commentary

The importance of training, in the overall effort to improve the effectiveness and efficiency of private security personnel, requires specific placement within a state regulatory agency of authority and responsibility for overseeing and evaluating training activities. States that have a private security regulatory board should assign this authority and responsibility to that agency.

It is recognized that it sometimes may be advisable to assign this authority and responsibility to the agency within the State responsible for accrediting schools, approving curriculums, and certifying instructors for public law enforcement officers. However, in such cases, it should be recognized that private security personnel have unique training needs. To place these personnel in public law enforcement courses is grossly inappropriate and does not comply with the intent of this standard. The few subjects that might be compatible are the exception, rather than the rule. For example, one of the most consistent criticisms of Ohio's private security train-

ing is that the approved course in that State is the same as that required for public law enforcement officers.

Some assistance in developing a model for State regulation of training for private security personnel can be found by examining the statutory provisions in selected States concerning authority and responsibility for public law enforcement training. The following excerpts from the Illinois police training act provide one example:

506. (Selection and certification of schools.) Section 6.

The Board shall select and certify schools within the State of Illinois for the purpose of providing basic training for probationary police officers, and advanced or in-service training for permanent police officers, which schools may be either publicly or private owned and operated.

507. (Rules and minimum standards for schools.) Section 7.

The Board shall adopt rules and minimum standards for such schools which shall include but not be limited to the following:
a. The curriculum for probationary police officers which shall be offered by all certified schools shall include but not be limited to courses of . . .
b. Minimum courses of study, attendance requirements and equipment requirements.
c. Minimum requirements for instructors.
d. Minimum basic training requirements which a probationary police officer must satisfactorily complete before being eligible for permanent employment as a local law enforcement officer for a participating local governmental agency.

115

510 (Rules and regulations.) Section 10.

The Board may make, amend and rescind such rules and regulations as may be necessary to carry out the provisions of this Act. A copy of all rules and regulations and amendments or recissions thereof shall be filed with the Secretary of State within a reasonable time after their adoption. The schools certified by the Board and participating in the training program may dismiss from the school any trainee prior to his completion of the course, if in the opinion of the person in charge of the training school, the trainee is unable or unwilling to satisfactorily complete the prescribed course of training.

The record of State involvement in public law enforcement training is impressive. California and New York, in 1959, led the States in enacting legislation to establish standards for law enforcement training. As of Jan. 1, 1976, 45 States had some form of legislation concerning training standards, and 40 States had mandatory training for recruit officers. Furthermore, State-legislated law enforcement training standards have been endorsed by groups, such as the International Association of Chiefs of Police and the American Management Association, in their efforts to professionalize the police.

If similar State involvement was to occur in private security training, rapid upgrading of the profession would be achieved. In assuming the authority and responsibility for private security training standards, States should undertake the following: (1) accreditation of schools, (2) approval of curriculums, and (3) certification of instructors. States should inspect facilities before accreditation to ensure they are adequate, only job-related curriculums should be approved, and quality controls should be placed on instructors to promote maximum training effectiveness. The duration and content of the training programs should be developed with the assistance of the private security industry.

Although each of the above elements is recognized separately, they are interrelated. There is little value in modern, well-equipped facilities if course content and instruction are poor. Nor can the best qualified instructors or the most relevant curriculums alone produce effective instruction. Without the proper interaction of these components, everyone is poorly served: The employee does not receive proper training, the employer does not receive an appropriate return on the economic investment in training, and the public does not receive competent service.

The capability of the State to set and maintain effective law enforcement training standards has been established in most States. The same approach could be followed regarding private security training. Each State should begin to set specific standards, appropriate to State and local needs, to provide cost-effective training for private security personnel. By doing so, States can help ensure that facilities, curriculums, and instructors are adequate to provide high-quality training for these personnel.

Selected References

1. *Illinois Revised Statutes,* chapter 85, sections 501–514.

2. Leonard, V. A., and Harry W. More. *Police Organization and Management* (3d ed.). Mineola, N.Y.: The Foundation Press, Inc., 1971.

3. The International Association of Chiefs of Police. *The Police Yearbook 1975.* Gaithersburg, Md.: International Association of Chiefs of Police, Inc., 1975.

4. Wilson, O. W., and Roy C. McLaren. *Police Administration* (3d ed.). New York: McGraw-Hill, Inc., 1972.

Related Standards

The following standards and goals may be applicable in implementing Standard 2.9:

2.1   Training in Private Security
2.4   Training Related to Job Functions
2.5   Preassignment and Basic Training
2.6   Arms Training
2.10 State Boards to Coordinate Training Efforts
4.3   Certified Training of Alarm Sales and Service Personnel
8.3   Noncredit and Credit Seminars and Courses
8.4   Degree Programs for Private Security
11.2 Registration Qualifications
11.3 Qualifications for Armed Security Personnel

Standard 2.10

State Boards to Coordinate Training Efforts

Appropriate State boards and agencies should coordinate efforts to provide training opportunities for private security personnel and persons interested in preparing for security employment, through utilization of physical and personnel resources of area vocational schools and colleges and universities.

Commentary

Research conducted for this report reveals that few States have coordinated efforts to make training available to private security and/or persons interested in entering the field. This problem can be corrected by a statewide, coordinated effort to provide such training, using the physical and personnel resources of area vocational schools, colleges, and universities, in addition to the training provided by private companies and proprietary schools.

This standard may seem to conflict with Standard 2.9, which proposes placement of the responsibility and authority to accredit training schools, approve curriculums, and certify instructors with State private security regulatory agencies. However, it is believed that both standards are appropriate and should be separate. Standard 2.9 provides guidance to ensure quality training; the main thrust of this standard is to provide a catalyst for the coordinated efforts of State boards and agencies in providing that training.

Because no exemplary models are available, Figure 2.1 illustrates the type of coordinated effort called for in this standard.

As Figure 2.1 shows, various agencies should be responsible for the administration, coordination, and delivery of private security training. The private security regulatory board, which would include individuals who are aware of training needs, should be in charge of administration. As stated in Standard 2.9, this board should have the authority and responsibility for accrediting schools, approving curriculums, and certifying instructors. To maximize physical and personnel resources, however, other agencies and boards should lend their expertise at the coordination level. Their activities should include ensuring that private security training is available, eliminating duplication of training programs within geographical areas, and assisting in course scheduling, as well as providing guidance to the private security regulatory board in certain administrative matters. For example, if such agencies and boards believe a given training school is not providing reliable and valid training, they should advise the private security regulatory board.

Finally, at the delivery level, a wide variety of resources should be used. Colleges, universities, vocational schools, and law enforcement schools should act in concert with private security company and

117

Figure 2.1.

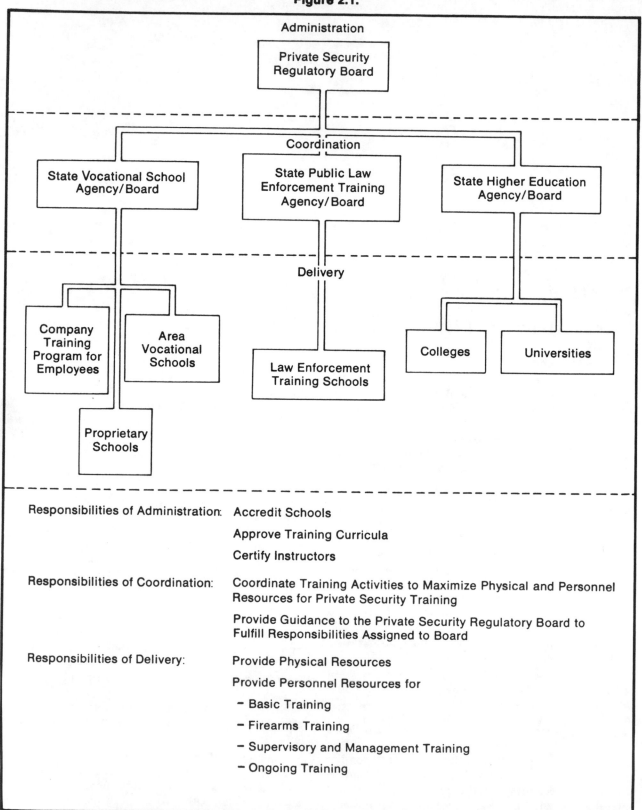

Responsibilities of Administration: Accredit Schools

Approve Training Curricula

Certify Instructors

Responsibilities of Coordination: Coordinate Training Activities to Maximize Physical and Personnel Resources for Private Security Training

Provide Guidance to the Private Security Regulatory Board to Fulfill Responsibilities Assigned to Board

Responsibilities of Delivery: Provide Physical Resources

Provide Personnel Resources for

– Basic Training

– Firearms Training

– Supervisory and Management Training

– Ongoing Training

proprietary schools in providing phsyical and personnel resources for private security training. Basically, these schools should provide opportunities for the following:

- Preassignment Training.
- Basic Training.
- Firearms Training.
- Supervisory and Management Training.
- Ongoing Training.

Consideration should be given to allowing prospective employees to enroll in preassignment, basic, and, if appropriate, firearms training to enable them to qualify for registration by the private security regulatory board before they enter the employment market. This action should benefit both the prospective employee and employer. Because the prospective employee would have successfully completed the required training, the employer can assign him to a job immediately after completion of other registration requirements. Considering the present high turnover rate, low salary scales, and limited opportunities for career advancement, this concept may seem idealistic. However, until the opportunity exists, the concept of preparatory training should not be automatically rejected.

The coordinated efforts of various State agencies and boards can significantly enhance the success of private security training. For government agencies to merely establish private security training standards and not fully use all available physical and personnel resources would be self-defeating.

Selected References

1. Bradel, Don. "Statewide Quality Control for Law Enforcement Personnel," *The Police Chief,* August 1975.

2. Logan, John F. "Law Enforcement Education and the Community College," *The Police Chief,* August 1975.

3. McManus, George P. (project director). *Police Training and Performance Study.* Washington, D.C.: Government Printing Office, 1970.

4. Troy, Walter W. "A Practical Training Program for Security Personnel," *Industrial Security,* April 1963.

5. Zlochower, Sol. "Delivery: Deliverance—New Method of Delivering Training in Southern Illinois," *The Police Chief,* August 1974.

Related Standards

The following standards and goals may be applicable in implementing Standard 2.10:

1.2   Commensurate Salaries
2.1   Training in Private Security
2.2   Professional Certification Programs
2.4   Training Related to Job Functions
2.5   Preassignment and Basic Training
2.6   Arms Training
2.8   Training of Supervisors and Managers
2.9   State Authority and Responsibility for Training
4.3   Certified Training of Alarm Sales and Service Personnel
8.3   Noncredit and Credit Seminars and Courses
8.4   Degree Programs for Private Security
9.1   State Regulation

Chapter 3
Conduct and Ethics

INTRODUCTION

It has been said that personnel are a business's most valuable asset. How they conduct their activities, to a large extent, determines the success or failure of an enterprise. Competent personnel who perform their duties in a conscientious, ethical manner do much to promote a favorable image and build public confidence. On the other hand, dishonest or unethical personnel create a poor public image and destroy existing trust or confidence in an organization.

Because private security personnel are entrusted with the protection of valuable assets and human lives, ethical standards and a high degree of integrity should be required. An analogy can be drawn with the medical profession. A person engaging the services of a doctor has a right to expect the doctor to exercise good moral and ethical conduct in protecting his life. The consumer of security services should be able to expect the same qualities in the protection of his property and life. Yet, whereas the medical profession and other groups entrusted with protecting life and property have formulated and adopted professional codes of ethics, the private security industry has made little progress in this direction.

As a logical starting point, Goal 3.1 recommends codes of ethics for both private security employers and personnel. Industrywide adoption and enforcement of these codes can promote an awareness by employers and employees of their obligations to consumers and society and can add significance to their effective performance and sense of pride. The guides for conduct provided in a code of ethics also would allow private security personnel to carry out their duties with discretion and in a professional manner, thereby advancing the professionalism of the entire industry.

Adoption and enforcement of a private security code of ethics would afford many additional benefits. Current personnel turnover rates (sometimes as high as 300 percent) need to be reduced if private security is to be a productive force in preventing crime. By promoting a climate of professionalism in which one can experience personal satisfaction and worth, a code of ethics can help the industry retain efficient, capable personnel, as well as attract new personnel of a higher caliber. Because a code of ethics is a step toward increased professionalism, public law enforcement agencies would view private security personnel with greater respect and trust, thus enhancing cooperative services between the two.

This goal, a unifying code, encouraging attainment of professional status, furnishes a basis for the remaining standards in this chapter. The manner in which private security personnel perform their duties has a direct bearing on the attainment of professional status. Therefore, Standard 3.2 states that private security personnel should perform their security functions within generally recognized guidelines for the protection of individual rights. Incidents of excessive force, false arrest and detainment, illegal search and seizure, impersonation of a public officer, trespass, invasion of privacy, and dishonest or unethical business practices not only undermine confidence and trust in the private security industry, but also infringe upon individual rights.

Although not bound by many of the formal legal restraints applicable to public law enforcement officers, private security personnel have an inherent responsibility to uphold the basic principles of American personal liberties. Suspects should be civilly treated and informed of their rights. Security personnel should know the limits of their authority and not abuse these limits. Due to fundamental differences between the private security and public law enforcement areas, it is not recommended that private security personnel be required to conduct their activities within the same guidelines as public law enforcement officers. However, specific guidelines should be established to ensure the protection of individual rights and the elimination of abuses of authority. Employers should research areas that are subject to abuses of authority and develop appropriate policies and procedures to guide the conduct of their personnel in these areas. Because of the complex nature of the industry and varying State and local regulations, procedures may necessarily differ according to the area in which security personnel are operating, possibly even within the same company. But if guidelines are absent, certain personnel, through confusion or irresponsibility, may continue to abuse their authority.

Another important aspect in ethically conducting private security operations is the reporting of crime (Standard 3.3). Existing data suggest that private security personnel do not report a large percentage of known and possible perpetrators to the appropriate criminal justice agencies. Although private censure is sometimes more expedient, it is, in reality, unfair. Unless all criminal violators are reported to the criminal justice system and prosecuted, appropriate reduction of crime is not likely. In addition, violations of individual rights are more apt to occur when a crime is not reported to the proper agency. Perhaps most importantly, use of the criminal justice system can serve as a common denominator to bring public and private crime prevention efforts together for increased efficiency and effectiveness.

Standard 3.4 focuses on the responsibilities of private security employers to provide their employees with suitable working conditions and adequate equipment. It is neither realistic nor ethical to assign workers to duties without supplying them the equipment and resources to perform their services safely and efficiently. Even the best selected and trained employee is at a disadvantage if equipment and working conditions are not conducive to effective job performance. It is just as unreasonable to assign a guard to function effectively within a darkened building as it is to expect a surgeon to operate without proper lighting.

All equipment issued should be the best available; productivity and safety cannot be sacrified for cost. This is particularly applicable to firearms. Unsafe or inoperable firearms are a danger to both the employee and those with whom he comes in contact. Firearms and other equipment should be periodically checked to ensure safety and to protect against malfunctions. The employer who overlooks these responsibilities is also overlooking professional ethics.

Finally, the industry has a responsibility to maintain records of criminal violations if it is to make honest decisions about effectiveness. Private security management has a moral obligation to its clients to use every method available to effectively deter crime. A good records system is one such method. Used as a planning tool, records can predict future needs and allow efficient tactical and operational plans to be made. They can also pinpoint areas that need immediate attention so that increased surveillance and patrol can be allocated accordingly.

Records are a yardstick of performance. Used to measure effectiveness, they can reveal whether the private security industry is meeting its goals and objectives. If achievement falls short in certain areas, every effort should be made to determine the cause and search for effective remedies.

The private security industry can serve as an effective complement to public law enforcement agencies, providing necessary crime prevention services that cannot be afforded by local governments. It has been estimated that one of every four retail corporations in the United States subscribes to some protective service. Untold numbers of small businesses, individuals, and other agencies also use security services. Yet, numerous ills plague the industry. If the private security industry is to continue as a viable crime prevention resource and best serve its consumers and society, steps need to be taken to remedy these ills. Acceptance and enforcement of the standards in this chapter are a partial remedy. The professionalism to be attained from honest and ethical conduct should lead to better protection of both consumers and the public, while at the same time promoting a better working relationship with public law enforcement agencies in pursuit of the increasingly important goal of crime prevention.

Goal 3.1

Code of Ethics

A code of ethics should be adopted and enforced for private security personnel and employers.

Commentary

A code of ethics is a statement that incorporates moral and ethical principles and philosophies. It is a necessary prerequisite for any profession, providing guidance to its members so that their activities can be measured against a standard of behavior. The need for a private security code of ethics is apparent. Private security personnel come into almost constant contact with human frailties and make decisions that can affect the welfare of many. For example, a private investigator may receive information that is unrelated to an investigation but damaging to a person's character and reputation. The investigator should keep the information confidential to protect the person. This ethical philosophy can be reflected in the code of ethics.

The need for a code of ethics is supported by the American Society for Industrial Security (ASIS). In a recent study conducted for this report (Appendix 1), 51 percent of ASIS members rated an industrywide voluntary code of ethics as "very important" and 27 percent as "somewhat important." Additional support and justification for establishment of a code of ethics for private security employers and personnel

are contained in the following excerpt from an article appearing in the July 1974 issue of *Security Management:*

> Without a code of ethics, a company will lose its most talented employees who will either become dishonest within the company or leave to find a better climate for personal achievement or growth.
>
> Without a code of ethics, every tough decision is agonized, and one must expend energies coping with crises on a treadmill rather than taking a real leap forward.
>
> Even worse, without a code of ethics you must spend yourself in self-defense, losing face and fortune, when you're finally caught.
>
> Most important for the security industry, however, is the fact that without a code of ethics for ourselves, our own work is an hypocrisy and we have no *raison d'etre* that would in any way contribute to the betterment of our communities. We would merely be automatons, reacting automatically to repetitive stimuli, unworthy indeed of ever achieving the status of a profession.

Some private security associations have adopted codes of ethics. They include the American Society for Industrial Security, Council of International Investigators, National Council of Investigation and Security Services (draft), National Burglar and Fire Alarm Association, Inc., and World Association of Detectives, Inc.

The Law Enforcement/Private Security Relationship Committee of the Private Security Advisory Council has developed and adopted the following codes for management and employees. The adoption

123

of the committee codes for private security management and employees is recommended.

Code of Ethics for Private Security Management

As managers of private security functions and employees, we pledge:

I   To recognize that our principal responsibilities are, in the service of our organizations and clients, to protect life and property as well as to prevent and reduce crime against our business, industry, or other organizations and institutions; and in the public interest, to uphold the law and to respect the constitutional rights of all persons.

II To be guided by a sense of integrity, honor, justice and mortality in the conduct of business; in all personnel matters; in relationships with government agencies, clients, and employers; and in responsibilities to the general public.

III To strive faithfully to render security services of the highest quality and to work continuously to improve our knowledge and skills and thereby improve the overall effectiveness of private security.

IV To uphold the trust of our employers, our clients, and the public by performing our functions within the law, not ordering or condoning violations of law, and ensuring that our security personnel conduct their assigned duties lawfully and with proper regard for the rights of others.

V   To respect the reputation and practice of others in private security, but to expose to the proper authorities any conduct that is unethical or unlawful.

VI To apply uniform and equitable standards of employment in recruiting and selecting personnel regardless of race, creed, color, sex, or age, and in providing salaries commensurate with job responsibilities and with training, education, and experience.

VII To cooperate with recognized and responsible law enforcement and other criminal justice agencies; to comply with security licensing and registration laws and other statutory requirements that pertain to our business.

VIII To respect and protect the confidential and privileged information of employers and clients beyond the term of our employment, except where their interests are contrary to law or to this Code of Ethics.

IX To maintain a professional posture in all business relationships with employers and clients, with others in the private security field, and with members of other professions; and to insist that our personnel adhere to the highest standards of professional conduct.

X   To encourage the professional advancement of our personnel by assisting them to acquire appropriate security knowledge, education, and training.

Code of Ethics for Private Security Employees

In recognition of the significant contribution of private security to crime prevention and reduction, as a private security employee, I pledge:

I   To accept the responsibilities and fulfill the obligations of my role: protecting life and property; preventing and reducing crimes against my employer's business, or other organizations and institutions to which I am assigned; upholding the law; and respecting the constitutional rights of all persons.

II To conduct myself with honesty and integrity and to adhere to the highest moral principles in the performance of my security duties.

III To be faithful, diligent, and dependable in discharging my duties, and to uphold at all times the laws, policies, and procedures that protect the rights of others.

IV To observe the precepts of truth, accuracy and prudence, without allowing personal feelings, prejudices, animosities or friendships to influence my judgements.

V   To report to my superiors, without hesitation, any violation of the law or of my employer's or client's regulations.

VI To respect and protect the confidential and privileged information of my employer or client beyond the term of my employment, except where their interests are contrary to law or to this Code of Ethics.

VII To cooperate with all recognized and responsible law enforcement and government agencies in matters within their jurisdiction.

VIII To accept no compensation, commission, gratuity, or other advantage without the knowledge and consent of my employer.

IX To conduct myself professionally at all times, and to perform my duties in a manner that reflects credit upon myself, my employer, and private security.

X   To strive continually to improve my performance by seeking training and educational opportunities that will better prepare me for my private security duties.

Employers, private security personnel, and professional organizations should not stop at adopting and publishing these codes, but should seek to enforce the codes to the best of their ability through peer pressure, disciplinary procedures, and, as appropriate, criminal and civil actions. Indeed, a combined effort of all parties involved is required if the codes are to truly represent a standard of excellence for the industry. Employers should insist that all employees perform in accordance with the principles stated in the code of ethics for personnel. Both employers and employees should adhere to the principles themselves and exert peer pressure against their colleagues who may not be abiding by the codes.

Under certain circumstances, if the codes are continually violated or if serious violations occur, enforcement can be referred to the courts. For example, if an employee is not just failing to protect equipment but is, in fact, stealing that equipment, the matter should be referred to the courts by invoking the appropriate criminal statutes. Professional associations can also assist by requiring adherence to codes as a prerequisite for membership and by invoking appropriate sanctions against individuals who violate moral and ethical principles contained in the code. Finally, the public can assist by reporting unethical conduct to the appropriate persons, companies, agencies, or associations.

The adoption of industrywide codes of ethics for private security employers and personnel is a necessary and worthwhile goal. It can be a significant advancement toward improved crime prevention, better protection of public rights, and professionalization of the industry.

Selected References

1. American Society for Industrial Security. "ASIS Code of Ethics."

2. Association of British Investigators. "The Code of Conduct of the Association of British Investigators."

3. Association of Investigators & Security Organization of India. "Norms of Ethics and Conduct."

4. Astor, Saul D. "Ethics and Professionalism in the Security Industry," *Security Management,* July 1974.

5. Council of International Investigators. "Code of Ethics."

6. International Association of Chiefs of Police. "Law Enforcement Code of Ethics."

7. Mahoney, H. T. "The Bicentennial and the ASIS Code of Ethics," *Security Management,* January 1976.

8. National Burglar and Fire Alarm Association. "Code of Ethics."

9. National Council of Investigation and Security Services. "Code of Ethics" (draft).

10. Private Security Advisory Council Staff Consultants. "Private Security Codes of Ethics for Security Management and Security Employees," prepared for the Law Enforcement/Private Security Relationship Study Committee of the Private Security Advisory Council, April 1976.

Related Standards

The following standards and goals may be applicable in implementing Goal 3.1:

1.1	Selection of Qualified Personnel
1.2	Commensurate Salaries
1.3	Preemployment Screening
1.5	Equal Employment Opportunity
2.1	Training in Private Security
2.2	Professional Certification Programs
2.5	Preassignment and Basic Training
2.6	Arms Training
3.2	Conduct of Private Security Personnel
3.3	Reporting of Criminal Violations
3.4	Employer Responsibilities
3.5	Maintaining Data on Criminal Activities
4.3	Certified Training of Alarm Sales and Service Personnel
7.4	Private Security Advertising Standards
11.2	Registration Qualifications
11.3	Qualifications for Armed Security Personnel

Standard 3.2

Conduct of Private Security Personnel

Private security personnel should perform their security functions within generally recognized guidelines for the protection of individual rights.

Commentary

The development of a standard relating to the moral and ethical conduct of private security activities and investigations is a complex problem. Most personnel are law abiding, and most activities performed are lawful and ethical. However, responsible persons acknowledge that there have been abuses; thus, the purpose of this standards is to set an objective for the future.

The *RAND Report* (Vol. IV), *The Other Police, Private Security and the Public Interest,* and other research reports plus numerous newspaper and magazine articles have graphically pointed out the existence of abuses throughout the industry. It would serve no useful purpose here, therefore, to present a series of horror stories to emphasize the problems. However, accepting such accounts of abuse as prima facie evidence of a need for this standard should not be construed as support for the unfair generalization that all private security personnel perform their duties in an unethical or illegal manner.

The job functions of private security personnel place them in a special position because their activi-

ties and investigations affect many people. Private security personnel may have the authority and responsibility to control the movement of people and sometimes detain and arrest them. The opportunities for abuses of authority are numerous. One clear example of potential abuse involves the interviewing of suspects. Public law enforcement officers are required to read all suspects the Miranda Warning as follows:

Custodial Interrogation (Miranda Warning)

After each part of the following warning, the officer must determine the suspect understands what he is being told:

1. You have the right to remain silent. You do not have to talk to me unless you want to do so.
2. If you do want to talk to me, I must advise you that whatever you say can and will be used as evidence against you in court.
3. You have a right to consult with a lawyer and to have a lawyer present with you while you are being questioned.
4. If you want a lawyer but are unable to pay for one, a lawyer will be appointed to represent you free of any cost to you.

Court cases cited in the *RAND Report* (Vol. IV) indicate that private security personnel are not controlled by the guidelines listed above unless (1) there is State involvement in the interrogation, or (2) security personnel are directly commissioned by

State, county, or local governments to act as police-men. Private security personnel usually are free to interview suspects without warning about the possible consequences resulting from information obtained during the interview.

To protect individual rights in interviewing suspects and all other activities, it has been suggested that private security personnel conduct their activities within the same guidelines as public law enforcement officers. However, this approach ignores two significant differences: (1) private security personnel do not, unless specifically authorized, have the same enforcement powers as public law enforcement officers, and (2) their primary function is to protect private property, which has a different historical base for legal decisions.

Guidelines for conducting investigations and other activities should be developed if individual rights are to be protected. Without such guidelines, continued improper actions could be accepted as permissable. This report, therefore, recommends that private security employers research the issues and develop reasonable performance guidelines to protect individual rights in all areas. Examples of areas needing research and guidelines follow:

1. General private security functions:
   a. Arrest,
   b. Detention,
   c. Use of force (including firearms),
   d. Impersonation of and confusion with public law enforcement officers, and
   e. Directing and controlling traffic.
2. Specific investigatory functions:
   a. Search and seizure of private property;
   b. Wiretapping, bugging, and other forms of surveillance;
   c. Access of private security personnel to public law enforcement information and procedures for the safeguarding of the information;
   d. Obtaining information from private citizens and safeguarding of the information; and
   e. Interrogation.

This outline is intended as a frame of reference only. Conflicting State laws and varying civil and criminal court decisions prevent establishment of a universal set of guidelines to protect individual rights. Also, additional subclassifications may be necessary within any given area. For example, search and seizure of private property may require one set of guidelines for an area within a plant that contains classified government documents and a different set of guidelines for other areas of the same plant. Accordingly, the private security industry should research all areas where abuses may occur and develop guidelines as they apply to individual operations.

If this standard is to succeed, all parties of interest need to do their part. Employers need to research the issues as they pertain to their operations; prepare written policies and procedures to insure compliance by employees; train employees; and, as appropriate, initiate company disciplinary actions and/or court actions against employees who do not comply. Employees need to set an example for others by their own actions, invoke peer pressure against those who do not follow the guidelines, and cooperate with employers and agencies in the criminal justice system. The public has a responsibility to report violations to employers, to private security regulatory boards, or to law enforcement officials.

In summary, private security personnel should conduct their activities within generally recognized guidelines for the protection of individual rights. It is recognized that there is no simple, universal approach to defining this subject, but with adequate research of the issues, adoption of reasonable policies and procedures, and enforcement by all parties, this standard can significantly improve the moral and ethical conduct of private security personnel. In the final analysis, this standard can provide a positive cause-effect relationship toward the ultimate goal of crime prevention.

Selected References

1. Brennan, Dennis T. *The Other Police*. Cleveland, Ohio: Governmental Research Institute, 1975.

2. Institute for Local Self Government. *Private Security and the Public Interest*. Berkeley, Calif.: Institute for Local Self Government, 1974.

3. Kakalik, James S., and Sorrel Wildhorn. *The Law and Private Police*, Vol. IV, R–872/DOJ. Washington, D.C.: Government Printing Office, 1971.

4. Stessin, Lawrence (ed.). *Protection Management*, Issue 2118. New York: Man and Manager, Inc., Nov. 15, 1975.

Related Standards

The following standards and goals may be applicable in implementing Standard 3.2:

1.4 Employer Exchange of Information
1.7 Availability of Criminal History Records
2.3 Job Descriptions
2.4 Training Related to Job Functions
3.1 Code of Ethics
3.3 Reporting of Criminal Violations
3.5 Maintaining Data on Criminal Activities
6.1 Interaction Policies
6.3 Policies and Procedures
8.4 Degree Programs for Private Security
11.7 Suspension and Revocation

Standard 3.3

Reporting of Criminal Violations

All felonies and serious misdemeanors discovered by private security personnel should be reported to appropriate criminal justice agencies. Private security personnel should cooperate with those criminal justice agencies in all subsequent actions relating to those crimes.

Commentary

It is generally recognized that the private sector does not report all criminal violations to appropriate criminal justice agencies. The following three examples illustrate this point.

The *RAND Report* (Vol. I) stated:

Almost half of the respondents stated that there are some criminal activities that are handled by the employer and not reported to the police. Of these, employee theft accounts for almost 60 percent, 8 percent involve shoplifting (recall that few respondents worked in retail security), 15 percent involve minor misdemeanors, and 17 percent are cases of fighting, often involving drinking.

"Survey of Consumers of Private Security Services in the Greater Philadelphia Area" (Appendix 3) revealed that 45 percent of respondents indicated that "certain types of criminal activities (employee thefts, loitering, assault, etc.) that security personnel encounter are not reported to public law enforcement agencies."

Private Security and the Public Interest, a study conducted in California, reported that "80 percent of the employers/supervisors indicated there were certain types of criminal incidents which were not reported to the police. These included petty theft, shoplifting, and assault."

Considering the above information, it would appear that a large percentage of criminal violators known to private security personnel are not referred to the criminal justice system. A logical conclusion would be that there is a "private" criminal justice system wherein employer reprimands, restrictions, suspensions, demotions, job transfers, or employment terminations take the place of censure by the public system.

It is recognized that most criminal incidents uncovered by private security personnel occur on private property and management has certain rights and obligations to decide what actions should be taken. Also, in many instances private action is more expedient, less expensive, and less embarrassing to the company. Fear of lawsuits or protecting the offender from a criminal record may be important. However, violations of due process, right to counsel, and other individual rights are more likely to occur under such a system. The criminal justice system is established for the purpose of resolving criminal offenses and can be a viable resource for the private security sector in this regard. Perhaps even more important, reporting incidents of criminal activity can be an important step toward coordinating the activities of the private security and law enforcement sectors through a common denominator—the criminal justice system. Employers should also be willing to support the process by compensating employees, especially private security personnel, for the time they spend in preparing for and appearing in court.

This standard aims at coordinating activities between private and public law enforcement agencies for the improvement of crime prevention. It is not within the purview of the private security industry to establish a microcosmic version of the criminal justice system. Management is ill equipped to provide probation systems or comprehensive rehabilitation programs for persons convicted of crimes, but the criminal justice system does have those resources. Some companies have drug and alcohol rehabilitation programs, but these are limited in number and scope. In short, internal handling of criminal punishment may resolve the immediate problem but offers no long-range benefit to the company, the individual, or the public. If all felonies and serious misdemeanors are reported to the appropriate criminal justice agencies, the criminal justice system can initiate appropriate actions and, thus, help reduce reported incidents.

Although private security personnel should provide the major resources in preparing cases for prosecution, public law enforcement agencies can help by offering technical expertise in such areas as fingerprints, preparation of crime scene diagrams, analysis of evidence, and so forth. They also can help locate witnesses and others who can provide valuable input into the cases. Of course, it is assumed that sufficient probable cause exists before individuals are referred to the criminal justice system. If all parties exhibit a cooperative spirit, private security companies and law enforcement agencies can work together toward a more effective process of crime reduction for both the private and the public sectors of society.

Although some would view this standard as unrealistic, considering the backlogs in many courts and the general public attitude that the criminal justice system is failing in its responsibilities, the research indicates that the concepts of this standard have not been adequately tested. Therefore, until greater use is made of the criminal justice system, such generalizations cannot be considered valid arguments. This standard sets realistic parameters for that use. The vigorous application of this standard should result in increased crime prevention benefits through the result of cooperative efforts between the private security industry and law enforcement agencies.

Selected References

1. Institute for Local Self Government. *Private Security and the Public Interest.* Berkeley, Calif.: Institute for Local Self Government, 1974.

2. Kakalik, James S., and Sorrel Wildhorn. *Private Police in the United States: Findings and Recommendations,* Vol. I, R–869/DOJ Washington, D.C.: Government Printing Office, 1972.

3. Private Security Task Force. "Survey of Consumers of Private Security Services in the Greater Philadelphia Area." (See Appendix 3 to this report.)

4. ———. "Private Security and Citizen's Arrest Authority." (See Appendix 9 to this report.)

Related Standards

The following standards and goals may be applicable in implementing Standard 3.3:

1.7	Availability of Criminal History Records
2.3	Job Descriptions
3.1	Code of Ethics
3.2	Conduct of Private Security Personnel
3.3	Reporting of Criminal Violations
6.1	Interaction Policies
6.3	Policies and Procedures
9.4	Regulatory Board Hearing Procedure
9.6	Regulatory Board Access to Criminal Record Information
10.8	License Denial, Revocation, or Suspension
11.2	Registration Qualifications
11.3	Qualifications for Armed Security Personnel
11.7	Suspension and Revocation
11.8	Sanctions

Standard 3.4

Employer Responsibilities

Employers should provide a working environment, including adequate and serviceable equipment, conducive to the efficient performance of security functions assigned.

Commentary

Most occupations require a suitable working environment and adequate equipment if their functions are to be performed satisfactorily. Employers must meet certain safety requirements in regard to personnel—i.e., hard hats for personnel in heavy equipment areas, facial protectors for welders, and so forth. Yet, safety related to the mission and activities of private security personnel, who often face life-or-death situations, is often overlooked. Identification and recognition of the dangers inherent in the performance of security services are two primary steps the employer should take to protect his employees.

The private security employer has a moral responsibility to provide a safe working environment. For example, instances in which police officers have been attacked by persons using darkness for cover are well known. In one recent case, a police officer was killed by burglars hiding in a darkened area. A store had been burglarized on several occasions and yet the store owner, although knowing that the officers were watching the area closely, disconnected a mercury-vapor lamp at the rear of the store. This officer's life might have been spared had the store owner provided proper lighting of the area. The same principle would apply to private security personnel.

The employer has an equal moral responsibility to provide safe equipment. This is particularly true for firearms. It is not intended here to infer that firearms are necessary in the performance of all private security assignments, but, if they are, firearms need to be adequate and serviceable in relationship to the security functions assigned. Several instances are recorded in which private security personnel have been issued fake, inoperative, or model firearms. In some instances, the personnel were not even aware of this situation.

Government reaction to this type of problem is reflected in the Pennsylvania Lethal Weapons Act, which was signed into law in October 1974. Section 10 of the act states:

Prohibited Act—No individual certified under this act shall carry an inoperative or model firearm while employed and he shall carry only a powder actuated firearm approved by the commissioner.

The complexity of security services precludes a detailed listing of all conditions and equipment necessary to perform diverse security functions, but one example follows. If private security personnel are assigned to patrol a warehouse after dark, the employer should provide (1) an adequately lighted building, (2) communications equipment necessary to make contact with other personnel in the area or with the police, and (3) emergency lighting equipment in case of power failure resulting from natural causes or an overt act. Safe vehicles, fencing, locks, alarm systems, and an adequate number of personnel to accomplish the mission are further examples of items requiring employer consideration.

On a broader scale, the employer should provide the necessary training to enable private security personnel to react appropriately to routine and emergency situations. Along with this training, the employer should provide an officers' manual listing guidelines for handling all general and specific situations. Finally, as indicated by a study of private security organizations in St. Petersburg, Fla., adequate supervision is needed to coordinate training and performance as new situations arise.

Employers who provide a reasonable working environment and adequate equipment are directly affecting the ability of private security personnel to perform their assigned security services. Employers, employees, and citizens can only be adequately protected when these conditions are met.

Selected References

1. McDermott, Thomas F. "Security Guard Business: Progressive Action Needed in Security Guard Business," *DVI*, April 1975.

2. Martensen, Kai R. *Private Security Survey and Ordinance for St. Petersburg, Florida*. Sunnyvale, Calif.: Public Systems Incorporated, 1975.

3. Shanahan, Donald R. *Patrol Administration.* Boston, Mass.: Holbrook Press, Inc., 1975.

4. Wathen, Thomas W. *California Plant Protection Officer's Manual*. Sherman Oaks, Calif.

Related Standards

The following standards and goals may be applicable in implementing Standard 3.4:

1.1   Selection of Qualified Personnel

1.2   Commensurate Salaries

2.2   Professional Certification Programs

2.3   Job Descriptions

2.4   Training Related to Job Functions

2.6   Arms Training

2.7   Ongoing Training

2.8   Training of Supervisors and Managers

3.1   Code of Ethics

5.2   Adequate Security Lighting

6.5   Mistaken Identity of Private Security Personnel

6.6   State Regulation of Private Security Uniforms, Equipment, Job Titles

8.4   Degree Programs for Private Security

Standard 3.5

Maintaining Data on Criminal Activities

The private security industry has a responsibility to maintain internal data on criminal activities to develop, improve, and assess effectiveness of crime reduction programs.

Commentary

The constantly increasing recorded crime rate in the United States has caused justifiable concern to government and to the American people. Many attribute the recent growth in private security services to a perceived or actual need by businesses for additional protection that public law enforcement cannot give because of limited resources. Also, citizens' perceived and actual fears about crime have led to increased concern for protection. The increase in numbers of home burglar alarm systems is probably greatly a result of this concern. Nowhere has research indicated that private security assistance in crime prevention is not necessary. To the contrary, it is reasonable to assume that businesses would not expend funds for private security if it were not cost effective. However, the security industry has a responsibility to maintain appropriate data to give management a basis for determining the value of private security services and to pinpoint specific needs.

The importance of keeping accurate crime statis-

tics by law enforcement agencies has long been recognized and was one of the fundamental principles of the Peelian Reforms written in 1829 by Sir Robert Peel, who organized the London Metropolitan Police Department. Peel wrote "Police records are necessary to the correct distribution of police strength." This principle is as pertinent today as when it was written.

Accurate record systems are as important for the private security industry as for public law enforcement agencies. Records can assist in determining patrol areas, work schedules, use of preventive measures, and other factors for the effective use of private security personnel and physical resources. For example, if accurate records point out a significant increase in thefts at a given location, surveillance measures and other special actions should be initiated. As another example, a large number of assaults occurring in a parking lot could be combated by assigning a roving patrol in the lot during the times employees are reporting to or leaving work. Imaginative planning, based on an accurate record system, can be an effective crime prevention tool. Public law enforcement agencies have developed crime analysis techniques that can be modified and adapted for use by private security firms.

The main purpose for maintaining internal data on criminal activities is to develop, improve, and assess effectiveness of crime reduction programs.

It is not intended as a record system on individual employees but rather as a data base for proper management planning. The scope of the system could depend on many factors, such as size of facility, criticalness and vulnerability of resources being protected, and location of facility. The overall purpose of the data effort should be geared to meet a management objective rather than be an end in itself.

In summary, accurate records of criminal offenses are essential to private security services for establishing a data base for assignment of personnel and physical resources and giving management a frame of reference to determine effectiveness.

Selected References

1. Brennan, Dennis T. *The Other Police.* Cleveland, Ohio: Governmental Research Institute, 1975.

2. Day, Frank D., Robert Gallati, and A. C. Germann. *Introduction to Law Enforcement and Criminal Justice* (16th printing). Springfield, Ill.: Charles C. Thomas, 1972.

3. Ely, David. "Always Home," *Playboy,* August 1975.

4. Federal Bureau of Investigation. *Uniform Crime Reports for the United States 1974.* Washington, D.C.: Government Printing Office, 1975.

5. Green, Gion, and Raymond C. Farber. *Introduction to Security.* Los Angeles: Security World Publishing Co., Inc., 1975.

6. "Home, Safe Home," *Newsweek,* Sept. 1, 1975.

7. Kingsbury, Arthur A. *Introduction to Security and Crime Prevention Surveys.* Springfield, Ill.: Charles C. Thomas, 1973.

8. Post, Richard S., and Arthur A. Kingsbury. *Security Administration.* Springfield, Ill.: Charles C. Thomas, 1970.

9. Private Security Task Force. "Private Security and Citizen's Arrest Authority." (See Appendix 9 to this report.)

10. Ursic, Henry S., and Leroy E. Pagano. *Security Management Systems.* Springfield, Ill.: Charles C. Thomas, 1974.

Related Standards

The following standards and goals may be applicable in implementing Standard 3.5:

2.3 Job Descriptions
3.1 Code of Ethics
3.2 Conduct of Private Security Personnel
3.3 Reporting of Criminal Violations
5.2 Adequate Security Lighting
5.3 Computer Security
5.6 Environmental Security in Comprehensive Planning
5.9 Crime Impact Forecast

Part 3
Crime Prevention Systems

Chapter 4
Alarm Systems

INTRODUCTION

Two persons out of every hundred are victimized by burglaries each year. The annual cost exceeds $1 billion. In the 5 years from 1969 to 1974, the number of reported burglaries in the United States rose by 53 percent. An average of 8,000 burglaries are committed daily.

These are startling figures and many American citizens and businesses, seeking more protection than our criminal justice system can supply, have turned to alarm systems. Correspondingly, there has been a dramatic increase in the number of alarm system companies. It has been estimated that the alarm industry is expanding at a rate of 10 percent a year.

Substantiated figures show that alarm systems do affect crime. In communities where such systems are used extensively, the burglary rate has been significantly reduced. Further, most insurance companies offer lower premiums to businesses that are protected by alarm systems. Various federally insured institutions, such as banks, are required by law to install systems.

Because alarm systems have become an irreplaceable tool in crime prevention and are a significant part of the private security industry, the standards in this chapter aim at developing guidelines for their most effective use. To better understand the intent of the standards, a basic knowledge of alarm systems and their characteristics is needed.

Defining Alarm Systems

The use of alarm systems dates back to 390 B.C. and the Roman Empire when squawking geese alerted the Romans to surprise attack by the Gauls. Carl Kellem of the National Crime Prevention Institute, Louisville, Ky., has adapted this historical account to make physiological analogies to geese in describing the three fundamental parts of modern intrusion detection systems (alarm systems) (see Figure 4.1):

1) **Sensor**—that function of the intrusion detection system which detects or senses a condition which exists or changes, be it authorized or unauthorized. This definition can be related directly to the animal senses of touch, hearing, sight, smell and taste. This definition includes all actions that occur since the senses have no means of distinguishing authorized or unauthorized actions. This is easily pointed out in one of the most common and simplest sensory devices —the magnetic contact on a door. This device is activated each time the door is operated and has no means of determining whether the operation of the door is authorized. The next fundamental part is assigned that function.

2) **Control**—that function of the intrusion detection system which provides the power, receives the information from the sensors, evaluates the information and transmits the required information to the annunciation function.

The control function is related directly to the physiological functions of the brain and nervous system and also to the circulatory system. The nervous system collects and evaluates information from the various senses and transmits signals to the muscles for appropriate action. The circulatory system provides the power source (i.e., nutrients and oxygen from the blood) to maintain the ability of the system to function.

3) **Annunciation**—that function of the intrusion detection system which alerts a human to initiate a response that will result in an investigation of the sensor environment.

This could be bell, buzzer, light flashing, etc. This function is analogous to the squawking of geese, barking of dogs or man calling for help.

When these three fundamental parts are combined, they form an alarm system that, upon detection of an intrusion, transmits and articulates a message for help. Numerous types of alarm systems are available—some simple, some highly complex. A user's choice of systems is limited only by the dollars he has available.

Devices for the sensor function of an alarm system range from simple magnetic switches to sensitive ultrasonic Doppler and sound systems. Other available equipment includes electronic, electromechanical, and photoelectric devices; microwave Dopplers; closed-circuit television cameras; and ionization detector systems. The more sophisticated devices are used primarily in large industrial or business complexes; simpler devices are used in residences or small businesses.

Incorporated in the control function is equipment necessary for power, energizing, signal transmission,

Figure 4.1. Burglary Alarm System Concept

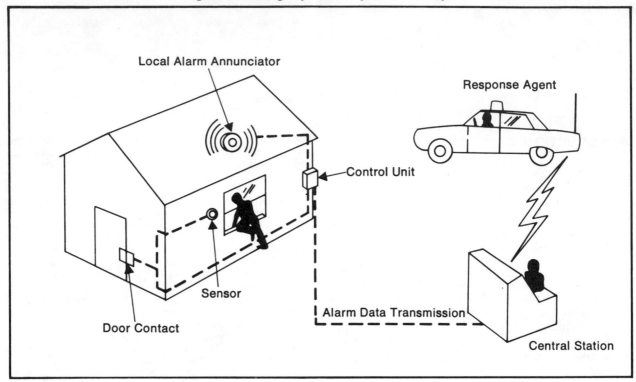

and circuitry. Depending upon the level of security desired, various devices are available for each component. For example, power to operate the alarm system can be supplied by either battery or public utility electricity, but a combination of both is necessary if the system is to function during public power failures. Possible energizing equipment includes shunt locks, key-operated control panels, and time delays. Signal transmission may be accomplished through the interaction of such equipment as relays, switches, amplifiers, telephone dialers, and so forth. A choice of telephone lines, radio waves, or coaxial cables is available to channel information to the annunciation system.

There are four basic systems of annunciation: local alarm, central station alarm, proprietary alarm, and police department alarm. All except local alarms function through either direct or indirect connections with the police. In the local alarm system, the alarm can be seen or heard only at the protected premises; police notification depends upon the presence of responsible persons in the vicinity of the alarm. Upon detection of an intruder, a device (bell, gong, horn, siren, flashing light) is activated, alerting anyone within hearing or seeing distance to initiate the response by notifying the police.

The central station alarm uses an independently owned and operated monitoring facility. An alarm device is installed in a location and wired directly to the central station. When an alarm is received at the central station, the signal is interpreted and appropriate action taken, i.e., maintenance or police notification. The monitoring facility also offers its subscribers services such as records of openings and closings, guard response, and key access, with charges corresponding to the number of services provided.

Although similar to central station alarm systems, in proprietary alarm systems the monitoring facility is maintained by the owner of the protected property. A private guard force monitors the system and responds to all alarms. A guard notifies police when they are needed.

The fourth type of annunciation system—police department alarm—initiates direct police response. There are two types of systems terminating in the police station: One is connected directly from the protected premises to an annunciator panel in the police station; the other is the telephone dialer. With the dialer, a signal is sent to the control, which dials a programmed number (law enforcement agency) and, when the phone is answered, plays a prerecorded message.

Although multiple combinations of these components are possible, in its simplest form an alarm system depends upon a detection device, a source of power, a means of interpretation, a method of transmission, and a means of articulating the alarm to someone who initiates a response.

The major goal of alarm systems is to prevent crime by reducing criminal opportunity. In many instances, the presence of an alarm system can serve as a psychological deterrent to crime—most would-be offenders stay away from premises they suspect are protected by alarm systems. Another goal is to reduce crime through apprehension of offenders. A reliable alarm system increases the likelihood of apprehension and prosecution of criminals. In addition to protection against burglary, alarms can also provide protection against other criminal intrusions, as well as smoke, fire, and other life- and property-threatening hazards. In short, alarms provide a valuable, viable means of achieving overall security.

The Problems of Alarm Systems

Although alarm systems have been proven effective in deterring and apprehending burglars, they are subject to certain inherent problems. A traditional and still-to-be-resolved problem is that of false alarms. From 90 to 98 percent of all alarms transmitted are said to be false. This high percentage can be basically attributed to three factors: (1) user error or negligence, (2) poor installation or servicing, and (3) faulty equipment.

More than half of all false alarms are estimated to result from user error or negligence. Users often do not understand how to properly operate their systems. Commonly, alarms are set off by users who fail to lock doors or windows or who enter a secured area when the system is engaged. Alarm systems are also activated accidentally by workers, custodians, domestic help, or even pets. Added to these false alarms are those from improper use. For example, merchants have been known to use their alarm systems to summon the police to deal with bad checks or suspicious individuals. Some users even set off their alarms to time police response to their premises.

The second factor leading to false alarms is poor installation or servicing. In order to function as intended, an alarm system must be properly installed and maintained. Equipment that is installed in an inappropriate environment or improperly positioned, set, or wired produces false alarms. Likewise, if equipment is not adequately maintained, the chances of false alarms increase. Too often installers and service personnel lack the necessary skills and knowledge for today's more sophisticated equipment.

The third common cause of false alarms is faulty equipment. If equipment is electrically or mechanically defective, the alarm can be activated when, for instance, the equipment breaks or shorts out the circuit. The use of cheap, substandard equipment that is especially vulnerable to breakdown or can be easily set off by a variety of extraneous conditions leads to frequent false alarms.

In addition to false alarms that can be traced to the above causal factors, there are a certain number of false alarms whose cause cannot be determined. Based on the results of various studies, roughly an average of 25 percent of all false alarms fall into this unknown category. It is possible that they may, in fact, be the result of user error; faced with probable sanctions, a user may deny responsibility for a false alarm. Another possibility is that a burglary or other unauthorized intrusion may have been successfully prevented, leaving no visible evidence of intrusion or attempted entry.

The continued high incidence of false alarms, whatever the cause, has led to other problems. In the use of automatic telephone dialer alarm systems, a large number of storm-caused false alarms simultaneously occurring can tie up police trunklines and switchboards, seriously hampering police capacity to respond to genuine emergencies. Malfunctioning of such systems can lock-in police communications trunklines for considerable periods of time. Although telephone dialers offer effective, low-cost protection, these problems have created negative police reaction toward their use.

Another problem is that of police attitudes toward alarm systems in general. Often the police, faced with repeated false alarms, tend to give alarms a low priority. The resulting significant response delays reduce the likelihood of apprehension and limit the value of alarms. Further, police officers, lulled by the high incidence of false alarms, may not conduct thorough on-the-scene investigations or be alert to the risks of valid alarms.

In addition to the problems of attitude, many police departments have documented the high costs of false alarms in terms of salaries, wear and tear on police vehicles, and loss of manpower for other activities. There is no question that false alarms waste valuable police resources and often divert coverage from more important areas. However, it should be noted that whatever the nature of a police response, these same factors are involved. The false alarm would be no more costly, for example, than checking out a disturbance call when there is no disturbance.

A more serious problem is that of the personal risks involved in false alarms. The high-speed response to false alarms unnecessarily endangers the personal welfare of policemen, as well as other drivers and innocent bystanders. False alarms often also bring to the scene alarm company respondents who are frequently armed, presenting a further threat to personal life and safety. The gravity of such situations is apparent; the problem involved, manifold.

Another problem of false alarms is the burden of expense to the users of alarm systems. When a system false alarms, servicing is usually required, resulting in increased costs that are eventually absorbed by the users. Further, some local governments directly impose fines upon users whose systems repeatedly produce false alarms.

Alarm companies also are faced with cost problems. Denied the special telephone rates granted to government organizations serving the public interest and faced with rapidly increasing circuitry costs, alarm companies find it difficult to provide alarm protection within the financial reach of small businesses and individuals. Also contributing to increased costs is the introduction of new, sophisticated equipment that requires both higher grade and more extensive telephone lines to achieve reliability of transmission and reduce probability of false alarms. The alternative methods of transmission—radio and television frequencies—are so expensive that they are presently unaffordable.

Cooperation and Research

As previously stated, alarm systems afford a valuable method of overall security. Their effectiveness in reducing crime provides a direct public benefit. They aid businesses by offering added protection at a cost lower than salaried security personnel and by cutting down on high insurance premiums. Private alarms also benefit public law enforcement officials by aiding in the apprehension of criminals and by enhancing the effectiveness of police patrol and surveillance. Considering these overall benefits, the standards in this chapter call for the cooperative efforts of all parties involved to overcome existing problems and the promotion of research to improve the efficiency and reliability of alarm systems.

If the problems of alarm systems are to be solved, the interrelationship of all factors should be recognized. A clear understanding of the roles of alarm system manufacturers, dealers, sales and service personnel, public law enforcement, and users can serve to illustrate the interdependency and interaction vital to increased reliability and effectiveness.

First, alarm system manufacturers need to develop dependable equipment. Performance standards for both individual components and installed systems should be adopted by all manufacturers. Agencies such as Underwriters' Laboratories, Inc., have made great strides in mitigating the problem of defective equipment. By submitting equipment to Underwriters'

Laboratories for inspection, alarm manufacturers and companies not only enhance their sales but also may obtain discounts from insurance companies and reduce frequent costly servicing of equipment prone to breakdown.

Manufacturers and alarm dealers should undertake further research to develop systems that are more false alarm resistant. The need exists for a more reliable human-discriminating sensor, as well as for the definition and development of new alarm communications media. Because urban and suburban residents and small businesses cannot afford high-cost protection, new ideas also are needed for low-cost alarm designs.

In light of recent power shortages, manufacturers should incorporate increased backup power in alarm system controls. This is especially important for alarm systems that terminate at law enforcement agencies. Users of such systems have an added responsibility to ensure continuous operation of their systems in the event of power outages.

Alarm dealers who do not manufacture their own equipment should make certain that the equipment they lease or sell meets performance standards. If they lack the capacity to install and/or service the systems they sell, dealers have an obligation to disclose where the user can obtain competent installation and maintenance services. To further ensure the effectiveness of the systems they sell or lease, alarm dealers should be required to instruct users and their employees in the proper operation of the system and the serious consequences of false alarms.

Although manufacturers have primary responsibility for reliable equipment, the assistance of others is needed if that equipment is to be correctly and effectively used. Beginning at the sales level, personnel should be trained in the concepts and operation of alarms. Often, because of inadequate technical knowledge or possibly the desire to consummate a sale, sales personnel tend to either oversell or undersell equipment, or they may sell equipment ill-suited to users' needs. Any of these errors can result in improper application of the system and subsequent serious functional problems. Similarly, alarm system installers and servicing technicians need to possess adequate skills and knowledge for proper installation and maintenance of a system. The installation and servicing of sophisticated space-protection equipment especially calls for up-to-date training for reliability to be achieved.

To prevent problems arising from improper sales, installation, and servicing, it is recommended that a certified training program be established for all alarm system sales, installation and service personnel. Such a program should stress basic skills and also should be oriented toward encouraging cooperation between sales and service personnel in an effort to reduce false alarms and to promote effective use of alarm systems. In addition to providing needed training and coordination, a certification program can afford consumers a basis for choosing reputable alarm system dealers and reduce the number of fly-by-night sales and installation companies that undermine the reputation of legitimate firms and contribute to the false alarm problem.

Assuming the use of dependable equipment installed in a compatible environment by well-trained and well-qualified personnel, there remains another factor to be considered—user error or negligence. As mentioned earlier, most false alarms are attributed to human error or carelessness. Through purchase or lease, users of alarm systems assume significant responsibility for proper operation and total effectiveness, yet often are unaware of essential operating procedures or the impact of false alarms. Properly educated by alarm dealers and/or installers, users should exercise every caution to ensure that correct operating procedures are followed and that systems are used only for emergency purposes. User cooperation is vital to any realistic hope of reducing false alarms.

Clearly, alarm system manufacturers, dealers, sales and servicing personnel, installers, and users share a responsibility for guarding against false alarms and increasing the effectiveness of alarm systems. However, their individual efforts to adopt measures for increased efficiency and reliability are limited without mutual cooperation.

The cooperation of public law enforcement agencies also is needed for the problems of alarm systems to be overcome. To attain this cooperation, alarm companies and law enforcement agencies should develop a mutual understanding of each other's problems and work together toward resolving these problems. A common definition of the term "false alarm" should be developed, and false alarm rates should reflect the total alarm performance record, including both valid and false alarms. While alarm companies work toward developing more reliable equipment and ensuring its proper installation, use, and maintenance, law enforcement officials should make similar efforts to improve alarm response rates and to help educate users by making known the difficulties police face when alarms are falsely triggered.

Finally, to solve problems of cost and transmission, the joint efforts of many agencies are required. Current extensive research aimed at developing new ideas for low-cost equipment and new means of transmission will be worthless unless facility rates are lowered. The Law Enforcement Assistance Administration has expressed an objective of encouraging the use of alarm systems at a cost that can be afforded by small businesses and individuals. To achieve this objective, the cooperation of telephone companies and regulatory agencies, such as the Federal Communications Commission and State Communications Commissions, is required.

Government Control of Alarm Systems

Government regulation becomes necessary whenever the public interest or welfare must be guarded. Because false alarms affect the public welfare, it is believed that local governments should take part in developing mechanisms to control the number of false alarms. One way to reduce the likelihood of false alarms is periodic inspection of alarm equipment. Accordingly, it is recommended that local governments require all alarm systems to be inspected annually. Alarm companies frequently are so busy with servicing problems that regular inspection of equipment becomes lax. Also, users without regular servicing contracts may fail to realize the importance of periodic inspection. Therefore, mandatory annual inspection would lead to detection of mechanical failures or malfunctions that might otherwise go unnoticed until they resulted in false alarms.

The recent crime rise has inspired the emergence of a number of disreputable companies who use fear of crime to make quick sales. Although most reputable alarm dealers service the systems they sell or lease, often the "quick-buck" companies disappear before maintenance arrangements can be made, leaving purchasers with no means of obtaining service for their equipment. To guard against this situation, a disclosure law should be enforced whereby sellers would have to make known prior to sales where alarm systems can be serviced. Further, if alarm systems are to terminate in law enforcement agencies, proof of servicing arrangements should be required in the form of legal agreements or contracts.

Many localities have successfully reduced false alarms by requiring alarm user permits. Under such a system, the user normally is assessed a fine after a given number of false alarms. This report contends that local governments should require alarm user permits but suggests that the penalty for excessive false alarms should be revocation of the permit rather than monetary payment. In this way, false alarms can be discouraged without also discouraging the use of alarm systems through excessive costs. Additionally, in establishing a permit system, revocation of the permit should not be based on alarms caused by conditions over which the user has no control, i.e., earthquakes, hurricanes, tornadoes, and so forth. The purpose of the permit should be to encourage user caution, not to penalize users for protecting their property.

The problems of telephone dialer alarm systems have prompted some communities to seek government regulation regarding their use. The problems in this area and the advantages of government regulation are recognized. However, because telephone dialer systems provide valuable protection to small businesses and others unable to afford more expensive alarm systems, serious consideration should be given to the consequences of government regulation before it is enacted. If the results of such legislation would force many users to discontinue alarm service, other methods of control would prove more advantageous. In no instance, however, should telephone dialer alarm systems be connected to a law enforcement agency's primary emergency telephone trunkline. These lines must be kept available for citizen emergency calls. Special trunklines should be installed to handle all telephone dialer calls, reducing unnecessary interference with police communications and improving police attitudes toward automatic dialer systems.

Through regulation in the suggested areas, governments can significantly help reduce the problems of false alarms. However, government ownership or operation of alarm systems should be discouraged. It is inappropriate for governments or law enforcement agencies to engage in the business of selling, installing, or servicing alarms. Governments competing with private enterprise in selling goods or services is an infringement of private rights. Furthermore, government-operated business involves questionable liabilities and the opportunity for serious misuse of public authority. Ultimately, government operation of private alarm systems could lead to an abandonment of the field by private enterprise.

Standard 4.1

Alarm Systems Research

Appropriate research should be conducted to develop new methods and techniques to transmit alarm signals and enhance alarm systems capabilities.

Commentary

It is a proven fact that alarm systems deter crime and enhance criminal apprehension. However, substantial research is needed to develop more cost-effective alarm transmission, to conserve resources, and to improve preventive capabilities.

Considerable resources are required to undertake effective research. Because funds required to meet this standard are beyond the means of many competent alarm systems manufacturers, government involvement is needed. As pointed out by the Small Business Administration's report to the U.S. Senate Select Committee on Small Business, there is a distinct need for government to "sponsor a central point of contact for manufacturers to evaluate and encourage research and development . . ." Such a facility could be especially beneficial in alarm systems research.

Various other reports likewise have indicated the need for government support in the establishment of a research facility. The *RAND Report* (Vol. II), for example, suggests the Federal Government fund a research center to evaluate the effectiveness and

costs of private security personnel and equipment. The Law Enforcement Standards Laboratory, in conjunction with the National Bureau of Standards, is to a limited degree doing such research, but no work is planned in the area of alarm transmissions.

Sound advice in establishing a research facility is offered in a document by the Alarm Industry Committee for Combating Crime. Among other things, it is suggested: "The clearing-house or private security center should give due regard to practical and economic considerations, as well as technical or hypothetical concepts, and should conduct its activities so that no competitive advantage is given to any person or organization in the private sector."

The need for research in alarm transmission is apparent. It has been suggested, however, that at this time research should not be focused on new systems, methods, and techniques but, rather, on improving the application of those systems currently in use. Carl Kellem of the National Crime Prevention Institute has stated, "There is very little need for new technology except in the area of alarm transmission. Right now we are not using all the technology available." What Kellem means is that there is a sufficiency of detection devices being developed, but, no matter how innovative the detection device, it must rely on the same transmission methods as all previous systems. These are wire, cable, or radio frequency. Realistically, there are probably no other plausible transmission methods except laser applications.

Use of the FCC-allocated 950-96MHz band may offer improved alarm transmission signals. As stated by Anthony Grosso, vice president of engineering of ADT Security Systems, "The costs have reached the point where ADT and possibly others feel the frequencies can be used for some applications." There appears to be interest, Grosso points out, in using lower range frequencies because of broader applications and because the equipment required would be less expensive. Grosso also indicates that some technical development by telephone companies in the alarm transmission field might be appropriate.

Another view, in regard to the use of radio frequencies, is that of Harold Gray, vice president and general manager of Pacific Fire Extinguisher Co.:

The complications of security alarm systems have, over these many years, involved all system components. More recently, the major problem has been the communication link between the protected premises and the central station, and/or the police communications center. With the low cost metallic circuits being withdrawn from service, by the nationwide telephone system, it has become necessary for other methods of transmitting signals to be applied. These applications are primarily in the area of multiplexing. The resultant investigation in this area of communication signalling has brought to light the possibility of using radio. The FCC over the past ten years has recognized the need for use of radio frequencies for alarm company use. They first allocated clear channel frequencies in the 450 MHz band for voice communication, and then subsequently allocated frequencies in the 960 MHz band for point-to-point signalling. Once these frequencies were available, the industry began to extend their research and development into this area. Today the various multiplexing and scanning systems are all designed to operate over either the telephone carrier system or over clear channel radio frequencies.

It is absolutely imperative that the use of radio frequencies be foremost in all consideration of future alarm signalling. All relative governmental agencies, such as FCC, LEAA, etc., should be aware of the need for these communication links.

Other alarm transmission methods developed by central alarm stations use a computer. One such method was described in *Security World* magazine. The article reported that, because multiplexing is still relatively new, the older McCulloh Loop configuration has been altered to tie in with a computer. "The computer is 'writing out' an alarm ticket giving the location of the alarm, specific point and kind of alarm, appropriate authority to notify, name of firm," and so forth. A second method for possible future development mentioned in the *Security World* article was direct-dialer communication to a computer.

Cable television also should be mentioned as a medium for alarm transmission. An unused channel could be leased from the cable television operator by the alarm company and subleased to the individual alarm subscriber.

As initially stated, research to develop new methods or techniques to transmit alarm signals should be encouraged. Past efforts in this area have been fragmented or have come about by driving necessity. Personnel, money, and facilities exist to achieve success in this field: They need to be combined to initiate research.

Selected References

1. Beerman, Bernard. Address to the Private Security Task Force. Chicago, Ill., July 11, 1975.

2. Grosso, Anthony J. "Central Station Signal Transmission Methods." An address before the City-Industry Alarm Task Force of Dallas, Tex., 1975.

3. Kakalik, James S., and Sorrel Wildhorn. *The Private Police Industry: Its Nature and Extent,* Vol. II, R–870/DOJ. Washington, D.C.: Government Printing Office, 1971.

4. Kellem, Carl. Personal interview. Louisville, Ky., Aug. 15, 1975.

5. Small Business Administration. *Crime Against Small Business.* Washington, D.C.: Government Printing Office, 1969.

6. "The Central Station," *Security World,* Vol. 7, No. 9, 1970.

Related Standards

The following standards and goals may be applicable in implementing Standard 4.1:

4.4   Compatibility of Sensors
4.6   Joint Cooperation to Reduce Transmission Costs
8.2   National Private Security Resource and Research Institute

Standard 4.2

Backup Power
for Alarms

All alarm systems terminating at a law enforcement agency should be equipped with a standby power source.

Commentary

Installation of a suitable backup power source for alarm systems operating on publicly supplied power and terminating at a law enforcement agency is the aim of this standard. The concern is not with law enforcement agencies—virtually all have some type of emergency power—or with wholly battery-operated systems or systems not connected directly to a law enforcement agency. This standard is directed at alarm users whose systems are wired directly into a law enforcement agency for monitoring service. These users should ensure that their systems have the capability to function continuously, even under the most adverse power conditions.

Proprietary and local alarm systems also have a need for backup power, but those systems terminating at a law enforcement agency have been identified in this standard, because, in most cases, public law enforcement officials receive criticism from citizens when alarms are activated, or not activated, as a result of a power failure. Also, in the case of alarm activation, law enforcement agencies have an immediate problem in determining if an officer is needed to respond to the location of the alarm. Many leaders in both the alarms industry and law enforcement have expressed concern regarding these matters.

A review of recent literature on security systems reveals a widespread awareness of the need for backup systems. Richard J. Scarvaci, chief engineer, special products, Globe-Union, Inc., accurately and succinctly summarized the situation:

Standby emergency power for security systems has become increasingly important in the past few years as power blackouts have highlighted shortcomings in what were previously thought to be highly reliable power systems.

Even momentary outages and voltage dips can be troublesome as sophisticated, less tolerant electronic equipment is added to security systems.

Two articles in *Security World,* Vol. II, No. 3, point out the backup power problem in regard to fire and burglar alarm systems. The first, written by James C. Shanahan, vice president of marketing of Gamewell, advocates reapprasial of existing backup power supply codes:

The electrical utilities in New York and New England have announced voltage reductions of a minimum of 5%. These same utilities have indicated that they anticipate they have to program intentional power blackouts in various communities at various times . . . this may be the time to begin thinking of revisions to both the NFPA standards and the UL standards for burglar alarm systems.

143

If there are going to be intentional, repetitive power failures, dry cell batteries which are not rechargeable will become less reliable for burglar alarm systems and there will be many schools, nursing homes, etc., without an automatic fire alarm system during these periods of power blackouts.

. . . a storm in New England . . . caused power failure in the Boston Metropolitan area that affected approximately 80,000 subscribers. The power was out in the Boston area up to 36 hours. Power was not available for many subscribers in the Hartford, Connecticut area for as long as five days.

The second article, written by Roy Longworth, general manager of fire and security group, Johnson Service Co., is primarily concerned with fire alarm systems backup power codes, but the same holds true for burglar alarms:

There is presently no national code requiring backup power sources, although some local codes require them for institutional, commercial, and industrial structures, in the event of a brownout or blackout, therefore, fire alarm systems in many buildings will fail unless a battery backup system has been installed. . . .

Observations from a survey by F. C. Heckman of security alarm systems further emphasize the need for backup power supplies:

. . . a good security control should have ample power supply reserves to run the entire system both on a continuous basis where comparatively little current is drawn, and on an alarm basis where heavy currents are drawn.

In addition, it is most advisable that the control have automatic switchover to standby power capabilities. Standby power can be in the form of dry cells or continuously charged standby batteries.

Certain problems may be encountered in upgrading current alarm systems to meet these needs. The quoted authors have not overlooked these problems. For instance, Longworth discussed the problem of battery life:

Batteries, however, must be checked on a regular basis to be sure they will function properly during a crisis. Battery life should be determined, and if batteries are nearing the end of their useful life, they should be discarded and replaced. Batteries should also be tested from time to time to be sure they will run through the required standby period.

Shanahan's article mentioned another problem area—obtaining a reliable system at a reasonable cost:

The problem with upgrading the fire alarm and security systems will be to determine the compromise required to supply a system at an economical price and still cover most power outages. It is not reasonable to assume that the standby power should be capable of handling a system for as much as five to seven days; however, 60–72 hours may be a very good compromise.

Such problems need to be met in order to provide a reliable backup power source for alarm systems terminating at a law enforcement agency.

Requirements to ensure the continued operation of law enforcement agency-linked alarm systems in the event of power lapses or failures should be established. Underwriters' Laboratories, Inc., states the following specific requirements for standby battery power in their standard entitled "Police Station Connected Burglar Alarm Units and Systems":

If a power supply with standby battery is provided, the battery shall have sufficient capacity to operate the system for periods as follows:

A. Bank alarms—72 hours.

B. Mercantile alarms in areas served by power facilities shown by experience to be dependable—4 hours.

Technical standards being prepared for model legislation for the International Association of Chiefs of Police include an identical backup power source standard.

Recent energy problems tend to indicate considerations of a longer backup capacity for mercantile alarms. But before any move to increase present requirements, consideration should be given to whether heightened requirements may lead to unit price increases that might, in turn, decrease the demand for alarm systems. If this should happen, increasing backup power capacity would be self-defeating.

Maintenance is naturally a concern with a backup system. The alarm servicing companies should budget more time and personnel for routine inspection of backup power equipment and battery replacement and recharging. The costs of this service would probably increase the servicing contract but can be held down if all users are required to have backup power.

Public power sources will probably continue to be unreliable through the 1980's. Because of such energy problems, backup power supply has become a serious issue calling for immediate action. Shanahan points out:

Revisions to standards require many months—sometimes several years—to accomplish, due to the economic impact on manufacturers, suppliers, and end-users. Therefore, the time has arrived when we should start to upgrade the standby power capability of both local fire alarm and security alarm systems.

Selected References

1. Alarm Industry Committee for Combating Crime, Standards Subcommittee. Report on August 21 meeting, Washington, D.C., 1975.

2. Heckman, F. C. "A Survey of Security Alarm Systems and Their Operational Characteristics." Unpublished master's thesis, Michigan State University, East Lansing, 1973.

3. Longworth, Roy. "Brownout Conditions and Building Fire Alarm Systems," *Security World,* Vol. II, No. 3, 1974.

4. Scarvaci, Richard S. "Adaption of Standby Power to Security Equipment," *Security Distributing and Marketing,* Vol. 5, No. 3, 1974.

5. Shanahan, James C. "Back-Up Power Supply Codes Being Reappraised," *Security World,* Vol. II, No. 3, 1974.

6. Underwriters' Laboratories, Inc. "Police Station Connected Burglar Alarm Units and Systems." Underwriters' Laboratories, Inc., 1975.

Related Standards

The following standards and goals may be applicable in implementing Standard 4.2:

4.8 Annual Alarm Inspection

7.1 Consumers Responsibility for Selection of Security Services

Standard 4.3

Certified Training of Alarms Sales and Service Personnel

There should be a certified training program for alarm sales personnel and alarm service technicians.

Commentary

A major cause of problems involving alarm systems can be traced back to inadequacies of the person selling, installing, or servicing the system. The alarm committee of the Private Security Advisory Council found:

Too often, individuals or companies attracted into the alarm industry because of constant publicity given to the crime problem, have little understanding, knowledge and experience of the specifics required in properly sustaining an alarm business. This may lead to improper selection of components to accomplish specific tasks, or improper installation, either of which may lead to frequent false alarms.

A contributing factor to the problem of inadequacies in alarm sales and servicing is the lack of effective codes, guidelines, or standards to ensure competence in these careers. Almost any individual can open an alarm systems business with no test required of his knowledge or ability to operate such a business. Although the system he sells may be reliable, he may have no experience or knowledge concerning correct installation and servicing, nor be able to obtain proper training in such matters through on-the-job activities.

Many basic arguments support establishment of a certified training program for installation, sales, and service personnel. First, new alarms are being installed every day. Installers have varying degrees of skill, depending on company training. Many are not knowledgeable of installation methods required for the more sophisticated systems on the market; many may even lack the necessary basic skills. This lack of training or skill not only results in ill will on the part of consumers and law enforcement agencies but also creates problems for alarm companies and manufacturers of alarm equipment. Norval Poulson of Certified Burglar Alarm Systems, Inc., described this problem as follows:

The equipment now being installed by many alarm companies is quite technical and far more sophisticated than the alarm system of the past 30 to 40 years. Many of the old-time employees are not trained—or are untrainable—on the new equipment. This is a serious problem facing both the alarm companies and the manufacturers of alarm equipment. Frankly many alarm companies are not purchasing newly-developed equipment because they realize they do not have the personnel, either in management or their service department, who can properly maintain and properly diagnose trouble in these sophisticated systems.

Alarm sales personnel, too, need to keep abreast of newly developed equipment, as well as possess a technical knowledge of the systems they sell. Many salesmen tend to be more sales oriented rather than technically oriented, but the consumer depends on the salesman's advice regarding which system to buy. If the salesman, through lack of technical knowledge, sells the wrong type of device, no amount of skilled servicing can make the system work properly.

Carl Kellem, instructor at the National Crime Prevention Institute and an electrical engineer, suggests that alarm dealers should be trained in security concepts, risk management, capabilities and limitations of protection devices, and seriousness of false alarms. For alarm installers and servicemen, he recommends minimum training in electrical fundamentals, seriousness of false alarms, and sensitivity of the proprietary equipment and information. He also believes that sales, installation, and service personnel should be encouraged to work together in order to build a better understanding of each other's jobs.

Another argument for certified training is that consumers need clear and understandable guidelines for selection of a reputable alarm company. Certification of alarm company personnel to a minimum level of training increases the ability of consumers to choose reliable companies to sell, install, and service their alarm systems.

A final argument in favor of a certified training program for alarm company personnel is that such a program would upgrade the industry's public image. This is an important consideration in today's marketplace.

A complex question in establishing a certified training program in the alarm systems field is who will implement it and how. One possibility would be government implementation and certification. An alternative to government certification is for the alarm industry to develop its own program and implement it on a local, State, or national level at a pace best suited to existing business conditions. Or the government regulatory agency involved might invite experts in the alarm industry to draft minimum guidelines for training. An alarm company applying for a business license or renewal would have to file a training program outline meeting these minimum drafted guidelines. By this method, the company, rather than the individual, would be certified, and occasional field inspection would be made to ensure compliance.

Representatives of the alarm industry were asked their opinions on a certified training program. Their responses were mainly negative. In their opinion, there already is enough licensing and certification, and the cost of such a program could be a threat to their business life. Without concrete proposals on the length, content, and cost of such a program, the alarm industry is not likely to lend its support.

Another approach to training could be through independent individual action. Certain standards for alarm sales, servicing, and installing personnel could be developed and offered as courses at local vocational or junior colleges. Persons completing the course work would possess more marketable skills and be an asset to the company hiring them.

The need to upgrade the level of skill of some alarm companies' sales, service, and installation personnel is evident, even though many highly professional alarm companies already have training programs that would surpass any minimum recommendations. It should also be noted that some training may be inappropriate for alarm companies that deal solely wtih specialty devices. But for the overall good of the public the alarm industry serves, a program of certification requiring minimum training should be adopted for alarm systems personnel.

Selected References

1. Alarm Industry Committee for Combating Crime. "Alarm Industry Committee for Combating Crime's Response to the Request of the National Institute for Law Enforcement and Criminal Justice for AICCC's Comments on Aerospace's Reports on Low Cost Burglar Alarm Systems and on a Citizen's Alarm System," 1975.

2. Kellem, Carl (instructor). Personal interview. National Crime Prevention Institute, Louisville, Ky., Aug. 15, 1975.

3. Poulson, Norval. "False Alarms: An Industry View," *Security World,* Vol. 6, No. 9, 1969.

Related Standards

The following standards and goals may be applicable in implementing Standard 4.3:

2.1   Training in Private Security

2.5   Preassignment and Basic Training

2.8   Training of Supervisors and Managers

2.9   State Authority and Responsibility for Training

2.10 State Boards to Coordinate Training Efforts

3.1   Code of Ethics

4.5   Training and Instruction of Alarm Users by Alarm Companies

8.3   Noncredit and Credit Seminars and Courses

8.4   Degree Programs for Private Security

11.2 Registration Qualifications

Standard 4.4

Compatibility of Sensors

Alarm companies and alarm users should only use those sensor devices in alarm systems that are operationally compatible with the area in which the system is located.

Commentary

Of the numerous types of alarm devices available, those referred to as sensors are cited because of the many problems that may occur with their use. For the purpose of this standard, sensors generally can be defined as detection devices for space protection and include those that work on the Doppler, ultrasonic, optical, or stress principle. This type of equipment is far more complex in makeup than simple contacts and switches, and a higher degree of skill is required for proper installation of such equipment. Thus, sensors are more susceptible to false alarming. However, George Lippert of Morse Products Manufacturing suggests in *Security Distributing and Marketing* that the problem of false alarming usually can be prevented by proper application and installation of the equipment.

For sensing equipment to function properly, the environment in which it is to be installed must be carefully studied first. Overlooking certain environmental factors at the time of installation could render the system useless. For example, installing vibration detectors in a bank vault located above a subway would be futile. Factors such as the state of repair of a building and the type of heating (radiators, air currents, and so forth) can affect the successful operation of sensory equipment. Table 4.1, as developed by F. C. Heckman, lists factors having a causal effect on the triggering of sensors. This list should be updated and used as an application guide for salespersons, installers, and purchasers of alarm systems.

Heckman states that security engineers contacted believed that, "through conservative design and utilization of only the best components, the sensitive amplifiers used in space intrusion detectors can be brought to a point where they will be as stable as the current state of the art will permit."

Improper installation is another factor that must be seriously considered with respect to sensor applications. As stated by Carl Kellem of the National Crime Prevention Institute, "The major problem we are having now with sensors and will in the future is the individual installing the system. He needs to have the knowledge to evaluate the capabilities and limitations of the system." Norval Poulson, in an article dealing with false alarms, broadens this definition, as follows:

148

Table 4.1 False Alarm Evaluation

False alarm causing Phenomena	Will Tend to Falsely Trigger				
	Radio Frequency	Ultrasonic	Sonic	Infrared	Stress
Lightning	Yes	No	No	No	No
Intermittent power failure	Yes	No	No	No	No
Intermittent power switching	Yes	No	No	No	No
AC sparks from switches and contacts	Yes	No	No	No	No
Shortwave transmitters (police, cabs, etc.)	Yes	Yes	No	No	No
Hot and cold air currents	No	Yes	No	No	No
Rotating machinery (fans, etc.)	Yes	Yes	Yes	No	No
Randomly moving objects (chandeliers, blinds, curtains, trees)	Yes	Yes	Yes	No	No
Small animals	Yes	Yes	Yes	Yes	No
Noises (telephones, radiators, etc.)	No	Yes	Yes	No	No
Structural member flexure	No	No	No	No	Yes
Wavering in large metal surfaces (walls, roofs, air and heating ducts)	Yes	Yes	Yes	No	No
Random heat sources (lights, radiators, sunlight)	No	No	No	Yes	No

Source: F. C. Heckman. "A Survey of Security Alarm Systems and Their Operational Characteristics." Unpublished master's thesis, Michigan State University, East Lansing, 1973, p. 33.

Improper installation includes poor workmanship, proper equipment improperly installed, and installation of equipment unsuitable for the specific application.

Further concerns of Poulson are described in the same article:

Another cause is what I call "over-extension of equipment." For example, a manufacturer may sell a photo-electric beam system with the claim that it is effective for 300 feet. Under ideal conditions, it may be, but under normal everyday working conditions, 300 feet is "over-extending" the equipment to the point where it will cause false alarms. A corollary of "over-extension" of equipment is the use of the "next best thing" when protecting problem areas for which there is no equipment available to do a proper job; "the next best thing" is sometimes a good source of false alarms.

An "economy" that is sometimes resorted to in order to offer the most competitive price is to ignore Underwriters' Laboratories specifications when making installations which do not require UL certification. By skimping here and there to be competitive an installation is produced which will in the long run be a source of false alarms.

Thomas M. Lewin agreed with Poulson in an article in *Security World* magazine: "Equipment should be operated within its design limitations. The limits of rated photo-electric beams and motion detection equipment, for example, are clearly defined. Stretching their coverage range invites false alarms." Lewin warned the alarm companies of an additional problem:

Insurance company underwriters may unintentionally create these same problems when they specifically request installation of certain types of alarm equipment. Physical conditions of the building or the eqiupment itself may render such systems extremely susceptible to false alarms. The insurance industry should make it a point to consult with operating alarm companies, and it is the responsibility of the alarm companies to keep insurance carriers informed about changes in protected premises and in the alarm systems protecting them.

The missapplication of sensor systems has resulted in various studies and recommendations by professional groups and research teams. One example of corrective recommendations is found in the *RAND Report* (Vol. I):

> The sensitivity adjustment of the sensory mechanism shall be so as to suppress false alarms as a result of short flashes of light, wind noises, vehicular noises, or other forces unrelated to genuine alarms.

In an attempt to alleviate application problems, the standards' subcommittee of the Alarm Industry Committee for Combating Crime prepared the following model legislation section for the International Association of Chiefs of Police:

Electronic Protection Units

4.10 Electronic intrusion-detection equipment includes a variety of operating principles that are used in combination with or in lieu of other protection forms. Included are such devices as photoelectric beams, ultrasonic devices, microwave devices and sound detector systems. False alarms will be minimized by strict adherence to the manufacturer's application and operation recommendations. (12.1)

4.11 Systems of invisible radiation, and sound and vibration detection systems, shall be acceptable only when the protected area is provided with a physical boundary. (12.4)

4.12 When a sound detection system is used to protect a premises, the following conditions and requirements shall apply. (12.10)

4.13 All such systems shall be limited to buildings of substantial construction in which a forcible entry through ceiling, roof, walls, or floor will create a significant amount of sound energy. Also, the construction shall be such as to reduce extraneous outside noise. (12.11)

4.14 The preceding paragraph is intended to restrict applications of such systems to buildings or areas constructed of masonry, metal, and glass. (12.12)

There is no question that a properly installed alarm system using sensors can greatly benefit crime prevention. Yet, until manufacturers can produce sensors with improved ability to discern stimuli correctly and until alarm sales and installation personnel upgrade their knowledge and skills in working with sensors, false alarm problems caused by errant sensors will continue to plague law enforcement officials, alarm users, and the alarm industry.

Selected References

1. Alarm Industry Committee for Combating Crime. Minutes of the AICCC standards subcommittee meeting, New York, Aug. 21, 1975.

2. Heckman, F. C. "A Survey of Security Alarm Systems and Their Operational Characteristics." Unpublished master's thesis, Michigan State University, East Lansing, 1973.

3. *July 1975 Progress Report of the Law Enforcement Standards Laboratory.* Washington, D.C.: National Bureau of Standards, 1975.

4. Kakalik, James S., and Sorrel Wildhorn. *Private Police in the United States; Findings and Recommendations,* Vol. 1, R–869/DOJ. Washington, D.C.: Government Printing Office, 1972.

5. Kellem, Carl. Personal interview, Louisville, Ky., Aug. 15, 1975.

6. Lewin, Thomas M. "How Serious Are False Alarms," *Security World,* Vol. 6, No. 9, 1969.

7. Lippert, George R. Untitled article, *Security Distributing and Marketing,* Vol. 2, No. 11, 1972.

8. Poulson, Norval. "What Can Be Done about False Alarms?" *Security World,* Vol. 6, No. 9, 1969.

Related Standards

The following standards and goals may be applicable in implementing Standard 4.4:

4.1   Alarm Systems Research

4.8   Annual Alarm Inspection

4.10 Alarm User Permit Systems and the False Alarm Problem

7.1   Consumers Responsibility for Selection of Security Services

7.2   Consumer Assistance Committees

7.4   Private Security Advertising Standards

Standard 4.5

Training and Instruction of Alarm Users by Alarm Companies

Companies and others installing alarm systems should be required to instruct or train users and their employees in the proper operation of the systems and to provide continued guidance when needed.

Commentary

The responsibilities inherent in the use of an alarm system do not end with proper selection and correct installation. A user must understand the system's operation, as well as the problems and dangers inherent in a false alarm. The problem of false alarms due to user error emphasize the need for improving user responsibility. A study in Cedar Rapids, Iowa, documented that 76 percent of all false alarms during the study period were the result of error or negligence on the part of the alarm owner.

Several other studies of false alarms have also documented the common problem of user error. One, entitled "Feasibility Demonstration of the Citizen's Alarm System," conducted by the Aerospace Corporation, found that alarm user error totaled 33.5 percent of all false alarms received at one central station in a 6-month period. Further, 58.4 percent of these false alarms were of unknown origin, and it can be safely assumed that some portion of that figure could be assigned to alarm user error.

An extensive study of false alarms was conducted by the Alarm Industry Committee for Combating Crime (AICCC). Involved in a 1-month pilot study were 178 central alarm stations servicing 152,425 alarms. During that period there were 35,992 false alarms. Forty-four percent, or 15,994 false alarms, were labeled internal alarms, defined as any alarm initiated from the protected premises and caused by anything other than equipment failure. Of this figure 66.5 percent, according to the AICCC, were caused by alarm user error. An additional 20 percent, or 7,212 unknown alarms, were logged by the central alarm stations during the study period. A portion of these alarms may be assumed to have been caused by alarm user error.

Another research report by the National Crime Prevention Institute, entitled "False Alarm Study," indicated that 61 percent of all false alarms of a selected bank's branches were caused by alarm user/employee error. The report further cited a survey of false alarms from general businesses and residences in which a 50 percent alarm-user-error rate and a 9 percent unknown-reason rate were discovered.

Data on the percentage of false alarms from unknown causes reported by various studies has been included, because alarm industry professionals have suggested that users may deny responsibility for false alarms in order to avoid sanctions imposed by local government authorities or central alarm stations.

Thus, it is probable that a portion of false alarms whose causes are listed in the unknown category are attributable to user error.

Assuming the figures on user error resulting in false alarms are correct and in view of the exceedingly high percentage of false alarms attributable to user error, the causes that contribute to these high percentages should be more closely examined. This was done by the AICCC in their study of false alarms:

	Percent
Failure to lock doors and windows	21.2
Custodial or other personnel improperly entering security areas	17.8
Improper operation by user	14.8
Failure to notify alarm company of change in procedure	12.7
Total percent of internal causes	66.5

This breakdown reflects that user-generated false alarms are caused by a lack of training and occasional negligence in the operation of the system. It also reflects the need for an ongoing training and communication program between the alarm company or central alarm station and alarm users.

Recognition of the need for proper training is cited by the Small Business Administration. In a report entitled "Crime Against Small Business," they recommend:

... that attention be directed to abatement of the serious operational problems of alarm systems including:
training of businessmen and their employees on procedures to reduce the number of false alarms caused by human errors.

The alarm companies are also aware of the need for user training. The previously mentioned AICCC study of false alarms stated:

An intensive study of the largest category, "Internal Alarms" has shown that a substantial portion of those alarms could very likely be eliminated with improved cooperation between alarm users and the alarm company.

In an attempt to deal with alarm user error, AICCC has recommended that central alarm stations initiate educational programs with their subscribers and report to AICCC on the success of their efforts.

When an individual or business concern decides to acquire an alarm system, the main concern is protection of the home or place of business. It is unlikely that the user truly understands the operation of the system or the effect it has on police, the alarm company or central alarm station, and fellow citizens. Therefore, at the time of installation, it is imperative that the proper attitudes and operating

skills be instilled in the alarm user. Accordingly, all companies and others installing alarm systems should be required to provide adequate instruction and proper training on the operation of the system.

In addition to instruction on the basic operations of the alarm system, all users should know the effect the system can have on others, particularly that a false alarm results in a serious loss of law enforcement coverage in the community. One example of the effect false alarms have on law enforcement coverage can be found in a study entitled *Private Security and the Public Interest*. According to the study, the false alarm rate in 1972 in Los Angeles, Calif., was 97 percent, or nearly 32,600 false alarms out of 33,600 alarms. Based on 40 man-minutes per call, the rates resulted in a loss of 22,400 man-hours that year, the equivalent of losing 11 full-time law enforcement officers.

Another negative effect false alarms have on law enforcement officers is building complacency in alarm response. This results in a lowering of priorities of the alarm response, increasing the danger to the officer, and decreasing the chance of apprehension of the suspects and recovery of property and goods in an actual criminal attack. But, even more important, it can lead to such tragic results as the Greenwood Bank incident of 1955, cited in the "False Alarm Study" of the National Crime Prevention Institute. Three officers responded to an alarm. The result—one officer killed and two officers wounded by the gunmen inside the bank. Complacency may well have been a cause of this tragedy.

Another danger involved in false alarms is the possibility that a law enforcement vehicle may be involved in a serious accident while attempting to respond promptly to the scene. Figures cited in the "False Alarm Study" show that:

In any case, alarms do result in vehicles trying to "get there" as fast as safely possible. With as many as 8,000 false alarms annually, every officer's safety is probably endangered many times. False alarms unnecessarily place his life and lives of other drivers in jeopardy. If such calls were valid calls for help, this overall response would be justified—but that is not the case.

From January through July, 1971, 37 SPD vehicle accidents occurred during "emergency responses" of which 17 were ruled "preventable" by the Accident Review Board. These incidents involved 23% of the 157 SPD accidents recorded during this period, and this compares favorably to 1970's figure of 37%. There are no available statistics of how many of these responses involved actual alarms.

Alarm users need to be informed that false alarms may result in the alarm company or central alarm station sending out a serviceman or, in some cases, an armed agent of the company. This response means increased costs for all alarm users and, in the case of armed alarm respondents, can pose a threat to life should confusion develop at the scene involving customers, police, and respondents.

As a part of their service, alarm companies or other installers should provide not only instruction at the time of installation but also continued guidance or training in the use and operation of the system as needed. Over the months or years following the purchase of an alarm system, the principal user may forget all he was taught at the time of purchase. Additionally, the third of fourth generation employee may receive inadequate training from the user in the operation of the alarm system. The user also may not be able to instill the proper mental attitude in his third or fourth generation employee toward alarm system procedure.

When this point is reach (it will be obvious because of frequent employee-actuated false alarms), the principal user should call the alarm company to request assistance. In response, the company should send a representative to provide a refresher course to the user and employees. This training should be, and is in many cases, provided free. If such service is now unavailable, capability to deliver it should be developed. If it is not feasible for an alarm company to provide this service free of charge, it should be included in the servicing arrangement at a minimal cost.

It is clear that if the problem of false alarms is to be effectively dealt with, alarm companies and others who install alarm systems need to take an active role in educating users in the proper use and operation of their systems. Glen D. King, executive director of the International Association of Chiefs of Police, summarized the role of alarm companies in a speech delivered to the National Burglar and Fire Alarm Association:

Your own part in this, it seems to me, lies in educating your customers about the system he has purchased and in making sure he understands what he has been told. You can't, of course, insure that the customer will communicate his knowledge of the system to employees who must come in contact with it, but you can stress the importance of this to the customer and even provide him with instructions that he can distribute to his workers. . . .

What I am proposing is that the alarm industry undertake a campaign to make users more aware of the need to prevent false alarms. The campaign should stress the fact that false alarms are not merely an annoyance for the police.

They are expensive in terms of wasted manpower. They cause telephone and radio congestion. They can contribute to a high accident rate because of emergency response to alarms. And, ultimately, they hurt the business with properly functioning alarm equipment.

Such a program would not have to be costly or elaborate. What I am suggesting is principally an increased emphasis

on educating the buyer of alarm equipment on ways to avoid false alarms.

Initial training as well as refresher and/or retraining programs could be implemented in a relatively short timespan by the alarm industry. The customer, although bearing final responsibility for the system, only understands the system and its implications to that degree to which he was initially trained.

Selected References

1. Alarm Industry Committee for Combating Crime. "False Alarm Study," Washington, D.C.: Alarm Industry Committee for Combating Crime.

2. Cedar Rapids, Iowa, Police Department. *Installation, Test and Evaluation of a Large-Scale Burglar Alarm System for a Municipal Police Department.* Cedar Rapids: Cedar Rapids, Iowa, Police Department, 1971.

3. Cohen, Robert. "Project No. 71-56." Seattle, Wash.: Research and Development Division, Seattle Police Department.

4. Institute for Local Self Government. *Private Security and the Public Interest.* Berkeley, Calif.: Institute for Local Self Government, 1974.

5. King, Glen D. Address before the 28th annual convention, National Burglar and Fire Alarm Association, Las Vegas, Nev., 1975.

6. National Crime Prevention Institute. "False Alarm Study," Louisville, Ky.: University of Louisville, School of Police Administration, undated.

7. Small Business Administration. *Crime Against Small Business.* Washington, D.C.: U.S. Government Printing Office, 1969.

8. Wadhwani, Romesh. *Feasibility Demonstration of Citizens Alarm System,* Vol. 1. Segundo, Calif.: Aerospace Corporation, 1975.

Related Standards

The following standards and goals may be applicable in implementing Standard 4.5:

2.1   Training in Private Security

4.3   Certified Training of Alarm Sales and Service Personnel

4.10   Alarm User Permit Systems and the False Alarm Problem

7.1   Consumers Responsibility for Selection of Security Services

Standard 4.6

Joint Cooperation to Reduce Alarm System Costs

Governmental agencies such as the Law Enforcement Assistance Administration; Federal, State, and local regulatory agencies, the alarm industry; law enforcement agencies; and the telephone companies should work together to reduce the cost of alarm systems and improve the efficiency and reliability of operation and transmission.

Commentary

Alarms offer a proven method for crime reduction and criminal apprehension. Unfortunately, at the same time as crime is rising, the costs connected with the provision of alarm systems and services also are steadily increasing. If alarm systems become so costly that only the wealthy and large companies can afford alarms for their homes and businesses, respectively, the poor and small businessman will suffer a serious injustice. To achieve the two-pronged objective of deterring crime and increasing the availability of alarm systems, many diverse groups will have to join together to search for meaningful approaches to reduce the cost of alarm systems.

The goal of reducing the cost of alarm systems and improving reliability of transmission appears to be hampered by the economic considerations of both telephone companies and central alarm station operators. The problem from the telephone com-

panies' point of view is that provision of high-grade metallic transmission lines to alarm operators is not cost effective. Telephone companies are moving to overcome this problem by increasing their fees for this category of service. To illustrate this point, Anthony J. Grosso, vice president of engineering, ADT Security Systems, pointed out that between 1972 and 1975 a rate increase of 300 percent occurred for metallic facilities used by alarm services in Florida. He further noted that 100 percent increases were imposed in Ohio, New York, and North Carolina.

Alarm operators are seeking rates comparable to those assigned to common carriers. Grosso pointed out that one telephone company agreed to a 25 percent reduction in local facility tariffs for common carriers, but because alarm companies are not interstate common carriers, they did not qualify for the reduction.

Cost problems sometimes are accompanied by unsatisfactory alarm transmission. Norval Poulson of Certified Burglar Alarm Systems cites industry problems with the telephone companies in terms of reliability of transmission:

For many decades alarm companies have used "signal grade" telephone lines for alarm transmission. These are lines of a lower grade not satisfactory for voice transmission. While signal grade lines were entirely adequate for the older alarm systems, the new sophisticated equipment . . .

is not always compatible with the lower grade line—and more false alarms occur.

Poulson further observed that telephone company personnel working on the lines sometimes interfere with the tagged alarm lines, resulting in false alarms.

The alarm industry is attempting to overcome some of these problems. The AC multiplex system was developed to take advantage of the more readily available voice-grade facilities. In 1969, Bell Laboratories, with alarm industry encouragement, began work on equipment that hopefully will provide low-cost McCulloh-type service. However, for alarm company operators to adapt their systems and equipment to a type using the less expensive telephone lines takes time and money. For the near future, alarm companies require lower line rates if they are to continue to provide affordable services. To obtain these lower rates, the full cooperation of telephone companies is needed.

To achieve the objective of low-cost, efficient, and reliable alarm systems the assistance and cooperation of more than telephone companies and alarm station operators is needed. The Federal Communications Commission (FCC) also should become involved, because it regulates the telephone companies and radio and television frequencies—alternates to leased telephone lines.

Although the relationship between the FCC and the alarm industry dates back 15 years, only recently has the FCC displayed an understanding of the alarm industry's problem. In a pamphlet entitled "Alarm Systems, the FCC, and You," by Jeremiah Courtney, credit is given to the Central Station Radio Committee and Frequency Advisory Committee for bringing about FCC understanding and obtaining the allocation of "five pairs of mobile radio service frequencies and a supply of microwave frequencies for alarm circuit use . . . allocated to central stations. . . ." Also, FCC cable accessed television rules may allow, as early as 1977, unused CATV channel for non-voice return alarm system service.

The Law Enforcement Assistance Administration (LEAA) is also involved with the alarm industry. Because various statutory mandates assigned to LEAA under the Omnibus Crime Control and Safe Streets Act of 1968, as amended, provide assistance to projects that prevent crime, the agency has a logical involvement in crime prevention systems.

In an address before the National Burglar and Fire Alarm Association, LEAA Administrator, Richard W. Velde announced that LEAA has established liaison with the FCC to assist in maximizing the effectiveness of the alarms industry in reducing crime. Two meetings have been held between LEAA and the FCC, and monthly meetings between the two organizations have been set up.

Grosso, acting on behalf of the alarm industry, developed the following list of activities where LEAA assistance could be used:

1. Encouraging availability of telephone lines.
2. Encouraging reduction in the cost of telephone facilities.
3. Reducing the time required by telephone companies to provide new facilities and repair existing facilities.
4. Encouraging technical development by the telephone company.
5. Assisting in procurement of new frequencies from the FCC.
6. Assisting in avoiding the imposition of costly technical restrictions by the FCC.

LEAA interaction with the FCC has not, as yet, involved these issues. However, there are indications that, in the near future, LEAA will move into a more active role with FCC and the alarm industry.

Not all problem areas have been presented, nor has every viewpoint involved in the goal to improve transmission capabilities at a reduced cost been covered in depth. Such a presentation is beyond the scope of this report; it would require legal and technical analysis of complex issues.

Although not all inclusive, this standard recognizes the multifaceted problem of achieving alarm system transmissions at reduced costs. Considerations of the several positions have been presented. Efforts by individuals and organizations in terms of time, money, and hard work have brought about a promising situation—a climate where reconciliation of problems is possible if appropriate executives can sit down in a neutral atmosphere and engage in formal and/or informal negotiations. Through such joint efforts, progress toward reduced costs and improved reliability of transmission should occur.

Selected References

1. Courtney, Jeremiah. "Alarm Systems, the FCC, and You." Central Station Electrical Protection Association, 1972.

2. Grosso, Anthony J. "Central Station Signal Transmission Methods." Address before the City-Industry Alarm Task Force of Dallas, Tex., 1975.

3. Poulson, Norval. "False Alarms: An Industry View," *Security World*, Vol. 6, No. 9, 1969.

4. "The Central Station," *Security World*, Vol. 7, No. 9, 1970.

5. Velde, Richard W. Address before the National Burglar and Fire Alarm Association, Las Vegas, Nev., 1975.

Related Standards

The following standards and goals may be applicable in implementing Standard 4.6:

4.1   Alarm Systems Research

8.2   National Private Security Resource and Research Institute

Standard 4.7

Special Trunklines Into Law Enforcement Facilities and Automatic Dialers

Consistent with existing technology, automatic telephone dialing services that are connected to alarm systems should not be keyed or interconnected with emergency law enforcement agency telephone lines.

Commentary

Telephone dialer systems are alarm systems that upon activation, normally use existing telephone lines to relay recorded messages to police or fire stations. In a master's thesis by F. C. Heckman, the following simple operational explanation of the automatic dialer system is given:

> . . . an automatic dialer is connected, usually through a telephone coupler which is rented from the phone company, to an existing regular telephone line. The dialer contains a tape cartridge which is programmed to dial a series of telephone numbers in the event the dialer is triggered. In addition to dialing the programmed numbers, the dialer also gives a prerecorded message. . . . Some use double channel tapes whereby separate rate calls and messages can be made in event of fire or burglary.

The telephone dialer system can provide a business with an alarm service at a cost lower than a central alarm station or a police department alarm. However, for various reasons, many police departments and municipalities have become disillusioned with the dialer. A proposed ordinance in Washing-

ton, D.C., would require dialers to go through telephone answering services; attempts have been made in other localities to ban dialers altogether.

It is the manner in which the automatic dialer transmits the alarm message that so disturbs law enforcement officials. When activated, the dialer plays a pretaped message to the number dialed. Thus, the system can tie up police telephone lines until the dialer completes its program, or until someone at the scene resets the system. Telephone communication can be disrupted considerably when several dialers attempt to deliver their messages simultaneously or when a malfunction occurs. The *RAND Report* (Vol. II) cited an example of one dialer making 22 calls to the Los Angeles police communications center in one day. Also, police communications officers experience frustration when they are not able to question the pretaped message in order to learn additional details regarding the emergency.

In an effort to counter this problem with the telephone dialer system, the *RAND Report* (Vol. I) made a recommendation consistent with this standard:

> No automatic protection device shall be keyed to a primary or secondary telephone trunk line to the public police department, i.e., such devices should be keyed to a special trunk line.

It is essential that the law enforcement agency's primary trunkline and special emergency lines be kept available for the fastest possible handling of person-to-person calls.

Various cities throughout the country have adopted some variation of the above recommendation. Excerpts from existing telephone dialer system ordinances are:

Dallas, Tex.:

Sec. 15C–2. Automatic protection devices—restrictions on keying.

(a) No automatic protection device that is installed after the effective date hereof by any person on premises of any kind in the City of Dallas shall be keyed either to a primary or secondary trunkline.

(b) After the effective date hereof, any alarm equipment supplier who installs automatic protection devices in the City for the purpose of sending pre-recorded emergency messages directly to the Fire Department or the Police Department shall first obtain necessary instructions, including a designated telephone number, from the particular Department concerned with the type of messages, in order to key such devices to a special trunkline into that Department.

(c) Within sixty (60) days after the effective date hereof, all automatic protection devices in the City that were keyed on that date to a primary or secondary trunkline shall be disconnected therefrom. The owner or lessee of any such device shall be responsible for the disconnecting of it.

(d) An owner or lessee of an automatic protection device who has it disconnected as required by (c) of this Section, may authorize an alarm equipment supplier who has a temporary permit or a license, as required by this Chapter, to key the automatic protection device to a special trunkline into the Fire Department or the Police Department, provided that the device meets operational requirements, as set forth in this Chapter.

Sec. 15C–6. Same—operational requirements.

Automatic protection devices installed on premises of any kind in the City that are keyed to a special or operator trunkline shall meet minimum operational requirements, as determined by the Director, as follows:

(a) The content of the type of recorded message to be transmitted by such device must be intelligible and in a format approved by the Chief of the Department concerned as appropriate for the nature of the alarm.

(b) No recorded message shall be delivered to the Police or Fire Department more than three times as the result of a single stimulus of the sensory mechanism.

(c) The length of time for transmitting the recorded message must not exceed fifteen (15) seconds.

(d) The time gap between delivery of each recorded message must be in the range from ten (10) to twelve (12) seconds.

(e) Such device must be capable of transmitting an alarm message to two or more recipients, so that upon installation, any message will be sent not only on a special or operator trunkline, but also on the line of an authorized person having a key to the premises who is available to respond to an emergency.

(f) The sensory mechanism used in connection with such devices must be adjusted to suppress false indications of fire or intrusion, so that the devices will not be actuated by impulses due to transient pressure changes in water pipes, short

flashes of light, wind noises such as the rattling or vibrating of doors or windows, vehicular noise adjacent to the installation or other forces unrelated to genuine alarms.

(g) All components comprising such a device must be maintained by the owner or lessee in good repair to assure reliability of operation.

Tenafly, N.J.:

B. Equipment—No dial alarm devices shall be finally registered until a test alarm has been made by the owner in conjunction with the Chief of Police or his representatives;

C. No dial alarm devices shall be permitted unless of a type approved by the Board of Police Commissioners in accordance with the rules promulgated under Section 10 of this Ordinance. Any such equipment must have the approval of the New Jersey Bell Telephone Company or its successor;

D. All dial alarms shall be coded to dial a special separate number which number can be obtained from the Chief of Police, and no dial alarm shall be coded to dial the number of the general police switchboard of the Borough to Tenafly;

E. Any dial alarm device shall be coded as well to notify a relative, neighbor, or other third party who will be disclosed in the registration of said equipment as required by this Ordinance;

F. All dial alarm devices shall be capable of disconnect to enable the owner to call the Police switchboard to indicate that a false alarm has occurred;

Ladue, Mo.:

Automatic dialers must be installed on a separate telephone line unless the device incorporates equipment capable of seizing the telephone line and a method to abort a false alarm. Automatic dialers cannot be keyed to the trunkline of the police department.

International Association of Chiefs of Police (IACP): Model ordinance

Section 12. Automatic dialing device—interconnecting to primary trunklines.

(a) No automatic dialing device shall be interconnected to a primary trunkline after the effective date of this ordinance.

(b) Within (90) days after the effective date of this ordinance, all automatic dialing devices interconnected to a primary trunkline shall be disconnected therefrom. The owner or lessee of such device shall be responsible for having the device disconnected within the (90)-day time period.

(c) Automatic dialing devices designed to transmit signals directly to the (police department) may be interconnected to a special trunkline into the department. Before such a device is interconnected to a special trunkline, the person performing this operation shall first obtain instructions from the (police department) concerning the procedure to be followed. The (police department) shall designate the number to be used for this purpose.

Further, the IACP model ordinance lists standards for automatic dialing services:

Section 15. Automatic dialing device—standards.

Automatic dialing devices installed on any premises within the (city) which are interconnected to a special trunkline transmitting signals into the (police department) or to a telephone line directly serviced by telephone company operators that will be responded to by members of the (police department) shall meet the following minimum standards, as determined by the (police chief):

(a) The contents of the recorded message to be transmitted by such device must be intelligible and in a format approved by the (police chief) as appropriate for the type of emergency being reported.

(b) Upon a single stimulus of the alarm device, an automatic dialing device may place two separate calls to the (police department) via the special trunkline. No such call shall be longer than one minute and fifteen seconds in duration. There must be at least three minutes between the completion of the first call and the initiation of the second, and the second call must be clearly identified as a second call.

(c) Messages transmitted during such calls, stating the location and nature of the alarm condition, shall not exceed fifteen (15) seconds in length.

(d) The time gap between delivery of messages must be less than five (5) seconds.

(e) All such devices shall be capable of transmitting an emergency message to two or more separate locations, so that upon activation any message may be sent not only on a special trunkline or a telephone line serviced directly by telephone company operators, but also to a location where an authorized person is available to respond to the emergency message, and to open the premises on which the device is installed.

(f) The sensory apparatus and hardware comprising such devices shall be maintained by the owner or lessee in such physical condition that false alarms will be minimized.

(g) This Section shall apply only to those automatic dialing devices interconnected to the communication center of the (police department), any other municipal office or to telephone company operators.

These ordinances represent a positive response to difficulties encountered by the police with telephone dialer systems. Thus, if a tremendous natural disaster, such as an earthquake, occurs or a single dialer malfunctions, only the special trunkline will be tied up.

Another feasible alternative involves sending the pretaped messages from all automatic dialers to central stations or answering services for routing to law enforcement agencies. This method may provide a workable alternative to total prohibition of dialer alarms by localities as a result of the concern over overburdened law enforcement communication facilities.

Before law enforcement officials or government authorities initiate any action involving automatic telephone dialers, consideration should be given to the result their actions may have on overall crime prevention in the community, especially the cost trade-offs between handling an automatic dialer alarm or investigating a burglary.

Selected References

1. "Alarm Ordinance." Ladue, Mo.

2. City of Dallas. "Ordinance #13139, Emergency Reporting Equipment and Procedures." Dallas, Tex., 1971.

3. Heckman, F. C. "A Survey of Security Alarms Systems and Their Operational Characteristics." Unpublished master's thesis, Michigan State University, East Lansing, 1973.

4. Kakalik, James, and Sorrel Wildhorn. *The Private Police Industry: Its Nature and Extent*, Vol. II, R-870/DOJ. Washington, D.C.: Government Printing Office, 1972.

5. ———. *Private Police in the United States: Findings and Recommendations*, Vol. 1, R-869/DOJ.

6. Research Section, Research Division, International Association of Chiefs of Police. "Model Burglar and Holdup Alarm Systems Ordinance." Gaithersburg, Md., 1973.

Related Standards

The following standards and goals may be applicable in implementing Standard 4.7:

4.2   Backup Power for Alarms

4.8   Annual Alarm Inspection

4.10 Alarm User Permit Systems and the False Alarm Problem

7.1   Consumers Responsibility for Selection of Security Services

Standard 4.8

Annual Alarm Inspection

Local governments should require all alarm system users whose systems ordinarily result in a law enforcement response to have their systems inspected at least once each year.

Commentary

False alarms not only reduce the efficacy of using alarm systems as a primary crime prevention tool, but also are a threat to both citizens and law enforcement officers. Users of alarm systems that alert other citizens or law enforcement officers to a criminal attack should do everything possible to ensure their systems will not false alarm due to mechanical failure or malfunction. In the absence of a servicing and maintenance contract, the user should arrange for annual inspection service.

Underwriters' Laboratories, Inc. (UL) has included an annual system inspection requirement in many of its standards; some UL standards even require inspection more frequently than once a year. UL standards require inspections of police station connected burglar alarm units, local burglar alarm units, central station burglar alarm units, holdup alarm units, mercantile and bank burglar alarm systems, and proprietary burglar alarm system units.

A representative example of the language used in UL standards requiring inspection follows:

43.1 All alarm installation and alarm receiving equipment shall be maintained under contract by the operating company and shall be inspected at intervals sufficiently frequent to insure continuously reliable service. In no case shall the interval between regular maintenance inspections exceed 1 year. (UL Standard 365, Police Station Connected Burglar Alarm Units and Systems, March 1975)

A document prepared by the Alarm Industry Committee for Combating Crime provides a sample of the language found in servicing and maintenance contracts:

The company agrees to install and maintain during the term of the agreement all necessary transmitters, wire connections and instruments necessary to convey signals from the subscriber's premises to the alarm company (to the police communications center) (or in the case of local alarm systems for proper operation of the system) and all sensing devices, appliances, cabinets, cables, conduits, foils, screens, springs, tubing, switches, wire and all other materials specified in the schedule of protection (the schedule of protection is part of the contract and it spells out the nature and extent of protection provided by the alarm company) and the alarm company will maintain such system in good working order. . . .

The Texas Municipal League's "Burglar Alarm Code for Texas Cities" extensively incorporates the standards of the Underwriters' Laboratories, Inc., and the American National Standards Institute. The League's code mandates annual inspection of alarm systems.

The International Association of Chiefs of Police, in their model burglar and holdup alarm system ordinance, includes a requirement of yearly inspection of alarm systems for annual renewal of the alarm user permit. Section 26, 2, D of this model ordinance states:

Every alarm user licensed under this Section shall be required to have its alarm system inspected at least once a year by a licensed alarm business, and post a certificate of such inspection on the premise where the alarm system is maintained.

The alarm industry, law enforcement agencies, and an independent testing laboratory support an annual alarm system inspection. However, the alarm system user would have to pay for the annual inspection. The cost of annual inspection should be determined with extensive citizen input. If the cost of an annual inspection is kept low and the user understands the reasons for inspection, this standard will enhance the crime prevention capabilities of alarm systems.

Selected References

1. Alarm Industry Committee for Combating Crime. Correspondence in response to the working outline of Task Force Report, Aug. 1, 1975.

2. International Association of Chiefs of Police, Legal Research Section, Research Division. "Model Burglar and Hold-up Alarm Systems Ordinance." Gaithersburg, Md.: IACP, 1973.

3. Private Security Task Force, Committee C Meeting, Louisville, Ky., Aug. 14-16, 1975.

4. Texas Municipal League. "A Burglar Alarm Code for Texas Cities." Austin, Tex.: Texas Municipal League, 1975.

5. Underwriters' Laboratories, Inc. "Standard 365 —Police Station Connected Burglar Alarm Units and Systems." Underwriters' Laboratories, Inc., March 1975.

Related Standards

The following standards and goals may be applicable in implementing Standard 4.8:

4.2 Backup Power for Alarms

4.4 Compatibility of Sensors

4.7 Special Trunklines Into Law Enforcement Facilities and Automatic Dialers

4.9 Alarm Systems Servicing Capability

7.1 Consumers Responsibility for Selection of Security Services

Standard 4.9

Alarm Systems
Servicing Capability

Every jurisdiction should have a disclosure law requiring persons in the business of alarm systems sales to make known prior to a sale where the alarm system can be serviced or where a service arrangement can be obtained. Proof that a servicing arrangement, such as a contract or agreement, is in existence should be submitted to a law enforcement agency by persons desiring to transmit alarm signals to that agency.

Commentary

The recent rise in burglaries across the country has brought a corresponding rise in the business of alarm systems sales.[1] A major problem confronting users of these systems is obtaining adequate servicing. When alarm systems malfunction, owners often discover that no servicing is available through either the original dealers or other concerns, thus rendering the systems virtually useless. Further, if an alarm company goes out of business, large numbers of

subscribers may be left with no means of maintaining their systems.

In order to protect consumers and prevent disruption of the important crime-deterring effect of alarm systems, persons selling alarm systems should be required to disclose whether a service capability exists for the systems sold. If sellers cannot service the equipment, consumers should be informed where such servicing can be obtained so that service arrangements can be made at time of purchase.

The need for prearranged servicing becomes apparent when the alarm user attempts to obtain repair or maintenance service from a company other than the original dealer or installer. Some of these difficulties that arise have been pointed out by members of the Alarm Industry Committee for Combating Crime:

When we get calls from people . . . how do we make a determination as to whether we want to service them or not? . . . We will not repair an alarm system where we don't know who installed it and how that man worked. . . .

. . . You must remember that an alarm system is not like a refrigerator or automobile where people know what to expect. You can go into a residence and find that the men who did the installation improvised in every possible way. There is no way we can figure out how the circuit went, particularly if the wires are concealed within the walls. . . .

There are reasons other than technical difficulties cited by the above for the reluctance of alarm com-

---

[1] Alarm system sales—any person, firm, or corporation that sells or leases and/or installs automatic protection devices that transmit over regular telephone lines; the alarm system being any assembly of equipment, mechanical or electrical, arranged to signal the presence of illegal entry or activity requiring urgent attention and to which police are expected to respond.

panies to service equipment other than their own. Carl Kellem of the National Crime Prevention Institute points out that to service other companies' systems requires available spare parts, and most companies are not willing to bear this additional expense. Therefore, unless the owner agrees to an extensive service and maintenance contract allowing replacement of most of the original equipment, alarm companies usually will refuse to service an alarm system they did not sell or install. Kellem points out that reputable alarm companies do not wish to service equipment sold or installed by other companies, because they do not wish to encourage alarm systems sales by companies that cannot or will not provide maintenance.

Reputable alarm companies believe that servicing marginal alarm systems sold by less creditable firms that neither have nor intend to develop servicing capability only helps to keep these sellers in business and encourages formation of new fly-by-night companies. Some of the problems posed by less creditable alarm companies are described in an article in *Security Distributing and Marketing* magazine:

About a dozen New Jersey burglar alarm installation companies will try and tighten up their own future security by creating intra-industry standards to thwart "fly-by-night" electronic entrepreneurs allegedly undermining the integrity of their firms.

An unexpected development from the two-hour session was a consensus expressed by the officials that something should be done to curb a proliferation of "shady fly-by-nights" trying to cash in on the present sales boom in residential burglar alarms and their installation by giving shoddy, cheap equipment, little, if any, service or maintenance, and a black eye to the legitimate firms.

. . . those companies "often open and close in the space of about three or four months and keep the security keys (a series of trade keys able to turn alarm systems on or off) which can open anybody's (system)."

"The traits are poor equipment—though you don't know it immediately—poor installation, a 'disappearing act' at service time, and high pressure sales pitches in high-crime areas."

The initial recommendation of this standard—a disclosure law—would protect both buyers and sellers of alarm systems from disreputable practices, as well as ensure continuous alarm service. Various community or governmental organizations should do their part by informing the consumer of possible servicing problems. Then, prior to sale, an alarm system company should inform the consumer of its servicing capabilities. If these steps are taken, a much more favorable climate will develop between the alarm industry, the purchaser of alarm equipment, and law enforcement officials.

This standard also recommends that proof of servicing capability for an alarm system intended to terminate at a law enforcement agency be required prior to connection of the system. This requirement is based on the belief that a citizen who desires additional protection, such as that provided by a direct connection to the police department, accepts an additional responsibility.

It appears that there is constitutional support for a standard requiring a service capability for systems connected to law enforcement agencies. The Nebraska case of *United States Brewers' Association, Inc.* v. *State* addresses police powers to make such a requirement:

The exercise of the police power must be directed toward and have a rational relation to the basic interest of society rather than the mere advantage of particular individuals. . . . A police regulation cannot arbitrarily invade private property or personal rights. There must be some clear and real connection between the assumed purpose of the law and its actual provisions. . . .

Actual examples of ordinances requiring service capabilities of alarm systems do exist. For example, a Dallas, Tex., ordinance requires alarm companies to ensure 24-hour-a-day, 7-day-a-week servicing capability, and to provide a maintenance manual and schematics to the purchaser of the alarm system and the director of public utilities. Similarly, a Ladue, Mo., ordinance states that all suppliers leasing, selling, or installing alarm systems must be able to repair the systems and provide purchasers with written material on how the devices operate.

In summary, a servicing disclosure law is necessary to reduce problems arising from lack of knowledge about the need for servicing, to help eliminate dealers capitalizing on the fear of crime to sell faulty or poor-quality alarm equipment, and to reduce unnecessary burdens on law enforcement agencies.

Selected References

1. Alarm Industry Committee for Combating Crime. Minutes of meeting, Aug. 26, 1975.

2. City of Dallas. "Ordinance #13139, Emergency Reporting Equipment and Procedures." Dallas, Tex., 1971.

3. Division of Public Safety. "Alarm Control Ordinance (Proposed)." Portland, Oreg.: Division of Public Safety, Multnomah County, 1975.

4. Kakalik, James S., and Sorrel Wildhorn. *Private Police in the United States: Findings and Recommendations*, Vol. I, R-869/DOJ. Washington, D.C.: Government Printing Office, 1972.

5. Kellem, Carl (instructor). Personal interview. Louisville, Ky.: National Crime Prevention Institute, Aug. 26, 1975.

6. McQueeny, James. "New Jersey Alarm Firms

Plan Crackdown on Fly-by-Nights," *Security Distributing and Marketing*, Vol. 3, No. 1, 1973.

7. Private Security Task Force. Committee "C" Meeting, Louisville, Ky., Aug. 14-16, 1975.

8. *United States Brewers' Association, Inc.* v. *State*, 192 Neb. 328, 22 N.W. 2d 544 (1974).

Related Standards

The following standards and goals may be applicable in implementing Standard 4.9:

4.8   Annual Alarm Inspection

7.1   Consumers Responsibility for Selection of Security Services

Standard 4.10

Alarm User Permit Systems and the False Alarm Problem

Local governments should establish and enforce an alarm user permit system to regulate and reduce false alarms. Verified excessive false alarming ordinarily resulting in a law enforcement response should be grounds for permit revocation, suspension, and other appropriate penalties.

Commentary

The most common problem with all types of alarm systems is false alarms. This drawback has lessened the alarm systems' role in crime prevention. But it is not a problem without a remedy, because experience has demonstrated that where strict control by municipal government over alarm users exists, statistics show a reduction in false alarming.

The sanctions exercised by governments over alarm users should focus on control of false alarming. The goal of the permit system is to bring about more effective crime prevention.

False Alarm Definition

To understand the advantages and desirability of the alarm system permit, there first must be comprehension of the false alarm problem. In the case of "false alarms," it is difficult to develop a simplistic definition of the problem. Bernard Beerman, counsel

for the Alarm Industry Committee for Combating Crime (AICCC), states:

The most volatile issue that affects the alarm industry today is the issue of false alarms. We believe that any report on private security must address itself to standards and goals on this issue. . . . A primary question which is raised and seldom definitively answered is, what is a false alarm? The alarm industry believes that the mere use of the term "false alarm" is inherently misleading.

There is no single definition of false alarms that is accepted by the various entities involved in or affected by alarm systems. This lack of an accepted definition makes discussion of the problem difficult among law enforcement personnel, alarm industry representatives, and alarm users. The sampling of definitions that follows illustrates how confusion may result when referring to false alarms:

The definition used for this study is: any alarm signal received that was not caused by a burglar is a false alarm. (Cedar Rapids Second Year Report)

While clearly it is possible to define a false alarm as one where an investigation indicates no criminal activity, the alarm industry believes such a definition is grossly misleading, . . . (Alarm Industry Committee for Combating Crime, False Alarm Study)

False alarm means an alarm signal necessitating response by the police department where an emergency situation does not exist. . . . (Multnomah County, Oreg., Alarms Ordinance)

A false alarm is an emergency alarm activated by inadvertence, negligence or unintentional acts to which the city police or fire department responds, including malfunction of the alarm system. The definition excludes alarms caused by: malfunctions of the indicator at the police station; testing or repair of telephone equipment or lines; acts of God, such as earthquake, flood, windstorm, thunder or lightning; an attempted illegal entry of which there is visible evidence; the resident acting under a sincere belief that a need exists to call the police or fire department; a call to police cancelling the alarm by giving proper code number, prior to arrival of the police or fire department. If a doubt exists as to the cause of a false alarm, the Chief of Police shall resolve it in favor of the alarm user. (Ladue, Mo., Alarm Ordinance)

"False alarm" means activation of an alarm system through mechanical failure, malfunction, improper installation, or the negligence of the owner or lessee of an alarm system or of his employees or agents. Such terminology does not include, for example, alarms caused by hurricanes, tornadoes, earthquakes or other violent conditions or acts of God. (Alarm Industry Committee for Combating Crime and Texas Municipal League)

False alarm—an alarm signal transmitted in the absence of an alarm condition. These may be classified according to causes. (Law Enforcement Assistance Administration)

The problem of definition is acutely encountered when attempts are made to establish monetary fines for false alarms. In monetary fine systems, the reasons for false alarms can be attributed to causes beyond the user's control, but, when no one on the scene of an alarm is capable of making an accurate assessment of cause, the usual practice is for police officers to list the cause as user error. Before any permit system is implemented, it is important that a definition of false alarm is agreed upon by all those who will be affected.

Because resolution of the controversy over what constitutes a false alarm is so difficult for law enforcement agencies, alarm companies, and alarm users, perhaps the word "fault" should be used to replace the term "false alarm." "Fault" seems to be a more suitable and useful label, because the disagreement over definition invariably leads to a discussion over what physical effect constitutes a legitimate initiating source. Stated another way, "whose fault is it that the alarm system functioned correctly at the wrong time?" An AICCC document lists four causes of alarms that bring clarity to the concept of allocation of "fault":

It was almost the universal consensus of the people in the industry that there are four major causes of alarms.

1. **Actual Alarms.** Any actual or attempted entry from anyone not in the employ of the alarm user; or damage to the property from any cause detected by the alarm system.

2. **External Alarms.** Any alarm initiated in a place other than the premises protected. For example: telephone line problems.

3. **Internal Alarms.** Any alarm initiated from the protected premises caused by anything other than equipment malfunction.

4. **Equipment Alarms.** Any malfunction of alarm equipment causing an alarm.

The term "false alarm rate" also needs examination and clarification. When the term is used, the alarm industry reacts negatively. The false alarm rate refers to the number of alarms that are not provable criminal attacks out of the total number of alarms received in a given period. For example, if there were one alarm in one month and it was false, the false alarm rate is 100 percent. This one false alarm may have come from one alarm system out of a thousand systems operating in a given location. Using the term without proper qualification and agreement will not foster cooperation and good will between law enforcement agencies and the alarm industry.

Need for Alarm User Permit

The justification for government control over alarm systems arises primarily from the thousands of man-hours and law enforcement dollars wasted in answering false alarms. Examples from the commentary of the Texas Municipal League's model ordinance vividly illustrate the cost of false alarms: In a 9-month period the Waco, Tex., Police Department handled 2,088 false alarms, expending 1,120 man-hours, at a cost of $7,100. In a 6-month period, the Corpus Christi, Tex., Police Department handled 2,300 false alarms, expending 2,320 man-hours, at a cost of $21,850. An article appearing in *Security Systems Digest* stated that the false alarm problem in Washington, D.C., was costing the city more than $100,000 a year. This sample of selective data suggests that municipalities across the country expend vast sums of money and valuable man-hours on false alarms.

The size, scope, and nature of the false alarm problem provide the rationale for the need for regulation. The alarm user permit system can provide a degree of control.

As an illustration of what an alarm user permit is and what it includes and provides for, the user permit section of the International Association of Chiefs of Police (IACP) model burglar and holdup alarm ordinance is presented in its entirety:

Section 26.   **Alarm User Permits.**

(a) Permit—Within (90) days after the effective date of this ordinance, every alarm user shall obtain an alarm user permit for each alarm system he operates within this (city) from the (police chief). This paragraph does not require that licensed alarm businesses obtain a permit under this Section when it leases or provides services to alarm system users. If a licensed alarm business does, however, use an alarm system to protect its own premises, it shall obtain a permit for such system as required in this Section.

(b) Alarm User Permit Application—

(1) The alarm user applying for the permit required in paragraph (a) of this Section, shall state on a permit application form to be prepared by the (police department) and approved by the city attorney: his name, the address of the residence or business or businesses in or upon which the alarm system has been or will be installed, his telephone number, the type of alarm system (local, direct connect, central station, etc.), the alarm business or businesses selling, installing, monitoring, inspecting, responding to and/or maintaining the alarm system and the name and the telephone number of at least one other person (in the case of a corporate alarm user applicant, at least two other persons) who can be reached at any time, day or night, and who is authorized to respond to an alarm signal and who can open the premises in which the system is installed.

(2) Any alarm user who installs a system (90) days or more after the effective date of this ordinance must submit with the application a certificate of a licensed alarm business stating that in the opinion of such business the alarm system complies with Section 21 of this ordinance. Such certificate shall satisfy the requirements of paragraph (d)(1) of this Section for the year in which the alarm permit is first obtained.

(c) Alarm User Permit Fee—

(1) There shall be a ($5) permit fee for the first year.

(2) There shall be an annual renewal fee of ($2).

(d) Every alarm user licensed under this Section shall be required to have its alarm system inspected at least once a year by a licensed alarm business, and post a certificate of such inspection on the premises where the alarm system is maintained. The certificate shall state that in the opinion of the alarm business:

(1) the alarm system complies with the applicable provisions of Section 21 of this ordinance if the system was installed (90) days or more after the effective date of this ordinance, or

(2) the alarm system is safe and reliable if it was installed prior to (90) days after the effective date of this ordinance.

(e) An applicant for an alarm user permit may file a request with the (police chief), requesting that he temporarily waive the requirements of paragraphs (c)(2) and (d)(1) of this Section in circumstances in which the public's safety, health or welfare is involved.

(f) The information contained in an alarm user permit application required by this Section and other information received by the (police chief) through correspondence or communications with an alarm user shall be securely maintained and restricted to inspection only by the (police chief or certain officers or city employees specifically assigned the responsibility for handling and processing alarm user permits) in the course of official duties. If the (police chief or any employee of the city) is found to have knowingly or willfully revealed the information contained in an alarm user permit application or in correspondence or communications with an alarm user to any other person for any purpose not related to this ordinance or official law enforcement matters and without the express written consent of the alarm user supplying such information, (the police chief or the city employee) shall be guilty of a misdemeanor as set forth in (refer to appropriate section of the municipal code or applicable state law).

(g) Any alarm system user who operates an alarm system without first obtaining a permit as required by this Section,

or who, after having a permit revoked, or suspended, and after exhausting his rights to hearing and appeal fails to disconnect his alarm system, shall be in violation of this ordinance.

Enforcement of Alarm User Permit

Enforcement of a permit system is the most perplexing problem. Any sanction incorporated in a user permit system should be aimed at the control of false alarms, not designed to punish the user. Punishment of a householder trying to protect his home or a businessman seeking to safeguard his factory will not serve to promote the goals of crime prevention.

Many user permit systems incorporate monetary penalties for false alarms. However, monetary penalties are not believed to be the best way to enforce a permit system for the following reasons:

1. Lacking a proper definition of false alarm, it is not proper to impose fines.

2. The person making the determination of the cause of the false alarm may be unqualified.

3. Fines may force a small businessman to give up his alarm system but not affect a large corporation.

4. Fines may cause a reduction in new alarm systems. This is contrary to the goals of crime prevention, i.e., as many systems in operation as possible.

5. No data exist proving user permit systems imposing monetary fines are any more effective than systems relying on suspension or revocation.

Revocation and suspension of permits used as an enforcement system to control the false alarm problem without forcing users into giving up their alarm systems is superior to the monetary fine approach. The punishment cost under this method is the price of a new permit after a given number of false alarms has been reached and the permit revoked. This concept appears agreeable to the alarm industry, providing the definition of false alarms is limited to those over which the alarm user has some control, e.g., false alarms caused by mechanical failure, malfunction, improper installation, or the negligence of the owners or lessees of alarm systems or of their employees or agents. Excluded from causes leading to revocation would be alarms caused by hurricanes, tornados, earthquakes, or other violent conditions or acts of God.

The examination of several user permit systems imposing revocation and suspension sanctions revealed that they allow an average of 3.75 free false alarms before action is taken against a user. Three of the four systems recommend notification of revocation/suspension by mail, with 15 days to file a report on corrective actions taken. All have an appeal procedure to continue use of the alarm system.

The Multnomah County, Oreg., ordinance requires a charge of $180 for the third suspension of a user's permit. The IACP model ordinance provides a penalty of up to $200 a day for continuing to use a system on a revoked permit. These stiff monetary penalties reflect the severity of the problem as seen by the authorities.

The revocation and suspension sanction method chosen for the IACP model ordinance was worked out over 2 years of negotiation and discussion between the alarm industry and IACP. Although acceptance was not by any means unanimous, IACP and the alarm industry have agreed to proceed with this system of sanctions as an initial model.

Many reasons have led various cities to adopt permit systems. However, regardless of the nature of the causitive reasons, positive results generally have been achieved with the application of closely monitored permit systems. An article in the July 1975 issue of *Police Chief* pointed out:

> After two years of experience, Pasadena, California, police personnel are delighted with the dramatic results of the 1972 Burglary and Robbery Permit Ordinance passed by the city council. In the five-month period between November, 1974 and April, 1975, there were only 786 false alarms (5.25 daily) as compared to 1,941 (12.85 daily) during a five-month period prior to the ordinance. This 60 percent reduction represents approximately $10,178 worth of police resources conserved. It is worth noting that during the 12-month period from April, 1974 to 1975, the number of alarm systems in use increased 27 percent.

The alarm industry, like any other industry, wants minimum regulation and would prefer to accept the user permit systems only after attempts to achieve low false alarm rates through the cooperative efforts of all involved have failed to resolve the problem. The alarm industry is also on record as opposing a system of fines, except as a last resort.

Steven Watts, Multnomah County, Oreg., Police Department, in a speech to the Western Burglar and Fire Alarm Association, stated the case for permit systems:

> I strongly believe that a program which brings the alarm industry and law enforcement together, and which incorporates a functional alarm ordinance into the community will cause the following to occur:
> 1. Total number of false alarms will decrease.
> 2. The inordinate number of police man hours expended in responding to false alarms will decrease.
> 3. The quality of alarm systems and companies will increase causing the number of arrests for burglary to increase.
> 4. The opportunity for crime to be committed will decrease.

The user permit system appears to be a necessity. It is the only effective tool for weeding out alarm systems that are improperly installed, inadequately maintained, and improperly operated. Without an alarm user permit system, a cycle can emerge where the law enforcement officer or agency reduces the priority of the response, resulting in less likelihood of capture of a suspect and an increased number of alarms that appear false.

Selected References

1. Alarm Industry Committee for Combating Crime. "False Alarm Study." Washington, D.C.: AICCC.

2. ————. Correspondence on working outline of Task Force Report, dated Aug. 1, 1975.

3. "Alarms Permit Ordinance Saves Police Department Time and Money," *The Police Chief*, Vol. XLII, No. 7, July 1975, p. 12.

4. Beerman, Bernard. Address to the Private Security Task Force. July 11, 1975, Chicago, Ill.

5. Cedar Rapids, Iowa, Police Department. *Installation, Test, and Evaluation of a Large-Scale Burglar Alarm System for a Municipal Police Department*. Cedar Rapids, Iowa, Police Department.

6. ————. *Installation, Test, and Evaluation of a Large-Scale Burglar Alarm System for a Municipal Police Department—Report of the Second Year of Operation*. Cedar Rapids: Cedar Rapids, Iowa, Police Department.

7. Cohen, Robert. "Project No. 71-56." Seattle, Wash.: Research and Development Division, Seattle Police Department.

8. "D.C. Police Prepare New Alarm Regulation," *Security Systems Digest*, Vol. 5, No. 12, June 5, 1974, p. 10.

9. International Association of Chiefs of Police, Research Section, Research Division. "Model Burglar and Holdup Alarm Systems Ordinance." Gaithersburg, Md.: IACP, 1973.

10. National Crime Prevention Institute. "False Alarm Study," Louisville, Ky.: University of Louisville, School of Police Administration.

11. Small Business Administration. *Crime Against Small Business*. Washington, D.C.: Government Printing Office, 1969.

12. *Terms and Definitions for Intrusion Alarm Systems*. Washington, D.C.: U.S. Government Printing Office, 1974.

13. Texas Municipal League. "Burglar Alarm Code for Texas Cities." Austin, Tex.: Texas Municipal League, 1975.

14. Wadhwani, Romesh. *Feasibility Demonstration of the Citizen Alarm System*, Vol. 1. Segundo, Calif.: Aerospace Corporation, 1975.

15. Watts, Steven B. Address to the Western

Burglar and Fire Alarm Association. Portland, Oreg., 1975.

16. ———. "Alarm Control Ordinance," Portland, Oreg.: Division of Public Safety, Multnomah County, 1975.

Related Standards

The following standards and goals may be applicable in implementing Standard 4.10:

4.2   Backup Power for Alarms

4.4   Compatibility of Sensors

4.5   Training and Instruction of Alarm Users by Alarm Companies

4.7   Special Trunklines Into Law Enforcement Facilities and Automatic Dialers

4.8   Annual Alarm Inspection

7.1   Consumers Responsibility for Selection of Security Services

7.2   Consumer Assistance Committees

9.1   State Regulation

Standard 4.11

Ownership and Operation of Alarm Systems

Ownership or operation of alarm systems should be the province of private enterprise, and government ownership or operation of alarm systems should be discouraged provided, however, that government should not be precluded from:

1. Operating such systems in temporary or emergency situations;

2. Owning or operating alarm systems that are located in publicly owned or leased buildings, annunciate in the same or other government buildings, and are responded to by government employees;

3. Providing private individuals and businesses with funds for the acquisition of crime prevention devices provided that such devices are purchased on the open market and remain the property of the consumer.[1]

Commentary

Almost all of the standards in this chapter en-

courage some degree of positive government involvement in the alarms industry. Government involvement is appropriate and needed to bring uniformity of regulation to the industry, to ensure the maintenance of a certain level of professionalism, to share the cost of research on alarm equipment and transmission methods when such activities would be of mutual benefit, and, in general, to further and foster a cooperative relationship between persons employed in the public and private sectors. This standard, although couched in negative phrasing, has a positive purpose in seeking to ensure that government refrains from providing alarm service in competition with the private sector. Such competition ultimately would result in the demise of the private sector's role in the alarm system field.

Chapter 6 states a similar concept in regard to prohibiting law enforcement personnel from holding certain private security jobs. Employment of a law enforcement officer as a private detective is prohibited because implicit conflicts are inherent in that job. The same is true of local governments providing alarm services, because the nature of such an arrangement leads directly to conflicts with private business and results in inappropriate use of tax dollars. This practice has occurred in the past, and all involved parties have become wiser from the experience. Governments should not continue or

---

[1] The National Advisory Committee on Criminal Justice Standards and Goals adopted a fourth exception, to wit: "Government ownership or operation of alarm systems is appropriate when the cost of a private alarm system puts it out of reach of a significant number of potential customers in an economically depressed, high-crime area."

In addition, some members of the National Advisory Committee objected to the standard in its entirety as expressing an economic and social philosophy, rather than criminal justice policy.

start this activity but should move on to the positive areas of involvement outlined in this chapter.

Concerning the question of government ownership of alarms, all parties agree on one point—there are valid exceptions to the rule. The first exception is a temporary and emergency situation that might require government involvement with alarms. In this regard, this standard is in agreement with the following position of counsel for the Alarm Industry Committee for Combating Crime (AICCC):

In situations where crime has reached critical and unmanageable levels, where national security is involved or where vital industries are threatened, there may be emergency justification for limited and temporary governmental involvement with alarm systems.

Also included in this area are portable tactical alarms (stakeout alarms) employed by many law enforcement agencies for temporary use in small businesses located in high-crime areas or warehouses suffering frequent criminal attack. Because these alarms are not permanent installations, they are excluded from the prohibition rule. In fact, these installations may inspire the person whose property has been protected to acquire an alarm system.

The second exception is the use of government-owned and -operated alarm systems located in publicly owned buildings that annunciate in the same or different building, resulting in a government employee response. This would protect existing practices by the General Services Administration and military installations, for example.

The third exception would allow cities to accept grants for experimentation when adequate and fair provisions are spelled out for disposition of the equipment and subscribers at the conclusion of the grant. Giving grants and providing funds to small businesses and citizens in high-crime and economically depressed areas for the purchase of protection devices would come under this exception. Allocation of government funds to private citizens for the purchase of alarm systems would be contingent on their acquisition from the public marketplace.

The International Association of Chiefs of Police (IACP) has gone on record as opposing government involvement with alarm system ownership and operation. At their 1975 annual meeting in Denver, Colo., the following official association position was presented:

Resolution

Police Involvement in the Alarm Industry

WHEREAS, There has been an increasing involvement of public law enforcement agencies in the security alarm industry, and

WHEREAS, The involvement of public agencies in competition with private enterprise is an infringement by government on the free enterprise system, therefore, be it

RESOLVED, That the installation, maintenance, and servicing of security alarms on or in private establishments is a service to be provided by private enterprise, and, be it further

RESOLVED, That the police role is to respond to such alarms and not to get into the business of providing security equipment or services that can be obtained from reputable private dealers, and, be it

FURTHER RESOLVED, That this resolution be recorded in the minutes of the Association and forwarded to the officers of the National Burglar and Fire Alarm Association for distribution to their membership.

What is important to note about the resolution is that the alarm industry and law enforcement agencies are in agreement on the issue because they realize that where competition exists genuine cooperation is impossible.

Other groups and individuals have come out against government ownership and operation of alarm systems. Among these groups is the Alarm Committee of the Private Security Advisory Council. This group of practitioners has taken a position similar to the IACP resolution:

Each of the Committee members and, indeed, we believe we speak for all of the people in the Private Security Sector, believes municipal operation of alarm systems under the guise of attempting in some way to control crime by more effective detection devices is totally inappropriate. . . . The Alarm Committee believes that it would be totally counterproductive to engage Government departments or agencies in such matters as sales solicitations, engineering, installation and servicing of alarm systems, maintaining keys and the host of other functions provided by the Private Security Sector. Wholly apart from financial considerations involved in adding thousands of people to municipal payrolls, problems relating to discriminatory treatment of customers of municipally sponsored systems would bog down the effective thrust of Government support in attacking crime to a degree that is clearly unwarranted. To involve municipalities in the operation of central stations or in the ownership of local or direct connect companies, would clearly be a step backward. The position of the Alarm Committee is that they are unequivocally opposed to municipal operation of central station systems.

Having recognized the valid areas of government involvement in alarms, it should be remembered that this standard's primary focus is on avoiding permanent government competition in the alarm business. Although recognizing the contribution to law enforcement alarm systems provide, this standard recommends that government should not attempt to provide services the private sector has proven they can adequately provide, and funds that would be allocated to purchase alarm systems that compete with private alarm companies should be applied to improvements of a more appropriate nature in the field of law enforcement.

In the preparation of this standard, points of conflict between the public and private sectors were identified and examined. But more importantly, points of agreement were likewise reviewed. On the question of government operation of alarms in competition with private alarm businesses, both a point of conflict and of agreement were found to exist. In its stand against the practice of government operation of alarm systems, the alarm industry was supported by the IACP.

This agreement is further evident in the Private Security Advisory Council's "Model Burglar and Hold-up Alarm Business Statute" (see Appendix 10). This document is the result of the public and private sectors working together to attain the types of industry improvements advocated in this chapter.

Among the industry groups opposing government ownership is the Alarm Industry Committee for Combating Crime (AICCC). This group is made up of representatives of national companies and associations of small regional companies providing alarm systems sales installation and service. In 1974, the AICCC (then composed of the Central Station Electrical Protection Association; National Burglar and Fire Alarm Association; American District Telegraph Company; Burns International Security Services, Inc.; Diebold, Inc.; Holmes Protection, Inc.; Mosler Safe Company; and Wells Fargo Alarm Services) expressed their opposition to government ownership of alarm businesses in a position paper:

The Alarm Industry Committee for Combating Crime believes that it is not in the public interest to permit government ownership of alarm system detection devices on private premises; that it is not in the public interest to establish governmental businesses subsidized to the extent of the cost of that equipment in competition with private enterprise; and that it is not in the public interest to permit governmental units or public bodies to sell goods or services to the public in competition with or to the exclusion of private enterprise for the following reasons: . . .

The AICCC listed reasons for their opposition, among them, the use of unofficial authority to sell the government's system, the selective allotting of alarm systems paid for by tax dollars, and the unfair competition created when government provides lower installation line, servicing, and maintenance costs than are available to industry. Further, the AICCC has certain philosophical and practical objections to government involvement in the alarm business in any but temporary emergency situations. Among these objections is the erosion of the principle of sovereign immunity. Private companies currently can be held liable in suits where an alarm system failed during a burglary. The AICCC asks whether the taxpayer would have to cover the judgment in a lawsuit against a government-owned alarm business. Another question posed is whether government-owned alarm system businesses would be subject to the same sanctions as nongovernmental businesses for excessive false alarming.

Also siding with opposition to government ownership is the monthly security publication *Security Distributing and Marketing*. A 1972 editorial discussing a federally funded alarm system project in Cedar Rapids, Iowa, took the following position:

On the surface, however, it certainly seems to us that the Committee [AICCC] has a point. . . . in fact, several of them. We agree wholeheartedly that (1) "the best interests of the public are not served when a municipality enters into a service business," and (2) that "the private alarm industry cannot survive if federally-funded alarm projects are abandoned to municipal ownership . . ." as was the case in Cedar Rapids.

Exactly 2 years later, a second editorial on the topic of government involvement bemoaned the fact that:

Of late, more and more cities appear to be getting into the act with city-owned and operated burglar alarm systems. . . .
Granted, the private alarm industry has its problems . . . with unscrupulous operators, high false alarm rates, lack of total direction and organization, etc. Federal grants aimed in the direction of clearing up these problems, I am sure, would be welcome by all.
But to see the taxpayer's hard-earned dollars being pumped into systems that appear to do nothing more than create favored special interest groups goes against the grain of every manufacturer and dealer installer trying to make a go of it.
In this editor's opinion, the competition within the industry is tough enough without making it worse by granting municipalities Federal funds for the purpose of putting these municipalities into direct competition with established alarm companies which have forgotten more about alarm systems than any police department will ever know! To do so is directly opposed to the concept of the American free enterprise system.

Three examples of what has occurred when government has gone into the alarm business are cited here to highlight some of the possible pitfalls.

Perhaps the oldest example is found in an AICCC counsel document. In the early 1930's, the Atlanta, Ga., Police Department not only installed annunciator panels for receiving alarm signals, but also began to provide citizens with alarm systems and service. Police encouraged a potential burglar alarm customer to send police headquarters a letter requesting installation of a system. It is AICCC Counsel's understanding that police officers engaged in the actual sale and installation of systems to citizens and that the citizens paid the officers directly and individually for their labor and for equipment costs. After the systems were installed, the city charged each user $7.50 a month to respond to alarms and to maintain and service the systems. Subsequently, after pressure from alarm companies, that fee was raised to $15 a month. Limitless witnesses from the private sector were available to testify that there was no way any entity could recover its costs in maintaining and servicing a substantial number of even the most simple and rudimentary alarm systems at the rate of $15 a month. It appears that the City of Atlanta had subsidized alarm systems to the private benefit of individual members of the police force at taxpayer expense.

A more recent example of what can happen when cities go into the alarm business can be found in a series of articles appearing in *The Louisville Times* in 1971. The following summarizes the main points of the articles as they relate to the alarm system operated by the Louisville, Ky., Police Department:

1. The high incidence of false alarms due to faulty alarms caused businessmen to unplug their alarm systems.

2. Cost overruns and disputes with the installing firm resulted in only 48 of 233 hookups being completed.

3. There were many problems with obtaining repair service.

A third example occurred in 1968 when a Federal grant was awarded to the city of Cedar Rapids, Iowa. It provided for the acquisition of an alarm system and subsequent study of the crime prevention effectiveness of burglar alarms. Although the results gained from the project were a worthwhile contribution to the growing body of knowledge about alarm systems, the low-cost competition (in the form of reduced transmission rates not available to private business) and the eventual disposition of this alarm system to the municipal government created a controversy. This controversy sparked the alarm industry to united action on the issue of government ownership.

Adoption of this standard has two major advantages to both law enforcement agencies and the private security industry. First, it sets a cooperative rather than a competitive relationship between the parties of interest. Second, it recognizes that there are situations in which public law enforcement agencies can reasonably, and in the public interest, actively participate in providing alarm services.

Selected References

1. Alarm Committee of the National Private Security Advisory Council. "Alarm Committee Report." Nov. 20, 1972.

2. Alarm Industry Committee for Combating Crime. "An Analysis of and Comment on the Cedar Rapids Project." Washington, D.C.: Alarm Industry Committee for Combating Crime.

3. Bargert, R. J. "The Cedar Rapids Project," *Security Distributing and Marketing*, Vol. 2, No. 9, October 1972, p. 3.

4. ———. "Let's Keep Private Industry Private," *Security Distributing and Marketing*, Vol. 4, No. 9, September 1974.

5. Beerman, Bernard (Counsel for AICCC). "Informal Working Paper." New Orleans, La., Jan. 8, 1976.

6. Cedar Rapids, Iowa, Police Department. *Installation, Test, and Evaluation of a Large-Scale Burglar Alarm System for a Municipal Police Department*. Cedar Rapids: Cedar Rapids, Iowa, Police Department, 1971.

7. ———. *Installation, Test, and Evaluation of a Large-Scale Burglar Alarm System for a Municipal Police Department—Report of the Second Year of Operation*. Cedar Rapids: Cedar Rapids, Iowa, Police Department, 1971.

8. Clifford, Frank. "Theft-Alarm Clients Are Buzzed Off," *The Louisville Times*, Vol. CLXXVI, No. 10, Nov. 11, 1971.

9. ———. "Cops and No Robbers," *The Louisville Times*, Jan. 26, 1971.

10. International Association of Chiefs of Police. Annual meeting, Denver, Colo., September 1975.

11. National Burglar and Fire Alarm Association. "Background Information on the Cedar Rapids Project in Support of a Resolution Submitted to the International Association of Chiefs of Police." National Burglar and Fire Alarm Association, 1974.

Chapter 5
Environmental Security

INTRODUCTION

Despite the efforts of upgraded and expanded agencies of the criminal justice system, crime in the United States continues to rise both in numbers and in seriousness. Even the value of police as a crime deterrent seems to be in question. The existing practices aimed at rehabilitation of offenders are not producing meaningful accomplishments. To find approaches with high potential for success for a resolution of the crime problem, criminal justice professionals are turning to new areas and to new technologies.

One approach developed through scientific research impacts crime through adjustment of the environment. Called by some as environmental security, this embryonic field applies various technologies to either structure the environment to discourage crime or to deter and prevent crime from occurring. Although most people are familiar with the use of locks and bars as a means to prevent crime, newer and more sophisticated environmental security techniques have been developed. These techniques involve placement of buildings on project sites, introduction of specific types of business establishments and community programs to certain neighborhoods, using theories regarding human behavior to determine which categories of people can best live in proximity to other groupings, and a myriad of other environmental management approaches.

One approach that has recently gained attention and consideration throughout the country is known as crime prevention through environmental design (CPTED). The basic aim of CPTED is to anticipate and prevent crime through physical and environmental planning. It seeks the cooperation of private security and public law enforcement sectors to assist planners, architects, builders, and other local officials to identify and eliminate points of criminal opportunity before they are built into a community. CPTED also seeks to identify positive structural and layout designs that can be incorporated into buildings and projects to discourage would-be criminals. Within this framework, CPTED uses physical security measures and community awareness to provide a safer atmosphere.

Although integrally related in nature, the private security industry has not become involved with the concept of CPTED. Most of the standards in this chapter were developed to initiate such involvement. The following overview of the development of CPTED provides added meaning for the standards.

Development of CPTED

CPTED as a concept is a recent development, although its roots extend back to the early 1960's. It has evolved from the work of individuals who recognized certain relationships between the environment and people. They studied these relationships and hypothesized about their general applicability.

Among the earliest contributors to the body of knowledge forming CPTED was Elizabeth Wood. Her background work in Chicago's public housing prompted Wood to develop a "Social Design Theory," which stressed the importance of physical design considerations in achieving social objectives. Recognizing the need for both privacy and community involvement, Elizabeth Wood recommended that public housing facilities be designed both inside and outside with areas for exercise, play, and loitering that would be private yet allow for surveillance by the tenants. To encourage a sense of community, she advocated the inclusion of meetingplaces, stores, churches, and pub-type establishments on project grounds.

Jane Jacobs, a contemporary of Wood, was interested in making the streets a safe part of the environment. Throughout her career as a journalist, she pointed out that because streets were for everyone it was necessary for everyone to feel that antisocial acts would be observed and reported or countered by those present on the street. Like Elizabeth Wood, Jane Jacobs was aware that a sense of community was necessary for a safe environment. She suggested that store owners, whose businesses brought people out on the streets should be active in ensuring the security of persons on the street through surveillance. She endorsed street play for children based on the theory that mothers watching the street provided added protection for the streets and that passers-by on the street would increase the children's safety. She also emphasized the benefits to be gained from short blocks and the need for clear delineation between public, semipublic, and private use areas.

In early 1968, Shlomo Angel did a study of crime occurring on the streets of Oakland, Calif. He theorized that high-density-use areas had more potential witnesses and other elements for likelihood of apprehension—thus lower crime rates. Lower crime rates also appeared in low-density areas that theoretically did not provide enough potential victims and had inadequate crime targets. It was the intermediate or critical-intensity zone that Angel believed was most susceptible to crime.

To reduce this crime potential, Angel proposed "evening squares" which would serve as commercial, self-contained oases. These sections would have no access to adjacent areas and would be located on main thoroughfares, provide directive pedestrian routes, maximize surveillance capabilities, and require active law enforcement coverage. Although his ideas were geared to the design of the City of Oakland and were not universally applicable or desirable, his work was important because it contained the embryonic use of design, citizen involvement, and law enforcement coverage to create a safe and secure environment.

In 1964 at St. Louis, Mo., two architects, Oscar Newman and Roger Montgomery, and two sociologists, Lee Rainwater and Roger Walker, met with members of the St. Louis Police Department to discuss the infamous Pruit-Ingoe housing project. From this meeting evolved the concept of defensible space. When this hypothesis is implemented it fosters territorial recognition through design; maximizes surveillance through hardware, design, and routing; reduces fear and crime; enhances the safety of adjoining areas; and reduces the stigma of public housing.

Not until 1970, with the aid of a Law Enforcement Assistance Administration (LEAA) grant and extensive preparatory work, was Oscar Newman able to conduct a major defensible space study. From this work, two New York housing projects were revitalized—Clason Point Garden and Bronxdale. The National Institute of Law Enforcement and Criminal Justice (the research arm of LEAA) was so encouraged by Newman's thesis that the Institute moved to expand its commitment to studying the relationship between design of the environment and crime.

Various LEAA-funded studies have resulted in specific recommendations for increasing security in existing structures and for design considerations for new structures. The purpose of these recommendations is to affect social behavior in such a manner as to reduce crime and the fear of crime. LEAA has published these studies to assist citizens, community leaders, builders, State and local government officials, architects, urban planners, and law enforcement personnel to understand the concept of crime reduction through environmental design.

With the development of a body of knowledge on how design can affect social behavior and perception of crime, it became possible to develop a new, total, social engineering strategy. The new strategy evolved as crime prevention through environmental design (CPTED).

LEAA funded a study by the Westinghouse Electric Corporation, entitled "Elements of CPTED." The report staff was comprised of experts in the fields of criminology, psychology, architecture, urban design, engineering, sociology, and others. The results of this study indicate that a CPTED program has the capability of raising the level of personal security and the quality of urban life through a reduction of common, predatory, stranger-to-stranger crime. The CPTED methodology developed by Westinghouse includes the following steps:

1. The identification of the crime-environment problem of a specific design mode;

2. The design of a strategic model (containing a set of coordinated and interrelated design strategies) that appropriately responds to the identified crime problem through pertinent design concepts;

3. Adaptation of the strategic model to a specific site, resulting in a tactical model (containing a set of coordinated and interrelated design directives that identify the environmental elements to be manipulated);

4. The implementation of the tactical model; and

5. The evaluation of the model.

To evaluate the effectiveness of this concept, LEAA has since funded CPTED projects in several locations. Hartford, Conn., is the site for testing the residential mode; Portland, Oreg., is testing the commercial mode; and Broward County, Fla., is the site for a test of the school mode.

Where these projects have been undertaken, the interdisciplinary team has worked together with local government officials and law enforcement agencies— each lending their expertise to solve a particular area of the total problem. The role of the architect has been illustrated through the work of Newman and Montgomery; however, other roles are equally important. The urban planner considers the wisest allocation of resources, law enforcement agencies provide public security forces, builders supply the materials, and government obtains citizen participation and coordinates and oversees the entire program.

In sum, CPTED is many disciplines brought together under one new label, with their focus on crime prevention. The existence of CPTED was made possible by the additions to the knowledge about design effects on crime. As yet, there is no well-defined discipline that is CPTED, and perhaps there never will be. It is not solely defensible space. It is not solely urban planning. It is not solely the application of private security know-how to crime prevention. CPTED represents the application of multidisciplinary skills and knowledge in a unique, new configuration supported by responsible research directed at the reduction of crime in a community.

Private Security Involvement with CPTED

In the preparation of the standards in this chapter, it was necessary to examine the CPTED concept for the purpose of identifying the role of the private security industry in its past and/or future development. A review of existing literature revealed very few references to any relationship between the security industry and CPTED, either direct or indirect. One fact became clear: Here was a developing concept with a goal of crime prevention and reduction that was leaving out one of the largest sources of crime prevention knowledge—the private security industry.

By not including the security profession in the early development of CPTED projects, problems in practical implementation may occur. The private security field can play an important role in the successful application of CPTED concepts. For maximum effectiveness, this role should be developed through the security industry's involvement in the following areas:

Direct involvement:
- Introduction to CPTED concepts,
- Participation in CPTED total plans,
- Advising others, and
- Teaching CPTED.

Indirect involvement:
- Advising and practicing with others.

The starting point for increased involvement, of course, is becoming knowledgeable about the concept of CPTED. The private security industry should avail itself of every opportunity to increase its understanding of CPTED. Through literature, conferences, and meetings with experts in CPTED's disciplines, valuable insights can be gained. An annotated bibliography of interdisciplinary materials related to CPTED is available through Westinghouse Electric Corporation for reference purposes. Also, the Private Security Advisory Council of LEAA has a standing committee on environmental security that meets regularly. In addition, many capable individuals working with these concepts would be willing to explain to small informal meetings how their disciplines relate to CPTED.

Another step toward increased involvement is participation in the planning stage of CPTED programs. If invited to participate in a CPTED program, private security representatives should comply; if not invited, they should ask to participate. CPTED planners should use the knowledge of the private security industry regarding crime prevention techniques because this area is an important consideration in developing the total design. Further, if the security industry does not participate in CPTED planning, it is conceivable that private security executives will have to face a rise in crime through displacement as CPTED is applied in nearby areas.

Once private security experts have developed a working knowledge of CPTED and have some practice in using CPTED methodologies, they will be in a position to offer advice on CPTED on a consulting basis. This activity would ensure that the security industry's voice is heard in CPTED planning, which would benefit the total crime prevention efforts of the community.

Private security personnel also should be involved in teaching security methods used in business and industry. Schools of architectural and urban planning should seek to contract with them as instructors for the purpose of introducing students to the concepts and practices of the security industry. In this way, future architects and planners can be prepared to give adequate consideration to security measures in their designs and practices.

The indirect relationship between the private security industry and CPTED is characterized by informal involvement and advice to others. Informal involvement includes practices such as the employment of surveys to ascertain the applicability of CPTED-related strategies to standard security measures. Informal advice to others is the passing along of CPTED concepts in professional meetings with peers or employers. Word of mouth carries great weight when it comes from respected individuals or professional societies with which the security executive is familiar.

CPTED is an emerging discipline. In order to be fully effective, it will require that private security executives keep pace with new study results and developing programs. It is a new concept that builds on the strengths of older proven disciplines.

The standards in this chapter encourage government, businesses, and citizens to become more aware of crime prevention techniques through physical design. They emphasize specific need for improvements in such areas as door and window security, lighting, and computer security, as well as stress the importance of incorporating considerations for CPTED into planning, education, and regulation. These standards do not represent the only aspects of private security involvement with CPTED. They do represent what is believed to be the most immediate needs of the private security field in relation to CPTED concepts.

References

1. *Crime Prevention through Environmental Design—Schools.* A program sponsored by the Law Enforcement Assistance Administration, U.S. Department of Justice in cooperation with the Broward County, Fla., School Board.

2. *Crime Prevention through Environmental Design—Commercial.* A program sponsored by the Law Enforcement Assistance Administration, U.S. Department of Justice in cooperation with the City of Portland, Oreg.

3. Newman, Oscar. *Architectural Design for Crime Prevention.* U.S. Department of Justice, Law Enforcement Assistance Administration. Washington, D.C.: Government Printing Office, 1973.

4. Tien, J. M., T. A. Repetto, and L. F. Hanes. "Elements of CPTED." Arlington, Va.: Westinghouse Electric Corporation, 1975.

5. U.S. Department of Justice, Law Enforcement Assistance Administration. *Residential Security.* Washington, D.C.: Government Printing Office, 1973.

6. Urban Systems Research and Engineering, Inc. *Crime Prevention through Environmental Design (CPTED) Annotated Bibliography.* Arlington, Va.: Westinghouse Electric Corporation, 1975.

Standard 5.1

Improvement of Door and Window Security

Governments should examine those standards developed for protection of doors, windows, and other openings. Those standards that provide the most economical level of effective protection and deterrence should be considered for incorporation into building codes.

Commentary

Physical security measures play an important role in preventing many crimes. Nationally, crime against property averages 90 percent of all reported crime. By determining likely points of attack, action can be taken to physically secure or harden these points. Estimates indicate that in the majority of all burglary cases entry was gained through doors or windows.

The Texas Municipal League, quoting Underwriters' Laboratories' "Field Service Record" for 1967, showed doors and windows as the points of attack in 66 percent of the surveyed burglary attempts. In the 1974 "Field Service Record" survey, the figure jumped to 80 percent. A 1973 Dallas, Tex., study of burglaries of businesses showed an 85 percent rate of entry through doors and windows. In Scarsdale, N.Y., approximately 89 percent of burglaries reported between 1967 and 1971 involved doors or windows as the points of attack.

In addition to knowing the likely target, it is helpful to have some knowledge of the potential burglar. It is generally believed that more than half of all burglaries are committed by persons under the age of 25, within a half mile of their homes. These burglars use simple handtools to overcome barriers as quietly and as quickly as possible. Many youthful burglars simply search for an unlocked door or open window.

Knowing the modus operandi of these burglars provides a solid basis for taking measures designed to foil or frustrate entry attempts. The Texas Municipal League's model code points out that a burglar delayed only 4 minutes generally gives up the attempt. Coupling this information with the high probability that the would-be burglar will attempt entry through either a door or a window, it is apparent that if increasingly high burglary rates are to be curbed, door and window security needs to be improved. Citizens and businesses should be informed by government of proper door and window security measures and urged to reduce this opportunity for crime.

Door and window security is a sound, simple, proven way to make a facility more secure; yet, builders consistently use inferior low-security hardware and materials, manufacturers continue to make locks that can be easily and quickly opened, and citizens do not voluntarily act to make their facilities more secure. Because of low security standards by builders and widespread public indifference, society must pay an ever-growing law enforcement services bill; the costs in handling the over three million burglaries a year contribute significantly to the overall cost of police protection. Further, the quality of life in this society is significantly lowered by fear of crime.

Establishment of door and window security standards can provide a positive step toward increased security at lower costs for all involved. In light of the failure of individuals, organizations, manufacturers, and others to take voluntary measures, local governments should examine security standards for doors, windows, and other apertures and select those most burglar resistant and cost effective for incorporation into building codes.

The following examples of building security code contents can assist government agencies interested in enacting door and window security requirements. It is not suggested that these examples represent the best; they are presented as a source of useful reference for governments wishing to move forward in this area.

The "Commercial Burglar Prevention Ordinance" of the City of Oakland, Calif., (now available in pamphlet form) was the first security code of its type. The new pamphlet contains an overview of the ordinance in layman's language, the formal wording of the ordinance, a security checklist to determine compliance, and an example depicting the ordinance requirements as applied to a small business establishment. City officials indicate that the code has contributed significantly to reduction in crime in Oakland, leading to a 4.4 percent decrease in burglary between 1969 and 1973 compared with the 38 percent national increase between 1969 and 1974.

The Texas Municipal League's "Building Security Code" contains a discussion of the burglary problem, legality of security codes, and the text of the model code. Also, its extensive bibliography would interest persons working on an ordinance or desiring to increase their knowledge of protection.

Several other publications that contain helpful information for those considering the establishment of building security codes are available. *Security Planning for HUD-Assisted Multifamily Housing* is published by the U.S. Department of Housing and Urban Development. Chapter 4 of this booklet presents commonsense information on target hardening that could be transposed into ordinance form.

A National Institute of Law Enforcement and Criminal Justice publication entitled "Federal Security Code" is a model ordinance covering antiburglary measures for commercial, single-family residential, and multiple-family dwellings (including hotels and motels). A most significant part of the document provides a cost estimate guide for the recommended security features. The individual can use these generalized guideline figures when considering the purchase of more security.

Another useful reference source is the voluntary national standard for physical security of door assemblies and components prepared by the Law Enforcement Standards Program of the Law Enforcement Assistance Administration. Included in this report are tests for doors and assembly components that can be replicated locally. The requirements are fully delineated.

Other standards for doors, windows, and locks have been or are being prepared by various independent testing laboratories. The following list is a mixture of recommendations from existing literature for target-hardening of doors and windows. A combination of the standards and recommendations should be utilized for more effective door and window security for both residences and businesses.

Door frames: 2-inch-thick wood or metal with a rabbeted jamb or hollow metal with a rabbeted jamb filled with a solid material able to withstand spreading.

Doors: 2-inch-thick solid wood or covered with 16-gauge sheet steel if wood is 1⅜ inch or less or 24-gauge steel bonded to kiln-dried wood core; minimum of 60-watt illumination above doors.

Door locks: dead bolt or dead latch type with a 1-inch throw and antiwrenching collar or secondary dead bolt with a 1-inch throw or minimum ½-inch throw for residential protection, pick-resistant cylinder and antiwrenching collar.

Windows: display windows should be of burglary resistant material plainly labeled as such; side and rear windows should be painted over and protected by ½-inch round steel bars 5 inches apart or 1- by ¼-inch steel flat bars 5 inches apart, the bars being secured in 3 inches of masonry or ⅛-inch steel wire mesh no larger than 2 inches square bolted over the window; where windows are not used for ventilation glass brick should be used; windows should not be able to be lifted out of the frame. (Applies to windows up to 18 feet above ground level or within 40 inches of an interior door handle.)

Window locks: clam shell (crescent) thumbscrew pin in hole or as applicable to the type of window.

Other doors: sliding doors, garage, and loading dock doors should be considered.

Other openings: any opening larger than 96 square inches should be covered by steel bars or mesh screen.

Because statistics show doors and windows are the most frequent points of attack in a burglary, the ordinances, models, and standards that do exist generally concentrate solely on these two areas. In the available reference materials, the protection of other openings has not been given enough emphasis. Any opening to a structure should be considered as a potential entry point and, as such, protected. Authorities concur that all openings of 96 square inches or larger need protection. Examples of these potential points of entry are skylights, hatchways, air ducts and vents, and elevators. Excerpts from various ordinances and studies on the protection of other openings follow:

Skylights: best protection is installation of metal bars, grills, or mesh; bars should be steel not less than ¾ inch in diameter not more than 5 inches apart; mesh should be at least ⅛ inch thick with spaces no larger than 2 inches, secured firmly by machine or roundhead bolts that cannot be removed from the outside; or special burglary resistant glass should be used.

Elevators: where feasible an elevator operator should be used; CCTV, continuous open listening device connected to a security control station, or special keys or cards held only by those requiring access can be used.

Hatchways: if good, cover with 16-gauge steel screwed to wood, secure with slide bars or bolts from the inside or padlock.

Air ducts and vents, transoms: those more than 8 by 12 inches on roof side or rear should have round or flat iron or steel bars secured by nonremovable bolts.

Note—all the above can be protected by various electrical and mechanical alarm devices.

Governments considering incorporating security requirements into building codes should carefully study local needs to ensure that adequate protection would be afforded at a reasonable cost. The expense of implementing these measures is small compared to the potential loss to the individual, the community, and society from criminal attack.

Selected References

1. City of Oakland Police Services. "Commercial Burglary Prevention Ordinance." Oakland, Calif.: City of Oakland Police Services.

2. Gray, Donald. "Direct Connection of Alarm Systems to Police Departments—Problems and Advantages." Address to the National Burglar and Fire Alarm Association, San Francisco, Calif.: 1973.

3. Law Enforcement Assistance Administration, U.S. Department of Justice. *Physical Security of Door Assemblies and Components.* Washington, D.C.: Government Printing Office, 1975.

4. National Institute of Law Enforcement and Criminal Justice. "Federal Security Code with Minimum Building Security Guidelines and Cost Estimates for the Security Features," initial draft. Washington, D.C.: Law Enforcement Assistance Administration, 1971.

5. National Sheriffs' Association. "National Neighborhood Watch Program." Pamphlet funded by a grant from the Law Enforcement Assistance Administration, Washington, D.C., n.d.

6. Texas Municipal League. "A Building Security Code for Texas Cities," Austin, Tex.: Texas Municipal League, 1975.

7. Tien, J. M., T. A. Repetto, and L. D. Hanes. "Elements of CPTED." Arlington, Va.: Westinghouse Electric Corporation, 1975.

8. Underwriters' Laboratories, Inc. "1974 Field Service Record Certificated Central Station Type Burglar Alarms." Burglar Protection and Signaling Department, Bulletin #35, 1974.

9. U.S. Department of Housing and Urban Development. *A Design Guide for Improving Residential Security.* Washington, D.C.: Government Printing Office, 1973.

10. —————. *Security Planning for HUD-Assisted Multifamily Housing.* Washington, D.C.: Government Printing Office, 1974.

Related Standards

The following standards and goals may be applicable in implementing Standard 5.1:

Standard 5.2

Adequate Security Lighting

Where appropriate, property should be adequately lighted to discourage criminal activity and enhance public safety.

Commentary

Since man first discovered fire, he has had a method of bringing light into the dark of night. Light makes man more secure in his environment. As pointed out in the National Crime Prevention Institute's course on lighting:

... fourth century Jerusalem lit its crossroads with wood fires, and in the tenth century the Arabs paved and lighted miles of streets in Cordova. . . .

It has always been accepted that the governmental unit—kingdom, city, state, county, etc.—has the responsibility for good lighting.

In response to growing street crime problems, many cities have funded major relighting programs during the past 10 years. These major projects were made possible because of advances in technology, notably the mercury- and sodium-vapor streetlamps. These lamps combine sodium or mercury gases with other gases to give off light when energized by an electrical current.

Relighting programs have evidenced significant success in reducing crime. For example, as a result of a relighting program, the City of Indianapolis, Ind., reported crime reductions of as much as 85 percent in specific neighborhood areas. An added plus accompanying the lowered incidence of crime was a reduction in accidents. A 40.9 percent reduction in crimes against persons, a 28 percent reduction in auto thefts, and a 12.8 percent reduction in burglaries were reported in St. Louis, Mo., one year after the implementation of a new lighting system. In Kansas City, Mo., an improved lighting system was installed in a sample area through a study funded by the Law Enforcement Assistance Administration (LEAA). Results showed crimes against persons down 48 percent, larceny reduced by 39 percent, and auto theft up only 3 percent compared with a previous 44 percent increase in the sample area. Results such as these encouraged the National Advisory Commission on Criminal Justice Standards and Goals to recommend that local government units consider the establishment of improved streetlighting programs in high crime areas.

Concurrent with the issuance of these crime-reduction-through-increased-lighting reports, some organizations have raised questions regarding the secondary impacts of relighting programs. In the Kansas City project, certain crime displacement problems were documented by LEAA. It was found that in commercial relighting some crime (mostly person-to-person) was pushed into the peripheral residential areas, and property crimes tended to shift to the daytime. The National Institute of Law Enforcement has pointed out that the newer types of lighting may affect the rest habits of individuals living in apartment buildings or houses located close to the street. The defensible space committee of the Private Security Advisory Council has suggested that lighting may conflict with aesthetic values; various citizen groups have registered opposition to the golden-yellow glow given off by sodium-vapor lamps.

Both the crime prevention benefits of improved lighting and the possible secondary problems should be considered by local officials when relighting programs are in the planning process. In particular, crime displacement problems should be anticipated and appropriate actions taken. Richard Rau of LEAA advises, "To avoid spill over into areas adjacent to lighted 'corridors' lighting must be on a neighborhood basis, not a street basis." Certain changes in previous law enforcement patrol procedures and tactics also should be considered as possible methods of dealing with any displacement.

The impact of lighting programs upon citizens also should be considered. The National Advisory Commission on Criminal Justice Standards and Goals stated, "Wishes of the residents and property owners should be considered at the outset." Citizens need to accept the program and be willing to play their role in its implementation. If a citizen observes suspicious criminal activity because of improved lighting but is afraid or unwilling to report it, then little has been accomplished. Public education, including the positive and negative aspects of lighting programs, can help gain citizen cooperation and input for effective and equitable lighting improvements.

Although major relighting efforts fall into government's realm of responsibility, the private sector should be aware of their obligation toward creating a safer environment through lighting. In addition to the moral and societal obligation, certain legal responsibilities may exist. To illustrate, *Criminal Justice Impact* reported that in a recent Illinois case (*Fancil* v. *Q.S.E. Foods, Inc.*) a police officer's widow won a wrongful-death suit. The store owner had disconnected his back door light despite the fact he had been burglarized several other times and was aware that law enforcement personnel checked his store in the evenings. The police officer was shot by a burglar concealed in the darkened area. In this instance, the store owner was found to be guilty of negligence through his failure to provide adequate lighting.

What is adequate lighting? The *Design Guide for Improving Residential Security* states adequate lighting should provide adequate visibility and surveillance. It should not create excessive glare or generate heavy shadows. Construction and installation should be of a vandalism resistant nature. Useful information on areas that should be adequately lighted is included in the following excerpt from the Oakland commercial burglary prevention ordinance:

Three out of four commercial burglaries are committed against buildings that either have no lights or inadequate lighting.

The interior of a store, especially the area near front windows, should be well lighted so as to be visible from the street.

All exterior doors as well as the rear of your store should have adequate overhead lighting with vandal-proof coverings.

The benefits to be gained from improved lighting are shared by everyone. Lighting not only creates an effective physical barrier against criminal acts, but also provides increased surveillance opportunities. Adequate lighting is a form of self-defense that can be employed by everyone from apartment dwellers to major manufacturers and corporations to prevent crime and promote public safety throughout the Nation. Although the private security industry has long recognized the crime prevention benefits of effective lighting for businesses and factories, the industry should educate itself to better understand the crime displacement effect of localized adequate lighting and should involve itself in community and government planning for effective lighting crime-prevention programs.

Selected References

1. "Darkness: Death Trap to Illinois Police Officer," *Criminal Justice* Impact, No. 1, Spring 1975.

2. Defensible Space Committee of the Private Security Advisory Council. Intercommittee working paper entitled "Initial Comments on the Secondary Effects of Defensible Space Concepts," 1975.

3. National Advisory Commission on Criminal Justice Standards and Goals. *A National Strategy to Reduce Crime*. Washington, D.C.: Government Printing Office, 1973.

4. National Institute of Law Enforcement and Criminal Justice, Law Enforcement Assistance Administration, U.S. Department of Justice. *Residential Security*. Washington, D.C.: Government Printing Office, December 1973.

5. Rau, Richard, Law Enforcement Assistance Administration, U.S. Department of Justice. Personal interview, Washington, D.C., Aug. 25, 1975.

6. Shakelford, Doyle, Jr. "Lighting for Crime," a course outline. Louisville, Ky.: National Crime Prevention Institute, University of Louisville, 1975.

7. Task Force on Community Crime Prevention, National Advisory Commission on Criminal Justice Standards and Goals. *A Call for Citizen Action: Crime Prevention and the Citizen.* Washington, D.C.: Government Printing Office, 1974.

8. U.S. Department of Housing and Urban Development. *A Design Guide for Improving Residential Security.* Washington, D.C.: Government Printing Office, December 1973.

9. Wright, Roger, Martin Heilweil, Paula Pelletier, and Karen Dickinson. *The Impact of Street Lighting on Street Crime.* Ann Arbor, Mich.: University of Michigan Press, May 1974.

Related Standards

The following standards and goals may be applicable in implementing Standard 5.2:

3.4   Employer Responsibilities

3.5   Maintaining Data on Criminal Activities

5.6   Environmental Security in Comprehensive Planning

5.8   Inclusion of Crime Prevention Measures into Existing Codes and the Consideration of Building Security Codes

7.1   Consumers Responsibility for Selection of Security Services

Standard 5.3

Computer Security

Possessers of computers should have a comprehensive protection plan for both physical site and data, regardless of whether the computer is used solely for their own needs or for providing computer services to others.

Commentary

More and more, computers are becoming part of our everyday environment. There are 140,000 computer systems currently in use in this country. *Introduction to Security* by Gion Green and Raymond C. Farber cites a study that states 7 percent of the United States work force of 84 million work directly with computers and an additional 15 percent work indirectly with them. It is projected that by 1980 computers and their related fields will represent 14 percent of the gross national product.

One of the largest computer users is the Federal Government. Computers are used in nearly every aspect of its operation, from simple bookkeeping procedures to complex space technology. Data collection on individuals alone demands tremendous computer capacities. A 3-year study by a subcommittee of the Judiciary Committee of the U.S. House of Representatives found 854 data banks in 54 agencies with more than 1.25 billion files on individuals. The personal data include police and military records and tax, intelligence, job, political, and religious information.

Other major computer users include banks and large public and industrial corporations. More than 60 percent of all banks are computerized, and large corporations, such as A.T. & T., Standard Oil, U.S. Rubber, and so forth, rely heavily on computers for their efficient overall operations. In addition, countless smaller private and public organizations use computers daily.

Computers represent a large investment for governments, banks, and other users. The following breakdown presented by Richard Cross, vice president, the Bank of New York, gives an idea of the extent of the fiscal investment of one corporation:

Equipment value	$3,150,000
Tape replacement	105,000
Monthly rental for backup time for minimal operations	550,000

Considering the enormous number of computers now in use, their importance to operational procedures, and their huge financial investment, the need for a comprehensive protection plan for both physical site and computer data is apparent.

Introduction to Security, points out that computers are vulnerable to many problems, including embezzlement, programing fraud, program penetration, operator error, input error, program error, theft of confidential information, simple carelessness, fire, riot, flood, and sabotage. Despite the apparent need for computer security, many agencies and businesses do not take adequate measures to protect their installations. Not only is physical security inadequate but also, in many cases, data is vulnerable to criminal attack and misuse. Dr. Ruth Davis, director of the National Bureau of Standards' Institute for Computer Sciences, lists an additional problem found in Federal Government computer operations. Dr. Davis advises that the "overwhelming majority . . . do not possess the security to meet data confidentiality conditions required by law." (*Security Systems Digest*)

With the lack of sufficient security, computer-related crimes are prevalent. Brandt Allen, in his article "Embezzler's Guide to the Computer," pointed out two very interesting facts about committing crimes with computers—it is relatively safe, and those who are caught usually are uncovered by chance or accident. To illustrate, he cites the case of a welfare department data center employee who stole $2.75 million in a 9-month period by issuing checks to fictitious persons. The scheme was uncovered "when a policeman discovered a batch of over a hundred of the fraudulent checks in an overdue rental car he found illegally parked." Brandt also includes the case of a "15-year boy who completely cracked the security system of a major London computer time-sharing service. . . . He used no special technical gadgets and started with no special knowledge of the computer's inner workings —instead he relied only on ingenuity and a teletype terminal in his school."

To effectively deal with such crimes, data security capabilities need to be strengthened and developed. Data security training programs should be set up for both public law enforcement and private security personnel. All available expertise should be called upon to develop materials and techniques that lead to maximum protection of security sites and data.

Assistance in security planning is available from the personnel and publications of large computer companies. IBM defines data security as "the protection of information from unauthorized disclosures, modification, or destruction whether accidental or intentional." IBM states that the keys to data security are reducing exposure to an acceptable level and ensuring a recovery capability.

The following points apply to security of the computer site and should be developed and expanded in training and practice:

1. Physical Security:
   Site selection,
   Fire and other damage controls, and
   Access control.
2. Controls and Procedures:
   Audit for security,
   Separation of responsibilities, and
   Machine room policies.
3. Recovery and Backup:
   Record protection,
   Disaster provisions, and
   Installation backup.
4. Computer Hardware and Software Facilities:
   Identification devices,
   Programmed devices, and
   Software integrity.

Law enforcement agencies are becoming increasingly aware of the growing need for expertise in combating computer crimes. Examples of training law enforcement personnel in this area are pointed out in *Datamation,* a computer journal. One involved computer training for the Los Angeles County district attorney's major-fraud-section personnel. A second example was a 2-week computer security program implemented by the FBI at Quantico, Va. This program consisted of two separate courses— one aimed at agents presently in the field and the other offered as an elective at the FBI national academy. There is a need for expanding programs like this to make them available to private security personnel as well as public law enforcement personnel. More courses, such as those discussed, are needed as a starting point for improved computer security.

In the private sector, some courses also are offered. The American Society for Industrial Security, several colleges and universities, companies such as IBM, and various privately operated programs have presented various aspects of computer security in workshops, seminars, and conferences. Class offered at local educational institutions and discussions with computer programmers and operators can teach security executives the principles, languages, and methods of computers. Following this, they can search the literature to ascertain types of crimes involving computers and to find additional information about current developments in computer security. Security executives could become involved in advance computer training concerned with data protection. Development of competency in computer usage and security is perhaps the most valuable protective function security professionals could perform for clients possessing computers.

The expanding use of computers places responsibility on users to provide a comprehensive protection plan for both the physical site and the computer data. This commentary gives ample evidence that disregarding computer security is inappropriate and often causes difficulties for persons with no control over the situation. Also, law enforcement agencies should increase their knowledge and activity for protecting against computer crimes.

Selected References

1. "Computer Security Discussed at Recent Assn. Meetings," *Security Systems Digest,* Vol. 6, No. 16, July 1975.

2. Cross, Richard. "Tighter Security for Computers," *Industrial Security,* Vol. 14, No. 6, August 1971.

3. Farber, Raymond C., and Gion Green. *Introduction to Security.* Los Angeles, Calif.: Security World Publishing Co., Inc., 1975.

4. International Business Machines Corporation, Data Processing Division. Data Security. White Plains, N.Y.: IBM.

5. ———. *The Considerations of Data Security in a Computer Environment.* White Plains, N.Y.: IBM.

6. "Privacy: Congressional Efforts Are Coming to Fruition," *Science,* Vol. 188, May 1975.

Related Standards

The following standards and goals may be applicable in implementing Standard 5.3:

3.5   Maintaining Data on Criminal Activities

5.5   Development of Environmental Security Expertise

Standard 5.4

Crime Prevention in Design

Architects, builders, and/or their professional societies should continue to develop performance standards of crime prevention in design with advice from law enforcement agencies and the private security industry.

Commentary

In 1973 the National Advisory Commission on Criminal Justice Standards and Goals, in its book *Community Crime Prevention,* made the following recommendation:

The Commission recommends that agencies and professions involved in building design actively consult with and seek the advice of law enforcement agencies in physical design to reduce the opportunity for the commission of crime. These agencies and firms should make security a primary consideration in the design and construction of new buildings and the reconstruction or renovation of older structures. Interaction with law enforcement agencies and security experts should be sought during preliminary planning and actual construction to determine the effects of architectural features and spatial arrangements on building security and security costs. . . .

In its report to the U.S. Senate, entitled *Crime Against Small Business,* the Small Business Administration made a similar recommendation:

We recommend that the architectural profession develop standards of security in design. In doing so, they should

draw upon the experience of the commercial central stations, the manufacturers of security devices, the police, the construction industry and building code officials, and other relevant agencies at all levels of government.

One example of what has been accomplished by architectural practitioners is illustrated by Oscar Newman's study, *Defensible Space,* published in 1972. In this study of New York's public housing, Newman set forth ideas and applied strategies for "getting persons to and from their living quarters without the fear (or occurrence) of crime or harassment." (*Progressive Architecture,* October 1972) Newman's work has led to an awareness of the relationship between physical design and crime.

Progress has also been made by the Westinghouse Electric Corporation. In 1975 Westinghouse established a methodology for planning crime prevention that included the use of strategies based on interdisciplinary fields, such as architecture, law enforcement, and sociology. This methodology is presently being evaluated by the Law Enforcement Assistance Administration (LEAA) in four test areas—schools, transportation, commercial business, and residential housing.

The Westinghouse and Newman studies discuss examples of what can be done when architectural and crime prevention concepts are combined in environmental design. Since the early 1960's, this body of knowledge has grown, culminating in the concepts of defensible space and crime prevention through environmental design (CPTED), as discussed in the introduction to this chapter. Others contributing to the development of these concepts include Jane Jacobs, Elizabeth Wood, John G. Kerns, and Schlomo Angel and agencies, such as LEAA, National Bureau of Standards, Southern California Association of Governments, and the Environmental Security Committee of the Private Security Advisory Council.

The concepts of crime prevention in architecture and design need to be disseminated to all involved with planning, design, and construction. Because materials on CPTED have not yet fully evolved, evaluations of these concepts are lacking. A substantial investment of money and time is needed to evaluate all new crime prevention concepts and security hardware. As the art of CPTED advances, evaluations and appropriate modifications should be made.

An important part of the CPTED concept involves the assistance of both public law enforcement and private security experts when architects, governments, and businesses are planning, designing, or building new works. Their knowledge of crime activity and preventive measures is essential to successful CPTED applications.

Although previously uninvolved with environmental design, the private security industry has undergone considerable upgrading and specialization in the last 20 years. The security industry, along with law enforcement agencies, has been developing additional knowledge about types of crimes and their perpetrators. Much of the knowledge, skills, and specialization is not yet known outside of the career field; thus, the average urban planner, architect, and builder is unaware of the security industry as a resource in CPTED planning. Only through the recent efforts of the LEAA has some of this knowledge become available to the public. This knowledge can contribute significantly to CPTED activities and the private security industry should be consulted regularly.

In addition to the role and services private security directors and contract companies can provide, specific situations may indicate a need for a security consultant. Hollis DeVines, director of Schlage Security Institute, Schlage Lock Company, explains his criteria for a security consultant:

In selecting hardware, a security, consultant should be called—that is, a consultant who has credentials to prove his ability. . . . I see too many "security consultants" springing up suddenly, and many of them do not seem to know what they are doing. When an architect designs a building, security measures would be considered at the very beginning

—and he always engages the services of other engineers. These men have proved their efficiency, and I feel a security consultant should qualify in the same category.

Some security problems get to be quite monumental, and there is a need for a person who keeps abreast of what items are on the market. Also he must have a good knowledge of the criminal and the way the criminal operates. This is the man I am referring to as the "Security Consultant."

The assistance of security consultants should be obtained for more specialized areas, depending on specific local needs. A list of areas in which private security and/or law enforcement representatives can provide expertise follows:

- Alarm systems.
- Antiburglary strategies.
- Antirobbery strategies.
- Crime displacement.
- Employee theft control.
- Law enforcement/security force in support of design.
- Personnel control techniques and systems.
- Security hardware for access points.
- Security lighting techniques.
- Shoplifting control design.
- Special security needs (i.e., computers).

Much has been done, in a relatively short time, by architects and builders to develop new strategies for the war on crime. Their efforts should be commended. It is hoped that others in these professions and their associations will join the effort to counter the rising crime rate. By becoming more knowledgeable about crime prevention, they can contribute to a safer environment for all.

Selected References

1. "Alternatives to Fear," *Progressive Architecture,* October 1972.

2. DeVines, Hollis. "Building Security" (comments), *Urban Design, Security and Crime Proceedings of a National Institute of Law Enforcement and Criminal Justice Seminar, April 12 and 13, 1975.* Washington, D.C.: U.S. Department of Justice, Law Enforcement Assistance Administration, 1973.

3. Newman, Oscar. *Defensible Space.* New York: Macmillan Company, 1972.

4. Small Business Administration. *Crime Against Small Business.* Washington, D.C.: Government Printing Office, 1969.

Related Standards

The following standards and goals may be applicable in implementing Standard 5.4:

5.6 Environmental Security in Comprehensive Planning

5.10 Crime Prevention Courses as a Job Requirement

8.2 National Private Security Resource and Research Institute

Standard 5.5

Development of Environmental Security Expertise

Those companies selling security services should develop the expertise necessary to offer environmental security planning services.

Commentary

Security companies often provide a variety of services—everything from guard service to security planning encompassing internal/external loss prevention plans made up of human and mechanical deterrents. However, a review of the National Institute of Law Enforcement and Criminal Justice publication, *Directory of Security Consultants,* and the literature of security service companies shows that very few offer services incorporating the concept of crime prevention through environmental design (CPTED).

Security service companies are not at fault, because it is a relatively new concept. Although its roots were established in 1961 in Jane Jacobs' book, *The Death and Life of Great American Cities,* not until the early 1970's did CPTED begin to take shape in viable concepts. Today, alarming increases in crime and strong public concern for safety have led more and more researchers and planners to look at CPTED in the search for new and better methods of protection. In fact, the Law Enforcement Assistance Administration currently is funding four major projects to test its effectiveness in different areas.

Although meaningful, evaluative results are not readily available because of the youth of CPTED projects, early reports indicate the significant crime-reduction potential of CPTED. For example, the article "Security: A 24-Hour, Seven-Days-A-Week Affair" discusses the benefits of the planned community of Deerwood, Fla. Included within its security system are a variety of mechanical devices, a security guard force, liaison with law enforcement agencies, and citizen involvement. The article indicates that the community so far has been successful in keeping crime out, with the resulting dividend that "The excellent security record of the Deerwood community has, of course, been a major sales factor for the condominiums."

If such indicators are correct, the concept of CPTED likely will be used more and more in both government and private planning. Companies selling security services should, therefore, develop the necessary expertise to offer environmental security planning services. This would not only increase the salability of services but also ensure viable crime prevention techniques in new communities and business developments. The developing environmental security expert will know the special problems relating to private security services and will be able to offer advice to other members of the interdisciplinary team, thus reducing risks for private security guards

191

and police officers, and providing for better consumer protection and greater public safety.

Expertise in environmental security could be offered not only for design but also for site selection. A crime impact statement could be prepared evaluating the impact of the new site in terms of crime attraction, displacement, types of crimes, and so forth. It should include proposals to involve the company and contiguous citizens and businesses in crime prevention programs.

All security executives should study CPTED concepts for application to their own situations. Companies providing security services should consider hiring an architect, urban planner, or sociologist/criminologist to be resonsible for CPTED. The development of CPTED expertise in this manner would considerably enhance the level of security services offered and contribute to safer environments for everyone.

Selected References

1. Drennon, William W. "Security: A 24-Hour, Seven-Days-A-Week Affair," *Journal of Property Management,* Vol. 38, No. 3, May/June 1973.

2. Fechter, John V., and Elizabeth Robertson. Center for Consumer Product Technology, National Bureau of Standards. "Directory of Security Consultants." Prepared for the National Institute of Law Enforcement and Criminal Justice, Law Enforcement Assistance Administration, U.S. Department of Justice. Washington, D.C.: Government Printing Office, October 1975.

3. Rau, Richard M. "Crime Prevention Through Environmental Design: A Historical Perspective." Washington, D.C.: National Institute of Law Enforcement and Criminal Justice, Law Enforcement Assistance Administration, U.S. Department of Justice, May 1975.

4. Tien, J. M., T. A. Repetto, and L. F. Hanes. "Elements of CPTED." Arlington, Va.: Westinghouse Electric Corporation, 1975.

Related Standards

The following standards and goals may be applicable in implementing Standard 5.5:

5.3   Computer Security

5.4   Crime Prevention in Design

5.7   Crime Prevention Courses in Schools of Architecture and Urban Planning

5.9   Crime Impact Forecast

Standard 5.6

Environmental Security in Comprehensive Planning

Environmental security should be a part of comprehensive planning from the design phase to the completion of construction projects.

Commentary

What do mud houses in Sudan, Neolithic settlements in Turkey, and rowhouse streets in 19th century American cities have in common? As Oscar Newman explains in his book *Defensible Space,* they all employ elements of security through building design. Man has learned, through the ages, numerous ways to protect his being and belongings—building design is one basic way.

The lessons learned over the years can now be applied on a more professional and advanced level. As discussed in Standard 5.4, the concept of crime prevention through environmental design is emerging as an effective tool in crime prevention. As a result of pilot projects and indepth research, new technology and information is becoming available for incorporation into building design. Standard 5.5 encourages the private security industry to gain expertise in environmental security. The objective of this standard is to recommend ways in which this expertise can be used for the maximum benefit of all concerned.

The proprietary security executive whose employer is planning a new facility should involve himself in the project from the planning and design stage to the end of construction. If not specifically asked (or in the case of consultant or contract security company, not hired) to function as part of the planning team, he should request that his input be considered; it is at this point that basic decisions are made and the involvement of security is clearly established. The goals and objectives established in the planning stage provide direction for all remaining phases of the project. At this stage, the security executive needs to familiarize the planning team with past security problems of the locale, offer methods to overcome these problems, point out the benefits of the expected results, and estimate what resources are required to attain the desired security objectives.

In the next step of the planning process—selection of the building site—the security executive's input again is needed. As pointed out by Richard B. Cole, president of Loss Prevention Diagnostics, Inc., ". . . security in design can assume new dimensions when it is considered in site selection." The security executive should consider the proposed site based on area crime statistics obtained from the local law enforcement agency. He should then conduct informal talks with other security executives in the area of the proposed site, and, finally, should visit the proposed site to contribute his personal expertise in the evaluation of its crime potential.

Once a final decision has been made regarding the site, the design phase allows the security executive to recommend parameter barriers and internal controls for the protection of equipment, inventory, and personnel. This phase can be accomplished by reviewing past criminal confrontations and considering how design might have deterred them. The security executive should then present a proposed list of security hardware necessary for protection of the new facility, with appropriate justification.

In some instances, security equipment can be effectively incorporated with other necessary equipment. For example, if management is considering an electronic control center for the facility's environmental process (heating, air conditioning, fire systems, and so forth), the security executive should point out that electronic control systems are available which incorporate the monitoring of separate environmental, manufacturing, and security processes into one control center, thus lowering initial costs and future maintenance requirements. Among the many advantages of these systems is the long-term reduction in security and maintenance personnel achieved through the use of computers and electronics for manpower.

Careful consideration of security needs in the design phase of a building will also provide more effective security at lower cost in the long run. As pointed out by Al Buckner in his article, "Designing Security into Retail Facilities":

> Security can be built in at little or no additional cost if it is considered prior to construction. The construction alone can provide your security staff the tools which will enable them to multiply the effectiveness of their function—many times over.

Buckner further points out that careful design of a facility can cut back on manning requirements. This can be a powerful argument in favor of acquiring the latest hardware when a guard's salary, insurance, benefits, and retirement fund for a 20-year period are considered against an initial capital investment.

When the project is in the construction phase, the security executive should visit the site and reevaluate and refine the proposed security system, in addition to traditional construction security measures. Also during construction, the security executive should prepare training materials for all personnel encompassed by the total security plan. Selection and training of security personnel should occur during construction so that employees can be familiar with the security measures incorporated into the design. Such training might include instruction about which route to use when entering and leaving the building, where various devices are located for summoning security personnel and how they work, use of elevators, and how the design can assist in surveillance and create territoriality that results in immediate identification of a person as an intruder.

When construction is finished, security personnel should be the first group to enter the site to provide implementation of the incorporated security measures. Additional security measures should be implemented to relate to those construction activities not as yet completed. Finally, if necessary, security training should cover any changes in procedures needed as a result of modifications in construction or equipment.

There is no guarantee that security principles appropriately applied during the planning, design, and construction phases will ensure a crime-free environment. However, when security is an integral component in the planning site selection, design, and construction phases of a new facility or community, coupled with a well-trained security force and security-minded employees or residents, the final results will cause a lowered incidence of external and internal crime, increased profits for the business, and a more satisfactory quality of life for the community.

Selected References

1. Buckner, Al. "Designing Security into Retail Facilities," *Security World,* Vol. 4, No. 8, September 1967.

2. Cole, Richard B. "Designing for Security," *Progressive Architecture,* November 1970.

3. Newman, Oscar. *Defensible Space.* New York: Macmillan Company, 1972.

Related Standards

The following standards and goals may be applicable in implementing Standard 5.6:

3.5   Maintaining Data on Criminal Activities
5.1   Improvement of Door and Window Security
5.2   Adequate Security Lighting
5.4   Crime Prevention in Design
5.8   Inclusion of Crime Prevention Measures into Existing Codes and the Consideration of Building Security Codes
5.9   Crime Impact Forecast
5.10 Crime Prevention Courses as a Job Requirement

Standard 5.7

Crime Prevention Courses in Schools of Architecture and Urban Planning

Schools offering courses in architecture or urban planning should include in their curriculums courses on architectural design for crime prevention.

Commentary

"Attention by the profession of architecture to designing security into plans and specifications is virtually nonexistent" concluded the Small Business Administration in its report, *Crime Against Small Business*. If schools of architecture had included courses in crime preventive techniques in their curriculums, this statement would not have been made. This same admonition could be applied to urban planning.

In the past, little relationship has existed between the fields of architecture and/or urban planning and the field of security services. However, as increasing numbers of citizens and businesses have become the victims of crime, experiencing serious losses and personal fear, the need for additional protection has become both vital and critical. The demand for a safer environment is being voiced throughout the Nation and, as a result, the involvement of physical security in structural design is receiving special emphasis. Architects and urban planners, heretofore unfamiliar and unconcerned with security measures, now need to consider them in building design and community planning.

Schools teaching architecture or urban planning should assist in familiarizing these individuals with security requirements by offering courses in architectural design for crime prevention. These courses should cover the historical development of crime prevention in design up to crime prevention in environmental design (CPTED) and defensible space. The following points, suggested by the National Institute of Law Enforcement and Criminal Justice, should be included in the course of study:

1. Promoting opportunities for surveillance,
2. Strengthening the differentiation of private from public space,
3. Fostering territoriality,
4. Controlling access,
5. Separating incompatible activities,
6. Providing alternative outlets for potentially delinquent and criminal energies.

The curriculums should also include a study of the effect of architecture on deterrence and displacement of crime. To bring about the broadest perspective possible, these subjects could be team-taught, using a combination of architects, urban planners, sociologists, criminologists, psychologists, law enforcement officers, and private security consultants. Course content for the study of crime deterrence should include specific tactics, alarm systems, barriers, lighting, and security patrols—all traditional and proven protective devices.

Course content for the study of crime displacement would be more difficult to quantify because little data are available; nevertheless it is an important and necessary subject for the architecture or urban planning student. If, through design, certain crime is prevented, will some even more heinous crime take its place? Will persons coming to and from the site or building now be subject to a greater level of criminal attack because of displacement, causing people not to use the site or building? Questions such as these should be confronted in architectural and urban planning courses. These subjects traditionally have been in the purview of the criminologist, law enforcement officer, and sociologist; now students of architecture and urban planning also must understand and be able to work with them.

Various divisions of the U.S. Department of Justice have been instrumental in publishing monographs and studies dealing with subjects ranging from target hardening to Oscar Newman's defensible space efforts with New York City's public housing. A review of these publications would prove helpful in crime prevention courses. Individual buildings and residential developments that have incorporated security-in-design concepts should be used for case studies, and law enforcement and private security personnel should be used as guest lecturers or instructors.

Standard 5.10 recommends that a certified course in CPTED be provided for architects or urban planners as a job prerequisite or as partial preparation for a license. Educators can ensure their students meet this requirement by making CPTED courses a degree requirement. Another approach would be to make these courses mandatory for accreditation of schools of architecture and urban planning.

To avoid charges such as that leveled by the Small Business Administration, crime prevention concepts need to be given general exposure in urban planning and architectural schools, perhaps as a required interdisciplinary course. If educators fail in implementing this measure, increases in human misery and economic loss will continue as a direct result of their oversight. Further, the security executive will have the continuing burden of attempting to convince planners and architects of the same lessons over and over again.

Selected References

1. Fielding, Byron. "Safety and Security in Multiple Family Complexes," *Journal of Housing,* No. 6, June 1971.

2. National Institute of Law Enforcement and Criminal Justice, Law Enforcement Assistance Administration, U.S. Department of Justice. *Residential Security.* Washington, D.C.: Government Printing Office, 1973.

3. Small Business Administration. *Crime Against Small Business.* Washington, D.C.: Government Printing Office, 1969.

Related Standards

The following standards and goals may be applicable in implementing Standard 5.7:

2.8   Training of Supervisors and Managers
5.5   Development of Environmental Security Expertise
5.10 Crime Prevention Courses as a Job Requirement
6.1   Interaction Policies
8.3   Noncredit and Credit Seminars and Courses
8.4   Degree Programs for Private Security

Standard 5.8

Inclusion of Crime Prevention Measures in Existing Codes and the Consideration of Building Security Codes

Crime prevention measures should be an identifiable part of existing or proposed regulatory codes. Building, fire, and safety code should be reviewed by regulatory bodies and private security representatives to avoid conflict with implementation of effective crime prevention measures.

Commentary

Throughout the 50 States there exists a myriad of codes and regulations at the local, State, and national level covering fire, building, and safety. They spell out "dos and don'ts" that affect the lives of everyone. Often provisions within these codes conflict; occasionally they complement one another. For example, San Francisco currently adheres to four different electrical codes relating to alarm systems.

The latest development in regulations and codes is to draft building security codes. Some successes in crime reduction have been documented where security codes have been implemented. However, it is preferable to incorporate crime prevention measures into existing building, fire, and safety codes. Additional codes only create another bureaucratic burden for the businessman and the citizen. Further, it appears likely that the future direction of building codes is toward developing a single code covering building, fire, safety, and possibly other environmentally related topics.

There are two very serious concerns to consider when discussing the incorporation of security provisions into existing codes. The first concern is the fear that crime prevention measures would become a stepchild among the traditionally strong fire, electrical, and plumbing provisions and be lost in the verbal foliage of the code. The second concern is the problem of conflict between crime prevention measures and fire, building, and safety codes. For example, security principles may clash with various safety code tenets and may generate construction expenses in excess of estimated budgets and aesthetics that do not correspond to conventional building codes. Also, as any security executive knows, the principles of good security frequently run counter to fire regulations. The Howard Johnson sniper case that occurred in New Orleans, La., in January 1973 illustrates this conflict. A gunman gained entry to a motel through a door that connects the building's garage with the upper-story guest room area. As required by fire regulations, as an emergency exit from a building-connected garage, the door was equipped with a crash bar that allowed access to the motel fire stairwell. If the crash bar designed to allow exit from the garage in the event of fire had not been used, the sniper may have been prevented from reaching the guest area.

The establishment of a review body should enable such conflicts to be reasonably and rationally resolved and should dispel the concern of those who envision security measures facing in impact by the terminology of the code. This review body should be established by local government and be responsible for reviewing current fire, building, and safety codes and mediating any conflicts created by the incorporation of crime prevention regulations. This body would also ensure that the wording of the code clearly identifies each requirement. Membership of the review body should consist of representatives from each of the areas being regulated and include private security representatives.

The private security members should be selected by screening the area's firms to find those individuals with the greatest expertise in current security hardware, alarms, and crime prevention techniques. These representatives would be able to identify current prevention techniques that might conflict with fire, safety, and building codes. Further, the private security representative could give advice on new developments in security hardware, as well as suggesting techniques that would be compatible with other code provisions.

Through this interaction with government, private security's expertise can be used to benefit the public. Participation of the private security industry in activities, including reviewing fire, building, and safety codes, would help develop mutual respect and cooperation between government bodies and the industry. When conflicts between proposed security measures and existing building, fire, and safety codes occur, the presence of a private security expert would tend to ensure a fair crime-prevention representation in the evaluation of the conflicting prerogatives.

Although incorporating crime prevention measures into existing fire, building, and safety codes is favored, this may be thought impossible in the immediate future for some jurisdictions. In these jurisdictions, a separate crime prevention or security code should be enacted.

The drafting of such a document does not present an insurmountable problem. In 1975, at least one State (California) and nearly two dozen cities in 12 States became involved in developing or implementing building security codes, the purpose of which was to safeguard buildings and occupants against vulnerability to crime. Sample codes are available for reference from these communities. Additional guidance can be obtained from *A Building Security Code for Texas Cities,* published by the Texas Municipal League. According to the League, security building codes are legal documents developed "to require construction methods that result in increased security and the addition of security hardware and other protective devices which make a structure less

vulnerable." They also point out that security building codes have their roots in "building and related codes (i.e., fire, life safety, etc.) that have been operative for decades." Building security codes also have been advocated by organizations, such as the National Institute of Law Enforcement and Criminal Justice and the Schlage Security Institute.

Existing security codes vary in their explicitness of definition and requirement for security hardware and its application, particularly regarding doors, windows, and locks. Some building security codes specify lighting requirements. Others offer detailed specifications for construction of doorframes.

The scope of security building codes also varies. Hollis DeVines, director of the Schlage Security Institute, points out two examples: In Indianapolis, Ind., single-family dwellings are included in the security building codes; in Montgomery County, Md., the code is retroactive for motels, hotels, and multi-family dwellings. Other codes specify only commercial buildings. The National Institute for Law Enforcement and Criminal Justice's Federal Security Code has provisions that are so broad that they apply "to all existing and future buildings or structures."

Although building security codes vary as to types of buildings included and types and applications of security hardware required, the drafting bodies have had a common characteristic—lack of private security representation. Not even the National Advisory Commission on Criminal Justice Standards and Goals in their recommendation, "9.2 Security Requirements for Building Codes in Community Crime Prevention," included private security experts in the list of persons to be consulted in preparing building security codes. The private security industry's everyday business is crime prevention. To exclude these professionals from groups drafting building security codes is a grave oversight.

Crime prevention measures should be incorporated into existing building, fire, and safety codes to reduce crime and serve the common good of the community. By including private security representatives in the development of regulations, the government allows those with expertise in crime prevention to exercise their civic responsibility.

Selected References

1. City of Oakland Police Services. "Commercial Burglary Prevention Ordinance." Oakland, Calif.: City of Oakland.

2. DeVines, Hollis. "Building Security Codes and Ordinances" (an address), *Urban Design, Security and Crime Proceedings of a National Institute of Law Enforcement and Criminal Justice Seminar,*

April 12 and 13, 1973. Washington, D.C.: U.S. Department of Justice, Law Enforcement Assistance Administration, 1973.

3. National Advisory Commission on Criminal Justice Standards and Goals. *Community Crime Prevention*. Washington, D.C.: Government Printing Office, 1973.

4. National Institute of Law Enforcement and Criminal Justice. "Federal Security Code with Minimum Building Security Guidelines and Cost Estimates for the Security Features," initial draft. Washington, D.C.: Law Enforcement Assistance Administration, May 14, 1971.

5. Texas Municipal League. *A Building Security Code for Texas Cities*. Austin, Tex.: Texas Municipal League, 1975.

Related Standards

The following standards and goals may be applicable in implementing Standard 5.8:

5.1   Improvement of Door and Window Security

5.2   Adequate Security Lighting

5.6   Environmental Security in Comprehensive Planning

Standard 5.9

Crime Impact Forecast

Crime impact statements should be included in the planning phase of all new public and private building and development projects.

Commentary

The crime impact forecast is a new concept. Its development and use stem from the environmental design approach to crime prevention. As envisioned, the forecast will be a planning instrument used to determine what changes in crime patterns may result from building and development projects. Its use can ensure that government and private business give consideration to public protection when planning new building projects. Crime impact forecasts should be included in the planning phase of all new public and private building and development projects.

The crime impact forecast is a written statement that projects expected results of a new building or development project in terms of criminal activities. As suggested in a Westinghouse Electric Corporation study, "Elements of CPTED" (crime prevention through environmental design), it should include the following projections:

1. Time of crime,
2. Tactics of crime,
3. Target of crime,
4. Place of crime, and
5. Type of crime.

Other equally important points that should be covered in the statement are those outlined by Michael B. Barker, chairman of the Environmental Security Committee of the Private Security Advisory Council:

. . . should include additional information which would be of use to local decision-makers. For example, 1) the impacts on the use of public spaces in the vicinity of the proposed facility; 2) the expense to local government to offset any adverse impacts (against which any tax benefits should be measured); 3) the adequacy of the public infrastructure with respect to security, i.e., police access, street lighting, etc.; 4) the extent of private security services which the owner himself will supply, and their relationship to the pertinent public security agencies.

Further, justification for the crime impact forecast is the present lack of understanding by the architect or urban planner in the elements of design that can deter or prevent crime. This factor is discussed in Standard 5.7.

Certain design elements may require modifications in order to best protect the residents and/or businesses of the surrounding area and to ensure the protection of the new building or development. Such changes should be made at a point that would require little or no additional expenditures; therefore, it is important that the crime impact forecast be prepared for the design phase of planning.

Crime is committed by humans, not laboratory specimens under controlled environmental conditions. It is not possible to accurately predict which person will commit what crime and when. But, enough is known about crime so that reasonable projections can be made as to what generally will occur when the environment is altered. A crime impact forecast can be made, but it is just that—a forecast. Because of the nature of crime, there should be no attempt to attach legal significance to the crime impact forecast or liability to those preparing it.

The responsibility for drafting the impact statement would vary, depending on whether the forecast is for public or private building or development projects. If the project concerns public buildings or developments, the local law enforcement agency would be the appropriate body to prepare the crime impact forecast, with input from urban planners. In the case of private buildings or developments, private security people should prepare the forecast.

Because the crime impact statement for public projects would be an extension of government's responsibility to provide its citizens a safe environment, it should be open to public scrutiny. Considering the highly emotional issue crime presents, the forecast could become a controversial community issue. The crime impact forecast could be used to rally community opposition to a public building or development to achieve some personal gain. Thus, a needed project whose benefits would outweigh other considerations could be forced aside because of negative community response. Persons interested in local political offices could use the forecast as a stepping-stone for their ambitions by attracting attention to themselves through raucous opposition to a project. Therefore, before government undertakes any construction, it should ensure that satisfactory responses are ready for each problem posed by the crime impact forecast. In this way, when the first shovelful of dirt is turned, law enforcement officials would be able to begin implementing new tactics to counter changes in crime patterns.

Private business should use its crime impact forecast as a planning tool. The forecast should be drafted to assure that the safety of the public and employees and the business's profits and inventories are protected through effective crime prevention measures.

In drafting a private business's crime impact forecast, the security executive should consult with local law enforcement agencies to develop a plan that would protect employees and neighborhood residents equally, so that the public interest is served.

In time, the crime impact forecast will become part of all new building and development projects. However, immediate efforts of private security and law enforcement personnel, architects, and urban planners are necessary if that goal is to be reached. Questions regarding content, applicability, controls, and other areas need to be resolved through the cooperative efforts of all these professionals. A few such questions are offered for consideration:

1. For what types of planned construction would the crime impact forecast be applicable?

2. Should the crime impact forecast be incorporated into existing environmental impact statements at the State and Federal levels?

3. What type of sanctions would be used to ensure that the crime impact forecast was made?

4. Would requiring forecasts result in a new breed of experts and consultants who would perform this service for private business, and would they need to be licensed and regulated?

Selected References

1. Barker, Michael M. Written correspondence with Clifford W. Van Meter, Oct. 3, 1975.

2. Tien, J. M., T. A. Repetto, and L. F. Hanes. "Elements of CPTED." Arlington, Va.: Westinghouse Electric Corporation, 1975.

Related Standards

The following standards may be applicable in implementing Standard 5.9:

3.5   Maintaining Data on Criminal Activities

5.5   Development of Environmental Security Expertise

5.6   Environmental Security in Comprehensive Planning

6.3   Policies and Procedures

Standard 5.10

Crime Prevention Courses as a Job Requirement

Architects and urban planners should be encouraged to attend seminars or classes in crime prevention through environmental design (CPTED). Proof of successful completion of a CPTED seminar or course could then become a necessary prerequisite for employment or the obtaining of a license.

Commentary

Since the early 1960's, a quiet evolution has been taking place in the field of crime prevention. It emerged from the work of individuals who recognized certain relationships between the environment and people and who studied this relationship and hypothesized about its general applicability to the prevention and reduction of crime.

Early activities in the field include the defensible space efforts of Oscar Newman and George Rand with the New York Public Housing Authority, a Westinghouse study entitled "Elements of Crime Prevention through Environmental Design," numerous professional papers, and Law Enforcement Assistance Administration publications on the effect of design on crime.

In addition to numerous texts, articles, and reports on crime prevention through modification of the environment, the Federal Government has an Environmental Security Committee as a standing committee of the Private Security Advisory Council. And there have been seminars conducted in several States for the purpose of making these new concepts available to architects and urban planners in the field.

The urgency for activating all available weapons against crime makes it essential that architects and urban planners become versed in these concepts. Acquisition of this knowledge can be achieved by making it a requirement for obtaining or renewing a license or as a prerequisite for a job as an architect or urban planner.

This requirement would necessitate that the architect or urban planner successfully complete a course in CPTED. The precise content of that course should be designed by professionals in the various fields. The selected references in this chapter, as well as the CPTED annotated bibliography by the Westinghouse Corporation should be consulted for source material.

The first courses and seminars should concentrate on informing architects and urban planners regarding the new CPTED concepts. When schools and universities have incorporated this material into their curriculums, the scope of the courses and seminars could be broadened with the inclusion of extensive, crime-related materials. The immediate goal of this standard, however, is to rapidly bring the basic CPTED concepts to the architects and urban planners already working in the field.

Selected References

1. Newman, Oscar. *Architectural Design for Crime Prevention*. U.S. Department of Justice, Law Enforcement Assistance Administration. Washington, D.C.: Government Printing Office, 1973.

2. Tien, J.M., T.A. Repetto, et al. "Crime Prevention Through Environmental Design (CPTED) Annotated Bibliography." Arlington, Va.: Westinghouse Electric Corporation.

3. Tien, J.M., T.A. Repetto, and L. F. Hanes. "Elements of CPTED." Arlington, Va.: Westinghouse Electric Corporation, 1975.

Related Standards

The following standards and goals may be applicable in implementing Standard 5.10:

5.4   Crime Prevention in Design

5.6   Environmental Security in Comprehensive Planning

5.7   Crime Prevention Courses in Schools of Architecture and Urban Planning

8.4   Degree Programs for Private Security

Part 4
Relationship of The Industry With Others

Chapter 6
Law Enforcement Agencies

INTRODUCTION

The recent escalation of crime in the United States and the resultant fear of personal harm, loss of property, and public disorder have caused considerable resources to be directed to law enforcement activities. In response to mounting demands for more and better protection, total Federal, State, and local expenditures for police services climbed to more than $6.5 billion in 1973 and are continuing to increase.

Clearly, Americans are experiencing a growing concern for personal and public safety. Just as clearly, already strained government budgets alone cannot provide the resources necessary to effectively deal with the upward trend in crime. In New York, Detroit, and many other cities, police manpower is being reduced because of community budgetary limitations. In other locales, planned increases or expansions of services are being halted. Police expenditures now constitute the largest single item in many municipal budgets.

A grave dilemma is arising across the Nation. In the face of ever-rising crime rates, communities are finding that the limits of their fiscal resources have been reached. Additionally, it is now apparent that police alone cannot control crime. As aptly pointed out by Louis Radelet, Michigan State University professor of criminal justice, in the Dec. 8, 1975, issue of *Crime Control Digest,* "The police alone are futile in the prevention of crime . . . . They need to work in partnership endeavors with community forces." One such force possessing the potential to significantly contribute to the reduction of national crime is the private security industry.

Considering the mutual interests and common linkages between the public law enforcement and private security sectors, a close working relationship could enhance the efficiency and effectiveness of both forces, adding impetus to the efforts to curb crime in our society.

The crime preventive role of the private security industry, and the benefits it provides to both the private and public sectors, have been recognized by the Law Enforcement Assistance Administration and serve as the catalyst for this report. The purpose of this chapter is to serve to promote increased cooperation and the development of mechanisms to improve working relationships between public law enforcement agencies and the private security industry in their mutual objective of crime prevention.

If this objective is to be realized, interaction between the two agencies must be strengthened. As stated in Goal 6.1, "Effective interaction between the private security industry and law enforcement agencies is imperative for successful crime prevention and depends to a large extent on published clear and understandable policies developed by their administrators." In examining the existing interaction between the two forces, very limited interaction was found, with the exception of informal contacts at the upper supervisory and management levels. If the public law enforcement and private security spheres are to work in unity and not at cross-purposes, interaction is required at all levels.

Significantly, research has indicated that most public law enforcement agencies believe that the establishment of close, well-defined working relationships with private security agencies would be valuable. Clear written guidelines aimed at improved understanding and cooperation on the part of both agencies are needed to promote and maintain effective interaction.

In order to aid interaction, public law enforcement personnel need to be knowledgeable of private security operations within their jurisdiction. To this end, law enforcement agencies should survey private security components within their jurisdiction and designate at least one officer as liaison to provide guidance and to coordinate services (Standard 6.2).

The exchange of information resulting from such a liaison would not only aid reciprocal cooperation but also provide a framework for the subsequent establishment of written policies and procedures covering the delineation of respective roles, interchange of information, and cooperative actions. As outlined in Standard 6.3, the formulation of such policies and procedures can eliminate the confusion and uncertainty that act as barriers to improved understanding and cooperation. For example, police administrators are often unaware of how private security services can assist them. Similarly, private security firms do not know how to obtain specific assistance from law enforcement agencies. Clear policies and procedures can provide the sense of direction necessary for decisive judgments and improved interaction between private security and law enforcement agencies.

Another area that can strengthen the bond between the two fields is education. Misunderstanding of the respective roles of law enforcement officers and private security personnel often leads to a lack of acceptance or respect of one another. Standard 6.4 proposes a multilevel training program for public law enforcement officials, covering the respective roles of the two agencies and the nature of their mutual contacts. This training can provide a basis for future cooperative actions, as well as dispel common stereotypes and misconceptions.

Those first four standards are aimed primarily at establishing the administrative groundwork for a close working relationship between the private security and public law enforcement sectors. The remaining five standards in this chapter deal with eliminating possible sources of conflict that may serve as barriers to professional interaction.

One source of conflict is the use by private security of title terms, verbal representations, and visual items that cause the public to mistake their personnel for law enforcement officers. Although private security personnel often are uniformed and may be armed, their powers differ significantly from those of public police. Therefore, for the protection of the public and security officers, private security companies and organizations should ensure that their personnel and equipment are easily distinguishable from public law enforcement personnel and equipment. Too close a resemblance to public police not only causes confusion for the public and resentment from public law enforcement agencies but also may lead to the imposition of liability from practices,

such as "impersonating a public police officer." Therefore, it is recommended that each State develop regulations on the use or wear of private security uniforms, equipment, company names, and personnel titles that avoids any possible conflict with those of public law enforcement forces.

An area that has created much controversy and has suppressed interaction between public law enforcement and private security agencies is the practice of public law enforcement officers moonlighting in private security jobs. As the demand for increased protective services has continued to grow, especially in the industrial area, many public law enforcement officers have turned to private security activities for secondary employment. This practice has created many problems, including the private security industry's belief that such a situation creates unfair competition.

Other problems associated with moonlighting are discussed in detail in the last three standards of this chapter. To guard against situations in which moonlighting may generate unfair competition, involve the use of public resources for private gain, or create serious conflicts of interest, it is recommended that public law enforcement officers be restricted from employment in certain types of private security activities, such as private investigatory work where such improper actions are almost inevitable. It also is suggested that law enforcement administrators develop and enforce clear policies limiting secondary employment for law enforcement personnel to positions that do not create conflicts of interest or involve the misuse of public property.

In summary, closer unity of private security services and public law enforcement agencies offers the potential for improved crime preventive measures that will greatly benefit society. In order to form a mutually productive working relationship, increased cooperation and opportunities for interaction should be exhibited by both forces.

Goal 6.1

Interaction Policies

Effective interaction between the private security industry and law enforcement agencies is imperative for successful crime prevention and depends to a large extent on published clear and understandable policies developed by their administrators. Policies should be developed to serve as guides for modification by appropriate agencies.

Commentary

Over the past decade, the resources devoted to both public law enforcement and the private security industry have increased as the awareness of the need for greater crime prevention and control has grown. National leaders have called upon every private citizen, institution, and business to join their efforts with the criminal justice system to prevent crime. Although a closer cooperation between the private security and public law enforcement spheres offers a special opportunity for improved crime prevention, the relationship has often been ignored, overlooked, or restrained.

Recently, however, the potential of a meaningful working relationship between law enforcement and private security personnel has been recognized. To promote a positive, ongoing relationship, formalized open interaction between the two agencies needs to be developed. On the national level, the International Association of Chiefs of Police and the American Society for Industrial Security (ASIS) have taken significant steps to provide a forum for such interaction. And in the fall of 1974, the Private Security Advisory Council formed a standing committee to study the law enforcement-private security relationship. Some of the goals and objectives of this standing committee are reflected in its minutes of March 7, 1975:

Goal 2. Outline proposals to improve understanding and cooperation between Private Security personnel and public law enforcement officers.

Objective 2–2. Develop guidelines for cooperation between private security and public law enforcement.

A study of the existing interaction between the private security industry and public law enforcement agencies reveals the need for clear guidelines. Surveys conducted by both the RAND Corporation and the Institute for Local Self Government, Berkeley, Calif., indicated that fewer than 25 percent of responding private security personnel had contact more than once or twice a year with law enforcement agencies. However, a third survey, recently completed by ASIS, is in direct opposition to these findings. The results of the three surveys are shown in Table 6.1.

Table 6.1. Interaction of Private Security and Public Law Enforcement

Frequency of Contact with Law Enforcement Agencies	Rand 1972 %	Institute 1974 %	ASIS 1975 %
Daily			47
Once or twice a week	7	5	
Weekly			24
Once or twice a month	14	17	10
Monthly			11
Once or twice a year	30	23	
Whenever necessary	15	10	
Never	27	29	
Declined to answer		16	1
Do not know			7
Unaccounted for	7		

Source: Private Security Task Force, "American Society for Industrial Security (ASIS) Survey Results." (See Appendix 1 to this report.) Institute for Local Self Government, *Private Security and the Public Interest*. Berkeley, Calif.: 1974. The *RAND Report*, Vols. I and II, Washington, D.C.: Government Printing Office, 1972.

The contrast between the results of the first two surveys and the ASIS survey can be explained by the fact that respondents to the latter were from upper supervisory and management levels. The contacts they frequently mentioned were informal meetings with law enforcement personnel at the local clubs, associations, luncheons, and so forth, and indicate interaction primarily at the upper management level. Although these interactions are higher desirable, the results of such contacts should be formulated into clear policies that increase interaction between security guards and law enforcement officers at the lower levels of the two fields. Because the ultimate missions of the two fields are parallel and, to some degree, overlap, effective interaction at all levels should be sought.

To achieve this interaction, certain obstacles need to be overcome. One such obstacle—the problem of lack of mutual respect—was discussed at a meeting of the Private Security Advisory Council's Law Enforcement/Private Security Relationship Committee. Some of the concerns discussed at this meeting follow:

1. Private security believes:
   a. Law enforcement does not respect them,
   b. Law enforcement is primarily concerned with arrests and not with crime prevention.

2. Law enforcement believes:
   a. Private security is nonprofessional, and
   b. Private security is client-oriented and not society-oriented.

What is important here is that, as long as lack of respect for each other's profession exists, effective interaction remains an untapped resource. But the frank and open discussion that took place at the committee meeting is a significant step toward solution of the problem. Identification of weaknesses and areas of misunderstanding are the necessary initial steps to achieving greater mutual respect and cooperation. For example, some comments disclosed that law enforcement lack of respect is directed primarily at the lowest level of private security personnel. A major portion of this lack of respect is based on a substantial difference in salary levels. Therefore, general upgrading of private security training and salaries may offer one means of increasing respect.

Another obstacle to the development of interaction can be attributed to existing laws. Laws often hinder the degree to which law enforcement agencies and the private security industry can interact, particularly in the area of exchange of information. Law enforcement and private security agencies need to voice the need for changing such laws. Their respective legal staffs should meet with others in the

Table 6.2 American Society for Industrial Security (ASIS) Survey Results Regarding Access to Criminal Justice Records

Question 22:   With what frequency do you utilize public criminal justice record systems? (i.e., license check, arrest records, etc.)

	Percentage
Never	16
Daily	27
Weekly	30
Monthly	18
Yearly	4
No response	5

Question 23:   Indicate your accessibility to public criminal justice records for private security business.

No response   7%

	Level				
	1	2	3	4	5
Not accessible	19%	18%	26%	14%	16%	Very accessible

Question 24:   Indicate the types of information you need to know from the criminal justice system.

	Yes %	No %	No response %
a. Arrest verification	74	11	15
b. Conviction verification	84	4	12
c. Alleged misconduct	49	20	31
d. Driver license check	57	18	25
e. Vehicle check	65	13	22
f. Other	10	0	90

Source: Private Security Task Force, "American Society of Industrial Security (ASIS) Survey Results." (See Appendix I of this report.)

criminal justice system to define and resolve the legal constraints on information interaction.

Specifically, private security firms should have appropriate access to criminal justice information and statistic systems. The information in Table 6.2, taken from the ASIS survey, indicates the need for such information.

Obstacles to interaction between the two fields are not limited to laws and lack of respect. Other obstacles exist. Through positive interaction, all such obstacles can be identified and policies developed to help surmount them. Only through the formulation of clear, understandable policies can effective cooperation occur.

One area in serious need of formal guidelines to promote effective interaction is that of crime reporting. In this respect, several questions are raised. Should private security personnel be required to report crime like ordinary citizens? Should they report all crime to police? Who should be given credit for an important arrest, the law enforcement or private security party? These are questions that need to be resolved through the mutual efforts of the law enforcement and private security sectors.

A significant figure from the "Survey of Consumers of Private Security Services in the Greater Philadelphia Area" highlights the lack of interaction between the private security industry and law enforcement agencies in regard to crime reporting. (This survey was the first major attempt to document user-reactions to the private security industry.) In the survey, question 19, asking if criminal activities were unreported to law enforcement agencies, drew a 45 percent affirmative answer.

In some areas, existing interaction has brought about desirable results. In one Virginia community, for example, law enforcement and private security professionals meet monthly to discuss topics of mutual concern. A list of cooperative actions appearing in the *RAND Report* (Vol. I) included:

1. Call-in service for guards;
2. Shoplifter bulletins;
3. Installation of alarms in police stations;
4. Providing law enforcement information, and
5. Serving as law enforcement's added eyes and ears.

In an article in *The Police Chief,* Raymond M. Atherton, chief, special agent, Standard Oil Co. of California, mentions a study that "identifies 39 types of businesses, educational, and industrial organizations having plant protection, security, or other specialized units responsible for maintaining liaison with law enforcement agencies." In the same issue of *The Police Chief,* an article by Thad F. Brown, deputy chief, Los Angeles Police Department, identifies some 40 areas of assistance that private security personnel can provide to law enforcement agencies. These citations indicate that the number of complex interrelationships of services and agencies, alone justifies the need for development of clear interaction policies.

Although the positive efforts and good will of those employed in law enforcement and private security will promote some level of interaction, there is still a need for clear policies to provide an ethical, legal, and professional framework to channel such interaction. Henry Armstrong, in his article in *Security Management,* sums up the situation well:

First of all we should reach an acceptable understanding as to who and what industrial security men are, then we should consider appropriate ways of improving the liaison between police and industry officers. Finally, we should recognize how effective liaison between the two groups can help the individual communities . . .

Law enforcement and private security sectors working together enhance each other's role and ability. Citizens indirectly benefit through more "eyes" on the streets, better and faster handling of persons committing criminal acts, and closer observation of those persons who may intend to commit criminal acts. In short, effective interaction can produce a greater degree of safety and security for the community.

Selected References

1. Armstrong, Henry C. "3 Primary Topic Affective Police and Security Officer Liaison," *Security Management,* January 1964.

2. Atherton, Raymond M. "Units Maintaining Liaison," *The Police Chief,* November 1964.

3. Brown, Thad F. "Types of Assistance Available," *The Police Chief,* November 1964.

4. Institute for Local Self Government, *Private Security and the Public Interest.* Berkeley, Calif.: Institute for Local Self Government, 1974.

5. Kakalik, James S., and Sorrel Wildhorn. *Private Police in the United States: Findings and Recommendations,* Vol. I, R–869/DOJ. Washington, D.C.: Government Printing Office, 1972.

6. Kakalik, James S., and Sorrel Wildhorn, *The Private Police Industry: Its Nature and Extent,* Vol. II, R–870/DOJ. Washington, D.C.: Government Printing Office, 1972.

7. Minutes: Nov. 6 and 7, 1974, meeting of Law Enforcement/Private Security Relationship Committee of the Private Security Advisory Council to the Law Enforcement Assistance Administration.

8. Minutes: Mar. 7, 1975, meeting of Law Enforcement/Private Security Relationship Committee of the Private Security Advisory Council to the Law Enforcement Assistance Administration.

9. Private Security Task Force. "American Society for Industrial Security (ASIS) Survey Results." (See Appendix 1 to this report.)

Related Standards

The following standards and goals may be applicable in implementing Goal 6.1:

2.1   Training in Private Security
3.2   Conduct of Private Security Personnel
3.3   Reporting of Criminal Violations
5.7   Crime Prevention Courses in Schools of Architecture and Urban Planning
5.9   Crime Impact Forecast
6.3   Policies and Procedures
6.4   Multilevel Law Enforcement Training in Private Security

Standard 6.2

Survey and Liaison
With Private Security

Law enforcement agencies should conduct a survey and maintain a current roster of those private security industry components operating in the agencies' jurisdictions and designate at least one staff officer to serve as liaison with them.

Commentary

Existing relationships between the public law enforcement and private security sectors range from close working arrangements to limited and sometimes strained contacts. Often law enforcement agencies are unaware of the extent or nature of private security operations within their jurisdictions. Many times private security services are unaware of correct crime reporting procedures or do not know the proper agency to contact for assistance. Regular liaison between law enforcement and private security agencies within a jurisdiction can eliminate these problems and lead to a mutually productive working environment and, further, to greater crime prevention and reduction capabilities.

For law enforcement agencies, the benefits of the establishment of formal liaison enhance the delivery of police services. Through liaison, the potential for positive cooperative measures can be explored, and those that are found to be feasible can be implemented to obtain greater law enforcement effectiveness. The private security sphere would also benefit from the increased guidance and flow of information resulting from regular liaison. The Institute for Local Self Government stated in their report on the California private security industry, "Lacking the prerogatives of full police power, many private security operations find public law enforcement liaison to be an absolute necessity."

Recognizing the important potential benefits of intercommunication between law enforcement agencies and the private security industry, this standard recommends that law enforcement agencies conduct periodic surveys of the nature and extent of private security operations in their jurisdictions. These surveys would be a first step toward effective liaison. Because in some areas, such as New Orleans, St. Louis, and Cleveland, public law enforcement personnel are outnumbered by private security personnel four to one, it is suggested that law enforcement agencies conduct the surveys to determine the amount of private security resources available to assist them.

The suggested survey would be uncomplicated and inexpensive. Companies selling private security services and equipment would be identified by consulting the local telephone book, chamber of commerce, and so forth. Identification of stores, factories, and buildings with their own private security systems poses more of a problem. However, time and legwork can yield identification of all private security operations in the jurisdiction, and a roster can be prepared and updated periodically.

Private security associations could perform a similar activity. They could prepare a roster of all local, State, and Federal law enforcement agencies operating within the jurisdiction, including phone numbers and persons to be contacted for assistance or information, and distribute this roster to all local private security operations.

Depending upon the size of the jurisdiction, at least one staff officer should be designated by law enforcement agencies to act as liaison with private security concerns. This officer would be responsible for conducting the survey, as well as establishing and maintaining an open line of communication with all private security operations in the jurisdiction. Such action is in line with the recommendations of the Institute for Local Self Government for improving law enforcement-private security relationships:

Local law enforcement agencies having private security activity within their jurisdiction should establish an authority (either a mini bureau or an individual security coordinator, depending on size) for reviewing private security activities.

Much of the success or failure of law enforcement/private security relations in a given area depends on the selection of liaison personnel. For this reason, the individual assuming this duty should possess certain skills and knowledge. As private security liaison, a law enforcement officer should be able to deal with owners of private security companies or representatives of national and/or international private security operations. The officer should, therefore, be of a high enough rank to be on an equal footing with the private security contacts. Private security executives may hesitate to confide in a patrol officer, regardless of competence, simply because they feel the officer is at too low a level in the power structure to effect any action.

The law enforcement officer selected for liaison also needs to be knowledgeable about the functioning of the private security industry. This representative should not only develop a working knowledge of all laws and registration requirements applicable to private security operations, but also understand the workings of a contract guard company, an armored car company, an alarm company and central station, and their related technical problems, as well as be familiar with the operations of proprietary security organizations.

One other realistic consideration should be given to the selection of the law enforcement officer responsible for liaison. The job should be given to an officer in midcareer who is aware of his or her advancement potential in the agency. An individual near retirement or near the highest probable level of advancement may be inclined to accept a position with a private security operation desiring the contacts, knowledge, and skill the officer can offer.

The exact duties of the liaison officer and the amount of time required can be more clearly discerned after contact with the private security industry yields an awareness of their local needs. Initially, however, the officer should prepare, with direct input from the chief law enforcement official, long- and short-term goals for liaison and procedures to be followed to achieve them. In developing these goals, the chief and the liaison officer should discuss and determine what the agency can and cannot do to aid the private security industry.

Private security operations also are encouraged to select at least one individual to work in a liaison capacity with law enforcement agencies. Here again a great degree of care should be exercised in the selection of liaison personnel. If mutual trust and rapport are to be achieved, the person selected should be knowledgeable about phases of the private security operation and have a working knowledge of law enforcement activities and operations. The liaison representative should use restraint in requests for assistance from law enforcement personnel as a measure to avoid withdrawal of the agency from the program.

When the law enforcement liaison officer and agency are ready to begin the survey of private security operations, three objectives should be met: (1) gather together all available information on private security resources operating in the jurisdiction; (2) prepare an inventory of police services available to private security concerns and methods of obtaining them; and (3) determine how the survey is to be conducted.

In small jurisdictions, a survey of private security elements would involve little more than picking up the phone and calling the local private security agencies and proprietary security operations to invite their administrators into the station for an informal meeting. An actual example of this was noted in a law enforcement agency response to a question posed in a Task Force survey as to whether it had conducted a survey. The answer was "yes," with the qualifier that the town was so small that they personally knew all the private security operations.

In larger jurisdictions, such as New York, Chicago, or Los Angeles, more elaborate survey preparations may be necessary and a more detailed survey instrument desirable. One method would be for law enforcement agencies to enlist the aid of various local private security organizations in developing a list of all private security operations in the jurisdiction. Regardless of the method chosen for conducting the survey, the following data should be obtained: (1) type and size of security operations, (2) whether security personnel are armed, (3) a list of all client services, (4) a list of key company personnel, and (5) special services needed from law enforcement agencies.

Other information that can be gained in the course of a survey was outlined by Robert L. Parsons in his master's thesis on law enforcement and retail management cooperative efforts:

> The administrators of each respective agency must begin to learn from each other: (1) their own respective problems; (2) their actual operational set-up; (3) areas in which reciprocal advantage can be obtained by cooperative efforts, and (4) the actual effects of the shared problem—the commission of burglary and robbery—against their own operations.

When the survey is completed and the data analyzed, the law enforcement agency should arrange channels of communication. These activities might include a meeting between the law enforcement and private security agencies. This meeting might include several persons and an address by the chief law enforcement official or might simply be an individual meeting of the liaison officer and private security executive at his place of business. Private security organizations could similarly organize an informal or formal meeting with law enforcement personnel, possibly including addresses by various executives of the private security industry. When this step is completed, the groundwork will have been laid for interaction, cooperation, and increased protection of the community.

Selected References

1. Institute for Local Self Government. *Private Security and the Public Interest*. Berkeley, Calif.: Institute for Local Self Government, 1975.
2. Parsons, Robert L. "Some Advantages of Cooperation between Retail Management and Law Enforcement Officials in the Prevention and Control of Robberies and Burglaries of Retail Establishments," a master's thesis. East Lansing: School of Police Administration and Public Safety, Michigan State University, 1968.

Related Standards

The following standards and goals may be applicable in implementing Standard 6.2:
6.1   Interaction Policies
6.3   Policies and Procedures

Standard 6.3

Policies and Procedures

For law enforcement agencies and the private security industry to most effectively work within the same jurisdiction, policies and procedures should be developed covering: (a) the delineation of working roles of law enforcement officers and private security personnel, (b) the continuous prompt and responsible interchange of information, and (c) cooperative actions between law enforcement agencies and the private security industry.

Commentary

Policies provide the necessary guidance for achievement of an organization's goals and objectives. Effective management calls for the establishment of a sense of direction; written policies provide this direction. Without established policies, confusion and uncertainty arising will hamper progress and desired objectives are not met.

Procedures provide further direction. Policies concern broad performance directives; procedures furnish specific guidelines for performance. Policies and procedures are the steps necessary to achieve objectives. For example, with the objective of increasing arrest rates, a police agency would adopt a policy of providing prompt response to all calls. Several procedures would then be established to ensure prompt response. These procedures might

include the use of deployment forces, personal alarms, computerized data retrieval, and so forth—all these steps provide prompt response and, at the same time, achieve the desired objective of increasing arrest rates.

In this standard, the desired objective is closer unity between law enforcement and private security forces. The realization of this objective relies on the development of clear policies and procedures of operation. These policies and procedures need to cover the aspects of respective roles, interchange of information, and other cooperative measures between law enforcement and private security agencies. Once clear policies and procedures are provided in these areas, both law enforcement and private security personnel can better understand their overall commitment, and prescribed actions can be taken to promote coordination of efforts.

Although good working relationships have been found to exist at certain levels in the private security and law enforcement areas, (see ASIS survey, Appendix 1), the need for closer unity and increased interaction will always be present. Government officials, private security personnel, and researchers have voiced the need for establishing policies and procedures that provide a framework for interaction between these two entities. One of the primary recommendations of the *RAND Report* (Vol. I)

214

was that, "There should be a predetermined clear-cut policy for public/private police interaction."

Numerous other reports and surveys have also recognized the importance of establishing policies and procedures covering various aspects of the private security/law enforcement relationship. *The Other Police* reported that results of a survey of municipal officials working in 17 communities in the Cleveland, Ohio, area showed that these officials most frequently indicated (in agreement with the RAND report quoted above) that "There should be a predetermined, clear-cut policy for municipal-private security interactions."

A survey conducted by Dr. Richard Post, former chairman of the Department of Criminal Justice, University of Wisconsin, Platteville, indicated that 82.6 percent of the law enforcement officials responding believed that the establishment of a close, well-defined working relationship with the private security industry would be valuable. In his article, "Relations with Private Policy Services," Dr. Post concluded that "Policy must be developed at the municipal and county level to insure a clear understanding of the role and responsibilities of private protective services in the protection of the individual and his property."

The Institute for Local Self Government in its report, *Private Security and the Public Interest,* gives further support to the development of policies and procedures. The Institute recommends:

Local law enforcement agencies should coordinate their activities with private security services operating within their jurisdiction. Extensive study should be made of the possible ways their services might assist the police in suppressing criminal activity.

There should be a predetermined policy as to the mutual cooperation between public and private security forces; definite policy interactions should be established and maintained; procedures for crime reporting should be established to insure total reporting. Mutual cooperation between public and private forces should be sought.

Private security guard, watchmen and patrol agencies should be required to maintain around the clock communication links with the local law enforcement agency.

Just as various reports and studies point out the need for policies and procedures for relationships between law enforcement and private security agencies, other research indicates the lack of existing written policies and procedures. Vernon G. Jahr, in his master's thesis entitled "The Relationship between Law Enforcement and Industrial Security," found that approximately 60 percent of the respondents to his questionnaire stated their companies did not have formal written policies regarding relationships with law enforcement agencies, and the same 60 percent believed there is a need to establish more definitive policies regarding interaction.

Further, another of his survey questions revealed that 96 percent of the respondents favored cooperative liaison with law enforcement agencies.

Responding to questions posed by Jahr during the data collection process for his thesis, 30 law enforcement agencies in 30 States provided the following information:

• Eight of 30 had policies and/or procedures for defining the working roles of law enforcement agencies and private security services.

• Seven of 30 had policies covering interchange of information with the private security industry.

• Six of 30 had procedures for cooperative actions with the private security industry.

Clearly the need for interaction between the private security and law enforcement spheres is acknowledged by professionals in both fields. In developing the necessary policies and procedures for the most effective working relationship, all possible duties, responsibilities, and interrelationships of the public and private agencies involved should be considered in order to provide written directives covering all areas of operation.

Thad F. Brown, deputy chief, Los Angeles Police Department, in his article, "Types of Assistance Available," listed 40 types of service the private security industry could provide law enforcement agencies—for example, accident data, baggage information, credit card information, fugitive leads, inplant surveillance, and property identification. Interaction on these items can lead to not only a better relationship but also a potential for indepth security, because private security and law enforcement professionals share a common enemy.

Although the ultimate responsibility for the development of policies and procedures rests with management personnel, input from all levels should be encouraged and evaluated. This input can be gathered through surveys conducted by both fields during the liaison phase. Further, a law enforcement liaison officer with a good understanding of private security operations can hasten the process of developing goal-oriented policies and procedures that are understandable and acceptable to both sectors.

Delineation of Roles

The roles of both law enforcement officers and private security personnel should be clearly defined. A clear understanding of duties, responsibilities, and limitations is essential to goal-directed performance. In the absence of policies and procedures, the individual may be forced to develop a personal policy that differs from what is expected or desired. Clearly written policies and procedures clarify the delineation of roles and lead to unity of purpose and coordination of effort at all performance levels.

To achieve a delineation of roles, law enforcement and private security administrators within a jurisdiction should inventory and develop the services they are capable of delivering. This process should be done at the executive level, where decisionmaking power rests. Executives from both fields should examine this inventory for:

1. Duplication of services,
2. Crime prevention and deterrent activities,
3. Crime detection and investigatory services,
4. Jurisdiction and authority, and
5. Areas lacking the needed law enforcement and private security services.

Duplication of services is not in itself negative when referring to protection. It does, however, pose a question as to whether duplication can be eliminated without the public or private entity suffering a decrease in crime-prevention or other services.

Crime prevention and deterrent activities have long been the dominion of the private security industry. Law enforcement agencies have only recently entered this area, offering programs such as the marking of property, and providing residential security inspections. Police administrators should evaluate the prevention and detection programs operated by the jurisdiction's private sector to ascertain if these programs have caused displacement of criminal activities requiring reassignment of law enforcement personnel, and if police cooperation in these programs would ensure greater success.

Local crime detection and investigatory services should be inventoried to determine if there are local agencies possessing detection or investigatory capabilities that could complement law enforcement criminal investigations, particularly in areas such as securities, computers, or multistate offices. Likewise, law enforcement agencies should provide information or supply supportive services (such as use of crime laboratories) if such cooperation would result in the arrest of persons suspected of committing crimes against the public (as opposed to aid in private cases such as divorce).

Jurisdiction and authority limitations should be determined and made known to line officers as rapidly as possible. Law enforcement officers often must carry out duties on private property, and they need clarification of legal issues when that property is protected by private security systems and when private security personnel initiate the call for service. The issue is further complicated in States where private security officers hold quasi-legal status.

When the inventory of services is completed, a comprehensive overview should make it clear as to who is handling what situations and how they are to be handled. Police and security executives should then ask: Where are the weak spots? What additional services should be offered? Who can best fill in the weak spots in the battle against crime? When the answers to these questions are ascertained, policies and procedures understandable by all parties should be formulated.

Interchange of Information

Because crimes often are solved by a good informant or a vital piece of data on a particular modus operandi, a two-way flow of information needs to be initiated in the interests of cooperative action. Every law enforcement officer is aware of suspects who are set free because the information necessary to place or sustain charges was not available. There also are tragic stories of citizens shot by private security guards hired and armed by employers unaware of previous convictions against the guards for offenses such as assault with a deadly weapon or even murder. In a climate and at a time when sources of information and intelligence are being shut off by legislation, it has become urgent for law enforcement and private security agencies to pool their efforts to ensure an ongoing and useful interchange of information.

In an address to the Greater Atlanta chapter of the American Society for Industrial Security, Chandler Eavenson, manager of corporate security, Rich's, Inc., pointed out, "As of June 1975 there were some 80 pieces of legislation relating to various aspects of privacy pending in the U.S. House and nine in the Senate. Since then some 30 additional bills have been introduced." Enactment of many of these bills would gravely threaten interchange of information. Private security and law enforcement interests should initiate necessary actions to ensure this vital information exchange is maintained.

Information and intelligence are of primary importance to the operation of any law enforcement or security agency. The American Society for Industrial Security survey (see Appendix 1) showed that 75 percent of the respondents used public criminal justice records at least monthly and 84 percent stated a need for conviction data, 74 percent for arrest data, 57 percent for driver license checks, and 65 percent for vehicle checks.

Because the law enforcement and private security fields generally provide services and not tangible products, it is very important that they maintain an adequate information gathering and processing system. Such a system is valuable not only for showing the public or employer what has been accomplished but also as a valuable tool for planning and future allocation of resources. Results of good information gathering can provide an overall crime picture, and adjusted crime occurrence map of the jurisdiction, an indicator of real versus perceived enforcement requirements, and a management tool for both law enforcement agencies and private security services that could be helpful in obtaining additional manpower, funding, citizen participation, and specialized training.

The private security industry currently considers the area of intelligence to be primarily a one-way transaction, with law enforcement agencies as the recipients. Because of the controls under which law enforcement agencies operate, the situation is not by choice. The degree of intelligence information passed to the private sector should actually depend on the intelligence needs of the specific private security functions in the jurisdiction. When these needs are determined in a survey (as proposed in Standard 6.2), the chief law enforcement official and the agency's attorney should carefully study them to determine to what extent these needs can be lawfully met. In no instance should law enforcement agencies expect or request intelligence from private security firms that would put both groups in the position of breaking any existing laws.

Finally, as suggested in Standard 5.9, law enforcement and private security functions should work together to draft crime impact statements. This action would provide a good exercise in jointly working on combined information toward a specific goal.

Cooperative Actions

The relationship between the private security industry and law enforcement agencies has been hampered by certain existing suspicions and prejudices held by both. As outlined by the Law Enforcement/Private Security Relationship Committee of the Private Security Advisory Council, some of these prejudices include the following:

1. Private security believes:
   a. Law enforcement stops at property lines.
   b. Law enforcement accepts a one-way communication from the private security industry but does not reciprocate.
2. Police believe:
   a. Private security will not prosecute.
   b. Private security is just trying to use law enforcement.

These problems are not common to all jurisdictions, but wherever they exist, in total or in part, they restrict cooperative efforts. Development of policies and procedures for cooperative actions should help destroy these existing misconceptions. Further, increased understanding brought about through cooperation can lead to the greater efficiency and effectiveness of each agency's operations.

The exact nature of the policies and procedures to be developed depend on local circumstances. Dennis T. Brennan, in his book, *The Other Police*, outlines some of the types of cooperative arrange-ments found in the Cleveland area. A listing of these programs is offered for illustrative purposes.

Municipal Police

- Respond to calls for aid.
- Permit installation of direct dail or central station alarms.
- Exchange information.
- Complete private security investigations.

Private Security Forces

- Report suspicious persons and circumstances.
- Assist in traffic control around private property.
- Act as extended "eyes and ears" of police.
- Assist in making arrests.

An inherent fact in these cooperative efforts is the meeting of private security and law enforcement personnel to work out a meaningful commitment for the common goal of crime reduction. This positive interaction means that law enforcement administrators have made a decision to assist private security concerns. Such cooperation and interaction would result in increased protection provided to the individual being serviced and also greater security for the community. When the private security sector agrees to cooperate with law enforcement agencies, it reflects a willingness to take on a secondary obligation other than the client for no monetary reward.

Once a course of cooperative action is decided upon by private security and law enforcement administrators (whether the activity involves investigations, arrests, alarm responses, or surveys), lower echelon personnel on both sides should receive policies and procedures in understandable, concise form. Further, as a part of building jointly cooperative efforts, education in each other's role is most important. Middle-level supervisors can assume the important role of ensuring that cooperative efforts are understood and carried out.

As Glen D. King, executive director of the International Association of Chiefs of Police, told the 28th annual convention of the National Burglar and Fire Alarm Association, "Greater cooperation between law enforcement and local security professionals can greatly enhance the effectiveness of this law enforcement team." Cooperative efforts are only limited by the imagination, good will, and innovativeness of law enforcement agencies and the private security industry.

Selected References

1. Brennan, Dennis T. *The Other Police.* Cleveland, Ohio: Governmental Research Institute, 1975.

2. Brown, Thad F. "Types of Assistance Available," *The Police Chief,* Vol. 31, No. 11, November 1964.

3. Eavenson, Chandler. "Recent Developments and Trends in the Field of Privacy Legislation." Address delivered Nov. 18, 1975, Atlanta, Ga., Greater Atlanta Chapter, American Society for Industrial Security.

4. Institute for Local Self Government. *Private Security and the Public Interest.* Berkeley, Calif.: Institute for Local Self Government, 1974.

5. Jahr, Vernon G. "The Relationship between Law Enforcement and Industrial Security and a Report of Industrial Crime," a thesis. Long Beach Department of Criminal Justice, California State University, 1975.

6. Kakalik, James S., and Sorrel Wildhorn. *Private Police in the United States: Findings and Recommendations,* Vol. I, R–869/DOJ. Washington, D.C.: Government Printing Office, 1972.

7. King, Glen D. Address to the 28th annual convention of the National Burglar and Fire Alarm Association, Las Vegas, Nev., March 20, 1975.

8. Law Enforcement/Private Security Relationship Committee of the Private Security Advisory Council to the LEAA. Minutes, Appendix—Goals and Objectives, Summit, N.J., Nov. 7, 1974.

9. Post, Richard. "Relation with Private Police Services," *The Police Chief,* Vol. 38, No. 3, March 1971.

10. Private Security Task Force. "American Society for Industrial Security (ASIS) Survey Results." (See Appendix 1 to this report.)

Related Standards

The following standards and goals may be applicable in implementing Standard 6.3:

2.3 Job Descriptions
3.2 Conduct of Private Security Personnel
3.3 Reporting of Criminal Violations
5.9 Crime Impact Forecast
6.1 Interaction Policies
6.2 Survey and Liaison with Private Security
6.4 Multilevel Law Enforcement Training in Private Security

Standard 6.4

Multilevel Law Enforcement Training in Private Security

There should be multilevel training programs for public law enforcement officials, including but not limited to:

1. Role and mission of the private security industry,

2. Legal status and types of services provided by private security companies,

3. Interchange of information, crime reporting, and cooperative actions with the industry, and

4. Orientation in technical and operating procedures.

Commentary

The "American Society for Industrial Security (ASIS) Survey Results" (Appendix 1) indicates that 83 percent of the respondents believed that a set of standards was needed for the formalization of law enforcement/private security relationships. However, the Private Security Advisory Council's Law Enforcement/Private Security Relationship Committee determined that law enforcement agencies often are not informed of the role, mission, and nature of the private security industry. If there is to be formalization of any type of relationship, the first step should be a training program that reaches all ranks of law enforcement and private security personnel. The program should define the respective roles of each group, as well as their contacts with each other.

To provide the optimum dissemination of information about private security functions, training requires a multilevel approach. Law enforcement personnel at various responsibility levels have differing informational needs. A model training program on private security should consist of recruit- and supervisory-level instruction, and ongoing instruction for all law enforcement ranks.

The goal of recruit training is to provide a general familiarization with private security services. The length of this training should be tailored to the local situation, with time allotted, as necessary, to ensure adequate coverage of all subjects.

Recruit-level training generally should provide data explaining the role, mission, and function of the private security industry. Particular emphasis should be placed on industry components within the law enforcement agency's jurisdiction. Training should include information on State and local laws applicable to private security, such as jurisdiction and authority. In this respect, the Institute for Local Self Government, in its study *Private Security and the Public Interest,* recommends instruction on private security's rights, privileges, and duties and, most importantly, on its limitation of authority.

A format for development of instructional areas

that should be covered in recruit training follows. Instruction subareas can be developed as appropriate.

- The private security industry: Who and what it is.
- Role and mission of the security industry.
- State and local laws affecting the security industry.
- Authority of private security personnel.
- Field-level relationships with private security personnel.

When this phase of instruction is completed, the law enforcement patrolman will be able to deal more effectively with private security personnel encountered during daily duties.

The goal of training in private security for law enforcement supervisors is to prepare them to deal with security management counterparts or executive-level private security personnel, as well as to handle private security request and referral activities. Training for law enforcement supervisors should enhance the knowledge already gained in recruit-level training. Law enforcement supervisors and detectives would be working with upper-management-level private security personnel and need to know how to relate to these individuals and their needs. They must be prepared to handle requests for information interchange, crime reporting on requests for investigatory services, and cooperative actions. These topical areas should adequately meet day-to-day, operational interactions of local law enforcement and private security personnel.

A format for supervisory instruction follows. Only general headings are given, because development of various subheadings may vary for specific jurisdiction. Much of the course content also may depend on the developed policies and procedures of a particular law enforcement agency relating to private security services.

- Interchange of information.
- Crime reporting and channeling.
- Cooperative actions.
- Role and mission of the private security industry.
- Management-level relationships with private security personnel.

Interchange of information is a course designed to improve the flow of information between law enforcement and private security agencies. The course should inform law enforcement supervisors about the types of information obtainable from private security sources and the information law enforcement agencies can legally make available to private security services.

Crime reporting and channeling refers to activities reported to law enforcement agencies by private security sources. This area is both important and delicate, because most private security personnel

want to protect their employer's reputation. Businesses may have policies that pertain to the reporting of crime. Where legal and possible, law enforcement agencies should honor these policies. Instruction in this area, among other things, would cover how to properly give credit for reported criminal activities and the procedures for reporting criminal activities to the appropriate criminal justice system section for action.

Instruction in cooperative action could be combined with material covering management-level relationships. The two areas are closely related but do have basic differences. Cooperative action should primarily outline department policy on the extent to which the agency could jointly work with private security operations. Successful examples of cooperative actions, and suggestions for locally implementing those actions, could be included. Management-level relationships, on the other hand, should cover joint planning, ethics, and other appropriate subjects.

Role and mission of the private security industry should expand the general informational course offered at the recruit level. It would serve as a refresher course for the supervisor and should develop in greater detail the specific private security operations within the jurisdiction.

The goal of orientation in technical and operating procedures is to provide a necessary, although limited, understanding of the types of security equipment currently used in the jurisdiction and of some fundamentals on how private security systems operate. All law enforcement officers should receive this training. The depth of course content should be limited to orientation in the type of alarm systems and other security systems the law enforcement officer may be reasonably expected to encounter. Further, the training should impart a general knowledge about private security operating procedures, i.e., if an alarm sounds, does the alarm company respond to it? This portion of the training should not attempt to disclose all procedures of all private security operations within the jurisdiction, because such disclosure conceivably could imperil the security of various businesses and companies.

Ongoing training refers to nonformal, nonclassroom training for all law enforcement personnel who are active in day-to-day operations. The areas selected for ongoing instruction dealing with private security should include the impact on law enforcement of (1) new laws pertaining to private security services, (2) new private security technology, and (3) new private security procedures. Instruction in these areas can be achieved by rollcall training, special order, training bulletins, or monthly commander's call.

A training technique that should be maximized at all levels is the use of private security personnel as instructors. In addition to the use of existing expertise, this practice can enhance law enforcement officers' perception of their counterparts. Also, formal presentations by private security personnel should be followed by informal learning situations, giving all levels of personnel from both sectors a chance to get to know each other on a less restricted basis and to freely exchange ideas. Finally, law enforcement should consider including private security personnel as students where feasible and permissible. Face-to-face encounters between private security personnel and law enforcement officers can help enhance the relationships at all levels within a jurisdiction.

The multilevel approach of training law enforcement personnel to understand the work of the private security industry is very important. By removing common misconceptions and stereotypes, the two forces can achieve the understanding necessary for coordinated crime-reduction efforts.

Selected References

1. Institute for Local Self Government. *Private Security and the Public Interest*. Berkeley, Calif.: Institute for Local Self Government, 1975.

2. Law Enforcement/Private Security Relationship Committee of the Private Security Advisory Council. Minutes. Summit, N.J., Nov. 7, 1974.

Related Standards

The following standards and goals may be applicable in implementing Standard 6.4:
6.1   Interaction Policies
6.3   Policies and Procedures

Standard 6.5

Mistaken Identity of Private Security Personnel

Title terms, verbal representations, and visual items that cause the public to mistake private security personnel for law enforcement officers should be eliminated; security employers should ensure that their personnel and equipment are easily distinguishable from public law enforcement personnel and equipment.

Commentary

Citizens seldom realize that their own powers of arrest and detention are equal to those of security officers. Uniforms give security officers the appearance of authority, which often gains the consent and cooperation of others. But this raises a question: Does wearing a uniform imply authority of a privately employed agent of a private entity or the authority of a uniformed agent of a governmental agency?

Arguments for uniforms are as numerous as those against them. *The RAND Report* (Vol. I), discussing the pros and cons of uniforms, states: ". . . when a uniform is an aid to obtaining voluntary compliance with legitimate requests, as it is for a plant guard, it serves a very useful security purpose and should be permitted." This report further points out that uniformed private security personnel benefit by the "confusion derived from the psychological advantage of a uniform or badge in deterring illegal acts such as shoplifting or in obtaining obedience to commands much more readily in those situations where the officer is entitled to obedience, such as when expelling trespassers."

Additional support for the use of uniforms by private security personnel can be found in *Private Security Survey and Ordinance for St. Petersburg, Florida* by Public Systems, Inc. It stated, ". . . uniforms are very necessary as they signify authority, which is sometimes needed in situations confronting private security personnel." The same report also stated that "a uniform is an aid in obtaining voluntary compliance with legitimate requests."

There can be no doubt that uniforms are necessary to private security personnel. However, the use of uniforms, badges, insignias, titles, vehicles, and other equipment similar to those used by law enforcement agencies has often caused problems of mistaken identity. These problems usually can be traced to four causal factors. First, the public fails to closely examine or educate themselves in the identity of uniformed persons and equipment and who they represent. The public often cannot differentiate between local law enforcement uniforms and equipment purchased with their own tax dollars and privately uniformed and equipped security guards. A second factor adding to confusion is caused by public law enforcement practices. Law enforcement agencies have consistently purchased uniforms that differ from jurisdiction to jurisdiction. The sole exception is the State law enforcement agencies. Third, the private security industry contributes to mistaken identity problems by using uniforms and equipment similar to those used by local law enforcement. The industry realizes the effect of uniforms on the public and, therefore, imitates as closely as possible local law enforcement uniforms. Finally, the problem of mistaken identity is magnified by unscrupulous security personnel and private detectives and investigators who impersonate and misrepresent themselves to the public.

Several investigatory reports have touched upon the problems created when private security personnel wear uniforms similar to those of public law enforcement officers, or when they operate vehicles of a similar color bearing a similar logo. *The Private Security Industry of Virginia* stated ". . . guards typically are clothed in uniforms of policeman blue or gray, carry guns, wear badges and shoulder patches. This camouflage technique has an appropriate title: 'Scarecrow in Blue.'" Continuing in this vein, the *Report on the Private Security Industry in Florida,* prepared by the Florida Senate Judiciary Committee staff, held, "Almost every agency stated that their guards wore a police-type uniform with a metal badge. This may explain at least partly why impersonating a police officer is one of the most frequently recurring problems in the security guard industry." Finally, the *RAND Report* (Vol. I) cited improper uniform or identification as the second most commonly reported complaint made to State private security regulatory agencies.

In the effort to reduce identity problems, many municipalities across the Nation have developed ordinances that attempt to establish specific guidelines for private security uniforms, items of equipment, and titles or words conflicting with local law enforcement standards. Some examples of local ordinances follow:

City of St. Louis, Mo.

XII. UNIFORMS

A. A complete and distinct uniform in the formal sense is not required, but if and when such a formal uniform is worn it shall not be of such a cut, design, color, or decoration as to allow the wearer to be mistaken for a St. Louis police officer.

B. The Commander, Watchman Division, has the authority to exempt a licensed watchman, upon written application, from the wearing of a uniform and/or the insignia provided by the Board when the wearing of such insignia is not conducive to the efficient performance of the duties of the watchman, or when compelling and unusual circumstances require the watchman to perform his duties in ordinary civilian clothes.

C. At the discretion of the commander or acting com-

mander of The Watchman Division, licensed private watchmen performing beat duties may be allowed for limited periods to wear plain clothes or other ordinary civilian attire for outside duties. For such limited periods, exemption by the Board is not necessary.

D. THE USE OF A COMPANY BADGE IS PROHIBITED TO THOSE AGENCIES PERFORMING THEIR SECURITY SERVICES AT MULTIPLE LOCATIONS AND PREMISES IN THE CITY OF ST. LOUIS. SUCH AGENCIES ARE RESTRICTED TO WEARING THE BADGE ISSUED BY THE WATCHMAN DIVISION OF THE ST. LOUIS METROPOLITAN POLICE DEPARTMENT.

City of Chicago, Ill.

II. POLICY

Members will take enforcement action against persons who, while in the uniform of a guard service or other security agency;

A. Wear the Chicago flag shoulder patch on shirts or coats.

B. Display the checkered pattern in any color on the hat or attached to the hat or cap.

C. Display the words "Chicago Police" or "Chicago Patrolman" or any other combination of such words on any shoulder patch or other part of the uniform.

III. CITY ORDINANCES CONCERNING THE OFFICIAL UNIFORM

A. The Municipal Code of Chicago, Chapter 11, Section 47 states:

"No person shall falsely assume or pretend to be a policeman or a member of the Department of Police of this city, or, without being a member of the Department of Police of this city, wear in public the uniform adopted as the police uniform.

No person shall counterfeit or imitate, or cause to be counterfeited or imitated, any bedge, sign, signal or device adopted by the Department of Police. Nor shall any person use or wear any badge, sign, signal or device adopted or used by said Department or any similar in appearance, without authority to do so from the Board."

B. Chapter 173, Section 9 of the Municipal Code of Chicago forbids any special policeman to wear any insignia, cap, device, button, or uniform unless approved by the Superintendent of Police.

Lake Oswego, Oreg.

Section 12. The Lake Oswego Code is amended by the addition of the following section:

14.675 Uniforms and vehicles
Uniforms and vehicles used by a licensee or permit holder shall not be the same as or deceptively similar to those used by the Lake Oswego Police Department or any other public law enforcement agency in the area. All uniform and vehicle designs and identifying marks shall be approved by the Chief of Police prior to use.

Bakersfield, Calif.

7.14.180 UNLAWFUL TO WEAR UNIFORM SIMILAR TO POLICE OR FIREMEN—APPROVAL OF UNI-

FORM. It shall be unlawful for any person to wear, or cause or permit to be worn, any uniform in the operation of a private patrol system that is similar to the uniform used by the Bakersfield Police or Fire Departments, and no uniform shall be worn unless the same shall have been first approved by the Chief of Police.

7.14.190 UNLAWFUL TO WEAR BADGE SIMILAR TO POLICE OR FIREMEN—APPROVAL OF BADGE. It shall be unlawful for any person to wear or display, or cause to be worn or displayed, any badge or insignia similar in design to that used by the Bakersfield Police or Fire Departments, and no badge or insignia shall be worn, displayed or used in any manner unless the same has been first approved by the Chief of Police.

7.14.200 RANK AND INSIGNIA. It shall be unlawful for any person to use, wear or exhibit any rank or insignia of rank, or cause or permit to be used, worn or exhibited any rank or insignia of rank, by any person operating, or employed by a person operating a private patrol system, except such as may be approved in writing by the Chief of Police.

7.14.201 COLOR SCHEME AND INSIGNIA ON VEHICLES. It shall be unlawful for any private patrol operator to paint any vehicle used in his operation with such a color scheme that is similar in design or color of vehicles used by the Bakersfield Police Department, the California Highway Patrol, or the Kern County Sheriff's Department. No painted badges, starts or decalcomania of badges, stars or other insignia will be affixed on such vehicles used by a private patrol operator unless such badges, stars or insignia have first been approved by the Chief of Police.

One interesting feature that the above ordinances, and many others, have in common is that the chief of police is the official who determines what uniform, equipment, and accessories private security personnel can wear in the jurisdiction. Given the concern for the problem, the number of abuses cited in reports and by the media, suggests that this prerogative is not being exercised by local chiefs of police. It appears that too much latitude is being given to private security services in terms of similar uniforms, titles, and markings, or that perhaps enforcement of these laws is lax or ineffective.

It is recommended that verbal and visual items causing mistaken identity be eliminated. The intent is not to take private security guards out of uniform, but simply to replace those items creating problems with others that would not create problems. Some specific suggestions for distinguishing private security forces without causing confusion follow.

Security personnel should be required to wear name tags for two reasons. First, when a citizen is confronted by a uniformed individual, establishment of the identity of this individual in the clearest possible fashion is a basic premise supported by all professionals. A name tag clearly identifies a uniformed person otherwise indistinguishable from others similarly attired. Second, a uniformed individual is less likely to misrepresent himself if required to wear a tag bearing his true name. Private security personnel not wearing name tags would become suspect of attempting to conceal their identity.

Another way to clearly identify persons in uniform is to require shoulder patches of a uniform color, size, and design. The wording on the patch should be limited to the name of the private security employer. No design should be allowed. In the past, certain companies have used on shoulder patches words such as "police" or the name of the community in which they do business. Designs similar to State or city seals have been used. These practices tend to confuse the public, because law enforcement officers wear similar patches.

In regard to equipment, private security vehicles should bear no resemblance to those used by law enforcement agencies within the same jurisdiction. Similar colors and color patterns, emergency light arrangements, and positioning, shape, and wording of any company logo should not resemble those used by local law enforcement agencies. All other equipment should be evaluated for possible conflicts.

One other item necessary to the private security uniform is a tag that clearly indicates the individual's capacity, such as "security officer," "security technician," and so forth. When a title is spelled out on the uniform, little doubt remains as to the status of the uniformed individual.

The terms "police," "law enforcement," "special police," and the name of the local city, county, or State should not appear on uniforms, insignias, or vehicles of a private security company.

These changes would hopefully make private security personnel readily distinguishable from law enforcement officers, thus reducing public confusion and other problems resulting from mistaken identity, and improving the relationship between law enforcement and private security agencies.

Selected References

1. Chicago Police Department. Department of Special Order 67–51, "Unlawful Impersonations of Chicago Police Officers." Chicago, Ill.: Chicago Police Department, Sept. 8, 1971.

2. City of Lake Oswego, Oregon. Ordinance Number 1503, "An Ordinance Regulating Security Patrols; Repealing 14.610, 14.620, Adding New Provision and Declaring an Emergency." Lake Oswego: March 20, 1973.

3. Institute for Local Self Government. *Private Security and the Public Interest.* Berkeley, Calif.: Institute for Local Self Government, 1975.

4. Kakalik, James S., and Sorrel Wildhorn. *Private Police in the United States: Findings and Recommendations,* Vol. I, R–869/DOJ. Washington, D.C.: Government Printing Office, 1971.

5. Martensen, Kai R. *Private Security Survey and Ordinance for St. Petersburg, Florida.* Sunnyvale, Calif.: Public Systems incorporated, 1975.

6. Office of the Chief of Police, Metropolitan Police Department, City of St. Louis. Special Order 74–S–2, "Licensing, Supervising, Inspecting and Controlling Private Watchmen." St. Louis, Mo.: Office of the Chief of Police, April 3, 1974.

7. Research Department, Division of Justice and Crime Prevention. *The Private Security Industry in Virginia.* Virginia: Division of Justice and Crime Prevention, 1972.

8. Senate Judiciary Committee Staff. *Report on the Private Security Industry in Florida.* Tallahassee: Senate Judiciary Committee, September 1974.

Related Standards

The following standards and goals may be applicable in implementing Standard 6.5:

3.4   Employer Responsibilities

6.6   State Regulation of Private Security Uniforms, Equipment, Job Titles

Standard 6.6

State Regulation of Private Security Uniforms, Equipment, and Job Titles

Each State should develop regulations covering use and wear of private security uniforms, equipment, company names, and personnel titles that do not conflict with those in use by law enforcement agencies within the State.

Commentary

Standard 6.5 establishes guidelines for the private security industry regarding the use of uniforms and other visual and verbal items that may lead to mistaken identity of their personnel. This standard recommends that States develop regulations to control the use of these items so that they do not conflict with those items used by public law enforcement agencies.

Because the responsibilities and powers of private security and law enforcement agencies significantly differ, the public should be able to clearly distinguish between private security personnel and law enforcement officers. When uniforms, metal or metal-like badges, titles, equipment, and other items of identification are so similar that confusion results, the public interest cannot be best served. Furthermore, this situation is detrimental to the relationship between the private security and law enforcement sectors. The Law Enforcement/Private Security Relationship Committee of the Private Security Advisory Council described the problem as follows:

Public law enforcement is . . . disturbed by the feeling that private security personnel attempt to imitate public police officers. The uniforms of private security personnel are often similar to those of the public law enforcement; the private security officer wears a metal badge which in many respects is similar to that worn by a police officer; and vehicles used by private security are marked in such a way that they are similar to police cruisers. This "intended" imitation is seen as creating confusion on the part of the public who find it difficult to distinguish between public and private officers. This fact tends to irritate the police officer. The police officer considers himself a professional and does not want private security officers mistaken for the police.

Presently, where State and local ordinances exist on the subject of private security uniforms, badges, titles, and so forth, considerable variation and application has been noted. In the study *Private Security and the Public Interest,* by the Institute for Local Self Government, 17 regulatory agencies from different States reported the breakdown shown in Table 6.3.

Although it appears there is adequate regulation, a survey of California law enforcement officers showed that about one-third were bothered by "misidentification of private security activities for public police actions," "uniform and badge similarity," or "playing cop." Further, regulation and licensing personnel surveyed for the Institute's study mentioned improper uniforms or badges as one of the most frequent problems.

Table 6.3. Ordinance Survey: Uniform, Badge, Vehicle, and Insignia Regulation

Category	Percent Regulating
Uniforms	16
Uniforms and badges	14
Uniforms, vehicles, and badges	9
Uniforms, badges, vehicles, and insignia	9
Uniforms, badges, and rank	4
Uniforms, badges, and titles	4
Uniforms, badges, and insignia	4
Uniforms and vehicles	4
Uniforms and insignia	3
Uniforms, badges, vehicles, insignia, and rank	3
Vehicle and insignia	1
Uniform and rank	1
Not cited	28

Breakdown by single category

Category	Percent Regulating
Uniforms	71
Badges	47
Vehicles	26
Insignia	20
Rank	9

Source: Institute for Local Self Government. *Private Security and the Public Interest*. Berkeley, Calif.: Institute for Local Self Government, 1975.

The Institute for Local Self Government is not alone in its findings. In a random sampling of law enforcement agencies conducted for this report, 20 of 29 respondents stated they had received complaints from the public about mistaking private security personnel for law enforcement officers. A study of private security in Florida revealed that "... impersonating a police officer is one of the most frequently recurring problems in the security guard industry." Two Virginia studies came to similar conclusions. A 1972 study of private security operations pointed out that, "Common observation attests to the lax enforcement of these provisions" (State laws on impersonation of a law enforcement officer) and cited the case of a Richmond guard firm using the Virginia State seal in violation of the law. A second study conducted 2 years later by a private security industry task force found:

A potential problem that has been brought out is that of impersonation of a public police officer by a private security officer. The Code of Virginia prohibits the wearing of any uniform of the state police or the use of the state seal or the wearing of a uniform which might "deceive the casual observer" by any person who is not a public police officer; however since some security companies design their uniforms and badges so similar to those of public police, it is apparent that the statute is not rigidly enforced.

In contrast to these findings, 80 percent of the respondents to a survey conducted by the American Society for Industrial Security stated that from seldom to never were their personnel mistaken for public police. To the question, "To differentiate private security personnel and public police personnel, which of the following do you prefer?" its respondents answered as follows:

	Percentage
Style of uniform	19
Color of uniforms	23
Cloth badges	5
No response	5
Distinctive color of hat	1
Other	10
Multiple responses	37

Because of the many problems arising from the close similarity of private security and public law enforcement uniforms, badges, titles, and so forth, many individuals and organizations have recommended that State regulation be required and strictly enforced to reduce public confusion and to eliminate abuses. For example, in its model licensing and regulatory statute, the Private Security Advisory Council advocates "security officer" name tapes. Square patches instead of badges are recommended for private security uniforms in St. Petersburg, Fla. Also, a mandate for cloth badges is recommended for improvements in private security services in *The Other Police.*

Other recommendations include those made in a California report, *Private Security and the Public Interest,* by the Institute for Local Self Government and those included in a study of private security in Florida by its Senate Judiciary Committee. The California report recommends, "Statutory proscriptions should be adopted by local jurisdictions regulating the allowable color and type of uniform, insignia, and vehicles, and the use of public police titles." The Florida study proposes a regulatory bill:

. . . trade names or designations, badges, or uniforms that could be confused with law enforcement in the vicinity are forbidden under the bill. The words "police," "sheriff," "deputy sheriff," and the use of the official seal or a facsimile of any governmental entity is forbidden.

The following is part of a San Mateo, Calif., ordinance that incorporates many of the above recommendations:

Article V.   USE OF OFFICIAL POLICE TITLES AND SIMILAR SUBTERFUGES.

No person shall in connection with any private business, employment or activity use the title "Chief of Police," "Police Chief," "Chief of Detectives," "Detective" or any other title or description whatsoever tending to indicate any official connection with any other governmental agency, unless accompanied by additional language clearly displaying with the initials or symbols the identity of the private agency

or employer on whose behalf the user, of the title or description is acting or purporting to act.

Article VI.   REPRESENTATIVE OF THE POLICE DEPARTMENT—PROHIBITED.

No person, other than regular police officers of the city, shall, for any purpose whatsoever, represent himself, or falsely represent another, to be a member of the police department of this city or use any sign, word, language, or device calculated to induce a false or mistaken belief that he is acting or purporting to act on the behalf of the police department of this city or within the scope of any purported duty thereof.

Article VII.   BADGES AND REPRESENTATIONS.

No person other than a regular police officer of this city, acting within the scope and course of his official duties, shall use any sign, badge, title or description, or make any express or implied representation, particularly in connection with any activity directed toward the collection of any money or debt or the repossessing, recovering, or taking of anything of value, or for the purpose of any private gain whatsoever, calculated to induce the belief that he is a member of the police force of the city, or connected therewith in any way.

Article VIII.   UNIFORMS.

No person shall wear any uniform designed to resemble so closely the uniform worn by the San Mateo police department, San Mateo County Sheriff's Office, or the California Highway Patrol as to reasonably induce the belief that he represents or is employed by the police department, the sheriff's office or the California Highway Patrol.

Article IX.   VEHICLES.

No person shall use any vehicle which is colored or has affixed thereon any sign, badge, title, or device that would reasonably induce the belief that said vehicle was being operated by the police department, sheriff's office, California Highway Patrol or any agency of local, state or federal government. Private patrol or security service vehicles shall have a sign displayed in a conspicuous place on the left and right hand side of the vehicle showing the name of the company or the operator of the private patrol or security services and the business telephone number. The letters shall be no less than two and one-half inches in height and shall be, in contrast to the color of the background, and plainly affixed thereto.

The State of Michigan has one of the best regulations covering uniforms, badges, and so forth, for private security personnel. The State police handle the administrative and enforcement duties. Excerpts from that act state:

Sec. 16.   A person shall not manufacture a badge or shield which purports to indicate that the holder is a licensed alarm system contractor, alarm system agent, private security guard or agency, or any of those persons as listed, in section 2. A person shall not display for sale a badge, shield, identification card, or certificate of license, by which the holder might mislead the public into thinking that the holder is a licensed alarm system contractor, alarm system agent, or private security guard, or agency. A person, firm, company, partnership, or corporation shall not distribute an identification card or certificate of license in this state except as provided by this act. A person shall not knowingly buy or receive from a source a form of spurious identification as an alarm system contractor, alarm system agent, or a private security guard or agency. A violation of this section is a misdemeanor, and an unauthorized identification card or certificate of license shall be confiscated by a law enforcement officer of the state. Each day the violation continues shall constitute a separate offense.

Sec. 19. (1) The particular type of uniform and insignia worn by a licensee or his employees, must be approved by the department and shall not deceive or confuse the public or be identical with that of a law enforcement officer of the federal government, state, or a political subdivision thereof in the community of the license holder. Shoulder identification patches shall be worn on all uniform jackets, coats, and shirts and shall include the name of the licensee or agency. Shoulder identification patches or emblems shall not be less than 2 inches by 3 inches in size.

(2) A badge or shield shall not be worn or carried by an alarm system agent, private policeman, special policeman, watchman, or employee, or licensee of an alarm system contractor, patrol service agency, or private security guard agency, unless approved by the director of the department of state police.

(3) A person licensed as an alarm system contractor, alarm system agent, or a private security guard or agency is not authorized to carry a deadly weapon unless he is licensed to do so in accordance with the laws of the state.

The Michigan act further specifies that the State seal must not be used on cap ornaments, that badges must not be issued to private detectives, and that any badge worn on the chest must be approved by the State police. The name for an agency or an advertisement may not be used on vehicles, nor can emblems that are likely to deceive the public be used on vehicles. Letterheads and so forth must be approved by the State police. The Michigan statute provides a model for solving the problems of mistaken or misrepresented identity.

This report recommends that the following actions be initiated to deal with these problems:

1. States should deny the use of advertisements that are designed to mislead or confuse the public and in which personnel titles or job or agency functions could be confused with those of law enforcement agencies.

2. All private security uniforms that are not cut along civilian clothing patterns should be of a color designated by the State. The color should be different from law enforcement colors. This stipulation may necessitate a change in uniform color by some law enforcement agencies.

3. Private security personnel should have a patch of designated size, shape, and color bearing only the name of the employer. This patch should be affixed to both shoulders of any coat, shirt, or jacket.

4. A tape identifying the security function performed by the individual should be worn on the uniform. This tape should match the color of the shoulder patches.

5. All security personnel in uniform should wear name tags matching the color of shoulder patches and job description tapes.

6. In no case should the word "police" or the name, emblem, or seal of a State, county, or city appear on any uniform item or commercial paper, with the exception of proprietary operations where such a name belongs to the company or corporation.

A most important consideration involves badges worn by private security personnel. Metal or metal-like badges are used by law enforcement officers as a readily understood symbol of authority and power, clarifying the right of the officer to act in various situations. The metal badge further identifies the law enforcement agency that the bearer represents. When private security personnel also wear metal or metal-like badges, the false impression is created that their authority is equal to that of public law enforcement officers. For this reason, no metal or metal-like badge should be issued to private security personnel.

If, however, private security representatives maintain that metal badges are intrinsic to their function, any metal badges permitted should be of a configuration unlike those used by law enforcement officers. If badges are worn, they also could be made of cloth.

Perhaps the shape of the badge could correspond to the amount of training received. For example, at the completion of basic classroom training, the badge worn could be a large Roman numeral I. Classroom and appropriate on-the-job training would merit a badge in the shape of a Roman numeral II. Completion of classroom, on-the-job, and supervisory training would merit a large Roman numeral III. The benefits of a system of this type would be:

1. Immediate identification of the individual's amount of training:

2. Avoidance of confusion with law enforcement's use of military rank;

3. Avoidance of conflict with any known law enforcement metal or metal-like badge or shield;

4. Further identification of the wearer by the marking of a control number; and

5. An incentive for achievement by the private security employee, i.e., desire to hold a II or III badge.

Total configuration of the recommendations for private security uniforms could appear as shown in Figure 6.1.

Figure 6.1. Suggested Private Security Uniform Configuration

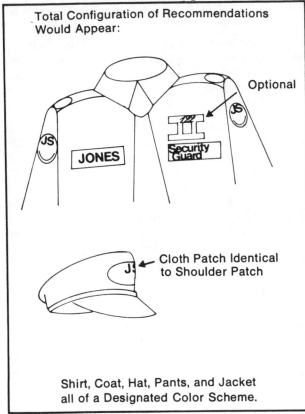

Total Configuration of Recommendations Would Appear:

Optional

JS

JS

JONES

Security Guard

Cloth Patch Identical to Shoulder Patch

Shirt, Coat, Hat, Pants, and Jacket all of a Designated Color Scheme.

A State uniform regulation for private security personnel should be aggressively enforced and should be backed by appropriate penalties for those private security firms and individuals not in compliance after the expiration of a grace period. A period of sufficient length (perhaps 24 months) should be given for the phasing out of uniforms and equipment not in compliance. In time, this type of regulation would eliminate public confusion and possibly spark law enforcement into adopting similar guidelines for their dress. The ideal result would be to ensure the type of uniformity existing in England and Scotland, where an individual can travel from John-O-Groats (northernmost Scotland) to Dover (southernmost England) and find law enforcement officers dressed in the same uniform, leaving no doubt as to identity.

Selected References

1. Brennan, Dennis T. *The Other Police*. Cleveland, Ohio: Governmental Research Institute, 1975.

2. Department of State Police. *Private Detective and Private Security Guard Licensing Acts*. East Lansing, Mich.: Department of State Police, 1974.

3. Institute for Local Self Government. *Private Security and the Public Interest*. Berkeley, Calif.: Institute for Local Self Government, 1975.

4. Martensen, Kai R. *Private Security Survey and Ordinance for St. Petersburg, Florida*. Sunnyvale, Calif.: Public Systems incorporated, 1975.

5. Private Security Advisory Council, Law Enforcement/Private Security Relationship Committee. "Abstract." 1975.

6. Private Security Task Force. "American Society for Industrial Security (ASIS) Survey Results." (See Appendix 1 to this report.)

7. "Report of the Private Security Industry Task Force to the Virginia State Crime Commission," Sept. 4, 1974.

8. Research Department, Division of Justice and Crime Prevention. *The Private Security Industry in Virginia*. Virginia: Research Department, Division of Justice and Crime Prevention, 1972.

9. Senate Judiciary Committee Staff. "Report on the Private Security Industry in Florida." Tallahassee: Senate Judiciary Committee Staff, 1974.

10. State of Michigan, 78th Legislature Regular Session of 1975. "Enrolled House Bill No. 4210."

Related Standards

The following standards and goals may be applicable in implementing Standard 6.6:

2.3   Job Descriptions
6.5   Mistaken Identity of Private Security Personnel
9.1   State Regulation

Standard 6.7

Law Enforcement Personnel Secondary Employment

Law enforcement administrators should ensure that secondary employment of public law enforcement personnel in the private security industry does not create a conflict of interest and that public resources are not used for private purposes.

Commentary

Secondary employment (commonly referred to as moonlighting) by law enforcement personnel is one of the foremost problems facing the contemporary law enforcement administrator. Yet, as common as it is, the extent of secondary employment is virtually impossible to accurately measure. Only a limited number of studies, in isolated areas, have been undertaken to determine the number of policemen moonlighting. An early study, cited in *The Police Chief,* gives some idea of the problem:

A 1956 survey of 11 cities found an average of 24 percent of the police working at outside jobs. The more definitive and recent studies of the Bureau of Labor Statistics sets the police percentage at 14.2. This is well above the 1963 rate for the nation as a whole, 5.7 percent. Thus, it would seem that except where controls or enforced prohibitions exist, more than a few policemen are exposing their departments to potential embarrassment if not censure.

A more recent survey, cited in *The Other Police,* found that in the county containing Cleveland, Ohio, between 20 and 35 percent of the municipal and county peace officers (or 830 to 1,450 of the total 4,150) alone hold secondary jobs in the private security industry.

The problem of accurately measuring the number of law enforcement personnel who moonlight was stated by Dennis T. Brennan in *The Other Police:*

A 1970 study done for the United States Justice Department asserts that any survey of public police agencies about moonlighting would almost certainly underestimate its extent due to non-reporting by policemen disobeying departmental regulations.

In spite of the lack of statistical data setting out the specific number of law enforcement personnel who have secondary employment across the Nation, there seems to be no question that a large percentage of police officers do in fact moonlight and that many problems arise because of this activity.

General Problems of Secondary Employment in Any Position

Initial problems associated with moonlighting arise because of law enforcement officers' primary obligation to their departments. Circumstances may develop in secondary employment that would prohibit officers from giving their full time and energy to the department. An officer employed in a secondary occupation may be unavailable in a public emergency, thus breaching his or her official oath and creating a serious problem.

Dividing loyalties between the police department and a secondary occupation may affect a moonlighting officer's obligation to the department. A law enforcement officer's job is important and delicate and demands alertness at all times. Secondary employment can have an adverse effect on an officer's obligation to the department and to the public. Alertness may be jeopardized by lack of adequate physical and mental rest between shifts. Impaired judgment and reflexes brought on by months of 16-hour work days can jeopardize the lives of law enforcement partners and fellow officers. The public may also be placed in danger if the officer has not had sufficient rest time to be alert for his primary job—law enforcement.

Finally, a law enforcement officer has an obligation to help upgrade the department's image. Secondary employment in certain areas—for example, a business associated with alcohol—could have a degrading effect on the law enforcement department's image.

The second set of general problems deal with the question of liability. If a law enforcement officer is injured while moonlighting and is unable to function in his or her primary occupation, a question arises as to who would pay compensation—the law enforcement agency, the secondary employer, or both. It is unfair to expect taxpayers to help compensate for an injury sustained during off-hours employment.

A question also arises over who is liable for a law enforcement personnel's actions against persons or property of others during moonlighting time. Because a law enforcement officer may take an oath to perform 24-hours-a-day duties, some argue that the municipality and law enforcement agency may be held liable for the officer's acts.

Serious Problems Created by Secondary Employment in Private Security

More serious problems may occur when private security work becomes a moonlighting law enforcement employee's secondary job. These problems also might arise with other secondary occupations but can best be discussed by referring to examples found in the private security industry.

One of the more serious problems is created by the temperament and training of law enforcement officers. A study by the American Justice Committee, cited in *The Other Police*, gives an example:

There may be problems of misunderstanding of crime prevention work by police moonlighters not tempermentally suited to such relatively passive work. No longer riding in a patrol car with a partner trained in criminal apprehension, some policemen moonlighting at fixed posts admit to feeling especially vulnerable to armed criminals. According to an AJC compilation of official 1974 Cuyahoga County homicide information, five off-duty Cleveland policemen—all moonlighting in private security—were recorded as assailants, whereas only four on-duty policemen (three Cleveland and one East Cleveland) were recorded as assailants. The on-duty killings in 1974 by policemen represent roughly four times greater total manhours, and thus a far lower frequency of use of killing force than the police moonlighters. (For comparison, it should be added that two private security persons were recorded as assailants and that one on-duty policeman, as well as one private security person, were recorded as victims.)

Other problems arise when two job functions have to be performed at the same time. This conflict between obligations might occur when a law enforcement officer has an oath to uphold the law 24 hours a day. For example, an off-duty law enforcement officer with a secondary job requiring that he protect certain private property may observe a public wrong being committed across the street. He must then decide whether to disregard his obligation to his secondary employment or forget his primary obligation as a law enforcement officer. Whatever decision is made, one employer is not receiving the job performance the officer is paid for.

A third serious problem arises because of the appearance of law enforcement officers as authoritarian figures and is particularly prevalent when a policeman moonlights in private security work. Normally, private security personnel have the same legal powers as do ordinary citizens. Off-duty law enforcement officers are often hired for private security jobs because their appearance, with their law enforcement equipment, badges, and uniforms, indicate they are vested with greater powers than ordinary guards. Thus, the public is led to believe that the company rules and regulations enforced by an off-duty law enforcement officer are supported totally by local laws.

A similar image problem arises because law enforcement officers performing private security functions may subject their departments to public degradation and unnecessary criticism. For example, taxpayers may see uniformed law enforcement officers directing traffic or checking personal property at private businesses, such as quick-order restaurants, discount shopping centers, or banks, and believe that their taxes are being used for officers to aid private business and not the public.

The fourth major problem dealing with incompatible private security employment of law enforcement personnel is that the possibility of direct conflicts of interest are more likely to arise. A document prepared by the Private Security Advisory Council's Law Enforcement/Private Security Relationship Committee pointed out how this conflict of interest can affect competition in the private marketplace:

The public law enforcer utilizes his uniform, equipment, and experience for those "after hours" assignments that he chooses to pursue. The competition angle is obvious, the mere fact that the public law enforcer has "public" assets to utilize makes him a more desirable investment for industry to employ, thus stepping on the toes of the private sector. Besides accepting these moonlighting details, a number of public law officers have actually formed guard businesses of their own.

The problem of unfair competition is not only limited to private security businesses. It also places private citizens seeking employment as private security guards at a distinct disadvantage.

It should be noted that there is one possible exception to the rules governing unfair competition: situations in which private security guard services are locally unavailable because of geographical or economic considerations. In such cases, citizens may need to turn to a law enforcement agency to provide off-duty private security services. In this case, the chief law enforcement officer should evaluate the request and act accordingly.

A situation in a midwestern community points out the serious conflicts of interest that can occur when law enforcement personnel moonlight in private security work. In August 1975 at a city council meeting, a local law enforcement officer recommended that the community's industrial park be required to meet specific security requirements he had drawn up in his official capacity. Some time after the requirements were presented, it was discovered that only one company could provide the level of security necessary to meet the officer's standards. The officer was found to be co-owner of that company.

Another serious problem is that of the temptations for public law officers to engage in official misconduct. Disclosure or exploitation of confidential information is a security problem facing any law enforcement department. The problem is even more serious when law enforcement personnel are also working for private businesses that could use the same information.

Law enforcement agencies are daily practicing a form of financial brinksmanship with tax dollars by allowing their personnel to take secondary private security employment. Unless questions concerning liability for false arrest, injury, or death are resolved before a law enforcement officer accepts a private security position, the taxpayer may end up underwriting the cost of a damage award against a law enforcement agency stemming from an incident occurring in the course of the law enforcement officer's secondary employment.

A law enforcement officer's secondary private security employment should be divorced from any relationship with his official law enforcement capacity. Where States and municipalities have licensing and registration requirements pertaining to private security services, they should be adhered to by law enforcement personnel. In this way, there can be little likelihood that the officer's agency, and indirectly the taxpayer, could be held liable for damages resulting from the officer's misconduct during the secondary employment.

The best way to deal with the liability question is through ordinance or statute—i.e., no law enforcement officer shall be insured against false arrest or general liability by the law enforcement agency while secondarily employed off duty; a law enforcement officer shall be considered as having only those powers of arrest and detention accorded to any other citizen while off duty. Wording such as this would eliminate liability on the part of the law enforcement agency for the actions of its officers who are also employed in private security work. Finally, it would clearly spell out to the law enforcement officer where liability rests for his acts.

Steps should be taken by law enforcement administrators, government bodies, and citizens to ensure that they would not be liable for actions of law enforcement officers while engaged in secondary employment. These steps should include eliminating practices that endanger tax dollars, passing corrective ordinances or statutes, and voicing objections to questionable law enforcement practices.

The case of *Burke* v. *State,* 47 S.E. 2d 116 (1957) reaffirms that it can be considered a breach of law enforcement duties to serve private clients, investigate private disputes, and support a client's case in or out of court. The law enforcement officer cannot serve two masters, and the information obtained as a law enforcement officer should not be disclosed to a private client, or vice versa.

The serious problems inherent in moonlighting, particularly in the field of private security, were aptly recognized by Sydney Cooper, a New York City police commander, when testifying before the Knapp Commission's hearing on police corruption: "The 'rent-a-cop' business is a growing and corruptive influence on many metropolitan police forces around the country."

Solutions to the Problem

Although very few specific State statutes restrict law enforcement personnel from moonlighting, Connecticut and Kansas specifically deny a private security license to a person vested with police powers. These States have recognized the many problems inherent in allowing such moonlighting.

Even though other States do not specifically

restrict law enforcement personnel from moonlighting in private security work, many private security regulatory statutes do not grant special status to law enforcement personnel. According to a 1975 survey of legislation (Appendix 6), 33 States regulate some aspect of the private security industry. Of these, 32 States do not treat off-duty law enforcement officers differently from anyone else. The private security legislation concerning law enforcement officers and private policing is similar to that found in Illinois, where an off-duty law enforcement officer who desires work as a guard or detective must obtain a certificate of registration in the same manner as any citizen.

The courts also have recognized the problem inherent in moonlighting and have upheld the validity of regulations prohibiting off-hours employment that would conflict with a law enforcement officer's duties or would otherwise be incompatible with the officer's primary employment. *Flood* v. *Kennedy,* 12 N.Y. 2d 345 (1961), upheld a municipal rule of New York City that precludes policemen from engaging in outside occupations except when suspended without pay or on vacation or other leave. Chief Judge Desmond's opinion states that "the rule is essential or at least appropriate to implement the Commissioner's control of a tightly disciplined group of employees with special duties and obligations to protect the safety and order of the city and to be available to cope with emergencies."

State v. *Denny,* 118 Ind. 449(1963), points out that the chief function of the police officer is to aid in the enforcement of local police regulations and that they are paid for such services by local taxpayers. The case also held that police powers and equipment were not to be used for any purpose other than municipal use. Other cases concerning this problem include *Hopewood* v. *Paducah,* 424 S.W. 2d 134(1965), which limits the total number of hours that a policeman can work during one week, and *Jurgens* v. *Davenport,* 249 Io. 711(1958), which upheld a restriction against outside employment and a city ordinance that stated a police officer could not receive compensation from any outside source. There are countless other cases that directly or similarly relate to those cited.

A 1964 opinion rendered by the Iowa Department of Public Safety also condemns and restricts public law enforcement officers from moonlighting in the private detective business. In addition, the opinion does not allow the use of police equipment, police uniforms, or of similar uniforms in the business of private security. A Michigan attorney general's opinion concurs with this second point.

Associations, such as the National Council on Crime and Delinquency, believe that law enforcement officers should not be authorized to engage in the private security sector. *The Other Police* suggests that State legislation should be enacted or revised to determine and set nonovertime law enforcement wage scale; to limit total hours police officers may work in outside employment; to have moonlighting police officers controlled by the private employer, who should also provide private legal defense and liability insurance; to mandate the local safety director to specify what types of law enforcement equipment and assignments are unacceptable when moonlighting; and to make the law enforcement administrator responsible for ensuring that no police officer works in an area incompatible with his public police duty.

An article in *The Police Chief* illustrates how one law enforcement agency—the Seattle, Wash., Police Department—handles this problem:

A recently revised general order requires a Seattle officer to apply for permission to work outside the department. A standard form is submitted to the individual's division head for initial approval. If the applicant has an adequate work record, the request is forwarded to the Staff Division for final approval or disapproval. One of the prime considerations at this point is the man's sick leave record. An above average incidence of sickness may result in disapproval.

A permit authorizes only the employment specified and under conditions listed. Compensation and hours are scrutinized. Permits are valid for only one year or less.

In all cases, an officer remains primarily obligated and responsible to the Department. This means that police action must be taken by an officer even while engaged in off-duty employment if a situation arises which requires such a course. Further, all police duty, including additional assignments on days-off and after hours, takes total precedence over a second job . . . .

The Seattle Department further requires assurance that the applicant will be defended and insured against all law suits stemming from police action he might take while working at an extra job. Two forms are acceptable. The employer can agree in writing to defend the officer and to assume liability for any judgment or the officer may substitute proof that he has $100,000 work of false arrest insurance which covers off-duty employment.

Finally, a limit is imposed on the number of hours a Seattle policeman may work during a week. The total hours on regular assignment and outside employment cannot exceed 64.

All law enforcement administrators have an obligation to develop and maintain controls over the behavior of their personnel. Clear policies should be developed concerning secondary employment. Law enforcement administrators should formulate and enforce policies that provide appropriate restrictions and regulations covering secondary employment in private security work by their department personnel. Specifically, controls should be exercised in regard to law enforcement personnel employed as guards, principals, or managers of private security operations. Chief law enforcement officers must ensure that none of their personnel is performing private investigatory functions. By taking active steps in this direction, law enforcement administrators would be protecting the public interest, as well as the law enforcement department and its employees.

Selected References

1. American Society for Industrial Security. "General Security Attitude Questionnaire." Denver, Colo.: 1975.

2. Brennan, Dennis T. *The Other Police*. Cleveland, Ohio: Governmental Research Institute, 1975.

3. Correspondence from Iowa Department of Public Safety to John Duffy. April 21, 1964.

4. Correspondence from Frank J. Kelley, attorney general of the State of Michigan, to Col. Frederick E. Davids, director of the Department of State Police, State of Michigan. March 26, 1970.

5. Ellis, James H. "Some Features of Moonlighting." *The Police Chief*, January 1965.

6. Ernat, David J. "The Crux of Police Adminis-

trators." An unpublished paper prepared for the Department of Law Enforcement Administration, Western Illinois University. Macomb: February 1976.

7. Private Security Advisory Council, Law Enforcement/Private Security Relationship Committee. "Abstract." 1975.

8. Private Security Task Force. "Summary of Private Security Legislation." (See Appendix 6 to this report.)

9. Research Department, Division of Justice and Crime Prevention. "The Private Security Industry in Virginia." 1972.

Related Standards

The following standards and goals may be applicable in implementing Standard 6.7:

6.8 Law Enforcement Officer Employment as a Private Security Principal or Manager

6.9 Private Investigatory Work

10.1 Licensing of Security Businesses

11.1 Registration of Private Security Personnel

Standard 6.8

Law Enforcement Officer Employment as a Private Security Principal or Manager

No law enforcement officer should be a principal or manager of a private security operation where such association creates a conflict of interest.

Commentary

Law enforcement officers who are principals or managers of private security operations may impede the improvement of the law enforcement/private security relationship by creating unfair competition and conflicts of interest. Law enforcement officials with secondary employment in these positions can easily upset the balance between the law enforcement and private security sectors that is necessary for cooperative efforts, interchange of information, and delineation of roles. Because the scope and potential for behavior damaging to the public are much greater in such employment than, for example, with an individual law enforcement officer working as a private security guard, this question merits special scrutiny.

More than just the questions of use of a duty uniform and/or service weapon or the exercise of police powers is involved when a law enforcement official becomes a principal or manager of a private security operation. Every on-duty decision made by the official needs to be examined for any indication of improper motives. If an official acts in a manner appropriate with the facts in a given situation, but is later questioned because of his private security interests or position, the reputation of both the individual and the employing law enforcement agency may be irreparably damaged, despite the fact that the official acted in genuine good faith as a law enforcement officer.

The Private Security Advisory Council's Law Enforcement/Private Security Relationship Committee, discussing those items hindering the development of the most productive possible relationship, cited the following:

> . . . a number of public law officers have actually formed guard businesses of their own. Problems that are created by this new venture are numerable:
> - Dual roles are not separated. Their use of official uniforms creates an "on duty" look. There is no indication that they are in fact off duty and working *special duty*.
> - Misunderstanding of crime prevention work.
> - Conflicting interest.
> - Temptation to perform his public police task so as to conform less to justice's requirements and more to his off-duty work schedule.
> - Temptation to disclose or exploit confidential police information.
> - May use his official position for personal gain.
> - Insurance complications.

A review of several specific problems concerning the propriety of law enforcement officials acting as

236

principals in private security operations illuminates those areas in which unfair advantage and conflict of interest lie.

First, law enforcement officials who are principals or managers of private security operations may be tempted to use law enforcement resources in their private business activities. Among these resources would be criminal justice information, law enforcement technical services (e.g., crime lab, ballistics), clerical assistance (e.g., typing, reproduction, case preparation), and, on a larger scale, as mentioned in the previous standard, law enforcement equipment.

Law enforcement officials who are principals or managers of private security operations may be tempted to withhold law enforcement services, may fail to act, or may act in such a manner as to favor their private security interests. An example of withholding services or failing to act would be the law enforcement official who, when notified by a firm of a suspected embezzlement, informs the firm that the law enforcement department does not make that type of investigation and recommends the private security operation. An example of acting to favorably affect the private security interest could occur when a law enforcement officer at a policy or decision-making level governs law enforcement action to best serve the private interest.

An atmosphere of unfair advantage is often engendered by the law enforcement official's use of his police identity to generate more private business. When prospective clients learn that one or all of the principals and/or managers of a private security operation are off-duty law enforcement officials, they may get the impression that they will receive the attention of the private security staff plus the resources of the public law enforcement agency.

Finally, a law enforcement official who is a principal or manager of a private security operation could solicit business from victims of crime. In an attempt to prevent a recurrence, these victims may ask law enforcement officials how to better protect themselves. The law enforcement officer with private security connections could then recommend the private operation at interest.

These examples are areas in which the problems of conflict of interest or unfair competition can be created. These problems are potentially more damaging to law enforcement agencies and the public than are the problems created when law enforcement personnel merely work as employees of private security firms, unconcerned about the firm's profit levels. These types of acts contribute to the growing climate of mistrust, loss of faith, and disrespect for public institutions. Police executives must act in a manner that ensures that such cases do not occur.

Selected References

1. Private Security Advisory Council, Law Enforcement/Private Security Relationship Committee. "Abstract." 1976.

Related Standards

The following standards may be applicable in implementing Standard 6.8:

6.7   Law Enforcement Personnel Secondary Employment
6.9   Private Investigatory Work
10.1   Licensing of Security Businesses

Standard 6.9

Private Investigatory Work

Law enforcement officers should be strictly forbidden from performing any private investigatory work.

Commentary

One particular job within the private security industry is consistently inappropriate for law enforcement personnel to hold as secondary employment: private investigator. It is almost impossible for a law enforcement officer to perform private investigatory functions as secondary employment without creating a conflict of interest.

A study by the Institute for Local Self Government, *Private Security and the Public Interest,* reached the same conclusion. The study specifically states: "There should be a prohibition against moonlighting by public law enforcement personnel. Active public police officers should be prevented from functioning as private detectives."

An explanation of successful investigatory work clearly indicates why it is such a highly objectionable secondary job for law enforcement officers: Good investigators must be able to gather information. They need to develop sources. Sources can be people or agencies and institutions. Good investigators need to be resourceful when obtaining needed information.

Information available to a private investigator depends on the individual's ability to ferret out facts from all possible sources. A good investigator will try to develop a contact inside a law enforcement agency to obtain arrest and conviction data, information from field investigations, fingerprint checks, or National Crime Information Center checks. A law enforcement officer working off-duty as a private investigator might be tempted to use law enforcement information and, thus, would be able to deliver better service than a private investigator without access to such information. This action would be both improper and unprofessional.

Other aspects of good private investigatory work include surveillance and undercover work. The public nature of law enforcement appears to make private surveillance by a public law enforcement officer inappropriate. A citizen might file a defamation-of-character suit against a city, law enforcement agency, or officer by claiming that surveillance conducted by an off-duty law enforcement officer working as a private investigator gave others the impression he was the target of a law enforcement criminal investigation.

With regard to undercover work, a solid case might be lost because an officer, in pursuit of public duties, by chance comes into contact with those persons he has been deceiving during his off-duty time. A case might be lost in the courts because the requirements for adequate safeguards of an individual's rights were not adhered to by the officer, believing that, because he was acting in a private capacity, they need not apply to him.

A situation especially subject to conflict of interest is created by private investigators' use of informants. Informants are as necessary a tool to a private investigator as they are to a law enforcement officer. A law enforcement officer moonlighting as a private investigator would certainly be tempted to use his law enforcement informants, because the cultivation of an informant is a lengthy and expensive process. In his private work the law enforcement officer would have neither the time nor the money to develop a second set of informants.

Because of these potentials for conflicts of interest, States, such as Connecticut and Kansas, have disallowed by statute those persons empowered with law enforcement authority from obtaining private-investigator licenses. In other States, the practice has been banned on the basis of an attorney general's opinion. For example, in Iowa, where just such a question was asked, an assistant State attorney general responded:

Finally, you have asked whether or not the Department of Public Safety may issue a private detective license to a person holding a special police commission or a special deputy sheriff commission.

In answering this question, it is well established that the duties of a special policeman or special deputy sheriff are to maintain law and order, prevent and detect crime, and enforce the law. *Burke* vs. *State*, 47 S.E. 2d, 116, 76 Ga. App. 612. But a detective agency license would authorize the policeman or deputy sheriff to serve private clients, investigate private disputes, and support his client's case, in or out of court. This investigation, disclosure of confidential facts, and assistance to his client would, in many cases, be a breach of his duties as a policeman or deputy sheriff. The policeman cannot serve two masters; and the information obtained as a policeman should not be disclosed to a private client, or vice versa. Accordingly, it is my opinion that the offices of a private detective agency and of a policeman are incompatible and that a policeman should not be licensed or authorized to engage in the private detective business.

One encouraging example is that of a law enforcement administrator who has taken action to eliminate this practice. *The Houston (Texas) Chronicle* reported that the acting chief of police was attempting to force at least 10 of his personnel to give up their private security businesses. Among those was an officer operating as a private investigator who, because he handled missing persons cases while on-duty, might have a conflict of interest.

Law enforcement officers should not be denied secondary employment in any jobs where a conflict of interest or unfair competition are not created. Private investigatory work is one of the few jobs where conflict of interest is present because of the nature of the job and is, therefore, inappropriate for a law enforcement officer. The only effective way to ensure that the integrity of law enforcement agencies and law enforcement officers is maintained and citizens' rights protected is to ban law enforcement officers from employment as private investigators.

Selected References

1. Institute for Local Self Government. *Private Security and the Public Interest.* Berkeley, Calif.: Institute for Local Self Government, 1974.

2. "Police Resist Order to Drop Private Eye Firms," *Houston Chronicle,* Sept. 24, 1975.

3. Zeller, Joseph W., assistant attorney general, State of Iowa. Written correspondence with Robert D. Taha, deputy commissioner, Department of Public Safety, State of Iowa, March 7, 1969.

Related Standards

The following standards and goals may be applicable in implementing Standard 6.9:

6.1   Interaction Policies

6.7   Law Enforcement Personnel Secondary Employment

6.8   Law Enforcement Officer Employment as a Private Security Principal or Manager

11.1   Registration of Private Security Personnel

Chapter 7
Consumers of Security Services

INTRODUCTION

As the incidence of crime in the United States continues to rise, the need has become evident for citizens, acting individually or collectively, to participate in the creation of a safer environment. This view is supported by the Administrator of the Law Enforcement Assistance Administration (LEAA), Richard W. Velde, who would ideally unite all forces in the public and private sectors in a partnership to reduce crime. Velde views the potential role of the citizen as a security resource that must be nurtured:

> Another major area that can and must be tapped for crime control and prevention is, of course, the individual. The citizen can have a significant impact on crime either through his institutions or organizations, national or local, or as a home owner who leaves his garage door open or a car owner who leaves the key in his automobile.
> When we talk about law enforcement, we should not confine our discussions only to what we as law enforcement officials can do for the citizen. We also should ask: What can the citizen do for law enforcement? In my view, the citizen has a great potential for preventing crime and that potential can be drawn on through an effective community crime prevention program.[1]

Consumers of private security goods and services are one part of society that can play a major role in combating crime.

Alert and concerned consumers can play an important role in improving the quality of products and services in the marketplace. More than ever before, the consumer's voice is having a forceful impact upon American businesses. Consumer movements have produced tangible results in the form of government legislation, consumer protection offices, and various consumer education programs.

The purpose of this chapter is not to generate new consumer-oriented legislation but rather to stimulate greater consumer responsibility in the selection and acquisition of private security products and services. By assuming a more positive and constructive role,

consumers can help effect improvements in those products and services, leading to more effective crime reduction results for both themselves and the public.

Because their choice of security services affects the safety and well-being of the public, consumers of private security services have an added responsibility to seek high-quality services and to carefully evaluate alternative systems and services prior to acquisition. Quality and performance standards should not be sacrificed for cost if inferior private security services are to be discouraged and the goals of crime prevention attained.

As is true of the relationship between private security and public law enforcement sectors, a two-way communication between the private security industry and its consumers is necessary for maximum productivity in crime prevention. It is urged that the expertise and assistance of private security professional associations and organizations be applied toward this goal through their development of consumer assistance committees. These committees could collect and disseminate data concerning private security products and services, handle consumer inquiries, and perform other public services.

The goal of promoting increased consumer responsibility in the selection and acquistion of private security products and services also can be enhanced through the assistance of private and governmental consumer agencies, such as consumer protection bureaus and better business associations. By developing private security expertise, these agencies can provide valuable services to consumers in a variety of areas, including the development of comparative data on private security systems and services, the establishment of complaint referral procedures, and the review of private security legislation.

Finally, in order to strengthen the relationship between the private security industry and its consumers, it is recommended that the security industry set standards for advertising that accurately portray to the public the nature and quality of services provided. Advertising by private security businesses should include the business license name, specify training levels of personnel, indicate the amount of

---

[1] Velde, Richard W., address at the annual meeting of the International Association of Chiefs of Police, Denver, Colo., Sept. 16, 1975.

supervision security personnel will receive, reflect compliance with insurance and regulatory requirements, and other items. Through this action, private security businesses can assist consumers in selecting the service that will best fit their particular private security needs. Honest and informative advertising is an effective, positive tool for building a reliable image and fostering credence for the industry in the marketplace. Dishonest or misleading advertising, on the other hand, only succeeds in degrading the industry as a whole and may lead to increased government regulation of private security advertising.

The standards in this chapter offer direction for positive interaction between the private security industry and consumers of its services. Active involvement by consumers has produced desirable results in other areas of the marketplace; similar results are possible in the private security sector. Clearly, it is in the best interest of both the private security industry and consumers to execute their respective responsibilities in an environment of mutual aid and cooperation.

Goal 7.1

Consumer Responsibility for Selection of Security Services

The consumer of private security services has a responsibility to evaluate systems and services prior to acquisition in order to ensure the best crime reduction results for himself and other members of the public affected by those systems and services.

Commentary

In today's marketplace, the consumer is better able to select the correct lawnmower than obtain the proper private security services. To select the correct lawnmower, the consumer can refer to any one of a half-dozen consumer magazines, government consumer publications, or a neighborhood hardware store. Should this same consumer desire private security services, the task of making an informed choice is both more complex and difficult.

The roadblock to making an informed choice is the scarcity of consumer information on private security. Few consumer magazines have carried articles on how to select security services. Even the two or three national security publications have published only a few dozen articles over the past 10 years aimed at assisting consumers. A search for government publications dealing with selection of security services would prove fruitless, with one exception— the recently published *Director of Security Consul-*

tants. And there is no neighborhood security dealer to offer friendly advice.

The lack of informative data does not diminish consumer responsibility in the choice of security services. There can be no lessening of this responsibility, because the consumer's decision affects the public's safety and general well-being. Ensuring that the consumer is able to properly and adequately meet that responsibility is the purpose of this and other standards in this chapter.

Checklists for obtaining security services are presented that should serve to encourage further work in expanding the material presented and in developing additional viable, extensive, and cost-effective guides. These checklists are targeted on the acquisition of guard and alarm services and home protection. The consumer considering the purchase of security services should find these lists a helpful starting point.

Some preliminary considerations need to be mentioned before the checklists are given. First, the decision to acquire security services should be followed by the consumer's evaluation of his personal needs. Based on the responses to a study prepared for this report (Appendix 3), the five main reasons for engaging security services are:

1. To prevent (and detect) potential criminal activity,

2. To protect property,

3. To detect fire and safety hazards,

4. To check entry and exit of personnel and vehicles, and

5. To reduce actual criminal activity.

Robert Schurr's article, "The Guard Force (Direct Hire or Contract)," outlines several relevant points. To determine the need for and the size of a guard force, he suggests the consumer consider the following factors: (1) what is to be protected, (2) to what degree must it be protected, (3) how much can be spent, and (4) what are management's expectations. These suggestions also apply to the acquisition of protective devices and alarm services.

Acquiring Alarm Systems

When considering the acquisition of alarm system protection or other protective-device systems, the consumer should attempt to become as familiar as possible with available systems. This can be accomplished by: (1) contacting a security consultant, (2) consulting security and general interest periodicals, (3) reviewing books on the physical security and alarm systems industry, (4) obtaining brochures from alarm sales companies, and (5) contacting organizations, such as the National Burglar and Fire Alarm Association (NB&FAA).

The NB&FAA has published a consumer guide, entitled *Considerations When Looking for a Burglar Alarm System*. This pamphlet outlines a good procedure for the consumer to follow once familiar with available alarm systems. When the consumer has educated himself as much as possible, a procedure primarily consisting of the NB&FAA prescribed process should be followed:

1. Locate reputable alarm companies by contacting:

   a. Local law enforcement agency,

   b. Underwriters' Laboratories, Inc., and

   c. NB&FAA.

2. Set appointments with reputable dealers for:

   a. Visit between the sales representative and appropriate management personnel, and

   b. Visit between the sales representative and all appropriate members of the family, and

   c. Conduct a security survey to determine alarm needs.

3. Consider all available systems to determine:

   a. Type of alarm devices required, and

   b. Type of total alarm system required.

4. Check local laws for:

   a. Type of alarm systems permissable,

   b. Length of time an alarm can sound, and

   c. Penalties for false alarms.

5. Study any contract or sales agreement prior to purchase for:

a. List of points of protection,

b. Itemization of equipment to be installed, and

c. Service arrangements and fees.

6. Consumer role in the use of an alarm system is:

   a. Thorough working knowledge of the system by all persons in contact with it, and

   b. Responsibility for ensuring that public law enforcement officers are not endangered by improper use.

A consumer of alarm systems protection following the procedure outlined would greatly reduce the likelihood of falling prey to the less-than-reputable alarm companies that are a problem in the industry. Further, the consumer's dollar will have been spent on a reasonably cost-effective system, with no overselling or underselling of the acquired system.

Acquiring Guard Services

In some situations, guards may be more appropriate than a mechanical detection device. However, the consumer faces a different set of problems when acquiring guard services. Among these problems is the question of whether to employ a guard or contract for this service. Consumers in the study conducted for this report (Appendix 3) were fairly split: 51 percent hired contract guards, 30 percent employed their own guards, 19 percent used both contract and proprietary guards, and 44 percent had changed their source of guard services.

In the consumer's quest for guard services, a review of available literature on these services is necessary for familiarization. Security periodicals, various studies listed in this report, local law enforcement agencies, better business bureaus, and books on security will provide valuable background data that can influence the consumer's decision on guard services.

Among the problems a consumer can anticipate with a guard force, either employed or contracted, are the complaints and criticisms listed in two studies: the Private Security Task Force Philadelphia Study (PSTF Philadelphia Study) (Appendix 3) and a survey of the California Peace Officers Association, contained in *Private Security and the Public Interest*. The top five criticisms from each study follow:

PSTF Philadelphia Study

1. Inadequate training,

2. Poor wage scale,

3. Undependability of personnel,

4. Inadequate supervision, and

5. Inadequate background checks on personnel.

Private Security and the Public Interest

1. Generally inadequate training,
2. Generally unqualified personnel,
3. (Inadequate) initial screening and background check,
4. Low wages, and
5. "Playing cop" or misuse of authority.

Other frequently occurring problems, cited in *Private Security and the Public Interest,* are failure to perform services as agreed, unlicensed services, and impersonation of law enforcement personnel. The study also determined that, of the complaints placed against regulated private security activities, 60 percent were opposed to private investigators, 35 percent were opposed to private patrol operators, and 5 percent were opposed to private patrol employees.

When the consumer has completed the familiarization process, and has perhaps received a security consultant's recommendations on manning requirements, the question of whether to contract for security guard services or to create a proprietary guard force must be resolved. To aid the consumer in this task, some of the positive and negative aspects of contract and proprietary guard services, based on the Schurr article and an article entitled "Company Guards vs. Subcontractor Guards," are listed below. They are neither comprehensive nor intended to favor either of the choices.

Advantages of Contract Guard Services

1. Selectivity—employer retains only those persons personally approved.
2. Flexibility—more or fewer personnel, as required.
3. Absenteeism—replacement of absentees on short notice.
4. Supervision—supplied at no cost to the client.
5. Training—supplied at no cost to client; may be superior to inhouse training program.
6. Objectivity—judgment not clouded by personalities.
7. Cost—20 percent less than inhouse, not counting administrative savings (e.g., insurance, retirement pension, social security, medical care).
8. Quality—may be of higher caliber than an inhouse guard.
9. Administration and budgeting—brunt borne by guard company.
10. Unions—very little problem, because contract guards are usually not unionized.
11. Variety of services and equipment—guard company may be specialists in various criminal justice skills or expensive equipment unavailable to inhouse security.
12. Hiring and screening costs—borne by guard company.
13. Better local law enforcement contacts—may know more law enforcement personnel.
14. Sharing expertise and knowledge—may have developed security skills, as a result of many jobs, that can be shared with the client.

Disadvantages of Contract Guard Services

1. Turnover—extremely high industrywide.
2. Divided loyalties—serving-two-masters quandary.
3. Moonlighting—low salary for guards may force them into secondary jobs, resulting in tired and unalert personnel.
4. Reassignment—some agencies send in the best men at inception of contract, and then replace with others as new contracts open.
5. Screening standards—may be inadequate.
6. Insurance—determining liability and ensuring individual guards are bonded and insured.

Advantages of Proprietary Guard Forces

1. Loyalty—a positive quality.
2. Incentive—promotion possibilities within the entire company structure.
3. Knowledge—of operation, products, personnel of the company because of permanent employment.
4. Tenure—less turnover than contract guards.
5. Control—stays inside company structure.
6. Supervision—stays inside company structure.
7. Training—can be specifically geared to the job performed.
8. Company image—may become a status symbol.
9. Morale—a hoped-for state maintained by security manager.
10. Courtesy—can render courtesies to VIP's because of familiarity with company personnel.
11. Better law enforcement liaison—security manager can informally develop law enforcement liaison with less conflict.
12. Selection—company selection procedures can apply.
13. Better communication—more direct.

Disadvantages of Proprietary Guard Forces

1. Unions—may go out with the company union, refuse to cross picket lines, and so forth.
2. Familiarity—may become too familiar with personnel to be effective on the job.
3. Cost—expensive (salary, benefits, Workmen's Compensation, social security, liability insurance, work space, equipment, training).
4. Flexibility—hard to replace absent personnel.

5. Administrative burdens—must develop an upper-level staff to handle these personnel.

If the decision is made to hire a contract guard service, based on the consideration of criteria such as those above, the next step is to ensure that the contractor selected is reliable. To aid in this judgment, 12 points, based on those presented in an article entitled "To Make an Informed Choice of a Security Contractor," are listed:

1. Is the security contractor licensed and bonded, as required by law?

2. Is there proof of adequate insurance to protect the client?

3. Can the contractor show a positive relationship with law enforcement?

4. Can the contractor provide multiple services?

5. What is the background and experience of the security contractor's staff?

6. Can the contractor provide a list of past and present clients?

7. Does the contractor have a specific evaluation process of client's problems?

8. What minimum personnel standards does the contractor maintain?

9. Does the contractor have formal and periodical training of personnel?

10. Does the contractor have supervisory personnel available on an immediate 24-hour-a-day basis and offices in each locality where business is solicited?

11. What type of reporting procedures are used to keep the client informed?

12. Is the contractor able to provide free information on costs of specific services?

After ascertaining the answers to these and other questions, the consumer should invite bids from those security firms considered finalists. Then, once the choice is made, a contract as favorable as possible to the consumer should be drawn up. Points to consider in a guard service contract could include, but not be limited to, those appearing in *The Other Police, Private Security and the Public Interest,* and an article by Charles Schnabolk, "Protection against a Guard Force":

1. Clients should be discouraged from using armed personnel unless absolutely necessary for personal safety.

2. Clients should be encouraged to incorporate training requirements into their contracts and to attend initial training sessions.

3. Clients should be advised of the quality of personnel received for the amount of money expended (i.e., a guard service receives $2.25 per hour from the client; the guard will receive, at maximum, only about 70 percent of this amount).

4. The contract document should clearly spell out the definition of each category (of personnel), and the client must be careful in describing the functions required.

5. A client copy of the guard's employment background and a reference check with at least one previous employer should be required.

6. Moonlighters should be accepted only if their total weekly work hours do not exceed 65 hours.

7. A thorough medical checkup of acceptable guards should be required.

8. Make sure all Federal and local civil rights regulations are followed.

9. The contractor must replace any guard within 12-hours notice.

10. The service may be terminated on a 30-day notice.

11. Agency must designate a detail supervisor who shall submit regular reports to the client's representative concerning his supervisory check on assigned guards and concerning any unusual circumstances reported in writing by guards.

12. Consumer can specify some components of employee preassignment and ongoing training that are appropriate to the consumer's facility.

13. Client may view results of graded training (both preassignment and ongoing).

14. Minimum and maximum total hours per day and per week should be determined for each guard to ensure post familiarity, as well as employee efficiency.

15. All weapons used should be the property of the contract agency.

16. All weapons used should be approved by the client.

The contract should ensure that no arrests, detentions, or complaints in the client's name take place without prior consultations.

If agreeable arrangements can be achieved between the consumer and the contract security firm (as a result of the entire acquisition process outlined here), the consumer stands a good chance of getting the most for dollars spent, while ensuring that his obligations to public safety have been met.

Acquiring Residential Protection

Perhaps the area where the consumer is best able to make effective decisions on obtaining security is that of residential protection. A large body of literature on this subject exists in physical security books, periodicals of all types, government publications, and pamphlets by business and industry. Almost all of this data are hardware oriented. Residential security consists primarily of hardening of doors, windows, and walls and installation of alarms, secure locks, special glass, adequate lighting, and appropriate landscaping. The material available for securing a residence is so voluminous that, rather than a specific checklist, a bibliography of selected resources follows:

Pamphlets

1. "Considerations When Looking for a Burglar Alarm System." National Burglar and Fire Alarm Association Inc., 1730 Pennsylvania Ave., N.W., Washington, D.C. 20006 (June 1975).

2. "How to Buy a Lock." Schlage Lock Company, P.O. Box 34186, San Francisco, Calif. 94134 (1972).

3. "How to Protect Your Home against Burglary and Robbery Plus Important Facts about Rip-Off Protection Federal Crime Insurance." Department of Housing and Urban Development, Federal Insurance Administration, Washington, D.C. 20410.

4. "Ives ABC's of Protection for Your Family and Home." The H. B. Ives Company, 50 Ives Place, New Haven, Conn. 06508.

5. "National Neighborhood Watch Program, How to Protect Your Home." The National Sheriffs' Association funded by a grant from the Law Enforcement Assistance Administration, U.S. Department of Justice, Washington, D.C.

6. "Residential Burglary and What to Do About It." California Council on Criminal Justice, Attorney General, State of California, Sacramento, Calif.

7. "Safe at Home?" Master Lock Company, Alarm Products Division, Milwaukee, Wis. 53210 (1975).

8. "Wanted" Citizens Who Care Enough to Stop Commercial Burglary in Oakland." Oakland Police Department in cooperation with Citizens Crime Prevention Committee, 455 Seventh, Oakland, Calif. 94607.

9. "Your Home Is Secure . . . Isn't It?" Schlage Security Institute, P.O. Box 3324, San Francisco, Calif. 94119 (1971).

Government Publications

1. National Sheriff's Association. "National Neighborhood Watch Program Phase III." Pamphlet funded by a grant from the Law Enforcement Assistance Administration, Washington, D.C.

2. "Residential Security" (monograph). A staff report funded by the National Institute of Law Enforcement and Criminal Justice, Law Enforcement Assistance Administration, U.S. Department of Justice. Washington, D.C.: Government Printing Office, December 1973.

3. U.S. Department of Housing and Urban Development. "A Design Guide for Improving Residential Security." Washington, D.C.: Government Printing Office, 1973.

Films

1. "No Place to Rest His Head." Director, Architecture and Engineering Division, U.S. Department of Housing and Urban Development, Washington, D.C.

2. "Horizon—Defensible Space." For information —Regional Office, Law Enforcement Assistance Administration.

Magazines

Back issues of general category periodicals.

Books

1. Kingsbury, Arthur A. *Introduction to Security and Crime Prevention Surveys.* Springfield, Ill.: Charles C. Thomas, 1973.

2. Lipman, Ira A. *How to Protect Yourself from Crime.* New York: Atheneum, 1975.

3. Nonte, George C. Jr. *The Complete Guide to House, Apartment and Property Protection.* S. Hackensack, N.J.: Stoeger Publishing Company, 1974.

The content of this report should form a good, basic document for consumer review, because the standards and goals highlight many significant points relating to private security services.

The consumer is expected to exercise care in any marketplace where the credo is "let the buyer beware." A consumer needs to take more care when searching for security services for a business or residence than when seeking services that affect only himself. The consumer's selection of security services can affect any person coming in contact with the service. However, until private and public consumer agencies and professional security organizations and associations fill the information gap, the consumer selecting private security services will encounter difficulties meeting his responsibility. The information contained in this standard should assist the consumer in meeting his responsibility in the selection of security services and serve as a springboard for development of useful guides and information.

Selected References

1. Brennan, Dennis T. *The Other Police.* Cleveland, Ohio: Governmental Research Institute, 1975.

2. Davis, Albert S. "Company Guards vs. Subcontractor Guards," *Industrial Security,* Vol. II, No. 6, January 1976.

3. Institute for Local Self Government. *Private*

Security and the Public Interest. Berkeley, Calif.: Institute for Local Self Government, 1975.

4. National Burglar and Fire Alarm Association, Inc. *Considerations When Looking for a Burglar Alarm System.* Washington, D.C.: National Burglar and Fire Alarm Association, Inc., 1974.

5. Private Security Task Force. "Survey of Consumers of Private Security Services in the Greater Philadelphia Area." (See Appendix 3 to this report.)

6. Schnabolk, Charles. "Protection against a Guard Force," *Security World,* Vol. 8, No. 5, May 1971.

7. Schurr, Robert. "The Guard Force (Direct Hire or Contract)," *Security Management,* Vol. 19, No. 6, January 1976.

8. "To Make an Informed Choice of a Security Contractor." (Source unknown.)

Related Standards

The following standards and goals may be applicable in implementing Goal 7.1:

5.2   Adequate Security Lighting
5.5   Development of Environmental Security Expertise
5.7   Crime Prevention Courses in Schools of Architecture and Urban Planning
7.2   Consumer Assistance Committees
7.3   Development of Expertise by Private and Governmental Consumer Agencies
7.4   Private Security Advertising Standards

Standard 7.2

Consumer Assistance Committees

Private security professional associations and organizations should form permanent committees or sections to develop useful guides for the evaluation and acquisition of goods and services and to provide clearinghouses for professional response to consumer inquiries.

Commentary

Mrs. Virginia Knauer, Special Assistant to the President for Consumer Affairs, says she receives some 4,000 letters of complaint a month, out of a total of 12,000 letters. . . .

The New York State Consumer Frauds and Protection Bureau, for example, handled more than 200,000 complaints and recovered more than 1.5 million dollars for consumers in a six-month period. . . .

. . . the New York City Department of Consumer Affairs opened what is believed was the nation's first government-financed neighborhood consumer complaint office. In the first two months of operation it reportedly processed 450 complaints from consumers, recovered $7,000 in refunds and uncovered five cases of fraud termed "important."

These quotes, from Goody L. Solomon's book, *The Radical Consumer's Handbook,* points to a trend in American society—the active and concerned consumer. These figures indicate that consumers will no longer tolerate being "taken" in the marketplace. They also highlight the need for consumer-oriented data that is accurate, unbiased, and, above all, helpful for arriving at an intelligent choice of goods and services.

Contributing to the volume of consumer complaints are the realities that the consumer is frequently unable to achieve adequate prepurchase familiarization of materials and that some businesses providing goods and services have inadequate consumer inquiry and complaint procedures. The private security industry is not free of these types of problems. A study conducted for this report of consumers of private security services (Appendix 3) found that 44 percent of the respondents had changed their source of security services. An average of 29 percent of the respondents did not know if the security workers and supervisors had any training for the jobs they performed. Overall, 72 percent of the consumers indicated that they would be willing to invest additional funds if qualifications of personnel and/or quality of services were improved.

These figures point to the need for private security associations and organizations to become active in the field of consumer assistance. These associations and organizations have the expertise and ability within their membership to render an invaluable aid to society through the development of a consumer assistance capability. However, a very strong caution is given: To avoid possible violations of any antitrust regulations, associations and organizations should obtain legal advice both prior to, during, and after development and operation of consumer assistance programs. One taboo to avoid is the creation of standards that force membership in the association by business entities in order to obtain association approval of and recommendation to consumers of their private security goods and services. Private security groups should take care to impartially examine the goods and services provided by all business entities, members and nonmembers alike. Positive recommendations to consumers should not be reserved for members only. With these cautions in mind, a review can be made of the composition of consumer assistance committees and of the types of actions these committees can take to aid consumer selection of private security goods and services.

An important consideration in formulating a consumer assistance committee is that such a committee be permanent. This is the only way to demonstrate genuine commitment. The members of the committee should represent a cross section of the association or organization, in terms of geographical location and size of business operations served. Moreover, its members should be recognized by their peers as experts, respected both inside and outside of the association, and capable of dealing with and relating to people.

When ready to proceed, the committee members should establish communication links with consumers in order to be truly effective, because committee objectives will depend largely upon consumer needs. These needs can only be directly learned from the consumer. Three methods are suggested to gather necessary data:

1. **Surveys.** Survey instruments could be developed that indicate consumer problems and needs. Questionnaires could be sent to users of security goods and services, based on customer lists supplied by the membership of the association or organization.

2. **Personal Meetings With Consumers.** Consumer assistance committees could learn firsthand of the problems, needs and questions of consumers by holding meetings with past and present clients of the membership. These meetings also should be publicly advertised to attract potential consumers.

3. **Government and Private Data on Consumer Complaints.** Data from government consumer bureaus, better business bureaus, and prosecuting officials could help determine the nature of consumer complaints about the goods and services provided by the association or organization members.

When the data collection process is complete, goals and objectives of the committee can be formulated.

One objective of the committee should be preparation of some type of printed material concerning the goods and services provided by the membership.

A sample checklist of items for inclusion follows:

1. Information about association or organization.

2. The goods and services provided.

3. Discussion of why the goods and services are needed.

4. What the goods and services can reasonably be expected to do.

5. How to properly obtain goods and services.

6. How to determine what is received for the amount being paid and information on costs and expenses that can be anticipated after acquisition.

7. What to do and who to contact if goods and services are unsatisfactory.

8. Consumer's role, responsibility, and obligation in the acquisition of goods and services.

9. Who to contact in the association for further information.

When a draft of the consumer material is completed, two actions logically follow. First, the draft should be distributed to the association or organization membership for review and approval. Interested and knowledgeable persons outside of the association or organization might also be given a draft for their reactions. Second, when the material is published, steps should be taken to ensure its dissemination. Quantities of the publication should be distributed to the association or organization membership for display and distribution at their business locations. Moreover, the publication, and where it can be obtained, should be well advertised.

Another objective of the consumer assistance committee should be the development of a capability to handle consumer inquiries. A committee member or an association staffer should be designated to handle all written correspondence from consumers. The committee might recommend the designation of consumer representatives from the association or organization membership to service the geographical area covered. The duties of the consumer representative could range from handling consumer complaints against association or organization members to speaking to groups about the nature and role of private security in crime prevention. The level of resources allocated to providing response to the needs and inquiries of consumers should not, however, surpass the need indicated in the consumer surveys.

Private security professional associations and organizations have great potential to provide an important service to the consumer. Several private security associations and organizations already have put both time and money into programs and publications to educate, inform, and assist consumers. The everyday business of the private security professional is the prevention, detection, and deterrence of crime. The professional, through his association and organization memberships, can be of great assistance in helping consumers select the proper goods and services from the private security industry. This assistance will, in turn contribute to greater public safety.

Selected References

1. Private Security Task Force. "Survey of Consumers of Private Security Services in the Greater Philadelphia Area." (See Appendix 3 to this report.)
2. Solomon, Goody L. *The Radical Consumer's Handbook*. New York: Ballantine Books, 1972.

Related Standards

The following standards and goals may be applicable in implementing Standard 7.2:

7.1 Consumers Responsibility for Selection of Security Services

7.3 Development of Expertise by Private and Governmental Consumer Agencies

Standard 7.3

Development of Expertise by Private and Governmental Consumer Agencies

Governmental consumer protection bureaus, better business associations, and private consumer groups should develop sufficient knowledge of the private security industry to enable them to intelligently evaluate complaints and advise consumers.

Commentary

In a review of the history of the consumer movement, Goody L. Solomon points out, in *The Radical Consumer's Handbook,* that the late President John F. Kennedy created a national Consumer Advisory Council and issued a buyer's "Bill of Rights." The bill included the following:

1) **The Right to Safety:** "To be protected against marketing of goods which are hazardous to health or life."

2) **The Right to Be Informed:** "To be protected against fraudulent, deceitful, grossly misleading information, advertising, labeling, or other practices, and to be given the facts to make an informed choice."

3) **The Right to Choose:** "To be assured, wherever possible, access to a variety of products and services at competitive prices and, in those industries in which competition is not workable and government regulation is substituted, to be assured satisfactory quality and service at fair prices."

4) **The Right to Be Heard:** "To be assured that consumer interests will receive full and sympathetic consideration in the formulation of government policy, and fair and expeditious treatment in its administrative tribunals."

The work of this Council laid the cornerstone for private consumer action committees and State and local government consumer bureaus.

For continuing support of this mandate, public and private consumer agencies should develop expertise in the private security industry as it grows in size and importance. A study by Arthur D. Little, Inc., estimated 1975 revenues of $3 billion for "security products and services," based upon a growth rate of 12 percent per year. A study by Frost and Sullivan, Inc., estimated revenues of $2.5 billion in 1974 for "loss prevention products and services." Based upon their projected growth rate of 10 percent annually, 1975 revenues would have been $2.8 billion. Figures of this magnitude indicate that the private security field is indeed big business and, as such, can affect many people's lives.

There are three relevant areas concerning the development of private security expertise that would enhance the role and mission of government and private consumer bureaus and associations: consumer information, complaint referral actions, and legislation. Consumer information should be developed providing prepurchase advice and listings of reliable private security firms. Expertise in methods of civil and legal recourse for complaints against private security firms should also be developed. Familiarization with local, State, and Federal legislation and studies of private security recommendations are important prerequisites to planning and initiating any needed action programs aimed at achieving improvement in the security market.

One of the most important functions that consumer bureaus and better business associations can undertake is preparing useful consumer information. Development of comparative data on private security goods and services, such as comparisons among various alarm systems, is perhaps the most important contribution that could be made. This service would be particularly useful in the area of guard and investigative services, because no evaluative method has yet been devised to compare these services. Perhaps the second most necessary information is local listings of reliable private security firms, based on professional association memberships, including number of registered complaints, out-of-court settlement data from insurance companies, and other data deemed appropriate. The development of this type of consumer information can, over time, im-

prove the goods and services of the private security industry.

The next area in which private security expertise needs to be developed concerns complaints referral by consumer bureaus and better business associations. The nature of the referral would depend on the type and the monetary amount of the complaint. Even more basic is the process of informing consumers that a complaint procedure exists. Although avenues for redress may vary from State to State, the possible directions a person with a complaint may take fall into five general categories:

1. Source of goods and services,
2. Consumer protection methods,
3. Regulatory,
4. Enforcement, and
5. Judicial.

Figure 7.1 provides an overview of interrelationships that may exist between the categories. Obviously, considerable expertise will be required to ensure that the proper referral is made.

Figure 7.1. Consumer Options for Complaints

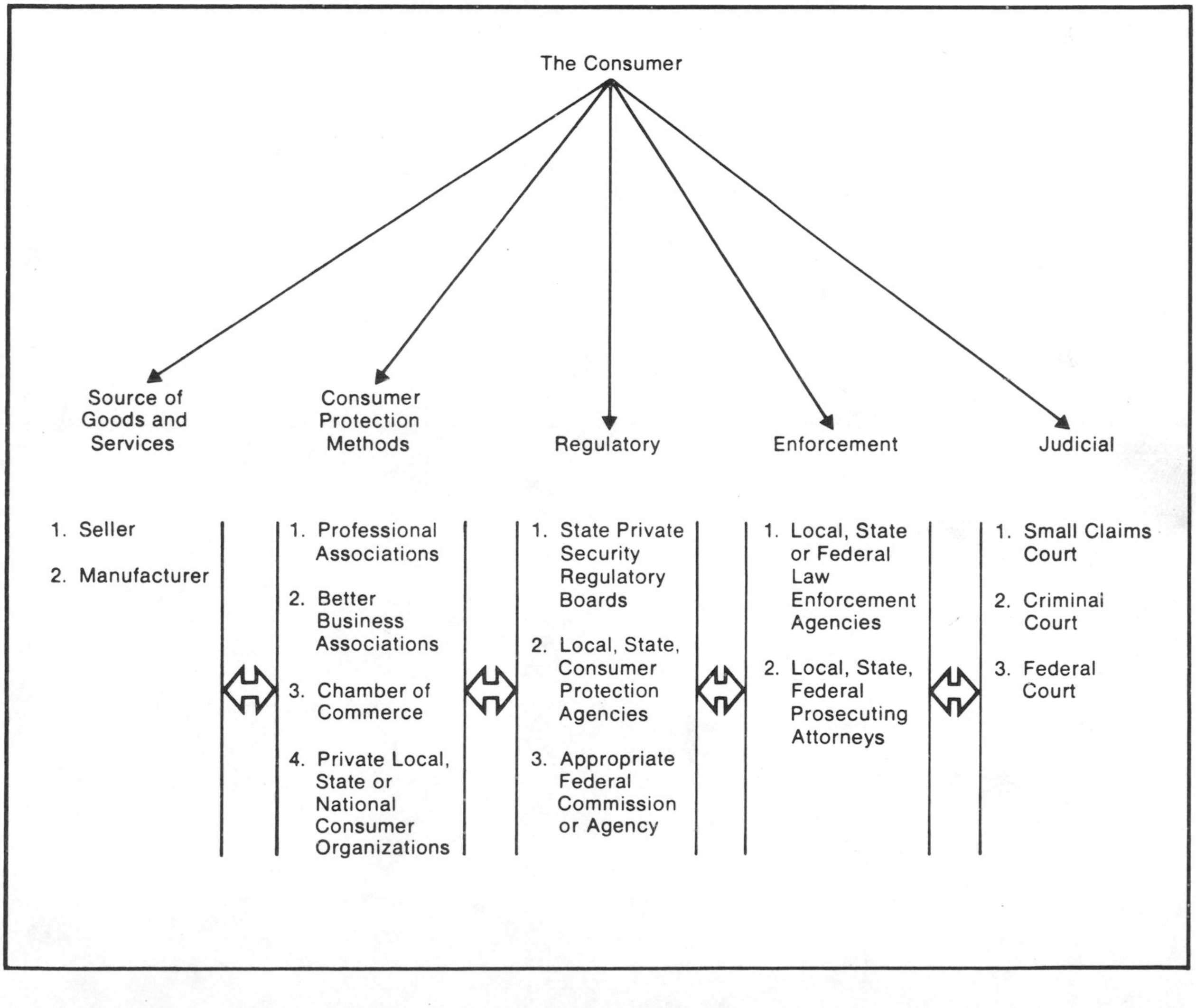

The third need for development of knowledge of private security activities is in legislation. In 1975, 33 States had private security legislation, and all States presently have some local private security ordinances. Consumer bureaus and better business associations should prepare compendiums of legislation in each State to better inform, advise, or refer consumers. Having developed a knowledge of legislation, the recommendations for private security legislation contained in several national and State studies of the industry should be reviewed. Recommendations for improving existing legislation then can be made to appropriate bodies. However, if research reveals that laws and ordinances already exist, the thrust of efforts should not be toward developing new laws but rather toward applying and enforcing the existing legislation.

Consumer bureaus and better business associations have, in a very short time, substantially contributed to improving the quality of life in the United States. It is in keeping with the avowed purposes of these organizations that they now undertake the task of developing expertise and services in the private security field.

Selected References

1. Frost and Sullivan, Inc. *The Industrial and Commercial Security Market,* New York: FSI, March 1975.

2. Little, Arthur D., Inc. *Outlook for the U.S. Safety, Fire Protection and Security Business.* Cambridge, Mass.: ADLI, January 1973.

3. Solomon, Goody L. *The Radical Consumer's Handbook,* New York: Ballantine Books, 1972.

Related Standards

The following standards and goals may be applicable in implementing Standard 7.3:

7.1 Consumers Responsibility for Selection of Security Services

7.2 Consumer Assistance Committees

7.4 Private Security Advertising Standards

Standard 7.4

Private Security Advertising Standards

The private security industry should adhere to advertising standards that accurately portray to the public the nature and quality of the service to be provided.

Commentary

Regulation of Advertising by the FTC (Federal Trade Commission) states that:

For markets to operate effectively, buyers must have accurate information about the quality and other characteristics of the products offered for sale. Otherwise there can be no basis for confidence that the market will enable consumers to make purchases maximizing their welfare within the limitations of their resources. The production of information about products is therefore of fundamental importance to the effective operation of a market system.

These words ring with reason and well introduce the purpose behind this standard. The consumer of security services has to rely heavily on information supplied by the industry itself because of the paucity of readily available resource materials. The accuracy and completeness of information and advertising have a direct relationship on how the consumer perceives the private security marketplace and how effectively consumer dollars are spent for security services.

The lack of information on private security services can make the consumer vulnerable to advertising claims. Consumers could be misinformed about the nature and quality of private security services and led into unwise choices of services by advertising practices relying on the fear of crime.

A consumer may not know what to look for when considering private security guard services and be misguided about their quality and nature. Some guard company brochures heavily stress that the company has personnel capable of performing many different security functions, from special event duty to retail store security. This advertising of across-the-spectrum capability may be of interest to a consumer, but it does not furnish the consumer with data on the qualifications of personnel for specific security functions, the amount of supervision guards receive, whether governmental regulatory requirements have been met, or if insurance or bonding is in effect. A consumer of private security guard services should review advertising copy for the following positive indicators:

Does advertising:
• Give the business license number?
• Offer a list of references (past and present clients)?
• Give specific information on the training guard personnel receive?

• Give the ratio of supervisors to workers?

• Reflect adequate levels of insurance in force or with whom insured?

• Reflect that pertinent government regulations have been met?

The consumer faces problems of a different nature when dealing with burglar and robbery alarm advertising. First, the product advertised is a tangible one. Unlike the human element of the guard industry, the alarm industry product conforms to certain levels of appearance, performance, and operability—marketable qualities that are highlighted in advertisements. Alarms, unlike guards, are technical products that are unfamiliar to the average consumer.

Second, because they are technical, an alarm product's qualities can be stated in technese—the fusing of technical terms with glowing adjectives, i.e., "our XT–5 annunciator audiovisual articulator has proven its superiority in kilowatt after kilowatt hour of actual use with glowing results." The uneducated consumer may give undue scientific merit to claims articulated in technese.

Finally, alarms and alarm systems have a reference quality that guard services do not. Independent testing laboratories list those devices and systems that meet published evaluation criteria. This gives the consumer some type of assurance that the device, or its components or systems listed by testing laboratories, will meet certain standards. Mention is usually made in advertisements of qualifying equipment. A caution to the consumer: An advertisement could be prepared in such a manner that an entire alarm system appears to have met a testing laboratory's requirements, where, in fact, only the plug at the end of the cord holds certification.

A trait common to advertising for both alarm and guard services is capitalizing on the fear of crime. Subtly or shockingly playing upon fear of crime to create business opportunities should be strictly avoided in all private security advertising. For example, one subtle means of playing on consumers' fears is the use of crime statistics; such use should be avoided. Any person with knowledge of the history of criminal justice statistics can give examples of how statistical data are manipulated to show only what the reporting agency wants these data to show. On the other end of the advertising spectrum, private security advertisements depicting simulated violent acts or designed to be unsettling also should be avoided.

A final advertising abuse is the use of words that can be misleading, such as the name of a State in the corporate name of a private security organization. These practices lead consumers to believe that the organization has quasi-governmental connection.

Private investigative agencies have been most commonly associated with this type of advertising.

Abuses in or confusion created by private security advertising is likely to result in government control. A study of private security services in St. Petersburg, Fla., included a recommendation for advertisement content and a model private security advertising ordinance. Included in the model ordinance was a provision that private security advertisements carry information regarding the location for filing citizen complaints. Both the *RAND Report* (Vol. I) and the study, *Private Security and the Public Interest*, offer recommendations for private security advertising practices. According to a study of legislation (see Appendix 6), nine States regulate private security advertising and six States take punitive action for false advertising.

To avoid further government encroachment into the area of private security advertising, the industry should develop and adhere to advertising standards that are helpful to consumers and that attempt to win them by providing the most accurate and complete data possible. Interesting, informative, intelligent advertising can succeed as well as that which misleads or utilizes fear of crime. A study of a private security advertisement section in *Fortune*, by the *Fortune* marketing research department, found that 71 percent of the respondents took some form of positive action in response to the advertisements, most of which had imaginative well-written copy, relying not on the negative aspects of crime but on the positive aspects of the service or product being sold.

As stated in *Regulation of Advertising by the FTC:*

As a result of increases in the complexity and variety of products and in the value of people's time (time being the principle resource consumed in search) it can be surmised that there has occurred a major shift from consumer to seller in the comparative advantage of supplying consumer product information.

The private security industry should heed this message and enhance its image and credence in the marketplace by drafting and adopting advertising standards.

Selected References

1. "Crime Does Pay" (special industrial security advertisement section), *Fortune*, Vol. XC, No. 3, September 1974.

2. Fortune Market Research Department. "Special Study on Industrial Security." December 1974.

3. Institute for Local Self Government. *Private Security and the Public Interest.* Berkeley, Calif.: Institute for Local Self Government, 1975.

4. Kakalik, James S., and Sorrel Wildhorn. *Private Police in the United States: Findings and Recommendations,* Vol. I, R–869/DOJ. Washington, D.C.: Government Printing Office, 1972.

5. Posner, Richard A. *Regulation of Advertising by the FTC.* Washington, D.C.: American Enterprise Institute for Public Policy Research, November 1973.

6. Private Security Task Force. "Summary of Private Security Legislation." (See Appendix to this report.)

7. Martensen, Kai R. *Private Security Survey and Ordinance for St. Petersburg, Florida.* Sunnyvale, Calif.: Public Systems Incorporated, 1975.

Related Standards

The following standards and goals may be applicable in implementing Standard 7.4:

3.1 Code of Ethics
6.5 Mistaken Identity of Private Security Personnel
6.6 State Regulation of Private Security Uniforms, Equipment, Job Titles
7.1 Consumers Responsibility for Selection of Security Services
7.2 Consumer Assistance Committees
7.3 Development of Expertise by Private and Governmental Consumer Agencies

Chapter 8
Higher Education and Research

INTRODUCTION

Although the growth of the private security sector has paralleled and often exceeded that of public law enforcement, there is a paucity of information and research for or about the industry and its operations. Educational and degree programs, specifically geared to the needs of private security employment, are also minimal. If the problems of the private security industry are to be overcome, allowing it to emerge in its proper role as an effective force against both private and public crime, these deficiencies in research and education need to be corrected.

This report highlights some of the problems of the private security industry and addresses methods by which the industry and other concerned groups can improve the quality of security services and/or performance. Most chapters are directed toward a more or less distinctive audience—i.e., chapter 1 chiefly concerns private security employers, chapter 7 is directed toward consumers. The standards in this chapter, however, have broad applications for all the persons for whom this report is intended, namely, members of the private security industry, governmental agencies, educators, and citizens in general. Their increased awareness of the need for basic research and expanded educational opportunities in private security subjects is required for the implementation of the standards in this chapter.

Although, at first glance, the general population would appear to play a passive role, a closer examination discloses that citizen encouragement of mechanisms to implement this report and advocation of educational programs can directly assist the purpose of the standards. Citizen groups have effectively furthered many worthwhile changes in government; their support should not be overlooked by the private security industry. Moreover, industry improvements increase overall protection against crime and repay citizens for their interest and involvement.

To ensure continuing research and the development of further knowledge in the private security field and to enhance its effectiveness in crime prevention and reduction, this report recommends that review and implementation mechanisms be set up on a State-by-State basis (Standard 8.1). The resulting organizations would be charged with review and implementation of the standards and goals of this report. Although the formation of such bodies would depend largely upon government action, it is not intended to exclude others from unilaterally supporting or independently implementing the recommended standards and goals.

Some may argue that Standard 8.1 is superfluous. However, available data indicates that many individuals fail to recognize the relationship between the private security industry and the criminal justice system. Also, many persons in private security do not care to be identified with the traditional criminal justice system. Nevertheless, the two forces have a common denominator that tends to support their lateral position—the suppression of criminal activity. The inclusion of Standard 8.1 emphasizes the belief that State review and implementation of standards and goals offer a unique opportunity for further exploration and increased use of the private security industry in crime prevention and reduction.

The Federal Government has made significant contributions to criminal justice planning through the implementation of State Planning Agencies. Citizens' crime commissions, colleges, universities, and other agencies also have given substantial support to criminal justice planning. However, there has been little emphasis on research as it relates to private security services. The absence of reliable research has made planning and decisionmaking difficult in the field. Therefore, Standard 8.2 proposes the development of a national private security resource and research institute and encourages the administrative and financial assistance of the Law Enforcement Assistance Administration in its establishment. This institute would significantly enhance the activities advocated in Standard 8.1, further the development of a body of knowledge for use in educational institutions, and provide a foundation for the development of new and improved strategies to optimize private security capacity in crime prevention and reduction.

Standards 8.3 and 8.4 were formulated in response to the alarming lack of comprehensive, private security educational programs in the United States.

Basically, their intent is to institute a cooperative plan under which educational institutions can contribute significantly to the professionalism of the private security industry. Standard 8.3 addresses the need for noncredit and credit seminars and courses designed to meet the unique needs of private security personnel. Standard 8.4 broadly outlines the need for associate, baccalaureate, and graduate degrees designed to prepare people for entry into the field and to enlarge the professional, educational experiences of those already so employed.

The national experience in making educational opportunities available for public criminal justice professionals may form a model for private security education. A decade ago there were limited opportunities throughout the country to help public criminal justice officials meet their preemployment or professional development needs. Since that time, a wide-ranging, academically sound program has been developed. It is hoped that educational institutions will respond correspondingly to private security needs, thereby contributing to a safer society for all.

Standard 8.1

State Review of Private Security Task Force Report

Each State should provide a mechanism to review and recommend implementation, as appropriate, of the standards and goals contained in this report.

Commentary

The Private Security Task Force was one of five major task forces formed under the Standards and Goals II program of the Law Enforcement Assistance Administration (LEAA) to develop national standards and goals for the prevention and reduction of crime. The recommendations of these task forces were reviewed by the National Advisory Committee on Criminal Justice Standards and Goals. If the deliberations and work reflected in this report are to accomplish more than serve as a reference book, each State needs to provide a statewide mechanism to encourage and facilitate meaningful and workable action programs for these standards and goals. State Planning Agencies (SPA) and/or other statewide organizations already in existence can be used or new organizations developed for this purpose.

The composition of the State organizations necessarily varies. However, if the proper balance of viewpoints is to be achieved, the members of the organization should be representative of the industry, government, and general population. Although it is almost impossible to set a model for the composition of the

organization, representatives from the following groups are suggested:

- Proprietary security agencies.
- Contractual security agencies.
- Alarm systems industry.
- Urban planning and/or architecture.
- Public law enforcement agencies.
- State registration and licensing authority (if one exists).
- State attorney general's office.
- General public.

The exact number of members and support staff would need to be determined at the State level.

Two States, California and Virginia, already have organized State private security task forces to make recommendations for the improvement of private security services. Perhaps these same groups could assume the responsibility of reviewing the standards and goals contained in this report and make further recommendations to support the better use of private security resources for crime prevention and reduction.

Although the remaining States do not have private security task forces, some States, such as Pennsylvania, have formed committees for criminal justice standards and goals. It would appear reasonable that such committees could well assume the task of reviewing this report and implementing its suggestions. In other States, the SPA might be the catalyst for the beginning of State private security task forces.

Naturally, to make effective recommendations based on this report's standards and goals, States need reliable base data. A private security survey was conducted by the Maine Criminal Justice Planning and Assistance Agency to provide information requested by the Private Security Task Force. The information gathered in this survey could serve as a starting point for a private security data base in Maine. If similar, current information is available in other States, it also could provide valuable base data for their evaluation of private security needs and recommendations for implementation of appropriate standards and goals. A national private security resource and research institute, as proposed in Standard 8.2, would significantly enhance the efforts of States.

It is recognized that the scope of work and priorities of each State organization would differ, based on their specific needs. First, urban and rural States may set different priorities because of varying needs. For example, a rural State may not view regulation as important but may see a high-priority need for training. Second, some States already have licensing and/or registration requirements that are effective, rendering unnecessary the national standards for licensing and regulation. Third, some of the problems identified in this report may not exist within a given State. For example, the standards regarding consumer protection associations or organizations may not apply if there are no substantiated complaints about private security services. It is doubtful that all of the standards could, or should, be adopted by each State. Processes used by the States to react to the previous standards and goals program of the LEAA can well serve as models for the present effort. These processes have resulted in States accepting, modifying, or rejecting the standards and goals in terms of their individual needs.

State committees or SPAs would be restricted in their effect because, like the national Private Security Task Force, they would be advisory in nature. However, they can have several advantages over the national Task Force. One advantage would be their greater impact on State legislative processes. [Because this report has recommended that government regulation be conducted at the State level, this affords a definite advantage in any given State.] Also, because State organizations have more direct access to local and State law enforcement agencies and associations and various private security associations, they can provide a more effective catalyst for improving the relationship between the two sectors. Finally, being more familiar with local conditions and resources, organizations at the State level can provide more effective guidance for review and/or implementation of the standards in this report.

In summary, it is strongly urged that each State provide a mechanism to review and, when appropriate, to implement the standards and goals contained in this report. Through this process, a significant contribution can be made toward the improvement of the private security field and its efforts in crime prevention. In the absence of activity by appropriate State organizations, this report could become merely another contribution to the literature on private security and not an action document intended to assist in the reduction and prevention of crimes.

Selected References

1. Evaluation Unit, Maine Criminal Justice Planning & Assistance Agency. "Report to Private Security Task Force—National Advisory Committee on Criminal Justice Standards and Goals/MCJPPA." Augusta: Maine Criminal Justice Planning & Assistance Agency, Sept. 30, 1975.

2. Private Security Industry Task Force. "Report of the Private Security Industry Task Force to the Virginia State Crime Commission." Virginia: Private Security Industry Task Force, Sept. 4, 1974.

3. Task Force on the Regulation of Private Police, Public Safety Planning Council. "Task Force Report to the Council." Sacramento, Calif.: Public Safety Planning Council, Aug. 24, 1974.

Related Standards

All standard and goal statements in this report can serve as a basis for implementing this standard.

Standard 8.2

National Private Security Resource and Research Institute

The Law Enforcement Assistance Administration should encourage the development of a national private security resource and research institute. In addition, all universities, companies, organizations, associations, and individuals concerned with private security should increase their efforts in private security research.

Commentary

In 1927, Felix Frankfurter, the late U.S. Supreme Court Justice, wrote that the problems of crime and crime control are "overlaid with shibboleths and cliches." He went on to emphasize that it is essential to "separate the known from the unknown, to divorce face from assumption, to strip biases of every sort of their authority." Frankfurter's words are equally applicable to present-day problems of crime and crime control and are especially revelant to the role of the private security industry.

Throughout the work of the Private Security Task Force, the lack of research for and about private security services was appallingly apparent. Scant attention has been focused on research to alleviate obvious problems and enhance the effectiveness of private security in crime prevention and reduction. Unless a reliable research base is available, adminis-

trators will continue to be handicapped in their decisionmaking roles.

To help alleviate the problem of lack of base data, all entities concerned with private security should initiate and increase their research in the field. Also, a national private security resource and research institute should be established to act as a center and resource for these research activities.

The potential of a national resource and research institute to contribute to more effective use of private security services is evident. Admittedly, the competitive nature of the industry may, at first glance, seem to make the concept of a national resource institute unrealistic. However, 10 years ago there was an almost total lack of research in the criminal justice system. Since that time, the Law Enforcement Assistance Administration (LEAA) has made significant contributions to criminal justice research through State Planning Agencies, technical assistance programs, standards and goals programs, and the establishment of the National Institute for Law Enforcement and Criminal Justice Research. A national private security resource and research institute is envisioned as an extension of those activities.

LEAA has already provided leadership and support for research related to private security services, primarily through the Law Enforcement Standards Laboratory and the National Institute of Law En-

263

forcement and Criminal Justice. For example, the National Institute, at the request of the Private Security Task Force, provided computer printouts (including annotated summaries) of several hundred research projects. Many of those documents have been referenced throughout the report. The following list indicates some of the private security research activities that have already been completed as a direct result of LEAA support. (The annotations were provided to the Task Force by the National Institute of Law Enforcement and Criminal Justice.)

Title: *Burglar Alarm Requirements Analysis— Equipment Systems Improvement Program Report*
Author: N. H. Mines
Accession Number: 09900.00.014970
Annotation: The requirements that need to be met to reduce the number of false alarms to an acceptable level as more systems are installed.
Available Through: National Criminal Justice Reference Service, P.O. Box 24036, S.W. Post Office, Washington, D.C. 20024, (Available from the NCJRS through a library using the Interlibrary Loan System.)

Title: *Commercial Robbery in a Medium-Sized City—Columbus, Georgia—Equipment Systems Improvement Program Report*
Author: L. G. Gunn
Accession Number: 09900.00.014958
Annotation: Study of armed robbery of business establishments, using the series of events surrounding the crime and the action and reaction of the participants.
Available Through: National Criminal Justice Reference Service

Title: *Deterrence of Crime in and Around Residences*
Accession Number: 09900.00.009632
Annotation: Papers dealing with overall impacts of architectural design on criminal activity, legislation as a deterrence factor, and community involvement.
Available Through: Superintendent of Documents, U.S. Government Printing Office, Washington, D.C. 20402

Title: *Minimum Building Security Guidelines and Cost Estimate for the Security Features—Initial Draft*
Accession Number: 09900.00.010758
Annotation: Guidelines to secure commercial and residential property (including multiple-family dwellings, hotels, and motels) against burglary, and including replacement cost estimates.
Available Through: National Criminal Justice Reference Service

Title: *National Institute of Law Enforcement and Criminal Justice—Summary of Institute Research Results and Recommendations on Housing Security for the Elderly*
Accession Number: 09900.00.016706 (available in microfiche only)
Annotation: A study of LEAA statistics indicated that the elderly generally are no more likely to become the victims of crime than are other population groups, although they do report more cases of pocket-picking and purse-snatching.
Available Through: National Criminal Justice Reference Service

Title: *Need for and Projected Contents of a Suggested Property Security Code*
Author: J. K. O'Rourke
Accession Number: 09900.00.000279
Annotation: Property security regulations for existing structures and new construction, and existing structures and new construction regulation enforcement.
Available Through: National Institute of Law Enforcement and Criminal Justice, Law Enforcement Assistance Administration, Washington, D.C. 20531

Title: *Project for Security Design in Urban Residential Areas—Annual Report, June 1, 1970–June 24, 1971*
Author: Oscar Newman
Accession Number: 09900.00.008815
Annotation: New York University's project for security design reports completion of its monograph, defensible space-architectural design for crime prevention.
Available Through: National Institute of Law Enforcement and Criminal Justice

Title: *Protective Device Systems*
Author: E. S. Krendel
Accession Number: 09900.00.010034
Annotation: Shortcomings in present security systems for retail businesses and residences, with a suggested functional (not gadget-oriented) attack on these weaknesses.
Available Through: National Institute of Law Enforcement and Criminal Justice

Title: *Residential Security*
Accession Number: 09900.00.011166
Annotation: Assessment of security measures, focusing on deterrents to burglary, discussing cost-effectiveness, physical security and design, group action, and public policy.
Available Through: National Institute of Law Enforcement and Criminal Justice

Title: *Role of Campus Security in the College Setting*

Author: S. Gelber
Accession Number: 09900.00.008966
Annotation: Role of the campus security officer in terms of historical origins, legal structures, and operational functions.
Available Through: Superintendent of Documents

As envisioned by the Private Security Task Force, the national resource and research institute would serve as a catalyst for the distribution of private security information, as well as a repository for available literature. The graduate theses and dissertations received from Professor A. F. Brandstatter and Dr. Leon Weaver of Michigan State University, along with journals, texts, research reports, and other publications gathered by the Task Force, could provide a nucleus for this effort. Building upon these resources, the potential for additional research to meet the needs of private security is almost limitless. The following list is intended to reflect potential research areas, and not to set priorities, nor to limit the scope of research.

1. Development of job-related tests for private security employment.

2. Accurate determination of the number of persons employed in the private security industry.

3. Development of private security job descriptions.

4. Development of model training programs for private security personnel.

5. Development of private security policy and procedure manuals.

6. Development and evaluation of private security equipment and systems.

7. Material for architects and urban planners to use in design of new buildings or in remodeling of existing buildings to promote the use of crime prevention through environmental design (CPTED) concepts.

8. Model guides to improve the relationship of the private security industry and law enforcement agencies.

9. Checklists for consumers of security services to use in selecting and evaluating services.

10. Checklists for managers in proprietary companies to evaluate their security programs.

11. Development of associate baccalaureate and graduate curriculums in security.

12. Model statutes for the licensing, regulation, and operation of private security regulatory agencies.

13. Evaluation of effectiveness and use of detection-of-deception (polygraph) and psychological stress evaluation (PSE) techniques.

14. Legal issues in the private security field.

15. Development of model records systems for private security companies.

Many of these research activities should be implemented on an individual basis by entities concerned with private security; however, no single university, company, organization, association, or individual can supply the resources to conduct all of the research needed in even a single area. Thus, the concept of a national resource and research institute provides a focus for these research activities. The exchange process is schematically illustrated in Figure 8.1.

Figure 8.1. Exchange Process for the National Resource and Research Institute

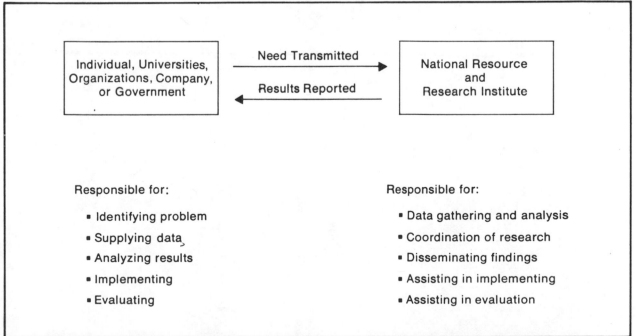

The organizational structure of the national resource and research institute can be conceptualized in a variety of ways: (1) centered at one college or university, or several colleges and universities under a consortium arrangement; (2) as a research component of a professional association; (3) as a not-for-profit corporation supported by both government and private funding sources; (4) as a separate unit under the National Institute for Law Enforcement and Criminal Justice Research, or (5) as a combination of two or more of the foregoing concepts.

The main concern of this standard, however, is not how the institute should be organized, but why it should be organized and what it should accomplish. If the private security industry and its services are to be more effectively used in crime prevention, reliable information about and research for the industry needs to be available. The institute can be the catalyst for literature collection and dissemination, applied and/or pure research, and other functions normally associated with a research operation.

The Law Enforcement Assistance Administration can play a major role in the development of the institute by providing guidance, technical assistance, and, if appropriate, funding.

Selected References

1. Lipson, Milton. *On Guard*. New York: Quadrangle/The New York Times Book Co., 1975.

2. McClarin, Roy C., and O. W. Wilson. *Police Administration* (3d ed.). New York: McGraw-Hill Book Company, 1972.

3. President's Commission on Law Enforcement and Administration of Justice. *The Challenge of Crime in a Free Society*. Washington, D.C.: Government Printing Office, 1967.

Related Standards

The following standards and goals may be applicable in implementing Standard 8.2:

2.3   Job Descriptions
2.4   Training Related to Job Functions
2.5   Preassignment and Basic Training
2.6   Arms Training
4.1   Alarm Systems Research
4.6   Joint Cooperation to Reduce Transmission Costs
5.1   Improvement of Door and Window Security
5.4   Crime Prevention in Design
8.3   Noncredit and Credit Seminars and Courses
8.4   Degree Programs for Private Security

Standard 8.3

Noncredit and Credit Seminars and Courses

Colleges and universities should develop and offer noncredit and credit seminars and courses to meet the needs of private security personnel.

Commentary

As established throughout this report, there is a need for education and training in the private security field. Participants at the First National Conference on Private Security (held at the University of Maryland in December 1975) resolved that "shared or cooperative training programs utilizing resources of private security, public law enforcement, education and training institutions [should] be pursued to meet the training needs of private security." In this respect, one of the most obvious contributions educational institutions can make is to develop and offer noncredit and credit courses for private security personnel.

Educational institutions throughout the United States have physical and personnel resources that can be used to effectively provide programs with reasonable cost, location, and scheduling. For example, a college or university could: (1) offer courses to students at a reduced enrollment fee because they are residents of the college district, (2) schedule the courses at a central location convenient to students' residences and/or places of work,

and (3) offer the courses in day, evening, or combination sessions. Although such arrangements are most appropriate for community and junior colleges, they often can also be handled by private and State-supported, 4-year institutions. Of course within each geographical area, all educational institutions need to coordinate activities to maximize enrollments, limit costs, and meet the private security needs.

The American Society for Industrial Security, other professional organizations, and private schools occasionally offer short courses, but these programs are inaccessible for many because of cost, geographical location, and scheduling. The need for short courses, available to all levels of private security personnel, from guards and watchmen to security executives, cannot be met by courses seeking students from across the Nation. Small companies cannot pay the tuition, travel, and per diem costs, and they have difficulty replacing personnel while they attend the courses. Thus, short courses need to be offered by colleges and universities located near the students.

Academic Guidelines for Security and Loss Prevention Programs in Community and Junior Colleges outlines four phases of program development: (1) noncredit course(s), (2) credit course(s), (3) subordinate credits programs, and (4) autonomous programs. The first two phases—credit and noncredit courses—apply to this standard. Both should be made available to students, but individual institutions should determine the noncredit and/or credit status of their courses. However, need of courses should be the primary consideration.

In developing appropriate courses, the logical first step for institutions is to conduct surveys to determine private security needs. Surveys can be accomplished through an advisory board, telephone inquiries, or mailings. Although local educators are best qualified to make the final determination of the exact courses to be developed, a list of possible courses for inclusion on a survey follow:

Courses for Operational Personnel

- Arson investigation.
- Background investigation.
- Bomb threats.
- Civil disturbances.
- Cooperation with public law enforcement agencies.
- Employee security.
- Fire and safety.
- Firearms training.
- First aid.
- Internal theft investigations.
- Interviewing.
- Law and the private security industry.
- Note taking and report writing.
- Patrol methods.
- Physical security measures.
- Preliminary investigation.
- Public relations aspects of security services.
- Security training.
- Shoplifting prevention.
- Surveillance techniques.
- Visitor control.

Courses for Management Personnel

- Crime prevention through environmental design.
- Disaster and emergency planning.
- Establishing a bomb threat plan.
- Establishing a more effective employee security awareness.
- Law/management relationship in security services.
- Private security/law enforcement relationship.
- Protection of key personnel.
- Security administration and management.
- Security problems discussion seminar.
- Strengthening business security.
- The role of the security administrator in research and development.

(Most of these courses and more can be found in *Academic Guidelines for Security and Loss Prevention Programs in Community and Junior Colleges.*)

For this list, or any list, to be meaningful for course development, survey respondents should be requested to set priorities. If need in particular areas is established, several separate courses could become subjects contained in a longer seminar. For example, first aid, firearms training, and patrol methods might be covered in one seminar or workshop for operational personnel.

These short courses can fill the present short-range need for educational opportunities while the academic programs recommended in other standards are being developed. Later, these courses can support the regular academic classes and, at the same time, give educational institutions a mechanism to provide information to meet continually changing private security situations.

The opportunities for innovative use of seminars and short courses to meet private security needs are apparent. Educational institutions, in cooperation with the private security industry, should take the initiative to provide the physical and personnel resources to implement this standard.

Selected References

1. Calder, James D. (chairman, resolutions committee). "Resolutions of First National Conference on Private Security" (final draft). College Park: University of Maryland, December 1975.

2. Kingsbury, Arthur A. (project director). *Academic Guidelines for Security and Loss Prevention Programs in Community and Junior Colleges.* Washington, D.C.: American Society for Industrial Security/ASIS Foundation, Inc., 1972.

3. ———. "Macomb College Looks at Security Education," *Industrial Security,* August 1970.

Related Standards

The following standards and goals may be applicable in implementing Standard 8.3:

1.1   Selection of Qualified Personnel
1.2   Commensurate Salaries
2.1   Training in Private Security
2.2   Professional Certification Programs
2.4   Training Related to Job Functions
2.5   Preassignment and Basic Training
2.6   Arms Training
2.7   Ongoing Training
2.8   Training of Supervisors and Managers
2.9   State Authority and Responsibility for Training

Standard 8.4

Degree Programs for Private Security

The private security industry and the Law Enforcement Assistance Administration (LEAA) should cooperate in the encouragement and development of:

1. Certificate, associate of art, or associate of science degree programs designed to meet local industry needs;

2. Undergraduate and graduate programs designed to meet private security needs.

Commentary

Although there is presently no comprehensive involvement by colleges and universities to provide educational opportunities for private security personnel, it should also be recognized that there is little evidence that the security industry or government agencies have encouraged their development. This standard is based on the premise that the industry, LEAA, and educational institutions can cooperate for mutual benefit.

Certificate and associate degree programs designed to meet the needs of the private security industry are a recent, but potentially significant, resource for improving the delivery of security services. *Academic Guidelines for Security and Loss Prevention Programs in Community and Junior Colleges,* published in 1972, identified 5 certificate programs, 2 associate programs, and 58 junior or community colleges offering at least one security course. Research (see Appendix 4) revealed 6 certificate programs, 22 associate programs, and 49 junior or community colleges offering at least one security course. The number of junior and community colleges offering some form of private security education has grown from 65, in 1972, to 77, in 1976. However, a closer look beyond these positive indicators of the growth of private security education reveals a need for much greater effort. Only five States (California, Illinois, Michigan, New York, and Virginia) have five or more programs at the junior and community college level; 24 States do not have even one institution that offers one course. Thus, although there has been growth in educational programs, the future offers great challenges to junior and community colleges to help develop the skills, knowledge, and judgment needed by private security personnel through appropriate courses.

Senior colleges are also involved in private security degree programs. However, educational programs at the baccalaureate and graduate levels designed to prepare persons for private security employment are totally inadequate. A survey (Appendix 4) located only five bachelor of science programs: Biscayne College, Niagara University, Northeastern University, Northern Michigan University, and Wichita State University. Two 4-year schools— Eastern Kentucky University and John Jay College of Criminal Justice—offer associate degrees. Western Illinois University has a formal minor in security administration, with options for (1) students majoring in law enforcement administration, and (2) students majoring in other than law enforcement administration. Thirty-two 4-year institutions, without formal private security degree programs, have at least one course that could be classified under security administration. In summary, the survey revealed only forty 4-year institutions offering courses designed specifically for private security personnel.

The situation regarding graduate degrees is even more discouraging. No educational institution offers a graduate degree in the private security field, although Michigan State University offers graduate courses that may be designated as one of several concentrations by a masters candidate, and many students have written graduate theses on private security subjects. As a result of circular revision in 1973, an area of specialization in security administration at the baccalaureate level once offered at Michigan State has been discontinued. This is especially significant, because Michigan State is generally recognized as a leader in private security education at the baccalaureate and graduate levels. "A Study of the Placement and Utilization Patterns and Views of the Criminal Justice Graduates of Michigan State University" revealed that 15 percent of all graduates identified security administration as their area of specialization. Further, Arthur F. Brandstatter, director of the school of criminal justice at Michigan State, in response to a questionnaire, indicated 310 graduates specialized in security administration at the baccalaureate level and 44 at the master's level. The need for private security degree programs is further supported by John J. Conrad, chairman, department of law enforcement administration at Western Illinois University, who indicated that approximately 10 percent of all baccalaureate graduates of his program were presently employed in the private security field.

Certain critics have voiced the opinion that because degree programs in business administration, criminal justice, law enforcement, and other related fields have provided appropriate educational backgrounds in the past to persons in private security, there is no need, at this time, for specific private security degree programs. This position is in error. Private security degree programs will not only enhance the professional movement in private security but also promote needed research and technological advancements.

Three significant resolutions passed at the First National Conference on Private Security are pertinent to the future development of educational programs. These resolutions are:

1. A multi-disciplinary and scholarly approach should be the core concept for the development of degree programs in private security.

2. There is a need to assess the manpower, training, and education requirements (managerial as well as technician level), both present and future, for the purpose of planning and developing academic programs.

3. There is a body of knowledge about the private security field sufficient to support realistic and meaningful 2-year, 4-year, and graduate-level college and university programs.

The following commentary is divided into two subareas—(1) associate degree programs, and (2) baccalaureate and graduate programs—to correspond with the differentiation made by most educational institutions.

Associate Degree Programs

A useful starting point in program planning is the Suggested Curriculum for Associate Programs contained in *Academic Guidelines for Security and Loss Prevention Programs in Community and Junior Colleges* (see Figure 8.2). A number of educators have indicated that this curriculum could serve as an excellent guide. Detailed course descriptions and other relevant information about designing and implementing programs can be found in the publication.

It would be inappropriate to recommend a set curriculum, because any program of private security education should be developed to meet the needs of local industry. Also, before developing and implementing degree programs, a review should be conducted of the assistance that colleges and universities should provide for training suggested (Chapter 2) and for seminars and courses (Standard 8.3). Immediate local industry needs can be better met by these forms of education. In any event, educational programs in appropriate forms should be designed with the specific needs of local industry in mind.

When developing degree programs, it may be difficult to identify the target population and to determine appropriate course content. However, it is strongly suggested that certificate, associate of arts, and associate of science degree programs be developed that include subject matter as the following:

• Conducting security surveys.
• Historical, philosophical, and legal bases of the security field.
• Information security.
• Interviewing and report writing.
• Loss prevention techniques.
• Personnel security.
• Physical security.
• Principles and practices of fire prevention and safety.
• Supervision and leadership.
• Unique security problems of hotels/motels, banks, manufacturing facilities, and so forth.

Figure 8.2. Suggested Curriculum for Associate Programs

FIRST YEAR

First Semester	Credits	Second Semester	Credits
English I	3	English II	3
General Psychology	3	Introduction to Sociology	3
Criminal and Civil Law I	3	Criminal and Civil Law II	3
Introduction to Security	3	Security Administration	3
Elective	3	Elective	3
	15		15

Electives:		Electives:	
Accounting I	3	Accounting II	3
Economics I	3	Economics II	3
Science I	3	Science II	3
Administration of Justice	3	Civil Rights & Civil Liberties	3
Principles of Interviewing	3	Report Writing	3
Industrial Relations	3		

SECOND YEAR

First Semester	Credits	Second Semester	Credits
Fundamentals of Speech	3	Criminal Investigation	3
Social Problems	3	Criminology	3
Human Relations	3	Labor & Management Relations	3
Principles of Loss Prevention	3	Current Security Problems	3
Elective	3	Elective	3
	15		15

Electives:		Electives:	
Document & Personnel Security	3	Commercial/Retail Security	3
Business Mathematics	3	Field Practicum	3
Emergency Preparedness	3	Industrial Fire Protection	3
Environmental Security	3	Security Education	3
Physical Security	3	Special Security Problems	3
Safety & Fire Prevention	3		

Baccalaureate and Graduate Programs

The lack of viable baccalaureate and graduate degree programs is both a handicap and an advantage. On the negative side, no curriculum model is presently available comparable to that which exists for associate degrees; therefore, each institution would have to develop its own curriculum without an historical frame of reference. This handicap, with proper research and planning, can turn into an advantage because no precedents exist that might need to be removed or modified during the developmental process. The following "Task Force Viewpoints for Developments of Baccalaureate and Graduate Programs in Private Security" (not listed in order of importance) are offered for consideration by educators:

Planning Phase

1. Each academic department of law enforcement/criminal justice should determine the number of graduates who are employed in the private security industry.

2. The academic departments of law enforcement/criminal justice should be the catalyst for development of security administration degree programs, but colleges of business need to be consulted and

their courses incorporated into any degree programs. The disciplines of sociology, psychology, and law also should be included in the degree program.

3. New courses should be designed to incorporate the body of knowledge about private security subjects, rather than an effort made to adapt existing law enforcement/criminal justice courses to meet private security needs. For example, one or two law courses should be developed to relate pertinent legal aspects of the private security industry, rather than requiring security administration students to take a law course designed to prepare students for public law enforcement careers.

4. An advisory board, consisting of private security personnel, should be appointed to assist colleges and universities during the planning phase. This board should also remain active after the program is initiated.

5. Boards of higher education in each State should closely monitor all degree proposals in security administration to preclude proliferation of degree programs and to coordinate transfer arrangements between educational institutions.

6. Baccalaureate and master degree programs should be designed to prepare students for entrance-level or middle-management positions and not merely duplicate course offerings in certificate and associate degree programs. Some overlap and duplication may be necessary, but it should be kept to a minimum.

Implementation Phase

Each institution should determine the most appropriate way to implement private security curriculums, depending on available personnel and physical and financial resources; the following three-step process is recommended:
1. Introduce private security courses; then, if needed,
2. Develop private security minor; then, if needed,
3. Develop baccalaureate and/or master degree program(s).

Model for Minor

An innovative model for a minor in security administration exists at Western Illinois University. It is a coordinated program with the College of Business and the Department of Health Sciences. Plan A is for students whose major is other than law enforcement and Plan B is for students who major in law enforcement administration.

Plan A

Minor in security administration for students whose major is other than law enforcement. Total hours—28 quarter hours.
1. Core Requirements. (24 quarter hours)

Survey of Criminal Investigation. Criminal investigation theory and procedures; case preparation, methodology, and techniques; problems in criminal investigations. (4 quarter hours)

Administration of Justice III. Summation of previous courses in administration of justice with emphasis on constitutional rights; related responsibility of police; special emphasis on amendments to the Constitution as related to the rights of the individual. (4 quarter hours)

Security Administration I. Overview of security systems found in retail, industrial, and governmental agencies; legal framework for security operations; detailed presentations of specific security programs. (4 quarter hours)

Security Administration II. Emphasis is on theft. Comparison of white-collar and blue-collar crime; techniques of detection, apprehension, and prevention; subject areas of employee dishonesty, cost considerations, pilferage, and embezzlement. (4 quarter hours)

Fire Protection. Organization and function of fire prevention organizations; inspections; techniques of hazard analysis; economics of fire protection; survey of fire protection equipment and application to hazards found in businesses and industrial situations. Development of Standard Operating Procedures Manuals. Responsibilities under Occupational Safety & Health Act of 1970. (4 quarter hours)

Disaster and Civil Defense. A course of instruction to prepare one for leadership and action in case of nuclear and natural disasters, as well as man-made disasters. Techniques of survival, operation of radiological instruments, shelter management training, medical self-help, and rescue operations are covered. (4 quarter hours)
2. Electives (4 quarter hours)

Accounting Theory I. Fundamentals of accounting theory and practice, with emphasis on introductory financial accounting techniques applicable to income determination and asset accounting. (4 quarter hours)

Physical Distribution. A study of the physical distribution function of marketing, including transportation, storage, warehousing, materials handling, inventory control, plant location, and government regulation. (4 quarter hours)

Management and Organizational Behavior. An introduction to the study of organization theory. The managerial process is introduced, as well as topics related to human behavior in the organizational setting. (4 quarter hours)

Personnel Management. This course focuses on the selection, development, maintenance, and use of personnel in business and in industry. (4 quarter hours)

Plan B

Minor in security administration for students whose major is law enforcement. (See Plan A for course descriptions.) Total hours—28 quarter hours.

1. Core requirements. (16 quarter hours)
   Security Administration I—4 quarter hours.
   Security Administration II—4 quarter hours.
   Fire Protection—4 quarter hours.
   Disaster and Civil Defense—4 quarter hours.
2. Electives. (12 quarter hours)
   Accounting Theory I—4 quarter hours.
   Physical Distribution—4 quarter hours.
   Management and Organizational Behavior—4 quarter hours.
   Personnel Management—4 quarter hours.

Model for Baccalaureate

It is believed that the most effective approach would be an interdisciplinary degree with emphasis on courses in security administration and business administration. In general, the degree structure should be as follows:

- 10 percent of courses in sociology and psychology.
- 10 percent of courses in law enforcement/criminal justice.
- 20 percent of courses in security administration.
- 20 percent of courses in business administration.
- 40 percent of courses in general education.

Model for Masters

- 20 percent of courses in sociology and psychology.
- 40 percent of courses in security administration.
- 40 percent of courses in business administration.

It is recognized that many of the suggestions regarding curriculum design are arbitrary; however, it is believed that security administration degree should be interdisciplinary. These course outlines also serve as a basis for discussions between the various departments in colleges and universities.

The Roles of LEAA and the Private Security Industry in Implementing This Standard

LEAA can make significant contributions toward implementing this standard. One of the highest priority efforts that LEAA should initiate is a national manpower study to determine the need for private security educational programs. This study should survey businesses and government agencies to determine their anticipated needs for persons with security administration degrees, from certificates to master's; salary levels; skills, knowledge, and judgment requirements; and opportunities for promotion. The study results would be an invaluable aid to educators in determining need for programs and which degree would most appropriately meet employment opportunities. LEAA can also assist by providing research grants to aid educational institutions in developing degree programs. However, it is not the intent of this report that Law Enforcement Education Program funds be made available for students majoring in security administration.

Individuals, companies, and professional associations should alert colleges and universities of their interest in obtaining educational opportunities for private security personnel. Once these opportunities are available, the industry should continue its assistance by providing guidance on curriculums, identifying qualified instructors, and, as appropriate, offering tuition assistance to employees. The industry should also provide career incentives—higher salaries and promotions—to persons who avail themselves of the educational opportunities. Moreover private security interests need to be willing to assist in the following four specific ways:

1. Cooperate to the fullest extent during the manpower survey to provide reliable information that would be of benefit to educators preparing degree programs.
2. Provide security-related equipment and material to the educational institutions for use in classroom and research activities.
3. Establish policies and procedures to encourage their personnel to act as resource persons, guest speakers, and, as appropriate, members of teaching faculties on a part-time or full-time basis.
4. Provide internship experiences for students majoring in security administration. An internship program would provide students an opportunity to be participants/observers in security activities that would help to achieve their career objectives, and also provide the business an opportunity to learn from the educational experiences of students. The concept of internship has been well established in the legal, teaching, and medical professions.

With the encouragement and support of both the industry and LEAA, it is believed that sound academic programs can be developed by colleges and universities to meet the needs of all private security personnel. The teaching process and the supporting research efforts would further the development of a body of knowledge that can be used to enhance the effectiveness of private security services, ultimately benefiting both the industry and the public.

Selected References

1. Calder, James D. (chairman, resolutions committee). "Resolutions of First National Conference on Private Security" (final draft). College Park: University of Maryland, December 1975.

2. Conrad, John J. (editor). "Department of Law Enforcement, Western Illinois University, Newsletter #1, Academic Year 1975–1976."

3. Fauth, Kenneth G. "The Need for Security Education at the Postsecondary Level," unpublished doctoral dissertation. Bloomington: University of Indiana, 1975.

4. Friend, Bernard D. "Profile of the Physical Security Officer Specialization or Professionalism," unpublished master's thesis. East Lansing: Michigan State University, 1968.

5. International Association of Chiefs of Police. *Law Enforcement and Criminal Justice Education Directory 1975–1976.* Gaithersburg, Md.: International Association of Chiefs of Police, 1975.

6. Kingsbury, Arthur A. (project director). *Academic Guidelines for Security and Loss Prevention Programs in Community and Junior Colleges.* Washington, D.C.: American Society for Industrial Security/ASIS Foundation, Inc., 1972.

7. ———. "Security Education," *Security Management*, September 1974.

8. Larkins, Hayes Carlton. "A Survey of Experiences, Activities, and Views of the Industrial Security Administration Graduates of Michigan State University," unpublished master's thesis. East Lansing: Michigan State University, 1966.

9. Moore, Merlyn Douglas. "A Study of the Placement and Utilization Patterns and Views of the Criminal Justice Graduates of Michigan State University," unpublished doctoral dissertation. East Lansing: Michigan State University, 1972.

10. Private Security Task Force. "Survey of Colleges and Universities Offering Educational Programs for Private Security." (See Appendix 4 to this report.)

Related Standards

The following standards and goals may be applicable in implementing Standard 8.4:

1.1 Selection of Qualified Personnel
1.2 Commensurate Salaries
2.1 Training in Private Security
2.2 Professional Certification Programs
2.4 Training Related to Job Functions
2.5 Preassignment and Basic Training
2.6 Arms Training
2.7 Ongoing Training
2.8 Training of Supervisors and Managers
2.9 State Authority and Responsibility for Training
2.10 State Boards to Coordinate Training Efforts
3.2 Conduct of Private Security Personnel
3.4 Employer Responsibilities
4.3 Certified Training of Alarm Sales and Service Personnel
5.7 Crime Prevention Courses in Schools of Architecture and Urban Planning
5.10 Crime Prevention Courses as a Job Requirement
8.2 National Private Security Resource and Research Institute
8.3 Noncredit and Credit Seminars and Courses

Part 5
Governmental Regulation

INTRODUCTION

Increased government regulation of business and industry has come under fire as a threat to America's system of free enterprise and a suppressor of the health and growth of national economy. Social critics, as well as staunch supporters of existing institutions, have voiced a need for regulatory reform to curb inflation and restore competition, efficiency, and innovation in the American marketplace. Professional groups and concerned citizens have urged that government regulation be reduced in light of the high costs and mountains of paperwork involved. This widespread concern with overregulation prompted President Gerald R. Ford to request that Congress establish a National Commission on Regulatory Reform.

Despite this justifiably strong concern, specific regulation in appropriate fields is both necessary and advantageous. A society without rules produces anarchy. The complexity of our industrial environment particularly demands that the public be protected against certain abuses in the marketplace. Consumers need to be assured that the products and services they pay for meet reasonable standards, and the public's health and safety must be safeguarded. The province of government's regulation is protecting the public interest.

The real issue is not whether government regulation is needed; most people agree that government should set rules that protect the public interest. However, who should be regulated and to what extent are debatable questions. The current proliferation of regulation, its high costs and more stringent requirements, have prompted many to reevaluate the benefits of regulation. It becomes important for proponents of new legislation and regulation to carefully consider the impact upon consumers, the industry to be regulated, and the public.

The rationale supporting regulation in the field of private security is based on four major factors:

1. Private security services primarily exist to protect life and property from criminal attack. With a mission of this importance, it is vital that some control other than laissez-faire capitalism should be present to ensure that these services can be reasonably expected to provide that which is claimed.

2. A major percentage of all private security services used by business involved guards and investigators. These persons are placed in positions in which they have direct contact with the public for the purpose of preventing crime. In fulfilling their mission, actions may be taken that could violate constitutional guarantees of individuals in the areas of detention, arrest, search, seizure, self-incrimination, confessions and statements made under duress, and a wide variety of other serious matters.

3. Because of the potential of dangerous criminal attack, certain private security personnel—armed guards, armed investigators, armored car personnel, alarm respondants, and others—carry weapons capable of killing. Even security personnel who do not carry firearms may be equipped with night sticks, billies, or other weapons that can kill or certainly inflict great bodily harm. Controls are needed to ensure that these weapons are only used under conditions conforming to the exact letter and spirit of the law.

4. Because uniforms and equipment of private security operations may resemble those used in public law enforcement, controls are needed to protect the public from situations in which private security personnel may inappropriately adopt the posture or appearance of public law enforcement personnel.

Over the many years that private security companies and units have been operating in this country, it has become painfully apparent that although many companies and operations in this field adopt standards that engender respect for the law and for the protection of the public, other companies and operations do not. Traditional civil remedies are neither adequate nor responsive to resolving the abuses that can occur as a result of improper actions by private security personnel. A judgment against a company incapable of paying the amount awarded is meaningless. Also, the time, effort, and dollars involved in pursuing civil remedies are often not available to low-income individuals, who are frequently the victims of improper actions by security personnel.

The standards recommended in these chapters were developed with these considerations in mind. This report recognizes the dangers of overregulation and does not advocate regulation merely for the sake of regulation. Nor does it promote the special interests of any or all segments of the private security industry. Rather, the standards in the following chapters were developed in response to the many problems the industry, as a whole, needs to overcome if it is to ensure the delivery of ethical, competent, and responsible services. These standards not only can protect the public and consumers of security services, but also can have a significant impact on the industry's attaining the professional stature necessary for acceptance, growth, and improved crime reduction efforts.

The lack of standardized regulation and accountability in the private security industry has led to serious indictments against it. Charges of incompetence, misconduct, and poor-quality services are common throughout the news media. Public concern has been aroused by recent exposes that have focused on the large numbers of poorly trained, incompetent, and unregulated personnel. News accounts, such as the following two, have further contributed to growing public alarm:

A tragic example of lax supervision of private police occurred here in July. Sidney Bennett Jr. was hired as a private security guard and given a gun. His employer, National Industrial Security Corp., did not know Bennett had confessed to the 1970 sniper killing of two Chicago police officers but was freed when he was found mentally incompetent.

Three days after he was hired, Bennett was accused of fatally shooting a 19-year-old youth without provocation (while on duty) and was indicted for murder. (Chicago *Sun-Times,* Sept. 28, 1975)

In October, it [California Bureau of Collection and Investigative Services] revoked the licenses of 41 persons engaged in security guard work. Of these 28 related to robbery or burglary on the part of the licensee, two were for other forms of dishonesty and 11 involved improper use of weapons including two cases where deaths resulted. (Pasadena *Star-News,* Nov. 26, 1975)

Understandably, accounts in the press have caused the private security industry to be viewed with skepticism and have resulted in lowered public confidence in security services. Many persons contend that without regulation, the expanding multitude of private security personnel constitutes a threat to the public. Exremists even envision an uncontrolled private police army. If these attitudes are to be dispelled and their underlying causes eradicated, steps need to be taken to obtain uniform performance throughout the industry for the protection of the public. Government regulation is an important and necessary step in this direction.

The overriding major objective of government regulation is to protect the public who have daily contact with security personnel. Because private security personnel often make decisions that affect the public, perform functions that overlap those of public law enforcement officers, and frequently are armed, only persons of high integrity and appropriate competency should be permitted employment in private security work. False arrests, brutality, wrongful death of innocent bystanders, and other abuses can be prevented by eliminating the unfit from the field. The nature of private security work involves an implicit responsibility to the public that should be fulfilled by each individual employee and the industry as a whole.

Another important aim of regulation is to protect the consumer of security services. It is the contractor of security services who is most often the victim of dishonest or otherwise incompetent performance. Unethical business practices and failure to perform contracted services are common complaints. In addition, a dishonest or incompetent security employee may cause the consumer significant business losses that could have been averted by better qualified personnel. Without regulation, consumers have little or no assurance that the services they purchase will be delivered in an ethical, competent, and responsible manner.

In a very real sense, the private security industry affects the nature and extent of crime in our society. To continue to operate as a viable source of protection, it must be well equipped to meet future demands. The standards developed, if implemented, can improve the industry's operation and lead to greater professionalism. It is believed that reasonable government regulation can further assist the industry by giving due consideration to the interests of both the consumer and the public.

As stated previously, it is recognized that problems of overregulation can and do exist. Also noted are the demands for regulatory reform. However, it must also be realized that, in certain instances, regulation is the only prudent way to protect important consumer and public interests. Clearly, the magnitude and nature of private security problems require a uniform application of standards. In an occupation where one error of judgment or incompetence can cause serious social and economic consequences, every effort needs to be expended to embrace forceful remedies.

THE REGULATORY PROCESS

There is a wide-ranging diffusion of private security legislation—some good, some of limited value, and most lacking uniformity and comprehensiveness.

As pointed out in Chapter 9, California has 63 municipal and 8 county ordinances regulating some aspect of the private security field—each diverse and each a separate entity. Of the 34 States that have some form of statewide licensing and/or registration, only 11 have a separate private security regulatory board established solely for this purpose. And in about half of these, agencies reported being understaffed. In some States, funding is inadequate and legal restraints limit investigative powers.

The standards in the following chapters are devoted to the establishment of a regulatory scheme that can be uniformly administered and realistically adopted for the private security industry. Mechanisms for preventive control, accountability, regular review, and remedial sanctions are incorporated for its total effectiveness.

Certain distinctions need to be made to prevent ambiguities in implementing the standards. Chapter 10 deals with licensing, defined as an arrangement whereby one obtains permission from a recognized authority in order to engage in a particular occupation or activity. For the purpose of this report, licensing is limited solely to the business that sells security services. Accordingly, Chapter 10 concerns the licensing of contract security companies that provide services for a fee, but not those agencies with their own security units for the protection of their own assets. The goal of Chapter 10 is to protect consumers of private security services and to give them confidence in the industry so that they will increase their use of its services.

Chapter 11 concerns registration. Commonly, registration refers to merely filing one's name. In this report, however, registration is carried one step further so that it also means obtaining permission. The goal of Chapter 11 is to protect the public; thus, the standards are aimed at individuals who perform private security functions, whether for contractual or for proprietary security forces. Several members of the Private Security Task Force hold that regulation of all proprietary security personnel for the protection of the public is unnecessary. Their view is that registration of proprietary security personnel should cover only armed security workers. Others believe that registration should be all inclusive, because the problems that affect the public are just as prevalent in proprietary as in contractual

security services. The public being protected by the registration standards includes employees working within a firm employing its own security force, as well as individuals who come in contact with private security workers.

The regulatory board coordinates licensing and registration. As described in Chapter 9, each State should establish a regulatory board and staff whose responsibility would be to regulate the private security industry within the State. It is important that regulation be performed at the State level if uniformity is to be achieved and the proliferation of city and county ordinances eliminated. Some matters, such as alarm installations, may require local control, but local performance standards should conform with those established at the State level. Federal regulation is not recommended, but endeavors should be made to develop uniform and reciprocal regulation among States.

NEED FOR EVALUATION

The regulatory process proposed in these chapters may provide solutions to many of the severe problems of the private security industry. However, as licensing and registration progress, it is hoped that regulatory agencies would evaluate the results in terms of benefits and costs. If legislation and regulation increase costs to the point of discouraging the use of private security resources or to the point of eliminating small but reputable businesses, regulators should carefully weigh these consequences against the added benefits. If the costs outweigh the benefits, other more creative and intelligent means of regulating the industry should be sought.

This report does not state that government regulation is the ultimate answer to the varied problems of the private security industry. However, the need for improvement is commonly acknowledged and government regulation affords a realistic hope for realizing that improvement. If regulation fails to produce the desired results, other methods should be tried. If the public is to be truly protected both by and from the private security industry during this period of unequalled growth and expansion, the most appropriate, cost-effective methods must be identified and implemented to achieve these goals.

Chapter 9
Regulatory Board

INTRODUCTION

The standards in this chapter are designed to assist in the establishment of a regulatory body to oversee the necessary regulation of various security services and functions. This body would be responsible for enforcing specific laws, would promulgate necessary rules and regulations for the implementation of the laws, and would make recommendations for necessary legislative changes. It should be the goal of the regulatory body to engage in conduct that would protect the consumers of security services, protect the public from possible abuse by security employees, and ultimately assist in the overall crime prevention effort.

A common complaint directed against government regulatory bodies is that they are often corrupted by regulated interests. To guard against this possibility, as well as to encourage cooperative efforts, the regulatory board should be made up not only of representatives from private security but also of others not directly involved with the private security industry. It is recommended that public law enforcement representatives also be appointed to the regulatory board, because interactions between the police and private security sectors are often affected by board decisions.

Current concern over invasion of privacy, emphasized by the Watergate scandal, has prompted a deluge of pending legislation restricting the release of confidential information. In some States, legislation is already in effect, denying access to criminal history information. However, State regulatory boards should be allowed to examine past arrest and conviction records to assist in background investigations, and, therefore, granted statutory authority for access to the information it regards necessary for licensing and registration.

Often, the consumer and/or public are unaware of the existence and purpose of private security regulatory boards, so valid complaints are never heard and abuses may continue, without penalty. To ensure that acts of misconduct, incompetence, and impropriety are properly adjudicated, the regulatory board should establish a hearing and appeals procedure and publicize its existence and purpose.

The regulatory board should also establish licensing and registration fees. This report recommends that these fees be based on the number of licensees and registrants to be processed and cover operating costs only. It has been suggested in the research that registration fees for operational-level personnel earning minimum wages should be less than those for higher-level personnel with higher salaries. However, the method of establishing licensing and registration fees should be determined by each State according to specific circumstances.

Every effort has been made to propose standards that would not become an economic or operational hardship on small businesses in the private security industry. The standards are considered those necessary for the protection of the public.

Standard 9.1

State Regulation

Regulation of the private security industry should be performed at the State level with consideration for uniformity and reciprocity among all the States.

Commentary

Over a period of years, numerous local jurisdictions have passed varied private security regulatory ordinances and rules. In California, 63 cities and 8 counties have separate and diverse ordinances. In Virginia, four counties and six major cities are known to have separate ordinances regulating some aspect of the private security industry. Similar examples can be found in many States. A study of these ordinances shows a lack of uniformity and comprehensiveness.

Because many security service businesses operate locally, logic suggests that local government units would play a crucial role in successful regulation. However, local regulation proliferation and diversity creates many problems for security service employees and businesses. For example, a security officer working in an urban area might have to register with many jurisdictions before commencing work. Diverse requirements also hamper security service businesses where it is important for security employees to be readily transferred, sometimes on an emergency basis, to different assignments through-out a State. Similarly, a merchant with several branch stores in a city and surrounding jurisdictions, who maintains a proprietary security unit at each location, would face similar problems, because meeting more than one set of requirements can easily restrict the movement of his security employees between stores. Finally, diverse regulation poses constant problems for an armored car or armed courier business transporting valuables throughout a State.

Although there is a definite need for statewide uniform regulation replacing varied local regulatory schemes, certain regulatory functions may be performed best at the local level. The quality of alarm installation, alarm user activity, and false alarm responses are a particularly local concern (Chapter 4), and regulation of such performance standards may require local assistance, e.g., passage of user permit ordinances. In setting performance standards on a local basis, however, statewide uniformity should be the ultimate goal. Additional assistance also may be provided on the local level by fingerprint and preliminary background checks. A State regulatory board should be able to delegate certain functions to the local level when they can be more efficiently performed there, but overall, licensing, registration, and rulemaking should be conducted on a uniform, statewide basis.

As statutes, rules, and regulations are established for private security control at the State level, every consideration should be given not only to uniformity within the State but also to uniformity with other States. As licensing and registration requirements become more uniform, efforts also can be made to add reciprocity actions. With more uniformity, the licensing of a security service business or registration of security personnel in one State could be accepted in another State as prima facie evidence of competence.

The benefits that accrue to States that create uniform regulation and reciprocity are great. The necessity of a complete background check is eliminated when a previously registered individual moves into a new State, or a business previously licensed, seeks to do business within a new State. The burdens and the costs of administering private security regulation are greatly reduced where reciprocity exists.

Regulatory agencies are not the only benefactors of reciprocity and uniformity among the States. Licenses, registrants, and consumers also benefit. Companies operating in numerous States may incur vast expenses, ultimately passed on to consumers, when attempting to comply with the diverse statutes and ordinances across the country. With uniform regulation, these costs would be reduced for both the company and the consumer. Similar problems exist for businesses operating in several contiguous States, causing difficulty in the deployment of employees to contract jobs in adjoining States. Here again, reciprocity and uniformity would benefit the licensee and the consumer. Finally, with increased family mobility, uniformity and reciprocity significantly benefit the individual registrant seeking to move to a new job in another State.

Reciprocity is of particular concern to armored car and armed courier services. They have a recurring need to assign crews to transport valuables throughout one State or in a number of States. So as not to impair interstate commerce, businesses licensed in one State, and their registered personnel, should be granted reciprocity by other States while in transit, making pickups, or completing deliveries of interstate shipments.

This report stresses that private security regulation should be performed at the State level; the need for uniformity and reciprocity is secondary to the need for each State to determine its own needs. Each State should analyze the private security services offered within its boundaries, consider the problems and abuses, balance various factors, and shape regulation accordingly. Uniformity among the States is important, but, again, such nationwide uniformity is secondary to individual State needs.

Selected References

1. Institute for Local Self Government. *Private Security and the Public Interest.* Berkeley, Calif.: Institute for Local Self Government, 1974.

2. Kakalik, James S., and Sorrel Wildhorn. *Private Police in the United States; Findings and Recommendations,* Vol. I, R-869/DOJ. Washington, D.C.: Government Printing Office, 1972.

3. Research Department, Division of Justice and Crime Prevention. "The Private Security Industry in Virginia." Virginia: Summer 1972.

Related Standards

The following standards and goals may be applicable in implementing Standard 9.1:

2.10 State Boards to Coordinate Training Efforts

4.10 Alarm User Permit Systems and the False Alarm Problem

6.6 State Regulation of Private Security Uniforms, Equipment, Job Titles

10.1 Licensing of Security Businesses

11.1 Registration of Private Security Personnel

Standard 9.2

Regulatory Board for Private Security

State level regulation should be through a regulatory board and staff responsible for the regulation of private security activities within that State. This board should have sufficient personnel to perform adequately and promptly their tasks of screening and investigating.

Commentary

Regulation of the private security industry is presently conducted by a variety of State agencies. Of the 34 States that licensed some aspect of the industry in 1975, only 11 had specific private security regulatory boards. The remaining States conducted their regulation through such diverse agencies as the State police department, the secretary of state's office, the attorney general's office, the department of public safety, the department of licensing, the Governor's office, the department of consumer affairs, or the department of commerce. Two States had established special boards to act strictly in an advisory capacity on security matters for their regulatory agency.

If regulation is to serve its purpose of protecting the consumer and the public, then careful thought should go into the decisions made concerning licensing, registration, rulemaking, and legislative recommendations. The procedures and policies of the State private security regulatory agency can best be set by persons familiar with this diverse and complex field. It is difficult to imagine that the necessary emphasis will be placed on private security regulation when that regulation is conducted by a section of a much larger agency, such as a secretary of state's office, assigned a variety of administrative duties.

It is, of course, recognized that a few States have established excellent private security regulatory sections within larger administrative agencies. Where that is true, there is no need to set up a separate regulatory board. However, if a separate board is not established, it is recommended that a private security advisory board be created to assist the regulatory agency in establishing its private security procedures and policies.

There is a trend in some States to consolidate administrative agencies under one unit. However, a separate regulatory board and staff, with expertise in the regulated area, often can best serve the public interest. It is felt that proper and meaningful private security regulation can be performed best by an agency whose sole responsibility is that regulation. An example of what often happens when a separate agency is not created can be cited in Colorado, where private security regulation is delegated to the secretary of state's office. Within that agency, the detective-licensing and -control duties have been assigned to the licensing section, whose major function is the control of games of chance conducted for charitable purposes. Detective licensing is only a peripheral part of that division's duties; operating funds are budgeted for the division's games-of-chance control duties, with the detective licensing duties being absorbed as a minor part of the program.

In setting up a private security regulatory board, legislators should recognize the need for adequate initial funding to meet staff needs; establishing a board in name only gains nothing. According to a 1970 RAND Corporation survey, one-half of the private security regulatory agencies surveyed indicated insufficient personnel to adequately perform their functions. Data showed that private security regulatory agency staffs averaged 3.7 persons, ranging from a high of 14 full-time staffers to one agency with only 1 part-time staff member assigned to this duty. The staffs were made up of about half clerical and half investigative personnel. The ratio of staff members to licensees/registrants ranged from 1:378 to 1:6, with an overall average of 1:109. A 1976 survey (Appendix 7) showed that the average regulatory agency staff consisted of 4.5 persons, ranging from 28 to 1 shared-time worker.

Such surveys indicate that agencies are especially understaffed in the investigative area—initial background investigations, complaint investigations, and general investigations for enforcement purposes. Because investigation is a particularly important function of the private security regulatory board, adequate funds need to be available to maintain a permanent investigatory unit to ensure maximum compliance with the regulatory legislation. A substantial clerical support unit also is necessary to process the volume of paperwork involved in the screening process for licensing and registration.

An inadequate-sized staff also affects the regulatory agency's ability to thoroughly and promptly handle licensing and registration. Individuals wanting to establish a business or become employed in the private security industry should not be required to wait several months for their applications to be processed. The regulatory board should be sufficiently staffed so that licensing and registration do not become a restraint on trade nor deter capable individuals from becoming security professionals.

It is recognized that many factors need to be weighed by legislators prior to establishing a regulatory board and staff. In some States, laws may require that all licensing be administered within a particular agency, or State constitutions may set forth other restrictions. In some sparsely populated States, the number of private security personnel may not warrant funding a separate board and staff. In other States, an adequate job may be done by existing agencies. Where possible, however, a regulatory board and staff whose sole responsibility is the regulation of private security activities should be set up to best perform this necessary function.

Selected References

1. Kakalik, James S., and Sorrell Wildhorn. *Current Regulation of Private Police: Regulatory Agency Experience and Views*, Vol. III, R–871/DOJ. Washington, D.C.: Government Printing Office, 1972.

2. Private Security Task Force. "Regulatory Agency Survey." (See Appendix 7 to this report.)

3. Private Security Task Force. "Summary of Private Security Legislation." (See Appendix 6 to this report.)

Related Standards

The following standards and goals may be applicable in implementing Standard 9.2:

9.3   State Regulatory Board Membership
9.5   Regulatory Board Funding
10.1   Licensing of Security Businesses
10.2   License Applications
10.3   Qualifying Agents
10.5   License Renewal
10.8   License Denial, Revocation, or Suspension
11.1   Registration of Private Security Personnel
11.2   Registration Qualifications
11.3   Qualifications for Armed Security Personnel
11.6   Registration Renewal
11.7   Suspension and Revocation
11.8   Sanctions

Standard 9.3

State Regulatory Board Membership

The State regulatory board should include, as a minimum, representatives of licensed security service businesses, businesses using proprietary security, local police departments, and consumers of security services; members of the general public; and individuals who are registered with the board and presently employed in the private security field.

Commentary

The proper composition of the State private security regulatory board is important for successful regulation. The board should not only act in an advisory capacity but also its responsibilities should encompass many other important aspects—enforcing minimum qualifications established by law; promulating administrative rules and regulations; considering special situations where rules might be modified in the interests of fairness and efficiency; voting to suspend, revoke, or deny licenses and registration cards; making recommendations for statutory changes; establishing standards; certifying training programs; and supervising the administrative operation of its staff. Because of this variety of duties, as well as the diversity and complexity of the field being regulated, individuals with differing backgrounds need to be included on the board.

A 1975 survey of private security regulatory legislation showed that nine States had separate regulatory boards with powers beyond that of advisers. Board memberships ranged from three to eight persons, averaging five per board. Eight of the boards were required to include certain experienced private security licenses; six were required to have a police or law enforcement representative; six required that a public representative be included; four States required that the attorney general or designate be on the board; and one required that a proprietary security representative be appointed.

No recommendation is made as to the specific number of individuals who should be appointed to the regulatory board. It is strongly suggested, however, that certain areas of competency of representation should be present on each board. Because the private security industry is composed of diverse segments and many different services are to be regulated, it is suggested that a representative from each security segment should be appointed to the board. The list includes guards, watchmen, patrolmen, canine handlers, polygraph operators, investigators, electronic surveillance personnel, alarm personnel, armored car personnel, and armed couriers. Also, small local security companies have interests different from those of large national companies; contract security companies differ from companies that use proprietary security systems. Including representatives from each segment of this diverse and complex industry, however, would result in an extremely unwieldy and perhaps inoperable board.

To narrow the cumbersome list of representatives, it is urged that the six general areas that are affected by the actions of the regulatory board should be represented on the board:

1. Contract security companies.
2. Proprietary security organizations.
3. Police.
4. Consumers of security services.
5. The public.
6. Registered security employees.

Representatives from these areas each have a different perspective of the industry and its regulation. Additionally, the suggested board composition prevents domination by private security industry interests. Domination of regulatory boards by the industry being regulated is a growing concern of the Federal Trade Commission and the public. Thus, to assure compliance with applicable laws and reasonable concerns, care should be taken not to allow the board to be dominated by security industry representatives or any other group.

Private security is often divided into two broad categories—contract and proprietary. Although both categories are concerned with loss prevention contract security companies provide their services to others for a fee, while proprietary security services are provided by employees for their employer. Many distinctions have been made in regulatory statutes based on this division, and many arguments over the validity of these legislative distinctions have been presented. Nonetheless, contract security companies and proprietary security organizations do have different problems and are affected in different ways by legislative provisions. Each should have a representative on the board.

Of major importance in crime prevention is the relationship between law enforcement and private security agencies. At present, this relationship ranges from close cooperation in some jurisdictions to strong animosity in others. This standard, as written, uses the term police representative rather than law enforcement. Although the term law enforcement is generally considered to be limited to local police, sheriffs, and deputies, it also includes prosecutors who are considered the chief law enforcement officials of their respective jurisdictions. However, it is the interaction between private security personnel and the police that would be most affected by the board decisions and policy; therefore, a representative of the police should be appointed to the private security regulatory board.

The interests of consumers and the public are often diffused and forgotten when issues are considered by regulatory boards. Representatives of these two segments have different perspectives on private security regulation that can be valuable in the board's decisionmaking process. The needs and concerns of these two important segments should not be ignored in the administrative process of regulating private security.

A security employee also should be included on the board. It is assumed that management- and executive-level persons would be appointed as representatives for licensed security service businesses and those using proprietary security. However, the individual who works at a guard post, responds to an alarm, confronts shoplifters, or investigates employee theft often has a different perspective on regulation than the security executive or manager; the views of the registered employee should be represented on the board.

No recommendation is made for a specific method for appointment of the regulatory board. Selection of this procedure is best left to the individual State. In the nine States that have separate regulatory boards, membership appointment is generally made by the Governor, with one State requiring that two appointments be made by the speaker of the house and president pro-tem of the senate. The person responsible for appointing the regulatory board may vary according to State procedures; however, whoever makes these appointments should be apprised of the importance of the selection. With appropriate representatives of the six major areas, the regulatory board should be able to function efficiently, effectively, and without undue influence from the area being regulated.

Selected References

1. Kakalik, James S., and Sorrell Wildhorn. *Private Police in the United States; Findings and Recommendations*, Vol. I, R–869/DOJ. Washington, D.C.: Government Printing Office, 1972.

2. Private Security Task Force. "Summary of Private Security Legislation." (See Appendix 6 to this report.)

Standard 9.4

Regulatory Board Hearing Procedure

The State regulatory board should establish a hearing procedure for consideration and resolution of the complaints of applicants, licensees, registrants, consumers, and the public. To assist in the implementation of this role, the board should be granted the means necessary to require appearance of witnesses and production of documents.

Commentary

The Federal Constitution and State constitutions require that no person be deprived of life, liberty, or property without due process of law. Thus, any action undertaken by the private security regulatory board needs to be performed with every consideration for administrative due process. The elements of administrative due process are summed up by Gellhorn and Byse in *Administrative Law*: "Determinations that finally dispose of life, liberty, or property must be preceded by adequate notice and opportunity for a fair hearing."

Adequate notice and fair hearing are generalities that have been interpreted in numerous cases over the years. Their definitions vary depending upon the facts in each case. It is inappropriate to discuss these legal requirements in detail, but the regulatory board should be prepared to defend its actions and prove that any persons affected by board decisions received adequate notice and an opportunity to be heard.

The Uniform Law Commissioners' *Revised Model State Administrative Procedure Act, 1970* (APA) has been enacted in a number of States. Where the APA has not been enacted, the private security regulatory board should consider using it as a guide for establishing its procedure. Certain portions of Sections 9 and 14 of that model act are particularly applicable to this standard.

SECTION 9. Contested Cases; Notice; Hearing; Records.

a. In a contested case, all parties shall be afforded an opportunity for hearing after reasonable notice.

b. The notice shall include:

(1) a statement of the time, place, and nature of the hearing;

(2) a statement of the legal authority and jurisdiction under which the hearing is to be held;

(3) a reference to the particular sections of the statutes and rules involved;

(4) a short and plain statement of the matters asserted. . . .

c. Opportunity shall be afforded all parties to respond and present evidence and argument on all issues involved.

d. Unless precluded by law, informal disposition may be made of any contested case by stipulation, agreed settlement, consent order, or default.

e. The record in a contested case shall include:

(1) all pleadings, motions, intermediate rulings;

(2) evidence received or considered;

(3) a statement of matters officially noticed;

(4) questions and offers of proof, objections, and rulings thereon;

(5) proposed findings and exceptions;

(6) any decision, opinion, or report by the officer presiding at the hearing;

(7) all staff memoranda or data submitted to the hearing officer or members of the agency in connection with their consideration of the case.

f. Oral proceedings or any part thereof shall be transcribed on request of any party.

g. Findings of fact shall be based exclusively on the evidence and on matters officially noticed.

SECTION 14.   Licenses.

a. When the grant, denial, or renewal of a license is required to be preceded by notice and opportunity for hearing, the provisions of this Act concerning contested cases apply.

b. . . .

c. No revocation, suspension, annulment, or withdrawal of any license is lawful unless, prior to the institution of agency proceedings, the agency gave notice by mail to the licensee of facts or conduct which warrant the intended action, and the licensee was given an opportunity to show compliance with all lawful requirements for the retention of the license. If the agency finds that public health, safety, or welfare imperatively requires emergency action, and incorporates a finding to that effect in its order, summary suspension of a license may be ordered pending proceedings for revocation or other action. These proceedings shall be promptly instituted and determined.

In only a few cases would the regulatory board consider individually the file of a specific applicant for a license or registration. The most likely procedure would be that the staff of the board would make recommendations to the board for its perfunctory approval. When, however, a license or registration is to be denied, revoked, or suspended, the board needs to carefully weigh all of the factors that resulted in the staff recommendation. If the board believes the recomendation has validity, then notice should be given to the applicant and a hearing set up. At the hearing, the board can make its determination based upon the facts presented by the applicant and the regulatory board staff.

In order to fulfill its role, the regulatory board should be well informed, obtaining information from sources such as government agencies, private security employers and employees, and private citizens. There may be times, however, when needed information is not given voluntarily, thus requiring some method of compelling disclosure. The private security regulatory board should be granted the means necessary to require the appearance of witnesses and the production of documents.

Three methods often used to obtain factual information by various administrative agencies are listed by Gellhorn and Byse. The methods are: (1) Issuing subpenas, which direct the recipients to testify or to produce documents they possess; (2) inspecting records or premises, either periodically or randomly; and (3) requiring the filing of reports. Care should be taken, however, in granting the

regulatory board strong investigative powers, particularly unlimited subpena powers. The power to use a subpena as an investigative tool can be misused. Accordingly, its use should be carefully limited to proper legal purposes.

Once the private security regulatory board has made its decision following the hearing, the individual who has had a license or registration denied, suspended, or revoked should be allowed to appeal the decision. The regulatory board's decision should not be final. This method for appeal varies from State to State. Many States have adopted the Uniform Administrative Review Act that sets up an independent review for all administrative decisions; other States allow appeal to local courts for parties aggrieved by administrative decisions. Whatever method is chosen for appeal, an independent body should be allowed to review the actions of the regulatory board.

The hearing procedures previously discussed were concerned with licensees, registrants, or applicants aggrieved by board decisions. However, it is just as important that specific procedures be established by the board for processing and maintaining records of complaints made by consumers and the public. Many complaints can be handled by an initial consultation. Others, however, may require a thorough investigation that may ultimately result in a revocation or suspension hearing. Processing of complaints are best handled by the investigative section of the board.

Establishment of a procedure for hearing complaints is a priority item, but, if consumers of private security services and the public are unaware of the board's existence or proper steps to take in the event of a complaint, the hearing procedure has little value. Therefore, the private security regulatory board should maintain a high level of visibility. Every effort should be made to publicize the purpose of the board and the procedure for filing complaints against licensees or registrants.

Selected References

1. Gellhorn, Walter, and Clark Byse. *Administrative Law: Cases and Comments*. Mineola, N.Y.: The Foundation Press, Inc., 1970.

2. Rogge, O. J. "Inquisitions by Officials: A Study of Due Process Requirements in Administrative Investigations." 48 *Minnesota Law Review* 557 (1964).

3. Uniform Law Commissioners. *Revised Model State Administrative Procedure Act*. 1970.

Related Standards

The following standards and goals may be applicable in implementing Standard 9.4:

Standard 9.5

Regulatory Board Funding

The State regulatory board should be funded by nonconfiscatory license and registration fees and such general revenue funds as may be necessary for the effective operation of the board.

Commentary

The purpose of licensing and registration, as recommended by this report, is to protect consumers of security services and the public. Too often, however, the primary function of the regulatory agency becomes revenue generating rather than regulatory. It is reported in *The Other Police* that the Ohio division of licensing advertised that it returned money to the State treasury by collecting more on fees than it spent on its own operation. Licensing and registration are not designed to be a means of generating revenue; every effort should be made by the regulatory board to ensure that fees collected are used solely to defray operating costs.

In a field where regulation is needed to protect the public from harm and constant investigation is necessary to ensure compliance, generating revenue should not be a basis for consideration of the amount of fees. In fact, in most States it is unusual to find a surplus in this activity, because it is difficult to set fees that cover all costs and still allow entry into the regulated profession. In States with

a small number of potential licensees and registrants, it may be prohibitive to set fees that alone would cover administrative costs. The fees should be moderate enough that all responsible individuals or entities can afford to enter business but substantial enough to cover most of the administrative costs. Where the cost of effective regulation cannot be covered solely by fees, it is necessary to seek additional funds from State general revenue funds.

A 1975 survey of private security regulatory legislation (Appendix 7) indicated that licensing fees ranged from $10 to $500, with a mode of $200. Alaska charged a percentage of gross business receipts. The survey further indicated that the fees charged for registration of individuals ranged from $2 to $300, with a mode of $100. The *RAND Report* (Vol. III) survey, conducted in 1971, found that the average license fees were $145 for contract guard agencies and $154 for investigative agencies, with renewal fees generally slightly lower.

It is impossible to recommend a specific fee schedule because of the varying factors that need to be weighed by each State before establishing fees. An effort should be made to predict the number of licensees and registrants to be processed and the approximate cost of operating the agency—from processing to investigating. These figures would vary from State to State and result in different fee charges. It must again be emphasized that the primary concern in setting fees should not be one of generating revenue but one of attempting to cover regulatory costs.

Selected References

1. Brennan, Dennis T. *The Other Police.* Cleveland, Ohio: Governmental Research Institute, 1975.

2. Kakalik, James S., and Sorrell Wildhorn. *Current Regulation of Private Police: Regulatory Agency Experience and Views,* Vol. III, R–871/

DOJ. Washington, D.C.: Government Printing Office, 1972.

3. Private Security Task Force. "Regulatory Agency Survey." (See Appendix 7 to this report.)

Related Standards

The following standard may be applicable in implementing Standard 9.5:

9.2   Regulatory Board for Private Security

Standard 9.6

Regulatory Board Access to Criminal Record Information

The State regulatory board should be granted statutory authority for access to all criminal history record information so that it can conduct the necessary criminal history record check of all applicants for licenses and registration.

Commentary

In recent years the American public has become concerned about the power that may be improperly wielded by governmental agencies straying beyond the bounds of their proper missions. Stories of invasions of privacy, attempted use of investigative agencies for political purposes, misuse of criminal history data, and dissemination of erroneous and incomplete personal and financial information have created a general sense of urgency and concern, resulting in the introduction of a number of recommended privacy laws, regulations, and administrative rules.

As of June 1975, there were 80 pieces of legislation pending in the U.S. House of Representatives relating to various aspects of privacy and 9 pending in the U.S. Senate. One of these bills, introduced by Senator John V. Tunney (D., Calif.) and Representative Don Edwards (D., Calif.) and known as the "Criminal Justice Information Control and Protection of Privacy Act," would severely restrict access by law enforcement agencies to arrest record information, by allowing dissemination of such information for investigative purposes only after a reasonable suspicion test has been met. This bill further provides for: (1) Sealing and purging of police investigative information after expiration of the statute of limitations, (2) placing restrictions on the exchange of intelligence data, and (3) allowing an aggrieved person to bring a civil action for violations. Many other bills are under consideration to further restrict the dissemination of criminal record information.

One of the first laws to be enacted in this area was the Privacy Act of 1974 (5 U.S.C. 552a), which became effective on Sept. 27, 1975. The act protects individuals from the misuse of Federal records by providing for access, challenge, and correction of those records affected. The new statute also established a 2-year Privacy Protection Study Commission to consider extending these new Federal principles.

U.S. Department of Justice regulations, issued pursuant to sections 501 and 524 of the Omnibus Crime Control and Safe Streets Act of 1968, as amended (42 U.S.C. 3701 et seq.), provide that conviction data and criminal history record information, relating to the offense for which an individual is currently within the criminal justice system, may be disseminated without limitations. The regulations require that after Dec. 31, 1977, most access to non-conviction record information would require authorization pursuant to a statute; ordinance; executive order; or court rule, decision, or order.

In enacting legislation, rules, and regulations pertaining to matters of privacy, three often-cited interests must be balanced: (1) The right of individual citizens not to have reputations damaged by improper dissemination of inaccurate or incomplete information, (2) the desire of law enforcement agencies not to have legislation that unnecessarily interferes with the administration of their departments, (3) the right of the public and press to have access to records maintained by law enforcement agencies that are public in nature. In addition to these is a key societal interest that is often forgotten: The right and need of the public to protection—to be free from crime and the fear of crime.

In the urgency to end certain abuses and invasions of privacy, society should not become blind to the need for the maintenance, use, and dissemination of criminal history record information, particularly as applied to private security employees. Private security personnel are hired to prevent crime and control loss, hold positions of trust, and often are assigned sensitive duties protecting valuable assets. Often they are armed, and their actions can have impact on the personal freedoms of others.

Because of the importance of these protective positions, the State regulatory board should be given statutory authority to evaluate the criminal arrest and conviction records of security personnel to determine if these records would adversely affect the performance of security services and to determine the trustworthiness of applicants for licensing and registration. For proper evaluation, the records should show arrests as well as convictions. The issuance of certificates of license or registration cards is, in effect, a seal of approval. Granting permission for persons to perform protective services without fully and carefully evaluating their criminal records would be a disservice to employers of security personnel, consumers of security services, and the public, who are so often affected by the actions of security personnel. Access to and subsequent evaluation of criminal arrest and conviction records may help eliminate certain employee risks, improve the caliber of persons performing security services, and assist the private security industry in preventing crime.

The importance of safeguarding the privacy rights of individuals is recognized and the desire to prevent criminal records from following people for the rest of their lives, even after they have paid penalties, is understood. Due to the prevalent process of plea bargaining, now universally employed in the United States, it is vital to examine arrest charges in order to determine essential information regarding an individual's criminal proclivities. The optimum way to protect both the individual involved and the public from improper police arrest charges is not to bury the arrest record but to initiate meaningful reforms against those police officers who engage in improper arrest and initial booking charges. It would be folly for a regulatory board to make a decision for certification based upon a criminal record that showed only two misdemeanor convictions for theft, when, in fact, the individual was arrested five times for burglary, with three charges dropped prior to conviction and two charges reduced (through plea bargaining) to larceny misdemeanors. The same would hold true of a conviction record for damage to property that was plea bargained down from arson, or of two misdemeanor assault convictions that were the only conviction record for an individual arrested five times for rape and attempted rape.

It is also unfair to the individual under review to exempt him from all security services if he has any conviction record. It may be that an individual, who has several minor arrests and convictions, can perform honorably and successfully in a specific security assignment. But unless the regulatory board has full access to an individual's complete arrest and conviction record, the board may, out of a need to protect the public, adopt unnecessarily rigid rules, prohibiting approval of any individual with a misdemeanor conviction.

Two possible safeguards should be included in legislation permitting access to criminal records by the regulatory board. One would be to properly inform the applicant for a license or registration that it will be necessary to obtain a criminal record check, including arrests and convictions. The applicant should then complete a written authorization for release of the information to the regulatory board. Second, a penalty should be imposed upon any regulatory board employee who releases criminal record information to unauthorized persons. With these safeguards, certain privacy concerns can be eliminated and the regulatory board can have access to the much-needed criminal history record information.

Selected References

1. Burstein, Harvey. "Protection vs. Privacy," *Security Management,* November 1975.

2. Clark, John V. "Right to Privacy Legislation," *Security Management,* May 1975.

3. Crown, John. "Too Many Individual Rights?" *The Atlanta Journal,* Nov. 17, 1975.

4. Eavenson, Chandler. "Recent Developments and Trends in the Field of Private Legislation." Address delivered Nov. 18, 1975, Atlanta, Ga.,

Greater Atlanta Chapter, American Society for Industrial Security.

5. Prepared Statement for the Subcommittee on Constitutional Rights, Committee on the Judiciary, U.S. Senate Concerning the Criminal Justice Information Control and Protection of Privacy Act. Gaithersburg, Md.: Research Division, International Association of Chiefs of Police, Inc., July 25, 1975.

6. Neier, Arych. *Dossier: The Secret Files They Keep on You.* Briarcliff Manor, N.Y.: Stein and Day, 1975.

7. 28 CFR Part 20, Criminal History Records.

8. *Federal Register,* Vol. 41, No. 55, Mar. 19, 1976.

Related Standards

The following standards and goals may be applicable in implementing Standard 9.6:

1.1   Selection of Qualified Personnel
1.3   Preemployment Screening
1.7   Availability of Criminal History Records

Chapter 10
Licensing

INTRODUCTION

As defined for legal purposes, *Corpus Juris Secundum* says that a license is a right or permission granted by some competent authority to perform a particular action, to exercise a certain privilege, to carry on a particular business, or to pursue a certain occupation that, without such license, would be illegal. In common usage, the term "license" often indicates the written document by which the right or permission is conferred, but strictly speaking "license" refers only to the right or privilege conferred and "certificate of license" refers to the written document that evidences such right.

Licensing is therefore an arrangement under which permission must be obtained from a recognized authority in order to engage in a particular occupation or activity. Usually, the issuance of the license is more than a formality and noncompliance with licensing requirements may result in a fine or jail sentence.

The courts, in cases such as *Northern States Power Co.* v. *Federal Power Commission* (7th Cir.), have held that license grants can be justified only on the theory of a resulting benefit to the public. An additional restriction imposed by the courts, and stated in *Allen* v. *Killoran,* is that license requirements may be imposed on occupations or privileges that may affect the public health, morals, or welfare. In spite of these apparent restrictions, the courts have upheld statutes licensing a variety of occupations. As of 1968, the Council of State Governments estimated that there were approximately 1,912 State licensing statutes. Among the 70 or more licensed professions listed in *Corpus Juris Secundum* are abstractors of titles, architects, attorneys, automobile dealers, barbers, cigar dealers, coal dealers, contractors, doctors, electricians, insurance agents, junk dealers, masseurs, miners, pilots, plumbers, real estate brokers, retailers, travel agents, and undertakers.

A 1975 survey of State legislation (Appendix 6) indicated that many States have also chosen to license certain private security services. Investigative agencies and guard companies, in particular, are subject to State license requirements, with 34 States licensing investigative agencies and 32 requiring a license for guard companies. Additionally, five States license armored car companies, eight license detection-of-deception examiners, three license central station alarm companies, five license guard-dog services, three license couriers, and one licenses counter-intelligence services.

Licensing is established to protect the consumer of security services. Therefore, any person or legal entity engaged in the business of providing security services for a fee should be required to be licensed. The standards in this chapter are designed to ensure that consumers receive the services they pay for and that they are delivered in a professional manner. Guidelines are established for license applications, qualifying agencies, notification of change in the licensee's status, license renewal, and display of the license certificate. In addition, it is recommended that a license be denied, revoked, or suspended in the event of violation of any of the licensing requirements or for other serious abuses, such as fraud or misrepresentation.

References

1. *Allen* v. *Killoran,* 56 F. Supp. 173, 176 (1944).

2. *Corpus Juris Secundum,* "Constitutional Law," Vol. 16A, Sec. 659, p. 1382.

3. *Corpus Juris Secundum,* "Licenses," Vol. 53, Sec. 1, p. 445.

4. *Northern States Power Co.* v. *Federal Power Commission,* 181 F. 2d 141, 144(1941).

5. Private Security Task Force. "Summary of Private Security Legislation." (See Appendix 6 to this report.)

Standard 10.1

Licensing of Security Businesses

Appropriate licensing should be required for any person or legal entity engaged in the business of:

1. Selling, installing, or servicing alarm systems;

2. Providing respondents to alarm signal devices;

3. Providing secured transportation and protection of valuables from one place to another under armed guard;

4. Providing guard or patrol services;

5. Providing investigative services; and/or

6. Providing detection-of-deception services, for the benefit of others.

Commentary

A primary objective of requiring a license is the protection of the consuming public. It has been stated that consumers need to be protected from their own ignorance. This axiom is especially applicable in the private security field. Its diversity and complexity make it difficult for consumers to be knowledgeable in choosing competent, reliable businesses that provide security services. When dealing with a licensed security entity, consumers are at least assured that the business or individual has met minimum standards and is qualified to provide the security services being purchased.

This standard is specifically designed to cover a wide range of businesses, including single individuals, acting as one-man operations, as well as corporations, partnerships, and associations. Any person or legal entity engaged in the business of providing a security service should be licensed. The standard is not designed, however, to include the licensing of security departments of private businesses whose general purpose is the protection and security of their own property, employees, and grounds. Private corporate entities should not have to obtain a license to protect their own assets. Licensing should be designed to protect consumers of security services. Therefore, if a business is not offering or providing a security service for the benefit of others, it need not be licensed. Employees of security departments of private businesses, however, are covered in the registration standards.

Licensing appears to be a remedy for many problems encountered by consumers of security services. Failure of security businesses to perform contracted services is one such problem according to the *RAND* Report (Vol. I) and other private security studies. For example, a study conducted by the Florida Senate Judiciary Committee included the mailing of questionnaires to 310 security agencies in that State. The respondents listed one of the major problems in the security industry to be the failure of security companies to provide the services contracted for, and their most common suggestion for remedying this problem was to require licensing.

A 1972 study conducted in Virginia by the Division of Justice and Crime Prevention pointed out:

> . . . there are a large number of personnel of the security industry lacking skill, training, and motivation. In total they are poorly equipped to render safe or professional protective service. The victim of poorly prepared, inadequate security personnel is most often the one who has contracted the security services. Contractual complaints appear frequently.

During the past several years, there has been an increasing emphasis upon community crime prevention and self-help methods of crime prevention. As the statistics, showing an increased crime rate, continue to climb, there also will be an increase in the number of individuals and businesses turning to private security for protection—consumers who may be frightened, concerned, and ignorant about security matters. These circumstances have created an area for unprecedented opportunity in consumer abuse, fraud, and misrepresentation. As has been noted, licensing is one method for preventing such consumer abuses. Security businesses have a direct effect upon the safety of the public. The licensing of those businesses appears to result in a benefit to the public, particularly the consuming public. Licensing ensures the delivery of ethical, competent, and responsible services.

This standard covers six types of security services that involve some aspect of crime prevention and control and that should be licensed for the protection of consumers:

1. Sell, install, or service alarm systems;
2. Provide alarm respondents;
3. Provide secured transportation of valuables from one place to another;
4. Provide guard services;
5. Provide investigative services;
6. Provide detection-of-deception services.

Because of the diversity of these services, a general license that allows a person or legal entity to engage in providing all of these security services should not be issued. The regulatory board issuing a license should specifically determine those security services the licensee is qualified to provide. The certificate of license should specifically state which of the listed activities the licensee is qualified to perform. Under this provision, consumers can have reasonable assurance that the business is capable of performing the security services enumerated on the license.

Selected References

1. Kakalik, James S., and Sorrel Wildhorn. *Private Police in the United States:* Findings and Recommendations, Vol. I, R–869/DOJ. Washington, D.C.: Government Printing Office, 1972.

2. Private Security Advisory Council. "Model Private Security Licensing and Regulatory Statute." Washington, D.C.: Law Enforcement Assistance Administration, 1975.

3. Research Department, Division of Justice and Crime Prevention. "The Private Security Industry in Virginia." Summer 1972.

4. Council of State Governments. *Occupations and Professions Licensed by the States, Puerto Rico and the Virgin Islands* (1968).

5. Senate Judiciary Committee Staff. "Report on the Private Security Industry in Florida." September 1974.

Related Standards

The following standards may be applicable in implementing Standard 10.1:

6.7 Law Enforcement Personnel Secondary Employment
6.8 Law Enforcement Officer Employment as a Private Security Principal or Manager
9.1 State Regulation
9.2 Regulatory Board for Private Security

Standard 10.2

License Applications

License applications should include sufficient information about the applicant to enable the regulatory agency to determine if ethical, competent, and responsible services can be provided. Such required information should include:

1. The full name and business address of the person or legal entity applying;

2. The name under which the applicant intends to do business;

3. A statement as to the general nature of the business in which the applicant intends to engage;

4. A statement of the specific security services to be provided by the applicant;

5. The full name, residence address, and two classifiable sets of fingerprints of the following:

    a. The applicant applying as an individual

    b. The qualifying agent and resident managers of each office within the State if the applicant is a corporation or partnership

    c. Each shareholder owning a 10 percent or greater interest in the applicant, each officer, and each director when the corporation is not listed on a national securities exchange or registered under section 12 of the Securities and Exchange Act of 1934, as amended, and

6. A verified statement of the qualifying agent's experience qualifications.

Commentary

To ensure that licensing achieves its principal purpose of protecting consumers of security services, certain information needs to be available to the regulatory agency. The information should be sufficient to enable the regulatory board to perform sufficient background checks and make other actions and decisions to determine if an applicant is able to deliver ethical, competent, and responsible services.

The first two requirements—full name and address of the person or legal entity applying and the name under which the applicant intends to do business—are general administrative questions that should be asked of applicants for any type of license, in order to determine with whom the regulatory agency is dealing. Security service businesses often operate under a trade name different from that of the actual owner, so it is important to have both the name of the applicant and the name under which the applicant intends to do business. The name and address also are needed so that initial processing can be started, and, once the license is granted, an address must be on file so that complaints can be easily investigated.

Throughout the licensing and registration standards, requirements differ depending on the security service offered for sale. For this reason, the regulatory board needs to have a record of the general nature of the business being performed by the applicant. The statement as to the services to be provided should be functionally specific so that the regulatory board can determine that the qualifications and requirements for each service being offered are met.

Requiring the name, address, and fingerprints, of the officers, directors, partners, 10-percent shareholders, resident managers, and qualifying agent may at first seem excessive. Yet, because each person listed has a critical role in the conduct of the security service business, the regulatory board needs to educate itself on the individuals background through investigations. The information obtained from these investigations may help the board determine if organized crime has any interests in the business, or if threatening conflicts of interest or other improprieties exist. The individuals involved only need to supply fingerprints once, because they could be maintained on file at the regulatory board for updating at renewal time.

It is not intended, however, that officers, directors, partners, and 10-percent shareholders of publicly held corporations, listed on a national securities exchange or registered with the Securities and Exchange Commission, be listed for scrutiny or investigation by other agencies. It is the officers, directors, and partners of the small privately held companies who should be checked by the private security regulatory board.

Because no residency requirement has been placed upon the qualifying agent, large national companies may have one person acting as their qualifying agent in several States. Although this individual may supervise the branches within the licensing State, some additional clearances within each State are needed. To assure closer scrutiny of the local branch officers, the name, address, and fingerprints of the resident manager of each office within the State should be required.

To effect and attest the qualifying agent's security-related experience, the regulatory board should require that a statement concerning qualifications be verified by the agent and accompany the license application. The statement should include the names and addresses of each person who employed the qualifying agent in a security-related job, a brief functional description of each security-related job corresponding with each employer previously listed, and the period of time each job was held. Because some educational training may be substituted for experience, this statement should also list any security-related education received, the school where such education was received, and the dates of attendance. This statement should be on a form that would impart the legality of an oath.

The information needed in connection with the license application is both necessary and reasonable. This information would allow the regulatory board to conduct a proper and sufficient investigation to determine if the applicant can provide ethical, competent, and responsible security services to consumers.

Selected References

1. Private Security Advisory Council to the U.S. Department of Justice, Law Enforcement Assistance Administration. "A Report on the Regulation of Private Security Guard Services including a Model Private Security Licensing and Regulatory Statute." May 1976. (See Appendix 11 to this report.)

2. Private Security Task Force. "Summary of Private Security Legislation." (See Appendix 6 to this report.)

Related Standards

The following standards may be applicable in implementing Standard 10.2:

9.2   Regulatory Board for Private Security

9.4   Regulatory Board Hearing Procedure

Standard 10.3
Qualifying Agents

License applicants should be required to name one individual who will act as the licensee's qualifying agent. The qualifying agent should meet the following qualifications:

1. Be at least 18 years of age;

2. Be an active participant in the business of the licensee;

3. Not have been convicted of any felony or crime involving moral turpitude or have any criminal charges and/or indictments pending, unless pardoned or granted a special exemption by the regulatory agency;

4. Not be under any present adjudication of incompetency; and

5. Be experienced in some area of security relevant to the license being sought.

Commentary

In order to protect consumers of private security services, certain minimum standards should be established in the licensing process. In establishing these minimum standards, however, the impact upon the licensed business should be considered. Any licensing process should be neither disruptive nor unnecessarily inconvenient to the business being licensed.

To require every partner, officer, stockholder, and manager to meet a list of qualifications would be impractical. One practical method for ensuring that certain minimum standards are met is to require that at least one participant in the business meet the necessary qualifications. The designated individual, acting as the applicant's qualifying agent, should be an active participant in the business.

The qualifying agent should be of legal age to ensure legal competence to contract and act for the business. As 18 is now the generally accepted age of responsibility, an 18-year-old could reasonably be named as a qualifying agent. It is recognized that, because few individuals of that age can meet the experience requirements, few qualifying agents would be that young.

Second, the individual representative of the business for licensing purposes should not be a nominal figure or a front-man with no actual control. The purpose of establishing minimum qualifications is to assure consumers that there is a qualified, knowledgeable, and competent individual actively participating in the affairs of the security service's business. Therefore, the business should certify that the qualifying agent is a person who engages in the everyday affairs of the business, acts in some supervisory capacity, and participates in the managerial decisionmaking process of the applicant. Because of varying business practices, this person need not be the officially designated manager.

The third qualification deals with any criminal incidents in the agent's background. It is recognized that assisting the rehabilitation of convicted offenders by removing restrictions upon their ability to obtain employment is in the public interest. Gainful employment is vital to any exoffender's chance for returning freely to society. But, it also should be recognized that the business being licensed is one that provides security services. An article in the August 1975 issue of *Top Security* Magazine sums up the beliefs of many: "Whilst it is one thing to give a man a second chance it is another thing to put him in a position where he can fall to temptation again."

The best method for aiding exoffenders, yet safeguarding consumers, is to give the regulatory agency the power to grant special exemptions based upon the careful consideration of criminal convictions and the adverse effect they might have upon the business of providing security services. In making its determination, the regulatory agency should consider the following factors outlined in the New Jersey Statute, P.S. 1968, c. 282 (C.2A:168A):

1. the nature and duties of the occupation, trade, vocation, profession or business, a license for which the person is applying;
2. nature and seriousness of the crime;
3. date of the crime;
4. age of the person when the crime was committed;
5. whether the crime was an isolated or repeated incident;
6. social conditions which may have contributed to the crime; and
7. any evidence of rehabilitation, including good conduct in prison or in the community, counseling or psychiatric treatment received, acquisition of additional academic or vocational schooling, successful participation in correctional work-release programs, or the recommendation of persons who have or have had the applicant under their supervision.

The fourth qualification—not to be under any present adjudication of incompetency—is intended to preclude persons from acting as a qualifying agent if they are awaiting adjudication for previous acts that, in the opinion of the regulatory board, would render these persons incompetent to perform the duties, and/or meet the qualifications, of a qualifying agent. Each regulatory board should determine the specific actions that would be considered appropriate to rendering persons incompetent.

The final requirement that the qualifing agent should meet relates to prior experience and education in an area of security relevant to the license being sought. The type and amount of experience and education required should be determined by the regulatory board and based upon the specific security services being offered. In a field as important and sensitive as security, at least one person within the business organization should be adequately qualified to advise on pertinent security procedures. Adequate experience should include work as an employee with any type of business or governmental unit providing security services. Governmental units would include work with various Federal law enforcement agencies or military security units. Adequate education might include as a minimum a security or law enforcement associate degree from a 2-year college or a bachelor's degree with a security or law enforcement major or minor. A combination of experience and education might be most effective and should be accepted as meeting the experience requirement.

Many States require additional qualifications for licensees, often including U.S. citizenship, State residency, good moral character, no dishonorable discharge from the military service, minimum education, and written examinations. These additional qualifications do not serve the purpose of protecting consumers or are too difficult to administer for the resulting benefit.

Selected References

1. "Ex-Convicts Take Aim at Jobs as Guards," *Top Security,* Vol. 1, No. 4, Aug. 1975.

2. New Jersey Statute, P.S. 1968, c. 282 (C.2A: 168A).

3. Private Security Advisory Council to the U.S. Department of Justice, Law Enforcement Assistance Administration. "A Report on the Regulation of Private Security Guard Services including a Model Private Security Licensing and Regulatory Statute." May 1976. (See Appendix 11 to this report.)

4. Private Security Task Force. "Summary of Private Security Legislation." (See Appendix 6 to this report.)

5. Research Department, Division of Justice and Crime Prevention. "The Private Security Industry in Virginia." Summer 1972.

Related Standards

The following standards and goals may be applicable in implementing Standard 10.3:

9.2   Regulatory Board for Private Security
9.4   Regulatory Board Hearing Procedure

Standard 10.4

Notification of Changes in Status of Licensee

The licensee should be required to notify the regulatory board within 14 days of any change in the status of the licensee previously reported in the license application.

Commentary

Licensing cannot maintain its viability if the regulatory board is not aware of changes occurring within the licensed entity. Therefore, some provision should be made to notify the licensing authority of changes as they occur. These changes would include: a change of address of the principal place of business or a branch office; a change of the name under which the licensee does business; if the qualifying agent ceases to act for the licensee; any addition or deletion of officers, directors, partners, resident managers of offices in the State, or shareholders who own a 10 percent or greater share in the licensee. Because a license is granted to the security business based upon the qualifications and background investigations of these individuals, when there is a change in the status of any of them, the original basis for granting the license is altered.

The regulatory board should be notified whenever one of the above listed officials ceases to serve in the official capacity, for whatever reason—death, resignation, or removal from office. The regulatory board also should be notified of the name and address of the individual designated to replace a former official or added to one of the official positions. Such persons should file fingerprints with the agency so that a background investigation can be conducted. Failure to notify the regulatory agency of these changes should result in the suspension or revocation of the license.

One reason for the license applicant to appoint a qualifying agent is to ensure the regulatory agency that at least one individual within the organization meets the necessary minimum qualifications. If this qualifying agent later ceases to act for the licensee, there is no longer any guarantee of a qualified individual assisting in the operation of the security service business. Therefore, it is necessary to promptly obtain a substitute who meets the qualifications outlined in Standard 10.3.

No time limit is specified for obtaining a new qualifying agent, and it is not intended that the licensee be forced to replace an individual within the 14-day notification period. However, a replacement for the qualifying agent should be found within a reasonable period, consistent with good business practice for personnel replacement. The Model Private Security Licensing and Regulatory Statute of the Private Security Advisory Council suggests a maximum time period of 6 months for the replacement of the qualifying agent; this time-frame appears reasonable.

Selected References

1. Private Security Advisory Council to the U.S. Department of Justice, Law Enforcement Assistance Administration. "A Report on the Regulation of Private Security Guard Services including a Model Private Security Licensing and Regulatory Statute." May 1976. (See Appendix 11 to this report.)

Related Standards

The following standards may be applicable in implementing Standard 10.4:

10.2   License Applications
10.3   Qualifying Agents
10.5   License Renewal

Standard 10.5

License Renewal

The license to engage in a security service business should be renewed every year.

Commentary

Once a license has been issued, the level of contact between the regulatory board and the licensee drops dramatically. Only if some change requiring notification occurs within the licensee or a complaint is made during the currency of the license is a licensee likely to come into contact with the regulatory board.

In order for licensing to be effective, a license cannot be a perpetual grant. The security service business should seek periodic renewal of its grant to do business, giving the regulatory board an opportunity to learn of any unreported changes in the business, to update the board's records, and to evaluate the licensee's performance with particular emphasis on any complaints, arrests, or convictions. License renewal forces periodic contact between the licensee and the regulatory board.

Of the 34 States licensing some aspect of the private security industry in 1975, 22 required annual renewal and 12 required renewal every 2 years. No State granted a 5-year license. A 1-year license period is recommended as most appropriate. The prime factor for requiring a yearly license renewal is monetary. An annual renewal assures the agency of a continuing flow of funds that should be delegated to the regulatory board for its continued operation.

Rather than requiring the refiling of information previously submitted and the fingerprinting of the same individuals, the license renewal process should be automatic, entitling the licensee to a renewal of the privilege to do business unless adverse information has been filed that reflects upon his ability to perform competent and ethical services. This automatic renewal process is possible because of several safeguards.

One safeguard for the continued evaluation of the licensee's competence is through periodic field investigations to verify the accuracy of information on file about the licensee and to check on any changes that should have been reported. Another safeguard is the complaint procedure. When complaints are received from consumers or the public, resulting investigations would involve contact between the regulatory board and the licensee.

A simplified renewal procedure need not preclude an updated background check of the individuals involved with the licensee. Fingerprints of the officers, partners, resident managers, qualifying agent, and 10-percent shareholders on file may be randomly resubmitted for updated criminal record checks during different renewal periods.

If the regulatory board maintains various safeguards that enable it to evaluate licensees' performance, the renewal process may be routine and automatic. The regulatory board should remember, however, that by renewing the license of a security service business it gives its seal of approval to that business.

Selected References

1. Kakalik, James S., and Sorrell Wildhorn. *Private Police in the United States: Findings and Recommendations,* Vol. I, R–869/DOJ. Washington, D.C.: Government Printing Office, 1972.
2. Private Security Task Force. "Summary of Private Security Legislation," 1975. (See Appendix 6 to this report.)

3. Stenning, Philip C., and Mary Cornish. *The Legal Regulation and Control of Private Policing and Security in Canada.* Ministry of the Solicitor General of Canada, May 1974.

Related Standards

The following standards may be applicable in implementing Standard 10.5:

9.2   Regulatory Board for Private Security

10.2   License Applications

Standard 10.6

Display of License Certificate

The licensee should be required to display the license certificate in public view in the licensee's principal place of business as well as displaying a copy of the certificate in each branch office.

Commentary

Consumers of security services should be able to walk into any security service business and determine immediately if it is licensed. It should not be necessary for consumers to search for evidence of a license, or to ask about the status of the business. Display of the license certificate also is one indication to consumers that the licensee is capable of providing ethical and competent security services. When no certificate of license is on display, consumers should realize they may be dealing with a disreputable business. Thus, the certificate of license, or a facsimile, should be prominently displayed in every office of the security business.

Required display of the certificate also can aid the complaint procedure. No matter how thorough the regulatory board is in screening applicants, a problem may occasionally occur involving a licensee. If consumers can tell the regulatory board the official name of the licensee and its license number because of the prominent display of the certificate of license, the board's procedure for processing and investigating consumer complaints can be aided.

Although the specific format of the certificate of license is unimportant, it should contain certain information: licensee's name and, if different, the business name under which it operates; addresses of locations where the licensee is authorized to operate; dates of issuance and expiration; and license number. Both consumers and the regulatory board will be aided if this information is readily observable in each security services office.

Selected References

1. Private Security Task Force. "Summary of Private Security Legislation." (See Appendix 6 of this report.)

Related Standards

The following standards may be applicable in implementing Standard 10.6.

10.1 Licensing of Security Businesses
10.4 Notification of Changes in Status of Licensee

Standard 10.7

Bonding and Insurance

When appropriate, due to the nature of the work, the applicant should file a surety bond and proof of public liability insurance with the regulatory agency before a license is issued.

Commentary

If an employee of a security services business acts wrongfully or negligently or the business fails to perform a service contracted for, the person injured needs some assurance of obtaining redress for damages suffered. Any business engaged in activities that may inflict injury should be prepared to restore any injury it causes. Adequate bonding and personal-liability and property-damage insurance are common means of compensating persons injured by business-related abuses. Bonding and insurance can create a measure of recourse for an aggrieved third party or consumer and discourage dishonest business practices and abuses of authority. Mandatory bonding and insurance also can have the practical effect of screening out uninsurable applicants.

Although it may be argued that bonding and surety requirements add to the operating costs of the small private security business, not requiring these provisions leaves the public at a grave disadvantage. The potential for improper, illegal, or harmful conduct by security operations and security personnel has

been discussed at length. A single act of one guard may evoke the same amount of damage, regardless of the size of the security organization. The failure of an alarm or detection device may result in the same loss, whether the company that provided the equipment was a national organization or a small local company. A small, marginally operating company does, indeed, have a legitimate right to conduct its business, but the right of the public to be protected from wrongful torts must prevail when the business involves the protection of life and property and the potential for denial of constitutional guarantees. Although the small businessman may be the most economically impacted by requirements for insurance, surety bond, or similar protection, the public may find it has, in fact, no recourse against such a company if the company's capital worth is less than the amount of awarded damages.

Of the 34 States presently licensing some aspect of the private security industry on a statewide basis, 85 percent require a minimum surety bond conditional so that any person injured by the willful, malicious, or wrongful act of the security service licensee, agents, servants, officers, or employees can bring a personal action for damage sustained. A few States supplement the bond by requiring personal-liability and property-damage insurance designed to protect the injured party; some States offer the applicant an option of bonding or insurance.

309

No State licensing statute makes reference to fidelity insurance, designed to protect licensees from the dishonest acts of their employees. The Private Security Advisory Council's model act eliminated any reference to surety bonds but requires an applicant to have comprehensive general liability coverage for bodily injury, personal injury, and property damage, with endorsements for assault and battery and personal injury, including false arrest, libel, slander, and invasion of privacy. Surety bonding is one more method of ensuring that the consumer and the public are protected and, therefore, it is recommended that both public liability insurance and surety bonding be carefully considered as licensing requirements for all security services businesses.

Although most often associated with building contracts and performance guarantees, a surety bond can cover much more. Commonly defined, a surety bond is an obligation whereby one (the surety) becomes responsible for the debt, default, performance of an obligation, or miscarriage of the bonded individual (the principal). The extent of the surety's liability is dependent on the terms of the bond. The surety bond generally required by most States for security service licensees is often referred to as a license bond. It is set up so that one may recover for actionable injuries, loss, or damage as a result of the willful, malicious, or wrongful acts of the principal, his agents, or employees. The surety bond may also be conditioned upon the faithful and honest conduct of the principal's business.

Surety contracts are in many respects similar to insurance contracts of fidelity bonds yet have significant legal differences. Unlike a surety bond, a fidelity bond is a contract of insurance, synonymous with fidelity or guarantee insurance, whereby one agrees to indemnify another against breaches of contract or against any loss arising from the lack of integrity or fidelity of employees and persons holding positions of trust. The bond generally covers fraud, dishonesty, larceny, embezzlement, negligence, and other named forms of misconduct. The bond is generally designed to protect an employer from losses sustained by the dishonest acts of an employee.

Surety bonds often provide greater protection for injured parties because a bond may cover any wrongful act, willful or negligent, whereas public policy generally prohibits people from insuring against their own willful acts. Substantively, a surety bond may be broader in coverage than public liability insurance, and, procedurally, recovery under a bond may be simpler. To recover insurance proceeds, the injured party must look primarily to the wrongdoer and prove that the cause of loss was specifically covered by the policy, that the loss occurred as a result of the type of transaction that was insured, that the loss was caused by the person

or entity who was insured, and that the person causing the injury or damage was acting in the scope of his employment. In addition, bond premiums are often less expensive than insurance premiums, because a surety bond, unlike public liability insurance, allows the surety to seek reimbursement of any claims from the bonded security service business. Insurance companies, however, cannot expect the insured to directly repay claims, except through increased premiums.

Surety bonds for large amounts may restrict the entry of smaller, less affluent security businesses ·into the market. This primary disadvantage arises because the surety company expects to be repaid for any claims, and therefore, carefully considers the financial responsibility of the company seeking to be bonded. This disadvantage should be carefully weighed against the advantage of allowing an injured party a method of recovering for damages sustained as a result of the actions of the security business or its employees.

In addition to study of the feasibility of requiring a surety bond, serious study also should be made of requiring each license applicant to file proof of public liability insurance. However, many private security companies are finding it difficult to obtain adequate liability coverage. In fact, this problem is so great that several large companies are self-insured. Compulsory insurance may therefore create serious problems, perhaps driving out many good businesses or even drying up the availability of liability insurance. Yet, there are advantages for mandatory insurance that make serious, careful, and extensive research into the liability insurance situation necessary.

Once it is determined that liability insurance should be required within a State, the type of policy required should be considered. Bruce W. Brownyard, in an article in *Security Management Magazine*, listed a number of important areas for coverage beyond the standard liability policy. These coverages should be considered as a minimum:

1. Comprehensive General Liability (basic bodily/personal injury and property damage coverage),
2. Assault and Battery Endorsement (intentional as well as accidental assaults),
3. Personal Injury Endorsement (false arrest, libel and slander, invasion of privacy, etc),
4. Broad Form Property Damage Endorsement (damage to property in the care, custody or control of the security firm),
5. Errors and Omissions (error or failure in performance resulting in bodily/personal injury or property damage).

The levels of surety bonding and liability insurance required by present State legislation vary considerably. Eleven States require surety bonds of

$3,000 or less, 12 States have set a level of $5,000, and 12 others have a requirement of $10,000. Only two States surveyed in 1975 required public liability insurance, with the levels set at $50,000. Each State private security regulatory board should consider the situation within its State before determining the specific monetary level that should be required. Specific levels of minimum bonding and insurance requirements are not cited in this standard; however, it is believed that current minimums should be increased so that ample funds would be available to sufficiently reimburse injured parties.

In summary, carefully structured bonding and insurance requirements offer a means of alleviating problems of abuse by private security businesses and employers. At the same time, they provide a necessary avenue of recourse for the citizen who may be victimized by unscrupulous firms and practices or who may suffer other forms of injury or damage as a result of actions by private security businesses or employees. Therefore, each State should examine the effects of bonding and insurance requirements and adopt uniform regulation in this area so as to best protect the public interest without forcing competent but smaller security operations out of the marketplace.

Selected References

1. Black, Henry Campbell. *Black's Law Dictionary*. St. Paul, Minn.: West Publishing Company, 1968.

2. Brownyard, Bruce W. "Are You Buying Security . . . or Trouble," *Security Management Magazine*. November 1974.

3. *Corpus Juris Secundum,* "Insurance," Vol. 44, Sec. 1, p. 473, and Sec. 72, p. 555.

4. *Corpus Juris Secundum,* "Principal and Surety," Sec. 2, p. 515.

5. Kakalik, James S., and Sorrel Wildhorn. *Private Police in the United States: Findings and Recommendations,* Vol. I, R–869/DOJ. Washington, D.C.: Government Printing Office, 1972.

6. National Commission on Crime and Delinquency. "Standard State Act for Private Security Services."

7. Peel, John Donald. *The Training, Licensing and Guidance of Private Security Officers*. Springfield, Ill.: Charles C. Thomas, 1973.

8. Private Security Advisory Council to the U.S. Department of Justice, Law Enforcement Assistance Administration. "A Report on the Regulation of Private Security Guard Services including a Model Private Security Licensing and Regulatory Statute." May 1976. (See Appendix 11 to this report.)

9. Private Security Task Force. "Summary of Private Security Legislation." (See Appendix 6 to this report.)

10. Research Department, Division of Justice and Crime Prevention. "The Private Security Industry in Virginia." Summer 1972.

Related Standards

The following standards may be applicable in implementing Standard 10.7:

10.2   License Applications

10.8   License Denial, Revocation, or Suspension

Standard 10.8

License Denial, Revocation, or Suspension

A license may be denied, revoked, or suspended if the licensee; its qualifying agent; resident manager; or any officer, director, or shareholder owning a 10 percent or greater interest in the licensee (provided the licensee is not listed on a national securities exchange or registered under section 12 of the Securities and Exchange Act of 1934, as amended) does the following:

1. Violates any provisions of the regulatory act or of the rules and regulations promulgated under the act;

2. Commits any act resulting in the conviction of a felony or a crime involving moral turpitude, where such conviction reflects unfavorably on fitness to engage in a security service business;

3. Practices fraud, deceit, or misrepresentation;

4. Makes a material misstatement in the application for or renewal of the license; and/or

5. Demonstrates incompetence or untrustworthiness in actions affecting the conduct of the security services business.

Commentary

To be effective, regulation needs to include strong sanctions. The revocation or suspension of a permit to engage in business is a sanction that can be very effective. Being aware of this serious consequence, a licensee would take great care not to violate any listed restrictions.

Because the enforcement of this sanction can result in the denial or loss of the privilege to do business, due-process requirements should be met. The various acts that may result in license denial, revocation, or suspension should therefore be delineated and enforcement standardized. Also, administrative procedures should be established to give notice to the applicant or licensee of the intent to deny, suspend, or revoke a license and of the procedure for requesting a hearing prior to that denial, revocation, or suspension.

Although its wording is permissive, this requirement should be strictly enforced and applied. Unless there are important and valid extenuating circumstances, a license should be denied if there is sufficient proof that the listed individuals have committed any of the enumerated acts. When a provision of this requirement is violated, the investigation and review process should be promptly initiated and completed. Early suspension should be invoked if evidence indicates such action is necessary for the protection of the public. Only through prompt and strict enforcement can denial, revocation, and suspension maintain their validity as useful sanctions and deterrents.

Several factors should be considered by the regulatory board before a decision to deny, suspend, or revoke a license. The board must first consider to what extent the action under consideration affects the conduct of the business. It also should determine if the action is an isolated incident or one that has occurred repeatedly. Additionally, the regulatory board should consider which individual committed the act and determine what action has been taken by the applicant or licensee to remedy the situation.

In considering these various factors, the regulatory board should remember that the purpose of licensing is to assure consumers that the licensee is capable of providing ethical, competent, and responsible security services. If the action of the licensee does not affect the continued performance of this type of service, then no reason may exist to revoke or suspend the license. However, if the action has an affect and no extenuating circumstances exist, then denial, revocation, or suspension should occur. The five actions outlined in this standard can ad-

versely affect the conduct of a security service business, but they can be controlled by the judicious, yet unsparing, use of the sanctions of license denial, suspension, and revocation.

Selected References

1. Private Security Task Force. "Summary of Private Security Legislation." (See Appendix 6 to this report.)

Related Standards

The following standards may be applicable in implementing Standard 10.8:

3.3   Reporting of Criminal Violations

9.2   Regulatory Board for Private Security

9.4   Regulatory Board Hearing Procedure

Chapter 11
Registration

INTRODUCTION

In Chicago a confessed murderer, judged mentally incompetent for trial, was hired as a security guard. Three days later, while on duty, he shot and killed a person. A private security guard in an Oakland, Calif., theater shot and killed a person allegedly causing a disturbance. In a Phoenix, Ariz., nightclub parking lot, a security guard shot a 17-year-old boy during a fight. Although these incidents are extreme, their occurence is rising. Several pages could be filled with similar examples of abuses involving security personnel that resulted in death or serious bodily harm.

The *RAND Report* (Vol. I) provides an estimate of the frequency and nature of less serious incidents in which security personnel overstep their authority or are threatened with criminal charges or civil suits. The most frequent types of incidents seem to be assault and unnecessary use of force, false arrest or imprisonment, defamation, improper detention, trespass, and invasion of privacy. The above report concluded that, based on certain evidence and analysis, a variety of potential and actual problems exist involving security personnel.

Another area where problems arise is in the protection of the property of the employer or contracting party. Security personnel's access to many valuables, including money, important assets, and trade secrets, poses serious problems. In an interview conducted for CBS' "60 Minutes," Dec. 21, 1975, Philadelphia district attorney Emmett Fitzpatrick, whose office conducted a 1975 investigation of the private security industry, summed up what may occur:

> One of the biggest problems that we have with private security guards is that they end up stealing things. They have access to all kinds of goods within the business establishments themselves; and hardly a month goes by that we don't have a complaint from a security agency somewhere, or from a store, that the security agents within the store have been caught stealing things.

Obviously, action should be taken to reduce the number of potential and actual problems involving private security personnel. This reduction can come about only when security personnel are above reproach in character, background, and honesty. Several suggestions have been made for improving the personnel caliber, with previous standards recommending thorough screening of job applicants by employers, increased wages, and improved training. These recommended policies already have been instituted by many reputable organizations. Yet, because of the intensely competitive nature of the industry, marginal companies are unable or refuse to institute programs needed for improvement. Government registration of private security personnel is, therefore, necessary to help set minimum qualifications to protect all persons affected by the acts of security personnel—consumers of security services and the public.

The standards for registration, as presented in this chapter require that every individual performing private security functions be registered with the State regulatory agency. Because the purpose of registration is to protect the public, certain qualifications should be met before registration is granted. These qualifications should include minimum age, physical, intelligence, character, and training requirements. Qualification for armed personnel should be higher than those for unarmed personnel and should include additional training in the use of firearms. Obviously, any individual who carries a firearm needs to be properly trained in its use, if serious mishaps are to be prevented, and must fully understand the legal aspects connected with the use of the weapon. And to ensure that all required persons are registered, any person permitting a nonregistered individual to perform private security services should be subject to criminal penalties.

Because of emergency situations, provisions should be made for issuance of temporary permits pending issuance of permanent registration cards. Temporary permits, however, should be valid only for 30 days and should not be issued until applicants have had favorable local law enforcement background checks. After applicants have met all other requirements, including training, permanent registration cards should be issued. These cards would belong to individuals and would not be tied in with any single employer. Renewal of registration for armed per-sonnel should be annual, for unarmed registrants, only every five years.

Standard 11.1

Registration of Private Security Personnel

Every person who is employed to perform the functions of an investigator or detective, guard or watchman, armored car personnel or armed courier, alarm system installer or servicer, or alarm respondent should be registered with the private security regulatory board.

Commentary

Every person employed to perform one of the listed security functions should meet certain minimum qualifications, with no distinction based on an employer/employee relationship. It does not matter whether the person is employed by a contract company or a company using a proprietary security organization. The security function, not the employer/employee relationship, creates the problem that needs to be remedied by registration.

The effectiveness of this regulatory plan would be nullified if personnel working for proprietary security organizations are excluded from registration. Both contract and proprietary security personnel are drawn from the same labor market, with personnel having similar education and rates of pay. The work performed and problems confronted by each are similar, and, most importantly, the potential threat to the public from abuses of authority, such as assault, unnecessary use of force, false imprisonment or arrest, improper search and interrogation, impersonation of police officers, and mishandling of weapons, is just as likely to occur with proprietary personnel as with contract personnel.

It is recognized that many large corporations with proprietary security organizations have exemplary training programs and employ highly qualified persons. However, just as in the contract security sector, many businesses using proprietary guards do not provide training, are not selective in their hiring practices, and do not carry adequate insurance to protect the public from possible abuses by their employees.

Some proprietary security professionals have maintained that proprietary guards should not be regulated unless they are armed. Many of their objections are self-serving; however, their basic position is that a businessman has a right to protect his assets. This right is not in disagreement. But, just as the businessman is required to have his elevators inspected, his building engineer certified, his accountant accredited, and his lawyer accepted by the State bar, the unarmed proprietary security guard needs regulatory controls to prevent a variety of abuses.

Proprietary guards, just like contract security guards, come into contact with the public—employees, visitors, tradesmen, vendors, trespassers, and others. These citizens have constitutionally guaranteed rights that guards can, and on occasion do, violate. A recent case, in which a guard hand-cuffed an individual to a railing for 6 hours, did not involve deadly force but clearly illustrates the potential of other possible substantive damages inflicted on a person by a guard. Guards in supermarkets, liquor stores, and retail establishments have been alleged to have physically assaulted customers; guards have conducted unconstitutional searches of vehicles, lunch boxes, and persons at factories and warehouses; guards have obtained confessions under threat or duress from employees charged with theft. Although a college-educated, physically powerful proprietary security director may not become a victim of a proprietary guard employed at another place of business, that same guard may improperly act toward a 16 year-old boy or an uneducated, minority group member.

It may be that the proprietary security director forgets that proprietary guard forces are employed by dancehalls, drive-in movies, innercity liquor stores, automobile junkyards, apartment houses, and so forth. Regulation of these businesses without regulation of large, well-staffed corporations is prohibited under the due-process clause of the Constitution.

The public would be the principal beneficiary of the registration of private security personnel. If proprietary personnel are exempted from this registration, public protection would be vitiated, because the number of proprietary personnel far exceeds the number of contract personnel. There is no reason to assume that a person employed by a proprietary security organization would act any differently toward the public than a person employed by a contract security organization.

There can be beneficiaries of the registration program other than the public. A prime beneficiary is the employer of security personnel. It is becoming very difficult, and, if the trend toward strict privacy legislation continues, it may become impossible for employers to learn anything about an applicant's past, particularly the applicant's character. However, with registration required, the prospective employer would need only to ask to see the applicant's security service registration card to be assured that certain minimum qualifications had been met. The possession of a valid card would indicate that the individual had been investigated, been judged dependable, and met certain training requirements.

In 1975, 12 of the 34 States regulating some aspect of the private security industry required registration of security employees of contract security organizations. Generally, the States required that the employer register the employee immediately upon hiring, and, if the person failed to meet the necessary qualifications, the employment relationship would be terminated. Often, because of delays in processing registration applications, a person conceivably could work several weeks, or even months, before receiving regulatory agency approval. In one State, processing took over 9 months.

It has been estimated that between 300,000 and several million persons could be involved in the registration process. Although no specific figures are available, statistics provided by the Bureau of Labor Statistics, the U.S. Bureau of the Census, private security regulatory agencies, and industry representatives indicate that a conservative estimate of the number of security personnel that would need to be registered is more than a million.

Before making a final recommendation for security personnel registration, various aspects of the problem were carefully considered: the large number of persons to be registered and the bureaucratic problems this could create, the desire not to over-regulate, the abuse cited concerning security personnel, and the positive role the industry can play in crime prevention. Balancing all factors, it was determined that a registration program should be established.

A registration program with minimum qualifications, including training and background screening, cannot end all abuses and automatically eliminate crime. Effectively operated and strictly enforced, however, it can begin to weed out undesirables and can help professionalize this important segment of the business community, leading to more effective private security services and improved crime prevention.

Selected References

1. Brennan, Dennis T. *The Other Police*. Cleveland, Ohio: Governmental Research Institute, 1975.

2. Cumbow, T. L. "Security—a Challenge," Rossford, Ohio, September 1975.

3. Institute for Local Self Government. *Private Security and the Public Interest*. Berkeley, Calif.: Institute for Local Self Government, 1974.

4. Kakalik, James S., and Sorrel Wildhorn. *Private Police in the United States; Findings and Recommendations,* Vol. I, R–869/DOJ. Washington, D.C.: Government Printing Office, 1972.

5. Private Security Task Force. "Summary of Private Security Legislation." (See Appendix 6 to this report.)

Related Standards

The following standards and goals may be applicable in implementing Standard 11.1:

Standard 11.2

Registration Qualifications

Every applicant seeking registration to perform a specific security function in an unarmed capacity should meet the following minimum qualifications:

1. Be at least 18 years of age;

2. Be physically and mentally competent and capable of performing the specific job function being registered for;

3. Be morally responsible in the judgment of the regulatory board; and,

4. Have successfully completed the training requirements set forth in Standard 2.5.

Commentary

The 1967 *Task Force Report: The Police* of the President's Commission on Law Enforcement and Administration of Justice stated that "policing a community is personal service of the highest order, requiring sterling qualities in the individual who performs it . . . Few professions are so peculiarly charged with individual responsibility." Although the quote is directed toward law enforcement personnel, it is equally applicable to private security personnel, who likewise often must make instantaneous decisions affecting lives and property.

As pointed out in the preceding standard, the nature of the role of the private security industry demands that steps be taken to upgrade the quality of its personnel. Research has indicated that far too many security personnel, charged with protection of life and property, are either incompetent or of questionable character. Yet, existing personnel selection requirements and procedures do not screen out the unfit. If costly and dangerous losses both to business and society are to be prevented, measures for improvement need to be devised.

Chapter 1 of this report makes a number of recommendations for improving the quality of private security personnel. These recommendations reflect reasonable standards that should be established. However, despite the validity of the recommendations, it is recognized that certain actions may never be instituted unless mandated by law. Therefore, in order to improve the quality of security personnel, it was felt that certain minimum qualifications should be established for registration.

Recognizing the desire to attract high school graduates who might make a career in the private security field, a minimum age requirement of 18 is suggested, thus enabling businesses to compete for qualified young people. It is believed that personnel who do not possess the necessary maturity so often associated with age would not meet other requirements. No attempt is made, however, to impose a maximum age restriction. Any individual who can meet the physical and mental qualifications established by the regulatory board should be allowed to perform security functions, regardless of age.

Physical qualifications are not specifically enumerated, because each particular job function requiring registration calls for different physical qualifications. For example, performing the duties of a guard may require a higher level of hearing and better eyesight than are necessary for an alarm servicer. Similarly, certain physical deformities or limitations may adversely affect performance as an alarm respondent but have no appreciable effect upon performance as an investigator.

The area of physical qualifications should be carefully studied by the private security regulatory board. These qualifications should become part of their rules and regulations after careful consideration of the relationship between specific duties to be performed by the registrant and any physical problems. Provisions should be made to consider questions of physical competence on an individual applicant basis.

The need for private security personnel to have emotional stability and sound judgment is apparent because of their important roles in maintaining order and protecting lives and property. Whether a person is guarding a remote rock quarry, patrolling a residential area, or investigating business losses, a certain level of mental competence is required. This does not infer that a specific level of educational accomplishment alone would qualify the individual; some people with high school diplomas possess neither commonsense nor emotional stability. Persons whose background investigations indicate they possess sound judgment and emotional stability should be allowed to register as security personnel, regardless of their level of formal education.

Measuring or determining mental competence is not easy, particularly when such determinations must be made for thousands of applicants in the initial stages of registration. Two recommended methods that perhaps can be gradually worked into the registration process are psychological tests and interviews by trained professionals. The present limitations of these methods are recognized, but their validity and usefulness may be increased through continued research. Private security regulatory boards, therefore, should study these methods and keep abreast of research so that the best available means of measuring mental competence can be determined and applied.

The need for morally responsible security personnel cannot be argued, but questions over what, in fact, constitutes being morally responsible are likely. One solution for adding preciseness to the term would be to require that no person who has been convicted of a felony or misdemeanor that reflects upon ability to perform security work should be allowed to register. However, in many cases, the regulatory board may find that an individual has a long list of criminal charges that have never resulted in a conviction but the nature and number of charges may indicate that the person is not morally responsible.

Finally, this standard incorporates the specific training recommendations set forth in Standard 2.5. As was pointed out in Chapter 2, training can significantly improve the competence of security personnel to aid in crime prevention and control. Training is one of the most common areas in the private security industry needing the most improvement. However, unless requirements are mandated by law, the majority of private security personnel may never receive the necessary training. The benefits of training to employers, private security workers, consumers of security services, and the public are too great to be left to the option of employers or individual workers.

It would, of course, be preferable if all security personnel met stringent, professional requirements. However, this report recommends that the initial government-mandated qualifications should be minimum. It is impossible to determine the number of people who would have to register with the private security regulatory boards. It is also impossible to accurately assess the impact of strict qualifications upon the industry. If the requirements are too high and cannot be met by those applying for registration, a serious shortage of available manpower could occur, adversely affecting the industry and those who seek to use it for protection. Thus, the requirements set forth in this standard are minimal but designed as an initial step for eliminating undesirable applicants. The regulatory board should constantly evaluate the requirements. If a particular requirement is too restrictive and is keeping competent and ethical persons out of the field, that requirement should be eliminated. Likewise, if serious problems are occurring that could be corrected by a different or more stringent requirement, it should be added. Although constant evaluation requires maintenance of records and careful analysis, such efforts are necessary in order to balance the interests of the private security industry and society.

Selected References

1. Brennan, Dennis T. *The Other Police*. Cleveland, Ohio: Governmental Research Institute, 1975.

2. Harrigan, James F., Mary Holbrook Sundance, and Mark L. Webb. "Private Police in California: A Legislative Proposal," *Golden Gate Law Review*.

3. Institute for Local Self Government. *Private Security and the Public Interest*. Berkeley, Calif.: Institute for Local Self Government, 1974.

4. Kakalik, James S., and Sorrell Wildhorn. *Private Police in the United States: Findings and Recommendations,* Vol. I, R–869/DOJ. Washington, D.C.: Government Printing Office, 1972.

5. National Advisory Commission on Criminal Justice Standards and Goals. *Report on Police.* Washington, D.C.: Government Printing Office, 1973.

6. Oglesby, Thomas W. "The Use of Emotional Screening in the Selection of Police Applicants," *Police,* January–February 1958.

7. President's Commission on Law Enforcement and Administration of Justice. *Task Force Report: The Police,* Washington, D.C.: Government Printing Office, 1967.

Related Standards

The following standards and goals may be applicable in implementing Standard 11.2:

1.1 Selection of Qualified Personnel

1.3 Preemployment Screening

1.6 Application of Employment

1.7 Availability of Criminal History Records

1.8 Minimum Preemployment Screening Qualifications

2.1 Training in Private Security

2.4 Training Related to Job Functions

2.5 Preassignment and Basic Training

2.6 Arms Training

2.9 State Authority and Responsibility for Training

3.1 Code of Ethics

3.3 Reporting of Criminal Violations

4.3 Certified Training of Alarm Sales and Service Personnel

9.2 Regulatory Board for Private Security

9.4 Regulatory Board Hearing Procedure

Standard 11.3

Qualifications for Armed Security Personnel

Every applicant who seeks registration to perform a specific security function in an armed capacity should meet the following minimum qualifications:

1. **Be at least 18 years of age;**
2. **Have a high school diploma or pass an equivalent written examination;**
3. **Be mentally competent and capable of performing in an armed capacity;**
4. **Be morally responsible in the judgment of the regulatory board;**
5. **Have no felony convictions involving the use of a weapon;**
6. **Have no felony or misdemeanor convictions that reflect upon the applicant's ability to perform a security function in an armed capacity.**
7. **Have no physical defects that would hinder job performance; and,**
8. **Have successfully completed the training requirements for armed personnel set forth in Standards 2.5 and 2.6.**

Commentary

Some of the most serious problems in the private security industry are caused by the use of weapons. Throughout this report, various tragic examples have been cited in which injury or death resulted from weapons abuse. Other private security studies have cited similar incidents. Although no statistics are available to determine the frequency of these incidents, it remains unquestioned that the carrying of a firearm includes the potential for serious and dangerous consequences.

Armed security personnel take on an awesome responsibility. Split-second decisions with lethal weapons can result in death or serious injury, and the lives of armed security workers are constantly endangered. Walter M. Strobl stated, in "Private Guards Arm Them or Not," "the very fact that a weapon is visible will cause the criminal to assume a more violent attitude that could trigger the most violent actions."

Many responsible individuals within the private security industry have long argued against arming security personnel. Proprietary security executives have encouraged executives within their organizations to abandon the use of weapons, and contract organizations have discouraged consumers from requesting armed personnel. One large contract company actually offers incentives to sales personnel who set up contracts that do not require armed personnel; this action should be commended and encouraged.

It is a sad true reflection on our society that some situations require the arming of certain security personnel. It would be foolish in situations in which lives are under constant threat to forbid the use of firearms. But it is not unwise to place firm restric-

323

tions on the use of firearms and equally firm requirements on those who are allowed to carry them. For this reason, higher qualications are established for those who seek registration as armed security personnel than for those who would be unarmed.

A minimum age requirement of 21 years for persons desiring to be registered as armed personnel was first considered. However, it is believed that there is little correlation between maturity, good judgment, and age. An applicant who can meet all of the other requirements should be allowed registration, regardless of age. Therefore, this report recommends that a minimum age requirement of 18 years should be established for registration of armed personnel.

In the area of educational requirements, a higher level should be required for armed registrants than for other security personnel. The basic education qualifications can be met by a high school diploma or by an equivalent written examination designed to measure basic educational aptitudes.

The qualification for mental competence can enable the board to determine if the applicant is able to understand and perform security functions in an armed capacity. A written examination designed to measure the knowledge and skills required or the psychological makeup of the applicant should be used. This qualification is given along with the education requirement, because it is recognized that such formal education or equivalent does not automatically indicate a person is psychologically capable of carrying a weapon.

Although almost totally ignored by both existing State regulatory boards and by private security employers, psychological testing to screen out the obvious cases of emotionally unstable or unsuitable persons should be an important and integral portion of the competency requirement. This step could prevent psycopaths or other seriously mentally ill persons from being certified as armed guards.

It is difficult to list the specific acts that would indicate that an individual was not morally responsible to carry a weapon. Sometimes a person may meet the listed qualifications, but a review of his records may indicate a very questionable background. A long list of criminal charges or a series of jobs that ended in firing would perhaps be incidents to watch for. Because of the requirement for a hearing before denial, this requirement is not believed to be too general. Any applicant denied registration on this ground would have an opportunity to be heard and to show if the decision was arbitrary and capricious.

Any person who has been convicted of a felony involving the use of a weapon should not be registered in an armed capacity. No exception should be made, regardless of extenuating circumstances, pass-age of time, or indications of rehabilitation. The responsibility of carrying a firearm is too grave to take the chance that a person previously misusing a gun would not do so again.

Although no flexibility is recommended for felony convictions involving weapons, convictions for other offenses should be carefully studied before denying registration. It is in the public interest to assist the rehabilitation of convicted offenders by removing restrictions upon their ability to obtain employment. But it also must be recognized that the exoffender is being registered to perform a security function in an armed capacity. Therefore, if an applicant has a conviction record, the regulatory board should carefully consider whether such convictions reflect upon the applicant's ability to perform a security function in an armed capacity. In making its determination, the regulatory board should consider the following:

1. The specific security function the applicant is registering to perform;
2. The nature and seriousness of the crime;
3. The date of the crime;
4. The age of the applicant when the crime was committed;
5. Whether the crime was an isolated or repeated incident;
6. The social conditions that may have contributed to the crime; and
7. Any evidence of rehabilitation, including good conduct in prison or in the community, counseling or psychiatric treatment received, acquisition of additional academic or vocational schooling, successful participation in correctional work-release programs, or the recommendation of persons who have, or have had, the applicant under their supervision.

The next qualification concerns physical requirements. Such requirements should not be unduly restrictive and should not include height and weight specifications or other requirements that have little relation to performance in an armed capacity. Physical standards, however, cannot be totally disregarded. Obviously, good eyesight and hearing are vital to anyone who carries a weapon. In order to protect the individual and the public, specific vision and hearing requirements should be carefully considered and delineated by the regulatory board.

Finally, this standard incorporates the specific training recommendations set forth in Standards 2.5 and 2.6. As pointed out in Chapter 2, training can greatly improve the competence of security personnel to aid in crime prevention and control but needs perhaps the most improvement of any private security area. However, unless requirements are mandated by law, the majority of private security personnel may never receive such training. The benefits gained through training to employers, private security workers, consumers, and the public are too great to be left to the option of employers or individual workers. Competence and proficiency in the use of a firearm should be demonstrated by those who seek to be registered as armed security personnel. This can best be shown by successful completion of the required arms training recommended in Standards 2.5 and 2.6.

In summary, any individual allowed to carry a weapon needs to be able to make decisions that require mature, calculated, and sound judgment. The armed security worker should also possess the physical and emotional makeup to act with split-second timing, if necessary, and be thoroughly trained in the use and legal implications of the weapon to be carried. Considering the life-or-death potential involved, every effort must be made to prevent any but the most qualified and capable individuals from performing in an armed capacity. Although there is no magic panacea to ensure that a life will not be taken accidentally or unnecessarily, the risks involved demand strict qualifications for registration of armed personnel.

Selected References

1. Brennan, Dennis T. *The Other Police*. Cleveland, Ohio: Governmental Research Institute, 1975.

2. Harrigan, James F., Mary Holbrook Sundance, and Mark L. Webb. "Private Police in California: A Legislative Proposal," *Golden Gate Law Review*.

3. Institute for Local Self Government. *Private Security and the Public Interest*. Berkeley, Calif.: Institute for Local Self Government, 1974.

4. Kakalik, James S., and Sorrel Wildhorn. *Private Police in the United States: Findings and Recommendations,* Vol. I, R–869/DOJ. Washington, D.C.: Government Printing Office, 1972.

5. New Jersey State, P.S. 1968, c. 282 (C.2A: 168A).

6. Strobl, Walter M. "Private Guards Arm Them or Not?" *Security Management,* January 1973.

Related Standards

The following standards and goals may be applicable in implementing Standard 11.3:

1.1   Selection of Qualified Personnel
1.3   Preemployment Screening
1.6   Application of Employment
1.7   Availability of Criminal History Records
1.8   Minimum Preemployment Screening Qualifications
2.1   Training in Private Security
2.4   Training Related to Job Functions
2.5   Preassignment and Basic Training
2.6   Arms Training
2.9   State Authority and Responsibility for Training
3.1   Code of Ethics
3.3   Reporting of Criminal Violations
9.2   Regulatory Board for Private Security
9.4   Regulatory Board Hearing Procedure

Standard 11.4

Permanent Registration Card

So that employers, consumers of security services and the public know that an individual is registered to perform specific security job functions, armed or unarmed, a permanent registration card should be issued and strictly controlled by the regulatory board. This card should not be issued until the applicant has met the minimum qualifications for registration in an armed or unarmed capacity.

Commentary

There are times when persons who come in contact with security workers need to see some form of identification. For example, a person being asked questions by an alleged investigator should be able to ask for some form of official identification. Official proof of identification should also be requested before allowing alarm sales, installation, or service personnel into a home or place of business. A policeman who sees a uniformed guard carrying a gun is justified in asking for identification and authorization to carry a weapon. Finally, an employer should be able to ask a security applicant to show a valid registration card and thereby know the person has met the minimum qualifications of the private security regulatory board, has had a background check, and has been trained to perform the specific job listed on the card. There are many

similar situations in which a registration card would benefit registrants, employers of security personnel, consumers of security services, and the public who may come in contact with security workers.

The registration card should include the registrant's name, signature, and address; the specific security functions the holder is qualified to perform (i.e., guard, investigator, alarm respondent, courier); whether the registrant may be armed; and the expiration date of the card. A recent, full-color picture also should be required on cards for security personnel who enter homes, act as plainclothes investigators, or carry weapons.

Several States also require that the name of the registrant's employer be included on the card. When this is done, however, a person has to refile with each job change. This additional burden is not advantageous; a registrant should be allowed to change jobs without experiencing undue difficulties.

Provisions should be made by the private security regulatory board for controlling registration cards. When a registrant is suspended or registration revoked, the card should be returned immediately to the regulatory board. Strong sanctions, such as strict misdemeanor charge, should be placed on any person who fails to return the card upon notification of suspension or revocation. An individual no longer qualified to perform security functions, for whatever reason, should not be allowed to carry a card that indicates that qualification still exists.

The employer of registered security personnel is not responsible, in any manner, for distribution and control of registrants' cards. An employer should, however, be notified by the regulatory board when a security employee is no longer registered. This procedure would assist employers, who may be held responsible for allowing a nonregistered person to perform a security function.

The official registration card should not be issued until the applicant has completed all of the required training. At the end of a training program, the person certified as responsible for the program should file with the private security regulatory board a list of those persons who successfully completed the training and those who failed. The list should state the specific security functions the individuals have been trained to perform and those individuals who have successfully completed arms training. Once the board is satisfied that an individual has completed the training requirements, met all other qualifications, and received a proper fingerprint check, it can issue an official card allowing the registrant to perform certain security functions within the State.

Selected References

1. Brennan, Dennis T. *The Other Police*. Cleveland, Ohio: Governmental Research Institute, 1975.

2. Institute for Local Self Government. *Private Security and the Public Interest*. Berkeley, Calif.: Institute for Local Self Government, 1974.

3. Kakalik, James S., and Sorrel Wildhorn. *Private Police in the United States: Findings and Recommendations,* Vol. I, R–869/DOJ. Washington, D.C.: Government Printing Office, 1972.

Related Standards

The following standards and goals may be applicable in implementing Standard 11.4:

 2.6   Arms Training
11.1   Registration of Private Security Personnel
11.2   Registration Qualifications
11.3   Qualifications for Armed Security Personnel

Standard 11.5

Temporary Permit

Pending the issuance of the permanent registration card, provision should be made for the issuance of a nonrenewable temporary permit to allow an applicant to perform a specific security job function, in an unarmed capacity only, for a maximum of 30 days. This permit should be issued immediately upon completion of a favorable preliminary check of the applicant with the local law enforcement agency and other available sources.

Commentary

In many States that regulate the private security industry, the processing of applications for licensing or registration can take several months; in several States, this process can take a year or longer. Much of this delay is due to the time required for fingerprint checks by State and Federal officials. Other delays may be caused by insufficient staffs and heavy workloads.

Whatever the reasons for delay, the consequences can create serious problems. Cases have been cited in which an individual with a serious criminal record takes a security job, works for a few months while fingerprints are being checked, then quits before the results of the check are returned to the employer from the regulatory board. In the meantime, the individual takes a security job with a second com-

pany. By the time the information on the serious criminal record becomes available, the first employer is no longer concerned, because the individual has left. Without employer exchanges of information, the second employer may not become aware of the criminal record until after the person has once again quit and moved on to new employment. It is conceivable that an individual following this procedure could hold security positions for several years, even indefinitely, without being officially registered or having a current employer learn of the criminal record. Such a situation presents the potential for grave abuses.

A person of poor character or little competence can do much harm while performing various security functions during an interim period, waiting for approval or denial of registration. For this reason, some security professionals have suggested that no person be allowed to begin performing security functions until all registration qualifications have been met.

Denying any type of temporary permit, however, creates an important problem for applicants. A waiting period seems inevitable before a person can receive a registration card and begin employment. Until the process for obtaining criminal history record information is streamlined, the waiting period may be several months long. Oftentimes those who desire security employment have a need to supplement their incomes, are on a temporary lay-off from their regular positions, or are unemployed. Asking these people to wait for a prolonged period during the registration process may be unfair. Therefore, it has been suggested that temporary cards be issued while registrations are being processed, thus eliminating the prolonged period when applicants are unable to work.

Contract security companies and businesses that use proprietary security organizations also can experience serious problems if they are forced to wait long periods before personnel can begin employment. They are often faced with immediate, short-term demands for increased numbers of private security personnel. These situations may include special sporting events, conventions, natural disasters, riot conditions, shipments of valuable merchandise, large sales, or similar unusual and temporary events. In these instances, finding a sufficient number of unemployed, registered individuals to perform security functions would be generally impossible unless temporary employment or some form of temporary registration is allowed.

On a more permanent basis, a shortage of registered persons may arise that can create a problem for employers trying to maintain a certain security manpower level. James Ellis, former president of the Private Police Association of California, estimated that about 35 percent of guards are part-time workers, and the annual turnover rate is as high as 300 percent. The *RAND Report* (Vol. I) indicated turnover rates as high as 200 percent. The California Institute for Local Self Government's study of California security personnel showed a turnover rate of approximately 80 percent per year. Whether the high or low figure is accepted, the turnover rate in the private security industry is serious. If this high turnover continues, it will be very difficult for employers to find available registered security personnel to meet their manpower needs.

It is not the purpose of this standard to delay or deny entry into security employment to qualified, competent individuals of good character, to unnecessarily complicate the hiring process, or create a shortage of qualified personnel. Therefore, in considering the various problems that can arise because of registration delays, it is recommended that temporary permits should be issued. Such permits would allow applicants for registration to work for 30 days while the regulatory board completes the registration process.

In order to protect consumers and the public and to improve the overall capability of security personnel to help combat crime, some initial screening should take place before a person can begin to work in security, either temporarily or permanently. It is therefore recommended that no person be allowed to begin performing any security function until the private security regulatory board has completed at least a preliminary check of the applicant with the local law enforcement agency and other available sources.

This type of check should include a name check and a local fingerprint check. According to law enforcement officials, this type of local check could be completed in several hours or days. If the applicant has recently moved into the jurisdiction, other sources might be checked—such as former employers, references, or other State regulatory boards with which the applicant may have been registered. It should be the goal of the board to complete the necessary preliminary check and to issue the temporary card within a few days.

The temporary permit being recommended should be nonrenewable. Therefore, a person who wants to continue private security work should begin to meet the training requirements for registration while the regulatory board is conducting its investigation.

Allowing persons to perform security functions before minimum background checks have been completed totally vitiates the purpose of registration. In the time it takes to complete a background check, a security worker can cause much harm. So that employers of security personnel, consumers of security services, and the public can have some assurance of the character of these personnel, no person should be allowed to begin security work until at least a local background check has been completed. There is no guarantee that this would automatically eliminate all personnel problems in the industry. It is, however, a necessary starting point for improving the quality of security personnel and eliminating potential problems.

Selected References

1. Brennan, Dennis T. *The Other Police.* Cleveland, Ohio: Governmental Research Institute, 1975.

2. Harrigan, James F., Mary Holbrook Sundance, and Mark L. Webb. "Private Police in California: A Legislative Proposal," *Golden Gate Law Review.*

3. Institute for Local Self Government. *Private Security and the Public Interest.* Berkeley, Calif.: Institute for Local Self Government, 1974.

4. Kakalik, James S., and Sorrel Wildhorn. *Private Police in the United States: Findings and Recommendations,* Vol. I, R–869/DOJ. Washington, D.C.: Government Printing Office, 1972.

5. Peel, John D. *The Training, Licensing and Guidance of Private Security Officers.* Springfield, Ill.: Charles C. Thomas, 1973.

Standard 11.6

Registration Renewal

Individuals who are registered as armed security personnel should be required to renew their registrations annually. All other registrants should be required to file for renewal of registration every 5 years.

Commentary

Once an individual has met the necessary requirements and been approved for registration as a private security worker, it is conceivable that the regulatory board could have no further contact with that registrant. For registration to be completely effective, methods should be designed to keep the regulatory board informed of the registrant's performance and any changes in his background that might affect ability to perform security functions. One method for increasing contact between the regulatory board and the registrant is to require periodic renewal of registration.

Issuing a registration card that allows a person to carry a weapon while performing security functions is a critical decision that can have a grave impact. Because of the serious consequences that can arise when a person carries a weapon, registration for armed personnel cannot be perpetual. It is therefore recommended that persons who are registered to perform security functions in an armed capacity be required to seek annual renewal.

When an individual seeks this renewal, the regulatory board should determine if the registrant still meets all of the requirements for carrying a weapon. Renewal investigations should be thorough and complete and determine if the armed registrant has completed yearly training and the required range qualification. When administratively feasible, armed registrants seeking renewal should undergo updated fingerprint checks to verify that no unreported criminal actions or convictions have occurred. All of these actions, of course, result in more administrative work, but granting a renewal of permission to carry a weapon is too important to become merely an automatic, revenue-generating device.

There is less need for a yearly renewal of registration for unarmed personnel. Certain safeguards can help the regulatory board maintain some contact with them. One safeguard for the continued evaluation of a registrant's competence is the use of intense field investigations. Investigators also can verify the accuracy of information on file about the registrant and check on any unreported changes.

Another safeguard comes with the complaint procedure. When complaints are received by the regulatory board from anyone—consumers of security services; supervisors, managers, or employers of security personnel; or the public with whom security personnel come in contact—resulting investigations would involve contact between the regulatory board and the registrant. In this context, the board should require employers of registered security personnel to report any complaints about individual registrants, any questionable incidents involving them, or any criminal charges filed against them that the employer is aware of.

It has been pointed out that a yearly renewal system would earn additional funds for the board's operation from the renewal fees. Estimates of the current number of private security personnel range from 300,000 to several million. By requiring the registration of contract and proprietary personnel, the figure could realistically reach a million. According to a survey of 33 States that regulated certain private security personnel, a total of 300,000 personnel were registered in 1975. This figure includes only contract guards and detectives. It does not include proprietary security personnel; contract alarm sales, installation, or service personnel; or armored car and armed courier personnel. Using additional figures from Frost and Sullivan (220,000 proprietary security personnel), the Alarm Industry Committee for Combating Crime (4,000 alarm installers), and the National Armored Car Association (30,000 armored car employees), the figure reaches 554,000. It is not hard to imagine, with the addition of 17 more States, that the number of persons to be registered would easily reach a million. The fees that could be generated from the annual renewal of these members would provide significant funding for the board. However, the administrative burdens of yearly renewal outweigh the monetary benefits. By instituting the safeguards previously outlined,

a 5-year renewal period should reduce paperwork, yet allow for some periodic contact with the unarmed registrants.

Selected Reference

1. Frost and Sullivan, Inc. *The Industrial and Commercial Security Market*. New York: March 1975.

2. Institute for Local Self Government. *Private Security and the Public Interest*. Berkeley, Calif.: ILSF, 1974.

3. Kakalik, James S., and Sorrel Wildhorn. *Private Police in the United States: Findings and Recommendations*, Vol. I, R–869/DOJ. Washington, D.C.: Government Printing Office, 1972.

4. National Armored Car Association. Position paper of the National Armored Car Association presented to the LEAA Private Security Advisory Council, July 8, 1975.

5. Private Security Task Force. "Regulatory Agency Survey." (See Appendix 7 to the report.)

6. ———. "Summary of Private Security Legislation." (See Appendix 6 to this report.)

Related Standards

The following standards and goals may be applicable in implementing Standard 11.6:

1.1 Selection of Qualified Personnel

2.6 Arms Training

9.2 Regulatory Board for Private Security

Standard 11.7

Suspension and Revocation

Registration cards and temporary permits may be suspended or revoked for good cause, after a hearing, when a registrant:

1. Is convicted of a misdemeanor or felony which reflects unfavorably on his fitness to perform a security function;

2. Has been formally charged with a criminal offense the nature of which may make him unable to meet the minimum qualifications of registration;

3. Fires a weapon without justification;

4. Engages in conduct detrimental to the public safety or welfare; or

5. No longer meets the requirements of registration or violates any provisions of the act.

Commentary

As was pointed out in the licensing chapter, regulation should include strong sanctions in order to be effective. The suspension or revocation of a permit to work is one type of sanction that can be very effective. Serious consequences arise when a person cannot continue to perform a particular job function. For example, the individual may be without any income, causing serious personal hardships. The employer may not have a registered person available to replace the suspended or revoked worker, leading to an ineffective security program until a replacement

can be found. Realizing these consequences, a registrant hopefully would take great care not to violate any of the listed restrictions, and, likewise, supervisors would take care not to allow any violations.

To be effective, this standard should be strictly enforced. Without important and valid extenuating circumstances, registration should be quickly suspended or revoked after a hearing if there is sufficient proof that the registrant has committed any of the enumerated acts. Only through strict enforcement can suspension and revocation maintain their validity as useful sanctions and deterrents.

Several factors should be reviewed by the regulatory agency before deciding on revocation or suspension. The agency should first consider to what extent the violation would affect future performance of security functions. This agency also should determine if the action is an isolated incident or one that has occurred repeatedly. In these deliberations, the agency should keep in mind that the purpose of registration is to protect the public. If the action of the regisrant under review does not affect the continued performance of this type of security function, there may be no reason to revoke or suspend registration. If the action has an affect and is not accompanied by extenuating circumstances in the registrant's favor, suspension or revocation should occur.

The incidents listed in this standard as cause for suspension or revocation are matters that can adversely affect the performance of security functions. The frequency of occurrence of these incidents can be controlled by the judicious, yet unsparing, use of the sanctions of license suspension and revocation.

The first listed incident is conviction of a misdemeanor or a felony. The regulatory board should carefully consider the particular misdemeanor or felony, as well as the surrounding circumstances, to determine if the conviction reflects unfavorably on the registrant's ability to perform security functions. Examples of convictions that reflect badly include retail theft, robbery, burglary, larceny, arson, assault, battery, carrying a concealed weapon, and discharging a weapon in public.

It is in the public interest to assist the rehabilitation of convicted offenders by removing restrictions upon their ability to obtain or maintain employment. Gainful employment is vital to any exoffender's chance for returning to a useful and active role in society. But it should be recognized that registered individuals are performing security functions—protecting persons and property. The convicted individual should not be allowed to work in a position that could allow a similar act affecting lives and property.

The regulatory board should also consider suspending registration when an individual is formally charged with a criminal offense that may reflect unfavorably on fitness to perform a security function. Several months may pass between a formal charge and conviction. During that time, the board will want to consider the circumstances of the charge and determine if the incident reflects unfavorably on the registrant's ability to properly perform security functions.

The regulatory board should establish an administrative procedure for learning when a registrant is charged with or convicted of a crime. Employers should be required to inform the board whenever they learn of a formal charge or conviction. A staff member may need to be assigned the task of checking court records. As burdensome as this task might be, some type of procedure needs to be established to learn of such convictions or charges.

The third listed incident that might result in suspension or revocation of registration is the unjustified firing of a weapon. Anytime a firearm is used, it can result in death. Large numbers of security personnel are performing functions in an armed capacity. Forty-nine percent of respondents to the 1970 Rand Corporation survey of private security employees said they were armed. An even larger number, 55 percent, of security personnel answering the 1974 California Local Self Government survey indicated they sometimes carried firearms while on duty. The 1975 Cleveland Administration of Justice Committee study found that 60 percent of the greater Cleveland area security personnel sometimes carried firearms while on duty. With the large number of security personnel carrying firearms, abuses seem inevitable. The California Bureau of Collection and Investigative Services reported that, in October of 1975, it revoked the licenses of 11 persons because of improper use of a weapon. Tragically, two of these incidents resulted in deaths.

For the regulatory board to learn about weapon firings and to evaluate if they were justified require some form of mandatory reporting procedure. An example of a possible procedure can be found in the law enforcement field, where many police department procedural manuals set out specific requirements for reporting any firing of a weapon, intentional or accidental.

Private security personnel who fire a weapon while on duty, either accidentally or intentionally, except on a firing range, should report the circumstances to a supervisor immediately. Within 8 hours, the involved personnel should file a written report with the appropriate employer representative. The employer should then file an investigative report with the private security regulatory board within 36 hours. This report should include a synopsis of the situation, conclusion, and recommended action. Based on this report, the board should take whatever action it considers appropriate—conduct an investigation, hold a hearing, or accept the firing as justified.

To determine if a weapon firing was justified, the regulatory board should carefully consider the surrounding circumstances and facts. However, the board should limit its consideration to what reasonably appeared to be the facts known or perceived by the individual at the time of firing. For example, if a security worker fires a weapon, perceiving that there was personal danger from an armed assailant, the action is justified, even if later testimony proves the assailant's weapon was a starter's pistol. However, if a security worker fires at an individual quickly walking across the plant grounds, firing is not justified, even if it is later proven that the individual fired at had committed, unknown to the security worker, a crime inside the plant. Facts unknown at the time of firing, no matter how compelling, should not be considered.

There are only two specific instances in which it generally can be held that firing a weapon is justified: (1) to protect one's life or the lives of others from imminent peril of death or from what reasonably appears as an immediate threat of great bodily harm, or (2) when reasonably necessary to effect the capture of a person who has committed a felony in the presence of the person firing the weapon. Carrying a weapon is an important responsibility;

firing a weapon is a serious action than can result in death. Any security worker who does not recognize this danger and fires a weapon without justification should not be registered to perform security functions in an armed capacity.

The fourth type of incident that could result in a suspension or revocation of registration, as stated in this standard, is engaging "in conduct detrimental to the public safety or welfare." This is a general statement, a catchall for conduct that does not result in conviction but is serious enough to have an adverse effect upon the performance of· a security function. One example is in the area of alcohol and drug abuse. An individual security worker under the influence of or actually using narcotics or intoxicants while on duty is clearly not properly performing assigned protective duties and is probably jeopardizing public welfare. If this worker were armed, there would be no question concerning the seriousness of the detrimental conduct. Additional examples of the type of actions that might be termed detrimental conduct include abuses of authority, general and constant negligence in the performance of security functions, falsification of facts within an investigative report, and release of confidential information.

The language within this section is general because it would be impossible to list every action that might be classed conduct detrimental to the public peace or welfare, and all varying factors and extenuating circumstances cannot be foreseen. This general terminology, however, is not included in the standard to enable the regulatory board to wield arbitrary power, suspending and revoking registration at will. If that happens, the aggrieved party could have a remedy through the judicial system. This item on detrimental conduct can give the regulatory board th necessary power to protect the public by suspending or revoking registration for a serious action not otherwise delineated in the statute.

The fifth action that could result in a suspension or revocation of registration, as stated in this standard, is that a registrant "no longer meets the requirements of registration or violates any provisions of the act." Individual circumstances will dictate the circumstances that would be considered before invoking this provision. For example, it could be determined that the registrant falsified proof of birth documents at the time of application and was, and is, not at least 18 years of age. Also, a person could become physically incapacitated and not able to perform a specific job function.

Because the enforcement of this standard can result in the loss of a person's privilege to work, due-process requirements should be met. The various actions that may result in registration suspension or revocation should be delinated and enforcement standardized. Administrative procedures should be established to give notice to the registrant of the intent to suspend or revoke his registration and to set up a hearing, if requested, prior to the revocation or suspension.

Within due-process and administrative guidelines, however, the regulatory board should strictly enforce this standard. The incidents enumerated reflect upon an individual's ability to perform security functions. For the protection of all employers of security personnel, consumers of security services, and the public, the registration of any security worker who engages in the conduct listed should be suspended or revoked.

Selected References

1. Brennan, Dennis T. *The Other Police*. Cleveland, Ohio: Governmental Research Institute, 1975.

2. Harrigan, James F., Mary Holbrook Sundance, and Mark L. Webb. "Private Police in California: A Legislative Proposal," *Golden Gate Law Review*.

3. Institute for Local Self Government. *Private Security and the Public Interest*. Berkeley, Calif.: Institute for Local Self Government, 1974.

4. Kakalik, James S., and Sorrel Wildhorn. *Private Police in the United States: Findings and Recommendations,* Vol. I, R–869/DOJ. Washington, D.C.: Government Printing Office, 1972.

5. National Advisory Commission on Criminal Justice Standards and Goals. *Police*. Washington, D.C.: Government Printing Office, 1973.

6. Peel, John D. *The Training, Licensing and Guidance of Private Security Officers*. Springfield, Ill.: Charles C. Thomas, 1973.

Related Standards

The following standards may be applicable in implementing Standard 11.7:

1.3   Preemployment Screening
3.2   Conduct of Private Security Personnel
3.3   Reporting of Criminal Violations
9.2   Regulatory Board for Private Security
9.4   Regulatory Board Hearing Procedure

Standard 11.8

Sanctions

Nonregistered persons who perform a security function requiring registration should be subject to criminal penalties. Any person authorizing or permitting a nonregistered person to perform a security function requiring registration should be subject to criminal penalties.

Commentary

No governmental regulation can be effective without some type of sanction to act as a deterrent. In fact, some courts have defined a law as "that which must be obeyed and followed by citizens, subject to sanctions or legal consequences." Without a penalty or punishment, there generally is no obedience to a law.

The principal sanction of licensing and registration is suspension or revocation. An individual or company licensed to engage in a security service business knows that violation of certain laws, rules, or regulations may result in the loss of the privilege to do business. Likewise, a registrant is aware that certain conduct can result in a withdrawal of the privilege to work in a security position. Actively enforced, these sanctions can act as strong deterrents.

These sanctions, however, do not affect a business that uses a proprietary security organization, administrative personnel within a contract agency who need not be registered, or an individual who fails to register. Without the type of sanction recommended by this standard, it would be very easy for a supervisor or manager, fearing no sanction, to put a nonregistered person in a security position requiring registration or for a nonregistered individual to perform a security function requiring registration.

This standard is worded to include "any person authorizing or permitting." This stipulation includes supervisors, managers, vice presidents, and even presidents. The president who says "That new contract must be filled now, so go out and hire as many temporary people as necessary, whether they are registered or not," is as guilty of authorizing a nonregistered person to perform a security function as is the supervisor who assigns a nonregistered person to a security post without checking on registration.

A stronger sanction should be imposed upon any person who authorizes or permits a person not registered as an armed security worker to perform in an armed capacity. Strong consideration was given to recommending that such action be a felony, but that was decided too severe a penalty. Nonetheless, the criminal penalty should be greater than that for allowing a nonregistered person to perform in an unarmed capacity.

The purpose of registration is to help improve

the overall quality of the security function being performed and, thus, improve crime prevention. Unless there are serious consequences for acting in contravention of the law, the security field will continue to be filled with marginal workers. It is therefore recommended that criminal penalties be imposed upon persons employing nonregistered persons to perform private security services and upon nonregistered persons who perform security functions.

Selected Reference

1. Black, Henry Campbell. *Black's Law Dictionary*. St. Paul, Minn.: West Publishing, 1968.

Related Standards

The following standards may be applicable in implementing Standard 11.8:

3.3   Reporting of Criminal Violations
9.2   Regulatory Board for Private Security

Appendix

Disregard any reference to the Appendix as cited within this text. The Appendix included within the complete Task Force Report has been omitted due to the statistical nature of the material.

Glossary of Terms

Alarm Respondent. A person employed by an organization to respond to an alarm condition at the protected site of a client, to inspect the protected site to determine the nature of the alarm, to protect or secure the client's facility until alarm system integrity can be restored, and to assist law enforcement according to local arrangement. The alarm respondent may be armed and also may be a servicer.

Alarm Sales Personnel. Persons in alarm sales who engage in client contact, presale security surveys, and postsale customer relations. This does not include selling self-installed alarm devices over the counter.

Alarm Systems. (See Part III, introduction to Chapter 4.)

Alarm System Installer. Trained technician who installs and wires alarm systems.

Alarm System Servicer (Repairer). Trained technician who performs scheduled maintenance and provides emergency servicing of alarm systems

Armed Courier Services. Providing or offering to provide armed protection and transportation, from one place or point to another place or point, of money, currency, coins, bullion, securities, bonds, jewelry, or other articles of value. This transportation is provided by means other than specially constructed bullet-resistant armored vehicles.

Armed Personnel. Persons, uniformed or nonuniformed, who carry or use at any time any form of firearm.

Armored Car Services. Providing or offering to provide protection, safekeeping, and secured transportation of money, currency, coins, bullion, securities, bonds, jewelry, or other items of value. This secured transportation, from one place or point to another place or point, is done by means of specially constructed bullet-resistant armored vehicles and vaults under armed guard.

Central Station. A control center to which alarm systems in subscribers' premises are connected, where circuits are supervised, and where personnel are maintained continuously to record and investigate alarm or trouble signals. Facilities are provided for the reporting of alarms to police and fire departments or to other outside agencies.

Central Station Alarm System. An alarm system or group of systems, the activities of which are transmitted to, recorded in, maintained by, and supervised from a central station.

Contractual Security. Security services provided by a private organization on a contractual basis for the protection of assets and personnel belonging to either a private or governmental client.

Couriers. Armed persons assisting in the secured transportation and protection of items of value.

Criminal Arrest Records (Criminal History Records). Information on individuals that is collected, processed, preserved, or disseminated by criminal justice agencies and consists of identifiable descriptions and notations of any arrests, detentions, indictments, informations, or other formal criminal charges regardless of disposition, and formal disposition if such resulted.

Criminal Conviction Records. Information on individuals that is collected, processed, preserved, or disseminated by criminal justice agencies and consists only of identifiable descriptions and notations of arrests, detentions, indictments, informations, or other formal criminal charges that resulted in actual conviction, and any disposition arising therefrom.

Criminal History Record Information. Includes both criminal arrest records and criminal conviction records.

Criminal Justice Information System. The system used for the collection, processing, preservation, or dissemination of information on individuals. This information, collected by criminal justice agencies, includes criminal conviction records and criminal arrest records. The system includes the equipment, facilities, procedures, agreements, and organizations used.

Criminal Justice System (Agencies). Courts and government agencies or subunits thereof performing any of the following activities pursuant to a statute or executive order: detection, apprehension, detention, pretrial release, posttrial release, prosecution, adjudication, correctional supervision, or rehabilitation of accused persons or criminal offenders.

Detection-of-Deception Services. Providing or offering to provide personnel, devices, or instruments to test or question individuals for the purpose of determining the veracity of their responses.

Detective. See Investigator.

Employment Records. Normal business information including employment application, health records, job performance records, and other records maintained on employees.

Felony. A crime of a graver or more atrocious nature than those designated as misdemeanors. The term has no very definite or precise meaning except where it is defined by statute. Under U.S. Criminal Code 335, 18 U.S.C.A. 1, a felony is defined as an offense punishable by death or imprisonment for a term exceeding 1 year.

Firearm. Any pistol, revolver, other handgun, rifle, shotgun, or other such weapon capable of firing a missile.

Guard. Any person who is paid a fee, wage, or salary to perform one or more of the following functions:
- Prevention or detection of intrusion, unauthorized entry or activity, vandalism, or trespass on private property;
- Prevention or detection of theft, loss, embezzlement, misappropriation, or concealment of merchandise, money, bonds, stocks, notes, or other valuable documents or papers;
- Control, regulation, or direction of the flow or movements of the public, whether by vehicle or otherwise, to assure the protection of property;
- Protection of individuals from bodily harm; and
- Enforcement of rules, regulations, and policies related to crime reduction.

Investigator. Any person who is paid a fee, wage, or salary to obtain information with reference to any of the following matters:
- Crime or wrongs done or threatened;
- The identity, habits, conduct, movements, whereabouts, affiliations, associations, transactions, reputation, or character of any person, group of persons, association, organization, society, other group of persons or partnership or corporation;
- Preemployment background check of personnel applicants;
- The conduct, honesty, efficiency, loyalty, or activities of employees, agents, contractors, and subcontractors;
- Incidents and illicit or illegal activities by persons against the employer or employer's property;
- Retail shoplifting;
- Internal theft by employees or other employee crime;
- The truth or falsity of any statement or representation;
- The whereabouts of missing persons;
- The location or recovery of lost or stolen property;
- The causes and origin of or responsibility for fires, libels or slanders, losses, accidents, damage, or injuries to real or personal property;
- The credibility of information, witnesses, or other persons;
- The securing of evidence to be used before investigating committees or boards of award or arbitration or in the trial of civil or criminal cases and the preparation thereof.

Job Functions. Those specific assigned duties or activities for which a person is employed.

Job-Related Tests. Tests designed to measure an individual's capability to perform duties, activities, and functions performed during employment.

Law Enforcement Assistance Administration (LEAA). An agency of the U.S. Department of Justice. Administers funds under the Omnibus Crime Control and Safe Streets Act of 1968, as amended.

Law Enforcement Liaison Officer. A law enforcement officer whose assigned duty is to serve as an agent between law enforcement agencies and the private security industry for fostering cooperating actions and providing referral capability for all private security requests.

Licensing. The act of requiring permission from a competent authority to carry on the business of providing security services on a contractual basis.

Local Alarm System. An alarm system that when activated produces an audible or visual signal in the immediate vicinity of the protected premises or object.

Manager/Administrator. Any person responsible for policy and procedural decisions relating to the operation of an organization.

Misdemeanor. A crime of a lesser degree than a felony. Although defined by statute in each State, a misdemeanor is most often punishable by fine or imprisonment of less than 1 year and in a place other than a penitentiary.

Operational. The duties, activities, and functions performed that lead to the accomplishment of a mission. Commonly referred to as line activities rather than staff activities.

Part-Time Employee. Any person who is employed fewer than 40 hours per week.

Principal. Any person who is an officer, director, partner, or shareholder owning a 10 percent or greater interest.

Private Security. Self-employed individuals and privately funded business entities and organizations who provide security-related services to a restricted clientele group for a fee, for the individual or entity that retains or employs them, or for themselves in order to protect their persons, private property, or interests from varied hazards.

Private Security Personnel. Individuals who are paid a wage or salary to perform the functions of a guard or watchman, detective or investigator, courier, or alarm system installer, repairer, or respondent. Includes both contractual and proprietary employees.

Professional Association. A group composed of individuals with similar occupations and organized for the purposes of furthering the goals and objectives of the occupation.

Proprietary Alarm System. An alarm system that is similar to a central station alarm system except that the annunciator (see Part III, introduction to Chapter 4) is located in a constantly manned guard room maintained by the owner for his own internal security operations. The guards monitor and respond to all alarm signals and/or alert local law enforcement agencies.

Proprietary Security. The method instituted, equipment owned, personnel employed by a private entity for the exclusive protection of its assets and personnel.

Qualifying Agent. An individual named by a license applicant, who engages in the everyday affairs of the applicant's security services business and who participates in the managerial decisionmaking process of the applicant. This individual must also meet certain statutory requirements.

Registration. The act of requiring permission from a State authority before being employed as an investigator or detective, guard or watchman, courier, alarm system installer or repairer, or alarm respondent.

Resident Manager. Any person responsible for policy and procedural decisions relating to the operation of an office of a security services business.

Secondary Employment. Work or a job that provides a supplemental income to the main income derived from the individual's primary employment. Also referred to in this report as moonlighting.

Security Services. Those means, including guards or watchmen, detectives or investigators, couriers, and alarm system installers, repairers, or respondents, that are provided on a contractual basis to deter, detect, and prevent criminal activities.

Security Services Business. An entity that provides or offers to provide security services on a contractual basis.

Supervisor. A person who directs or inspects the work performance of others and is primarily responsible for carrying out policies and procedures developed by managers and administrators.

Uniformed Personnel. Persons who wear distinctive attire that is intended to identify the wearer as a member of a specific group, as one who performs a specific function, and/or as one who holds special authority within an organization.

Watchman. See Guard.

Discussion Questions

SECTION 1
WHAT IS PRIVATE SECURITY?

1. There are many definitions and explanations of private security. Prior to reading the Report, how did your own definition differ from the Task Force's composite definition?

2. Would it be useful to study and examine the definitions of private security in order to develop improved utilization of this crime-fighting resource? Explain.

3. Describe the interaction between the missions of public law enforcement and private security.

4. Outline the services provided by private security as they apply to information, personnel and physical facilities.

5. What measures might be explored to provide security for individuals and businesses utilizing the "self-help" concept?

6. Identify four major methods of providing security services to the public and the businessman. What are examples of the application of each of these services?

7. Should special police, such as the railroad police, be included within the basic concept of private security? Explain.

8. Based on the Task Force's Standards and Goals, what are the criteria used to determine whether an individual with special police powers is a private security officer?

9. Discuss the areas in which the Report indicates that no distinction should be made regarding standards and goals.

10. How can a clear understanding of the private security sector's constituency and purposes increase the industry's effectiveness in the reduction and prevention of crime?

SECTION 2
DEVELOPMENT OF STANDARDS AND GOALS FOR PRIVATE SECURITY

1. Why has the increase in crime and the public's fear of becoming crime victims necessitated the development of security goals and standards?

2. Describe the "vicious circle" that results in ineffective security. Explain why standards can exert a positive impact upon this self-supporting problem cycle.

3. What role has the federal government played in upgrading and improving private security's effectiveness as a crime prevention agent?

4. What were the four important issues examined by the Private Security Task Force early in its work? What resolution was reached in each area?

5. Explain the approach utilized by the Task Force in developing consensus goals and standards.

6. Explore the limitations that circumscribed the parameters of the Task Force's work.

SECTION 3
THE ROLE OF PRIVATE SECURITY IN CRIME PREVENTION AND THE CRIMINAL JUSTICE SYSTEM

1. Outline supporting arguments for the improvement of private security as a crime prevention tool *vis a vis* total reliance on public law enforcement agencies.

2. Various barriers prevent effective interaction between public law enforcement and private security. List these barriers and explain why they exist.

3. How do restrictions on criminal justice infor-

mation dissemination hamper private security's optimum impact on crime?

SECTION 4
DEFINITIONS AND FUNCTIONAL DESCRIPTIONS OF PRIVATE SECURITY COMPONENTS COVERED IN THE REPORT

1. Name the four major components of the private security industry. Outline their basic organizations, operations and duties.

2. Which private security industry practitioners were not the subject of major Task Force scrutiny? Does the elimination of these components suggest that their function is not necessary to the basic purposes of private security? Explain.

SECTION 5
SUMMARY OF RESEARCH IN PRIVATE SECURITY

1. Give specific examples of private security research which have been conducted on local, state, regional, national and international levels.

2. What were four major research projects conducted by the Task Force and its staff?

3. Identify two products of the Private Security Advisory Council which were used by the Task Force as research documents.

SECTION 6
THE HISTORY AND DEVELOPMENT OF PRIVATE SECURITY IN THE UNITED STATES

1. Describe the Anglo-Saxon practices that influenced the early development of private security.

2. Discuss the various conditions which transformed the early colonial watchmen into fulltime, paid city police officers.

3. Identify the contributions that Allan Pinkerton, Edwin Holmes and Perry Brink made to the field of private security.

4. The railroads and the union movement each played a role in relation to private security. If private security had not existed, give your own theory of how the nation would have developed in these two vital areas.

5. What was the effect of the two World Wars on the development of private security in the United States?

6. How did the growth of federal, state and local investigation agencies change the nature of private security?

7. Describe the effect of recent technological change on the composition of the private security industry.

8. Briefly outline the significant features of growth and major trends in private security since 1850.

9. What is the breakdown by category and percentage of the major markets for private security products and services?

SECTION 7
UNIQUE SECURITY PROBLEMS OF SPECIALIZED AREAS

1. Describe the security services and security problems in each of the following areas:

   a. Airports

   b. Airlines

   c. Office buildings

   d. Shopping centers

   e. Elementary and secondary schools

   f. Colleges and universities

   g. Financial institutions

   h. Health care facilities

   i. Hotels and motels

   j. Private and public housing

   k. Manufacturing

   l. Museums

   m. Libraries

   n. Railroads

   o. Retail establishments

   p. Special events

   q. Cargo movement

   r. Mass transit systems

CHAPTER 1
SELECTION OF PERSONNEL

Introduction

1. The standards and goals in this Chapter are aimed at the employer of security personnel. Do you believe these standards meet the minimum, medium or maximum criteria for adoption by the security field?

2. List and explain various reasons why Selection of Personnel is one of the most important Chapters in the Report.

Goal 1.1
Selection of Qualified Personnel

1. What indicators are needed to identify individuals who should be hired by private security? What actions should be taken by private security administrators until the indicators are developed?

2. Explain how the lack of opportunity for career growth limits the attractiveness of the security field to job seekers.

Goal 1.2
Commensurate Salaries

1. What approach would you suggest for the determination of realistic salary levels for the security industry?

2. Where does the fault lie for substandard security industry salaries? What measures could be taken to overcome this problem?

Standard 1.3
Preemployment Screening

1. What are the civil rights implications inherent in detailed and exhaustive preemployment screening activities on prospective security personnel?

2. What is your personal position as to how much preemployment screening should be conducted regarding prospective security personnel? Explain.

3. Does the honesty test seem to be a fair requirement to demand of a prospective security employee? Explain.

Standard 1.4
Employer Exchange of Information

1. Can safeguards be set for employer exchange of information on security personnel which will not violate individual rights? Explain your answer.

2. Of the twelve items cited in the Report as relevant for information exchange on security personnel, explain which ones you believe are necessary, those you feel are unnecessary and those which seem to you as a violation of individual rights.

Standard 1.5
Equal Employment Opportunity

1. Have existing studies shown that private security is an equal opportunity employment industry? Explain.

2. Discuss what facts can be derived from the breakdown of age percentages identified in the New Orleans and St. Louis security surveys.

Standard 1.6
Application for Employment

1. Explain why you would use all, part or none of the thirteen items listed in the Report as recommended for a security employment form.

2. Four additional documents are recommended in this Standard to accompany the application. From your own point of view, discuss the desirability or undesirability of including these documents with the application form.

3. What advantages may be gained by obtaining a fingerprint card from prospective security applicants?

Standard 1.7
Availability of Criminal History Records

1. Identify the changes in the requirements established by the federal government dealing with the dissemination of criminal history information to private security agencies:
   a. Prior to publication of the February 14, 1975 rules.
   b. Following the publication of the May 20, 1975 rules.
   c. Following the publication of the March 19, 1976 rules.
   d. After December 31, 1977.

2. What are the major arguments favoring and opposing the release of criminal history information to private security?

Standard 1.8
Minimum Preemployment Screening Qualifications

1. Discuss the two categories of educational requirements recommended in this Standard and explain their mutual exclusivity.

2. Give your opinion on whether you support or oppose the National Advisory Committee on Criminal Justice Standards and Goals position on educational requirements.

3. Identify the supporting arguments for the minimum age prescreening requirement.

CHAPTER 2
PERSONNEL TRAINING
Introduction

1. Untrained guards are thought to be a product of marketplace budget limitations. What actions would you propose to produce appropriate guard training?

2. Even if adequate preemployment screening were instituted by the security industry, discuss why effective training would remain a critical security need.

Goal 2.1
Training in Private Security

1. Identify the points cited in the Report in support of effective guard training.

2. What information about security training has been learned from the studies conducted by the Task Force?

Goal 2.2
Professional Certification Programs

1. Certification has been described by its opponents as a technique maintained by the "possessors of the keys" to perpetuate their positions. Do you favor professional certification for security officers? Are there viable alternatives to professional certification in the security field?

2. Discuss actions which might be taken to overcome what the Report cites as the most difficult problem in developing certification programs.

3. If the American Society for Industrial Security operates a professional certification program, what is the likely response of the counterpart professional associations in the armored car, investigations and alarm fields? How would you recommend resolving this problem?

Standard 2.3
Job Descriptions

1. What is a job description?

2. Cite examples of how appropriate job descriptions in private security would be helpful to employers, employees and training officers.

Standard 2.4
Training Related to Job Functions

1. What actions would you recommend to test the validity of various security training programs?

Standard 2.5
Preassignment and Basic Training

1. Do you agree with the universal preassignment and basic training requirements recommended in this Standard? Explain your answer.

2. Give reasons why the Standard recommended for sworn police officers by the National Advisory Commission on Criminal Justice Standards and Goals (1973) would not be appropriate for application to current security personnel.

3. What major conclusions could be drawn from the data presented in Table 2.2 dealing with Current Private Security Guard Training Programs?

4. Explain the reasons that could be proposed in support of and in opposition to the use of a "grandfather clause" in private security training.

Standard 2.6
Arms Training

1. List five reasons why security guards should receive firearms training before being given weapons.

2. Do you believe that the firearms training program outlined in this Standard will adequately equip an armed security guard to deal with actual shoot-out situations? Explain.

3. What items should appear on a firearms policy form? What is the usefulness of such a form?

Standard 2.7
Ongoing Training

1. List six reasons found in the Report that support the practice of ongoing security training.

2. Describe the differences between ongoing training and inservice training. Explain why only one of these two training forms would be appropriate for security personnel.

Standard 2.8
Training of Supervisors and Managers

1. Should formal education ever be accepted in place of effective job-related training for supervisory and managerial employees? Explain.

2. Can qualities such as patience, wisdom, virtue, empathy, kindness, trust, knowledge and self-control be developed, or in some cases originated, through training?

3. What research is needed at this time in relation to supervisory and managerial training?

Standard 2.9
State Authority and Responsibility
for Training

1. In your opinion, should private security training be the same as the training required for public law enforcement officers? Explain your position.

2. What action have many states taken regarding public law enforcement officer training? Can there be a similar action taken by the states regarding private security training? Explain.

3. What is the probable three-fold effect of states setting specific standards to provide cost-effective training for private security personnel?

Standard 2.10
State Boards to Coordinate Training Efforts

1. Discuss the apparent conflict between Standards 2.9 and 2.10.

2. Explain the tri-level "Administration — Coordination — Delivery" approach to security training proposed in the Report.

3. A newly-hired employee states he has successfully completed a state-accredited college security program. What risks would an employer take in assigning this employee to a security job without training or testing?

CHAPTER 3
CONDUCT AND ETHICS
Introduction

1. Is it a valid analogy to compare the security and medical fields in matters of ethics? Explain.

2. How would the promotion of a "climate of professionalism" serve to reduce the security industry's turnover rate?

3. Security personnel are not bound by the Miranda and Escobedo decisions of the United States Supreme Court. Discuss whether it would be in the best interest of this country for private security to voluntarily adopt the requirements established by these court rulings.

4. Outline four reasons why a good records system can be effectively used by private security to deter crime.

Goal 3.1
Code of Ethics

1. Give five reasons why a Code of Ethics is essential for private security practitioners.

2. Does the first provision of the model Code of Ethics for Private Security Employees bind security personnel to the protection of the general welfare and the common good? Explain.

3. Describe measures which could be employed to enforce a private security ethics code.

Standard 3.2
Conduct of Private Security Personnel

1. Under what conditions would security personnel be controlled by the guidelines of the Miranda case?

2. In what areas of private security operations is research and consensus needed in order to develop generally recognized guidelines for conducting activities, investigations, interviews and functions?

Standard 3.3
Reporting of Criminal Violations

1. Identify three reports containing comments concerning private security's reporting of criminal violations to the police.

2. All felonies and serious misdemeanors discovered by private security personnel should be reported to the police. Explain why you agree or disagree with this Standard.

3. Explain why only certain criminal actions known by private security should be reported to the police.

Standard 3.4
Employer Responsibilities

1. Is there a safety advantage for private security personnel to carry dummy or unloaded weapons rather than genuine, loaded firearms? Explain.

2. Identify items, assistance and equipment that employers should provide for their security personnel. Explain why providing these items would result in more efficient performance of assigned duties.

Standard 3.5
Maintaining Data on Criminal Activities

1. What advantages can be gained by maintaining accurate records of criminal activities within a business?

2. Cite three examples of how proper criminal incident recording and statistical information could be useful to private security.

CHAPTER 4
ALARM SYSTEMS

Introduction

1. Identify the three fundamental parts of a modern intrusion detection system and explain the function of each.

2. Identify and explain the four basic systems of alarm annunciation.

3. Describe the three basic causes of false alarms.

4. What are the major problems caused by false alarms?

5. What actions should be taken by alarm system

manufacturers to increase the reliability and effectiveness of alarm systems?

Standard 4.1
Alarm Systems Research

1. Alarm systems date back to 390 B.C. Why is major research still needed in this field? Explain.

2. Should a research center devoted to the study of alarm systems be established? Discuss.

3. Identify several of the new techniques currently being tested in the alarm systems field.

Standard 4.2
Backup Power for Alarms

1. What types and amounts of backup power should alarm systems have?

2. Power outages and power reductions have a negative impact on alarm systems. Discuss some of the problems related to these conditions.

Standard 4.3
Certified Training of Alarm Sales and Service Personnel

1. In view of the personnel turnover in alarm systems sales and service, what practical approaches would you recommend for improved training of these individuals?

2. The high turnover of alarm sales personnel and the inappropriateness of some alarm systems lessens the crime prevention impact of alarm systems. What regulations would you recommend to resolve these two problems?

3. Outline four basic arguments in favor of establishing a certified training program for alarm company sales, installation and service personnel.

Standard 4.4
Compatibility of Sensors

1. List five types of non-contact alarm sensor units.

2. What type of alarm sensor is not recommended for installations that have:

   a. Structural member flexure

   b. Intermittent power switching

c. Random heat sources

d. Small animals in the area

e. Hot and cold air currents

3. What is the single most critical problem associated with sensor alarm systems?

4. In the commentary to this Standard, what is the meaning of F.C. Heckman's quote on sensor alarm installation?

Standard 4.5
Training and Instruction of Alarm Users by Alarm Companies

1. Who should bear the responsibility of instructing and training users of alarm systems? Why?

2. In view of the statistics cited on the major cause of false alarms, what action would you recommend to solve this problem?

3. There is a high attrition rate among users trained in the operation of alarm systems. How does this affect the problem of false alarms? Explain.

Standard 4.6
Joint Cooperation to Reduce Alarm System Costs

1. Some persons have suggested that alarm system costs could be reduced through lower line rates from the telephone companies and assistance from the Law Enforcement Assistance Administration. Explain your position on this issue.

2. If the telephone companies need higher rates to meet today's rising costs and alarm companies need lower line charges to remain in business, what recommendations would you propose to resolve this dilemma?

Standard 4.7
Special Trunklines Into Law Enforcement Facilities and Automatic Dialers

1. Contrast the problems caused by false alarms from home dialer systems with their potential for increasing crime prevention with widespread use.

2. Some police departments oppose automatic dialer alarm systems because of repeated false alarms. Do you believe that they take similar positions on other types of citizen calls that are false alarms? Explain the differences between these two categories of alarm messages and suggest a practical solution.

Standard 4.8
Annual Alarm Inspection

1. What are the arguments for and against mandated annual alarm system inspections?

2. Few cities in the United States require annual inspections of residence and business alarm systems. Why do you think mandated annual alarm system inspections are not required more often?

3. What actions could be taken to encourage the adoption of an ordinance mandating annual alarm system inspections in your community?

Standard 4.9
Alarm Systems Servicing Capability

1. Disclosure laws regarding service capabilities for new alarm systems are thought by some critics to favor the large, well-equipped alarm companies over the small companies. What is your position on this Standard?

2. Who should bear the financial burden of maintaining alarm system servicing: the purchaser, the manufacturer, the sales company, the community? Explain your choice.

Standard 4.10
Alarm User Permit Systems and the False Alarm Problem

1. What technique has been proven to be the most effective in reducing false alarms?

2. How should false alarms be counted?

   a. Number of false alarms vs. number of hours a given system is in operation.

   b. Number of false alarms for a given system.

   c. Number of false alarms in which there was no criminal intrusion.

   Give reasons for your selection.

3. Explain the concept of "Alarm User Permit." Give reasons why you believe it is a desirable or undesirable crime prevention device.

4. What are the techniques for enforcement of "Alarm User Permits"? Which approach do

you favor and why?

5. Describe the experience of two communities which have adopted and implemented the user permit system.

Standard 4.11
Ownership and Operation of Alarm Systems

1. This Standard is one of two in the Report in which the National Advisory Committee favored a variation from the position adopted by the Task Force. What is the basic difference between the Task Force and the National Committee positions? Give reasons supporting the position which you favor.

2. Describe the Atlanta, Louisville and Cedar Rapids experiences relating to government involvement in the alarm system field.

CHAPTER 5
ENVIRONMENTAL SECURITY

Introduction

1. Why have researchers turned to environmental security in their quest for effective crime prevention approaches? Explain.

2. Describe in detail the CPTED concept.

3. Outline three examples of environmental security experiments.

4. Is there any practical way in which the fragmented private security industry can become meaningfully and responsibly involved in CPTED? Explain.

5. Do you believe that CPTED will ultimately be found to have the same impact on crime prevention as more traditional approaches? Explain.

Standard 5.1
Improvement of Door and Window Security

1. In the Environmental Security section of the Report, why does the Standard on door and window security appear first?

2. Discuss the Texas Municipal League and Oakland Security Code experiences regarding door and window security.

3. List the basic minimums for door and window security.

Standard 5.2
Adequate Security Lighting

1. In view of the problems associated with the energy crisis, how can a reasoned compromise be achieved between the need for adequate security lighting and reduced energy consumption?

2. Who is responsible for maintaining sufficient outside lighting for the deterrence of crime? Explain your position.

3. What is the implication of the Fancil v. Q.S.E. Food, Inc. decision on private security personnel?

Standard 5.3
Computer Security

1. Computers were singled out for special mention in the Report. Explain why an entire Standard was devoted to this piece of equipment.

2. Do you believe that computer crime problems are over emphasized? Explain your answer.

3. Which is more critical: computer site security or computer program security? Explain your answer.

Standard 5.4
Crime Prevention in Design

1. It may be assumed that architects have always given thought to crime prevention in the design of businesses and residences. What additional action appears to be necessary in this field?

2. How can the CPTED concept be interrelated with the activities and operations of architects and builders?

Standard 5.5
Development of Environmental Security Expertise

1. CPTED is one of security's newest acronyms. How can security companies respond to this concept?

Standard 5.6
Environmental Security in Comprehensive Planning

1. If Neolithic settlements in Turkey included crime prevention in their community design, what new concepts can environmental security

in comprehensive planning offer to the present construction field?

2. When employing the environmental security concept, what major actions/inputs should occur at the three basic stages of design and construction?

3. For optimum benefits, design security should be coupled with a well-trained security force and security-minded occupants. When these three components are present, what are the likely results?

Standard 5.7
Crime Prevention Courses in Schools of Architecture and Urban Planning

1. What has been the history of the relationship between the fields of architecture and urban planning to security services? What are reasons for this situation?

2. List six subjects/topics that should be covered in security courses for architects and urban planners.

3. Describe the probable effect of including programs in crime prevention in curriculums for architects and urban planners.

Standard 5.8
Inclusion of Crime Prevention Measures in Existing Codes and the Consideration of Building Security Codes

1. How do you explain the prevalence of building codes containing fire prevention and control provisions and the scarcity of any city, county or state codes dealing with crime prevention?

2. Incorporating security provisions into existing state and local codes raises serious concerns. Explain.

3. If security provisions were added to state and local building codes, would there be a reduction of crime? Explain.

4. Discuss the review body proposed in the commentary to this Standard in terms of its formation, membership and function.

Standard 5.9
Crime Impact Forecast

1. Why is this Standard one of the most important proposals listed in the Report?

2. What projections should be included in a Crime Impact Forecast?

Standard 5.10
Crime Prevention Courses as a Job Recruitment

1. This Standard does not mandate that architects and urban planners take crime prevention courses. Do you favor compulsory or voluntary courses in this area? Explain.

2. What should such courses contain?

CHAPTER 6
LAW ENFORCEMENT AGENCIES
Introduction

1. Explain Professor Louis Radelet's statement that "the police alone are futile in prevention of crime . . ."

2. This Standard contains the findings of various studies and research projects dealing with the relationships between public law enforcement and private security. Outline the findings and discuss whether similar conditions exist in your community.

3. Private security personnel prevent crime, intercept lawbreakers and protect the lives and assets of their employers. How can they perform these tasks and not be thought of as police? How can they command respect if they do not have a quasi-military uniform? Discuss these problems in terms of the Reports' recommendations.

4. What possible dangers could result from a close relationship between private security and the public police? What measures could be taken to prevent these excesses?

Goal 6.1
Interaction Policies

1. An old law enforcement axiom states, "In the absence of formal policy, every patrolman becomes a chief." Describe the need for formalized policies covering effective interaction between private security and public law enforcement.

2. In Table 6.1, what explanation would you give for the similarity of findings in the 1972 Rand Study and the 1974 Institute for Local Self

Government Study. How do these findings compare with the information presented in the 1975 ASIS survey?

3. How will improved guidelines for private security crime reporting assist in crime prevention?

4. You are a security director working together with the local police chief. What would be the first three policy guidelines for private security/public law enforcement relationships that you would try to develop?

Standard 6.2
Survey and Liaison with Private Security

1. Name the major benefits to be derived from a regular liaison between private security and public law enforcement operating in the same community.

2. What type of police officer would be most suitable for liaison with private security agencies?

3. Would a liaison between police and private security be as meaningful in large metropolitan areas as in small communities? Explain your answer.

Standard 6.3
Policies and Procedures

1. Three major areas of policies and procedures are listed in this Standard as being necessary if police and private security are to work effectively within the same jurisdiction. Explain the advantages of each.

2. Give one example from each of the three reports listed in the commentary of this Standard regarding the need for improved/increased policies and procedures between police and private security.

3. Duplication of services by police and private security is viewed by some as a positive and by others as a negative. What is your position on this issue? Give reasons to support your stand.

4. Describe the roles that administrative, supervisory and operational personnel can play in implementing procedures for police and private security relationships.

Standard 6.4
Multilevel Law Enforcement Training in Private Security

1. Identify the four levels of security training programs recommended for police. Explain the advantages of these programs.

2. Given the multiplicity of subjects a police recruit must master to become a professional law enforcement officer, do you believe private security training can justifiably be added to the recruit curriculum? Explain your answer.

3. Under what conditions should private security personnel become directly involved in police training programs?

Standard 6.5
Mistaken Identity of Private Security Personnel

1. The similarity of some private security uniforms and police uniforms can be confusing. Describe in detail the type of uniform and accessories you would recommend for a private security officer.

2. Some private security companies uniform their personnel to look like policemen. Should regulations be adopted to end this practice?

3. Regulations designed to prevent private security uniforms from being similar to those worn by police may actually restrain trade and work economic hardship on small private companies. What suggestion(s) would you propose to resolve this problem?

Standard 6.6
State Regulation of Private Security Uniforms, Equipment, and Job Titles

1. Do you favor state or local control over private security uniforms and equipment? Explain your answer.

2. Discuss the findings and recommendations of the studies dealing with private security uniforms.

3. Is the cloth badge, as a replacement for metal badges, a solution to the private security vs. police identity problem?

4. If private security gave up all rank and titles similar to police, what recommendations would you make for suitable replacement designations?

Standard 6.7
Law Enforcement Personnel Secondary Employment

1. While police may complain of security guards who look and/or act like public law enforcement officers, security companies point out that sworn police sometimes "moonlight" as security guards while wearing their full police uniform. Do you favor this practice? Explain your answer.

2. What major problems are inherent in public law enforcement officers "moonlighting" as private security personnel?

3. When a "moonlighting" public law enforcement officer arrests a shoplifter in the store where he is employed as a guard, who has the liability for his actions: the store owner or the local police department?

4. A sworn police officer, "moonlighting" as a night watchman in a factory, looks out a window and sees an old man a half-block away being assaulted by two thugs. What should the officer do? Answer from the perspective of the old man, the factory owner, the officer's chief and a local taxpayer.

Standard 6.8
Law Enforcement Officer Employment as a Private Security Principal or Manager

1. Do owners of contract private security companies have the right to prevent a police officer from owning or managing a security company? Explain your answer.

2. What are the major objections to sworn police officers owning or managing a private security company?

3. Could a sworn police officer own and operate a security company under conditions acceptable to his department and other private security company owners? Explain.

Standard 6.9
Private Investigatory Work

1. Secondary employment situations involving investigatory work, create the greatest problems for a sworn police officers engaged in security work. Why?

2. How can a private citizen's individual rights be safeguarded against the actions of a sworn police officer covertly working as a private investigator?

3. What steps should be taken by police to cope with this problem?

CHAPTER 7
CONSUMERS OF SECURITY SERVICES
Introduction

1. What role can an individual citizen play in crime prevention?

2. What role can consumers of private security goods and services play in crime prevention?

3. Who should stimulate consumer responsibility in the selection and acquisition of private security goods and services: consumer, government, purveyors, professional security organizations? Explain your answer.

Goal 7.1
Consumer Responsibility for Selection of Security Services

1. What programs and activities would you recommend to educate consumers about the purchase of security goods and services?

2. List four factors that should be considered by the consumer when purchasing guard services, protective devices and alarm systems.

3. Your next door neighbor is considering the installation of an alarm system in his home. What recommendations would you make to him as to what his criteria and concerns should be? What resources would you suggest?

4. List six criticisms that have been leveled at contract security companies and their personnel.

5. As the owner of a small business, you are in need of security guards. Would you select a contract or proprietary force? Explain your answer.

6. Let's assume you have decided to hire a contract guard force. Develop a checklist for your plant superintendent to follow in selecting the appropriate security guard company. What would you want included in the contract for service?

Standard 7.2
Consumer Assistance Committees

1. Do you believe private security professional

associations and organizations are the best groups to develop guidelines for the evaluation and acquisition of security goods and services? Explain your answer.

2. How could a security consumer assistance committee develop meaningful and continuing communication with consumers of security goods and services?

3. Why have many professional security associations not yet developed appropriate consumer assistance committees?

Standard 7.3
Development of Expertise by Private and Governmental Consumer Agencies

1. Your neighbor complains to you that he has been "taken" by a purveyor of security goods and services. What suggestions and recommendations would you make to help him resolve his problem?

2. If consumer protection agencies and better business associations develop the necessary security data, what measures should they use to alert potential security consumers to available information and assistance? How could these agencies help consumers utilize their security information services?

Standard 7.4
Private Security Advertising Standards

1. Check the "yellow pages" of your local phone directory and cite examples of abuses of this Standard.

2. Do you believe that a security company's advertising should be subjected to honesty requirements? Should these requirements be more strict than those controlling other businesses such as exterminators, electricians, pharmaceutical companies? Give arguments supporting your answer.

3. Is it wrong for security advertisements to include pictures or copy stressing the menace and danger of crime?

4. Again using the classified section of your local phonebook, list examples of security and investigative companies whose names suggest involvement with some unit of government.

CHAPTER 8
HIGHER EDUCATION AND RESEARCH
Introduction

1. What recent national experience could be adopted as a model for private security education?

2. In your opinion, why have private security's educational and research programs not yet reached a level equal to the importance of private security in today's society?

Standard 8.1
State Review of Private Security Task Force Report

1. What role could you play in bringing about the consideration and adoption by your state of the recommendations contained in this Standard?

2. In what ways could state planning agencies be more meaningful and appropriate than a national private security task force?

3. In order to achieve a balance of viewpoints for task force membership, representatives of what groups should be selected? Explain the reasons supporting your selections.

Standard 8.2
National Private Security Resource and Research Institute

1. Compare the need for criminal justice research of ten years ago with that of private security today.

2. If the Law Enforcement Assistance Administration of the U.S. Justice Department reduces its role in the field of research and funding, what alternate sources would you recommend for private security research?

3. From the fifteen potential private security research areas listed, select the three you feel are most urgently needed. Give reasons supporting your selections.

4. What could be accomplished by creating a national private security research and resource institute?

Standard 8.3
Noncredit and Credit Seminars and Courses

1. What role should the following groups take in response to training and educational needs in the private security field?

    a. Educational institutions
    b. The American Society for Industrial Security

2. What could be done to encourage private security guards and their supervisors to take courses such as those listed in this Standard?

Standard 8.4
Degree Programs for Private Security

1. Outline the current status of private security degree programs and courses offered by U.S. colleges.

2. Do you believe the "Suggested Curriculum for Associate Programs" presented in Table 8.2 is appropriate or inappropriate for its intended objectives?

3. Identify and give supporting reasons for the program you believe to be most urgently needed in private security education:

    a. Courses and seminars
    b. Associate degree
    c. Bachelor degree
    d. Graduate degree

4. What roles should the Law Enforcement Assistance Administration and the private security industry play in implementing this Standard?

CHAPTER 9
REGULATORY BOARD

Introduction

1. Do you believe that government involvement in the regulation of private security is appropriate and desirable? Explain your answer.

2. Identify and discuss two major objectives of private security regulation.

3. List the main responsibilities and objectives of a government regulatory board.

Standard 9.1
State Regulation

1. Explain why a state-level private security regulatory board is more desirable than local control.

2. Outline the benefits that would result from reciprocity and uniformity of state private security regulatory boards.

Standard 9.2
Regulatory Board for Private Security

1. List the state agencies that currently regulate private security.

2. Do you favor or oppose having private security regulatory activity as a separate unit of state government?

3. Most private security regulatory agencies do not have sufficient numbers of adequately trained personnel. Why does this condition exist and what will resolve the problem?

Standard 9.3
State Regulatory Board Membership

1. In addition to the approach recommended in this Standard, it has also been suggested that private security regulatory board membership be composed of a small group of laymen. Others have suggested the board be limited to private security practitioners. Still others have favored an all-police board. Which approach do you support? Explain your answer.

2. Would you recommend the elimination of any of the six general areas of representation suggested for board membership in the commentary accompanying this Standard? Defend your position.

3. Would a regulatory board composed of (1) a police official who "moonlighted" as a private security employee, (2) a citizen whose home was protected by a leased central station burglar alarm system, and (3) a company security director who had a guard force composed of both contractor and proprietary security officers, be adequate to meet the intent of this Standard? Explain your answer.

Standard 9.4
Regulatory Board Hearing Procedure

1. What conditions and procedures do you think

would provide a fair and just hearing for a security officer charged by a state regulatory board with an impropriety?

2. What procedures should be established and what actions should be taken to insure that improper acts committed by security officers or security companies are brought to the attention of the state regulatory board?

3. When a state regulatory board discovers that a security company has committed an improper act, what steps should follow to bring the matter to a just conclusion?

Standard 9.5
Regulatory Board Funding

1. Explain the meaning of "nonconfiscatory license" and "registration fees."

2. In your judgment, would it be more desirable to use general state revenue funds or license and registration fees to provide for the administration and operation of state regulatory boards? Give reasons supporting your position.

Standard 9.6
Regulatory Board Access to Criminal Record Information

1. Discuss the necessity for a private security company and the state regulatory board to have access to criminal history record information on applicants for registration (See Standard 1.7).

2. The reports of the Privacy Protection Study Commission recommend controls over information access. Many others support the concept of reduced access to information about individuals. Give reasons in favor of the view allowing increased access by state regulatory boards to criminal history information on applicants for security licenses and registration.

3. What actions could be taken by state regulatory boards and state legislatures that would provide license and registration applicants with safeguards against improprieties involving access to criminal history information?

4. Plea bargaining reduces the validity of criminal history conviction records. Is this sufficient reason to allow state regulatory boards to have access to arrest records in addition to conviction records? Explain your answer.

CHAPTER 10
LICENSING

Introduction

1. Chapter 10 deals with licensing, Chapter 11 with registration. Explain the distinction between licensing and registration as used in the Report.

2. Licensing of contract security companies is the most common form of private security regulation in the United States. How frequently are contract security companies licensed in comparison with all other security operations and activities?

3. Does the issuance of a security license ensure that a company will provide efficient crime prevention services? Explain.

Standard 10.1
Licensing of Security Businesses

1. List the categories of security businesses which this Standard proposes should be licensed.

2. This Standard does not call for the licensing of proprietary security operations. Do you believe it would be useful to license proprietary security operations? Explain your answer.

3. This Standard proposes the licensing of many areas of security. Would it be best to issue a single license to a company planning to engage in more than one of these activities?

Standard 10.2
License Applications

1. This Standard lists six items that should be on a license application. Identify any area which you believe should be added to or deleted from the list. Give reasons for your recommended changes or state why you believe the list is appropriate in its recommended form.

2. Large security corporations would view a resolution requiring the name, address, fingerprints of all officers, directors, partners, ten per-cent shareholders, resident managers and qualifying agents as excessive. Explain why the Task Force believes this requirement is necessary.

3. Why is a "full investigation" necessary if a security company has provided the state regulatory board with all of the data required in license applications?

Standard 10.3
Qualifying Agents

1. What is a qualifying agent?

2. What is your opinion of the Task Force's recommendation that a qualifying agent need be only eighteen years of age?

3. Identify and describe the five requirements a qualifying agent must meet under the terms of this Standard.

Standard 10.4
Notification of Changes in Status of Licensee

1. If the licensee does not commit any improper acts or permit employees to commit such acts, why is it necessary for the licensee to report to the regulatory board within fourteen days any change in the status of the license?

Standard 10.5
License Renewal

1. Discuss the effectiveness of a one-year license renewal program.

2. Are there any safeguards, other than annual license renewal, that the regulatory board has to maintain a viable evaluation of the licensed company?

Standard 10.6
Display of License Certificate

1. The licensee certificate must be displayed in the licensee's principal place of business, but copies may be displayed in branch offices. Would it be preferable for the regulatory board to issue certified copies of the original license for branch offices?

2. What are the advantages of displaying a license in each of the branch offices operated by the licensee?

Standard 10.7
Bonding and Insurance

1. This Standard recommends mandatory surety bond and proof of public liability insurance for each company. Is this an example of government interference and control in private business? Explain your answer.

2. What is a surety bond? What is public liability insurance?

3. This Standard does not set specific amounts for public liability insurance. Discuss this matter in view of the current practices cited in the commentary. Recommend possible approaches a professional regulatory board might use to determine the minimum amounts of coverage.

4. What coverage should the regulatory board include in the required liability insurance?

Standard 10.8
License Denial, Revocation or Suspension

1. List the five areas recommended for license denial, revocation and suspension.

2. Do you believe that other restrictions should be added to or deleted from the recommended list? Explain your answer.

3. What should be one of the major considerations of the regulatory board when determining whether a license should be revoked?

CHAPTER 11
REGISTRATION
Introduction

1. Do you believe that a properly operated registration program will have any impact on the shooting of innocent persons by security guards? Explain your answer.

2. Do you believe the public receives a distorted image of a security guard's role in shooting incidents? Explain media influence.

3. Why is theft one of the biggest problems with security guards?

Standard 11.1
Registration of Private Security Personnel

1. Does this Standard apply equally to all types of security personnel, including guards, alarm respondents, armored car officers and investigators? Why is it necessary to register all of these personnel?

2. Does this Standard apply equally to propietary private security personnel and contract security personnel? What reasons support this uniform application?

3. Some large corporations argue that their proprietary guards are better screened and trained than state requirements demand, and therefore should not have to be registered. Do you agree? Explain your answer.

4. Should "moonlighting" police officers, working as security guards, be required to register with the state regulatory board? Explain your answer.

Standard 11.2
Registration Qualifications

1. Outline the minimum training requirements necessary for an unarmed guard.

2. Do you agree with the four requirements for unarmed guards recommended in this Standard? Explain your answer.

3. How can a state regulatory board effectively determine whether an applicant is "morally responsible"?

4. Do you believe the Task Force should require a certain minimum education level in its recommendations? Explain your answer.

Standard 11.3
Qualifications for Armed Security Personnel

1. Review the problem of improper shooting incidents by security guards. Do you believe this problem is serious enough to warrant this Standard?

2. What impact should a criminal conviction record have on the registration of an individual applying as an armed guard?

3. What specific acts would classify an individual as unsuitable for armed guard registration, but would not disqualify the person from becoming an unarmed guard? Explain your answer.

4. How can the state regulatory board determine in advance if an individual is emotionally or psychologically capable to serve as an armed guard?

Standard 11.4
Permanent Registration Card

1. What are the advantages of a permanent registration card?

2. What should appear on a permanent registration card?

3. How can the state regulatory board control improper possession of a permanent registration card?

Standard 11.5
Temporary Permit

1. Explain the difference between a temporary permit and a permanent registration card.

2. What are the arguments in favor of issuing a temporary registration card? Do these arguments seem convincing enough to justify this special practice? Explain your answer.

3. What minimum checks must be made of an individual before issuing a temporary registration card?

Standard 11.6
Registration Renewal

1. How often should armed security personnel be required to renew their registration? Unarmed registrants?

2. How can the complaint procedure of the regulatory board serve as an argument for a valid extension of unarmed guard registration?

3. Is it realistically possible for states to require registration of all security personnel? Explain.

Standard 11.7
Suspension and Revocation

1. In your judgment, how effective is the suspension or revocation of registration as a sanction against improper guard behavior? Explain your answer.

2. Discuss the reasonableness and appropriateness of the state regulatory board's control over the employment of security personnel who allegedly act improperly?

3. What special provisions should the state regulatory board institute regarding weapon firing by security personnel? What is the rationale for such regulations?

4. List the circumstances that should govern weapon firing by private security personnel.

5. What are the justifications for weapon firing recommended in this Standard? Do you agree? Explain.

Standard 11.8
Sanctions

1. Should a police chief, who knowingly allows his personnel to "moonlight" as non-registered security guards, be held accountable under this Standard? Explain your answer.

2. Should criminal penalties be imposed on a security company furnishing non-registered persons to provide security services?

3. Is it appropriate and desirable to set criminal penalties for security violations or would regulatory actions be sufficient? Explain your answer.

Index

References to Appendix materials appear in this Index, however, the Appendix has been omitted.